Understanding Organizational Behaviour

Second Edition

UDAI PAREEK

Distinguished Visiting Professor
Indian Institute of Health Management Research
Jaipur

OXFORD

UNIVERSITY PRESS

OXFORD

UNIVERSITY PRESS

YMCA Library Building, Jai Singh Road, New Delhi 110001

Oxford University Press is a department of the University of Oxford.
It furthers the University's objective of excellence in research, scholarship,
and education by publishing worldwide in

Oxford   New York
Auckland   Cape Town   Dar es Salaam   Hong Kong   Karachi
Kuala Lumpur   Madrid   Melbourne   Mexico City   Nairobi
New Delhi   Shanghai   Taipei   Toronto

With offices in
Argentina   Austria   Brazil   Chile   Czech Republic   France   Greece
Guatemala   Hungary   Italy   Japan   Poland   Portugal   Singapore
South Korea   Switzerland   Thailand   Turkey   Ukraine   Vietnam

Oxford is a registered trade mark of Oxford University Press
in the UK and in certain other countries.

Published in India
by Oxford University Press

ISBN-13: 978-0-19-569086-6
ISBN-10: 0-19-569086-9

Typeset in Baskerville
by The Composers, New Delhi 110 063
Printed in India by Radha Press, Delhi 110031
and published by Oxford University Press
YMCA Library Building, Jai Singh Road, New Delhi 110001

To my family

Rama, my late wife; our children, Sushama, Surabhi, and Anagat,
and their children
for their deep love and emotional support

Preface to the Second Edition

This completely revised edition of *Understanding Organizational Behaviour*, while retaining the basic framework of the first edition of the book, includes new material in the areas of organizational structure, leadership, and power. The relevance of organizational behaviour for developing countries, mainly India, continues to be the emphasis of the book and is highlighted throughout.

Three chapters have been added in this edition. Chapter 4, Organizational Structure, covers determinants of organizational structure, usual organization designs, emerging organizational designs, and corporate restructuring, that is, mergers and acquisitions. Chapter 22, Developing Leadership for Tomorrow, explores paradigm shift on leadership, profile of tomorrow's leaders, processes, mechanisms, and some models of leadership development. Chapter 23, Power and Politics, delves into the concept and bases of power and organizational politics.

The existing chapters from the first edition have all been extensively revised, enhanced, and updated. Chapter 2, Changing Context, has been expanded to include the implications of flattening of the globe and social responsibility and ethics. Chapter 5, Positive Perspective, includes interventions with positive approach. Chapter 6, Learning Process, also explores learning theories and learning styles. Chapter 7, Motivational Process, now also encompasses theories like Alderfer's ERG Theory, cognitive evaluation theory, and reinforcement theory. Chapter 10, Personality and Personal Effectiveness, has been widened to include psychometric theories, psychodynamic theories, and theories of emotion. Chapter 15, Decisional Process, also includes consensus competencies. Chapter 18, Effective Teams, explains the various factors that contribute to building effective teams. Chapter 21, Leadership Theories and Styles, has been expanded to include trait theories of leadership, behavioural theories, contingency theories, leadership function theories, and some recent theories. Chapter 28, Organizational Development, explores OD in the past, present, and future.

The book now has case studies included in every chapter to illustrate the issues and concepts discussed. Besides the major case studies in the first edition such as The Dabbawalas of Mumbai, this new edition includes case studies on Reviving Khadi in India, Cisco's Acquisition Strategy, McDonald's 'Beef Fries' Controversy, National Dairy Development Board, Role Negotiation at Bokaro Steel Plant, Turnaround at Damodar Valley Corporation, Acquisition of Arcelor, Netscape's Work Culture, and Change Management at ICICI.

The book provides chapter-end exercises with concept-review and critical-thinking questions. It suggests interesting classroom and field projects.

I am sure that with the enhanced content and up-to-date material on the subject, this revised edition will be more useful to students and faculty alike. I shall be happy to receive feedback on the book from users for ideas for its future revision.

I would like to thank all the individuals and institutions for their permission for the case studies accompanying the chapters, which have been acknowledged in the respective case studies. I am grateful to the editorial team at OUP for their constant encouragement, feedback, and meticulous editing. I am also thankful to my secretary, Beena Nair, for her secretarial help.

UDAI PAREEK

Preface to the First Edition

People have always been regarded as important in managing organizations. Their centrality has become sharper in today's changing world. There is widespread realization that while other resources (material, technology, finance, etc.) can be bought and acquired, human processes (commitment of employees, organizational culture, managerial styles, etc.) cannot be brought into an organization from outside. Human aspects are critical in each functional area of management, and equally so for the effective utilization of resources. In view of this, the study of Organizational Behaviour (OB) has assumed great importance. OB, as a discipline, therefore, is included in management studies, as well as in courses of specialized education, such as medicine, agriculture, engineering, technology, entrepreneurship, and development studies.

While several good textbooks on OB are available from the West, mainly from the US, they do not address some relevant problems of developing countries. Furthermore, the examples cited in these books are from Western companies and organizations. Organizations in the developing world are facing several challenges today. The young people who join organizations in developing countries wonder how they can remain rooted in their own cultures, while helping their organizations to become global. For example, which aspects of the Indian culture should be retained, nurtured, and adopted in the managerial practices to make them effective, and which aspects (that are dysfunctional) should be changed and how? In other words, they need to know how to make organizations 'indigenous' as also how to develop a counter-culture which will change the dysfunctional aspects of the culture.

With increasing competition, disappointing political leadership, and a shrinking job market, people in developing countries are becoming cynical, pessimistic, and negative in their outlook. This mindset needs to be changed. People in organizations must develop positive attitudes and values. The available OB books do not pay attention to these aspects.

Organizational behaviour can be better understood after one first experiences various OB phenomena, and then examines them against a conceptual framework. This way students can discover the depth of OB concepts rather than merely acquire theoretical knowledge from external sources.

About the Book

This book, designed specifically for management students, is an attempt to respond to a long-standing need for a textbook written primarily from the perspective of a third-world country, and particularly, in the Indian context. Managers as well as would-be managers of these countries would also find this book useful as it would help in preparing them to meet the challenges faced by organizations.

The human process, hitherto a neglected aspect in OB, is the unique feature of this book, since the focus on process orientation forms the basis of understanding the subject. This approach is emphasized in the book as it is important to understand some aspects of the changing social and economic context in which organizations function. This volume discusses OB in the context of the emerging issues in the societies of developing countries and in relation to all the organizational units: the individual, the role, the team, and the organization.

Contents and Structure

The book is divided into five sections. The first section discusses the context in which organizations function and which have implications for organizational behaviour. Here, the first and opening chapters are devoted to the human process to provide the basis of understanding OB. Process orientation is important to understand some aspects of the changing social and economic context in which organizations function. This is briefly covered in Chapter 2. Given their importance, the third chapter focuses on the society in which the organizations work and its culture. Then we have two main perspectives underlining organizational behaviour in this century—one of them is a shift towards positive thinking and behaviour (Chapter 4).

The second section emphasizes the second main perspective—learning as an important condition for effectiveness (Chapter 5). The other important topics in this section are motivation, perception, basic orientation, personality, personal effectiveness, attitudes and values, and styles of working with people.

The third section is devoted to the understanding of the role as an integrating concept between individuals and organizations, the dynamics of the roles, role effectiveness, enhancing commitment of individuals, role conflicts, coping with frustration and stress, leadership styles, and decision-making.

The fourth section covers the team and its dynamics, including interpersonal communication, conflict management, and developing collaboration and leadership for tomorrow.

The fifth and final section deals with the dynamics of organization as a total system, its climate and culture, organizational communication, organizational learning and learning organizations, managing change in organizations, and continuous self-renewal of organizations, which is known as organization development.

Pedagogy

In order to help the students 'experience' some OB phenomena, students are required to complete (answer) some instruments and participate in some exercises (games) before they study some chapters. Each chapter has review questions to help the students recollect the main concepts discussed in the chapter. Additional questions have also been included to stimulate creativity in students.

Students would be able to internalize the concepts by applying them in practice. The chapter-end classroom and field projects to be performed through activities, preferably in groups, provide opportunity for such practice. These projects will help the students to internalize learning by critically examining concepts in the classroom setting and then by applying them in real-life situations. The topics covered (a) are action-oriented, so that students can apply the concepts, (b) are embedded in known, established theories, and (c) relate to new developments (e.g., positive approach).

Each section has a glossary of the main terms used for quick reference. There are two types of questions at the end of most chapters—concept-review questions to help the students to review their learning of the concepts, and critical-thinking questions to help them to integrate the concepts with their previous learning.

To integrate the learning of an organizational unit (individual, role, team, organization), a comprehensive case study has been given at the end of each section, with study questions. These case studies (actual significant experiences) will help the students to see how the various concepts discussed in the sections are interrelated and integrated in life.

Although it meets the needs of the current syllabi of various institutions and universities, the book includes many other important aspects of OB, thus suggesting a different approach for the bodies designing OB curricula.

The book is accompanied by an instructor's manual, which offers general guidelines on teaching OB and use of various methods to enhance students' learning of OB concepts in the classroom.

I hope that readers will find this book useful for the varied purposes for which the contents have been envisaged.

UDAI PAREEK

Acknowledgements

I acknowledge the contributions made by my students at IIM Ahmedabad and other institutions where I taught many of the topics included in the book as well as by the participants of various management development programmes I conducted.

I am grateful to the anonymous reader of the manuscript for very useful comments and suggestions, which helped me to redesign some parts of the volume. I would like to mention the invaluable support of my secretary Binil K. Nair for his patient typing and retyping of the text and preparation of glossaries, references etc. In spite of some personal problems and inconvenience, Binil was always available for help.

I have used with modification some material I wrote earlier, as well as some material from other authors. Permission to use such material is acknowledged in the relevant places in the chapters and below.

1. ASCI Journal of Management for Section-end Case IV
2. Ashok Kumar for Section-end Case I
3. Bombay Psychologist for some material in Chapter 19
4. C.N. Snyder for suggestions to improve the section on 'Hope' in Chapter 8
5. Dharni Sinha for Section-end Case IV
6. Gandhian Institute, Varanasi, for some material in Chapter 3
7. IIMB Management Review for Section-end Case I
8. Indian Journal of Industrial Relations for some material in Chapter 6
9. Indian Journal of Social Work for Chapter 26
10. Indian Management for some material on frustration in Chapter 14
11. Indian Society for Applied Behavioural Sciences for material on process in Chapter 1
12. K.K. Verma for Section-end Case IV
13. Learning Systems, Mumbai, for material in several chapters
14. National HRD Network, Hyderabad, for the OCTAPACE text in Chapter 22
15. Oxford & IBH, New Delhi, for Section-end Case V
16. Rajasthan Institute of Public Administration, Jaipur, for some material in Chapter 14
17. S. Ramachandran for some material on values in Chapter 16
18. Rawat Publishers, Jaipur, for some of the material used in some chapters
19. Response Books, Sage Publications, New Delhi, for Chapter 21
20. Sage Publications, New Delhi, for Section-end Case III
21. Tata McGraw-Hill, New Delhi, for Section-end Case II, and some text in Chapter 18
22. Uma Jain, Academy of HRD, Ahmedabad, for the section on development of values in Chapter 10
23. Vikalpa for some material in Chapter 3

UDAI PAREEK

Contents

Part One
The Framework

Part Two
The Individual

**Part Three
The Role**

**Part Five
The Organization**

The Framework

- Organizational Behaviour: Scope and Processes
- Changing Context
- Societal Culture and Organizations
- Organizational Structure
- Positive Perspective

1
Organizational Behaviour: Scope and Processes

LEARNING OBJECTIVES

After studying this chapter, you will be able to
1. Understand the importance and scope of organizational behaviour (OB)
2. Discuss the conceptual foundations of OB
3. Appreciate the historical roots of and Indian contributions in the field of OB
4. Distinguish intraperson, interperson, and role processes
5. Identify group, intergroup, and organizational processes
6. Understand organization–environment interface and societal processes

Technology has been changing at an unprecedented rate over the last century. Changes that would take place in the past in about a century are now happening in about a decade. These changes have impacted various aspects of human life, with deep implications for the management of organizations. With possibilities of virtual groups and virtual organizations, the manager's job has become more challenging than ever before. These changes are also affecting the relationship of organizations with their members (persons working for organizations). More and more, there is movement towards a contractual relationship rather than the traditional employer–employee relationship. Organizations are in continuous flux, and their structures are undergoing change almost every third or fourth year. Speedy action and decision making have become extremely important. Such changes are affecting the stock markets as well. In this context, the importance of human processes has increased tremendously.

THE ORGANIZATION AND THE INDIVIDUAL

Although people were always regarded as important in managing organizations, their centrality has become sharper in today's changing world. While it is much easier to buy technology and to borrow and get resources, both financial and material, it is impossible to buy human processes such as faster decision making, effective negotiation, strategy formulation, and leadership development. Our understanding of human dynamics has thus become more complex as well as more crucial. This is the focus of organizational behaviour (OB), which can be defined as an interdisciplinary behavioural science that studies phenomena related to organizations and the dynamics (processes) of organizations and their various human units (individuals, roles, dyads, teams, interteams, organizations, and the organization–environment interface).

Human processes concern not only individual employees and other members associated with an organization, but also other human units of the organization. Individuals come to work in the organization and get integrated with (or remain alienated from) the organization as per the roles they occupy in it. The roles, therefore, require separate attention. Individuals do not work in isolation. The smallest unit in an organization is a dyad (two-member groups consisting of an employee and a supervisor). For most tasks, people work in teams. Enough attention, therefore, needs to be given to the formation of teams, their dynamics, and ways of making them more effective. The effectiveness of an organization also depends on interteam collaboration—the collaboration of teams in an organization with other internal teams, as well as with external teams. Each organization has its own dynamics: its culture, its climate, the process of its development and decay, and the process of its turnaround or dissolution. The organization also deals with the external environment. Its interface with the environment requires an understanding of political dynamics so that it can not only adapt itself to the changing environment, but can also impact and 'shape' the external environment.

OB and Behavioural Sciences

Organizational behaviour is concerned with this whole gamut of units (individuals, roles, dyads, teams, and entire organizations) and interfaces (interpersonal, interteam, and organization–environment). Each of these aspects deserves independent understanding and study so that interventions can be designed and implemented to make organizations more effective.

This wide range of concerns necessitates drawing on knowledge from several fields, especially from the behavioural sciences, and applying this knowledge meaningfully. The conceptual foundation of organizational behaviour is multidisciplinary. While an understanding of individual dynamics is helped by the study of psychology (psychodynamics, cognitive studies, human psychology, social psychology, etc.), a proper understanding of roles and groups is provided by sociology. Merton, in particular, has contributed much to the understanding of roles, later taken up by other scholars. Group dynamics, including the study of conflict and collaboration between groups, has been a major contribution of sociology and social psychology. Sherif and Sherif[1] have done pioneering work in this area. The study of the culture, values, and functioning of unique groups has been the main contribution of anthropology. Issues of power and politics are studied in political science. Exhibit 1.1 shows the respective sources of OB topics for different organizational units.

We thus see that the conceptual foundations of organizational behaviour are anchored in the behavioural sciences of psychology (including social psychology, clinical psychology, industrial psychology), sociology, anthropology, and political science. We have drawn on the major theories of these sciences. The premise in this book is that we cannot understand the dynamics of individuals, roles, teams, or organizations without understanding the relevant basic processes. Unfortunately, process has remained rather a neglected aspect of organizational behaviour until now. This volume therefore emphasises the importance of process, which we discuss later in this chapter.

Exhibit 1.1 *Behavioural Science Sources of OB Topics*

Organizational unit	Topic	Relevant behavioural science
Individual	Motivation	Psychology
	Perception	Psychology
	Personality	Psychology
	Personal effectiveness	Psychology
	Decision making	Psychology
	Interpersonal styles	Psychology
	Attitudes	Psychology
Role	Role effectiveness	Sociology and Psychology
	Leadership	Sociology and Psychology
	Work motivation	Sociology and Psychology
	Role stress and burnout	Sociology and Psychology
	Coping	Sociology and Psychology
Teams and interteams	Team effectiveness	Psychology
	Interpersonal communication	Psychology
	Conflict management	Psychology
	Consensus building	Psychology
	Developing collaboration	Psychology
Organization	Organizational culture	Psychology
	Organizational climate	Psychology
	Organizational communication	Psychology
	Organizational learning	Psychology
	Organizational change	Psychology
	Organizational development	Psychology
	Power and politics	Political science
	Cross-cultural organizations	Anthropology
Context	Societal culture	Anthropology
	Values	Anthropology
	Positive thinking	Psychology
	Learning	Psychology

ANCESTORS OF ORGANIZATIONAL BEHAVIOUR

Since OB is an interdisciplinary study, scholars and practitioners should be aware of the evolution of this new field, including the rich origins of relevant thoughts and practices in many cultures across the world.

Alagaraja and Dooley[2] have proposed a framework to identify and encapsulate simultaneous events that occurred in different parts of the world, enabling us to trace the early development of relevant conceptual foundations. They have divided the history of human thought into nine periods. In the period of the Old World Civilizations (1250–600 BC), leaders from the East such as Zarathustra, Buddha, and

Confucius deeply influenced our relation with the ultimate reality. Lao-tse and others in China used a method that closely resembles the contemporary case study method of problem solving.[3]

During the period of the Regional Civilizations (600–200 BC), Plato and Aristotle contributed to the fields of knowledge and philosophy. In India, the university of Nalanda was established and *Arthashastra*, the first political and administrative handbook for running a state, was produced. In China, Confucius was influential in changing the social structure: military talent replaced hereditary status. A class of professional administrators, military officers, and educators was created that offered vocational training to aspirants for employment in government service.

During the period of the Roman Empire (AD 200–600), the establishment of the Christian Church as the most dominant institution in the Roman Empire was the most significant event for humankind. The Church was organized on the lines of the Roman Empire, subordinating local churches to a hierarchy on an imperial scale. Indeed, the Christian Church derived its strength from its organizational skills. The concerns of the Church spread over every walk of life. The Ten Commandments, for instance, provided a means to assist human beings in their personal growth. The Roman Empire also made use of slave labour, which was the first form of captive human capital used for the purpose of generating income.

During the period of the New Order (AD 900–1321), Islam influenced the daily practices of its followers deeply. During this period, merchants and craft guilds helped in achieving economic success, sowing the seeds of the capitalist system of production. The guild system established quality standards for both products and practices.[4]

During the period of Western Christendom (AD 1321–1763), the Renaissance led to a revolution in thinking. Locke set out the principles of empiricism. The Pestalozzi theories laid the groundwork for modern elementary education and Rousseau expounded a new theory of education, emphasizing the importance of expression rather than repression in yielding a well-balanced, freethinking child.[5]

During the Industrial Revolution (AD 1763–1871), the creation of a new social class of workers was one of the most significant events. Herbart, acknowledged as the 'father of scientific pedagogy', stressed the study of psychological processes of learning as a means of devising educational programmes based on the aptitudes, abilities, and interests of students. Freud's contributions also led to the development of the field of psychology. The rise of Marxism led to the trade union movement. The foundation of training within organizations was established, as some people in the organization spent significant portions of time instructing others.[6]

Industrial relations between the employer and the employees were formalised at a much later stage, but the role of the government in providing a legal framework for the welfare of its citizens took root during this period. It appears that the earliest developments in the field of OB were non-Western contributions. Contributions from Western perspectives to the growth of the field as it is today became significant only much later. However, a global synthesis of cultures shapes the field's growth and development today.

Organizational Behaviour in the West

In the West, the precursors of OB can be traced to Europe. Robert Owen, a British industrialist of the early nineteenth century, attended to the various needs of workers: he improved working conditions, prevented child labour, shortened working hours, and provided meals for employees. In that same century, the German psychologist Munsterbeg and the American scholar Mary Follett wrote of the importance of motivation, participation, and democracy. However, these pioneering attempts and ideas remained largely neglected until the 1930s.

It was in the US that OB flourished early. At the turn of the twentieth century, Fredrick Taylor popularised the concept of scientific management using studies of time and motion. There was little concern for the human aspects. The main emphasis was on the manipulation of the workplace. Although these studies contributed to the development of industrial psychology, the human dimensions were neglected.

The beginning of OB may be said to lie in the 'Hawthorne studies'. In 1924, at the Hawthorne works of the Western Electric Company, US, studies were being conducted to determine the effect of intensity of light on productivity.[7] Productivity increased under both conditions of increasing and decreasing intensity of light. This was a baffling finding. The researchers then investigated the effect of rest pauses, with the same result: productivity increased under each trial. The chance findings of these Hawthorne studies matched with the workers' preferences of factors influencing productivity: size of group, supervisory behaviour, earning, novelty of situation, workers' interest in the experiment, and attention received. Thus, for the first time, the importance of 'behavioural' factors was discovered, and that too by chance.

The Hawthorne studies led to the human relations movement, which started in the 1950s. Its main emphasis was on the social environment to which people responded. It advocated that people were motivated more by social rather than economic needs. McGregor and Maslow became the main proponents and figureheads of the human relations movement. McGregor[8] is famous for his classification of managerial behaviour into two contrasting categories called Theory X and Theory Y. The assumptions underlying these two approaches are shown in Exhibit 1.2. Maslow[9] is famous for his theory of motivation (hierarchy of needs), which we shall discuss in Chapter 7.

In a way, OB really took off in the West in the 1950s. According to Khandwalla,[10] OB was a response to challenges in the form of 'dissatisfaction with the abstractions of the theory of the firm in economics,[11] dissatisfaction with the unsubstantiated verities of the principles of management school,[12] chance observation of group dynamics at work,[13] observation of substantial variation in the structure and functioning of business organizations,[14] the failure of 'rational' operations technologies,[15] the organizational implications of the existence of a hierarchy of needs,[16] and alienation at work'.[17]

Exhibit 1.2 *McGregor's Theory X and Theory Y*

Theory X	Theory Y
• People do not like work and try to avoid it • People do not like work, so managers have to control, direct, coerce, and threaten employees to get them to work towards organizational goals • People prefer to be directed, so as to avoid responsibility, and want security—they have little ambition	• People do not naturally dislike work—work is a natural part of their lives • People are internally motivated to objectives to which they are committed • People are committed to goals to the degree that they receive personal rewards when they reach their objectives • People will seek and accept responsibility under favourable conditions • People have the capacity to be innovative in solving organizational problems • People are bright, but under most organizational conditions, their potential is underutilised

Organizational behaviour has been influenced by the following trends:
- The systems approach
- The socio-technical system approach
- The democratic approach
- The contingency approach
- The interactional approach

Systems approach Systems theory views organizations as complex systems consisting of interrelated elements functioning as a whole. The various units (human, material, information, finance) interact with each other to produce products and profits; they do not function in isolation.

Socio-technical system approach Important work was done in England at the Tavistock Institute. The term 'socio-technical system' was coined there. Researchers and practitioners at the institute demonstrated that the technology of production was a major determinant in the organization of firms. It was demonstrated that technology would greatly influence the culture and structure of the organization. Trist and his colleagues of the Tavistock Institute demonstrated that changing technology from small-group work to three-shift working had a disruptive effect on workers' output and productivity.[18] This approach influenced OB in the US also.

Democratic approach Emphasis on democracy in the political field influenced thinking in all other aspects of life. Importance was given to democracy in the workplace, human dignity was valued, and participation and involvement of employees was seen as a good in itself as well as a means of increasing productivity.

Contingency approach Instead of insisting on a universal solution as the best way of doing things, the contingency approach came to be more widely accepted. According to this approach, the appropriate managerial behaviour in a situation depends on the elements of that situation. We shall discuss this approach in Chapter 21.

Interactional approach Generally there is a tendency to search for cause-and-effect relationships (what causes what), so that the 'causes' can be influenced to manipulate the effects. The interactional approach suggests that the relationship is not simple and one-way: there is continuous interaction between the so-called 'causes' and 'effects' and the 'effect' can also become a cause. For example, it is believed that employee attitudes influence their perception of work. But the employees' experience at work may also modify or shape their attitudes. There is a continuous interaction between the two.

Organizational Behaviour in India

Four developmental trends have contributed to the evolution of OB in India. The first trend was the increase in the scope of applied behavioural sciences (ABS). While education and social anthropology were always 'applied' sciences, departments of applied psychology were established in Kolkata (then Calcutta) and later in other universities. Applied psychology was, however, still confined to clinical, industrial, and educational psychology. Some departments of sociology initiated the study and teaching of social issues. However, very little work was done in applied political science until the establishment of the Centre for the Study of Developing Societies and the Centre for Policy Research. Public administration, management, and agricultural extension meanwhile emerged as new areas of higher education and research.

The second trend was the relaxing of boundaries between the different behavioural sciences. Reviews of research in psychology sponsored by the Indian Council of Social Science Research (ICSSR), New Delhi, are a good example of this (as also of the first trend). Compared with the first review,[19] which used traditional classification for the topics, the second used thematic classification, including social issues like poverty, inequality, population and family planning, and ecology, and drew on relevant writings from other behavioural sciences for topics like communication, influence, and political processes.[20] This trend was continued in the third[21] and subsequent surveys. In the third, topics like intergroup relations, rural development, and organizational effectiveness were included. The Behavioural Sciences Centre was established in New Delhi under the chairmanship of S.K. Mitra in 1962. The centre published three directories of research in behavioural sciences, a guide to Indian behavioural science periodicals, and a quarterly, *Indian Behavioural Sciences (IBS) Abstracts*. When ICSSR started the publication of abstracts of periodicals, the *IBS Abstracts* was discontinued.

The third trend, the psychodynamic process as the integrating force for behavioural science research and applications, had its beginnings in India with the coming of Rolf Lynton to Mysore, where he founded the institution Aloka in 1957 for youth leaders from Asian countries. This trend was strengthened with the institutionalisation of learning groups (L-groups) and training groups (T-groups). This was used as the core methodology to help people confront interpersonal and group issues at the Small Industry Extension Training Institute in the early 1960s, where the author joined Rolf Lynton to redesign training and group development.[22] IIM Calcutta, under the influence of McGregor, Bennis, and Baumgartel, arranged to send some of its behavioural scientists to National Training Laboratories (NTL). With social scientists going to NTL from various parts of the country as well, a sizeable group of NTL-trained persons was built up, who established the Indian Society for Applied Behavioural Science (ISABS) in 1971. ISABS is a highly specialized professional group of ABS experts engaged in advancing its cause. ABS is involved in developing ABS competence throughout the country. Dharni P. Sinha[23] has chronicled the development of ABS in India.

The fourth trend contributing to the development of ABS, dealing with social, group, or institutional issues, using process interventions, and involving the members of the concerned group in research, was that of action research. This had its beginnings in India in community development, but emerged more strongly in education with the coming of Stephen M. Corey to India in the late 1950s, at the invitation of the Ministry of Education. A large number of action research workshops were organized for teachers and headmasters throughout the country. The workshops entailed the three elements of ABS. A manual for facilitators of such workshops advocated the psychodynamic approach in classrooms. Incidentally, T-groups were convened in New Delhi in the late 1950s and early 1960s.

IMPORTANCE OF PROCESS

Organizations are mostly kept busy with routine matters and activities to meet their goals. Their main concern is what to do, rather than how to do it. In the pursuit of these goals, which constitute their main objective, they are primarily concerned with the substantive aspects. Universities are busy preparing curricula, and other institutions are busy preparing courses and material, which they consider important and useful for certain client groups. Research organizations primarily focus on matters such as the type of research that should be done, the methodology to be followed, and where the research should be published. Similarly, industrial organizations are primarily concerned with their main task, namely, production and marketing. Organizations seem to be so obsessed with their substantive area of work that they do not stop long enough to focus on other dimensions that may, in the long run, help them achieve their goals more effectively. One such dimension, which tends to be neglected, is process.

Process Defined

Process can be defined as the underlying human and behavioural dimensions of an organization and the various groups and individuals constituting it. Process can be contrasted with structure on the one hand and content on the other. When an organization faces a problem or crisis, a solution is usually sought in terms of changes that can be made in the organization. For example, suppose a university faces the problem of teachers not spending enough time in their offices and going home much earlier than expected, one solution is to promulgate new rules giving greater power to the department heads and enabling them to act as police officers. Similarly, if an organization faces the problem of a conflict between two departments or two individuals, a solution is sought in defining the respective roles more clearly, making each one responsible for specific aspects of the work. The implication here is not to undermine the importance of these aspects of organizational life, nor to suggest that structural changes are less desirable. But while such changes are being suggested, what is forgotten is that there are underlying behavioural dimensions and group dynamics and a mere structural adjustment may not be able to help the situation. It is unfortunate that structure is overstressed and process neglected, and it is still more unfortunate that a dichotomy is seen between them.

I am impressed with our market leadership. Now pay more attention to human dynamics and interpersonal behaviour in your teams.

Process vs Structure

The stress on process should not mean that the importance of structure can be undermined. In fact, structure and process are two sides of the same coin. Emphasis on one implies emphasis on the other, the only difference being that the emphasis has a different focus. Structural changes are part of the dynamics underlying organizational processes. An organizational problem that requires a change in structure as a possible solution can be addressed equally well with emphasis on the process, with the understanding that it will bring about the necessary structural change. Thus, an integration of structure and process can be achieved, rather than worrying about which of the two is more important.

Process vs Content

A similar dichotomy is present between content and process. When thinking of education, for example, the syllabus (as a catalogue of various items of knowledge that the students should acquire) assumes great importance. Much energy goes into discussing the content of knowledge that the students should acquire. Similarly, in the training of teachers, more emphasis is laid on what the teachers should know in order to teach better. Even when the teacher's behaviour is discussed, the emphasis is again on the syllabus—what the teacher should know so as to behave in a different way. Process is neglected. There is no discussion at all of how teachers and students interact in the school and in classrooms, what happens in various groups, how teachers behave and what they do in order to meet the various goals of the school, what relationship exists between the headmaster and the teacher, and how the headmaster interacts with students and with what results. Unfortunately, these aspects are taken for granted.

Needless to say, it is unfortunate that process and content are treated as dichotomous. They are interrelated, and each depends on the other. Emphasis on process should not mean de-emphasising content. In fact, the value of content increases with emphasis on process—process becomes content, since crucial questions about the acquisition of knowledge and its utilisation, changes in student behaviour, etc. become important aspects of the curriculum.[24] Emphasis on process would not only help in designing curricula, but also gear the entire school system to maximise learning. This holds true not only for education but for other fields as well. Conversely, emphasis on content usually implies emphasis on what is done rather than how things are done, but these are in fact interrelated.

The concept of process essentially concerns the question of 'how' and, to a great extent, the question of 'why'. It emphasises the behavioural and interactional dimensions of a situation. It also emphasises the dimension of values, which is often neglected. Thus, process is concerned with the overall dynamics that underlie most questions of change.

Perspective

Both the understanding and interventions of organizational behaviour processes need a perspective: for whom the knowledge and interventions are primarily meant to serve—the corporate sector or the people. Such perspective is also important while working with organizations, including the corporate sector. Prayag Mehta is a pioneer in attempting to reorient OB, which he feels has travelled a long way, 'mostly in the reverse gear'. OB processes need to be understood in the socio-historical perspective of a country. For example, for the Indian society the following historical events provide the perspective for OB.[25] These have implications for understanding and designing OB interventions.

- Anti-colonial heritage of freedom movement; planned development to raise people's standard of living—dominant role of the public sector; the Nehru-Mahalanobis model of development; the Industrial Policy Resolution of 1956; the Bombay Plan.
- Education Commission (1964–66); NCERT research projects such as Sociology of Education; common schooling and democratisation; education for the disadvantaged; Achievement Motivation, Classroom Behaviour—these were

all-India projects that diffused ideas, skills, and institutional development and promoted research and training activities in the related fields.

- Support for the Bombay Plan during the Shastri government; nationalisation of the banking industry in August 1969; sharp rise in food prices and social unrest during the middle of 1970s; the JP movement.
- Shift to New Economic Policy in July 1991; Stabilisation and Structural Adjustment Programme; increasing role of the World Bank and IMF; growth in GDP becomes the primary goal; primacy of the private sector and market; neo-liberalisation and corporatisation; rise of finance capital and MNCs.
- The Second Five-Year Plan stated that the basic criterion for lines of advance must be social gain, not profit.[26]

PROCESS LEVELS

While discussing the importance of process, it may be useful to consider it from the perspective of several levels. In an organization, several levels operate simultaneously, from the individuals who work in the organization to the whole of society, which constitutes the context in which the organization functions. Nine different levels can be identified between the micro level (the individual) and the macro level (society). Different processes operate at different levels, but they should not be treated in isolation. In fact, the various levels interact, and the processes at different levels have significance for one another. It may therefore be useful to think of linkages, and treat the processes at one level in the context of (and as linking with) the processes at the other levels. This implies treating process as a continuous phenomenon. The various levels at which processes operate are discussed hereafter.

In the discussion that follows, only one main process that characterises a particular level is picked up as the primary process at that level. Various other processes also operate at that level, and the discussion of a single process is only for convenience.

The Person: Existential Processes

The processes, which operate at the level of the individual working in an organization, can be defined as existential processes. Of primary importance at this level is the process of self-awareness, that is, to what extent the person is aware of what is happening to him or her, of social reality, of his or her relationships with others, and so on. It also relates to an awareness of the various aspects of one's life, which are primarily concerned with self-actualisation, or the achieving of personal goals.

If these existential processes are neglected, it is likely to adversely affect the respective individuals, as well as the quality of work in the groups they are working in and the organization as a whole. The organization should therefore take definite steps, such as organizing special programmes, to help individuals become aware of these processes and deal with them effectively.

The Interperson: Empathic Processes

The main process at the interpersonal level is the empathic process, the process of one individual reaching out to another and establishing a relationship with him or her. This has several significant aspects, and communication is one of them. How people communicate with one another is not only important in itself, but also because it has implications for relationship-building between two or more individuals. Similarly, collaborative and competitive processes, which respectively result in cooperation and conflict, represent another important dimension. Attention must be paid to such processes in order to increase the effectiveness of interpersonal relationships. All such processes are part of the general empathic process, which underlies all interpersonal dealings. The person who communicates with or establishes a relationship with another person is primarily concerned—or should be concerned—with the extent to which he or she has been able to empathise with the other person, and vice versa.

The Role: Coping Processes

Role processes (associated with the role an individual plays in an organization) have been comparatively neglected. The individual has a role to play in the organization, and this role enables each person to build up links with other persons in the organization. The role, therefore, is an important linking concept. The main process associated with the role is that of coping. Individuals have to deal with various problems that impinge on their roles. On the one hand is the conflict arising out of the relationship between the self and the individual's various roles; on the other hand are the pressures and stresses that the individual has to cope with in the relationships of his or her role with the roles of other individuals. Various role conflicts or role stresses have implications for the effectiveness of both the individual and the various groups working in the organization. If individuals cope effectively with these stresses, their effectiveness in the organization will be high, and vice versa.

The Group: Building Processes

Various groups work in the organization as distinct entities. These may either be functional groups (production people, marketing people, researchers, etc.) or

You have a long list of achievements in your CV. But could you share with us some concrete experiences on coping with problems at work?

hierarchical groups (headmasters, teachers, senior managers, middle managers, workers, supervisors, etc.). These groups, including those comprising entire departments, have their own dynamics. The main processes that characterise a group are concerned with the formation and building up of the group as an entity. The main aspects of building processes are norms and traditions that emerge in the group. These result in cohesion, as opposed to conflict. Such building processes contribute to the establishment of a strong group that can make an impact at work and can cope with various problems. Otherwise, groups may remain weak and ineffective.

The Intergroup: Collaborative Processes

The various groups in the organization work with each other: they shoulder common responsibilities as well as deal with problems in their own respective areas. The main process operating between groups is thus cooperation. When interacting groups have a shared goal in common, they cooperate. The dynamics of cooperation and conflict between groups deserve special attention. Several factors contribute to cooperation. Two important factors are the perception of how much power each group has and the minimum degree of trust between groups (manifested as confidence that one group will not use its power against another). The processes of competition and cooperation are very important in the building of groups and of individuals. Both have contributions to make, and both processes can be used in either an effective (functional) or ineffective (dysfunctional) way.

If competition is used to raise the level of excellence and to continuously pose challenges in terms of standards of performance and achievement, it is likely to contribute to the development of self-worth in members of the group. This may be termed as positive competition or Comp(+). On the other hand, if competition is used primarily for competing with other individuals or groups merely by preventing them directly or indirectly from attaining a goal seen as non-shareable, this has a degenerative effect on individuals in the group. This may be called negative competition, or Comp(−). Similarly, collaboration can also be either positive, that is, Coop(+), or negative, that is, Coop(−). Coop(+) is reflected in the tendency to collaborate with others to achieve a common goal and to contribute positively towards this effort. Coop(−) is shown in the tendency to collaborate either to escape hard work or to ingratiate oneself with the other party. The former builds self-worth; the latter erodes it.

Another related process in the group is problem solving. Groups face various problems. Two groups working together also face problems, which they have to cope with. The main underlying process in problem solving is also that of perception— whether each group perceives the other as contributing to its interests or lacks trust in the other. This influences the stand the two groups take towards any problem they face.

The Organization: Growth Processes

A dynamic organization is constantly evolving and growing in terms of its mission, areas of activity, size, etc. It is continuously learning, that is, utilising past experience in future action. Its channels of communication function effectively. A dynamic organization also develops conducive climate that helps employees to attain self-fulfilment and contribute their utmost to the achievement of organizational goals. It also deals effectively with change. A dynamic organization has to make the choice between resting on its laurels and self-renewal. The choice is a difficult one. The first (staying on the beaten track to success) provides security to the organization, while the second (change and self-renewal) involves some risk. On the other hand, the first may lead to stagnation and decay, while the latter may provide new meaning and satisfaction.

The Organization–Environment Interface: Influence Processes

An organization has interfaces with the societal environment, namely, the political, economic, and cultural conditions prevailing at a particular time in society. It is necessary to understand the framework of societal culture; otherwise the organization does not develop deep roots. In addition, the organization is also involved in a transactional process with the environment. The main process on this dimension is that of influence, and it is an important process for institution building. Here it is worth examining whether the organization exerts greater influence on the environment, or vice versa. This is an issue of proactivity versus reactivity: whether the organization merely reacts to the environment or proactively attempts to change the environment to some extent. The process of influence is also concerned with the autonomy of the organization: to what extent it is able to insulate itself against undue influences from outside, while keeping itself open to healthy influences.

Several related organizations work for a common goal, sometimes in a common field. For example, schools of the same kind may work together on common problems. On the other hand, several organizations with different goals and different fields of work may also have some common goals and come together to work on certain problems. In many cases, such interorganizational efforts involve the basic process of collaboration, of searching for common ground on which they can come together. Conflict and competition may also operate when organizations work within the same field, share resources that seem to be limited, and see their goals as non-shareable (i.e., if one organization achieves the goal, other organizations may not have a goal left to work on).

The Community: Processes of Social Awareness

The community has some special responsibilities and certain processes operate at that level. Some organizations may be concerned with the process of relating to and helping the community, such as educational organizations and those dealing with human development. The main process, which operates at the community level, is social awareness. Paulo Freire[27] has dramatically drawn attention to this aspect while talking about the need for 'conscientisation'. Conscientisation is the process of increasing awareness about social realities and increasing a positive self-concept in relation to such realities. This process needs the attention of not only those who are working directly for the welfare of the community, but also other organizations for which the community has any relevance.

The Society: Value Processes

The society is the main context within which all organizations work. Social processes are therefore an important concern for the organization. However, it is also necessary to consider these social processes from the point of view of society as a whole. The most relevant processes at the level of the society are related to values and power. Karl Marx drew attention to the basic dynamics of a society, namely, what controls the main instruments (i.e., the means of production) in the society. Similarly, what values prevail in the society is important. Values should be understood not only in the sense of what is considered important by a society, but also in terms of who is considered a model human being. Are human beings regarded and treated as passive recipients or as active agents? The process of self-awareness at the community level focuses on values.[28]

The various processes briefly indicated above are interrelated, and the circle is completed when the individual, as a part of his existential process, becomes aware of the social reality and of the value and power bases in society. This awareness may make the various levels discussed in this chapter more relevant and better related to one another. Understanding of a process and making use of this knowledge would involve, therefore, awareness of the main processes at different levels and the links between these processes. In addition to this, it may be useful to discuss these processes openly to see the implications they have both for making structures more effective and for making content richer. Such openness in dealing with a process may contribute to the effectiveness of both the individual and the other levels of an organization. It may also be useful to pay attention to structure and content so that structures are designed which can promote some of the important processes and contribute to the effectiveness of various levels. Similarly, content may also be designed to strengthen processes. To do this, the process itself may be treated as content and as a supportive dimension of structure. If such an approach is taken, process and content on the one hand, and process and structure on the other, do not remain dichotomies, but become integrated aspects of the same phenomenon. The various contradictions, which may exist in organizational life, can be resolved to a great extent by doing so.

SUMMARY

Unprecedented changes in society and technology have brought into sharp focus the importance of individuals and teams to the success of organizations. The study of individuals, their roles in organizations, teams, groups, the organization as a whole, and their dynamics is within the scope of organizational behaviour.

OB is a multi-disciplinary study drawing mainly on important behavioural sciences like psychology, sociology, social psychology, anthropology, and political science.

Significant contributions in the development of human thought all over the world, mainly in the East, were the 'ancestors' of OB, although OB as a discipline developed in the West. However, Indian OB scholars have made significant contributions too. The main contribution of OB is in understanding and using processes, which can also be defined as the underlying behavioural dimensions of any unit of the organization.

The main processes concern the individual (existential processes), interperson (empathic processes), the role (coping processes), the team (building processes), the group (collaboration processes), the organization (growth processes), the organization–environment interface (influence processes), the community (social awareness), and society (value processes).

GLOSSARY

anthropology   the science that studies societies and their patterns of living

cognitive   related to knowledge or opinion

contingency approach   the attitude that most aspects of an organization are contingent on (are influenced by) various other elements

dyad   two-member group

group dynamics   complex processes of working of groups

interactional approach   individual or organizational behaviour is determined by continuous interaction between individuals and situations

organization   quasi-permanent social unit having a specific structure and norms to achieve common goals

organizational behaviour (OB)   an inter-disciplinary behavioural science that studies phenomena and dynamics (processes) of organizations, their various human units (individuals, roles, dyads, teams, interteams, organizations), and the organization–environment interface

political science   the science that studies individual and group behaviour within a political environment

process   underlying human and behavioural dimensions of an organization and the various groups and individuals constituting the organization

psychodynamics   *see* **group dynamics**

psychology   the science that explains, measures, and attempts to change behaviour

role   the position one occupies in a social system, as defined by the functions one performs in response to the expectations of its 'significant' members and ones own expectations from that position

social psychology   the branch of psychology that integrates concepts from psychology and sociology

sociology   the science that studies human groups and their activities

system   an interrelated set of elements functioning as a whole

team   two or more persons working together towards a common goal(s)

EXERCISES

Concept Review Questions

1. What is organizational behaviour? Define and explain.
2. Why is OB important for the management of organizations?

3. What new developments in the present environment have made the role of OB more crucial?
4. From which behavioural sciences has OB drawn its subject matter?
5. What is the difference between process and content, and process and structure?

Critical Thinking Questions

1. Which intrateam processes are strong and which are weak in your class?
2. Which processes in your organization (workplace or institution) require to be strengthened? Consider one or two of them and give suggestions on how to strengthen those processes.

Classroom Projects

1. Analyse the structure of your institution. What are the accompanying processes?
2. Analyse a printed speech by a political leader or a CEO of a company in terms of content and process.

Field Projects

1. Attend a meeting at an NGO (for about 30 to 60 minutes). Take notes both on the content (what is discussed) and the process (how it was discussed, who spoke and who were silent, the pattern of participation, etc.)
2. Attend a meeting in an industry. Assess the quality of the content (quality and speed of decision making) and the quality of the processes (participation, consensus building). Is there a relationship between the two?

The Dabbawalas of Mumbai*

The *dabbawalas* of Mumbai carry hot lunches from the homes of employees (customers) to their places of employment. The aluminium containers, known as *dabbas* or 'tiffins', serve the dual purpose of keeping the food warm and preventing it from splashing out during the tiffin carrier's rushed and jostling journey. A typical tiffin carrier carries about 40 of these dabbas on a long, unwieldy tray on his head as he moves speedily through busy streets and cramped trains. The tray and tiffins have a combined weight of more than 60 kg. For distances over 4 km, the carriers often use bicycles; when carrying more than 40 tiffins, the carriers use handcarts.

Each dabbawala is employed by one of the city's 800 *mukaddams* (contractors). The contractors and tiffin carriers both belong to the Mumbai Tiffin Box Carriers Association. It was registered as a trust in 1967, but was an informal guild for some 50 years before this.

There are two primary reasons why the tiffin carrier operations started and succeeded in Mumbai. First, the Indian value system places great emphasis on home-cooked meals, served hot. The problem for roughly eight out of ten white-collar workers in Mumbai is that they do not have time to go home for lunch. The tiffin carrier brings the security of an inexpensive, clean, tasty, and often still-warm, home-cooked meal. Restaurant meals cost five to fifteen times more than home-cooked food and there is also the chance of falling ill, as many public eateries lack hygienic kitchens.

Second, Mumbai is the only city in India where the train traffic flows in the north–south direction and the pedestrian traffic flows in the east–west direction. Thus, tiffins are physically carried for relatively short distances from homes to train stations by one set of tiffin carriers, carried by train for longer distances between stations, and finally carried by other tiffin carriers from the train stations to the designated workplaces. Therefore, Mumbai alone can sustain a tiffin carrier network of this size and complexity because of its quick, efficient, and far-reaching suburban train service.

THE ASSOCIATION

Most of Mumbai's tiffin carriers and contractors come from the Pune region, roughly 150 miles away from Mumbai. A tiffin carrier does not have to pay the contractor to be hired. There is absolutely no paperwork involved. Trust and loyalty are the main

---

*This case has been developed by Ashok Kumar, Stephen T. Margulis, and Jaideep Motwani, and published in *IMB Journal of Management*. Reproduced with slight modification with permission.

underpinnings of recruitment. Typically, no formal training is provided to the tiffin carrier upon being hired. However, for the first 2 days, the tiffin carrier follows his contractor or another dabbawala who shows the new recruit his route, the homes/apartments he would visit to pick up tiffins in the morning and to which he would return tiffins in the afternoon, and explains the coding/identification system. A tiffin carrier will visit up to 40 homes each day and he must learn the location of all of them during his 2-day orientation. All the training is done orally.

A dabbawala is usually paid a fixed/straight salary of Rs 1,000 a month by his contractor. There are no other benefits provided to the tiffin carrier, except that he gets a week's vacation in March apart from public holidays. By contrast, contractors make between Rs 6,000 and Rs 8,000 a week. There is no policy regarding sick leave or absenteeism. A worker is expected to be at work. If a worker gets sick, other tiffin carriers in his group or his contractor may cover for him. The bond among tiffin carriers is as strong as the old school tie. They would not entertain any talk of dishonesty in the ranks. Trust is the essence of the business and a tiffin carrier typically sticks to his contractor.

The contractors basically run the business through two committees: the Mandal Committee and the Trust Committee. The members of the Mandal Committee are 11 elected contractors, each elected for 5 years. This committee collectively governs the Trust but its primary responsibilities seem to be dealing with brokering conflicts among contractors and addressing potential contractors. The Trust Committee, comprising 11 elected contractors, each elected for a 5-year period, is responsible for the operation of the *dharamshalas* (courtesy inns) back home in Pune. In addition, two contractors serve as staff to the Trust. The job of these two contractors includes (1) resolving disputes and problems arising in day-to-day operations that cannot be resolved by contractors and their groups, (2) enrolling new customers into the business, and (3) arranging and calling meetings of the Trust. The contractors, in turn, are responsible to The Mumbai Tiffinbox Carriers Association. The *mandal* or 'circle' (i.e., the association) organizes monthly business meetings. All contractors are required to attend the mandal's monthly meetings. The tiffin carriers can also attend the monthly meetings if they so desire. The Mandal Committee sorts out the internal problems/disputes between the contractors at these business meetings. Additionally, the tiffin carriers and contractors meet socially once a month. These meetings are organized by the Trust.

Structure

Some of the salient points of the Trust in terms of structural dimensions are:

Standards   In the Trust, the work appears to involve output standardisation, because workers are given explicit work goals (e.g., tiffins to retrieve each morning). If goals do not change and each person completes his task, this is an important coordination mechanism.

Moreover, it appears that workers share beliefs about what is acceptable behaviour and what is not. This implies that output standardisation is supplemented by norm standardisation. The latter is encouraged by the tiffin carriers' functional unit grouping. In a functional unit grouping, everyone within a specific work group has similar tasks to perform.

Hierarchy   There is a relatively flat hierarchy of authority. There are only three levels within the organization: some 5,000 workers, called carriers; some 800 supervisors or managers, called contractors; and the 11-member Mandal Committee. A flat organization such as this often implies a wide span of control. By contrast, here each manager manages a group of some four to ten employees. By Western standards, the span of control is narrow. However, we believe that this reflects an aspect of Indian culture—specifically, the tendency to have many supervisors in an Indian organization.

Specialisation   There is a relatively high degree of specialisation. There are a limited number of different jobs and each involves a relatively narrow range of tasks. The jobs correspond to the three phases of the work: the pick-up of filled tiffins from and the return of empty tiffins to homes; train transportation of tiffins between residential and commercial districts; and the delivery of tiffins to and pick-up of tiffins from receivers (workers). A consequence of high specialisation is increased task interdependence, hence the need for coordination mechanisms, such as standardisation, to accomplish end results.

Complexity   The Trust is low in all types of structural complexity. Vertical complexity is low because the organization is flat; horizontal complexity is low because there are a limited number of different jobs in the organization; geographical complexity is low because the organization is at one site only.

Staff   Professionalism is also low. There is very little formal education or employee training required for the work of contractors or carriers. As for personnel ratios, the administrative ratio is quite low, perhaps zero. There are only two line members (contractors) who have, as their additional responsibility, the completion of the staff functions of the organization.

Contextual Dimensions

There are four contextual dimensions—organizational size, organizational technology, external environment, and goals and strategies. Some of the salient features of the Trust in these areas are:

Organizational size   The Trust has some 5,800 members, making it a large-scale operation.

Organizational technology   The technical complexity is low, as the Trust's organizational technology is labour intensive (uniform inputs, pre-coded inputs, and few exceptions). Technical uncertainty is also low (variability in tiffins is low). The principal form of technical system interdependence is sequential interdependence across the three phases of work (mentioned earlier) and with pooled interdependence within phases. This specific form of organizational technology is associated with low structural complexity and output standardisation as an effective coordination mechanism, both of which we have observed.

External environment The external environment is regarded as relatively stable by the Trust even though there are competitors in their task environment that are cutting into their business. Customers are the primary focus and they are satisfied with the service they are receiving. Nevertheless, consistent with our description of changing values towards meals, the customer base is shrinking because street vendors and restaurants offer active competition.

Goals and strategies Although strategies and goals are a central concern of organizations, the only stated goal we gathered from interviews with contractors and tiffin carriers was to continually provide this service in the best possible manner. The lack of strategic interest is even reflected in their passive approach towards threats to the very survival of their business.

A TYPICAL JOURNEY

To understand how the exchange and delivery of food take place (in other words, the activities involved in the supply chain), one of the co-authors accompanied the tiffin carriers on their daily routes. Before describing the process in detail, we will present an overview. The process has three phases: the pick-up of the tiffin and its delivery to a train station, the train transportation of the tiffin to its final destination, and the delivery of the tiffin to the customer. This process occurs twice daily: from home to office and the tiffin's return from office to home.

We will now describe a typical journey by following the tiffin of Raj Ramaswamy, a fictional accountant, on its daily trip from his home to office and back.

Step 1 Raj's tiffin carrier, who we call tiffin carrier 1, knocks at approximately 10 a.m. on Ramaswamy's door. He is not wearing a watch. He quickly gets the tiffin from Mrs Ramaswamy and sprints down the stairs. His daily route covers 38 apartments (38 tiffins) spread over a 2-mile radius. Each tiffin has a different symbol as each is bound for a different destination.

Step 2 At approximately 10:30 a.m., Raj's tiffin is transferred to tiffin carrier 2, who has been collecting all the tiffins with yellow characters. As tiffin carrier 2 pedals off to a nearby train station with his collected tiffins, tiffin carrier 1 continues to go from apartment to apartment to get lunch boxes that will soon be collected by other carriers.

Step 3 At the railway station, different collectors have deposited hundreds of tiffins. From them, tiffin carrier 3 quickly removes all of those with a red dot, Raj's included. He loads his consignment on a 'tray', a wooden crate 2.5 m long. A typical tray loaded with 40 tiffins has a total weight of more than 60 kg. The carrier puts the tray on his head and runs to the platform just as the train rolls in. Raj's tiffin is now one of thousands riding this train into the city. Different characters on the tiffins tell the carriers at which stations en route they must pass on specific tiffins to other waiting carriers. The yellow alphanumeric character and the red dot on Raj's tiffin tell the carrier its destination is Churchgate Station, the hub of commercial Mumbai.

Step 4 At Churchgate Station, Raj's tiffin enters the last phase of its journey. Tiffin carrier 4, waiting on the platform, picks it out together with other lunch boxes marked with similar characters. The second and third characters of the symbol indicate its exact destination: the Express Towers building at Nariman Point. By 12:30 p.m., the carrier has carried his tray up four flights of stairs and left Raj's lunch box, along with the others, outside the customers' offices.

At 2 p.m. the morning's delivery service tracks down the above steps in reverse, using exactly the same symbols that moved the tiffin forward previously. Tiffin carrier 1, now at the receiving end of the line, brings Raj's tiffin back to his wife at 4 p.m., guided to her house by the last character of the symbol. Of course, the exact location of the house is part of the memory database of tiffin carrier 1.

Logistics Perspective

The logistics systems that have an exact one-to-one correspondence with the tiffin carrier system of Mumbai are the mail and parcel delivery systems in the United States of America and other countries. These systems have unique customer–supplier pairings for each delivery. Postal or parcel delivery systems are typically modelled as hub-and-spoke systems. Here, all letters/parcels are first flown to a hub and then flown to their destination from the hub. These are multi-billion-dollar systems that employ the latest technology for receiving and tracking deliverables. Major efficiencies are supposedly obtained through the hub-and-spoke structure of the logistical system. Despite large capital investments, highly sophisticated technologies, mature postal systems (zip codes and all), and other well-established identifications, these systems yield low delivery reliability and are unable to individualise operations. In contrast, the tiffin carrier system of India invests pennies, uses a very crude identification system, uses virtually no technology, and relies mainly on untrained, grossly under-educated (if not illiterate) personnel to obtain great delivery reliability and customer satisfaction.

The tiffin carrier system is a conjoined structure that falls squarely under arborescent systems. It involves the transfer of some 200,000 lunch boxes, collected every day from an equal number of sources, and delivered to some 80,000 destinations the same day within a time window of 3 hours. The error rate of this system is remarkably low (less than 1 per cent) and it accomplishes its goals at the rate of pennies per customer per day. In the US, large logistical systems that involve material transfer of the order of the lunch carrier system are generally reduced to a hub-and-spoke structure (e.g., Federal Express, American Airlines) to gain efficiencies of time. They are also supported by state-of-the-art technologies, including computerized decision-making that exploits artificial intelligence and a very sophisticated telecommunication system. Their operating costs are typically in millions of dollars. By contrast and as noted, the tiffin carrier system uses virtually no technology (other than the trains and bicycles), is limited to face-to-face communication, employs virtually no computers, and is about as informal as a system this size can be. What is particularly notable is the coding system to identify lunch boxes: it consists of just three to four symbols. Moreover, on-the-job training of operators is often accomplished within 2 days, which includes learning the delivery process and the specific locations of some 40 dwelling units of customers. Yet, it registers an outstanding performance on both counts—cost and reliability of delivery. That is, it operates literally at pennies a day per customer. It operates at a remarkably low error rate of less than 1 per cent, where errors include not only non-delivery within the time window, but also loss and breakage of lunch boxes. The tiffin carriers' error rate compares favourably with the error rates of lost suitcases at various airlines.

CONCLUSIONS

Our case study of a prosaic business supports two important principles. First, culture affects organizational form and functioning, human resource management, and the development of logistical systems; that is, it can result in systems that are not fully 'Western' in form and functioning. This leads to the second principle—a labour-intensive, technologically unsophisticated logistical system can be as efficient and as effective as a technologically sophisticated (Western) logistical system of the same design. The tiffin carriers are the unsophisticated counterparts of such sophisticated courier services as Federal Express and United Parcel Service, all of which are conjoined logistical system, i.e., where material is transferred from multiple sources to multiple destinations. We found that an organizational and logistical system that fits its cultural and geographic 'niche' can survive and, more importantly, prosper. And, in special cases where employee dedication results from family values, as is the case with the tiffin carrier system studied here, the performance could well be stunning!

Questions for Discussion

1. What are the main learnings from the case?
2. What team and inter-team processes are reflected in the operation of the dabbawala system?
3. How has the dabbawala system responded to the changing context of the life of office-goers in Mumbai?
4. Which behavioural sciences are relevant for understanding the dynamics of the dabbawala system?

NOTES AND REFERENCES

1. Sherif, M. and C.W. Sherif (1953). *Groups in Harmony and Tension*. New York: Harper and Row.
2. This section is adapted from Alagaraja, Meera and Larry Dooley (2002), 'Origins and historical growth of human resource development: A global perspective', in U. Pareek, A.M. Osman-Gani,

S. Ramnarayan, and T.V. Rao (eds), *Human Resource Development in Asia: Trends and Challenges*, pp. 101–8. New Delhi: Oxford & IBH.

3. Clark, D. (1999). *A Time Capsule of Training and Learning*, http://www.nwlink.com/~donclark/history/history.html.
4. Swanson, R.A. (ed.) (2001). 'Origins of contemporary human resource development', *Advances in Developing Human Resources*, 3(2): 120–121. Thousand Oaks, CA: Sage.
5. Swanson, R.A. and E.F. Holton (2001). *Foundations of Human Resource Development*. San Francisco: Berrett-Koehler.
6. Nadler, Leonard (1984). *The Handbook of Human Resource Development*. New York: John Wiley & Sons.
7. Roethelesbegger, G. and W. Dickson (1939). *The Manager and the Worker*. Cambridge, MA: Harvard University Press.
8. McGregor, D. (1960). *The Human Side of Enterprise*. New York: McGraw-Hill.
9. Maslow, A. (1954). *Motivation and Personality*. New York: Harper.
10. Khandwalla, P.N. (ed.) (1988). *Development: A New Role for the Organisational Sciences*. New Delhi: Sage.
11. Cyert, R.M. and J.G. March (1963). *A Behavioural Theory of the Firm*. Englewood Cliffs, NJ: Prentice Hall.
12. Simon, H.A. (1976). *Administrative Behavior*. New York: Free Press.
13. Roethelesbeggar and Dickson. *The Manager and the Worker*.
14. Dale, E. (1952). *Planning and Developing the Company Organisation Structure*. New York: American Management Association.
15. Emery, F. and E. Trist (1960). 'Socio-technical system', in C. Churchman and M. Varhulst (eds), *Management Sciences: Models and Techniques*, Vol. 2, pp. 83–97. London: Pergamon.
16. Maslow. *Motivation and Personality*.
17. Blauner, R. (1960). 'Work situation and individual trends in modern society', in W. Cutman and S.W. Lipset (eds), *Labour and Trade Unionism*. New York: Wiley; also see Argyris, Chris (1957), *Personality and Organisation*, New York: Harper.
18. Emery and Trist. 'Socio-technical System'.
19. Mitra, S.K. (ed.) (1972). *A Survey of Research in Psychology*. New Delhi: ICSSR.
20. Pareek, Udai (ed.) (1980), (1982). *Survey of Psychological Research in India*, 1971–1976. Part 1, 2. Bombay: Popular Prakashan.
21. Pandey, J. (2001). *Psychology in India Revisited: Developments in the Discipline*. New Delhi: Sage.
22. Lynton, Rolf P. and Udai Pareek (2000). *Training for Organisational Transformation*, 2 volumes. New Delhi: Sage.
23. Sinha, A.K., S. Singh, and A. Shukla (1986). 'Structure of locus of control in Indian executive is different', *Psychological Studies*, 31: 130–5.
24. Parker, J.C. and L.J. Rubin (1966). *Process as Content Curriculum Design and the Application of Knowledge*. New York: Rand McNally.
25. Freire, P. (1977). *Cultural Action for Freedom*. London: Penguin.
26. Government of India (1956), Second Five-Year Plan, pp. 22–23.
27. Freire, P. (1977). *Cultural Action for Freedom*. London: Penguin.
28. Freire, P. (1973). *Education for Critical Consciousness*. New York: Seabury Press, 1998.

2
Changing Context

LEARNING OBJECTIVES

After studying this chapter, you will be able to
1. Describe the changing profile of people associated with organizations
2. Discuss the impact of globalization on individuals and organizations
3. Explain the concept of and forces contributing to flattening of the globe
4. Review the wide impact of information technology on various aspects of life
5. Examine the various aspects of diversity and privacy in relation to organizations
6. Discuss the importance and implication of social responsibility and ethics

We are experiencing dramatic changes in the Indian society. There has of late been a drastic reduction in hierarchy, affecting relationships in the family as well as in organizations. In the past, there was a relational distance between parents and children. Today, parents are much closer to their children, and the relationship is friendly rather than hierarchical. This is also true in teaching institutions and organizations. Teachers and students in good schools, colleges, and institutions are now closer to each other than in the past. In many Indian organizations, people from different levels and different age groups now address each other by first names, indicating the breaking down of hierarchical feeling in relation to position or age. This has brought about more openness, with some uncomfortable consequences for 'senior' people, who may have different expectations. But, on the whole, it has led to better working relationships.

Today, an increasing number of young people are in need of work, yet there is a reduction in the number of jobs. Unemployment has also resulted from an outdated educational system, which has become irrelevant and does not cater to the changing needs of society. Higher education is in a crisis, and most universities produce students who are not prepared to undertake the responsibilities required in a fast-changing society. As a result, we have a strange and anomalous situation in which increasing unemployment is accompanied by an increasing number of unemployable individuals. Several organizations and institutions need highly competent people, who are in short supply, whereas the large number of people graduating from universities and other educational institutions do not fulfil the requirements for these roles. This has also resulted in unethical practices such as 'stealing' qualified and competent people from sister organizations. Several recruiting agencies also encourage people selected by them for a certain organization to join another organization after some time. Since the main system (of universities and colleges) does not respond to changing needs, parallel systems like those of the IITs and IIMs have emerged to meet these needs. The establishment of autonomous institutions is indicative of the failure of the main system of higher education.

The present context of work organization is changing very fast. Lawler[1] contrasted the 'old logic' with the 'new logic' with regard to this. Exhibit 2.1 summarises his main suggestions on the 'new logic'.

Exhibit 2.1 *Lawler's Propositions on Old and New Logic*

Old logic	New logic
• Organization is a secondary source of advantage	• Organization can be the ultimate competitive advantage
• Bureaucracy is the most effective source of control	• Involvement is the most effective source of control
• Top management and technical experts should add most of the value	• All employees should add significant value
• Hierarchical processes are key to organizational effectiveness	• Lateral processes are key to organizational effectiveness
• Organizations should be designed around functions	• Organizations should be designed around products
• Effective managers are the key to organizational effectiveness	• Effective leadership is the key to organizational effectiveness

Unfortunately, there is resistance to the radical thinking and solutions required to deal with problems both in organizations and in society. Traditional thinking still dominates (with the exception of some particularly effective organizations). Although the government is undergoing changes, in spite of its declared commitment to administrative reforms, it is dragging its feet on implementation. It is like the proverbial huge elephant that finds it difficult to run fast when in danger. So also, it is generally hoped that the traditional solutions will prove sufficient to a society coping with changes.

CHANGING PROFILES OF EMPLOYEES AND CUSTOMERS

As already mentioned, there has been a drastic change in the profile of people joining organizations (employees) and those benefiting from the services of organizations (customers). Both employees and customers are now better informed and better educated because of the available choices, which are increasing every day. Both are highly demanding and are beginning to almost dictate to organizations.

Employees are impatient—the best and brightest people look for organizations that will foster their personal growth and help them to feel empowered so that they have a sense of ownership, both psychological as well as actual (control over what needs to be done in the organization). Expectations are changing. Bright young individuals who join organizations want assignments that are challenging and that allow them to prove themselves. Young people today are taking major responsibilities in some organizations and are innovating new practices. Young people today want to take their own decisions. Their values are changing. While 'loyalty to the organization' was highly valued in the past, young people today value their own growth and the growth of their careers more. As a result, there is high mobility of employees and, unless an organization makes special efforts to provide an attractive working environment, they tend to move on to another organization that may seem to provide such opportunities. In India the demand for efficient employees is increasing, resulting in increased salary levels (see Exhibit 2.2).

Exhibit 2.2 *Expected Salary Hikes*

According to the BT-Gallup survey of 43 companies across six high-interest sectors, employees in these sectors can expect average salary hikes of 13–15 per cent (in nominal terms, not taking into account the inflation rate) this year. And that is just the average hike. In some cases, such as senior management of telecom and IT companies, the hike will be 20 per cent, translating into average pay hikes of more than Rs 29,000 and Rs 28,000 per month, respectively. Add to that the performance-linked pay—often more than 30 per cent of the total pay at senior levels—and it adds up to quite a bit. The significance of these hikes becomes evident when seen in the backdrop of projected salary movements in other countries, especially in the Asia Pacific region. Various salary projections made by different organizations in the recent past have indicated that India is likely to be the only country in the region where double-digit salary growth will happen for the next few years. China, which had been clocking double-digit salary growth in the recent past, is now expected to witness single-digit salary hikes.[2]

GLOBALIZATION

Globalization is the process of economic integration at the international level. Multinational companies (MNCs) are helping this process. The information technology and aviation industries have demolished geopolitical boundaries. It is no longer possible to have a 'national' IT or aviation company. With the whole world being converted into a single global marketplace, individuals and organizations buy raw material, technology, services, and resources from the provider who offers high quality with low price. In this respect the scarcest and most critical component is human resource. It is extremely difficult to get the requisite competence because of the high competition to acquire that, which is in short supply.

Threats of Globalization

Globalization has been promoted by MNCs, which are primarily Western, and mainly US-based. While globalization has opened up opportunities for products, services, and people to travel to different parts of the world, it has also created problems for developing countries. Because of technological advances, developed countries can manufacture products and provide services at a relatively low cost. As a result, local products and services, mainly offered by small and cottage industries, are going out of business, resulting in multiplying unemployment. Singh, discussing the consequences of globalization for India, notes that globalization is based on the Western world-view, which has been universalistic and positivistic, generalising and even totalising. 'It has tended to treat local, regional, and parochial cultures and their traditions in the non-Western world condescendingly at best and disdainfully at worst. With the emergence of the unipolar world under the domination of the Western capitalism, cultural impact of market and trade relations is further intensified. Culturally globalization involves some kind of homogenisation that basically means Americanisation. The general feeling shared in the developing world is that gains from globalization are going to be negligible, and the only visible impact is likely to be negative for female workers. Some also fear that globalization can further accelerate the pace of feminisation of poverty that in turn will deepen miseries of women, particularly from the underprivileged sections of the Indian society.'[3]

Globalization is being pushed, in fact 'imposed', by the World Bank under American influence, and the national governments under pressure are yielding to this arm-twisting by the World Bank and WTO. Globalization is here to stay. The main challenge before Indian organizations, and those in other developing countries, is how to harness the new trends, and yet retain our basic strengths and preserve our rich tradition of diversity reflected in our cottage industries and local crafts and lifestyles. Globalization is a threat to diversity. For example, we have variations in the taste of cooked foods (*dosa* or *chhole-poori*) in different places. Globalization, in the name of hygiene, may standardise the cooking process on a large scale and we may have the same taste of *dosa* or *chhole* in Shimla and Coimbatore!

Hart[4] has outlined the crisis facing globalization (the child of capitalism). According to him, major markets are slowing down, the environment is going down the drain, many countries are yet to benefit from globalization, and unemployment is rising. Protests against globalization are rising. While the multinationals account for a quarter of global economic activity, the benefits are not spreading wide enough. The multinationals have only a handful of shareholders.

One area that is threatened by globalization is health, mainly of women and children in the developing world. A 50-country survey of government action on women's health carried out in 1999 by the Women's Environment and Development Organization (WEDO), a network of women's groups and activists around the world, pointed out: 'All respondents ... cite economic reforms as paramount constraints in implementing the ICPD Programme. Health sector reform in particular is emerging in most countries as a challenge to expansion of reproductive health services.'[5]

Another survey found that widespread cost recovery schemes and privatisation of health care services 'keep the poorer populations (rural, women, old persons) away from hospitals and health centres. Of the 23 countries surveyed in five geographical regions, 46 were dependent on international aid, but aid donors were reluctant to fund health infrastructure, while structural adjustment requirements were curtailing domestic investment in them.'[6]

Moreover, according to the Asia Pacific Resource and Research Centre for Women 'The new global economic context has badly affected sexual and reproductive health worldwide causing a decline in health education, [increased] delivery of reproductive health services by private doctors, over-priced drugs and the ineffective self-treatment of reproductive tract infections to name a few.'[7]

Women's groups around the world are now well aware that health sector reforms are affecting women's access to health services and that many policymakers are either unwilling or unable to integrate reproductive health services into national health systems. Yet merely calling upon policymakers to do so is ineffective in challenging the interests behind the reforms. Neither does it clarify the reasons why governments have less money for health care, and why politicians believe free markets are the best way to provide health care, nor why the reforms are linked with other global financial and trade processes, agreements, and interests.[8]

Opportunities in Globalization

Globalization also offers great opportunities for growth and development. Britain and India offer dramatic illustration of the effects of deregulation. A series of changes in institutional rules in the 1980s and 1990s have led to Britain becoming one of the most open economies in the world. It is the fourth largest economy, after the US, Japan, and Germany. Deregulation led to dramatic changes in many of Britain's industries. Traditional industries such as steel, coal, and shipbuilding have almost disappeared, to be replaced by a thriving services industry. London is the leading international financial centre in the world. The BAA, formerly known as the British Airports Authority, manages airports in America, Europe, and Asia Pacific. However, well-known British firms such as ICI and Rolls Royce have significantly declined. British Airways, Marks and Spencer, and BT (British Telecom) are all struggling. On the other hand, Vodafone, having acquired an American and a German mobile-phone company, has emerged as the world's top mobile phone company. Deregulation can, therefore, lead to both creation and destruction. New industries may emerge and the old ones may die, and the new entrants may transform the other ones. There is an increasing trend of outsourcing human resource functions (see Exhibit 2.3).

Exhibit 2.3 *Deal between Unilever and Accenture*

Unilever has entered a 7-year HR outsourcing deal with Accenture, to service 0.2 million Unilever staff in 100 countries. The deal size is valued in excess of 1 billion US dollars. The contract covers transactional, administrative, and HR IT systems support for activities such as recruitment and resourcing, reward, training, and performance management.

This applies to Unilever globally and the implementation will take place between the last part of 2006 and 2009. It is learnt that 40 per cent of the global HR community of Unilever will be impacted by this programme, with a major part of the impact expected to take place in Europe and North America. The number is touted to be in excess of 3,000 HR personnel globally.

In India, out of HLL's total strength of 20,000 employees, 200 are in HR.

However, India could benefit from the fact that of the various Accenture centres that will be servicing Unilever under this programme, Bangalore will play a key role.

The outsourcing programme is part of the company's One Unilever initiatives to increase leverage of its scale, improve its marketplace competitiveness, deliver functional excellence, and create a more competitive cost structure allowing it to focus on its consumers and customers.

(Contd)

Exhibit 2.3 (*Contd*)

> Unilever intends to minimise the impact on people through staff transfer to Accenture, early retirement, exploring alternate roles, natural attrition, and voluntary programmes. By outsourcing functions such as human resources to Accenture, Unilever would benefit from increased efficiencies, decreased costs, and greater global standardisation.[9]
>
> India offers a more dramatic example of industry creation and change as a result of deregulation. The IT industry in India is made up of firms that provide hardware and peripherals, software and training. Firms specialising in software include firms that provide software products and those that provide software services. In 2002–03, the total turnover of this industry was roughly 18 billion US dollars. Software services accounted for 75 per cent of this turnover. Within software services, exports contributed to 60 per cent of the turnover. In other words, export-oriented software services sector dominate the industry. The software industry is comprised of firms that undertake software projects and firms that offer IT-enabled services (ITES) such as call centres, processing credit card, and back-office transactions.[10]
>
> Indian organizations show evidence of increasing global aspirations. Exhibit 2.4 gives some information about the global workforce in some Indian organizations.

Exhibit 2.4 *Global Workforce in Some Indian Firms*

Company	Total employees	Global employees		
		Total	Senior most	Junior most
Tata Motors	22,000	950	Senior R&D engineer	Shopfloor worker
Asian Paints	4,600	1,400	Country manager	Paint factory worker
Bharat Forge	5,300	1,800	CEO, Int. business	Shopfloor worker
Dr. Reddy's Laboratories	7,000	7,000	Executive vice president	Medical representative
Infosys Technologies	46,196	1,300	Head, consulting business	Intern
Mahindra & Mahindra	25,000	487	Country manager	Shopfloor worker
Ranbaxy Laboratories	9,000	1,600	CEO	Medical representative
Sundram Fasteners	1,700	500	Country manager	Shopfloor worker
Tata Consultancy Services	55,000	4,000	Head, consulting business	Intern
Wipro	46,000	270	Head, consulting business	Programmer

Following its vision to establish itself as India's first discovery-led global pharmaceutical company, Dr. Reddy's Laboratories' branded formulations are spread across 38 countries, organized into seven regions: India and other SAARC countries; Russia and the member states of CIS; South Africa; Central Eastern Europe, Middle East, and rest of Africa; member states of ASEAN; Latin America; and China. A little more than half of its revenues come from India and the remaining from international operations. Expatriates play a critical role in the business expansion of Dr. Reddy's—in business development, culture building, strategic planning, and operational support.

FLATTENING OF THE GLOBE

Drastic changes are taking place in the world, leading to what Friedman calls its 'flattening'.[11] Friedman's main criterion of globalization is the integration of the world—breaking of boundaries of the nations and countries. According to him there have been three phases of globalization. Historically, the first phase, Globalization 1, is pre-1800. Although Friedman attributes the starting date of the first phase to Columbus' discovery of the new world, there is enough evidence to show that there were large-scale movements across nations in the old and the ancient world—India, China, Greece, Egypt, etc. Anyway, Globalization 1 was nation-driven, the driving force being the muscle power—army, weapons, horsepower, etc. It was inspired by religions or imperialism. Globalization 1 reduced the world from large to medium size. The second phase, Globalization 2, from 1800 to 2000, was MNC-driven, the driving force being hardware—technology, from steamships and railways to telephones and mainframe computers. Globalization 2 reduced the world from medium to small size. The third phase, Globalization 3, is post-2000, driven by individuals, the driving force being software. It has reduced the world from small to tiny size, flattening the playing field at the same time. But Globalization 3 not only differs from the previous eras in how it is shrinking and flattening the world and in how it is empowering individuals, it is different in that Globalization 1 and 2 were driven primarily by European and American individuals and businesses. Even though China actually had the biggest economy in the world in the eighteenth century, it was Western countries, companies, and explorers who were doing most of the globalizing and shaping of the system. But going forward, this will be less and less true. Because it is flattening and shrinking the world, Globalization 3 is going to be more and more driven not only by individuals, but also by a much more diverse—non-Western, non-white—group of individuals. Individuals from every corner of the flat world are being empowered. Globalization 3 makes it possible for so many more people to plug and play, and you are going to see every colour of the human rainbow take part.

Globalization has been advanced by new ways of sourcing resources, distributing products and services, and accelerating information exchange. We shall examine these in this section.

Sourcing

Sourcing is the process of identifying, conducting negotiations with, and forming supply agreements with customers and vendors of goods and services. It is concerned with managing resources—augmenting, expanding, leveraging, inviting, or contracting them out. In this section we shall discuss four strategies of sourcing.

Outsourcing

Outsourcing is the regular use of an external third party, instead of internal resources, for functions like production of a single operation, a product or an entire line, shipping and order fulfilment, product design, network infrastructure support, etc.

Outsourced functions are normally outside an organization's core competencies and are done to reduce cost and lead time, improve quality, or achieve some other advantage.

Outsourcing is used by different companies to reduce costs by transferring portions of work to outside suppliers rather than completing it internally. It is an effective cost-saving strategy when used properly. In 2003, some 25,000 US tax returns were done in India. In 2004, the number was 100,000; in 2005, it was around 400,000. One can then assume that in a decade the American accountant has outsourced the basic preparation of tax returns. The positive side, according to Friedman, is that the accountant who wants to stay in business in America will be the one who focuses on designing creative complex strategies, like tax avoidance or tax sheltering, managing customer relationships.

It is sometimes more affordable to purchase a good from companies with comparative advantages than it is to produce it internally. For example, Videocon gets components for its Bazooka model from the semiconductor unit of Philips India, although the two companies are competitors in the market. Another example is of the two brands of tomato puree, one of Godrej Foods and the other Kissan brand of Hindustan Lever Ltd, produced at the Godrej factory in Bhopal—using tomato paste from their competitor, Nestle! These are like, but not strictly, outsourcing.

Outsourcing is a business decision that is often made to lower costs or focus on core competencies. Outsourcing involves transferring a significant amount of management control to the supplier. Buying products from another entity is not outsourcing, but merely a vendor relationship. Outsourcing always involves a considerable degree of two-way information exchange, coordination, and trust.

Functions typically outsourced include information technology, human resources, facilities and real estate management, and accounting. Some organizations even outsource personnel training. The logic is that training not being the core business of the organization, it cannot afford to develop high-quality trainers and training infrastructure and may find outsourcing training by signing a memorandum of understanding (MoU) with good training or management organizations advantageous. Several companies have signed such MoUs with the Management Development Institute, Gurgaon.

On the negative side, product quality suffers. However, the outsourcing organization has the freedom to move back an outsourced function if its profits suffer as a result of poor quality. In fact, many American companies like Dell have moved their customer services division back to the US because of poor quality. The decision to outsource is like any other decision—like the decision to expand a business overseas, to incorporate computer technology, or to hire new workers. If the company does it correctly, it benefits from higher profits.

It has been reported that for every dollar spent on outsourcing to India, the US reaps between US $1.12 and US $1.14 in benefits. Large software companies such as Microsoft and Oracle have increased outsourcing and used the savings for investment and larger domestic payrolls. About 70,000 computer programmers lost their jobs between 1999 and 2003, but more than 115,000 computer software engineers found higher-paying jobs during that same period.

The main criticism is that since 'outsourced' workers are not actually paid employees of the company, they are likely to have low loyalty to the organization, as also low work ethic. Therefore, quality levels of customer service and technical support of outsourced tasks are lower than those of the internally performed ones.

Outsourcing appears to threaten the livelihood of domestic workers. This is especially true for high-tech workers. Outsourcing is criticized as representing a new threat to labour, contributing to high worker insecurity, and reflective of the general process of US-led globalization.

There are also security issues concerning companies giving outside access to sensitive customer information. In April 2005, a high-profile case involving the theft of US $350,000 from four Citibank customers occurred when Indian call centre workers in Pune acquired passwords to customer accounts and transferred money to their own accounts opened under fictitious names. Citibank did not find out about the crime until the American customers noticed discrepancies with their accounts and notified the bank. In another case, Intel discovered and fired 250 Indian employees after they faked their expense reports. The firings followed from Intel's internal Business Practice Excellence programme of expenses claims. The report concluded that fraudulent practices such as 'faking bills to claim your allowances like conveyance [and] drivers' salaries were some common malpractices in India. Intel would not put up with such fraud. NASSCOM, which is a forum of IT and ITES companies, has attempted to address these fraud concerns in India by creating the National Skills Registry. This database contains personal and work-related information, enabling employers to verify a staff member's credentials and allowing police to track the background of workers. However, it is worth noting that outsourcing-related fraud is insignificant, and that such malpractices can occur in any country. For example, 40 million credit card numbers were stolen in June 2005 at CardSystems Solutions in Tucson, Arizona, US. In December 2005, nearly 50 people were indicted in connection with a scheme that bilked at least US $200,000 from Katrina Relief Fund at Red Cross claim centre in Bakersfield, California, which handled calls from storm victims.

While outsourcing is a useful device to get high-quality service at a lower cost, it should be done with care. It is also necessary to examine the loss to the organization from outsourcing. For example, outsourcing training may deprive an organization of internal competence at capacity-building, which could have indirectly boosted competencies related to the core business. The organization should also consider the 'loss of control' over operations caused by outsourcing. For example, by outsourcing recruitment, the organization may lose its 'feel' of the current cohort of young people and the opportunity of seeing potential employees in their own setting.

Outsourcing therefore requires detailed planning, not only from the point of view of quality and cost, but also from the point of view of knowledge management— competencies the organization wants to develop and retain. Outsourcing will certainly stimulate development of a new industry in specialized services. However, competence of organizations in developing and delivering specialised services will also be needed in the future.

The following guidelines are suggested for outsourcing to be successful.

1. Consider the reasons behind initial outsourcing. Outsourcing must be done principally to enhance the customer experience.
2. Examine the values prevalent in outsourcing supplier. If these are 'at odds' with the outsourcing company, then the customer-facing staff will never be able to develop crucial relationships with customers as they will be pulled in opposing directions.
3. Scrutinise customer metrics that reflect outsourcing company values and customer needs. Ensure that metrics are not simply those that are easy to do but those that truly reflect what is important to customers. The easy stuff does have value but not in isolation. As the outsourcing company, choose independent measurers. Their experience may help both parties. Consider paying for metrics independently of contract. This reduces potential for internal conflict in supplier. Review results with supplier in a 'no blame' manner but insist on positive action. Include in reviewing body all strata from supplier to gain best feedback. Ensure metrics immediately, reward good performance, and penalise poor performance. Review team reports and staff survey results with supplier at least biannually.
4. Appoint an internal relationship manager or team to oversee relationship. Insist on 'instant' accesses by your relationship manager or team to ensure openness. Work with HR of outsource supplier to ensure that your team has the types of people to whom your customers respond best.

Insourcing

Insourcing may be described as 'imbedding' specialists at client locations, where they perform specific tasks. In a way, insourcing is the opposite of outsourcing. Outsourcing and insourcing can both be described generally as the acquisition of internally required resources obtained from an external source. While in outsourcing the external resources are used at the latter's location, in insourcing the external agency operates at the client's location. For example, in freight transportation management, the following outsourced services are fairly common: freight bill auditing of both pre- and post-management reports; loss and damage claim handling; and transportation purchasing. Outsourcing firms perform these services, as well as others, at their locations; whereas the insourcing firm would deliver the functional programmes at the client's site. Outsourcing tends to be exclusive, that is, client interaction is typically limited to processing and rules questions raised by the vendor. On the other hand, insourcing is inclusive and these firms interact with their clients in order to lead the market through innovation and continuous programme improvement.

According to Friedman, insourcing came about because once the world went flat, the small could act big—small companies could suddenly see around the world. Once they did, they saw a lot of places where they could sell their goods, manufacture their goods, or buy their raw materials in a more efficient manner. But many of them either did not know how to pull all this off or could not afford to manage a complex global supply chain on their own. Many big companies did not want to manage this complexity, which they felt was not part of their core competency. Nike would rather spend its cash and energy designing better tennis shoes, not supply chains. This created a whole new global business opportunity for traditional package delivery firms like UPS.

In 1996, UPS (United Parcel Service) went into the business of 'synchronized commerce solutions'. It has spent 1 billion US dollars since then to buy 25 different global logistics and freight-forwarding firms so that it could service virtually any supply chain from one corner of the flat earth to the other. The business took off right around 2000 ... UPS engineers come right inside your company; analyze its manufacturing, packaging, and delivery processes; and then design, redesign, and manage your whole global supply chain. And, if necessary, they'll even finance parts of it, such as receivables and COD payments ... UPS oversees the whole journey from factory to warehouse to customer to repair. It even collects the money from customers if need be. This form of deep collaboration, which involves a huge amount of trust and intimacy among UPS, its client, and its client's customers, is a uniquely new flattener.[12]

It is a totally new business, but UPS is convinced it has an almost limitless upside. Though margins are still thin in this kind of work, in 2003 alone, insourcing pulled in 2.4 billion US dollars in revenues for UPS.

Multisourcing

Multisourcing is 'the disciplined provisioning and blending of business and IT services from the optimal set of internal and external providers in the pursuit of business goals.'[13]

Take the case of one international petrochemical firm that decided every department should first consider outsourcing certain services before any new expenditure could receive the go-ahead. Three years on, an independent audit revealed that the firm had no less than 500 separate outsourcing agreements that, on average, were costing 20 per cent more than the going rate.

In another instance, a government agency, with much fanfare, entered into a deal with an IT services provider, to which many of the agency's staff were subsequently transferred. Six months into the contract, it became apparent that some departments within the agency were still vehemently opposed to the idea and had found ways to order equipment and services from elsewhere. Thanks to a fixed-price contract, the agency was paying nearly double what it could have been for services it was no longer able to provide in-house. The deal had to be re-negotiated at even greater cost.

Opensourcing

Opensourcing is the act of releasing software under an open source/free software license. The intellectual common form of opensourcing has been common in the academic and scientific communities. Self-organized collaborative groups of scholars have created networks to share new information and knowledge for free.

One example of opensourcing is Wikipedia, the multilingual web-based free-content encyclopaedia. Volunteers write it collaboratively, allowing most articles to be changed by anyone with access to a web browser and an Internet connection. The project began in 2001, and is operated by the non-profit Wikipedia Foundation. Wikipedia has more than 3,700,000 articles in many languages, including more than 1,000,000 in the English-language version. Since its inception, Wikipedia has steadily risen in popularity, and has started several sister projects. Editors are encouraged to uphold a policy of 'neutral point of view' under which different perspectives are summarised without an attempt to determine an objective truth. Jimmy Wales, the co-founder of Wikipedia, has called it 'an effort to create and distribute a multilingual free encyclopaedia of the highest possible quality to every single person on the planet in their own language.' There are over 200 language editions of Wikipedia, around a hundred of which are active. Meanwhile, Jimmy Wales is expanding into Wiktionary, a dictionary and thesaurus; Wikibooks, textbooks and manuals; and Wikiquote, a book of quotations. He says he has one simple goal: to give 'every single person free access to the sum of all human knowledge.'

Although the free software movement was, and remains, inspired by the ethical ideal that software should be free and available to all, and it relies on open-source collaboration to help produce the best software possible to be distributed for free, linkages have been established between creators of open-source software and commercial firms. We shall give examples of four open-source ventures.

The most popular open-source venture is Apache, the open-source web-server community. It was created by Brian Behlendorf. Apache started with eight people who trusted each other, and as new people showed up at the discussion forum and offered patch files to be posted, trust expanded, and eight grew to over one thousand. Apache was the first open-source project to get attention from the business community and get the backing from IBM.

Because of Apache's proficiency at allowing a single-server machine to host thousands of different virtual website, it began to have a commanding share of the Internet service provider market. Apache was free—and a better technology. So IBM eventually decided that if it could not beat Apache, it should join Apache. At IBM's expense, its lawyers worked with the Apache group to create a legal framework around it so that there would be no copyright or liability problems for companies like IBM that wanted to build applications on top of Apache and charge money for them. The Apache collaborators did not set out to make free software. They set out to solve a common problem—web serving—and found that collaborating for free in this open-source manner was the best way to assemble the best brains for the job they needed done. The one thing the Apache people demanded in return for their collaboration with IBM was that IBM assign its best engineers to join the Apache open-source group and contribute, like everyone else, for free. Today Apache is one of few most successful open-source tools, powering about two-thirds of the websites in the world.

Behlendorf started a new company called CollabNet in 2004, to promote the use of opensourcing as a tool to drive software innovation within companies. 'Our premise is that software is not gold. It is lettuce—it is a perishable good,' explained Behlendorf. 'If the software is not in a place where it is getting improved, over time, it will rot.' What the open-source community has been doing, said Behlendorf, is globally coordinating distributed software development, where it is constantly freshening the lettuce so that it never goes rotten.[14] Behlendorf's premise is that the open-source community developed a better method for creating and constantly updating software. CollabNet is a company created to bring the best open-source techniques to a closed community, i.e., a commercial software company.

'CollabNet is an arms dealer to the forces flattening the world,' said Behlendorf. 'Our role in this world is to build the tools and infrastructure so that an individual— in India, China, or wherever—as a consultant, an employee, or just someone sitting at home can collaborate. We are giving them the toolkit for decentralized collaborative development. We are enabling bottom-up development, and not just in cyberspace … I like the way Irving Wladawsky-Berger, IBM's Cuban-born vice president for technical strategy and innovation, summed opensourcing up: "This emerging era is characterized by the collaborative innovation of many people working in gifted communities, just as innovation in the industrial era was characterised by individual genius." '[15]

Another example of opensourcing is the Linux operating system. In 1984, according to Wikipedia, MIT researcher and ex-hacker, Richard Stallman launched the 'free software movement' along with an effort to build a free operating system called GNU. To promote free software, and to ensure that its code would always be freely modifiable and available to all, Stallman founded the Free Software Foundation and something called the General Public License (GPL). The GPL specified that users of the source code could copy, change, or upgrade the code, provided that they made their changes available under the same license as the original code. In 1991, Linus Torvalds, a student at the University of Helsinki, building off Stallman's initiative, posted his Linux operating system to compete with the Microsoft Windows operating system and invited other engineers and geeks online to try to improve it—for free. Since Torvalds's initial post, programmers all over the world have manipulated, added to, expanded, patched, and improved the GNU/Linux operating system, whose license says anyone can download the source code and improve upon it but then must make the upgraded version freely available to everybody else. Torvalds insists that Linux must always be free. Companies selling software improvements that enhance Linux or adapt it to certain functions have to be very careful not to touch its copyright in their commercial products.

Delivering

A related issue is delivery of goods and services. Cutting-edge processes have been developed recently for delivering new products and services efficiently and faster. We shall review them in this section.

Supply chaining

Supply chaining is the process of horizontal collaboration of value creation among suppliers, retailers, and customers. There has been substantial research on collaboration in manufacturing. 'Supply chaining is both the effect and the cause of the flattening of the world—it is enabled by the flattening of the world and is an important flattener itself, because the more these supply chains grow and proliferate, the more they force the adoption of common standards between companies (so that every link of every supply chain can interface with the next), the more they eliminate points of friction at borders, the more the efficiencies of one company get adopted by the others, and the more they encourage global collaboration.'[16]

An excellent example of supply chaining is that of Wal-Mart of US. 'Just one company, Hewlett-Packard, will sell four hundred thousand computers through the four thousand Wal-Mart stores worldwide in one day during the Christmas season, which will require HP to adjust its supply chain, to make sure that all of its standards interface with Wal-Mart's, so that these computers flow smoothly into the Wal-Mart river, into the Wal-Mart streams, into the Wal-Mart stores.'[17] 'No company has been more efficient at improving its supply chain (and thereby flattening the world) than Wal-Mart; and no company epitomises the tension that supply chains evoke between the consumer in us and the worker in us than Wal-Mart.' Wal-Mart has introduced just-in-time inventory programme that reduced carrying costs for both the retailer and its suppliers. As its latest supply chain innovation, it has introduced RFID (radio frequency identification microchips), attached to each pallet and merchandise box that comes into Wal-Mart, to replace bar codes, which have to be scanned individually and can get ripped or soiled. 'In June 2003, Wal-Mart informed its top one hundred suppliers that by January 1, 2005, all pallets and boxes that they ship to Wal-Mart distribution centres have to come equipped with RFID tags ... RFID will allow Wal-Mart to track any pallet or box at each stage in its supply chain and know exactly what product from which manufacturer is inside, with what expiration date. If a grocery item has to be stored at a certain temperature, the RFID tag will tell Wal-Mart when the temperature is too high or too low etc. Thanks to the efficiency of its supply chain alone, Wal-Mart's cost of goods is estimated to be 5 to 10 per cent less than that of most of its competitors.'[18]

According to Nishith Srivastava,[19] the importance of supply chain in India can be gauged from the fact that logistics cost is in the range of 10–12 per cent of our GDP. As per the recent CMIE (Centre for Monitoring Indian Economy) database, over 1 trillion rupees of total capital is tied up in inventories in industrial sector. This is close to 22 per cent of aggregate industry sales. Besides this, all the industry brands are already in the Indian SCM sector. Srivastava feels that the entire process of supply chain management can be outsourced to India except the actual delivery part. Companies in India can emerge as a back-end support for all the activities starting from planning to execution, i.e., setting up the virtual infrastructure (technology based), providing back-end support for the operations, and finally handling the execution. Factors like low cost and IT expertise would act as a catalyst to make this concept a reality. According to him, India very soon will be a hot destination for supply chain process outsourcing (SCPO).

Srivastava says that the following aspects/processes can be moved/outsourced to India.

1. *Information integration:* This includes processes like shared demand information, inventory status, capacity plans, production schedules, promotion plans, demand forecasts, and demand schedules, etc.

2. *Workflow coordination:* Streamlining workflow activities among supply chain partners could be made possible by workflow coordination of a host of activities encompassing procurement, order execution, engineering change, design optimisation, and financial exchanges.

3. *Technology assimilation:* Entire supply chain integration can be based on a platform of technology-enabled network solution for sustained future prosperity. Supply chains should access the market through both physical and cyber-based channels to serve the needs of the consumer. Both channels should accentuate e-commerce features to distinguish the supply chain in the eyes of the customer. Thus, all these cyber-based support can be easily outsourced to India.

4. *IT-based tools for synchronisation:* IT companies in India are already creating customised IT solutions for supply chain industry in the US and Europe, which are used in various phases in a supply chain network in these companies.

However, as there has been a concern on outsourcing due to BPOs and emerging KPOs, companies and their executives would certainly not accept this concept immediately, but companies would acknowledge that this move could save lots of money as well as enhance their supply chain network.

Some recent books[20] have spelled out various forms of collaboration in manufacturing and have provided background and guidelines on how to use the concepts.

Offshoring

Offshoring is the process of moving a part of an organization from its country location to another country location. The very same product is produced in the very same way, only with lower cost because of cheaper labour, lower taxes, subsidised energy, and lower health-care costs. While outsourcing is arranging with another company to perform some specific in-house function such as accounting, research, training, etc., and then reintegrating their work back into the overall operation, offshoring is moving one whole factory offshore to another country. Offshoring became popular after China's joining the WTO. Friedman says that just as Y2K took India and the world to a whole new level of outsourcing, China's joining the WTO took Beijing and the world to a whole new level of offshoring—with more companies shifting production offshore and then integrating it into their global supply chains.[21]

In the 1980s many investors, particularly overseas Chinese who knew how to operate in China, saw an opportunity of using China's disciplined labour to manufacture products there and sell them abroad. According to Friedman, this dovetailed with the interests of China's leaders. China wanted to attract foreign manufacturers and their technologies—not simply to manufacture 1 billion pairs of underwear for sale in China but to use low-wage Chinese labour to also sell 6 billion pairs of underwear to everyone else in the world, and at prices that were a fraction of what the underwear companies in Europe or America or even Mexico were charging.

According to Friedman 'once that offshoring process began in a range of industries—from textiles to consumer electronics to furniture to eyeglass frames to auto parts—the only way other companies could compete was by offshoring to China as well (taking advantage of its low-cost, high-quality platform), or by looking for alternative manufacturing centres in Eastern Europe, the Caribbean, or somewhere else in the developing world.'[22]

In-forming

Google symbolises the power of in-forming, a new tool in flattening the globe. Google is a major search engine and has triggered development of several sites that are used by all types of people in diverse languages to search all types of information. Never before in the history of the planet have so many people—on their own—had the ability to find so much information about so many things and about so many other people.

Said Google cofounder Russian-born Sergey Brin, 'If someone has broadband, dial-up, or access to an Internet cafe, whether a kid in Cambodia, the university professor, or me who runs this search engine, all have the same basic access to overall research information that any one has. It is a total equaliser. This is very different than how I grew up. My best access was some library, and it did not have all that much stuff, and you either had to hope for a miracle or search for something very simple or something very recent. When Google came along, suddenly that kid had "universal access" to the information in libraries all over the world.

'That is certainly Google's goal—to make easily available the entire world's knowledge in every language. And Google hopes that in time, with a PalmPilot or a cell phone, everyone everywhere will be able to carry around access to all the world's knowledge in their pockets.'[23]

'The Internet is growing in the self-services area, and Yahoo! Groups exemplifies this trend,' said Jerry Yang. 'It provides a forum, a platform, a set of tools for people to have private, semiprivate, or public gatherings on the Internet regardless of geography or time. It enables consumers to gather around topics that are either impractical or impossible offline.'[24]

INFORMATION TECHNOLOGY

Information technology has invaded the world and is having the greatest impact on organizations. It has developed and grown at an unprecedented rate. Hardware is becoming obsolete almost every fourth year. The application of IT has exploded now into e-commerce, pushing globalization further.

Computational Capacity

IT is applicable in almost every human activity and organizational function. Its application has been greatly helped by developments in hardware and software, making it affordable for most users. The cost of computer processing has been falling by an estimated 30 per cent a year in real terms. Moreover, information technology has speeded up decision making and information sharing. The new culture of openness—the result of greater accessibility of information—has empowered individuals and groups. The central and state governments, for example, have given their attention to the right of information through use of information technology. The Web has made all new development in various fields accessible to all people in the world.

Diverse Application

In India, communication has been greatly facilitated by IT. The Internet and intranets have helped fast information sharing and processing. Cellular phones have multiplied at a fantastic rate. Teleconferencing has also helped in interpersonal and intergroup interactions and discussions. These have cut down delays and expenses in 'bringing people together' over long distances.

IT has also enriched education and training. Distance education, supported by IT, has great scope in India. Community-based IT facilities in the villages and interior parts of the country have tremendous potential for accelerating the rate of literacy and education in India. Panchayati raj can be made more effective with increasing connectivity of all village panchayats with the district-level and state-level functionaries.

Media and research have also benefited greatly from IT. E-publishing is making a large number of publications accessible to a larger number of people. Most journals now have electronic editions and a large number of new developments are being put on websites. It is now very easy to read the latest publications and download relevant writings and information.

E-business has been spreading quite fast too. Consumers can buy products through the Internet. The Indian Railways has made bookings so easy that a customer can get all information about alternative trains to a destination, book a place on the one of his/her choice, pay through a credit card, and get the ticket delivered at his/her doorstep. While business-to-customer (B2C) transactions have been a major focus of e-business, business-to-business (B2B) electronic transactions have also been increasing at a fast rate. It is estimated that B2B transactions are about five times more in volume than B2C.

Limitations

While IT has been impacting organizations and society in general, its use in India and other developing countries is highly restricted because of the high cost involved in replacing fast-changing technology. The gap between those who have access to technology and those who do not (because of its cost) is widening. Moreover, IT has reduced face-to-face and group interactions. Reading habits are changing. People are becoming more restricted in their reading habits (helped by the Internet) and wide exposure to liberal education has been declining. Answers have to be found to these issues in order to make IT serve more organizations and people better. Organizational behaviour experts face the challenge of harnessing IT and yet retaining the richness of interpersonal and intergroup interactions that make the world more human.

DIVERSITY

Diversity has emerged as an issue because of imbalanced representation of diverse groups in the workforce. India has not only been a diverse society, it has valued and celebrated diversity. The term 'synergic pluralism' has been suggested[25] to describe Indian culture, citing examples and legends of how diverse religious and ethnic groups coming from outside, such as Parsees, Jews, and Christians, were made welcome and encouraged to maintain their identities, even while integrating with the social mainstream. India is the only country in the world to have enacted legislation on reservation quotas for the underprivileged sections of the society (termed scheduled castes, scheduled tribes, or backward classes).

Diversity has become an issue because of several reasons. There is an increasing realization in India that we need to include in the workplace, in a planned way, people from those sections of the society that are under-represented. Legislation and various commissions monitoring implementation of the laws are pressurizing organizations to examine the composition of their workforce. The World Bank and the WTO are also putting pressure on paying attention to diversity. Even consumers in Western countries are bringing about such pressure. For example, they may boycott certain imported products whose manufacturers use discriminatory practices, or under-employ some sections of the society. With globalization and the entry of Indian companies into the global market, attention to diversity has increased. Moreover, there is increasing evidence that diversity is a competitive advantage for a firm, enhancing productivity and profitability.[26] Organizations paying attention to diversity are also more likely to attract and retain talented people.

Bases of Diversity

There are several bases of diversity: demographic (age, gender, education), social (religion, language, region, caste, tribes, physical and mental handicaps), and ideological (different ways of perceiving issues).

The demographic profile in India is changing very fast. Younger people are entering the workforce. Because of the spread of education, legislation, and social movements, more women and more members of minority communities are being employed by organizations. Organizations are finding that physically and mentally challenged persons can be valuable human resources for specific jobs.

Diversity is important at all levels. While in many organizations diversity is ensured at the lower levels (workers and office staff), there may be no diversity at the top or higher levels. Attempts are now made to consider diversity while composing the administrative board of an organization, though not much attention is being paid to the higher levels.

One diversity issue is the ratio of women executives at different levels of an organization. A CII study on women empowerment in the workplace has shown that instances of women leaving an organization is only 7 per cent against the whopping 59 per cent for men. Yet, only 45 per cent women reach the junior management level, and only 2 per cent become senior managers. Surprisingly, recruitment of women employees is at par with that of men in most companies.

So why do so few women reach the top? According to Anu Aga, chairperson of CII's national committee on women empowerment, it is not just plain discrimination; one of the biggest factors listed by the respondents in the study was family responsibilities. The organizations in the study, however, accepted that men were preferred in certain departments. As many as 75 per cent did not want women in production functions, while 24 per cent felt sales was not women's forte. And while the reasons for this ranged from security concerns to company policy, the most revealing one was the HR conception that women were just not competent enough.

Diversity is also linked with human rights. Exhibit 2.5 shows the role of the UN in promoting cultural diversity.

Exhibit 2.5 *Human Rights and Cultural Diversity*

Promoting and valuing cultural diversity is an important factor in maintaining peace, stability, and prosperity around the world. It has been a cornerstone of international law since 1945 that the best way of managing the complex inter-relationships between cultures within states is through the realisation of universal human rights. The 1948 Universal Declaration of Human Rights (UDHR), the source of subsequent UN human rights law, affirmed that universal human rights were the foundation of 'freedom, justice and peace in the world'.

Neither human rights nor the structures and processes that oversee them are Western inventions. People from all regions, and representing many political, economic, cultural, and religious traditions, drafted the UDHR. As more and more non-Western states have joined the UN, the UN as a whole has repeatedly reaffirmed and elaborated diversity of its people and that cultural differences are no excuse for human rights violations. The 1993 Vienna Declaration and Programme of Action affirmed that the universality of human rights was 'beyond question'. People's basic human needs transcend cultural differences. Speaking in Iran in 1997, UN Secretary-General Kofi Annan said:

'When we talk of human rights being a Western concept, doesn't the Iranian mother or the African mother cry when their son or daughter is tortured? Don't we all feel when one of our leaders is unjustly imprisoned? Don't we all suffer from the lack of the rule of law and from arbitrariness? What is foreign about that? What is Western about that?'

Human rights advocates from Nelson Mandela to Aung San Suu Kyi have echoed Mr Annan's point. Whatever their cultural, religious, ethnic, or national background, people all over the world want to realise their human rights and to enjoy participatory and representative government and the rule of law. Further, the universal human rights are set out in the UDHR. Much of today's international human rights machinery was initially proposed and championed by non-Western states.

Inclusive and participatory systems of governance can be critical to promoting cultural diversity. At the same time, there is no single model of realising universal human rights or of establishing good governance. It is right that the policies and structures of a state should address the cultural, religious, ethnic, and national characteristics.

Promoting Diversity

Diversity needs to be promoted in organizations in a planned manner. Several approaches can be adopted in this respect. Some values and behaviours promote diversity. Empathy, openness, democratic values, and supportive behaviour help to develop a mindset conducive to diversity. Special training programmes can also develop such a mindset. The Education Resources Centre in New Delhi under the Campus Diversity Initiative (CDI), for example, has been organizing 3-day programmes to develop a diversity-oriented mindset in colleges and universities all over the country. The programme consists of instruments,[27] exercises, dialogues, games, action planning, etc. The CDI programmes are based on the idea that diversity in organizations has to start with the individual, who needs to develop an internal locus of control, be optimistic, and examine his/her functional and dysfunctional behaviour in order to develop plans for changing himself/herself. Emphasis is placed on cooperation (intrateam) and collaboration (interteam). The sharing of images, by learning about and appreciating the strengths of other groups, etc., can break stereotypes. Training can be a powerful tool for promoting diversity.

Diversity will be promoted only if diversity in views and points of view is encouraged. P.P. Gupta, chairman of CMC Ltd, had a managing director with views quite different from his. During discussions, he included the MD to ensure that diverse views are shared before taking any decision. Organizations that encourage dissent and debate will develop a culture of leveraging diversity.

Mentoring can also help in changing mindsets towards seeing diversity as a competitive advantage. Bright young people need mentoring for dealing with emotional issues they face during their initial period in the organization. The mentors themselves should have a positive attitude towards diversity and need to use dialogue to help young people examine issues of diversity.

The organization can, of course, take steps to ensure recruitment of a diverse workforce. The HR department should take the leading role in this regard by monitoring compliance with diversity-related laws, periodically surveying diversity-related attitudes, organizing debates and discussions, including diversity as an issue in training programmes, etc.

RPG Enterprise uses its diversity and size to create knowledge links among its 35 group companies. The company holds an off-site conference every year, where managers from its 35 companies assemble to compare individual performance on 12 specific parameters—e.g., purchase management, energy saving, and pricing strategy. This exercise helps to identify the best performers in the group, so that others can benchmark these practices. The presentations are followed by site visits.[28]

The UK-based Holset Engineering Company, also known as Holset Turbochargers, a technology leader in the manufacture of turbochargers for the mid-range and heavy-duty diesel engine market, has operations in the UK, the US, China, India, Brazil, and Holland. A wholly owned subsidiary of Cummins Inc., Holset partners with several global manufacturers of diesel engines around the world. The company is committed to a very strong business case for diversity, both visible (like gender, race, nationality) and invisible (religion, skills, experience). The organization believes that the broadest scope of diversity in the workplace helps innovation, problem solving, and creativity, all critical ingredients for success in a highly competitive environment. Holset also believes that the organization should reflect the diversity in the population of the countries in which it operates. Naturally, expatriates become an essential part of Holset's corporate ideology.

PRIVACY

Privacy has emerged as an important social as well as organizational concern. A recent number of a well-known journal[29] has been devoted to this topic. Privacy has emerged as an issue because of the fast-expanding information technology that has made it possible to intrude into the privacy of individuals.

Concept of Privacy

Privacy has been defined as 'control over transactions between person(s) and other(s), the intimate aim of which is to enhance autonomy and/or to minimise vulnerability'.[30] There are two main theories of privacy: one that focuses on privacy as a process of regulating levels of social interaction, the other that focuses on the states (types) and functions of privacy.[31] Two categories of privacy are relevant for our purpose: employee privacy and consumer privacy.

Employee Privacy

The main issue of employee privacy relates to the employee records maintained by an organization. These are maintained in relation to selection, placement, promotion, assessment, etc. While the employees may approve such practices, there is concern about the handling and use of such information. In a survey, about 40 per cent of corporations reported that they lacked policies regarding briefing of employees about the types of records maintained on them, the use of such records, and disclosures to government enquiries. Stone-Romeo et al. have reported three studies on the invasion of privacy resulting from 12 common selection procedures.

Procedures such as electronic performance monitoring (EPM) can also involve computer-assisted surveillance. The American Management Association found that 19 per cent of companies taped phone conversations, 15 per cent stored and reviewed e-mails, and 34 per cent used video cameras to monitor employee activities.[32] Yet EPM is also used to monitor work performance. Stone and Stone have discussed such issues of employee privacy.

Consumer Privacy

Consumer privacy has been discussed as a conflict between the interest of businesses to collect and use personal information to their competitive advantage and the consumers' feeling that such collection and use of information is unfair and constitutes an invasion of privacy.[33]

Consumer privacy as a social issue has its roots in technological advancements.[34] 'Sophisticated software for mining increasingly large databases of personal information is used to create electronic profiles of individuals. These profiles allow customised marketing of goods and services (or, in principle, of ideologies, policies, and candidates).' The use of fair information practices (FIPs) has been advocated to balance both business and consumer interests by providing the consumer with control and voice. Three approaches to implementing FIPs have been suggested: legislation and regulation, industry self-regulation (such as third-party assurance), and technological solutions.

Regarding the fair exchange of personal information, the non-monetary exchange of personal information, based on FIPs, in return for better service, discounts, etc. is preferable.[35] However, consumers should share the financial benefits that result from the commercial use of their personal information. Consumer privacy is likely to become a still more important issue with increasing use of sophisticated methods of tracking and mining personal information in developing countries.

SOCIAL RESPONSIBILITY AND ETHICS

While work organizations, especially corporates, are using all facilities available in the society for their growth, they need to reciprocate by doing something for the societies where they exist and benefit from. This need is reflected in the concept of corporate social responsibility (CSR). CSR has been defined in several ways. A good definition of CSR is a company's commitment to operating in an economically, socially, and environmentally sustainable manner, while recognising the interests of its stakeholders, including investors, customers, employees, business partners, local communities, the environment and society at large.[36] Some definitions combine internal and external obligations: 'CSR is the continuing commitment by a business to behave ethically and contribute to economic development while improving the quality of life of the workforce and their families as well as of local community and society at large.'[37] Some other definitions also balance profit making and social concerns and action, like 'achieving commercial success in ways that honour ethical values and respect people, communities and the natural environment,'[38] or 'business decision making based on ethical values, compliance with legal standards and respect for communities, their citizens and environment.'[39]

Saxena and Gupta state that 'CSR should be defined by not just the concerns and aspects it covers presently, but also the issues that are likely to come up in the future, and as mentioned, by the importance that consumers gain in relation to the responsibility taken. The definition of CSR will appear complete if the issues of social justice, distribution of wealth, progress and assets generated out of business avoiding capitalism and strengthening of institutions serving and maintaining the society are also given due consideration.'[40]

Evolution of CSR

The concept of CSR has evolved steadily and the corporate sector has moved from simply being a profit-making business to playing a more active role towards the society—under the influence of social responsibility. In the West the private sector has apparently emerged as 'a key driver of the development paradigm'.[41] However, in India it is the public sector that initiated a systematic approach and developed strategies of CSR. CSR originated in the US in the early part of the twentieth century, when corporations came under attack for being too big, powerful, and guilty of antisocial and anti-competitive practices.[42] To silence critics, two broad principles emerged—the charity principle and the stewardship principle—and they are the foundation stones of the modern concept of CSR.

In the process of exhibiting social responsibility, corporates have undergone the phases of charity, trusteeship, involvement of labour force, recognition to trade unions with participative management, and social welfare interventions.

In recent years both the corporate sector and the civil society organizations, particularly international NGOs, have become more influential in shaping development debates and policies. While there is increasing awareness about the need to demonstrate social responsibility in the corporate sector, among NGOs there is growing acceptance that business is essential to economic growth, which in turn will fuel social development.[43]

Competitive Strategy and CSR

Research has shown that consumers give preference to companies that adopt CSR practices. According to the 2002 Edelmen StrategyOne Survey of Opinion Leaders, 76 per cent of those surveyed would switch to a company with strong CSR practices if price and quality are equal to non-CSR competitors. In the same survey, 75 per cent claimed they would give a CSR company the 'benefit of the doubt' if the company were subjected to negative publicity.

It has been stressed that CSR has the potential to be far more than a public relations ploy or a means to pluck some 'low-hanging fruit' from the corporate efficiency tree. Instead, it can be the strategic engine for long-term corporate profits and responsible social development.[44] In other words, a company's CSR initiative should be aligned with its competitive strategy. The Reinventing Education Programme sponsored by IBM is one of the best examples of how a company can align its CSR initiative with its competitive strategy to maximize the benefits to the society and also create new business opportunities. IBM has developed a teaching model in the Philadelphia school system that uses voice recognition technology to instruct non-English speaking children in their native language. Computers act as personal instructors for these children. This advancement in voice recognition technology has enabled IBM to develop new voice recognition products, which in turn are generating strong commercial interest.[45]

Corporates have experienced a range of bottom line benefits by adopting CSR initiatives like improved financial performance, enhanced brand image and reputation, increased sales and customer loyalty, increased ability to attract and retain employees, reduced regulatory oversight, and easy access to capital.[46]

Alacrity is the undisputed leader among apartment construction companies in Chennai. It has got to that position, with a turnover of more than 1 billion rupees, without ever having paid a bribe or dealt in black money or any other illegal operation. In India at least, a company that has proved it possible to do ethical business and still be a commercial success is an exception.

Launched in 1978, Alacrity is owned by its employees. The undertaking is based on the values of honesty, commitment, and accountability. Today the company is the undisputed leader not only in the fields of construction, but also energy management, health, and education in Chennai.

Alacrity has changed the rules of construction in this city. The company represents a house of trust for the common man. More than 60 per cent of the respondents in a recent market survey in Chennai named Alacrity as their most preferred company.

The company has constructed more than 30 per cent of Chennai's apartments, effectively minimising the problem of housing in this metropolis. Moreover, each housing project undertaken by this company subscribes to the rules of the Director of Development Control, the nodal government agency.

Recalling the nascent stages of this undertaking, Amol Karnad, chairman of the Alacrity group of companies, says, 'The central idea of starting this venture was to bring about a merger between the quality of social life and individual life.'

Not being satisfied with merely running an ethical business, this company has also provided employment opportunities and fair wages for a migrant labour force, thereby, showing that its concern transcends class barriers.

Although there have been problems by way of political pressure and acute competition, the organization has been successful in persisting with its values of discipline, renewal, and commitment. Says a customer who has benefited from the Alacrity experience, 'When you are investing the savings of your life, you need a builder you can trust and we have found one in Alacrity.'

Alacrity has effectively proved that value-based management does not curb profits and that economic growth and social development can go together.

A few brief examples of CSR being used as a competitive advantage are mentioned below while discussing the various dimensions of CSR.[47]

Dimensions of Social Responsibility

Organizations are becoming increasingly aware of their wider responsibilities towards the environment in which they function and are located. Social responsibility relates to several aspects of social life like health, education, community development, and human rights.

Ecology

The Indian cement industry, a potentially high polluter and the country's biggest excise payer after tobacco, has earned praise for its efforts to reduce air pollution and energy use in its manufacturing practices. However, the industry has been criticised for its bad mining practices, in a survey by the Centre for Science and Environment (CSE), a Delhi-based organization.

The countrywide survey, which covered 41 top cement producers across nine Indian states, representing 80 per cent of the sector, resulted in the sector being awarded the CSE's Three Green Leaves eco-award.

The Chennai-based Alathiyur Works, which was awarded the prestigious Four Green Leaves award, is the first plant in India to receive this honour. Gujarat Ambuja Cement Ltd's Gujarat plant bagged the second spot, while the third spot was shared by three companies—J K Lakshmi Cement Ltd, Prism Cement Ltd, and ACC's Gagal Cement Works.

While the cement industry may have scored higher points than the three other polluting industries previously rated for eco-friendly practices by the CSE under its Green Rating Project (GRP)—paper pulp, chlor-alkali, and automobiles—the market leaders in the industry were not the environment leaders. The industry has performed poorly where it has no economic returns, says the CSE. 'The cement industry's better environmental performance in energy and waste-utilisation is not because of environmental concerns but because of better economic returns,' stresses Sunita Narain, director of the CSE.

Grasim Industries Ltd, from the Aditya Birla Group, which has a 22 per cent market share in this booming industry, was rated 'mediocre' by the CSE. The next largest cement company, the prestigious Associated Cement Companies (ACC) Ltd, now jointly owned by multinational Holcim and the Indian Ambuja Group, scored less than 35 per cent marks as a group. However, the group's Gagal plant, located in Himachal Pradesh, was rated the third best plant in the country. The privately owned India Cements Ltd, the fourth largest cement seller in the country, was given the lowest rank. Global cement leader Lafarge could only manage sixth position. The study observes that while the cement industry does not fit the definition of a 'sustainable industry', an 'acceptable trade-off' can certainly be proposed. What the study attempts to do is to benchmark the performance of companies against such a trade-off.

The sector scores high because of certain initiatives taken to reduce air pollution and the fact that it is today one of the world's most energy-efficient sector, more so even than its counterparts in the US or Europe.

The rating found that energy is the sector's biggest production cost, and Indian companies have done a lot to reduce this cost. They have modernised their technology and have focused on producing more blended cement. According to the GRP's assessment, the Indian cement sector (after Japan) is the second most energy-efficient cement sector in the world.

The GRP also found that emissions of carbon dioxide—which leads to global warming—from Indian cement companies are significantly lower than European and American cement companies. 'This is an important message to give out to the developed world, where the general feeling is that India is not doing enough to combat global warming,' says Chandra Bhushan, head of the GRP and associate director of the CSE.

However, the cement industry has been indicted for its bad mining practices. The Indian cement industry spends as little as 4 per cent of its turnover on the cost of its raw material—limestone. 'Since all limestone mines are captive mines of cement plants, and mining regulations are poor, the cement industry is not investing in mine management,' says Bhushan. In fact, the overall sector score for mining is only 24 per cent efficiency, compared to 50 per cent scores in areas in which the sector has done well, such as technology and energy use.

Regulations on the location of mines are poorly implemented—many mines are located close to wildlife sanctuaries and reserve forests. The GRP survey found that 44 per cent of the mines it assessed were located in ecologically sensitive areas.

Mines have also depleted groundwater and led to acute water shortages in some areas, resulting in local communities protesting against the sector. 'Lax and completely ineffective regulations are really to blame for this state of affairs,' adds Bhushan.

The study recommends strong regulatory control over the sector. To begin with, regulators can do away with cheap mine leases and provide incentives for good mine management and disincentive for poor management. The economic benefits of mining must also belong to local communities, whose resources are exported by the sector.[48]

Henkel Spic India Ltd has adopted eco-friendly technologies in the manufacture of detergents, reducing water consumption in the company by 20 per cent. This contributes to the profits of the company, at the same time benefiting the society at large.[49]

The prestigious TERI (The Energy and Resources Institute) Corporate Awards offer a platform for Indian corporate houses to showcase how development concerns can be met with social commitment.

For their outstanding achievement in environmental management and social responsibility practices, 13 companies from among 178 applicants won the esteemed TERI awards in the categories of Environmental Excellence and Corporate Social Responsibility. The awards were announced in Delhi on 27 May 2005.

TERI instituted the Corporate Environmental Awards in 2000–01 to recognise corporate leadership in environmental management. The Corporate Social Responsibility Awards were established in 2001–02 in recognition of good corporate citizenship. TERI's Corporate Awards are known for the recognition they accord to innovative initiatives promoting sustainable development.

The six companies that won the TERI environment awards were Tata International Ltd, Shree Cements Ltd, Sanghi Spinners India, Kanoria Chemicals and Industries Ltd, Akzo Nobel Ltd, and Mecpro Heavy Engineering Ltd.

OIL India Ltd, ITC Ltd, Ballarpur Industries Ltd, ONGC Ltd, TATA Tinplate Company of India, Bhoruka Power Corporation Ltd, the ORCHID—an Escotel hotel are the seven companies that received awards for CSR.

The awards are divided into three categories based on the company's turnover: Category I includes companies with a turnover of less than or equal to 1 billion rupees per annum. Category II includes companies with a turnover of between 1 billion rupees and 5 billion rupees per annum. Category III includes companies with a turnover of 5 billion rupees or more per annum.

Among those nominated, Tata International and Shree Cements won the Corporate Environmental Award in Category III for their projects on hazardous waste recycling and a project to replace conventional fuel with petcoke.[50]

Health

Worldwide 46 per cent of business executives believe that their operations would be adversely impacted by HIV/AIDS over the next 5 years, says a World Economic Forum 2005 Global Health Initiative (GHI) study. By comparison, 'Business and HIV/AIDS: A Healthier Partnership', a forum of the World Bank, says just 7 per cent of Indian companies expect HIV/AIDS to have any serious impact on their operations. Another 18 per cent expect some negative fallout, while 80 per cent do not expect any adverse consequences from HIV/AIDS on their businesses.

The study is based on the responses of over 10,000 executives in 117 countries, including about 100 in India. Of the total of 2,221 companies surveyed worldwide, 42 were Indian businesses.[51]

However, as this report shows, with some exceptions the private sector has yet to adopt a widespread leadership role in the response to HIV/AIDS.

India has more cases of HIV—estimated to be about 5.1 million—than any other country, barring South Africa.

The report says that though 'South Asian and Southeast Asian firms report increasing concern over the effects of HIV/AIDS … and a relatively high proportion of respondent firms have policies to combat the disease, there is a growing tendency towards informal rather than formal responses.'

The report observes that 76 per cent of the Indian companies surveyed claim to have a prevention programme, while only 29 per cent have provision for any voluntary testing against the global average of 33 per cent. In 50 per cent of cases there was no provision for voluntary testing, 45 per cent had no facilities to distribute condoms, and 67 per cent had no treatment programme.

What is most discouraging is that 74 per cent of the Indian companies revealed they had no anti-discrimination policy to protect the interests of HIV/AIDS infected workers.

On the positive side, 14 per cent had an active policy to protect workers, with 10 per cent ensuring access to anti-retroviral treatment, 19 per cent to promotion of condom usage, and 29 per cent to providing voluntary testing facilities.[52]

Education

Holland Tractors has taken the responsibility to fund education and provide employment to one person from each displaced family from the land it acquired for the factory.

Intel's Teach to the Future project involves large-scale training of teachers on how to impart education through computers. It also helps in introducing the same skills at the academic level in teacher-training institutions. In the long run, introducing computers would benefit the company in terms of increasing sales and consumer awareness.

Community development

Nestle's initiative of effective milk collection system, provision of technical inputs, education, and advise to farmers, extension of loans to farmers for purchasing buffaloes and sinking tube-wells, and setting up of welfare projects like drinking water facilities, milk sheds, village schools, and check posts for the police in the area, supply of medicines to the tuberculosis clinic in the town, etc. enhanced business interests and also won the goodwill of the people.

HLL's Project Shakti, launched in the year 2001, integrates its business interests with national interests. Its challenge was to reach the other 500,000 smaller villages in remote parts of India, where there were millions of potential consumers, but no retail distribution network. HLL recruited women from these villages to act as freelance direct sales operators. HLL trained them, delivered its products directly at their doorsteps, and helped them in getting finance for acquiring and selling the company's products. The women would in turn sell the products to their neighbours. This innovative strategy has had a significant impact on the lives of the women. A typical woman entrepreneur, selected and trained under the project, has been able to earn a regular income of more than Rs 1,000 per month. This has improved the status of the women in their families and resulted in an overall betterment in living standards.

Tata Steel shows an interesting example of comprehensive approach to development. If the 'firsts' notched by Tata Steel during the initial years were all in the area of employee welfare, the most significant and pioneering development in recent times has been its social audit, the first ever undertaken by any company in India, in the private or public sector. On 22 May 1979 the TISCO Board approved a proposal to appoint a committee 'to examine and report whether, and the extent to which, the Company has fulfilled the objectives contained in Clause 3A of its Articles of Association regarding its social and moral responsibilities to the consumers, employees, shareholders, society and the local community.' The committee comprising Mr Justice S.P. Kotval, Prof. Rajni Kothari, and Prof. P.G. Mavalankar observed that while Clause 3A had been added only on 28 January 1970, 'It was not as if the Company was about to undertake these tasks for the first time pursuant to the resolution passed. Our examination of records shows that the Article merely translated into a legal obligation what the Company had undertaken to do ever since its inception in 1907 ...'

Russi Mody explains that Tiscare, Tata Steel's involvement not just with its workforce but with people in the larger environment, really springs from the concept that if industry is to make a contribution to society, it must be accepted by that society: 'It's no use your saying that I am good for you. They must say, please come, you are good for me. And towards that end we take the poorest sections of society and try and make them self-reliant. We don't give them charity. We help them to work. We find a market for their produce and so on. And since it is not a welfare activity but a social activity, we insist that all these activities should be at least 25 km away from Jamshedpur ...'

Tata Steel's involvement with the life and problems of the community, which began as early as 1916, has burgeoned into a gigantic, multi-million activity, touching the lives of some 0.4 million people. The Community Development and Social Welfare Department (CDSW), whose function was primarily to help the rural poor who were pouring into the steel township during the initial years, now organizes a comprehensive range of activities encompassing all spheres of community life. The emphasis is on facilitating the development of man. The objective of CDSW is to effect a transformation in the life of the community through programmes that include adult literacy, primary education, cultural programmes, sports training, social integration, small savings, good housekeeping, and economic development. Tata Steel supports self-help efforts of the local population by purchasing a variety of items from them. With time, increasing emphasis has come to be placed on vocational training and self-employment programmes to enhance family incomes.

The community centre is the nucleus of community life in the *bustee* (a self-contained cluster of houses in an urban area). The first such centre was set up at Sonari in 1958. Thirteen more have been added subsequently. Each centre has educational, production, training, and recreational facilities, including playgrounds, gymnasiums, libraries, machines, halls, etc. Not only has the department ensured adequate civic amenities to the bustees, but its involvement with the lives of the employees and their families goes to the extent of organizing classes for housewives on home economics, safeguarding employee pay packets from moneylenders and gambling, organizing courses for youths in carpentry, vehicle and electronic repairs, masonry, and so on. Intensive training courses are also organized for the bustee youth on personality and leadership development. The facilities are open to all and not just to the families of employees.

The volunteer groups, namely Sevadal, Mahila Sevadal, and Yuvakdal, symbolise the spirit of involvement of the community in its own development. As a departmental manager observed, 'These groups have been largely instrumental in bringing about the excellent sense of rapport that exists between the department and the people.'

If CDSW's medical vans provide an excellent support base to the outstanding hospital facilities in Jamshedpur, by treating over 1,000 people every day, the Tata Steel Rural Development Society (TSRDS), registered as a voluntary organization in 1979, reaches out to 0.1 million rural patients annually through its mobile clinics. In fact, TSRDS coverage extends to over 120 villages around Jamshedpur and some 110 villages in TISCO's mines and collieries. The society promotes self-help in the villages through agricultural extension, animal husbandry, community forestry, rural industries, and other programmes including training for upgrading of skills, community sharing of water resources through Pani Panchayats, putting up community halls, and digging wells, as a cooperative effort with the local community.

Jamshedpur is located in a tribal area. A joint committee for Adivasi affairs has been supporting the efforts of the CDSW particularly in the peripheral areas of the steel city. While initially the joint committee brought about the involvement of the grass-roots level leadership of the *adivasis* (aborigines) and of top Tata executives in implementing basic civic amenities in peripheral areas, Mody emphasised the need for improving the quality of life of the tribals. He stressed that it was necessary to inculcate a sense of pride and dignity in the tribals, instead of just providing them economic inputs. A full-fledged Adivasi Welfare Department was constituted in 1983 (harijans were also included in its scope in 1984). Its programmes benefit more than hundreds of thousands adivasis and harijans through some nine centres in suburban and rural areas. Nomads are being housed in resettlements and taught income generating projects like goat rearing, piggery, etc. Eight club buildings provide recreational facilities. Besides being provided educational and sports facilities, adivasi youths are being sponsored for sports and higher educational scholarships and even helped in getting jobs in TISCO.

In all the welfare activities of Tata Steel, the thrust is on creating imaginative avenues for help and self-help in the company's social environment. Commending this performance, the Social Audit Committee observed in its report in 1980: '... the social performance of this Company is of a high order and, in its magnitude, is perhaps unequalled in India.'

The event in recent history that best sums up Tata Steel's commitment to its larger and even global environment involves the eradication of small pox in India for the first time in June 1975.

When there was a breakout of a small pox epidemic in the Chotanagpur Division of Bihar in 1974, WHO sent Dr Larry B. Brilliant to launch an all-out operation for containing and eradicating the dreaded disease. Brilliant met Mody and placed his requirements before him: 50 doctors, 200 para-medical supervisors, between 600 to 900 searchers-cum-vaccinators, 50 vehicles, and innumerable other facilities within 72 hours! The somewhat intimidatory requisition was promptly met—as only TISCO can do—within the time Brilliant had laid down.' Within 6 weeks the epidemic had been brought under control. Other Tata companies joined in the second and third phases of the operation to contain and eradicate the small-pox menace. As the Social Audit Committee put it, 'This was humanitarian work of a high order, the like of which it would be difficult to find undertaken in India by any company—public or private.'

Mody summed up the feelings of the dedicated men and women who had joined in the fight against smallpox when he observed, 'Those who have been involved in the campaign from the beginning have had the rich experience of sharing the sorrows of the downtrodden and poor, of the neglected and forgotten segment of society. Perhaps by their efforts, a line in the history of mankind has been written ...'

One could say that a number of times over about quite a few of the initiatives taken by Tata Steel in the area of welfare and human resource development.[53]

Human rights

All companies, including multinationals, have a responsibility to carry out their business and production processes ethically. They should take into account people's human rights as well as the wider impact a company's operations may have on local communities and environment.

Exhibit 2.6 *Total Ban on Child Labour*

The Indian government has extended a ban on child labour to include the employment of children as domestic servants or in the hospitality sector, including roadside eateries, hotels and resorts, officials said. The government—which earlier banned the employment of children under 14 in factories, mines as well as other hazardous jobs—later also prohibited government workers from employing children as domestic help. The extended ban, which also applies to children under 14, is to be implemented October 10, said the ministry. Spas, motels and other recreational centres have also been barred from employing children. The penalty for flouting the law is a jail term ranging from three months to two years with or without a fine of up to 20,000 rupees. The ban was imposed after a recommendation by the Technical Advisory Committee on Child Labour, which said children in these industries were made to work long hours and undertake hazardous activities that were severely affecting their health and psyches.[54]

Human rights are an integral part of CSR, and the private sector has a clear and important role in the promotion of human rights and can play an important part in their observance. Companies are responsible for not acting in a way that impairs the human rights of their employees or of others on whom their activities have an impact, and should act in a way that actively promotes employees' enjoyment of human rights. It is also often in the company's own interest to work actively on CSR. Child labour and exploitative wages can tarnish a global brand, reduce sales, and harm a company's value. A company with a good human rights record is likely to attract quality employees and keep them motivated and to have a loyal customer base.

India has recently taken steps to eliminate child labour (see Exhibit 2.6).

The UN Global Compact was set up in 1999. It is based on nine core principles covering human rights, labour, and the environment, which are derived from various UN declarations and instruments. It encourages companies to build these principles into their business strategies. By committing to the compact, a company undertakes to uphold the principles and to make an annual report on its performance.

The UK and the US jointly launched the Voluntary Principles on Security and Human Rights for the Extractives Sector in Zones of Conflict in 2000. The principles provide practical guidance to companies on making sure that respect for human rights is central to their arrangements for protecting the security of their personnel and operations in areas of conflict.

The principles were developed in close consultation with oil and mining companies and NGOs working in human rights, labour, and CSR. The original participants were from the US and the UK. The UK participants are Shell, BP, Rio Tinto, Amnesty International, and the Prince of Wales International Business Leaders Forum (IBLF). The Dutch and Norwegian governments joined the process in 2002–03 along with several other companies and NGOs from the US, the Netherlands, and Norway.

In the short term, the principles encourage companies to understand better the environment in which they operate, to improve relations with local communities through dialogue, and to uphold the rule of law. Ultimately, the goal is to create a better environment for sustainable economic investment and ensure respect for human rights.

The principles are the first voluntary guidelines for the extractives sector on security and, as such, they are global and generic. They do not focus on a particular country nor do they present a one-size-fits-all approach to preventing human rights violations. They offer guidelines that can be adapted to local operating environments.

So far, participants have concentrated on integrating and implementing the voluntary principles. Many companies have taken significant steps to integrate them into security practices at their headquarters and on the ground. Human rights and CSR groups have given presentations on human rights training, working with local NGOs and protecting personnel at risk.

In Nigeria, Indonesia, and Colombia, the combination of high levels of foreign investment in oil, gas, and mining with domestic tensions has lead in the past to the types of violent incidents that the voluntary principles are intended to address. The governments of these countries are now working with companies to implement the principles.

This process has demonstrated how governments can help to create a space for business and NGOs to work together in an atmosphere of trust. The voluntary principles are now increasingly seen as a global standard for codes on CSR.

One important issue relates to labour rights, the rights of workers to fair conditions and standards in the workplace. They include the right to work, the right to fair wages, the right to safe and healthy working conditions and reasonable working hours. They are established in the Universal Declaration of Human Rights and International Covenant of Economic, Social and Cultural Rights and set out in greater detail in the Conventions of the International Labour Organization (ILO), the foundations of which pre-date the UN framework.

The UK encourages the private sector to go beyond general compliance with ILO core standards and to lead on issues such as improving employment conditions. Action is most effective when it is voluntary, when it builds on the existing framework of national and international regulations, and when action develops from a partnership between enterprises, governments, and other stakeholders.

Businesses have long acknowledged that competitive advantage can be improved by taking a responsible attitude towards labour rights. Many companies see these rights as a necessary part of developing their global operations. Respect for labour rights not only contributes towards sustainable development, it also enhances brand value. This improves public perception of companies as responsible operators, opens more doors, and creates goodwill. Compliance with labour standards can help improve staff efficiency and morale through policies recognising equal opportunities and diversity, as well as creating a culture of lifelong learning and skills development. Companies that respect labour rights become more conscious of the environment in which they operate and are therefore better at risk management.

At the fifty-ninth session of the UN Commission on Human Rights (CHR), the EU highlighted continuing violations of labour rights as a particularly troubling feature of China's human rights record. The EU tabled a resolution on Turkmenistan expressing grave concern at discrimination against minorities in employment.

Another human rights issue relates to contemporary forms of slavery, defined as 'the status or condition of a person over whom any or all of the powers attaching to the right of ownership are exercised'. Contemporary forms of slavery cover a wide range of human rights violations. A slave is forced to work, owned or controlled by an 'employer', treated as a commodity or bought and sold as 'property', and physically constrained, or has his or her movements restricted. In addition to traditional slavery and the slave trade, contemporary forms of slavery includes forced and bonded labour, the sale of children, child prostitution, child pornography, the exploitation of child labour, the use of children in armed conflicts, and the traffic in human beings. In many cases there are no clear distinctions between the different forms of slavery. The same groups of people are often the victims of several kinds of slavery. Extreme poverty often forms the backdrop to many cases of slavery today.

ILO has estimated that 179 million children are working in the worst forms of child labour—prostitution, bonded labour, trafficking, and hazardous work.[55] For many of them, it is difficult to seek help as they have no birth certificates or other official documents and therefore do not officially exist.

Forced labour is a major issue. Forced labour means forcing a person to work involuntarily, under the menace of penalties such as physical harm, constraint, being indebted to the employer, or having identity documents taken away. Forced labour includes trafficking of women and children for sexual exploitation and labour. The coercive recruitment of forced labourers occurs in many countries in Latin America, in parts of the Caribbean, in Asia, including India. In Europe, trafficking increased dramatically after the break-up of the former Soviet Union.

In most cases, main perpetrators are individuals, organizations and enterprises, feudal landlords and criminals, acting outside the law. Their governments have a clear responsibility to eliminate forced labour and punish those responsible.

The ILO deemed the use of forced labour in Burma to be so serious that in December 2000 it implemented measures against an ILO member for the first time in its history. The UK was, and remains, at the forefront of those supporting the ILO's effort to eliminate forced labour in Burma.

However, action by the Burmese authorities to eradicate forced labour has been slow and insufficient. Despite appointing a full-time ILO liaison officer in October 2002, the Burmese regime has refused to agree an acceptable plan of action with the ILO. Most of the recommendations of the ILO high-level team report of September 2001 remain to be acted upon. The liaison officer noted in March 2003 that although forced labour in central parts of the country has probably decreased, it remains particularly prevalent in areas with a large military presence, especially border areas, where forced labour is widespread and systemic. It is often accompanied by violence and demands for materials, provisions, or cash. The Burmese army routinely uses forced labour as porters. There are reports that forced labour has been used for clearing mines. Forced labourers are often taken away from their families for long periods of time, including at harvest time. There are also credible reports of homeless children and other civilians being forcibly recruited into the army.

A related issue is that of bonded labour. Many millions of people are held in bonded labour around the world. It is especially prevalent in South Asia. There are bonded labourers working in Pakistan's brick kilns and on farms in Nepal. There are young girls repaying loans taken by their parents by working in India's cottonseed fields.

Bonded labour, or debt bondage, has existed for hundreds of years. Today, it is one of the most widely used methods of enslaving people. A person becomes a bonded labourer when his or her labour is demanded to repay a loan. The person is then trapped into working for little or no pay until the debt is repaid. Sometimes whole families are bonded—children bonded in return for loans taken by parents. Bonded labourers are regularly threatened with, and subjected to, physical and sexual violence. They are kept under surveillance, which may include armed guards.

The practice of bonded labour is widespread in India with the figures for bonded labourers varying widely from 5 million to 40 million. This is despite the fact that the practice is illegal—bonded labour is outlawed under the Indian constitution and the Bonded Labour System (Abolition) Act 1976. Whatever the real figures are, it is clear that bonded labour is a serious problem that affects many people. Our High Commission in New Delhi monitors the issue closely and is in regular contact with the Indian National Human Rights Commission (NHRC). A 3-year project of the HRPF funds an Indian NGO, Volunteers for Social Justice. The aim of the project is to strengthen capacity among Indian NGOs to tackle bonded labour and to release and rehabilitate some of India's millions of bonded labourers.

The state of emergency and emerging conflict over the past year in Nepal hampered any previous progress by the Nepalese authorities in eradicating bonded labour. Despite this, 14,000 bonded labourers received land allocations last year and most of them have begun leading lives free of bondage. In January 2003, protests by ex-bonded labourers raised concerns over the size of the land grants—they consider these insufficient to produce a livelihood. The protesters also called for further identification of more groups of bonded labourers who were not identified in the first registration. The government has responded by organizing another registration. The Indian Embassy in Kathmandu continued to support a community radio project (BASE), owned and run by ex-bonded labourers, that broadcasts information on the rights of ex-bonded labourers and how to claim these rights. The international NGO Anti-Slavery International presented BASE (Backward Society Education) with the Anti-Slavery Award in 2002, in recognition of its work in this field.

Millions of Pakistanis remain bonded to employers through debts they can never clear—a decade after the official outlawing of bonded labour. Most bonded labourers work in agriculture, and also in brick kilns, carpet weaving workshops, and the mining, fishing, and service sectors. Inhumane conditions are rife. In Sindh and Punjab, bonded agricultural labourers and brick kiln workers claim they were kept in shackles at night to reduce the risk of them fleeing.

Minority communities are particularly at risk of being subjected to bonded labour, and non-Muslim tribes in Sindh are the most vulnerable. It has been difficult for the authorities to implement the law. Human rights activists point out that the tenancy laws need reconciling with the law on the abolition of bonded labour. Their concern is that tenancy laws permit rent advances to tenants and some landlords use this to legitimise debt bondage of agricultural workers. The Pakistan government has to implement fully the law outlawing bonded labour and provide safeguards on all advances to tenants in order to ensure that employers cannot violate people's basic freedoms of movement and work.

Ethics

A commitment to ethical conduct lies at the heart of CSR. To successfully adopt strong CSR practices, a company must define its ethical principles and reflect on how they impact the company's business practices. An important step in this process is reinforcing ethical conduct among employees through ethics training programmes.

Personal

Suresh Vazirani, chairman and managing director of Transasia Biomedicals, says that he has never paid a paisa in bribes, but that avoiding corruption takes up more of his time than any other issue. Transasia, India's leading manufacturer of high-tech diagnostic machines to check for life-threatening blood diseases, began marketing imported diagnostic equipment in 1985, only branching into manufacturing 8 years later with the help of international manufacturers, such as Sysmex, Wako, and Nittec in Japan, Finland's Biohit, and Trace in Australia. What marks out Transasia is the stance it takes against corruption. When Vaziarani wanted to install a fountain in the lunch area, two officials demanded a US $100 bribe for a 'licence'. It took 4 years in court, and US $4,000, to deal with the case.

Vazirani's interest infighting corruption stems from his 9 years as a volunteer with Moral Re-Armament (now Initiatives of Change), running industrial leadership training courses. There he would urge businessmen not to be corrupt, he recalls. 'That's all very well,' they would reply, 'but you've never run a business. You don't know what it's like.'

He and a friend decided to go into business in 1979 and as the company grew from a modest importer to a global player exporting to over 30 countries, so did the opportunities for corruption. Vazirani risked losing a 20-million-Deutschmarks (12.6 million US dollars) sales contract to Germany because a customs officer wanted a bribe to release imported components. Rather than pay, Vazirani left the components in the warehouse for 3 months. He went to the top customs officials and 'appealed to their sense of national pride'. The components were released just in time.

Recently, a politician suggested to Vazirani that it would be 'an opportunity' if they pocketed part of the World Bank aid the politician had received to improve health. 'Yes, and is it an opportunity if we land up in hospital needing urgent care ourselves?' replied Vazirani. At this, the politician changed his tune, realising that Vazirani was not to be bought.[56]

Another aspect of ethics is sexual harassment at work place. A shocking revelation in a CII study of women empowerment was the lack of a sexual harassment policy in a majority of companies. As many as 56 per cent companies admitted that there was no policy or regulation for sexual harassment faced by their women employees. A staggering 75 per cent did not even consider clients or vendors as potential causes of sexual harassment. However, companies in India are increasingly paying attention to this aspect (see Exhibit 2.7).

Exhibit 2.7 *Some Examples of Sexual Harassment Policy*

Satyam Computer Services
- Zero tolerance policy.
- No employee shall promise, imply, or grant any preferential treatment for engaging in sexual conduct.
- Employees to bring matter to the attention of their supervisor, any member of the human resource department, or any senior manager of the company.
- The company to promptly investigate any allegations in a confidential manner as far as possible and take appropriate corrective action.
- Any employee utilising the complaint procedure will be treated courteously. However, a person knowingly making a false claim shall also be subject to disciplinary action.

Spectramind
- Measures shall be taken to avoid, eliminate, and, if necessary, impose punishment for any act of sexual harassment, which includes unwelcome sexual behaviour.

Hughes
- Sexual harassment may include sexually oriented 'kidding' or 'teasing', 'practical jokes', even comments on gender-specific traits.
- Employees are strongly urged to notify their supervisor and, if appropriate, to contact Chief of Ethics/HRD.

Gillette
- Sexual harassment includes quid pro quo (this for that) favours and the creation of a hostile environment.
- All supervisors and managers are responsible for ensuring that the workplace environment is free of sexual harassment.

Citigroup
- If employees believe they are being subjected to harassment or unwelcome behaviour, they may use the employee hotline numbers that have been established for this purpose by their organization.
- These numbers may be found in each employees handbook or other business publications.
- Citigroup prohibits sexual or any other kind of harassment or intimidation, whether committed by or against a supervisor, coworker, customer, vendor, or visitor.

Bharti Telenet
- Policy applicable to all allegations made against an employee or a third party, irrespective of whether sexual harassment is alleged to have taken place within or outside company premises.
- If the complaint is oral, the same shall be put in writing by the recipient and sent to the president of the company for forwarding to the complaint committee.
- The complaints committee will hold a meeting with the complainant within 21 days of receipt of the complaint.
- The president of the company will ask for an annual report giving full account of such activities and forward a copy to the Ministry of Human Resource Development.

Business

Corporate ethics programmes in the US started in the early 1990s with the development of the US Federal Sentencing Guidelines (FSG). Most companies started ethics programmes to be compliant with the Guidelines. Over the past 10 years, it has evolved from a reactive to a more proactive approach to corporate ethics. In the past year, with the recent failure of many global companies due in large part to ethics violations, it has become obvious that proactively managing corporate ethics is good business and directly affects the bottom line.

Ethics matters because it makes good business sense to 'do the right thing'. Additionally good corporate ethics results in:

- Attracting better talent
- Retaining employees
- Attracting new customers
- Retaining customers
- Creating positive effect on return on investment (ROI)
- Creating positive effect on corporate reputation

SUMMARY

With sweeping changes taking place globally as well as within Indian society, Indian organizations are working in a changed and changing context. Both employees and customers are better informed and more demanding these days. Yet both unemployment and unemployables are increasing in India. Globalization, resulting in free import of foreign products and services, is both posing a threat to the Indian organizations, as well as opening up opportunities for them to go global. The world is becoming 'flatter', by providing level playing through sourcing (out-sourcing, in-sourcing, opensourcing), delivering (supply chaining), offshoring, and in-forming.

Information technology is having a widespread impact on organizations in several ways. Diversity is another emerging issue for organizations, in terms of gender, age, religion, ethnicity, race, community, and regional issues. With increasing sophistication of information technology, individual and group privacy are also emerging as issues that organizations must address. Corporate social responsibility in the fields of ecology, health, education, development, etc., and personal and business ethics are important issues, with behavioural implications.

Organizational behaviour, as a discipline, should take into account these emerging issues in this changing context.

GLOSSARY

B2B business-to-business is a marketing strategy that involves the transaction of goods or services between businesses

B2C business-to-customer is an activity of commercial organizations serving the end consumer with products and/or services

corporate social responsibility (CSR) a company's commitment to operating in an economically, socially, and environmentally sustainable manner, while recognising the interests of its stakeholders

diversity acceptance of, respect for, and exploring differences of race, ethnicity, gender, sexual orientation, socio-economic status, age, physical abilities, religious, political, or other beliefs

e-business business through the Internet

globalization the process of economic integration at the international level

information technology the study, design, development, implementation, support or management of computer-based information systems, particularly software applications and computer hardware

insourcing 'imbedding' specialists at client locations where they perform specific tasks

Internet the computer-based worldwide communications network

intranet computer-based internal communication systems

multisourcing the disciplined provisioning and blending of business and IT services from the optimal set of internal and external providers in the pursuit of business goals

offshoring the process of moving a part of an organization from its country location to another country location

opensourcing the act of releasing software under an open source/free software license

outsourcing buying a function or a service from outside sources

privacy control over transactions between oneself and others, the ultimate aim of which is to enhance autonomy and/or minimise vulnerability

supply chaining the process of horizontal collaboration of value creation, among suppliers, retailers, and customers

teleconferencing discussion among individuals sited over long distances through electronic media

EXERCISES

Concept Review Questions

1. What is globalization? What are the likely consequences of globalization for developing countries?
2. What are the factors contributing to the flattening of the globe?
3. How is information technology impacting society and organizations?
4. How can diversity be promoted in organizations?
5. Why has the issue of privacy become so important today?
6. Describe the main dimensions of CSR.
7. Discuss the importance of personal and business ethics.

Classroom Projects

Sweeping changes are taking place in our economy, society, and government. These changes have a significant impact on organizations and individuals. In small groups of five or six, discuss the changes you have been observing and reading about. List the changes that have significance for business organizations. You will have 15 minutes to prepare a list of such changes. Then report these in the class. The class will discuss them for 15 minutes.

Field Projects

1. Visit an organization and collect information on the composition of its workforce. Discuss with the HR head what action the organization proposes to take to deal with the issue of diversity.
2. Visit another organization and find out which functions/services they outsource and what has been the effect of such outsourcing.

Jain Group of Industries[*]

Shri Bhavarlal Jain (or simply, *Bhau*—the respected elder brother) is the founder-chairman of the 3.7-billion-rupees Jain Group of Industries (JGI). A first-generation entrepreneur, he has come up the hard way. JGI manufactures an impressive range of agriculture-related high-tech products including new seeds and tissue culture products, micro-irrigation systems and plastic tubing for water management, liquid fertilisers, tissue culture, high-yield fruits, and other farm products. Each product enjoys a pioneering status in its industry.

THE PRESENT

JGI is a value-ridden and value-driven company, inside out, which is its strength and weakness. As the financial year 1996–97 came to a close, it was obvious that the company was facing severe problems of cash flows. A great debate was on inside the company whether the company had over-extended its operations.

After a period of terrific growth when group sales jumped from 500 million rupees in 1991–92 to 3.7 billion rupees in 1995–96, the company's various projects were suffering from time and overruns and consequently, huge cost overruns. The finished goods inventory and accounts receivable were at an all-time high. These were the unmistakable early signs of the company in severe cash trouble and products being pushed into markets. Also under microscopic scrutiny was the issue of mergers and divestments for crucial synergy building within the group companies—in which case, the emerging entity would perhaps need a new name, identity, and brand. Senior managers had been requested to send in their suggestions for naming the new combined and trimmed *avatar* of JISL and JPCL.

Between all this, Bhau maintained a cool poise and reassuring confidence. He had seen similar situations before and had pulled out the company and he felt he would be able to successfully pull it off again. The only worrisome part was that this time the magnitude and scale of problems were altogether different. The key values persisted: 'To establish leadership in whatever we do. To leave this world better than we found it. Serving and striving through strain and stress; doing your noblest—that's success.' This vision had been backed by a strong personal work culture system. Placards hung around all over the office stating 'Work is life', 'Work for the pleasure of working ...'

*Case study prepared by Dr Arun Kumar Jain, and published in *Corporate Excellence*, New Delhi: AIMA, 1997, pp. 88–203. Reproduced with permission with slight modifications.

ORIGINS

A farmer's son, Bhau, with some help from relatives, completed his law degree from Mumbai university. He was selected to join one of the civil services. Instead he quit within a month to start a business with a dealership of kerosene and diesel oil of Esso Petroleum in 1962. The next few years were spent in making the ends meet and consolidating a fledging business—but the vision, will, and (unarticulated) strategy were evident and brilliant. Within a decade, Bhau had created a one-stop departmental store for agricultural inputs. At one point, the trading firm had 110 prestigious agencies and distributorships ranging from pumps, seeds, fertilisers, pesticides, PVC pipes to motorcycles, cement, and tractors. Inspired by the quote 'agriculture—a profession of the future', Jain later added micro-irrigation and sprinkler systems.

In 1978 came an opportunity to take over a bankrupt banana powder manufacturing unit at a price of 3 million rupees. Bhau's logic to buy this unit was 'If others can turn it around and make it profitable, why not me with all the assets, resources, and rural background?' Taking over the unit, it was decided that instead of making run-of-the-mill banana products, why not make papain—an industrial enzyme with wide applications in the food and pharmaceutical industries. The competition in the domestic papain market was intense and it was therefore decided to develop ultra-purified papain for the foreign markets, where a monopoly of two or three Western suppliers existed. An in-house R&D unit successfully developed the purification process, wherein the produce received immediate acceptance in the global market. Even today, JISL is the largest supplier of purified papain in the world. For Bhau, it was the taste of his first blood in international markets.

NEW FORAYS

In 1980, Bhau started manufacture of PVC pipes since demand outstripped supply. Initially a second-hand machine was procured and as demand and profits grew, more machines were added. The rigid PVC pipes have a strong resistance to all acids and other corrosive material, are non-toxic, and hence are a good substitute to iron pipes. In time, the strict adherence to quality and delivery has created a brand equity for Jain brand of PVC pipes. Jain Plastics and Chemicals Ltd, started in 1992, has become the largest PVC pipe exporters in India despite a crowded market.

Entry into Micro-irrigation

In 1988, Bhau set up Jain Micro-Irrigation Systems (with 50 per cent own equity and rest from the public) to manufacture micro-irrigation system products (such as sprinklers, flexible plastic tubes, and water and nutrition control components). This was a value-added product, eminently suitable for Jalgaon and Maharashtra climate. But it was new concept in an area that had to be sold to the users who have been brought up on the belief that more water and nutrients means more and better produce. The local farmer had to be educated on the benefits and cost effectiveness of this new technology that essentially minimised wastage since the nutrients went straight to the roots of the plants and did not spill around. The company sponsored and organized a 12-day study tour for interested and progressive farmers in Maharashtra at the time of the Agritech exhibition in Israel. JISL got a boost in 1990 when the Indian government created a subsidy programme for small irrigation systems compensating the farmer upto 50 per cent of the cost. The following year JISL's sales doubled. Major innovations included offering MIS as a complete package, including a survey of the soil and land, and installation of a micro-irrigation system. As a kind of showroom, JISL bought a remote, rocky, barren hill, converting it into an experimental model farm for educating the farmers about the latest innovations in agricultural technology.

The Jain Group has introduced further innovations in the PVC pipe industry. Specialised pipes under brand name Jain Rib-Loc are mainly used as low-pressure gravity pipes for water. Other uses for spiralled pipes are for drains, culverts, sewers, and farm work. These extremely light yet strong and cost-effective pipes are manufactured in collaboration with the world leader Rib-Loc of Australia. Well casing and screen pipes are easy to install and have been introduced for strength and durability and as a substitute for steel. These products are sold in domestic as well as in foreign markets.

Diversification

The company has diversified into fruit and vegetable processing under a joint venture name—Jain Chiquita Food Pvt. Ltd. The project cost for this diversification originally was 480 million rupees that has been overshot due to project delays for various reasons. The group has also moved into granite quarrying and polishing.

The Jain Group also attempted entry into high-tech support services such as information technology, banking, and finance. The latter project was dropped at the gestation stage itself. The company dealing with IT has been suffering from losses and may have to be divested sooner.

Apart from being flush with cash in the aftermath of a successful Euro issue in 1994–95, there are opportunities in processing. For instance, onion is a staple and heavily produced vegetable in the region. Presently, farmers often have to make a distress sale or even destroy the produce in case of oversupply. The huge project for dehydrated onions will not only take care of glut, but also help improve the quality of cash crops and substantially increase farm productivity, thereby, adding to the farmers' income. Farmers would be provided with disease resistant, high-yielding variety saplings produced at Jain Hill Labs through tissue culture in green houses. These plants will be nourished with liquid fertilisers and irrigated through MIS. The final produce will be bought back by JGI. Bhau explains the value chain: There is a link between the past and the future. We started off with seeds but did not stop there. We went further and began dealing in tractors and fertilisers. Throughout the process our customer remains the same. What we are doing is simply supplying integrated inputs. Now what we have started doing is buying back the output and adding value to it.

SUPPORT FRAMEWORKS FOR GROWTH STRATEGY

Research and Development

To give shape to the dreams of Bhau, JGI has created an impressive, state-of-the-art R&D facility, both at the company's farm and factories. On the experimental farm, plant geometry, agronomy, protection, and various other aspects of crop development are studied. The company also undertakes trails and experiments for its new range of products. The farm attracts thousands of farmers from all over the country. In each of the product categories, one theme runs across and that is achieving market leadership through innovation.

Joint Ventures and Strategic Alliances

A key feature of policy at the JGI has been to forge technology partnerships to cut the time barrier for product launches. Towards the end of 1994, JISL had entered into JVs with nine Israeli firms in a variety of agriculture-related areas such as the fabrication and installation of green houses, tissue culture, filtration systems used in micro-irrigation systems, etc.

In December 1994, JGI, along with nine Israeli collaborators, signed an MoU with the Government of Haryana to set up a modern hi-tech research and development farm for demonstrating the advanced Israeli technology. In setting up this facility, the Government of Israel has also promised support through their Centre for International Development and Co-operation in Agriculture.

IN GLOBAL MARKET

Exports have played a critical role in the fortunes of JISL, and as a result have been accorded top priority by the company. Between 1991–92 and 1993–94, while domestic sales grew by 102 per cent, it was exports that permitted the company to grow by a considerably higher 161.1 per cent.

This trend continued through 1994–95, when the total sales for the year went up to 1.44 billion rupees as compared to 922 million rupees during the previous year, representing an increase of 57 per cent. While during this period, the domestic sales increased by 28 per cent from 510 million rupees to 651 million rupees, exports showed an increase of 92 per cent from 412 million rupees to 793 million rupees.

Here the philosophy of leadership at JGI is clear: To consider the entire world as a potential market and to produce a quality that competes with the best in the world.

The company is currently the largest producer of papain in the world, meeting about 20 per cent of the world demand. This was marketed worldwide by Quest International (Ireland), a subsidiary of Unilever Plc.

The largest contributor to exports in the JGI stable presently is the EX-CEL brand of PVC sheets that has penetrated into the exacting markets of Europe and the US. These products account for about 60 per cent of the groups' total exports. The company has developed dealers and distributors in Europe, the US, and Southeast

Asia plus representatives and offices in Austria, Belgium, Hong Kong, and Singapore. The papain and PVC sheet division received the ISO 9001 accreditation by RWTUV, Germany.

By 1995, the company had also opened offices for the distribution of micro-irrigation components in North and South America. Since 1993–94, besides being India's top producer of PVC sheets, JISL was also the country's second largest exporter of PVC pipes.

Jain Irrigation signed an MoU with a South African firm for the manufacture and marketing of their newly invented sprinklers. While JISL in India would manufacture for the worldwide company, marketing abroad was to be done by an overseas joint venture company.

The Future

JGI faced a dilemma. Many of the new projects required a longish gestation period. Also the products were conceptual and often customers needed to be educated on the benefits of the innovation. For the lenders, it was still a million-dollar question, literally: Is it a temporary cash crunch, since most of the new projects should bear cash inflows in about 2–3 years time? Or, has the company over-stretched? Or, is it sheer bad management being unable to handle rapid growth? Or, simply bad investments?

In 1987–88, the turnover of JISL, the flagship company was 20 million rupees. In 1995–96, it exploded to 250 million rupees. In this stupendous growth phase, many past personal values have obviously become irrelevant or even a hindrance for corporate success. There is little doubt that at JISL the incoming generation of entrepreneurs would have to invest considerable time and effort on laying effective management and information systems and on acquiring and developing complex management skills to build upon the solid foundation and to ensure corporate longevity. The restructuring would need drip irrigated, concentrated, and focused nutrition to selected plants, and avoiding spillage and wastage of scarce resources.

The new projects of the Jain Group of Industries include

- Tissue culture (a joint venture with Rahan Meristem in banana tissue culture technology)
- Green houses and seedling nurseries (in collaboration with Azrom Metal Industries, Elder Electronics)
- Liquid fertilisers
- Solar heaters (in collaboration with Amcor Ltd, Israel, for transfer of technology for solar water heating)
- Granite
- Fruit processing (in collaboration with Hovev Agriculture)
- Vegetable dehydration (with technical support from Foodpro International Inc., US)

Questions for Discussion

1. What is the underlying philosophy of JGI?
2. What core values guide the working of JGI?
3. How is JGI responding to the needs of the society?
4. What is the main source of the company's value-centred strategy?
5. How has social concern and social responsibility become good business policy?

NOTES AND REFERENCES

1. Lawler, E.E. (1960). *From the Ground up: Six Principles for Building the New Logic Corporation.* San Francisco: Jossey-Bass.
2. *Business World,* 27 February 2006, p. 33.
3. Dhanagare, D.N. (2003). 'Globalisation: Towards an alternative view', *Sociological Bulletin,* 52(1): 4–31.
4. Hart, Stuart L. (2006). *Capitalism at the Cross Roads.* Upper Saddle River, NJ: Wharton School Publishing.
5. Sadasivam, Bharati (1999). 'After Beijing'. WEDO. http:/www.socialwatch.orglen
6. DAWN (1999). Annual report of Development Alternatives with Women for a New Era; Nair, Sumati, Preeti Kirbat, and Sarah Sexton (2005). 'Population Politics and Women's Health in a Free Market Economy'. *Development,* 48(4): 43–51.
7. ARROW (1999, 2000), Annual report of Asia-Pacific Resource and Research Centre for Women.
8. Richey, L.A. (2002). 'Is overpopulation still the problem?' Global Discourse and Reproductive Health Challenges in the Time of HIV/AIDS. CDR working Paper. 02.1.
9. *Business Times,* 9 June 2006.
10. McClellan, Michael (2003). *Collaborative Manufacturing: Using Real-Time information to Support the Supply Chain.* London: CRC Press.
11. Ideas and material in this and following sections have been borrowed from Friedman, Thomas M. (2005), *The World Is Flat: A Brief History of the Globalised World in the Twenty-First Century,* London: Allen Lane.
12. *Ibid.,* 144.
13. Cohen, Linda and Allie Young (2005). *Multisourcing: Moving Beyond Outsourcing to Achieve Growth and Agility.* Cambridge: Harvard Business School Press.
14. Friedman. *The World Is Flat,* p. 92.
15. *Ibid.,* 92.
16. *Ibid.,* 129.
17. *Ibid.,* 129.
18. *Ibid.,* 134.
19. Srivastava, Nishith (2005) Supply Chain Process Outsourcing (SCPO) in India, published 15 September 2005, *SupplyChainDigest Newsletter Logistics Edition,* http://www.scdigest.com/assets/News/05-09-15.htm.
20. See McClellan Michael (1993). He identifies various forms of collaboration (CPFR is one of four) and provides background and guidelines on how to use the concepts. One of the forms of collaboration is CPFR (collaborative planning, forecasting, and replenishment). CPFR has been a very effective tool in the retail world to reduce stock-outs and to get retail chains in a dialogue with the product manufacturers over product schedules and delivery.
21. Friedman. *The World Is Flat,* p. 115.
22. *Ibid.,* 115.
23. *Ibid.,* 152.
24. *Ibid.,* 184.

25. Pareek, Udai (1992). 'Coercive and Persuasive Power Scale', *Indian Journal of Industrial Relations*, 30(2): 175–89.
26. Luthans, Fred (2002). *Organisational Behaviour*. New York: McGraw-Hill.
27. Purohit, Surabhit (2000). *Self-Development: Instruments for Students, Teachers, Parents*. New Delhi: Tata McGraw-Hill.
28. Dhawan 1996, quoted in Shukla, Mandhukar (1997), *Competing Through Knowledge: Building a Learning Organisation,* New Delhi: Response Books.
29. *Journal of Social Issues*, 59(2) (2003).
30. Margulis, S.T. (1977). 'Conceptions of privacy: Current status and next steps', *Journal of Social Issues*, 33(3): 5–21.
31. Westin, A.F. (1967). *Privacy and Freedom*. New York: Atheneum.
32. Reported by Margulis, 'Conceptions of privacy'.
33. Culhan, M.J. and R.J. Bies (2003). 'Consumer privacy: Balancing economic and justice considerations', *Journal of Social Issues*, 59(2): 323–342.
34. Westin. *Privacy and Freedom*; Culhan and Bies. 'Consumer privacy'.
35. Culhan and Bies. 'Consumer privacy'.
36. Canadian Business for Social Responsibility, 2004. Summit on CSR. Toronto: Canada.
37. World Business Council for Sustainable Development (WBCSD). 'The designability and feasibility of 150 corporate responsibility standards'. Final report, May 2002, www.wbcd.com.
38. Business for Social Responsibility (BSR), a global organization with headquarters in San Francisco, US.
39. Gillis, T. and N. Griffin (2001). 'Doing good is good for business', *Communications World*, 18(b): 23–26.
40. Saxena, Karunesh and Gupta, Divya Kirti (2005). 'Corporate Social Responsibility: A Fad?', *Effective Executive*, pp. 37–42. Hyderabad: ICFAI University Press.
41. Henderson, H. (2000). 'Corporate social responsibility in international development: An overview and critique', *Journal of CSR and Environmental Responsibility*, 10(3): 25–43.
42. Fredrick et al. (1992) quoted in Saxena and Gupta (2005).
43. Henderson (2002). 'Corporate social responsibility in international development'.
44. Hopkins, M. (2003). *The Planetary Bargain: Corporate Social Responsibility Matters*. London: Earthscan Publications.
45. *Effective Executive*, November 2006.
46. Mehta (Proposal 84), referred in *Effective Executive*, November 2005.
47. See imarketing@alacrityhomes.com.
48. To read the entire report go to http://www.cseindia.org/.
49. www.cseindia.org, 16 December 2005.
50. The awards were chosen by a jury chaired by Justice J.S. Verma, former chairperson, National Human Rights Commission, and former Chief Justice of India, and several other eminent personalities. For more information read: 'Indian corporates felicitated for environmental excellence and CSR by Mr Kamal Nath TERI announces corporate environmental awards'. *TerraGreen*, 15 June 2005; *The Financial Express*, 5 June 2005; www.teriin.org, 27 May 2005.
51. See Bloom, David E., B.H. Graig, and P.N. Mahaney (2005), *The Quality of Life in Rural Asia*, London: Oxford University Press. The study had survey inputs from the Foundation for AIDS Research.
52. Indo-Asian News Service, 15 January 2006.
53. Seth, Suhel (2004). 'Jamshedpur is where India is shining'. *Asian Age*, 5 May.
54. *Business Standard*, 2 August 2006, New Delhi.
55. ILO (2002). *A Future Without Child Labour*. Geneva: ILO.
56. Excerpt from *A Change Magazine*, December 2003/January 2004.

3
Societal Culture and Organizations

LEARNING OBJECTIVES

After studying this chapter, you will be able to
1. Explain the concept of societal culture and its importance for organizational management
2. Discuss different approaches to the understanding of societal culture
3. Analyse the functionality or dysfunctionality of cultural characteristics
4. List some strengths and weaknesses of Indian culture
5. Examine the application of a framework of cultural analysis, based on human concerns to management of an organization
6. Develop ways of leveraging culture as well as 'changing' it

Management is the process of achieving results in organized groups. Organizations and groups function in a societal culture; in fact, they are part of the larger culture. Organizations also have their own cultures, which are shaped to a large extent by the larger societal culture. Schein defines culture as 'a pattern of basic assumptions invented, discovered, or developed by a given group as it learns to cope with its problems of external adaptation and internal integration that has worked well enough to be considered valid and, therefore, to be taught to new members as the correct way to perceive, think and feel in relation to those problems'.[1]

We shall define culture as the cumulative preferences of some states of life over others (values), response and predispositions towards several significant issues and phenomena (attitudes), organized ways of filling time in relation to certain affairs (rituals), and ways of promoting desired behaviour and preventing undesirable ones (sanctions). People living in a society by and large imbibe these norms and are guided by them. Organizations have their own rituals, sanctions, values, and attitudes. And the organization being part of a society, most of these are a replica of the societal culture.

Since management is concerned with the achievement of results in an organization, one legitimate concern is the use of cultural elements (attitudes, values, sanctions, and rituals) in the achievement of goals and results. The dilemma before management is whether to design and develop an organization according to the larger societal culture, or to develop a distinct organizational culture that will enable the achievement of results. This dilemma is sharper when the prevailing societal culture is apparently in conflict with the 'needed' culture for getting results. For example, the prevailing culture in a society may be affiliative (valuing good relationships and harmony highest), whereas a new industrial unit set up in the country may need a technological or achievement-oriented culture (valuing achievement of results through meticulous planning highest).

'After all, we need to reconcile the local culture with our modern management practices!'

Two opposing points of view are popular in this matter of organizational management and culture. One view is that management must adapt itself to the societal culture, and management systems and techniques should be rooted in the latter. Japan can be cited as an example of this. The opposite view is that management must establish new values and norms relevant to organizational goals and develop a culture of its own conducive to the attainment of its objectives. Many multinational companies with successful units in several countries are cited as examples. Probably both the views have some merit. Effective organizations cannot remain cultural islands; they must use the main cultural features of the society to design their systems and practices. On the other hand, organizations also need to be proactive, to influence the larger societal culture in ways needed for the society to progress. A significant number of people spend the greater part of their waking lives in organizations, and if they develop new values and norms of behaviour, these values and norms would probably spread to their families and other social institutions, resulting in some change in the large societal culture. How can management systems and processes be designed so that they are relevant to the societal culture, while also using the systems and processes to change some aspects of the larger culture? We shall discuss this in the Indian context. In this section, we shall also discuss three relevant questions about the relationship of social culture and management—how can we understand a societal culture? Is societal culture always functional or dysfunctional with regard to modernisation? How do we deal with the conflict between traditional cultures and modern management practices?

DIMENSIONS OF CULTURE

Culture is reflected in the external life of a society or an organization, as well as in the values and beliefs held by its members. Schein has proposed three levels of variables in a culture.[2]

- Artefacts and creations, which are visible but often not decipherable (technology, art, visible and audible behaviour patterns)
- Values, which indicate greater awareness (both those testable in the physical environment and those testable only by social consensus)
- The deepest level of basic assumptions, which are taken for granted, are invisible, and preconscious (relationship to the environment, the nature of reality, time and space, the nature of human activity, and the nature of human relationships)

The conceptual framework of values of Kluckhohn and Strodtbeck has been quite frequently used in understanding cultures.[3] This comprises five main orientations based on the meaning of human existence, the meaning of human labour and endeavour, the relationship of human beings to nature, time orientation, and our relationship to fellow human beings. These dimensions have been used to propose a continuum. Western (industrialised) culture is at one end, with a masterful attitude to nature, an active and optimistic view of humankind, a model of society built on competitive relationships, and an orientation to the future. At the other end is the traditional culture of non-industrial societies, with opposite orientations. Industrialising societies may be located anywhere on this continuum between these extremes.

Another useful and potential framework is one of power proposed by McClelland,[4] individual orientations being defined by the course of power (external or internal) and the target of power (others or self). This framework can be used to conceptualise typologies of culture. Borrowed from Freud, this framework has been used to study managers' effectiveness. This framework can also be used to understand some other typologies.

For example, the distribution of 'doing' orientation, 'being' orientation, and 'being-in-becoming' orientation can be seen as relevant here. A fourth orientation can be added to these—the 'enabling' orientation, in which active doing by the self is replaced by facilitating action by others. Exhibit 3.1 is an adaptation of McClelland's framework.

Exhibit 3.1 *Frameworks of Power*

Source of power	Target of power	Freud	McClelland	Kluckhohn & Strodtbeck	Typology of culture
External	Self	Oral	Dependent	Being	Expressive
Internal	Self	Anal	Autonomous	Being-in-becoming	Conserving
Internal	Others	Phallic	Manipulative	Doing	Assertive
External	Others	Genital	Serving	Enabling	Expanding

Based on a study of 116,000 respondents of IBM subsidiaries in 70 countries, Hofstede[5] proposed four cultural dimensions—individualism (taking care of oneself and one's immediate family) vs collectivism (distinguishing one's own group from other groups); power distance (the acceptance by less powerful groups of the unequal distribution of power in a system); uncertainty avoidance (a feeling of being under threat in situations and a tendency to avoid them); and masculinity (emphasis on assertiveness and the acquisition of material resources) vs femininity (emphasis on relationships, concern for others, and quality of life). He found developed countries had higher individualism, smaller power distance, higher uncertainty avoidance, and higher masculinity than developing countries.

It may be useful here to consider our main concerns in studying cultures. These relate to coming to terms with nature, our immediate environments (context), time, the collectives we are part of, and natural biological differentiation (sex, as opposed to gender). One other aspect deserving attention is that of coming to terms with power in the collective. The various dimensions of culture can then be derived from these six concerns:

1. **Relationship with nature** Kluckhohn and Strodtbeck have suggested this dimension. In the relationship of humanity and nature, either may be regarded as dominant. If nature is seen as powerful and dominating and human beings as helpless, a fatalistic orientation may result. The opposite orientation, that of scientism, may result from the belief that man can manipulate and change nature. The concept of locus of control is relevant here.

   Fatalism vs scientism If most members in a culture feel helpless in relation to nature, and perceive nature as dominating and beyond human manipulation, an orientation of fatalism may develop. In the contrasting orientation of scientism, nature can be changed and adapted for use by human society.

2. **Orientation to the environment** (**context**) If the environment is seen as structured and unchanging, this may result in a sense of satisfaction in some people. In that case any ambiguity in the environment may be disturbing. On the other hand, some people may like and enjoy ambiguity. This dimension called 'ambiguity tolerance',[6] or 'uncertainty avoidance',[7] is a useful dimension.

   Ambiguity tolerance This aspect, first studied by Adorno et al., has been used by Hofstede who calls it uncertainty avoidance.[8] If members of a collective feel uncomfortable with ambiguity and try to structure situations to avoid ambiguity, their tolerance for ambiguity is low, or 'uncertainty avoidance' is high. Detailed and rigid structures, procedures, uniform behaviour, and belief in absolute truths can help in avoiding ambiguity. When there is ambiguity tolerance, unstructured, vague, and unpredictable situations provide opportunities for using multiple approaches. The following beliefs characterise this dimension of ambiguity tolerance:

   - Several truths may coexist without causing disruptive conflicts. People not only tolerate this, but find the various 'truths' mutually enriching.
   - Deviant behaviours and ideas should be tolerated. These are seen as sources of creativity.
   - Time is seen and treated as cyclic, and as not deserving undue importance. Cultures with low ambiguity tolerance tend to overstructure time.
   - The role of rituals is to achieve order in a society or an organization.

   Another dimension relates to giving importance to the context in understanding the meanings of some phenomena or ignoring the context in a search for clear, universal meanings. The terms 'high context' and 'low context' cultures have been proposed.[9] In high-context cultures, events can be understood only in their contexts, meanings and categories can change, and causality cannot be unambiguously established. Such cultures are context sensitive. The opposite is the case in low-context cultures.

   Contextualism In a high-context culture, the meanings of events, phenomena, and behaviour are interpreted in the context in which they occur. One behaviour (e.g., eating from the same plate with a member of another caste) may be right in one context (in a temple) and not in another context (at home). Such apparent contradictions arise out of the contexts. In a low-context culture, all events and behaviour are judged by one standard, and there is an attempt to evolve universal rules or explanations.

3. **Time orientation** Kluckhohn and Strodtbeck have proposed this dimension relating to orientation to the past, to the present, or to the future. Also, time may be seen either as a collection of discrete units or as a flowing phenomenon.

Temporalness Cultures may differ in their orientation to time. This orientation, called temporalness here, is reflected in the importance given by members of a culture to the present. Past-oriented cultures think highly of and indulge in nostalgia over the past (usually the glory of the past) and are oblivious of the present. Members of a culture with present orientation get involved in the immediate tasks. However, they may not ensure the endurance and continuity of these tasks. They live in discrete time periods, without strong links with the past or the future. In such cultures, more attention is paid to the immediate, and members are able to easily switch from one task or group to another one.

4. **Orientation to collectivity** The relationship between the individuals and the collectives to which they belong has two dimensions—primacy and identity.

   If the individual is seen as more important than and independent of the collective, an orientation of individualism may result. If the collective is seen as primary, subordinating individuals, the orientation of collectivism may result. Hofstede has used this dimension in his study of cultures.[10] Collectives may be defined by their identities, and persons belonging to them may identify with them strongly. We call this a particularistic orientation, contrasted with the universalistic orientation, where the individuals do not have a strong 'in-group vs out-group' feeling.

Collectivism vs individualism This is one of the four dimensions thoroughly researched by Hofstede. According to Hofstede, individualism stands for a preference for a loosely knit social framework, where individuals are supposed to take care of themselves and their immediate families only.

   Its opposite, collectivism, stands for a preference for a tightly knit social framework in which individuals can expect their relatives, clan, or other in-group to look after them in exchange for unquestioning loyalty.[11] The fundamental issue addressed by this dimension is the degree of interdependence a society maintains among individuals. It relates to people's self-concept: whether they think in terms of 'I' or 'We'. In a collectivist culture, a person belongs to one or more cohesive collectives and is obliged to serve them, as much as the collectives are obliged to protect the interests of its members. The following beliefs and behaviours characterize 'collectivism':

- Relations are moral and not contractual. In individualist cultures, relations are treated more as contracts for a particular purpose. In collectivist cultures, mutual obligations between the individual member and the collectives are sacred and have moral overtones; neither party can get out of this mutuality.

- Individuals have strong obligations towards their collectives. This is a part of the moral nature of the relationship. Loyalty to the group is important in such cultures.
- Relations take precedence over tasks. In a collectivist culture, maintaining relationships and fulfilling personal and communal obligations are more important than completing tasks.
- Harmony must be preserved in a collectivity. Maintaining harmony is highly valued in a collectivist culture. This means being non-confrontational and avoiding conflicts.
- Opinions are predetermined collectively. In a collectivist culture, in most cases individual opinions are influenced by the decision taken by the collective.
- Some tasks are accepted as collective tasks.

Another dimension relates to the use of norms in a collectivity. If norms are determined by the collectivity and individuals feel obliged to follow these norms in deciding whether their behaviour is right or wrong, we have an other-directed orientation. If individuals evolve their own norms, and judge their actions against these norms, we have an 'inner-directed' orientation.

Particularism In a collective (society or organization), there are several groups with identities formed on some basis—ethnicity, religion, region, caste, speciality, etc. If such groups have strong identities, resulting in in-group/out-group feelings, we may have an orientation that is called particularist. This is different from the universalist orientation, in which the groups do not have insular tendencies or strong identities. In a particularist culture, there is a tendency to classify persons as belonging to one's in-group or belonging to an out-group. Sinha has studied this dimension in the context of Indian culture.[12] In a particularist culture, an individual feels secure in the in-group and tends to make the in-group stronger than out-groups.

Other-directedness vs inner-directedness Cultures and individuals can be inner-directed (their behaviour being directed by internal standards) or other-directed (their behaviour being directed by standards or opinions set by others). In an other-directed culture, a person is guided by the accepted standards or conduct of a collective, and saving face is critical to individuals in the collective. Often, a distinction is made between 'guilt cultures' and 'shame cultures'. In the former, inner worth and a notion of sin are said to guide behaviour; in the latter, honour and reputation are critical. As Geertz argues,[13] it is difficult to use the two words (guilt and shame) in their general connotation in the English language (guilt being the feeling of having done sometime reprehensible, and shame implying consciousness of guilt). But 'shame is the feeling of disgrace and humiliation which follows upon a transgression found out; guilt is the feeling of secret badness attendant upon one not, or not yet, found out'. Thus shame is other-directed and guilt inner-directed.

As Geertz suggests, shame cultures could be characterised by stage fright—a diffuse, usually mild, but in some situations virtually paralysing, nervousness before the prospect (and the fact) of social interaction, a chronic, mostly low-grade worry that one will not be able to bring it off with the required finesse.

The following values or beliefs characterise other-directedness:

- Loss of face is painful to the individual. Individuals do not like to be seen as violating norms that are obligatory in the society. If someone points out a case of such violation in front of others, the implicated person feels very bad.
- Conflict must be resolved without loss of face by either party. Since loss of face is so critical to individuals, an attempt is made not to create situations in which either party loses face. Conflict situations have the potential of loss of face by at least one party. Hence, in an other-directed culture, conflict-management strategies are dominated by a consideration for saving face on both sides.
- Indirect communication is better than direct communication. A corollary of the above is that confrontation is avoided for fear of loss of face.
- Pleasant and pleasing behaviour towards seniors is more desirable than telling the unpleasant truth. This is a special case of avoiding confrontation.

5. **Orientation to sex differences**   There are biological differences between men and women. If these differences are overemphasised, dividing social roles according to sex, what has been called masculinity may result. If the differences are not overemphasised in the social allocation of roles, we may have an orientation of femininity. Hofstede studied this dimension and called it masculinity–femininity. Androgyny may be a better term for the integration of characteristics usually attributed to the two sexes.

Androgyny   Different qualities have been attributed to the two sexes. Toughness, competitiveness, aggression, perseverance, achievement, and assertiveness have been attributed to men. Women have been seen as having qualities like compassion, empathy, harmoniousness, collaboration, aestheticism, and creativity. If a society emphasises differentiation of sex roles, and allocates social roles according to such differences, expecting men to work in areas of achievement and physical activity (manual labour and defence) and women to work in areas requiring 'feminine' virtues (nursing, housekeeping, etc.), we have a sexist orientation. Roles are largely determined by men and they impose 'masculine' values, emphasising competition and toughness in contrast with empathy and collaboration, on all activity. In such a society, competitive–aggressive characteristics are valued. The culture has been called 'masculine'[14] by Hofstede. In contrast with such a culture, if there is less differentiation of sex roles, and social roles are not allocated according to sex, the orientation called 'feminism' by Hofstede may develop. In such societies, both qualities attributed to men and women are valued and integrated. We shall call such a culture 'androgynous'. Western culture is an example of the sexist culture, whereas Indian and Indonesian cultures, for example, are androgynous cultures. One symbolic image of androgyny found both in India and Indonesia is the depiction of *Shiva* as *ardhanareeshwara* (half man and half woman).

In androgynous cultures, interpersonal trust is highly valued. Harmony and friendship are seen as desirable, and there is a high concern for the weak, the underdog. Mahatma Gandhi represented this orientation well.

6. **Orientation to power**   In a collective, power is not distributed equally. However, in some collectives, there may be uneasiness about unequal distribution of power, associated with attempts to redistribute it. Other collectives may tolerate the differences in power.

Power distance tolerance   Hofstede has studied this dimension which he called 'power distance'. He defines it as the extent to which the members of a society accept that power in institutions and organisations is distributed unequally. People in large power distance societies accept a hierarchical order, in which everybody has a place that needs no further justification. People in small power distance societies strive for power equalisation and demand justification for power inequalities. The fundamental issue addressed by this dimension is how a society handles inequalities among people when it occurs. In a society with high tolerance for power distance, inequality in power is seen as a normal and acceptable reality. The following characteristics define this orientation:

- Senior persons look after the interests of, develop, and properly guide their juniors. Seniors take the nurturing role.
- People respect and learn from their elders. In a society with intolerance for power distance, people are not accorded respect simply because of their age.
- Hierarchical relations are seen as necessary and useful to maintain order in a society or an organization.
- The corollary of the above is that people in power are seen as knowledgeable and capable of protecting the interests of their subordinates.
- Leaders are faithfully followed. Their wisdom is not questioned. In a society with low tolerance for power distance, leaders are questioned and there is criticism of their behaviour.
- Procedures and systems laid down by seniors are faithfully adhered to. Such cultures are usually ritualistic, following traditions faithfully.
- It is believed that higher status in the hierarchy can be obtained with help from elders. As a result, ascribed status is emphasised, rather than status acquired by one's own efforts.
- Manual work has low value and is usually allotted to persons in the lower strata of the society or organization.

The other aspect of power, as already mentioned, is the combination of the source and target of power, resulting in four types of cultures—expressive (where emotional, verbal, and artistic expressions are profound, with a variety of dishes and drinks), conserving (with emphasis on long and sustained training, conserving traditions, and cultivating arts and learning that require long training and perseverance), assertive (with emphasis on accomplishing things through the use of talents, high competition, and creation of wealth), and expanding (emphasising building organizations and institutions to sustain and increase growth).

Use of power As stated above, power (derived from external or internal sources) can be used to strengthen oneself or to make an impact on and strengthen others. This dimension has not been studied much and the comments here are more in the form of broad proposals that need to be expanded and studied.

The remarks made here are more in the form of tentative hypotheses.

(a) *Expressive cultures* evince strength in developing openness to outside influences, which are assimilated and integrated. Such cultures make tremendous contributions to expressive arts—literature, music, dance, etc. Expressive cultures are creative and provide opportunities to their members to experiment and innovate. Their weaknesses, however, relate to lack of attention to rigour, planning, completion of tasks with perseverance, and building of appropriate institutions.

(b) *Conserving cultures* help in preserving and refining the traditions and legacy of the culture. Such cultures develop cultivated art forms—such as classical dances and music. They develop a high sense of discipline and what has been called 'activity inhibition', which McClelland finds contributes to the building of effective executives. These cultures, however, emphasise conformity and discourage change and experimentation. Spontaneity is a victim of this conservation of traditions.

(c) *Assertive cultures* are high in economic activity, contributing to the creation of wealth. These cultures produce individuals who take risks, develop vigorous lifestyles, and 'get things done'. Their weakness is lack of emphasis on social aspects requiring rigour—scholarship, art forms, etc. Also, less attention is paid to building organizations.

(d) *Expanding cultures* contribute to the development of institutions and organizations which are able to sustain and consolidate the gains of the culture. Innovative and successful organizations abound in such cultures. Their weakness is lack of emphasis on expressive arts and rigorous activities—such as scholarship and cultivated classical art forms.

FUNCTIONALITY AND DYSFUNCTIONALITY OF CULTURE

The various dimensions of culture briefly discussed above can be used to prepare certain profiles. These profiles fall into broad categories on the modern–traditional continuum. One question before developing societies is whether their characteristics are dysfunctional with regard to a move towards modernity, with the implication that they may need to adopt characteristics of the cultures of developed societies. However, the experience in managing development has been that developing countries need not adopt (or copy) the culture of the 'developed' world. This implies that there are many functional aspects in their cultures which can be preserved and used for modernisation. Similarly, there are many aspects in the cultures of industrialised societies that are dysfunctional for the purpose of creating a future. In fact, developing countries can contribute a lot in evolving future societies capable of meeting new challenges. Yet, because of long periods of colonisation, developing countries have lost self-confidence and developed a negative self-image. It is not surprising that members of such societies do not see many strengths in their cultures and tend to use the framework of the colonising power.

However, sometimes the opposite view is taken by people in the developing countries as a reaction against these pressures. They eulogise the past and create delusions about the functionality of their cultures. This revivalist tendency, that the past was glorious and must be restored in order to achieve the glory again, is more dysfunctional than lack of awareness of one's own strengths. What is needed is a critical attitude, sifting the functional from the dysfunctional aspects of the culture.

Tradition and modernity can coexist—that's the statement our new CEO wants to make.

We shall briefly examine below the functionality and dysfunctionality of 10 aspects of the culture of most developing countries. A similar analysis can be done of industrialised cultures also. In most cases, the same aspect can be functional if used in one way (or within limits), and can become dysfunctional if used in another way (or beyond certain limits). In ascertaining the functionality and dysfunctionality of cultures, the 10 dimensions discussed earlier have been used. Some examples from Indian culture will be cited in the next section.

1. **Fatalism**   Fatalism as a mode of surrendering to circumstances is dysfunctional for managing change. In this mode, a person or a group has a high external locus of control (believing that control of the outcome of an action lies outside, in nature or in significant persons). However, this orientation can also make a group more realistic, and help it to hibernate and survive. In some societies, an absence of this mode of externality may lead to frustrations and dysfunctional conflicts. Fatalism helps people to perceive the constraints about which nothing can be done.

   Fatalism is obviously dysfunctional when it makes individuals and groups passive, reactive, and dysfunctionally tolerant of conditions that need to be changed. It can lower self-confidence and reduce exploratory tendencies to search for solutions to problems.

2. **Ambiguity tolerance**   Ambiguity tolerance helps a culture to develop several rich traditions that are not seen as necessarily conflicting. It develops tolerance for differences. There is also higher role flexibility in such cultures.

   In a culture with high tolerance of ambiguity, there is lower respect for structure and time. Many areas in which structuring is necessary may therefore be left unattended, causing confusion, delays, and anxiety.

3. **Contextualism**   High-context cultures develop much more insight into social complexities and have higher empathy for others who may differ in their behaviour from the known norms. Persons in such a culture are more sensitive to other persons and groups. They are also able to understand contextual factors faster.

In high-context societies and organizations, common norms and procedures take time to develop. There may also be confusion in interpreting events or behaviour, because different people may use different contexts to understand these.

4. **Temporalness** Emphasis on the present and a tendency to live in the present results in high involvement of individuals in their current activities. Emphasis on the here and now may help in dealing more effectively with current problems. Present-oriented cultures are likely to develop competencies for working with and using temporary systems.

   Present-oriented cultures find it difficult to undertake long-term planning. Their commitment to goals for future activities is generally low, that is, a long-term perspective is generally missing.

5. **Collectivism** The following are the strengths of this orientation, contributing to individual and organizational strengths:
   - Good relations are maintained and affiliation needs are satisfied.
   - There is high trust among the members of a collective, with high potential for collaboration.
   - Consensus is attempted more frequently—for example, in Indonesia, the tradition of *musyawarah* is a very useful one.
   - There is sharing of work and reward. In Indonesia, the practice of *gotong-royong* (shared work) is a good example of this.
   - Members have a high sense of belonging to the collective.

   Collectivism also produces several handicaps for the individual and the society:
   - People find it difficult to confront their seniors in matters requiring confrontation and exploration.
   - There is lack of initiative in individuals and groups.
   - There is lack of self-confidence and lack of effort towards individual development. Individuals, living under the umbrella of the collective, do not develop autonomy and individual identity.
   - Collectivism tends to develop ingratiating behaviour and individuals find it difficult to say no to their seniors.

6. **Particularism** Particularist cultures have strong in-groups and people belonging to them have a very high sense of identity with their groups.

   On the other hand, the 'in-group vs out-group' feeling reduces the objectivity of the members, who are generally prejudiced in favour of their in-groups and against out-groups. Favouritism and clique formation are encouraged, taking attention away from the achievement of results.

7. **Other-directedness** Giving importance to norms laid down by society may help to reduce 'improper behaviour' by individual members. The concern with saving face may also contribute to behaviour useful for the maintenance of the collective.

   The greatest dysfunctionality is in terms of lack of internalisation of values without developing criteria that are internally consistent to oneself. People in such cultures are afraid of taking risks if this involves any possibility of loss of face.

8. **Androgyny** Androgyny contributes to the values of the future human society. It helps groups to value (and develop) interpersonal trust, caring, harmony, concern for the weak, and collaboration.

   However, overemphasis on such values may reduce the effectiveness of competition, which is also needed in societies and organizations.

9. **Tolerance for power distance** There are some strengths in societies with high tolerance of power distance. Respect for seniority and age may help people to learn from experienced individuals. Conformity may be high, and is needed for the effective functioning of groups.

   However, high tolerance for power distance may result in stress on form rather than substance. There may be high centralisation, with little autonomy for lower-level units and individuals. Ascribed status is valued more, leading to lack of value for achievement. There may also be much higher dependence on authority.

10. **Psychosocial types** The least researched aspect is what we have proposed as four psychosocial types of culture—expressive, conserving, assertive, and expanding, already discussed earlier.

INDIAN CULTURE

Having a long history of thousands of years, Indian culture has several strengths that have sustained it and have been acknowledged in various periods in various parts of the world. These strengths not only sustained the culture, but helped it to become a unique one and to make significant contributions to other parts of the world. However, this is also a society with a long history of feudalism, casteism, and foreign oppression, and has acquired several weaknesses. If we are to transform India into a strong nation, capable of providing global leadership in the current century, it is necessary that we look at both its strengths and weaknesses, and then plan to reinforce the strengths and reduce and, if possible, eliminate its weaknesses. Pareek[15] has discussed these in detail, suggesting an agenda for action. These are summarised below:

Strengths of Indian Culture

The strengths of Indian culture can be grouped under three cognitive-values— behaviour clusters—universalism, ambiguity tolerance, and self-restraince.

Universalism In the first cluster are included four strengths—universalism (love and respect for all forms of life and for ecology), extension motivation (involvement in large goals), respect for learning and intellectual pursuits, and openness to learning from others.

Ambiguity tolerance The second cluster has three strengths—context sensitivity (high ambiguity tolerance), diversity (leading to synergic pluralism, according to the author [1989]), and androgyny (equal emphasis on and integration of cognitive and emotional aspects).

Self-restraince The third cluster includes three strengths—self-restraince (willingness to postpone gratification of immediate needs for long-term goals), role-boundness (giving more importance to the role than to the self), and equanimity (steering between two extremes and not being swayed by extreme emotions of joy or sorrow).

Weaknesses of Indian Culture

The weaknesses of Indian culture can be grouped into three clusters—narcissism, power concentration, and attributional thinking.

Narcissism Narcissism is reflected both in self-seeking behaviour as well as in an inward-looking tendency. In this cluster are included five weaknesses—in-group infatuation (concern for the self, i.e., self-seeking or confinement of interest to the family or kin), unreality orientation (orientation towards fantasy or substitutes of reality), non-involvement (attitude of indifference and reluctance to engage in confrontation), lack of detailed planning, and an oral culture (resulting in low reading and writing skills).

Power concentration The second cluster, what Hofstede calls power distance, has four characteristics—hierarchical orientation, critical orientation (excessive use of sanctions and 'don'ts', rather than the use of reinforcement and encouragement), non-confrontation, and a non-work culture.

Attributional thinking The third cluster of attributional thinking has two characteristics—fatalism (resulting in 'deadening efficiency in maintaining the status quo'), and pessimism–rumination (expecting failures and misfortunes, and indulging in recollecting and mulling over bad experiences).

TRADITIONAL CULTURES AND MODERN MANAGEMENT

There is often a conflict between traditional cultures and the demands of modern management. As already stated, two extreme views are taken on the subject, some advocating that management practices should be designed to suit the culture and others advocating that modern management practices should be uniformly adopted to suit the goals of the organization.

The argument that various systems in the organization should be designed to suit the culture of the organization as well as the culture of the society is a reactive position: it will keep the organization where it is. We spend a major part of our life (also the most important part of life, in which new things are learnt and new attitudes and skills acquired) in work organizations. Therefore, change can be effectively introduced through them. We should consider the major responsibility of work organizations as producing the kind of culture needed for future effectiveness of these organizations and of the society. Moreover, work organizations have an edge over other organizations in society—they have the advantage of getting better-educated citizens, those who think a little differently, and probably those who may be able to accept and disseminate new values. It is, therefore, a great pity if work organizations merely perpetuate the culture they have inherited or the culture that prevails in society.

Leveraging Culture

As we have already stated, each culture has its strengths and weaknesses, functionalities and dysfunctionalities with regard to developing modern organizations. Even those who argue for designing systems to suit the larger culture do not talk of strengths alone. While designing an organization or a system in an organization, we can build on the existing strengths of the culture, further reinforce these strengths, and use the positive aspect of the culture for organizational design. In the Indian context, for example, organizations should make that such positive qualities of the Indian culture, such as concern for others, a tendency to harmonise and synthesise various points of view, a positive regard for different points of view, and general respect for knowledge and expertise, are properly used while designing systems. For example, instead of promoting a zealously individualistic or competitive spirit in an organization, a spirit of collaboration may be developed. Systems may be designed to suit these needs. Unfortunately, when we talk of change and think of designing new systems, we usually have only Western models before us and implicitly argue either for or against such models. In the latter case, we take the position that the model does not suit our culture but often fail to explore alternatives available within it. It is important that we search our own cultural traditions and experiences to develop models as well as learn from the experience and cultural traditions of other countries. By taking a close look at our culture and learning from the available elements of various models, we may be able to make some conscious choices regarding the type of organization we want to build and the systems we want to develop in our work organization.

A proactive strategy would be to preserve, use, and consolidate the strengths of a culture in management practices and to use management to change the dysfunctional aspects of a culture. However, using management for changing a culture would require careful planning and monitoring. It may be useful to do a force field analysis of the facilitating and hindering forces in a culture, use and reinforce the facilitating forces and strengths, recognise blocks, produce counterforces, and pay enough attention to process.

A proactive action strategy would involve the following steps.[16]

Determine the direction It is necessary in the beginning to be quite clear about where the organization wants to go. The direction should be defined not only in terms of specific systems such as performance feedback, counselling, potential appraisal, career planning, etc., but also in terms of process movement towards, for example, greater openness, more collaborative action, and more consultation. An open discussion about new directions will help the organization to make the necessary psychological preparation for accepting the changed system. Also, thoughts about new directions should be widely shared.

Share the possible consequences of the journey   The introduction of a human appraisal system is like starting a new journey. The fact that the journey is not likely to be pleasant should be understood very clearly from the beginning. Usually consultants who work on the introduction of such a system not only communicate the possible consequences verbally to the client, but also make them clear in their written reports. For example, it should be made known that the appraisal system may increase general dissatisfaction to some extent, because individuals will begin to voice certain problems when the system is opened up. It should also be made clear that a more open system may result in some managers complaining that subordinates do not accept their statements and ask more questions. When a system is beginning to become open, people will also tend to test the limits of that openness. It should be understood that these processes are part of the 'teething problems' experienced in introducing the system. If these are not communicated and understood, the organization may be unduly disturbed when it faces such problems. Instead of taking these problems as a necessary part of the introduction of the system, it may take them as signs of failure and the system may be abandoned. Those who are introducing a new system should clearly anticipate such problems and be prepared to deal with them.

Start from where you are   Each organization has a tradition and some rudimentary forms of a particular system. The design of a new system will be different for each organization. While the same direction of movement may be selected by two organizations, the nature of the system to be designed as well as the way in which the organizations will implement the system may well differ. It would be useful for an organization to understand this and start from the level where it currently stands in terms of the sophistication of its system.

Take one step at a time   Organizations should prepare a careful plan to implement the various changes in steps or phases. The various elements of a system cannot be introduced simultaneously. For example, while introducing an appraisal system, a simple appraisal form may be introduced at first. After the form has been properly understood and used, counselling and feedback systems may be introduced, followed by an analysis of critical attributes of various jobs and a system of assessing these attributes. This kind of phasing may be done for various sub-systems.

Prepare for the journey   The introduction of a system requires preparation. Changes will be required in the orientation and attitudes of people in the organization and in the skills that are needed to implement and use the system. In the absence of these, the system is likely to fail. As the system is being introduced, these needs may be identified and steps can be taken to meet these needs. Various complications can arise if the skills and competence to run a system are lacking. It would be wrong to introduce, for example, feedback and counselling systems unless enough preparation has gone into developing the skills of giving feedback and counselling subordinates in the various managers. Problems may also arise if the necessary training does not precede the introduction of a system. However, in the name of such preparation, the introduction of a system should not be postponed indefinitely. If an organization argues that it will introduce a system only after the necessary conditions have been achieved, it may have to wait forever. Sometimes this may be used as a pretext for not introducing a system. Action to provide such preparation is necessary. But the preparation may also be phased. These phases may have to be implemented during various stages of the introduction of a new system and not all together in the beginning.

Be prepared for reversals   The introduction of a system would produce certain changes. There may be two kinds of consequences, which the organization should be clear about and be prepared for. Changes may produce some disturbing symptoms in the organization. The introduction of a new system may create confusion, give rise to suspicion, create doubts, and result in increased problems of communication. This may be a necessary part of the change, and change is rarely smooth, easy, and pleasant. However, any change that intervenes in the culture of an organization creates disturbances. Secondly, at several stages it may seem as if the preliminary work has been wanting and the organization is back to square one. Such reversals may appear especially when progress is not happening according to schedule. Managers may report that their feedback and counselling sessions have not been as good as they anticipated—the quality of counselling was probably assumed to be superior in the beginning but later found wanting. Such reversal should not arouse anxiety. It should be understood that reversals are likely to occur and the organization should be prepared to deal with them and move forward.

Develop internal expertise   It is necessary that while a system is being designed and implemented, there is enough internal expertise, which increases with the development of the system. A system cannot be implemented with the help of external expertise alone. Outside help may be useful both in the beginning and at a later stage, when some dimensions need special attention. However, the regular work should be done through internal resources alone. If enough attention is not paid to developing such expertise in the enthusiasm of accepting a new system, the system is likely to fail.

Continue moving   Persistence in the implementation of a system is important, with various sequences, planning for certain reversals, and phasing of the system. Such perseverance is possible only if the organization is able to prepare a long-term plan and to identify a person (or a small group of persons) to attend to the introduction of the system and its implementation. The main responsibility of these people should be to take necessary steps to deal with problems, and not let these come in the way of the final implementation of the system. The very fact that a system is followed up doggedly and steps are taken continuously to implement it can ensure its success. Yet, in many cases a system fails because reversals and problems create anxiety—these are seen as signs of failure and the system is pre-maturely abandoned.

Have a compass and a speedometer   Monitoring mechanisms are necessary for the implementation of a system. At each step, enough information should be collected about the progress of the system and the direction in which the system is heading. An individual or a small group of individuals may be given the responsibility of monitoring progress. For example, special interview schedules or questionnaires can be designed to gather information about the quality of employee feedback and counselling after performance appraisal forms have been submitted. Such information helps in taking corrective action. From time to time, a meeting of various groups may be held to discuss such problems and how they may be rectified.

To sum up, a proactive strategy requires planned and persistent work. Past experiences of failure and problems experienced in implementing other systems can confirm these needs. Advocates of a reactive strategy adopt these as defences, however, to argue that such systems are not suited to the indigenous culture and that systems should be evolved to suit the culture. But such a strategy may not help an organization take the necessary steps for change.

A MODEL OF CULTURE-CHANGING MANAGEMENT

A management working to change its culture needs to pay attention to four dimensions: structural elements, processes, strategy of change, and tactics to be employed. Eventually, cultural change must be built into the system so that the new culture becomes a part of the organization. This cannot be done without paying close attention to the processes underlying the structural elements. Simultaneous attention to structure and relevant processes would require a broad but clearly thought out plan of action (strategy). It is also necessary to break up the strategy into specific action steps (tactics). This four-fold S-P-S-T (structure-process-strategy-tactics) model can help to develop culture-changing management. These dimensions, with their various aspects are listed in Exhibit 3.2. Most of these are self-explanatory.

Exhibit 3.2   *SPST Model*

Stuctural elements	Processes	Strategy	Tactics
Stable structure	Incremental planning	Anchoring in and using strengths	Prepare in advance
Temporary systems	Action research approach	Sensitivity to stone walls	One step at a time
Linkage building mechanisms	Modeling	Competency building	Prepare for the journey (resources)
Information system	Mentoring	Critical concentration	Go together
Rewards	Process awareness and orientation	Developing key institutions	Stop and review progress
Regular budget	Counselling	Sanction and support	Keep up the spirit (reinforcement)
Guidelines	Organizational norms	System ownership	Keep going (perseverance)

S = Structural elements
- Stable structure
- Temporary systems
- Linkage-building mechanisms
- Information systems
- Rewards
- Regular budget
- Guidelines

P = Processes
- Incremental planning
- Action research approach
- Modelling
- Mentoring
- Process awareness and orientation
- Counselling
- Organizational norms

S = Strategy
- Anchoring and using strengths
- Sensitivity to stonewalling
- Competency-building
- Critical concentration
- Developing key institutions
- Sanction and support
- System ownership

T = Tactics
- Prepare in advance
- One step at a time
- Prepare for the journey (resources)
- Go together
- Stop and review progress
- Keep up the spirit (reinforcement)
- Keep going (perseverance)

SUMMARY

Culture is the cumulative preference of some states of life and some organized ways of dealing with basic concerns by members of a society. Culture evolves over a long period of time and is reflected in artefacts (symbols). Different scholars have proposed different dimensions to understand various cultures. Those proposed by Kluckhohn and Strodtbeck (five orientations based on human existence, human labour, relationship with nature, time, and relationship of individuals with fellow beings), McClelland (based on the use of power), and Hofstede (comprising four aspects: individualism vs collectivism, power distance, uncertainty avoidance, and masculinity vs femininity) are popular. Every culture has some strengths (functional aspects) and some weaknesses (dysfunctional aspects). This is true of Indian culture also. An effective strategy for progress would focus on leveraging the functional and reducing the dysfunctional aspects. A 'culture-modifying' management approach has been suggested above.

GLOSSARY

affiliative   friendly and close personal relations

ambiguity tolerance   *see* **uncertainty avoidance**

androgyny   integration of characteristics usually attributed to the two sexes separately; equal emphasis on and integration of cognitive and emotional aspects

assertive culture   emphasis on accomplishing things through the use of power, high competition, and creation of wealth

being   focus on the present

being-in-becoming   movement from the present towards change

collectivism   social framework in which people expect other members of their groups to look after them

conserving culture   emphasis on conserving traditions and cultivating arts and learning that require long training and perseverance

contextualism   giving importance to contextual factors in a culture

critical orientation   excessive use of sanctions ('don'ts') rather than the use of reinforcement and encouragement

culture   cumulative preferences of some states of life over others (values), response predispositions towards several significant issues and phenomena (attitudes), organized ways of filling up time (rituals), and ways of promoting desired behaviour and preventing undesirable ones (sanctions)

equanimity   steering between two extremes and not swayed by extreme emotions of joy or sorrow

expanding culture   emphasis on the building of organizations and institutions to sustain and increase growth

expressive culture   profundity of emotional, verbal, and artistic expressions, with a variety of dishes and drinks

fatalism   perceiving nature as dominating and beyond human manipulation

femininity   emphasis on relationships and concern for and interest in others

high-context culture   understanding events only in their contexts, so that meanings and categories can change and causality cannot be unambiguously established

individualistic culture   emphasis on taking care of oneself and one's immediate family

in-group vs out-group   distinguishing one's own group from other groups

in-group *infatuation*   concern for self, i.e., self-seeking, or interest confined to the family or kin

inner-directed orientation   behaviour being directed by internal standards

irreality orientation   indulgence in fantasy or substitutes of reality

locus of control   belief regarding who/what controls significant happenings in one's life

masculinity   emphasis on assertiveness and acquisition of material resources

non-involvement   attitude of indifference and non-confrontationality

other-directed   orientation norms are determined by the collective, and individuals feel obliged to follow these norms in deciding whether their behaviour is right or wrong

particularism   strong sense of identity, resulting in in-group vs out-group feelings

power distance   acceptance by less powerful groups of the unequal distribution of power in a system

role-boundness giving more importance to the role than the self

scientism belief that nature can be changed and adapted for the better use of human society

synergic pluralism diversity enriching the society

temporalness orientation to time

uncertainty avoidance feeling of threat in ambiguous situations and a tendency to avoid them

universalist orientation not having strong insular identity

EXERCISES

Concept Review Questions

1. What is the concept of culture? Why is societal culture important for management?
2. What are the dimensions of culture suggested by Kluckhohn and Strodtbeck?
3. What are the four dimensions of culture used by Hofstede in studying several societies of the world?
4. How can different aspects of culture be both functional and dysfunctional? Give examples.
5. What are the main strengths and weaknesses of Indian culture?
6. How can we use Indian culture for management?

Critical Thinking Questions

1. List two main strengths of your institutional culture. Also suggest how these strengths can be leveraged by the students.
2. List two main weaknesses of Indian culture and show how these are reflected in your own style of working.
3. Should management be culture-specific and adapt to the societal culture, or should it be proactive to modify the culture? Give reasons for your answer.

Classroom Projects

1. The Tata group of companies has pioneered industry in India. From the written reports available, analyse its cultural features. To what extent do these reflect the characteristics of Indian culture?
2. Analyse from published reports how Infosys has changed some of the characteristics of traditional Indian culture.

Field Projects

1. Interview two successful executives to find out what aspects of Indian culture they find functional and have used.
2. Interview a senior-level employee working with a joint venture such as Maruti and list the cultural practices of the non-Indian collaborating company.

Reviving Khadi in India*

KHADI LOSES ITS SHEEN

Khadi,[†] the home spun cloth that symbolised self-reliance and emancipation during the freedom struggle in India,[††] has lost its sheen over the years. And there are several reasons for the same. Post 1947, India opted for state-led large-scale industrialisation. With many Indian industrialists setting up huge textile mills, the mass production of fine cloth led to the availability of cloth at lower prices. People began to buy machine-made textiles and thus khadi began losing out to the mill fabric.

In January 1953, the All India Khadi and Village Industries Board was set up to provide employment to thousands of spinners all over India. In 1957, the Khadi and Village Industries Commission (KVIC) was established to take over the work of the board. KVIC was formed as a nodal agency to promote Khadi all over India through its exclusive outlets known as *khadi bhandars.*[†††] The Government of India has ever since continued its support to khadi.

However, there were a few problems. According to designers, the production of khadi was inconsistent and the cloth was prone to shrinkage and fabric stretch. Besides, fabric colours in khadi were also limited. Redtapism and bureaucracy prevalent in the Indian system further hampered the growth of the khadi sector. In spite of having a wide distribution network, there were problems, especially middleman. Corruption was rampant. There were many bogus khadi units operating in the country, which made it extremely difficult to claim rebates from the Government of India.

KVIC received huge financial assistance from the government in the form of subsidies and rebates. In May 2000, the Ministry of Small Scale Industries announced a special package of 12.16 billion rupees to the industry. In order to face the challenges

---

*This case was written by D. Preethi, under the direction of Sanjib Dutta, ICFAI Management Research (ICMR), 2003. Reproduced with permission from ICFAI Center for Management Research (ICMR), Hyderabad.

[†]Khadi is a cloth produced by interlacement of handspun yarn. The soft twist imparted by the hand gives the Khadi yarn the 'hairiness' that gives maximum comfort to the wearer. The loom used in weaving of khadi interlaces the threads in a manner that allows maximum air to permeate to body and soothes the body. Khadi is acknowledged to be one of the coolest and the most comfortable fabric.

[††]Instead of exporting raw cotton and importing fine Manchester-made cloth, freedom fighters in India led by Mahatma Gandhi wanted all Indians to spin their own cloth and boycott imports to weaken the British rule in India and make India self-reliant.

[†††]Khadi bhandars are exclusive outlets opened by the KVIC to retail all its products.

of globalization and to strengthen its position in the market, KVIC launched two separate brands—Sarvodaya and khadi in August 2001.

Sarvodaya comprised consumer goods like incense sticks, spices, honey, and pickles. The khadi brand included products like essential oils, herbal oil and soaps, face scrubs, dry fruit honey, designer garments, etc. The khadi brand was introduced exclusively for exports and upmarket. The fabric was being promoted as a fashion fabric. Many high-profile fashion designers were roped in to create garments using the fabric. KVIC allotted huge funds into research and development to improve the quality of khadi. It allotted around 0.4 billion rupees for promoting the fabric emphasising its unique selling proposition (USP)—eco-friendliness.

BACKGROUND NOTE

Khadi has its roots in the freedom struggle of India. Khadi was central to Gandhi's vision of self-reliance and self-rule. Gandhi wanted Indians to spin their own cotton thread and to weave khadi, thereby, providing employment to many Indians and contributing to the country's self-sufficiency. Post independence, khadi fabrics were woven on handlooms from hand-spun cotton, silk, and woolen yarn.

The production of khadi is labour-intensive, as the weaving has to be done manually. The pure cotton collected from cotton farms is first ginned and bales are made. These bales are then converted into rowing and distributed to different spinning units. In the spinning units, the cotton fibre is manually converted into yarn, using *charkas.*[†] The yarn is then woven into fabric using handlooms.

During the post-independence era, Indian industrialists set up capital-intensive textile mills. Due to mass production, these mills could offer fine cloth at lower prices. Synthetic material like polyester was available at a very low price compared to khadi. Thus, despite all policy incentives to popularise khadi, people bought machine-made textiles.

In order to popularise khadi among the masses, in 1957, the government set up the KVIC. It had the following broad objectives:

- The social objective of providing employment
- The economic objective of producing saleable articles
- The wider objective of creating self-reliance among the poor and developing a strong rural community spirit

Besides khadi, KVIC also dealt with other products such as toilet soaps, detergents, honey, pickles, spices, incense sticks, hand-made paper, leather, ceramics, and many other agro-based products. To keep the spirit of khadi alive and promote it as a national fabric, KVIC has set up many outlets across India. As a result, thousands of spinners who wove the fabric could sell their output through the vast network of KVIC retail outlets.

[†] *Charka* is the Indian version of the spinning wheel.

However, the situation did not improve much. The poor quality of garments sold through the KVIC outlets resulted in customer dissatisfaction. People even complained that the quality of khadi had deteriorated and hence it faded easily. In the 1990s, very few people bought khadi. Khadi was bought only during the annual discount sale. Synthetic material was quickly replacing the hand-made fabric. People who had got used to the high quality of imported materials felt that khadi was rough and coarse and associated it with shapeless *kurtas*,[†] mostly worn by politicians. And therefore, in spite of the government's financial assistance to thousands of traditional spinners in India, selling this product was tough.

REVIVING KHADI: FROM FREEDOM FABRIC TO FASHION FABRIC

In 1985, designer Devika Bhojwani pioneered the Swadeshi label of khadi ensembles. These were distributed through nearly 5,000 khadi emporia. To display khadi's potential, KVIC organized a fashion show in Mumbai in 1989. Nearly 85 dazzling garments created by Bhojwani were presented at the show. This was the first step towards changing khadi's earlier image of being unfashionable. Commenting on the poor state of khadi, Bhojwani said that failures in the khadi sector were a result of redtapism and bureaucracy prevalent in the Indian system. Even though the country had a wide distribution network, middlemen, commissions, and cuts had gradually weakened the system. She further said that though the government was taking the initiative to revive khadi, nothing much would improve until the implementation and the cost per garment and other such concerns were controlled.

In 1990, the Delhi-based designer, Ritu Kumar presented her first khadi collection—Tree of Life—which helped put khadi in the fashion circuit. With increasing interest of the Western world in use of handloom and khadi, many Indian designers began to use khadi for their designs. The government also made efforts to promote khadi. In September 2000, Vasundhara Raje, Minister for Small Scale Industries, initiated a movement to revive all the 7,000 KVIC shops in India and make khadi more fashionable and affordable. The KVIC board hired the services of leading fashion designers to help create a new range and brand of khadi wear.

In May 2001, KVIC set up the first air-conditioned shop in New Delhi. The decor was modern and the clothes were neat and fashionable. The outlet sold khadi garments designed by high-profile designers. On the opening of this outlet, well-known fashion designer Rohit Bal commented, 'Khadi is the Indian alternative for linen. It is as comfortable, and now we've proved that it is as fashionable.'

In January 2002, a high-profile textile exhibition, featuring khadi ensembles designed by prominent Indian designers, was launched in New Delhi to popularise the traditional hand-spun cotton. The idea of the exhibition was to promote the wholly hand-spun, hand-woven, and hand-patterned fabric as a unique luxury product. The exhibition displayed Western as well as traditional Indian attire made from the finest khadi available in the country. Besides, nearly 110 varieties of the fabric (from

---

[†] *Kurta* is a loose fitting shirt.

the sheerest to the coarsest) were showcased. Designer Rakesh Thakore, whose collection was showcased in the exhibition commented, 'If packaged well, khadi can be sold internationally.' The exhibition was sponsored by a Swiss charitable trust, Volkart Foundation,[†] in association with the Indian National Trust for Art and Cultural Heritage (INTACH).[††]

With many designers experimenting with khadi, the designs are no longer as simple as they used to be. A great deal of emphasis was given to the details of the designs and many new colours were introduced. Eco-friendly vat dyes were used. In March 2002, Preyasi,[†††] the official designer for KVIC, launched 'The Khadi Range Collection–2002'. In the collection, khadi was used to create apparel such as casual shirts, waist coats, skirts, wrap-arounds, trousers, parallels, and tops for women.

Government Support to Khadi

The government had been providing huge subsidies and grants to the khadi sector. Khadi was given a rebate[††††] of 1.49 billion rupees and 1.4 billion rupees in 1998–99 and 1999–2000, respectively. In 2000–01, funds to the tune of 1.29 billion rupees were released for the same. During the same time, concerted efforts were made to root out corruption in the payment of rebate. Regular vigilance raids were conducted in various parts of the country to detect malpractices in claiming of khadi rebates and to distinguish between genuine and bogus khadi and village industries. In May 2000, the Ministry of Small Scale Industries announced a special package of 12.15 billion rupees for KVIC. Of this, 0.3 billion rupees had been allocated for renovation of the existing outlets, while 0.4 billion rupees was sanctioned for promotional activities.

Though the government provided huge financial assistance to KVIC, the funds did not produce the desired result. It was also felt that the structure of KVIC needed to be changed to enable it to face the challenges of globalization. Therefore, in 2000, the global consulting firm Arthur Anderson was hired to suggest restructuring strategies for KVIC. According to the report, submitted to the Ministry of Small Scale Industries,

---

[†]Volkart Foundation, a Swiss charitable trust, is devoted to funding sustainable development. Marking its 150th anniversary in February 2001, the Volkart Foundation pledged 1 million US dollars as a cultural and social grant. The khadi exhibition, which formed a part of this, was meant for the revival of the old cotton business, as well as to highlight the non-violence movement.

[††]INTACH is an NGO that seeks to make strategic and timely intervention in order to conserve and promote India's natural and cultural heritage. INTACH has a nation-wide network of volunteers who spread awareness about heritage, prevent acts likely to degrade their region's cultural and natural wealth, and act positively to preserve and enhance local heritage. INTACH is the nation's largest NGO working in the field of culture.

[†††]Preyasi is a designer certified by the Ministry of Handicrafts and Textiles. It claims to be the world's best wardrobe management company. Since 15 years, Preyasi has been involved in delivering designer-wear and consultancy services to clients in over 48 countries. In 2001, it signed up with KVIC as their official designer to design and promote khadi garments in the national and international market.

[††††]Rebates are the discounts given by the khadi outlets to the consumers, which can be later claimed back from the KVIC.

KVIC should be a policy-making body and play a strategic role rather than being involved in the operations. It also suggested that KVIC should be made a market-oriented organization and given the freedom to decide on the issues of rebate. In order to improve the marketing and retailing aspects of the sector, it was proposed that an independent marketing company be formed, which would be disintegrated from the existing khadi and village industries structure. This company would also deal with improvements in the quality of products, packaging, and marketing. It also recommended that the special rebate on khadi products be made available in the first week of every month, instead of the usual 90-day period after the month of October.

The declining production, sales, rural employment opportunities, and share of khadi in the total business of KVIC had become a matter of serious concern for the government. This had assumed greater significance as the population and per capita consumption of clothes in India had considerably increased over the years. Keeping this in view, the government took many initiatives to promote the sector and exploit the full potential of khadi as a product category in all its forms. As a part of these initiatives, KVIC registered khadi as a brand name, thereby, protecting it legally.

For khadi to compete with other varieties of textiles and be more acceptable in the market, improvisation was needed and new products and designs had to be developed. Keeping this objective in mind, in October 2001, KVIC signed a memorandum of understanding with the Ahmedabad-based National Institute of Design (NID) to provide it design support in order to improve the diminishing market share of khadi. Under the agreement, a special cell was be set up at NID (financed by the KVIC) to provide design support services in khadi, village industries, packaging, marketing, communication, publicity, disseminating materials, and other design-related activities.

Khadi Goes for a Facelift

Over the years, the khadi boards of different states have been experimenting on blending of khadi with other materials and improving its quality. In July 2002, a collection of ensembles in 'tencel khadi' (a blend of tencel and khadi in the ratio 30:70) was created by Bangalore-based designer, Deepika Govind, in association with the Karnataka Khadi Board. Tencel is a lyocell fibre, natural in origin and, hence, environment friendly. It offers the comfort and luxury of a natural fibre as well as the performance and practicality of a man-made fabric. Tencel khadi showed lesser shrinkage (4–5 per cent) as compared to the high shrinkage seen in khadi garments (about 7 per cent). Due to tencel's softness, it would become easier to work with khadi and lend better drape quality to finished garments. Tencel khadi would provide excellent scope for exports.

In 2002, the Austria-based company, Lenzing AG, proposed to make khadi more eco-friendly by blending the bio-degradable 'modal fibre'[†] with khadi. This blend

---

[†]Modal is a speciality fibre, produced solely by the Austrian company, Lenzing AG. It is made exclusively from beechwood pulp and consists of 100 per cent cellulose.

would absorb 50 per cent more humidity than cotton. The blend, besides strengthening the khadi yarn, would make it easy to wash and maintain.

FUTURE OF KHADI

The salability of any textile depends on its USP and performance. For many years, the promotion for khadi had been on emotional and political grounds while its quality and variety had been ignored completely. Khadi has very little to offer in terms of fabric performance. It looks attractive when starched and kept in showrooms, but it does not remain the same after washing. Even finer counts and blends of khadi cannot withstand many washes and, thus, cannot be used for day-to-day purposes. It was becoming extremely difficult for khadi to compete with the high-tech, colour-fast, wrinkle-free, mill-made cottons and blends available today. According to analysts, khadi requires government sanction in every single activity and has therefore been stuck in a bureaucratic swamp, unable to increase its output or raise its quality. In 2002, khadi formed less than half per cent of India's textiles. In order to grow, the production of khadi needs to be decentralised.

A research and development wing should also be established by KVIC to experiment with new patterns and colours. Besides, weavers can also be given grants to enable creating new designs. KVIC must allot a special advertising budget to promote the fabric. KVIC plans to launch an advertising campaign in India and abroad to create awareness among people about khadi and its uses. For this, it allocated an advertising and promotional budget of about 0.4 billion rupees. It also plans to set up khadi shops at all the international airports in India. KVIC is also exploring the possibilities of using e-commerce to market its products. However, khadi, like any other craft of India, would need to face the challenge of quality and produce contemporary designs, which suit the tastes of the present generation.[†]

Khadi   The products include cotton, woolen, silk, and polyvastra khadi. Cotton khadi is 100 per cent cotton, hand-woven and hand-spun, and has a great demand abroad. Silk khadi comes in different varieties. Silk khadi and polyvastra khadi can be converted into shirting and sarees. Woolen khadi items consist of sweaters, mufflers, blankets, socks, and other winter wear.

Fibre   Fibre utility items are made out of sisal, banana, pineapple, palm, and other fibres. Some of the products include bags, table mats, wall hangings, carpets, floor mats, floor potholders, baskets, etc.

Leather   The leather product range includes sandals, shoes, purses, briefcases, jewel bags, vanity bags, attractive readymade garments, etc.

[†]The following material is sourced from kvic.org.in.

Cane and bamboo   These include fancy utility articles like furniture, sofa sets, partitions, wall mats, handicrafts made of cane and bamboo. They are produced in the northeastern parts of the country.

Incense sticks   Incense sticks are available in different varieties. There is a good demand for incense sticks in India and abroad.

Processed fruit products   Products like mango pulp, tomato pulp, juices, pickles, etc. are exported in large quantity, especially to the Gulf countries where there is demand for canned foods. The products are covered under the FPO (Food Product Organization) license.

Honey   Honey is a natural sweet syrup collected by honey bees. Honey can be procured from the forest or by installing colonies of bees and maintaining these in a systematic manner.

Hand-made paper   This product uses cloth rags and waste paper as raw material for production thus saving trees and preserving the ecological system. Hand-made paper products include stationery items like files, letter pads, envelopes, fancy bags, visiting cards, greeting cards, watermark certificate and decoration materials, photo album, etc.

Pottery and stonewear items   These include clay articles, fancy pottery items, and terracota produced in rural areas.

Papad and masala   Papad and masala are in great demand both in India and abroad. Mahila Griha Udyog Lijjat Papad of KVIC exports papad and masala in a large way to the UK, the US, the Gulf countries, and New Zealand.

Herbal Products   A number of herbal products like herbal shampoo, tooth powder, and health tonics are produced.

Questions for Discussion

1. How is the concept of khadi relevant to the Indian culture?
2. What were the strategies adopted by KVIC to popularise khadi among the modern youth?
3. Why is khadi popular in the West? Why was it not popular in India?

REFERENCES

1. Schein, E.H. (1985). *Organisational Culture and Leadership.* San Francisco: Jossey-Bass.
2. *Ibid.*
3. Kluckhohn, F. and F.L. Strodtbeck (1961). *Variations in Value Orientation.* Evanston: Rowe, Peterson.
4. McClelland, David C. (1975). *Power: The Inner Experience.* New York: Irwington.
5. Hofstede, G. (1980). *Culture's Consequences: International Difference in Work-Related Values.* Beverly Hills: Sage; Hofstede, G. (1991). *Cultures and Organizations: Software of the Mind.* New York: McGraw Hill.

6. Adomo, T.W. and E. Frenkel-Brunswick (1983). *The Authoritarian Personality,* abridged edn. New York: Norton.
7. Hofstede. *Culture's Consequences.*
8. Adorno and Brinswick. *Authoritarian Personality.*
9. Hall, E. (1997). *Beyond Culture.* New York: Anchor Books.
10. Hofstede. *Culture's Consequences.*
11. *Ibid.*
12. Sinha, J.B.P. (1980). *The Nurturant Task Leader.* New Delhi: Concept.
13. Geertz, C. (1973). *Interpretation of Cultures.* New York: Basic Books.
14. Hofstede. *Culture's Consequences.*
15. Pareek, Udai (1979). 'Culture and organization designing: Proactive or reactive stategy?' *Vikalpa,* 2(4): 303-08.
16. Pareek, Udai (2002). *Effective Organizations,* Chapter 26. New Delhi: Oxford & IBH.

4
Organizational Structure

LEARNING OBJECTIVES

After studying this chapter, you will be able to
1. Elaborate determinants of organizational structure
2. Discuss the implications of chain and span of control
3. Explain the usual ways of designing organizations
4. Elaborate emerging new forms of organizations
5. Discuss the basic issues in mergers and acquisitions

Organizational structure is the way in which the interrelated groups of an organization are constructed. The main concerns are effective communication and coordination. Several aspects determine the organizational structure. The important aspects are discussed here.

DETERMINANTS OF ORGANIZATIONAL STRUCTURE

Strategy

Chandler proposed that the structure of an organization depends on its strategy—a company must determine its strategy before it can organize properly.[1] He discussed how American corporations have dealt with a common economic problem—the effective administration of an expanding business. He proposed that corporations have two management tiers. Top leaders set the vision of the company, and managers execute the vision. Chandler summarised the history of the expansion of the largest industries of the US during the past hundred years. He then examined in depth the modern decentralised corporate structure as it was developed independently by four companies: DuPont, General Motors, Standard Oil, and Sears.

All the four organizations had to deal with their growing businesses. The firms that had a good strategy developed the proper organization. Without a good strategy, various reorganizations were required.

Some other researchers have also suggested that strategy determines structure. This is the theme of a recently published book[2] that elaborates the evolution of Intel's strategy and its supporting structure. Igor Ansoff's work is a major pioneering effort in strategic planning and corporate advantage.[3]

According to Chandler, the new economy is primarily based on more than just the new technology; a major factor is the technological revolution based on electronic communications. Although strategy remains the main factor, the strategies of individual enterprises have to be redefined in order to take advantage of the new electronic technology.

Issues of structure and strategy are at the root of both effecting and coping with change. Changing structures and formulating strategies require time and patience. The results will not be seen overnight and they will probably not be right the first time.

Technology

Technology can be defined in terms of the knowledge and the use of tools. Technology refers to the tools and machines that may be used to help solve problems. Tools may include both simple tools, like kitchen tools, and complex tools, like computers, information control manuals, maintenance manuals, etc.

Technology as tools refers to our knowledge of how to use resources to produce desired products, to solve problems. Technology in this sense includes technical methods, skills, processes, techniques, tools, and raw materials (for example, in such uses as computer technology, construction technology, or medical technology).

Technology influences the organizational structure. Woodward found that by knowing an organization's primary system of production, you could predict their structure.[4] For example, cheque processing at a bank is usually performed by a business unit that is highly formalised, has a great deal of specialisation and division of labour, and has a high centralisation of decision making. In contrast, the creative section of an ad agency is usually not formalised at all, has blurred division of labour, and has highly decentralised decision making.

Organizations that manufacture huge volumes of identical products, like machine parts, bottles, kitchen equipment, etc., use automation and assembly lines. Such organizations generally have mechanistic and bureaucratic structure with taller hierarchies and larger span of control. Organizations that make one-of-a-kind custom products or small quantities of products, like furniture, made-to-measure clothes, ships, aircraft, etc. tend to have organic structure—a flat structure. In such organizations people's skills and knowledge is more important than the machines used, and work process is unpredictable, hard to pre-programme or automate.

Organizations with continuous technology, like chemical companies, oil refineries, bakeries, dairies, etc., have organic structure at the top and mechanistic structure at lower levels. Employees have to do very little; machines do everything. Such organizations are generally tall and thin or even inverted pyramid—almost nobody at the bottom.

Size

Size refers to capacity, number of personnel, outputs (customers, sales), and resources (wealth). Blau's studies show that differentiation (of levels, departments, job titles) increases with size, but at a decreasing rate. In contrast, the percentage of the organization that is involved in administrative overhead declines with size, leading to economies of scale.[5]

Increasing size is also related to increased structuring of the organization's activities but decreased concentration of power. Managerial practices, such as flexibility in personnel assignments, extent of delegation of authority, and emphasis on results rather than procedures, are related to the size of the unit managed.

Environment

An organization operates in an environment, which is outside and is constituted by various significant forces. Some of these are competitors, customers, vendors, financial institutions, trade bodies, regulatory institutions, and the government. The main characteristics of the environment affecting its structure are environmental complexity, uncertainty, and time horizon.[6] For example, a research organization operates in an environment characterised by longer time horizons, longer feedback times, and higher uncertainty than those of a manufacturing organization.

Differentiation–Integration

Contingency theory is the most widely used and perhaps the most influential perspective in studying organizations.[7] It is succinctly summarised in the statement that 'there is no one best way to organise.'[8] Organizations should be structured differently in different environments to achieve the best 'fit' to their environments.

Although the contingency idea that organizations adapt to their environments had been established,[9] it was Lawrence and Lorsch who emphasised the notion that different parts of the *same* organization adapt in different ways, leading the organization to a state of internal differentiation. Integrative mechanisms are then required to ensure effective coordination of activities in such internally differentiated organizations. This seminal theory, deserving attention for organizational structuring, is called the differentiation–integration theory. It addresses the issues associated with intra-organizational alignment of organizational sub-units and the integration challenges associated with intra-organizational differentiation, that is, the degree to which the various departments or sub-units within the organization specialise to perform different activities.

There are two main functions of organizational structure: *division* and the subsequent *coordination* of tasks.[10] The first task in structuring an organization is to define the main task of the organization and subsequently divide it into a number of sub-tasks. Conventionally, the main task is divided by function into what can be called the first-order sub-tasks: R&D, operations, sales, marketing, human resources, and financial management. Within operations, the second-order sub-tasks, in turn, primarily consist of supply chain management and manufacturing operations; cost management can probably be thought of as a third important second-order sub-task. The third-order sub-tasks within manufacturing, in turn, consist of materials handling, production planning and control, quality assurance, final assembly, and packaging. In addition to being divided by functions, tasks can also be divided on the basis of projects, or processes.

The second main task of organization designers is to ensure that the sub-tasks are effectively coordinated; to use Lawrence and Lorsch's terminology, 'integration' is needed. Lack of integration may manifest itself in lack of cooperation, communication problems, and sub-goal pursuit. Thus, organization design must explicitly address and reflect a well-thought-out division of tasks (differentiation) as well as the effective coordination (integration) of both routine and non-routine activities.

Different choices regarding how tasks are divided give rise to different kinds of integration challenges. According to Lawrence and Lorsch the functionally organized sub-units, like manufacturing, R&D, and sales, operate in different kinds of sub-environments. To the extent that these various sub-environments—scientific, techno-economic, and market—differ from one another, the organization as a whole becomes internally differentiated. Differentiation follows, in accord with contingency theory, from the proposition that organizations and, in this case, the various sub-organizational units must adapt to the requirements of their specific environments. Organizational integration is not limited to functional integration. No matter what the basis for the division of tasks, inter-departmental coordination is always relevant.

Lawrence and Lorsch's central proposition was that when an organization is highly differentiated, it has to develop and employ various integrative mechanisms to ensure effective coordination of tasks. Lawrence and Lorsch suggested that high internal differentiation implies inter-departmental conflict and thus the need for integration. In the case of functional division of tasks and functional differentiation, functional integration is implied.[11]

Power and Control

One important variable determining the nature of organizational structure is power (and control). We shall discuss the variable in detail in Chapter 24. Power and control are related to decision making and allocation of resources. The control of resources may be only in one place (centralised), or it may be shared throughout the organization (decentralised). One aspect of control is related to how many people are involved in the control process. We discuss this aspect under chain and span of control.

Chain and Span

The hierarchical structure is characterised by a strong chain of command. Chain of command is the line along which orders and decisions are passed down from top to bottom of the hierarchy. There are several advantages of hierarchy (chain of command). It improves coordination by creating a clear communication line between the top and the bottom of the business. Employees know what is expected of them and when. It also helps in creating departments, and departments form teams.

The disadvantages of hierarchies are that departments become insular, working for themselves rather than for the organization, and do not see the 'whole picture'. Hierarchies can also be inflexible and non-adjusting, especially when businesses need to adapt to changing markets.

A term originating in military organization theory, but now used more commonly in business management, particularly human resource management, span of control describes the number of subordinates that report to each military officer. In a hierarchy, span of control is the number of people who report to one manager. The more people under the control of one manager, the wider is the span of control. Less people means a narrower span of control. A narrow span of control allows managers to communicate quickly with the employees under them and control them more easily, and makes workers' feedback more effective.

On the other hand, in a wide span of control there are less layers of management to pass a message through, so the message reaches more employees faster. It is economical because less number of employees are required. A more skilful workforce can operate with a wider span of control because they will need less supervision. A more skilful manager can control a greater number of staff.

A tall organization has a larger number of managers with a narrow span of control while a flat organization has few managers with a wide span of control.

In the hierarchical business organization of the past it was not uncommon to see average spans of 1 to 10 or even less—that is, one manager supervised 10 employees on average. However, in the 1980s there was a flattening of organizational structures, causing average spans to move closer to 1 to 100. This was made possible by the introduction of inexpensive information technology that replaced many middle managers (whose main task had been to collect information from operational managers, compile it, and present it to the top management). Computers also made feasible the task of managing larger groups.

The current shift to self-directed cross-functional teams and other forms of non-hierarchical structures have made the concept of span of control less salient. Although Urwick developed a theory based on geographical dispersion and the need for face-to-face meetings,[12] no convincing theories have been presented. This is because the optimum span of control depends on numerous variables including organizational structure, available technology, the functions being performed, and the competencies of the manager as well as the staff.

USUAL ORGANIZATION DESIGNS

Based on the determinants discussed above, the organization can be designed in different ways. The nature of the design will depend on a combination of various determining elements. Some usual organizational designs are briefly mentioned here.

Centralisation–Decentralisation

One broad basis to classify an organization is power and control. If the decision making is concentrated in one place, we have centralised organization. Such an organization is generally unifunctional and smaller in size. Decision making is concentrated at the top. If decision making is shared at various levels or various subdivisions of the organization, the organization is decentralised. Such an organization is generally multi-functional, multi-locational, and larger in size. The subdivisions function with a fair amount of autonomy.

Divisionalisation

The growth and expansion of an organization may make it less efficient because of its large size. One common response to this problem is to restructure the organization into a number of semi-autonomous operating divisions, based either on product or on geographical areas. Such divisionalisation results in the creation of the multi-divisional organization.

Major businesses usually have some sort of divisional structure. For effective functioning, each division has its own performance criteria. It is necessary to measure how well or badly each division meets these criteria. A number of bases are used, like profit margin comparisons, return on capital, or economic value added.

There are numerous examples of divisionalised structures. One example of a divisionalised company is RPG. With a turnover of 9,500 crore rupees, it is a divisionalised conglomerate with 20 businesses. Its core businesses comprise mature economy businesses such as power, tyre, cables, power transmission, plantation, carbon black, and also new economy businesses such as pharma, retail, IT, and entertainment. It has 2,000 managers, out of whom 170 are at general manager and above level.

Many corporate structures comprise divisions with clear product remit. Such divisions often have their own management boards, financial targets, and strategic plans. Often at the centre is a group management responsible for strategic and financial control and for ensuring that management resource is optimised, best practice is adopted, and synergies are realised between operating divisions. Fulfilment of that responsibility can only be encouraged, rewarded, and tempered if performance is measured and monitored on a sound, accepted, and comparable basis.

'Responsibility centres' provide the basis for one such approach. The Chartered Institute of Management Accountants has defined a responsibility centre as 'a segment of the organization where an individual manager is held responsible for the segment's performance'. Generally there are three types of 'responsibility centres'—expense centres, profit centres, and investment centres.

An expense centre is a location, function, or item or equipment in respect of which controls may be ascertained and related to cost units for control purposes.

A profit centre is a segment of the business entity by which both revenues are received and expenditures are caused or controlled. Such revenues and expenditure are used to evaluate segmental performance.

An investment centre is a profit centre in which inputs are measured in terms of expenses and outputs are measured in terms of revenues, and in which assets employed are also measured, the excess of revenues over expenditure then being employed.

Profit responsibility performance can be reflected in figures relating profit to turnover. However, performance may be subject to the fairness of apportioned costs and transfer prices. Investment responsibility performance can be judged on the basis of return on investment or residual income (excess earnings over the cost of capital). In each case the assets/capital included should be that over which the responsible management has control. More recently the term EVA (economic value added) has been used. EVA is simply the net operating profit after tax less the cost of capital (the weighted average cost of debt and equity) used in the business.

Measurement of divisional performance calls for some form of responsibility accounting. It can be made in terms of earnings to sales, return on investment (RI), residual income, or economic value added. Management's performance would be measured using RI/EVA and often management and employees would be rewarded based on this performance measure.

Departmentalisation

Departmentalisation refers to the process of grouping activities into departments. Division of labour creates specialists who need coordination. Grouping specialists together in departments facilitates this coordination. The following are the common forms of departmentalisation.

Functional departmentalisation: Grouping activities by functions performed
Product departmentalisation: Grouping activities by product line
Customer departmentalisation: Grouping activities on the basis of common customers
Geographic departmentalisation: Grouping activities on the basis of territory
Process departmentalisation: Grouping activities on the basis of product/customer flow
Owing to the complexity of tasks and the competitive environment in which organizations operate, they often use a combination of the above mentioned methods in departmentalisation. Recent trends are in the direction of increasing emphasis on customer departmentalisation, and supplementing rigid departmentalisation is being complemented by the use of teams that cross over traditional departmental lines.

Bureaucracy

Bureaucratic organizations have a certain degree of standardisation. They are hierarchical, with rigid rules and regulations. They are better suited for more complex or large-scale tasks. Government organizations generally have bureaucratic structures.

Matrix Structure

Matrix organizations utilize functional and divisional chains of command simultaneously in the same part of the organization, commonly for one-of-a-kind projects. In a matrix organization, teams are formed and team members report to two or more managers. Matrix structure is used to develop a new product, to ensure the continuing success of a product to which several departments directly contribute, and to solve a difficult problem. Superimposing a project structure upon the functional structure creates a matrix organization, which allows the organization to take advantage of new opportunities. This structure assigns specialists from different functional departments to work on one or more projects being led by project managers. The matrix concept facilitates working on concurrent projects by creating a dual chain of command—the project manager (programme, systems, or product) and the functional manager. Project managers have authority over activities geared towards achieving organizational goals, while functional managers have authority over promotion decisions and performance reviews.

Matrix organizations are particularly appealing to firms that want to speed up the decision making process. However, the matrix organization may not allow long-term working relationships to develop. Furthermore, using multiple managers for one employee may result in confusion as to manager evaluation and accountability. Thus, the matrix system may elevate the conflict between product and functional interests.

EMERGING ORGANIZATIONAL DESIGNS

With changing technology and expectations and increasing involvement of employees, new forms of organizations are emerging. We discuss some of the forms in this section.

New Organising Principles

The future organizations will need to have a different mindset when viewing the structure of their workforce. Some of the characteristics of such organizations are that they are horizontal (flat), customer-driven, global, infinitely adaptable, team-based, and networking. In some new organizations, employees can work anywhere—on planes, in hotels, in their homes, in cars, etc., with the help of cellular phones, laptops, integrated software working groups, and faxes. Location becomes less of an issue for most people—allowing culture and geographical lines to be crossed anytime. The new forms of organizations often exhibit the following characteristics:

1. Strong employee involvement—Utilising input to the system from those closest to the outcome preferred by the system, from those most in-the-know about whether the organization is achieving its preferred outcomes with its stakeholders. This way, the organization stays highly attuned and adaptive to the needs of stakeholders.

2. Organic in nature—Ascertaining less rules and regulations, sometimes no clear boundaries, and is always changing forms.

3. Authority based on capability—Ensuring the organization remains a means to an end and not an end in itself.

4. Alliances—Taking advantage of economies of scale, e.g., collaborations, networks, strategic alliances/mergers, etc.

5. Teams—Sharing activities to take advantage of economies of scale at the lowest levels of activities and ensuring full involvement of employees at the lowest levels.

6. Flatter, decentralised organizations—Minimising middle management, resulting in top management exchanging more feedback with those providing products and services and also in less overhead costs.

7. Mindfulness of environments, changes, patterns, and themes—Prioritising on reflection and inquiry to learn from experience; developing 'learning organizations'.

Lateral organization represents one of several alternative organization designs that managers can choose from for dealing with the information processing demands imposed by high levels of task uncertainty.[13] Organizations are open systems and hence subject to uncertainty, but have limited means by which to process that information.[14] Open systems, by their very nature, are responsive to environmental change, but often have complex internal arrangements to manage and process diverse environmental stimuli. Open systems develop structures that match their information-processing capacities with the demands imposed by task complexity, interdependence, and uncertainty. As organizations increase the breadth, complexity, and novelty of products and services, they correspondingly increase the number of decisions that must be made to operate effectively. This complicates resource allocations and transfers of personnel. Several scholars have suggested that organizations establish lateral integrative mechanisms to increase the capacity to handle the high information processing requirements of such diverse activities.[15] Lateral mechanisms tend to promote learning that balances integration with responsiveness.

Network Structure

The network structure is a modern structure and includes the linking of numerous, separate organizations to optmise their interaction in order to accomplish a common, overall goal. There can be intra-networking, a joint venture to build complex, technical systems such as the space shuttle. Or there may be inter-organizational networking, like a network of construction companies to build a large structure. Networking requires synergy, a high level of collaboration.

Team Organizations

Several organizations function with self-managed teams. Tata Cummins is one such organization, working with 8-member teams. There are no supervisors in the company. Many other organizations operate with self-managed teams. These teams usually include 5–15 people and are geared to produce a product or service. Members provide a range of skills needed to produce the product. The team is granted sufficient authority and access to resources to produce their product in a timely fashion. The hallmark of a self-managed team is that members indeed manage their own group, i.e., they manage access to resources, scheduling, supervision, etc. Team members develop their own process for identifying and rotating members in managerial roles. Often, authority at any given time rests with whoever has the most expertise about the current activity or task in the overall project. Often members are trained in various problem solving techniques and team-building techniques.

These teams work best in environments where the technologies to deliver the product or service are highly complex and the marketplace and organization environments are continually changing. Self-managed teams pose a unique challenge for the traditional manager. It can be extremely difficult for him or her to support empowerment of the self-managed team, taking the risk of letting go of his or her own control.

In 1998, Federal Express organized its 1,000 clerical workers into super teams of 5–10 people. These teams were trained and given the authority to make improvements in their work. Without any formal supervision, in just 1 year, these teams were able to bring down costs due to incorrect billing and lost packages by 13 per cent.[16]

Chip-maker Intel is organized into several dozen small councils, which not only manage the research and product development activities, but are also responsible for the traditional support functions (e.g., purchase policy, operating procedures, employee compensation). The performance of the teams is judged against the targets set by them. According to Intel CEO Andy Grove, the aim is to remove authority from an artificial place at the top and to place it where the most knowledgeable people are.[17]

'Pizza' structure is a special kind of team organization. In 1993, Eastman Chemical Co., a division of Eastman Kodak, changed itself into a circular 'pizza chart' organization. In the pizza chart, each function, geographic region, or 'core competence' is represented by a pepperoni on the pizza. The white space around the pepperoni is where the actual collaborative work takes place. Hierarchy is abolished, and functions are not supposed to have separate goals. People work in self-directed work teams; all managers are members of at least one such team.[18]

Team organizations also use networking in their operations. In 1993, Amtrex started to mould itself into what its CEO described as a 'horizontal, circular structure'. Most of its activities were reorganized around a number of teams: '100 per cent OK teams', 'customer care teams', 'teams for accelerated innovation', and so on. To ensure customer focus, the company re-engineered itself into a process-based organization and redefined each function as a part of the service chain. The company also invested heavily in information technology to network the various parts of its processes, so that relevant information was available all the time to anyone, anywhere in the organization.[19]

Spaghetti Organization

Some organizations have experimented with flexibility in the structure—or almost lack of structure. Lars Kolind, newly named CEO of Oticon A/S, a Danish manufacturer of high-quality hearing aids that had suffered significant losses since the mid-1985s, brought about a radical change in the company in 1990. He implemented a design change, what he now calls the spaghetti organization—so named because of its relative lack of structure. Shortly after implementation, the company suffered further financial losses. By 1993, however, the company achieved its greatest profit since it was founded in 1904. In 1994, Kolind won the EFMD (European Federation of Management Development) award.

Its traditional bureaucratic structure was replaced with a radically new design based on project teams, a new IT system that led to the virtual elimination of paper, reconfigured office spaces, and a shift in the business from focusing on technology to serving end-users. Kolind dubbed the new organization the 'spaghetti organization' because the multiple roles individuals played were intertwined. The new structure was celebrated in articles and Harvard case studies. In a 1992 article, *Fortune* called it 'the Terminator II-type organization', comparing it to the shape-shifting robot of the futuristic film. Kolind took Oticon public in 1995, and left in 1998.

Fishnet Organization

Another flexible organization design is what is called the fishnet. The fishnet is flexible; it can form and re-form varied patterns of connection. The middle manager may at one time be at the apex, at another in the middle. The fishnet organization rearranges itself quickly while retaining its inherent strength.

A 'fishnet' organizational structure is flexible, adaptable, and increasingly necessary in today's downsized corporations. The fishnet model allows any structure to be woven together electronically and altered as needed; the organization becomes an ad hoc cooperative web instead of a permanent competitive citadel.

Virtual Organization

The virtual organization form is based on organization members interacting with each other completely, or almost completely, via telecommunications. Members may never actually meet each other.

Virtual organization requires a different way of perceiving the world by those who wish to participate in it. There are four key characteristics of virtual organization as a process: (1) development of relationships with a broad range of potential partners—each having a particular competency that complements the others; (2) capitalisation on the mobility and responsiveness of telecommunications—to overcome problems of distance; (3) responsiveness and availability to decide between alternatives—timing is the key aspect of relationships for the actors; (4) trust between actors separated in space—essential for virtual organization to be effective.

Virtual organizations are seen as the emerging standard in business, resulting from technological advances and changing expectations on the part of consumers and collaborators.[20] With information processing and telecommunications networks continuing to expand, corporations that use these technologies to their full potential will succeed, and in the process raise the standard for competition higher than what traditional forms of organization can achieve.

American Airlines' SABRE reservation system is a good example of a virtual organization.[21] SABRE makes money for American by providing more information about its customers to members and by giving customers faster response and more choices. This is a core competency that American can use to enter profitable partnerships with other airlines.

A focus on change, being customer-driven and managed, and the presence of highly skilled workers, working in a collaborative climate, have been suggested as the distinguishing characteristics of virtual organizations.[22] They succeed when they develop relationships with their clients that last three to four product generations and include a broad variety of services related to a product. It has been suggested that each organization must focus on achieving world-class excellence in one area of its core competency.[23] By building a virtual web of relationships with other corporations, including competitors, suppliers, and clients, a corporation enables itself to efficiently and effectively pull together the resources needed to develop and deliver profitable solutions to client problems. By integrating their complementary core competencies, virtual corporations can reap the benefits of interdependence—reduced overheads, increased profits, greater commitment from members and customers, and increased array of opportunities for future collaborations.[24]

Learning Organizations

In a world where environments are continually changing, it is critical that an organization detects and quickly corrects its own errors. This requires continuous feedback to, and within, the organization. Continual feedback allows the organization to 'unlearn' old beliefs and remain open to new feedback, uncoloured by long-held beliefs.

In a learning organization, managers do not direct as much as they facilitate the workers' applying new information and learning from that experience. Managers ensure time to exchange feedback, to inquire and reflect about the feedback, and then to gain consensus on direction. The learning organization is continually expanding its capacity to create its future. For a learning organization, 'adaptive learning' must be joined by 'generative learning,' learning that enhances its capacity to create.[25]

Learning organizations are self-organizing systems, with the ability to continually change their structure and internal processes to conform to feedback with the environment. Some writers use the analogy of biological systems as self-organizing systems. The ultimate purpose of learning organizations is to stay alive and duplicate. They exist in increasing complexity and adapt their structures and forms to accommodate this complexity. Ultimately, they change structure dramatically to adjust to the outer environment.

A self-organizing system requires a strong current goal or purpose. It requires continual feedback with its surrounding environment. It requires continual reference to a common set of values and dialoguing around these values. It requires continued and shared reflection around the system's current processes. The manager of this type of organization requires high value on communication and a great deal of patience—and the ability to focus on outcomes rather than outputs. Focus is more on learning than on method.

CORPORATE RESTRUCTURING: MERGERS AND ACQUISITIONS

As the organizations grow in size and functions, they start restructuring their activities. In fact, organizational growth itself is triggered by acquisition of new units. Such forms of restructuring are increasing now. These take various forms like expansions (increase in size of the organization), acquisitions (buying out a new company), mergers (a combination of two or more companies into a single company), amalgamations (fusion of two or more organizations, for example, the merger of Brooke Bond India Ltd with Lipton India Ltd resulted in the formation of a new company Brooke Bond Lipton India Ltd), joint ventures (two companies agreeing to provide certain resources for achievement of a common goal), etc.

Merger and Acquisition Process

The merger and acquisition (M&A) process can be divided into a planning stage and an implementation stage. The planning stage consists of the development of the business and the acquisitions plans. The implementation stage consists of the search, screening, contacting the target, negotiation, integration, and the evaluation activities. In short, the process of acquisition can be summarised in the following steps[26]:

1. Develop a strategic business plan.
2. Develop an acquisition plan related to the strategic plan.
3. Search candidates for acquisitions.
4. Screen and prioritise potential candidates.
5. Initiate first contact with the target.
6. Refine valuation, structure the deal, perform due diligence, and develop financing plan—negotiate.
7. Develop plan for integrating the acquired business.
8. Obtain all the necessary approvals, resolve post-closing issues, and implement closing.
9. Implement post-closing integration.
10. Conduct the post-closing evaluation of acquisition.

The acquisition strategy of GE Capital illustrates the acquisition process. GE Capital uses a successful model called '81 Pathfinder' for acquiring firms. The model disintegrates the process of M&A into four categories that are further divided into subcategories. The four stages incorporate some of the best practices for optimum results.

The pre-acquisition phase of the model involves due diligence, negotiations, and closing of deals. This involves the assessing culture, devising communication strategies, and evaluating strengths and weaknesses of the business leaders. An integration manager is also chosen at this stage. The second phase is the foundation building. At this phase the integration plan is prepared. A team of executives from GE Capital and the acquiring company is formed. Also a 100-day communication strategy is evolved and the senior management involvement and support is made clear. The needed resources are pooled and accountability is ensured.

The third is the integration phase. Here the actual implementation and correction measures are taken. Processes like assessing the workflow, assigning of roles, etc. are done at this stage. This stage also involves continuous feedbacks and making necessary corrections in the implementation. The last phase involves the assimilation process in which integration efforts are reassessed. This stage involves long-term adjustment and looking for avenues for improving the integration. This is also the period when the organization actually starts reaping the benefits of the acquisition. The model is dynamic in the sense that the company constantly improves it through internal discussions between the teams that share their experiences and effective tools and refine best practices.[27]

The integration process itself can be a powerful tool to make mergers and acquisitions effective. It has been suggested that a unifying theme for every phase of a merger can be

- Built around the principle of employee engagement, helping to nurture an every-widening sense of ownership and commitment to the new combination
- Linked tightly to the strategic vision and objectives of the combination and conducted in such a way that they help leverage the human capital within the combining organizations
- Managed in such a way as to encourage dialogue, upward feedback, and the flow of knowledge, ideas, and fresh insights around the organization
- Made a source of personal and collective learning that can enhance the combination's capability and better equip it to handle future partnership arrangements

Behavioural Issues in Mergers and Acquisitions

M&A, involving large-scale organizational change, can be a significant source of anxiety.[28] In the majority of mergers and acquisitions, the combination of one plus one yields less than two.[29] With the growing trend towards M&As, recent research has shifted to the human side of M&A to understand the psychological and behavioural effects of M&A on employees.[30] M&A involves organizational change, integrating some or all parts of the original organizations' functions and activities. The recent wave of M&As has been dominated by horizontal mega mergers,[31] in which businesses pursue market synergy or consolidation. These require the greatest degree of organizational integration, including procedural, physical, managerial, and sociocultural integration.[32] Large-scale organizational change can have traumatic impacts on employees, such as layoffs, turnover, stress, and illness. We discuss below six theories related to psychological problems in mergers and acquisitions, and briefly mention some interventions to deal with the problems.[33]

Anxiety theory Generally, employees experience a high degree of anxiety regarding uncertainty of the impact of the M&A on their future jobs and careers, leading to increased worry and feelings about fair and objective human resource management, equal participation in decision making, and treating employees with dignity and respect. Separation anxiety can also result from seeing coworkers terminated.

Several interventions can be used to manage the anxiety created by M&A:
1. Top-down, formal communication that provides timely and accurate information about what will happen to the organization and employees' jobs
2. Early and ongoing communication
3. Speed-up of the integration processes
4. Employee counselling and stress management training
5. Social support from spouse, friends, supervisors, coworkers, relatives; organizations provide social support in various ways, including providing employee assistance programmes and conducting 'town meetings' where employees can voice their

views openly, listen to others, and take solace in the fact that others are experiencing the same emotions

6. Enhancement of employees' perceptions of control, for example, allowing them to participate in decision making during and after the M&A
7. Training of managers in listening skills and in helping their subordinates cope with M&A-related anxiety
8. The practice of golden parachutes, which ensures executives will receive compensation in the event that they lose their job as a result of the M&A

Social identity theory   According to the social identity theory, a part of an individual's identity is derived from membership in groups, for example, organizations and professions. During the M&A process, employees will react by trying to attain a positive position for their own group in the new organization. This can lead to strong ingroup/outgroup biases that can generate serious inter-organizational conflicts. The extent to which employees are willing to accept a new identity during an M&A is related in part to the relative status (success, budget, etc.) of their existing group compared to the M&A partner, and the degree to which they accept the status differential as legitimate.

Several interventions can support the creation of a new identity. These include

1. Articulating a new vision, common goals, and organizational symbols
2. Highlighting a common outgroup or competitor and using various cross-organizational structures and teams
3. Disengaging efforts such as termination ceremonies or 'grieving meetings' where people are encouraged to openly express their feelings and emotions as a means of letting go of the old identity

Acculturation theory   Four modes of acculturation as adapted to the context of M&A include deculturation (members of an organization do not retain their old culture or replace it with a new one), assimilation (members of an organization adopt the culture of another), separation (members of both organizations retain their original cultural identity), and integration (members in both organizations change to some extent).

Interventions to address acculturative stress involve assessing the potential for culture clash and then facilitating the process of bringing the different cultures together. A culture audit conducted as part of the M&A process can provide a realistic assessment of the cultural differences that exist between the organizations in the M&A. It can also enable proactive planning of interventions to address potential acculturation problems. Possible interventions include fostering multiculturalism, in which both organizational cultures are equally valued and integrated, and facilitating intercultural learning via intercultural presentations and workshops. Intergroup mirroring workshop may be useful, where members from both organizations are encouraged to surface both differences and similarities between organizational cultures. An important assumption of these interventions is that structured and purposeful interactions between the combining organizational members will lead to either intercultural tolerance or assimilation.

One example of how to integrate different organizational cultures is the integration process of GE Capital already cited earlier. The company has implemented a systematic process for cultural integration that includes a cultural workout, where managers from the combining companies discuss differences in the organizational cultures and develop plans to integrate the cultures. The results from the cultural workout are shared widely in both companies. GE Capital also assigns members from both companies to serve on short-term projects that address important business issues. This allows organizational members to see the value of working together.

Role conflict theory   The role conflict theory suggests that psychological tension occurs when individuals are engaged in multiple roles that are incompatible. Employees may experience high degrees of role conflict as a result of new job demands related to the merger, or may experience conflict between remaining loyal to old customers or coworkers and implementing the changes required by the M&A. The threat of job loss can interfere with employees' role as providers for their family.

Two-way communication, which consists of both active listening to the sources of role conflict and ambiguity and promptly responding to the role-related issues, may help to cope with such conflicts. Strong managerial leadership can help to develop and clarify employees' new roles in the merged organization. This may require one-on-one discussions with employees to negotiate and clarify role expectations.

Job characteristics theory   The job characteristics theory suggests that core job characteristics (skill variety, task identity, task significance, task autonomy, and task feedback) influence perceptions of the work environment and in turn influence motivation and job satisfaction. Broader job characteristics can include other dimensions of the work environment, such as career paths, work relationships, support networks, status differences, geographic transfer, and job security. These can all play a role in shaping employee attitudes and behaviour after a merger.

Redesigning of jobs in the post-M&A organization to sustain or increase employees' job satisfaction and organizational commitment may be helpful. Employees can be encouraged to participate in job redesign processes; this is likely to reduce possible resistance and maintain a positive attitude during the transition. Training employees to adjust to job changes is also useful.

Organizational justice theory   When workers see themselves as being treated fairly, they are more likely to develop attitudes and behaviours in support of change, even under conditions of adversity and loss. Employee reactions to an organizational change such as an M&A can be influenced by the following three types of fairness perceptions: (a) distributive justice—fairness of outcomes received compared to an individual's standard of fairness, (b) procedural justice—fairness of procedures used to determine the outcomes, and (c) interactional justice—how the organizational members are treated by those responsible for determining outcomes and procedures.

Employees' perceived fairness of how both surviving and displaced employees were treated during the post-merger integration period substantially influence their attitudes (psychological withdrawal) and behaviours (turnover). Several approaches have been suggested for managing organizational justice perceptions during organizational restructuring.

1. With regard to distributive justice, outcomes should be based on the needs of the organization and those of the employee. For example, employees should receive training based on the criticality of their role in the new organization and the deficit of skills for those roles.

2. Procedural justice perceptions can be increased by allowing equal participation of employees from both organizations in making important decisions, including employee displacement. Second, new human resource management policies and procedures in the newly merged organizations should use accurate, objective, and unbiased criteria and be consistent across both people and time.

3. Interactional justice requires handling displaced employees with fairness and respect, providing adequate explanations of the need for change, and acknowledging the adversities that employees are facing.

The integration process needs to be managed in a systematic way, developing integration plans to help guide the process and to ensure that issues are adequately addressed. Some companies that have been successful in M&A have used a full-time integration manager and an integration or transition team. The integration manager should be someone who is well respected, has proven management skills, and also has strong skills in facilitating organizational change. In addition, the integration manager should have the necessary functional knowledge to lead the integration.

SUMMARY

Organizational structure is the way in which the interrelated groups of an organization are constructed. The main determinants of organizational forms are size, technology, environment, power, and control. Differentiation–integration is the most widely used and perhaps the most influential perspective in studying organizations. Chain and span of command also determine the organizational designs. The usual organization designs include centralisation–decentralisation, and divisionalisation (restructuring the organization into a number of semi-autonomous operating divisions, based either on product or on geographical areas) and departmentalisation (grouping activities into departments). The other usual forms are bureaucracy (hierarchical organizations having a certain degree of standardisation and rigid rules and regulations) and network structure (linking of numerous, separate organizations to optmise their interaction in order to accomplish a common, overall goal). Emerging organizational designs are organic in nature, mindful of environments, and characterised by strong employee involvement, authority based on capability, teams, and alliances. The new forms include network structure and team organizations, which use networking in their operations. Other new forms are 'spaghetti organizations,' a radically new design based on project teams, intertwining multiple roles; fishnet organizations (flexible, forming and re-forming varied patterns of connection); virtual organizations (organization members interacting with each other completely, or almost completely, via telecommunications); and learning organizations (self-organizing systems, with the ability to continually change their structure and internal processes to conform to feedback with the environment).

Corporate restructuring can take various forms like expansions (increase in the size of organizations), acquisitions (buying out a new company), mergers (a combination of two or more companies in a single company), amalgamations (fusion of two or more organizations), joint ventures (two companies agreeing to provide certain resources for achievement of a common goal), etc. Merger and acquisition process involves several steps. Behavioural issues in mergers and acquisitions have addressed the psychological consequences on employees. Various theories have been proposed to explain such consequences and have suggested interventions to cope with them. Some of these are—the anxiety theory, the social identity theory, the acculturation theory, the role conflict theory, the job characteristics theory, and the organizational justice theory. The integration process needs to be managed in a systematic way, developing integration plans to help guide the process, ensuring that issues are adequately addressed.

GLOSSARY

acquisition   buying out a new company

assimilation   members of an organization adopting the culture of another organization

bureaucratic organization   an organization having a certain degree of standardisation, hierarchy, and rigid rules and regulations

centralisation   concentration of decision making in one place

chain of command   the line along which orders and decisions are passed down from top to bottom of the hierarchy

decentralisation   shared decision making among several levels and sub-units

deculturation   members of an organization not retaining their old culture or replacing it with a new one

departmentalisation   the process of grouping activities into departments

divisionalisation   structuring the organization into a number of semi-autonomous operating divisions, based either on products or on geographical areas

differentiation   dividing the main task of the organization into a number of sub-tasks

environment   outside significant forces and institutions

identity   self-image derived from membership in groups

integration   effective coordination of sub-tasks

learning organization   a self-organizing system, with the ability to continually change its structure and internal processes to conform to feedback with the environment

matrix organization   utilising functional and divisional chains of command simultaneously in the same part of the organization

merger   a combination of two or more companies in a single company

network structure   linking of numerous, separate organizations to optmise their interaction in order to accomplish a common, overall goal

organizational structure   the way in which the interrelated groups of an organization are constructed

separation   members of both organizations retaining their original cultural identity

size   capacity in terms of number of personnel, outputs (customers, sales), and resources (wealth)

spaghetti organization   an organization in which individuals play multiple roles, which are intertwined

span of control   the number of people who report to one manager

strategy   a long-term plan of action designed to achieve a particular goal

technology   the knowledge and use of tools

virtual organization   an organization in which members interact with each other completely, or almost completely, via telecommunications

EXERCISES

Concept Review Questions

1. What are the main determinants of organizational structure?
2. What are the implications of line and span of control?
3. What are the main characteristics of a matrix organization?
4. Discuss the various new forms of organizations.
5. What are the main theories of psychological aspects of M&A?

Critical Thinking Questions

1. Compare the main differences between public sector and private sector organizations from the point of view of characteristics of structure.
2. Discuss the differences between corporation and university structures.

Classroom Projects

1. Discuss the characteristics of the structure of your institutions and the strengths and weaknesses.
2. Search from the Internet material on the acquisition of Arcelor by Tatas and discuss the whole process of acquisition.

Field Projects

1. Visit any one company and study its structure and its relationship with the company's strategy.
2. Visit a recently merged or acquired organization, and discuss the process and strategy.

Cisco's Acquisition Strategy*

INTRODUCTION

For the fiscal 2000–01, California-based Cisco Systems Inc., a market leader in the networking business, reported a net loss of 1 billion US dollars. Apart from the slowdown in the global IT industry and supply chain management problems and several other reasons, industry analysts blamed Cisco's much touted acquisition strategy for its dismal financial performance.

Cisco had acquired 71 companies (mostly start-ups with unproven products) between 1993 and 2000. With such a large number of acquisitions made in a relatively short period, it was very important for Cisco to integrate the acquired companies and get along as a group quickly. To evaluate and integrate the acquired companies, Cisco followed a standardized methodology. Cisco's ability to integrate scores of newly acquired companies was appraised by several analysts. John Morency, executive vice president of Sage Research said, 'Cisco has the uncanny ability not only to make targeted purchases, but also to integrate the company and technology well into its products and into the company.'

Cisco's acquisition strategy was working well while the IT industry was in its boom phase. However, with the beginning of the slowdown in early 2000 and the overall global economic slowdown, the situation turned bad for Cisco. By late 2000, Cisco's management found that many of its acquisitions were not performing as expected. With the company posting a loss, analysts were quick to point fingers at Cisco's acquisition strategy. Criticising Cisco for acquiring several companies, especially during 1999–2000, Johnson, an analyst at Robertson Stephens, said, 'Most of the recent acquisitions have been nothing more than mass recruiting. When there's a field that Cisco doesn't have expertise in and wants to enter, it goes out and buys the company that has the best engineers in that area.'

Learning from its mistakes, Cisco's management soon revised its acquisition strategy, adopting a more cautious approach. Compared to 41 acquisitions in 1999–2000, Cisco acquired only five companies during 2001–02.

BACKGROUND NOTE

In late 1984, a group of computer scientists at Stanford University, led by Len Bosack and Sandy Lerner, founded Cisco in California, US. They designed an operating system software called IOS (Internet Operating System) that could route

*This case was written by Konakanchi Prashanth, under the direction of Vivek Gupta, ICFAI Center for Management Research (ICMR), 2004. Reproduced with permission of ICFAI Center for Management Research (ICMR), Hyderabad.

streams of data from one computer to another. The software was loaded into a box containing microprocessors specially designed for routing. This was known as the router.

Over the next couple of years, the scientists carried on with their full-time occupations in the daytime and spent evenings working on the router. What drew the team together was the confidence they had in the performance of their product and the challenge of working for a start-up company.

In March 1986, the first router was delivered. Cisco's router was far more technologically advanced than other routers available in the market and was much cheaper. By November 1986, Cisco was earning revenues of US $250,000 per month. By then, most of the scientists were involved full time in Cisco, having left their lucrative jobs elsewhere. Encouraged by the initial success, Cisco started seeking venture capital funding. The company also formed its management team. In 1987, Cisco appointed Bill Graves as CEO and Lloyd Embry as CFO. In the same year, the company received funding of 2.5 million US dollars from a venture capital firm, Sequoia Capital, in return for a 29.1 per cent equity stake.

Sensing the need for a more professional leadership, Cisco's board appointed John Morgridge as its CEO in November 1988. Morgridge roped in several key professionals and expanded Cisco's business in Europe and Japan. He emphasised team-building at Cisco and offered stock options to most of the employees, changing the policy of awarding stock options to only executive-level employees. Morgridge also made efforts to increase the diversity of Cisco's workforce. By 1988, Cisco's revenues reached 5.45 million US dollars. The company had 35 employees, 12 of them being engineers. By late 1989, Cisco's 174-strong workforce comprised 35 software engineers, with the rest from diverse fields including manufacturing, sales and marketing, customer service, finance, and administration.

In the early 1990s, events took a positive turn at Cisco. The increasing popularity of routers and certain top management changes, including the one involving the recruitment of John Chambers, as the senior vice president (Worldwide Sales and Operations), helped the company experience spectacular growth. Chambers stressed a shift in focus from being technologically driven to customer driven. The engineers were asked to make product modifications as per customer requirements. The sales team aggressively promoted the product and added several major corporate customers.

In June 1994, Chambers was appointed as the executive vice president of Cisco and was given the additional responsibility of managing manufacturing. Chambers felt that Cisco was relying too heavily on routers. He felt that Cisco should offer the widest possible range of networking products to its customers. At the same time, Chambers realised that Cisco could not fully depend on its R&D team to come up with new products that catered to the market demands on a regular basis.

Chambers was appointed as Cisco's president and CEO in January 1995. Given the competitive scenario in the IT industry in the mid-1990s, with rapidly shrinking product life cycles, Chambers felt that it was impractical for Cisco to rely completely on in-house development of products. This belief formed the basis for Cisco's acquisition strategy.

ACQUISITION STRATEGY

Led by Chambers, Cisco focused on acquiring start-up companies that were working on emerging technologies with a promising future in the networking business. As Cisco was a highly decentralised company, managers were empowered to take decisions on acquiring companies. However, it was made necessary to follow a standard procedure for acquisitions and ensure uniformity in execution all across the company. Cisco employed a three-step process. This began with making an evaluation of the target company and convincing its management regarding the benefits of merging. Next, the company to be acquired was examined in terms of how various divisions of the company and its employees fitted with Cisco. This was followed by an integration of the acquired company. It was estimated that on an average, Cisco took 100 days to complete the acquisition process.

Evaluating Target Company

While evaluating a target company, Cisco took several factors into consideration. First, it checked whether the target company shared a similar business vision. In most cases, the target company had to be on the verge of developing a new product (within the next couple of months), which had the potential to be commercially exploited and generate quick profits. Cisco selected smaller companies for acquisition, since it was easier to integrate their business processes into its own.

Cisco also examined whether all the stakeholders of the target company, including the shareholders, employees, and customers, would benefit in the long term if the acquisition was made. Another important consideration was proximity to Cisco's headquarters, to facilitate closer monitoring and minimise travelling expenses for Cisco's executives. Summing up the criteria Cisco looked into while evaluating a company, Mike Volpi, executive-in-charge of acquisitions, said, 'Cisco's strategy can be boiled down to five things. We look at a company's vision, its short-term success with customers, its long-term strategy, the chemistry of the people with ours, and its geographic proximity.'

Apart from the above, another important factor taken into consideration was whether the values and culture of the company fitted with those of Cisco. In doing this, Cisco's managers examined several aspects of the company. For instance, the target company needed to be adventurous and not averse to taking risks. This was judged by the previous decisions made by the company—if the company was really adventurous, it would have made a couple of wrong decisions in the past.

Cisco reviewed the decisions taken by the target company and the lessons they had learned from their past mistakes. Cisco checked if the company's actions were similar to those that Cisco would have taken in such a situation. This was an indicator of synergy in the style of functioning. Another important indicator of the target company's culture was the unity within the company. Cisco had to be convinced that the employees of the target company were united. Ascertaining the cultural compatibility was critical for Cisco because this made integration easier.

Cisco did not believe in forced acquisition. The company's management always tried its best to convince the target company about the benefits likely to accrue to both the companies. Cisco was not merely interested in acquiring the product expertise of the new company but also its employees. Mutual consent of the two companies for the merger was thus absolutely critical to the success of the deal.

Determining Compatibility

The next important step in the acquisition process was to closely examine the target company in terms of its compatibility with Cisco. An acquisition team, comprising key members from all the departments of Cisco, was instituted. The team's task was to assess the extent to which both the top management and the lower level management employees of the potential company could be accommodated in Cisco. Cisco's engineers closely studied the technological aspects of the company, while its finance personnel looked into the company's financial records. Usually, the team spent a fortnight at the target company to make an in-depth assessment. The team assessed such aspects as the company's knowledge pool (the calibre of its employees) and the way in which its management functioned.

People formed a critical focal point for the acquisition team. In fact, the prospect of attracting and retaining the valuable intellectual talent that the target companies possessed was considered to be very important. As Dennis Powell, Cisco's controller said, 'If we're going to lose the people who are important to the success of the target company, we're probably not going to have an interest. We're not interested in just bringing in a product by itself. If we don't continue development of that product, we will not leverage the success of the acquisition as much as we could.'

Cisco's acquisition team closely studied the culture of the target company. Commenting upon how he judged the target company's culture, Chambers said, 'I can tell by walking into a company whether we're going to get along or not. I look at the size of the president's office. My office looks like any other office. I look at an office that the president can play basketball in and the employees are stuck over in grungy areas. It isn't going to work. You look at how stock options are spread between leadership teams and employees. If all stock is at the top, we're not going to get along. If we're talking to the acquisition target and they don't talk about customers, we can tell it won't be a culture match and we may as well go home. You can tell if they're creating a win–win or a win–lose in negotiation. If they don't think win–win, it's not going to match. Is it a culture of empowerment? It doesn't mean one culture's right or wrong, because they are many culture's here in Silicon Valley. You just don't combine two dramatically different cultures.'

Once the acquisition team was satisfied, the decision regarding the acquisition was left to the top three executives of Cisco's board—Chambers, Morgridge (chairman), and Don Valentine (vice chairman). This was done in order to ensure that the acquisition was not prone to any bias on Cisco's part.

Integrating Acquired Companies

Once a potential target company was identified, evaluated, and appraised, a consensus was reached between the two managements and the acquisition deal was signed. The next major step was to integrate the new company with Cisco. For this purpose,

Cisco put in place an integration team, comprising 15–25 persons, headed by the chief integration officer (CIO). The CIO's primary role was to facilitate the smooth integration of the two companies.

Cisco's HR and business development team visited the acquired company and interacted with the employees to clarify any doubts relating to the deal. The team distributed pamphlets describing Cisco's organizational structure, employee benefits, and the strategic significance of the acquired company for Cisco. Cisco's integration team conducted negotiations with the top management and 'mapped' employees to determine where they would fit. These decisions were based on the experience of employees. Usually the product engineering and marketing departments retained their identity and enjoyed functional autonomy, while the sales and manufacturing departments were merged into Cisco's departments.

The IT integration team integrated the acquired company's systems, including its e-mail ID, ERP systems, customer care systems, and its website with Cisco's systems. The team was given a deadline of 60 days from the date of acquisition to complete this highly complicated task. The team started by installing a virtual private network (VPN) to facilitate closed-door interaction and exchange of ideas between the officials of both companies. All through the integration process, the company's telecom and networking groups assisted the IT integration team. In most cases, Cisco was able to achieve the IT integration task well before its deadline. The success of the IT team was reflected in the fact that in the case of 20 acquisitions, customers were able to place orders for the acquired company's products within a day of acquisition.

The employees of the acquired company went through a 30-day tailor-made orientation programme. The new managers were trained about Cisco's hiring practices, the sales personnel received training on Cisco's products, and the engineers were educated about the development projects being undertaken by Cisco.

When deciding about employee retention, Cisco followed a policy called Mario Rule—named after Mario Mazzola, the CEO of Crescendo. According to this rule, no employee of the newly acquired company would be fired without the mutual consent of its CEO and Chambers. Explaining the significance of the rule, Daniel Scheinman, Cisco's vice president – Legal and Government Affairs, said, 'It buys the trust of the people ... and their passion is worth a lot more than any of the downside legal protection.'

One of the most critical jobs of the integration team was to reduce the tensions between the employees of the two companies. It had to ensure that the new employees had an identity of their own at Cisco. This was done by assigning them designations, job responsibilities, and other benefits associated with Cisco's employees.

The extent of success of the integration process could be judged from the fact that Cisco was able to retain a significant number of employees of the companies it acquired. According to a study conducted in 1999, the employee turnover among the employees entering Cisco through acquisitions was just 2.1 per cent, as against the industry average of over 20 per cent. This was lower than even Cisco's overall employee turnover. Commenting on the integration process, Mike Volpi, Cisco's senior vice president – Internet Switching and Services, said, 'Certainly the process of integration that we built around the acquisitions was very good. Even looking back now with everything we've learned since, I really think we had a great integration process, and I think we've far outstripped any other, either competitors in our industry or any other player that's done that number of acquisitions, as far as our success rate. We really have a very good success rate for our acquisitions, and I think a lot of that had to do with why we bought, how we bought, and how we integrated.'

In September 1993, Cisco made its first acquisition of Crescendo Communications. After this deal, Cisco started acquiring companies at a rapid pace. In tune with its strategy to develop the capability to offer end-to-end networking solutions to its customers, Cisco made 71 acquisitions between 1993 and 2000. This enabled the company to diversify into several new product lines and segments and demonstrate leadership in most of them. Cisco was also able to offer the benefits of its expanded product range to its customers. According to the company sources, by 2001, about 40 per cent of Cisco's total revenue of 19 billion US dollars was contributed by the companies it acquired.

Loopholes in Strategy

Several analysts and media reports expressed doubts over the manner in which the acquisitions were evaluated and the pace at which the deals were closed. Though the company officials boasted of a high success rate for all acquisitions, analysts expressed doubts. Cisco mostly acquired start-ups that were yet to come out with a product. The revenues obtained from those products could not be known until they were fully developed and marketed. Analysts felt that what Cisco acquired was skilful technicians and a product that, if developed successfully, might generate better revenues in future. They considered this a very risky strategy.

In its attempt to offer end-to-end networking solutions to its customers, Cisco diversified into too many business segments. Of the several acquisitions Cisco made, a few were successful, while others proved to be a drain on company resources. According to a *Business Week* report, while companies such as Crescendo Communications, Grand Junction, and Cerent Technologies were integrated successfully, the acquisitions of companies like Pirelli Optical Systems, Montery Networks, Amteva, and Maxcomm Technologies were not successful.

Cisco's 2.2 billion US dollar acquisition of Pirelli Optical Systems, aimed at boosting the optical networking business, performed below expectations. Cisco acquired Montery Networks for 500 million US dollars in 1999 and sold the company in 2001 at a 108-million-dollar loss, as the company could not develop a commercially viable product. Another instance of poor judgement was Cisco's 170-million-dollar acquisition of Amteva Technologies in 1999 to strengthen its unified messaging business. Cisco had to sell it at a loss in July 2001.

Cisco's policy to acquire companies by making use of its own stock came under scrutiny. Its financial reporting was also questioned. The media reported that between 1996 and 2001, Cisco wrote off 5.4 billion US dollars as acquisition-related charges.

This made it difficult to figure out the investment made by Cisco for acquisitions and what the company earned out of these acquisitions. Expressing his doubts over the authenticity of Cisco's financial reporting, Harvard Business School Professor Michael Porter said, 'When the historians actually plough through all the data, we will likely find that even during its so-called heyday, Cisco wasn't nearly as profitable in terms of return on invested capital as many believed.'

Doubts were raised over Cisco's ability to integrate the cultures of the acquired companies with that of Cisco. Media reports talked about the formation of small groups, representing the employees of acquired companies, within Cisco. Employees were often identified by the name of the company from which they came. There were several instances of conflicts between different groups.

Problems were reported on the IT integration front as well. Commenting upon the IT integration problems, Michael Zadikian, a former Cisco executive said, 'There are interface compatibility problems, software mismatches, and integrating these businesses is still a problem. From the outside looking in it seems Cisco integrates well. Inside, it looks horrendous. The pieces don't fit together.'

Prior to going on the acquisition spree, Cisco had a highly innovation-driven culture. The employees, especially those in the R&D department were proud of their company and its core product. However, as Cisco began rapidly expanding, analysts felt that the culture, which once fostered innovation, was receding, leading to resentment among employees. Though Cisco continuously increased its R&D spend over the years, this was not sufficient to boost the morale of the employees, whose main task became integrating the acquired technologies, rather than working on new technologies. Lawrence J. Lang, a former employee of Cisco complained, 'It became a very frustrating place. Cisco was saying very clearly to people like me, "If you want to innovate, go join a startup." '

Cisco's efforts of building a quality workforce and retaining the employees of acquired company by providing them lucrative incentives like stock options worked well as long as the company performed well and the stock price was near its peak. However, in 2001, when the company reported losses, the situation changed with a few employees leaving the company. Instances of infighting were also reported at Cisco.

Analysts felt that the insistence of Cisco's top management on managers to make fast decisions on acquisitions negatively affected the company. It caused problems such as a massive pileup of inventories, forcing Cisco to write off 2.5 billion dollar's worth inventory in 2001, and confusion involving the acquired technologies and products and a lack of coordination within various Cisco units. This affected the company's service as customers had to wait for longer periods to receive their goods.

Cisco's management realised its mistakes when the company reported a huge loss of 1 billion US dollars in the fiscal year 2001. Due to the slowdown in the IT industry, Cisco decided to act tough. In March 2001, Cisco announced its first major lay-off of 8,500 employees, which accounted for 18 per cent of its total workforce. Apart from the operational and cost-cutting initiatives, Cisco decided to make modifications in its acquisition strategy.

Revising Strategy

According to the new plan, Cisco's managers were not allowed to decide upon acquisitions. This was a shift from its previous culture of empowerment. Cisco constituted an investment review board whose task was to thoroughly scrutinise all the acquisition proposals. Every month, the heads of various departments including marketing, finance, and operations met to discuss the proposals. They assessed the potential impact of a particular acquisition on Cisco. A well-defined operational plan was drawn up at these meetings to ensure a smoother marriage of the target company with Cisco. The managers who supported an acquisition were also made responsible for achieving the financial performance targets on that deal. The revised strategy thus significantly raised the accountability of those managers. The number of acquisitions made by Cisco drastically reduced from 23 in 2000 to 2 in 2001 and 3 in 2002 indicating the cautious approach adopted by the management.

Another significant development at Cisco was the top management's decision to place emphasis on team building. A number of committees were set up all across the company to ensure that various departments worked in close coordination with each other. In order to enhance the team spirit within the organization, Cisco laid down a rule that 30 per cent of the bonuses of Cisco's executives would be based on how they promoted teamwork and cooperation.

Cisco's efforts since 2001 seemed to pay off as the company not only reported improved financial results, but also a change in the attitude of employees. A recent survey conducted by *Business Week* on 30,000 Cisco employees revealed that 92 per cent of the employees were keen on working with Cisco for the next 5 years as against the industry norm of 50 per cent. Commenting on the improvements, Daniel A. Scheinman, Cisco's senior vice president – Corporate Development, said, 'There's been a huge progress. There's a sense of redemption and vindication.' By 2003, Cisco was well on the path to profits, with its 2002–03 net income amounting to 3.6 billion US dollars.

Elements of Cisco's Culture

Empowerment   Cisco's management believed in offering maximum autonomy to executives. Several decisions, including the ones relating to investments in new products and technologies, were decentralised.

Drive change   All Cisco employees were encouraged to be vigilant towards changes in market environment, like customer attitudes, competitors moves, etc. State-of-the-art IT systems were installed to observe even minor changes in the external environment. The R&D department was encouraged to come out with new products quickly. The sales personnel were required to be proactive.

Teamwork   A lot of emphasis was placed on teamwork. Employees were encouraged to be team players. Efforts were made to promote better relationships between executives. They were encouraged to work with each other as a team to improve the company's prospects. They were even promised attractive rewards if they did so.

Customer success   All employees had to pay attention to the customers. They had to anticipate what customers wanted and act accordingly. The grievances of customers had to be properly addressed. Products were to be made as per customer requirements. Employee compensation, especially the bonus of the executives, was arrived at on the basis of the extent to which their customers were satisfied. The company conducted customer satisfaction surveys for this purpose.

Quality team   In order to achieve customer success, Cisco needed a skilled work force. At Cisco, recruiting and retaining talented people was a top priority. This was required for the company to consistently maintain its top position in the market. Cisco's management took steps to ensure employee satisfaction and hence retained skilled employees. It awarded stock options for employees in the managerial cadre as well as for non-management employees.

Questions for Discussion

1. Cisco acquired 71 companies during the period 1993 to 2000. Briefly explain the process followed by Cisco in evaluating, judging compatibility, and integrating an acquired company. How did this standardised procedure of acquisition help Cisco to quickly integrate a large number of acquired companies?
2. According to Michael Porter, 'Cisco wasn't nearly as profitable in terms of return on invested capital as many believed.' Critically analyse Cisco's acquisition strategy in light of this statement. What according to you were the flaws in Cisco's acquisition strategy?
3. Examine the revisions made by Cisco in its acquisition strategy after the company reported a poor financial performance in the fiscal year 2000–01. What measures, according to you, must Cisco take to make its acquisition strategy flawless? Explain.

NOTES AND REFERENCES

1. Chandler, A.D. (1962). *Strategy and Structure: Chapters in the History of American Industrial Enterprise.* Cambridge, MA: MIT Press.
2. Burgelman, R.A. (2002). *Strategy Is Destiny: How Strategy-making Shapes the Company's Future.* New York: Free Press.
3. Ansoff, H.I. (1965). *Corporate Strategy.* New York: McGraw-Hill.
4. Woodward, Joan (1980). *Industrial Organization: Theory and Practice.* Oxford: Oxford University Press.
5. Blau, Peter and W.R. Richard (2003). *Formal Organizations: A Comparative Approach.* Stanford University Press.
6. Lawrence, P. and J. Lorsch (1967). 'Differentiation and integration in complex organizations', *Administrative Science Quarterly*, 12: 1–30.
7. Donaldson, L. (2001). *The Contingency Theory of Organizations.* California: Thousand Oaks; Scott, Robert (2003). 'Reflections on a Half Century of Organizational Sociology', *Annual Review of Sociology*, 30, 1–21.
8. Galbraith, J. (1973). *Designing Complex Organizations.* Reading: MA: Addison-Wesley.
9. Burns, Tom and G.M. Stalker (1961). *The Management of Innovation.* London: Tavistock.
10. Galbraith. *Designing Complex Organizations;* Lawrence and Lorsch. 'Differentiation and integration'; March, J.G. and H.A. Simon (1958). *Organizations*, p 32. New York: Wiley; Mintzberg, H. (1979). *The Structuring of Organizations: A Synthesis of Research.* Englewood Cliffs: Prentice Hall.

11. Lawrence and Lorsch. 'Differentiation and integration', Chapter 3.
12. Urwick, L.E. (1956). 'The managers span of control', *Haward Business Review*, May–June, 56–70.
13. Galbraith. *Designing Complex Organizations*.
14. Thompson, James D. [1967] (2003). *Organizations in Action: Social Science Bases of Administrative Theory*. New Brunswick, NJ: Transaction Publishers.
15. Galbraith. *Designing Complex Organizations*; Burns, L.R. (1989). 'Matrix management in hospitals', *Administrative Science Quarterly*, 34(3): 349–368; Davis, S. and P. Lawrence (1977). *Matrix*. Reading, MA: Addison Wesley.
16. Dummaine, 1990, as quoted in Shukla, Mandhukar (1997). *Competing Through Knowledge: Building a Learning Organisation*. New Delhi: Response Books.
17. Quinn, 1992, as quoted in Shukla, *Competing Through Knowledge*.
18. Byrne, 1993, quoted in Shukla, *Competing Through Knowledge*.
19. Misra, 1996, quoted in Shukla, *Competing Through Knowledge*.
20. Goldman, S.L., R.N. Nagel, and K. Preiss (1995). *Agile Computers and Virtual Organizations*. New York: Van Nostsand Reinhold; Davidow, W.H. and M.S. Malone (1992). *The Virtual Corporation*, p. 38. New York: Harper-Business.
21. Davidow and Malone. *Virtual Corporation*.
22. *Ibid.*, 7–8.
23. Goldman et al. *Agile Computers*.
24. Davidow and Malone. *Virtual Corporation*.
25. Senge, P.M. (1990). *The Fifth Discipline: The Art and Practice of the Learning Organization*. New York: Double Day.
26. ICFAI (2003) is an excellent source on strategies and theories of M&A (with main focus on financial aspects), from which this has been taken.
27. Ashkenas, B.E. and F. Mael (1989). 'Social identity theory and the organization'. *Academy of Management Review*, 14: 20–39.
28. Seo, Myeong-Gu and N. Sharon Hill (2005). 'Understanding the human side of merger and acquisition: An integrative framework', *Journal of Applied Behavioral Science*, 41: 422–443.
29. Marks, M.L. and P.H. Mirvis (1992). 'Rebuilding after the merger: Dealing with "survival success". *Organisational Dynamics*, 21(2): 18–32.
30. Hogan, E. and L. Overmyer-Day (1994). 'The psychology of mergers and acquisitions'. *International Review of Organizational Psychology*, 9: 248–281.
31. Gaughan, P.A. (1999). *Mergers, Acquisitions and Corporate Restructuring*. New York: John-Wiley.
32. Shrivastava, P. (1986). 'Postmerger integration', *Journal of Business Strategy*, 7: 65–76.
33. The various theories have been discussed, with research support in Seo, Myeong-Gu and N. Sharon Hill (2005), from which material in this section has been taken.

5
Positive Perspective

It was Fred Luthans who first stressed the need for a positive approach in OB, devoting a full chapter to the subject.[1] There is a growing movement of 'positive psychology', emphasising the need to recognise and build strengths, rather than attempting to find weaknesses and 'cure' them. The development of appreciative inquiry as an organizational development approach[2] illustrates such a trend.

HISTORICAL PERSPECTIVE

It may be useful to have a historical perspective on this shift, especially in the context of the Indian culture. Management, by and large, is the product of a Western tradition and the Industrial Revolution. Organizational behaviour, with its roots in psychology and sociology, has developed in the same tradition and has been borrowed by other cultures. Both management and OB have two basic roots that developed in the West.

In the Christian tradition, universal sin is emphasised and Jesus Christ is perceived as doing penance for the sin of humanity, as shown through the Crucifix. As a result, the Western culture is largely a guilt culture rather than a shame culture. While this has contributed to excellent efforts in community service, it has also emphasised the need to purge society of evil. The medical profession did this by treating patients for various kinds of illnesses, and clinical psychology followed the same tradition by 'curing' mental diseases.

The second root of management and OB is the Industrial Revolution in the West. The Industrial Revolution led to unprecedented achievements, but at the same time over-emphasised the qualities generally attributed to men (achievement, drive, hardiness, toughness, aggression, etc.), thus bringing about a male-dominated society. Some Western thinkers have recently started questioning such a biased emphasis on 'manly' qualities, and concepts such as that of 'emotional intelligence' have been proposed to balance this bias. As a result, several authors have addressed the need to develop a positive approach. For example, Seligman—who did pioneering research in helplessness—came up with the concept of 'learned optimism'.[3] More recently, 'flow' (as contrasted with 'rumination') has been emphasised.[4]

Until recently, clinical psychologists gave almost all of their attention to the diagnosis and treatment of pathologies, and social psychology became preoccupied with biases, delusions, deficiencies and dysfunctions of human behaviour. For example, a search of contemporary literature in psychology as a whole found approximately 200,000 published articles on the treatment of mental illness; 80,000 on depression; 65,000 on anxiety; 20,000 on fear; and 10,000 on anger; but only about 1,000 on positive concepts and capabilities of people. Over the years, the tendency has been to view positivity with doubt and suspicion—a product of wishful thinking, denial, or even 'hucksterism'.[5] A group of psychologists has now started to develop what is called 'positive psychology'. The aim of positive psychology is to shift the emphasis away from what is wrong with people to what is right with them, from vulnerability to resilience.

Contrasted with the Western tradition, Eastern tradition has always emphasised the need to integrate the 'masculine' qualities with those traditionally attributed to women. The concept of androgyny, now becoming popular in the West, has always been a part of Indian tradition. It is interesting to note that thousands of years back we already had the concept of *ardhanareeshwara*, depicting Lord Shiva as half man and half woman, symbolising that even God is not complete without an integration of the masculine and feminine. In India, great emphasis is thus laid on values and characteristics generally attributed to women, such as compassion, caring, peace, and non-violence. Mahatma Gandhi represented this basic tendency of the Indian psyche effectively in modern times. The same qualities are being emphasised today in the West in concepts like emotional intelligence.

Similarly, in Ayurveda the emphasis is on achieving well-being rather than merely curing illness.

Now American psychologists are also laying more emphasis on the understanding and promotion of positive attributes such as contentment, flow, optimism, and hope.[6] There is thus a fairly strong movement towards positive psychology.[7] 'The field of positive psychology at the subjective level is about valued subjective experience: well-being, contentment, and satisfaction (past), hope and optimism (future), and flow and happiness (present). At the individual level it is about positive individual traits—the capacity for love and vocation, courage, interpersonal skill, aesthetic sensibility, perseverance, forgiveness, originality, future-mindedness, spirituality, high talent, and wisdom. At the group level it is about the civic virtues and the institutions that move individuals toward better citizenship: responsibility, nurturance, altruism, civility, moderation, tolerance, and work ethic.'[8]

In India, the author proposed a new basic need or motive—the extension motive, which is the need to be relevant to others and to a larger cause,[9] discussed its role in development,[10] and designed instruments to measure it.[11]

In 1971, as part of another study, the effect of teachers' influence styles (teaching behaviour) on pre-adolescents' positive mental health was investigated in a project supported by the Indian Council of Medical Research.[12] The author has also proposed hope (as contrasted with fear) as a basic dimension of organizational variables such as motivational behaviour, interactional style, power, and developed instruments to measure these. He has proposed the concept of 'organizational ethos'[13] and has proposed the concept of the pioneer-innovative (PI) motive relating to development and industrialisation.[14] Others have recently suggested the concept of SQ (spiritual quotient), parallel to IQ and EQ (emotional quotient).

CATEGORIES OF POSITIVE APPROACH

Luthans has enumerated the five main elements of the positive approach in OB: confidence, hope, optimism, subjective well-being, and emotional intelligence (CHOSE).[15] In confidence he includes self-efficacy.[16] Subjective well-being (SWB) has been found to have a high correlation with job satisfaction. Optimism and emotional intelligence have been studied in detail—they are reported to have a positive relationship to the effectiveness of individuals and groups. Luthans has included hope as a separate category, but it can be clubbed with optimism although there is some distinction between the two. The concept of emotional intelligence is quite wide and may easily become an amorphous category.

In order to retain a sharp focus, five categories of the positive approach are suggested here: internality, self-management, optimism, trust, and collaboration (ISOTC).

Internality

Internality, or internal locus of control, is the general orientation of an individual that results in a belief that he or she can shape his or her destiny. In a group, it implies that the members of the group believe they can collectively influence the main events relevant to the group. We shall deal with this aspect in detail in Chapter 9. Internality is closely related to and can include self-efficacy. In internality, we shall include both internal locus of control and efficacy.

The concept of efficacy has been popularised by Bandura's studies[17] and the theory of self-efficacy. According to him, self-efficacy refers to 'how well one can execute courses of action required to deal with prospective situation'. It refers to an individual's confidence in his or her ability to mobilise motivation, cognitive resources, and courses of action to execute a task. The major sources of self-efficacy are the following:

1. Mastery experiences or performance attainment—Information about success increases a sense of efficacy.
2. Various experiences or modelling—When people see certain role models, they feel more efficacious.
3. Social persuasion—When people are persuaded by significant others to initiate an activity, they may experience a sense of efficacy.

4. Physiological and psychological arousal—This refers to the physical and mental state of an individual, such as whether the individual is in good health or tired and exhausted.

The concept of efficacy is one of potential effectiveness. While Bandura has applied his concept to the self, it can also be applied to other aspects, such as a role or a team. Chapter 13 deals further with role efficacy.

Self-management

Self-management is a part of emotional intelligence. There are two main elements of self-management: self-regulation or self-restraint, and perseverance.

'There is perhaps no psychological skill more fundamental than resisting impulse. It is a route of all emotional self-controls, since all emotions, by their very nature, lead to one or another impulse to act.'[18] Goleman has drawn attention to a remarkable study on pre-school children by Walter Mischel in the 1960s. The children were involved in an experiment that required choosing between having one marshmallow (a kind of candy) immediately or getting two after the experiment. The follow-up showed remarkable results: those who had resisted the temptation of having the one marshmallow immediately and waited to get two later exhibited different behaviour 14 years later as compared to those who took the marshmallow immediately. 'The emotional and social differences between the grabbed-marshmallow pre-schoolers and their gratification-delaying peers was dramatic. Those who had resisted temptation were more socially competent, personally effective, self-assertive and better able to cope with the frustrations of life.'[19] This characteristic of postponement of immediate gratification for a long-term goal is a part of self-management, an important component of emotional intelligence. It is evident in successful entrepreneurs and creators of wealth such as Narayan Murthy of Infosys.

Optimism

Seligman has made a strong case for optimism as the central element of effectiveness for both individuals and groups.

Instead of indulging in the recollection of misfortunes and bad experiences, which is called rumination, individuals should get deeply involved in the activities they do and find enjoyment in them. Such 'joy of work' contributes not only to involvement but also to effectiveness. This has been called flow.

As Luthans has indicated, a state of happiness is an important element in effectiveness and has extended this concept to subjective well-being (SWB), proposed and thoroughly researched over the past three decades.[20] The psychological concept underlying SWB is flow.[21] In optimism also we include flow. We shall discuss both these concepts further in Chapter 9.

Trust

Trust, as an orientation, is reflected in (a) a positive image of 'others', resulting in dialogue and delegation, (b) positive reinforcement—appreciation, recognition, and reward, (c) respect for the confidentiality of information shared by others and care to see it is not misused, (d) a sense of assurance that others will help when such help is needed and will honour mutual commitments and obligations, and (e) acceptance of what another person says at face value without searching for ulterior motives. Trust is an extremely important ingredient in organization building. Interpersonal trust, leading to collaboration, has been seen as a cyclic process involving expectations (both formation and fulfilment of expectations), risk (overcoming the fear that the 'other' party will act opportunistically), and vulnerability (the willingness to assume that the 'other' party will bear the vulnerability resulting from the acceptance of risk).[22] Rao has developed an effective instrument to measure interpersonal trust.[23]

Collaboration

Much work has been done by economists and sociologists on cooperative effort. But studies to understand these processes at the micro level, in individuals, and in work organizations, are in their infancy. Collaboration between individuals, between groups within organizations, between organizations, between industrial and business sectors, and between nations has increased and is in great demand today.[24]

Collaboration can be defined in terms of a person working with another person or other people for the attainment of a goal that is seen as sharable. In this definition, the basic criterion of collaborative behaviour is the perception of the goal. If the goal is seen as shareable, working with other people for the attainment of the goal is collaborative behaviour. When the goal is seen as unsharable, that is, in a situation where two people are involved but only one of them can attain the goal, working for the exclusive attainment of the goal (by implication, against the other person) is competitive behaviour. Both collaboration and competition have their uses. We shall discuss this concept in detail in Chapter 20.

POSITIVE THINKING

Recently behavioural scientists and management practitioners have realised the need to think in positive terms. New ways of positive thinking have emerged, having significant implications for improving relationships and management of groups and organizations. Of these, the most important is the concept of emotional intelligence, in which equal importance is given to soft aspects like caring, empathy, and concern, along with tough mindedness, competition, etc. Another significant concept proposed is that of mindfulness. Concern for others is reflected in the recognition of a human need called extension motivation. Extension motivation reflects the realisation that human beings are motivated not merely by self-interest, but also by the need to be of service to others. Another new concept in relation to roles is that of role efficacy, which has various positive aspects in an organizational role.

Emotional Intelligence

Great emphasis was given in the past, both by schools and by parents, to intellectual achievement exclusively in terms of higher marks in examinations. While this continues even now, it is becoming evident that though intellectual excellence is highly desirable, exclusive emphasis on it at the cost of other important aspects is both self-defeating (because, in the long run, intellectual excellence requires 'emotional maturity') and dysfunctional (as it produces anxiety and depression in children).

The traditional concept of intelligence was confined to two varieties of the academic kind: verbal and mathematical–logical. Now the emphasis on the positive role of emotions has increased. For example, the well-known statistical firm, Gallup, is now pleading the case for emotional engagement in its new book.[25] It has proposed that the fifth 'P' of marketing is 'people'. Its research shows that 'this drives customer loyalty twice or thrice more significantly than advertising, product servicing or whatever. Also the days of product superiority are almost over.'[26] Goleman has also drawn attention to this neglected aspect that he calls 'emotional intelligence'.[27] Gardner, however, proposed the concept of multiple intelligences.[28] His model of multiple intelligences included—in addition to the two already mentioned (verbal and mathematical–logical)—spatial ability (seen in artists and architects), kinaesthetic ability (seen in sports), musical ability, and two personal intelligences (interpersonal and intrapersonal). According to him, 'Interpersonal intelligence is the ability to understand other people; what motivates them, how they work, how to work cooperatively with them. Successful sales people, politicians, teachers, clinicians and religious leaders are all likely to be individuals with high degrees of interpersonal intelligence.' He further added that interpersonal intelligence included the 'capacities to discern and respond appropriately to the moods, temperaments, motivations, and desires of other people'.[29]

Salovey[30] was the first to use the term 'emotional intelligence', however. He suggested five main domains of emotional intelligence: knowing one's emotions, managing emotions, motivating oneself, recognising emotions in others, and handling relationships.

Goleman's popular book spells out various dimensions of emotional intelligence. One important element in emotional intelligence is optimism, well-researched by Seligman. Goleman has recently suggested five components of emotional intelligence at work: self-awareness (self-confidence, realistic self-assessment, and a self-deprecating sense of humour), self-regulation (trustworthiness and integrity, comfort with ambiguity, and openness to change), motivation (a strong drive to achieve, even in the face of failure, and organizational commitment), empathy (expertise in building and retaining talent, cross-cultural sensitivity, and service to clients and customers), and social skills (effectiveness in leading change, persuasiveness, and expertise in building and leading teams).[31]

The current concept of intelligence is biased in favour of qualities traditionally attributed to men—high energy, drive, achievement, and competitiveness. Emotional intelligence emphasises the importance of characteristics traditionally attributed to women—empathy, self-control, emotional facility, etc. It balances the tilt and can be said to recommend an androgynous nature, integrating qualities traditionally attributed to men and to women. The components of emotional intelligence are briefly listed in Exhibit 5.1 under three categories (masculine, feminine, and common). The components are grouped under six heads—two groups each for men and women, and two groups common to both. This is a tentative and broad classification, and it is not suggested that the categories are mutually exclusive. These components need to be adequately developed for effectiveness in various spheres of life, including in organizations.

It is interesting that most of the components of emotional intelligence are highly valued in Indian culture and traditions. Goleman has, in fact, commented that some of these attributes are found in larger measure in Asian cultures.

Exhibit 5.1 *Components of Emotional Intelligence*

Men	Women	Common
Achievement motive	**Extension motive**	**Self-determination**
Urge to excel and compete	Urge to help and care	Self-awareness
Sensitivity to opportunity	Compassion	Internality
Acceptance of responsibility	Empathy, synchrony	Optimism
Low fear of failure	Trust	Flow (as opposed to rumination)
Persistence, perseverance	Collaboration, synergy	
Power motive	**Self-determination**	**Social competence**
Urge to control and impact	Intuition	Reflection
Positive self-image	Value orientation (authenticity, integrity)	Ambiguity tolerance
Energy, discontent	Management of emotions	Commitment
Assertiveness	Resilience	Management of others' emotions
Self-reliance, independence	Goal involvement (self-restraint)	Networking

Purohit[32] has developed an instrument to measure emotional intelligence. It contains 48 items, eight items for each of the six aspects of emotional intellegence—self-awareness, self-management, internality, motivation, empathy, and social skills.

Mindfulness

Langer,[33] who proposed the concept of mindfulness and did extensive research on it, defines her version of mindfulness as a 'heightened sense of situational awareness and a conscious control over ones thoughts and behaviour relative to the situation'.[34] She explains that mindfulness is not about just paying attention. It is making a conscious effort to be 'in the moment' and to not ignore the environment.

In essence, mindfulness is about preserving our individuality. By choosing the mindset of limited resources, by choosing to focus on outcomes rather than doing (process), and by making faulty comparisons with others, we become little more than robots. The true individual is characterised by openness to the new, is always reclassifying the meaning of knowledge and experience, and has the ability to see his or her daily actions in a bigger, consciously chosen perspective.

Langer recognises the parallels in her work with an Eastern religion—the Buddhist understanding that meditation is about enjoying a mindful state that leads to 'right action'. However, her concept and its fine distinctions and insights are based on years of research. Mindfulness is not a normal state for most people. Often people operate mindlessly: driving while thinking about what to eat for dinner, shopping while talking on the cell phone, cleaning while daydreaming. Mindlessness, or 'zoning out', is often a way to make mundane tasks bearable.

The three types of mindlessness[35] can be useful, but all of them also have negative consequences.

Categorical thinking   This can be helpful in a world where we have too many choices and too much information to deal with on a daily basis, but it can also lead to stereotyping and to mislabelling. Snap judgements are sometimes necessary, but sometimes harmful.

'Zoning out', 'not thinking', or 'not paying attention'   People who are in this mental state do not shift perspectives or weigh their options. This can certainly be a problem when new situations arise, but often it is a way for people to 'save mental energy for when we need it'.

Performing routine tasks automatically   Using automatic actions can make tasks faster. For instance, touch typists often slow down if they start looking at the keys. The problem with acting without paying attention to what you are doing is that you risk relying on routine. People need to be able to recognise when they are on autopilot and decide when they need to really focus.

According to Langer the qualities of a mindful person will include
- Ability to create new categories
- Openness to new information
- Awareness of more than one perspective
- Attention to processes (doing) rather than outcomes (results)
- Trust of intuition

We live and experience reality in a conceptual form; we do not see things afresh and anew every time we look at them. Instead, we create categories and let things fall into them, which is a more convenient way of dealing with the world. Apart from the smaller things, such as defining a vase as a Japanese vase, a flower as an orchid, or a person as a boss, there are the wider categorisations under which we live, including religions, ideologies, and systems of government. Each gives us a level of psychological certainty and saves us from the effort of constantly challenging our own beliefs.

Mindfulness is a necessary mental set for a teacher.[36] The teacher is doing more than just having eyes in the back of his or her head. He or she is aware of what students are doing, aware of the environment, and aware of his or her own behaviour and attitude. Teachers that operate with mindlessness instead of mindfulness get themselves caught up in their routine, so that they do not quickly adapt when there is a problem.

Mindfulness is not just useful for teachers; it is useful for students as well. 'For generations, educational philosophers, policy makers, and practitioners have decried the mindlessness of schools and their tendency to stifle creativity, curiosity, and enthusiasm while nurturing passivity and superficial learning.'[37] If teachers do not help students make a conscious effort to understand mindfulness, then students will not learn, or possibly even notice, new and interesting information and ways of operating. Mindfulness involves being open to new ideas and experiences because learning is fun and interesting. 'A mindful approach is like "play"; a mindless one, "work".'[38] An instrument is also available on this topic. The Langer's Mindfulness Scale (LMS)[39] is a 21-item questionnaire intended for use as a training, self-discovery, and research instrument. It assesses four domains associated with mindful thinking: novelty seeking, engagement, novelty producing, and flexibility. An individual who seeks novelty perceives each situation as an opportunity to learn something new. An individual who scores high in engagement is likely to notice more details about his or her specific relationship with the environment. A novelty producing person generates new information in order to learn more about the current situation. A flexible person welcomes a changing environment rather than resisting it.

Creativity

As we have discussed earlier, undue emphasis has been given to intellectual abilities (mathematical–logical thinking and verbal reasoning). These have been the conventional measures of intelligence, giving credit for problem solving, which produces the 'right' answer, but under-estimating creativity and unconventional approaches to problems.

Creativity (or creativeness) is a mental process involving the generation of new ideas or concepts, or new associations between existing ideas or concepts. The products of creative thinking usually have both originality and appropriateness.

More than 60 different definitions of creativity can be found in the psychological literature.[40] However, the term generally refers to the activity that results in producing or bringing about something partly or wholly new, in investing an existing object with new properties or characteristics, in imagining new possibilities that were not conceived of before, and in seeing or performing something in a manner different from what was thought possible or normal previously.

Contrast has been made between convergent and divergent thinking. The concept of divergent thinking was developed in the 1950s by psychologist J.P. Guilford, who saw it as a major component of creativity.[41] Convergent thinking is good at bringing material from a variety of sources to bear on a problem in such a way as to produce the 'correct' answer. This kind of thinking is particularly appropriate in science, maths, and technology. Divergent thinking involves skills in broadly creative elaboration of ideas prompted by a stimulus and is more suited to artistic pursuits and studies in humanities.

Contrast has also been made between critical and lateral thinking. Critical thinking is primarily concerned with judging the facts and seeking errors. Lateral thinking is more concerned with ideas. A person would use lateral thinking when they want to move from one known idea to creating new ideas. The concept of lateral thinking was proposed by de Bono.[42]

An example of lateral thinking[43]: Consider the statement 'Cars should have square wheels.' When considered with critical thinking, this would be evaluated as a poor suggestion and dismissed as impractical. The lateral thinking treatment of the same statement would be to speculate where it leads. Humour is taken intentionally with lateral thinking. A person would imagine as if this were the case, and describe the effects or qualities. Someone might observe that square wheels would produce very predictable bumps. If bumps can be predicted, then the suspension can be designed to compensate. How could a car have predictable bumps? It could have a laser or sonar in the front. This leads to the idea of an active suspension. A sensor connected to the suspension could examine the road surface ahead on cars with round wheels too. The sensor determines when it is going to hit a bump, and feeds back to the suspension that would know to compensate. The initial provocative statement has been left behind, but it has also been used to indirectly generate the new and potentially more useful idea.

Individual creativity

Generally speaking the creative person is curious, sensitive, venturesome, independent, persistent, complex, imaginative, visionary, and moody and yet realistic. She/he is propelled by the desire to grow, innovate, pioneer, change the status quo and is not hampered by various sorts of fears and blocks that act as inner censors of bold ideas.

Certain motives play a significant role in the case of creative persons. While most people, particularly professionals, have a strong desire to succeed, to achieve, to get ahead, to be respected, and so on, creative persons have a strong desire to actualise their potential, do something new, unique, pioneering, or innovative.

There are many distinctive creativity-related abilities.[44]

- Problem sensitivity or sensitivity to subtle anomalies, gaps, contradictions, paradoxes, and so on. Problem sensitivity is the child's ability to ask naive but fruitful questions: Why does the sky look blue?
- The ability to restructure problems in interesting ways.
- The ability to ideate copiously. Suppose someone asks the uses of the aspirin pill. Most would promptly write down relief from aches and pains and fever. But some might consider its round shape and wonder whether it could be used as a button, or whether it could be used in a collage, or whether one could make a joke about it.
- Flexibility is a key creativity-related ability. In designing a factory, a chief consideration is efficiency and smooth production. Add an artist to the design team and aesthetic considerations would change the format, paths, greenery, and surface modulation.
- The ability to guess the causes of problems or situations is, of course, the ability that distinguishes a first-rate scientific mind from a mediocre one.

- Elaborative ability is the ability to take an idea or a thing and bend and stretch it in interesting ways. Management is full of tools and techniques; each of these is an elaboration of an insight.
- Originality is the crown of creative intelligence. All the dimensions of creative intelligence—fluency, flexibility, problem sensitivity, problem restructuring ability, guessing ability, and elaboration ability—can contribute to originality, either individually or in combination.

Several attempts have been made to develop a creativity quotient of an individual, similar to the intelligence quotient. Most measures of creativity are dependent on the personal judgement of the tester, so a standardised measure is difficult to develop.

J.P. Guilford, who pioneered the modern psychometric study of creativity, and his group constructed several tests to measure creativity.[45]

Building on Guilford's work, Torrance developed the Torrance Tests of Creative Thinking.[46] It involves simple tests of divergent thinking and other problem-solving skills that are scored on

- Fluency—The total number of interpretable, meaningful, and relevant ideas generated in response to the stimulus
- Flexibility—The number of different categories of relevant responses
- Originality—The statistical rarity of the responses among the test subjects
- Elaboration—The amount of detail in the responses

Nickerson provides a summary of the various creativity techniques that have been proposed.[47] These include approaches that have been developed by both academia and industry:

1. Establishing purpose and intention
2. Building basic skills
3. Encouraging acquisitions of domain-specific knowledge
4. Stimulating and rewarding curiosity and exploration
5. Building motivation, especially internal motivation
6. Encouraging confidence and a willingness to take risks
7. Focusing on mastery and self-competition
8. Promoting supportable beliefs about creativity
9. Providing opportunities for choice and discovery
10. Developing self-management (metacognitive skills)
11. Teaching techniques and strategies for facilitating creative performance
12. Providing balance

Organizational creativity

Managers and executives in most companies are aware that their creative *potential* greatly exceeds their creative *performance*. The problem is that they do not know what to do about it. Most creative acts, as they now occur in companies, are not planned for, and come from where they are least expected. It is not possible to predict them. A good example of the power of the unexpected occurred at Japan

Railways (JR) East. This company never anticipated that constructing a new bullet-train line through the mountains north of Tokyo would lead it to a new and very profitable business in beverages. The new train line required many tunnels. The one through Mt Tanigawa had water problems, and JR engineers began to draw up drainage plans. But a maintenance worker thought the water tasted so good, he proposed that instead of pumping it away into runoffs, JR East should bottle and market it as premium mineral water. His idea was implemented, and soon the water appeared on the market under the brand name of Oshimizu. It became so popular that JR East installed Oshimizu vending machines on every one of its nearly 1,000 platforms. Advertisements for the water emphasise the purity of Mt Tanigawa's snow pack, the source of the water, and the slow process by which it percolates through the mountain, picking up healthful amounts of minerals. The product line has grown to include juices as well as iced and hot teas and coffees. In 1994, sales of Oshimizu beverages were 47 million dollars.[48]

It has been suggested that three components are needed to enhance creativity in business: expertise (technical, procedural, and intellectual knowledge), creative thinking skills (flexibility and imaginative approach to problems), and motivation (especially intrinsic motivation).[49]

Robinson and Stern, based on detailed real-life examples from organizations around the world, like British Airways, Du Pont, Fujitsu, General Motors, Hallmark, Hewlett-Packard, IBM, Japan Railways East, Kodak, Universal Studios, the United States Forest Service, and even enterprises in the USSR, have suggested six essential elements that companies can use to turn their creativity from a hit-or-miss proposition into something consistent that they can count on[50]:

1. Alignment   An alignment ensures that the interests and actions of all employees are directed towards their company's key goals, so that *any* employee will recognise and respond positively to a potentially useful idea.

2. Self-initiated activity   A self-initiated activity allows employees to pick a problem they are interested in and feel able to solve it—for *whatever* reason. Their intrinsic motivation is much higher than what it could be if the project had been planned or picked for them by someone else.

3. Unofficial activity   An unofficial activity gives ideas a safe haven—where they have the chance to develop until they are strong enough to overcome resistance. Furthermore, official status for a project raises all kinds of barriers to creativity, which every planned project encounters throughout its life. Unofficially, employees are free to experiment, even far outside their job.

4. Serendipity   A serendipitous discovery is one made by fortunate accident in the presence of sagacity (keenness of insight). Creativity often involves making connections between things that may seem unconnected. Whether those involved recognise it or not, serendipity is present in every creative act. Only when serendipity is truly understood can companies take action to promote it.

5. Diverse stimuli   Organizations should do all they can to bring diverse stimuli to their employees, but they should also recognise that such efforts have limited

impact. Most stimuli arise in connection with daily life or with the work itself. It is far more important that an organization provides opportunities for its employees to tell others about the stimuli they have received and the possibilities these suggest to them. It is here that the real leverage lies.

6. Within-company communication A company's creative potential increases rapidly with its size. But without systems in place to promote unanticipated exchanges of information, this potential will never be realised. Worse, the assumption will continue to be made that creativity can only really happen in small companies.

It has been suggested that organizational creativity involves knowledge creation. Knowledge is of four types.[51] Tacit knowledge is what is in the minds of people in the organization, whereas explicit knowledge is what can be written down, filmed, or copied. Knowledge is created in four ways. Tacit knowledge is transmitted as such through socialisation. When an IIM graduate is sent to work as a salesman for 12 weeks, he learns tacit knowledge about salesmanship from an experienced person. In our guru–shishya system too, tacit knowledge was transmitted through socialisation.

Externalisation is the act of converting tacit knowledge into explicit knowledge, expressing a concept or an idea into something that another person can understand, often through a metaphor. When Henry Ford said he wanted 'to make a car for the masses', he used such a metaphor. When Ratan Tata said that he wanted 'a car with the interior space of an Ambassador, a running cost less than a Maruti, and a price that is affordable', he was externalising his tacit knowledge articulately before the Indica took concrete shape.

Combination, the third method of knowledge creation, involves combining different bodies of explicit knowledge. Formal education in an MBA school is an example. It combines pieces of explicit knowledge into an explicit form of educational material. Internalisation is the process of embodying explicit knowledge into tacit knowledge. When the young MBA who has put in 10 years of work experience realises that he learned only 30 per cent at college and the rest in the real world, he is referring to internalisation as his process of learning.

Organizational knowledge creation is a continuous and dynamic interaction between tacit and explicit knowledge. First, the socialisation mode starts with building a field interaction. This field facilitates the sharing of members' experiences and mental models. Second, the externalisation mode is triggered by dialogue and collective reflection. Third, the combination mode is triggered by networking newly created knowledge and existing knowledge from various parts of the organization. Finally, learning by doing triggers internalisation. Thus the knowledge develops in a spiral of expanding scope. The case of Matsushita Home Bakery illustrates this concept well (see Exhibit 5.2).

Exhibit 5.2 *The Case of Matsushita Home Bakery*

The case of Matsushita Home Bakery[52] is interesting for two reasons: what it really takes to deeply understand customer's needs, and the passing on of tacit knowledge. Due to a maturing of the home appliances market, Matsushita launched a programme called 'Action' in 1983. Three appliances divisions were integrated to save costs in the face of static sales, but sales did not improve and the integration itself came into question.

Ikuji Masumura, the strategy planner of the division, found that working women were increasingly simplifying home cooking, which resulted in poorer diets. His team came up with the concept of an appliance that could produce 'easy and rich' food. A multifunctional team was formed for the project and a charter was framed.

Using all known technologies, a prototype was developed for an 'automatic home bakery'. To improve it, a software developer, Ikuko Tanaka, was deployed. Her task was to watch, initiate, and practice what the master baker did while kneading the dough; simply put, her task was to absorb his tacit knowledge. Then she had to convert this tacit knowledge into explicit knowledge by explaining it to her engineers, who would change the propeller design or the motor speed to mimic the kneading action of the master baker. It took Tanaka 6 months of apprenticeship with the master baker to learn what she had to do.

Finally, when the product was launched in February 1987, Matsushita had a runaway success. The company went on to further develop the concept and extend its application to other products. There are two big lessons that this case teaches: first, that innovation must be customer-driven and, second, that it needs processes to convert an invention into an innovation. But there are instances where this rule has been broken.

Techniques for Creative Thinking

Creativity techniques are deliberate thinking processes designed to help find ideas and solve problems.

The most common creative process is analogical thinking—the transfer of an idea from one context to a new one. Perhaps 80 per cent of creative ideas are rooted in analogical thinking. One technique is asking how nature has solved a similar problem. Pringles Potato Chips were conceived via the analogy of wet leaves—which stack compactly and do not destroy themselves. Cartoonists and cartoon strips continually borrow ideas from movies, television commercials, children's stories, etc.

Brainstorming is a commonly used technique. It involves generating wild and even preposterous ideas and jotting down each one of them. Such wild ideas can often be 'tamed' into workable solutions.

While brainstorming is a general procedure, attribute listing is a specific idea-finding technique (one that could even be used while brainstorming). It involves identifying the key characteristics, or attributes, of the product or process in question and then thinking of ways to change, modify, or improve each attribute (in design engineering this is called the substitution method).

Morphological synthesis is a simple elaboration of attribute listing. After completing the list of attributes, changes in one attribute (such as 'products') are listed along the horizontal axis and changes in a second attribute (such as 'markets') are listed along the vertical axis. Idea combinations, or syntheses, will appear in the intersections, or cells, of the table.

Checklists have been written expressly to solve problems creatively. The best known is Osborn's 73 Idea Spurring Questions'.[53] A few are as follows:

Put to other uses?	New ways to use as is? Other uses if modified?
Modify?	New twist? Change meaning, colour, motion, sound, form? Other changes?
Magnify?	What to add? Greater frequency? Length? Extra value? Duplicate? Multiply? Exaggerate?
Minify?	What to subtract? Condense? Miniaturise? Lighten? Split up? Understate?
Rearrange?	Interchange components? Other sequence? Change schedule?
Combine?	How about a blend, an assortment? Combine units? Combine purposes? Combine appeals?

Innovation

Innovation has been defined as the introduction of a new thing or method. Innovation is the embodiment, combination, or synthesis of knowledge in original, relevant, valued new products, processes, or services.[54] Innovation typically involves creativity, but is not identical to it. Innovation involves acting on the creative ideas to make some specific and tangible difference in the domain in which the innovation occurs. While creativity implies coming up with ideas, it is the 'bringing ideas to life' that makes innovation a distinct undertaking.[55]

According to OECD, technological product and process (TPP) innovations comprise implemented technologically new products and processes and significant technological improvements in products and processes. A TPP innovation has been implemented if it has been introduced on the market (product innovation) or used within a production process (process innovation). TPP innovations involve a series of scientific, technological, organizational, financial, and commercial activities. A TPP innovating firm is one that has implemented technologically new or significantly technologically improved products or processes during the period under review.[56]

A 2005–06 MIT survey of innovation in technology found a number of characteristics common to innovators working in that field:

1. Innovators are not troubled by the idea of failure.
2. They realise that failure can be learned from and that the 'failed' technology can later be re-used for other purposes.
3. They know innovation requires that one works in advanced areas where failure is a real possibility.
4. Innovators are curious about what is happening in a myriad of disciplines, not only their own specialism.
5. Innovators are open to third-party experiments with their products.
6. They recognise that a useful innovation must be 'robust', flexible, and adaptable.
7. Innovators delight in spotting a need about which we are not even aware and then fulfilling that need with a new innovation.
8. Innovators like to make products that are immediately useful to their first users.

While innovation is 'doing' things differently, creativity is all about 'thinking' differently. Innovation is essentially the application of high creativity. It need not be restricted to just products. It applies to services and employee attitude, across all levels. Innovation is a fundamental mindset pursued seriously by an organization. It is imperative to imbibe the culture of innovation.[57]

The Wipro Centre of Excellence, with over 500 dedicated professionals, works on lean technology to software development, new ways of delivering business, and is striving towards creating intellectual properties in the wireless and mobile telephony segment, says Premji. Wipro bagged 29 major deals in the last quarter of 2006, as a result of innovation. Wipro has become the first company to develop an outsourcing model for remote infrastructure and remote business process outsourcing services.

Exhibit 5.3 is an example of an interesting innovation, which was born out of abject failure—an engineer's maiden business venture, a briquetting plant in Punjab, flopped miserably because his client base, brick kilns, remained closed several months in a year.[58]

Exhibit 5.3 *Sanjha Chulha*

A 40-year-old mechanical engineer from Chandigarh, Nibhoria has invented the Sanjha Chulha (translated it means a combined cookstove). Meant for large-scale use, this stove is fuelled by briquettes (cylinders of compressed crop waste) instead of the more expensive LPG. 'It not only allows large kitchens like that of a school to use a cheaper, easily sustainable alternative to fossil fuel,' he says, 'it also provides good business to the briquetting industry.' Using briquettes, he explains, cuts carbon dioxide emissions (since the crop waste is a renewable source of energy), cuts fuel bills, and provides a new source of income to the farmers, who can sell the crop waste to the briquette makers. His invention has won the 2005 Ashden Award, the green Oscar coveted the world over. In fact, the two factors that impressed the Ashden Award jury were the tremendous potential the Sanjha Chulha has for checking greenhouse gas and the potential for replicating this technology wherever crop waste is readily available.

So, how exactly does the Sanjha Chulha work? The design is simple. It has a combustion chamber into which briquettes are fed at a rate of about 15 kg an hour. Above it are hot-plates, designed to provide uniform heat. Three small electric fans control the flow of gases through the stove, providing the primary air flow to get the briquettes burning and the secondary air to burn the emanating volatile gases. A 400-litre water tank around the chimney absorbs heat from the exhaust gases and provides hot water for cooking and making tea.

Nibhoria further impressed the Ashden judges by coming up with a unique financial package for the Sanjha Chulha. 'When I did the costing and found that the stove would cost about 1.5 lakh rupees, I realised my target clientele—residential schools funded by the government (Navodaya schools)—would be averse to placing bulk orders,' he explains. So, he decided to sell the stoves on credit and allowed the users to pay in instalments from the savings they would make in their fuel costs.

The 'install, operate, save, and pay' mantra has worked well for the schools—25 Navodaya schools in Punjab have bought Sanjha Chulhas till now. Consider a typical residential school catering three meals per day for 450 people. Conventional stoves would use three LPG cylinders (42.6 kg) costing about Rs 900 every day. Replace them with the Sanjha Chulha, and the school spends only Rs 375 a day on briquettes. From the monthly savings of Rs 16,000 per stove, Nibhoria's Nishant Bioenergy takes 15 payments of Rs 10,000 over 18 months, allowing for school vacations.

The outlook for the Sanjha Chulha looks bright. 'Within the next few years, commercial enterprises will no longer be able to avail the government subsidy on LPG. I expect to see a huge increase in the demand for my stove then,' Nibhoria predicts. And that is enough to fire his enthusiasm for now.

Attention is being increasingly given to creativity and innovation. Several organizations in India have instituted rewards for creativity and innovation. EMPI has instituted the Indian Innovation Awards for organizations. Honey Bee, based in IIM, Ahmedabad, is promoting grass-root level technology innovations through rewards. Bhoruka Trust is awarding individual grass-root level innovations. EMPI also publishes a journal, *Innovations*.

Extension Motivation

Extension motivation will be discussed further in Chapter 7 and some other chapters. One of the basic needs for individuals is to be relevant to others, including the society. The relevance is reflected in the concern we have for others, perusing superordinate goals, helping others, sacrificing our own interest to that of others, etc. This is one of the basic needs, called extension motive. Not much work has been done on extension motive, although some work researches have been done on altruism.

Altruism is the practice of placing others before oneself. It is a traditional virtue in many cultures and is central to many religious traditions. In English, the idea was often described as the golden rule of ethics. In Buddhism, it is considered a fundamental property of human nature.

The concept has a long history in philosophical and ethical thought and has more recently become a topic for psychologists and sociologists. While ideas about altruism from one field can have an impact on other fields, the different methods and focuses of these fields lead to different perspectives on altruism.

Altruism can be distinguished from the feeling of loyalty or duty. Altruism focuses on a moral obligation towards all humanity, while duty focuses on a moral obligation towards a specific individual (e.g., God, a king), a specific organization (e.g., a government), or an abstract concept (e.g., country). Some individuals may feel both altruism and duty, while others may not.

Role Efficacy

We as individuals are connected with various systems by the roles we occupy and play in those systems. A person will be effective in a system if she gets integrated with his or her role. The integration of the person and the role comes about when the role is able to fulfil the needs of the individual, who in turn is able to contribute to the evolution of the role. The more we move from role taking (responding to the expectations of others) to role making (taking initiative in designing the role more creatively in a way such that the expectations of others as well as of the role occupant are integrated), the more the role is likely to be effective. Effectiveness of a person in a role in an organization will depend on his potential effectiveness, potential effectiveness of the role, and the organizational climate. The potential effectiveness can be called efficacy. Role efficacy can be seen as the psychological factor underlying role effectiveness. In short, role efficacy is the potential effectiveness of a role.

Role efficacy has the 10 dimensions mentioned below. We shall discuss in detail these aspects in Chapter 13. Here we only point out the importance of role efficacy as a positive variable increasing the effectiveness of the individuals working in systems.

1. Self-role integration (vs role distance): Integrating between self-concept and the role demands
2. Proactivity (vs reacting): Initiating action
3. Creativity (vs routine): Experimenting and trying new ideas/strategies
4. Confrontation (vs avoidance): Facing problems to attempt their solution
5. Centrality (vs peripherality): Feeling important or central in a system
6. Influence (vs powerlessness): Feeling that one's occupying a role can make some impact in the system
7. Growth (vs stagnation): Feeling that the one occupying a role grows and learns in the role
8. Inter-role linkage (vs isolation): Linking of one's role with those of others
9. Helping relationship (vs hostility): Giving and receiving help among roles
10. Superordination (vs deprivation): Linking of one's role with a larger entity/cause

Research shows that persons with high role efficacy seem to experience less role stress, anxiety, and work-related tension; they rely on their own strengths to cope with problems, use more purposeful behaviour, are active, and interact with people and their environment; they persist in solving problems, mostly by themselves and sometimes by taking the help of other people, show growth orientation, attitudinal commitment, positive and approach behaviour, and feel satisfied with life and with their jobs and roles in the organization. This is a profile of effective managers. Role efficacy is found to be related to the quality of work life (measured by influence, amenities at the work place, nature of job, and supervisory behaviour). Step-wise multiple regressions yielded supervisory behaviour as the most important dimension in role efficacy. Role efficacy has also been found as related to the type of roles, location of the work place, and the length of employment (and age).

INTERVENTIONS WITH POSITIVE APPROACH

Some interventions have been designed on the basis of positive categories. The main characteristics of these interventions are using strengths as the leverage for change, using future-oriented (rather than past-oriented) strategies, searching positive aspects (rather than diagnosing problems), working towards collaboration (rather than competition). Such interventions have brought about attitudinal change in organizations and individuals. We briefly discuss such interventions below.

Future Search

The future search (FS) conference was developed by Marvin Weisbord and Sandra Janoff. According to them it 'is a large group planning meeting that brings a "whole system" into the room to work on a task-focused agenda .... In a future search, people have a chance to take ownership of their past, present, and future, confirm their mutual values, and commit to action plans grounded in reality.'[59]

By 'whole system' Weisbord and Janoff mean 30 to 64 diverse stakeholders—a cross-section of people concerned with the activities of the organization or community undertaking the search. About one-third of them come from outside the system. For example, if a local community is doing the future, then the outsiders might include officials and citizens from nearby cities, state and local officials, representatives of national organizations or businesses involved in the community—key people who normally do not work together.

Once the diverse stakeholders come together, they begin exploring their shared past: What are the patterns of the last several decades? What are the stories? What does it all mean? Diverse participants often come up with clashing perspectives. In future search, differences like this are simply understood and acknowledged, not 'worked through'. Like a meditator who brings her wandering attention back to her rhythmic breathing, future search participants continually return their attention to their common ground—in this case, the shared milestones in their history.

Moving to the present, participants explore the trends—including global forces—at work in their lives. Together they create a detailed 'mind map' of these trends on a giant sheet of paper. They discuss concerns, prioritise the trends they have identified and explore common ways of viewing the 'mess' they have charted together. They tell each other what they are proud of and what they are sorry about. Often their perspective on themselves and each other shift dramatically during these exercises.

Diverse stakeholders then gather in subgroups to imagine themselves 5, 10, and 20 years in the future. They generate concrete images and examples of what is going on in their chosen future and the barriers they imagine they have had to overcome to get there. After coming together to share this information, participants develop lists of common futures (what they agree they want), potential projects (how to get there), and unresolved differences. After some reflection and second thoughts, each participant figures out what they personally want to work on. They get together with others of similar passion to plan action. Follow-up has suggested that people in such groups tend to continue working together.

Simply by changing the conditions under which people interact, future search procedures enable participants to bridge barriers of culture, class, age, gender, ethnicity, power, status, and hierarchy to work together as peers on tasks of mutual concern. Unlike many community organizers and organizational consultants, future search facilitators offer no diagnosis of problems, no prescriptions for fixing things, no preconceived issues, frames of reference, or action ideologies. They do not judge information as good or bad, complete or sketchy, useful or futile, appropriate or redundant. Whatever people do or say—their words, their behaviour, their wishes, and their reactions—belongs to them. Not knowing what issues and obstacles will arise, facilitators simply set a workable process in motion and let the system come up with its own information, meanings, and motivation. In short, they help participants self-organize.

Usually, future search conference is organized for two half and one full days. The typical future search agenda is as follows—

Day 1: Afternoon
- Focus on the past
- Focus on the present, on external trends

Day 2: Morning
- Focus on trends (continued)
- Focus on the present, owning our actions

Day 2: Afternoon
- Discuss ideal future scenarios
- Identify common ground

Day 3: Morning
- Confirm common ground (continued)
- Plan action

In a productive open space session at a recent learning exchange, the following ideas were generated on facilitating sticky reality dialogues[60]:

- Consider first giving the mixed groups a generous amount of time to develop the future scenarios with specific questions related to the situation, without telling them that they will be dramatising the scenario. When the time is up, give them the additional instruction that the report-out will be a dramatisation. This two-step process helps ensure developing details that can be used in the action planning, as well as additional common ground for initiatives, etc.

- After the mixed groups have identified the common ground themes from the scenarios, consider lining up flip charts of all of the groups so that they are next to each other. Then, ask the large group to identify the common themes. With each, ask whether they agree or disagree and place charts on the common ground wall or the parking lot. (This was proposed as an alternative to having the mixed groups combine their charts.) Then ask what is missing, and what does not seem to have a lot of energy (for moving to the parking lot).

- Ask for thumbs up, down, or sideways for each of the common ground items so that you are not making assumptions about agreeing/disagreeing and can proceed accordingly.

- In the steering committee meeting, explain and demonstrate integrative statements, using the meeting as a 'lab' for such understanding. Ask the steering committee members to listen for integrative statements during the FS and to build upon them actively during the session.

- Integrative statements are key.

The following ideas were generated on how to help groups develop action plans that will have a higher likelihood of being followed:

- Build into the steering committee process a session on what will happen after the FS and how it will be monitored/assisted/reported. During this session explain that there will be some predictable and unpredictable outcomes, so the group needs to know how it will proceed with both.

- Stress to the steering committee that their work will continue after the FS.
- Make sure there is plenty of time for action planning after common ground.
- Coach the action planning teams on how to work as a group, including choosing someone to champion the efforts and discussing how the group will monitor and follow-up on the actions they outlined; perhaps including this in the workbook and in the instructions, asking them to pose the questions 'What will this plan mean for each of us?' 'How will we track our work together?' 'What are our immediate next steps?'
- Consider offering in your contract a coaching session (even two or three) for each of the action planning teams to help them keep on track.
- Consider a follow-up 'pool' in your contract to be used as needed, with an exit clause if it is not needed.
- Explore establishing action groups as 'communities of practice', as appropriate, including use of technology to connect.
- After the FS, consider expanding the steering committee to include new people from the FS who express interest and add diversity.

A short account of future search conferences held in India is given in the case at the end of the chapter.

Appreciative Inquiry

Appreciative inquiry (AI) was developed by David Cooperrider and Suresh Srivastva in the 1980s.[61] The approach is based on the premise that organizations change in the direction in which they inquire. So an organization that inquires into problems will keep finding problems, and an organization that attempts to appreciate what is best in itself will discover more and more that is good. Then the organization can use these discoveries to build a new future where the best becomes more common.

AI contrasts the commonplace notion that 'organizing is a problem to be solved' with the appreciative proposition that 'organizing is a miracle to be embraced'. Inquiry into organizational life should have four characteristics. It should be appreciative, applicable, provocative, and collaborative.[62]

The appreciative inquiry approach is often worked out in practice by using the '4-D' model: Discover, Dream, Design, Delivery.

Discovery   This phase begins with the introduction of the AI theory and practice to the organization, impinging on its purpose. A 'core team' is formed to guide the work and to select topics for the inquiry. The topics must be affirmative and be stated in affirmative language. For example, an organization concerned with absenteeism might study employee motivation, while an organization concerned with conflict and its reduction might study collaboration. In the selection of affirmative topics, members are asked to focus on the things they want more of in their organization. In other words, they are asked what would make the organization a more desirable workplace.

Dream   In this phase, people describe their wishes and dreams for their work, their working relationships, and their organization. Participants (the group can be quite large, up to a thousand) are encouraged to consider what their organization's mission is. This may pertain to a department, a business unit, or the entire company. An attempt is made to connect the work of all members of the organization to a greater purpose and vision. Working together in small groups of eight, participants share and discuss the data and stories collected in the discovery phase. Even as these discussions ground them in the most positive aspects of their organization's past, they inspire them to imagine future possibilities for themselves and their organization in relation to the world at large.

Design   In this phase, members and stakeholders (including customers and suppliers) recreate the 'social and technical architecture' of the organization, so that everything about it reflects and responds to the most positive aspects of the organization's past and its highest potential. Whereas the discovery and dream phases generate and expand the organization's images of itself, the design and delivery phases ask members to make choices for the organization. Design statements must be written in the present tense.

Delivery   This phase, also called destiny, focuses on personal and organizational commitments, and the 'path forward'. Individuals work on applications and action plans, small groups work on areas that require collaboration, and teams may be established for new initiatives.

Among the most exciting applications of appreciative inquiry is the AI summit. An AI summit differs from other large-scale meeting processes in that it is fully affirmative. It focuses on discovering and developing the organization's positive core and converting it into strategic business processes such as patient care, marketing, and human resources. Its goal is to launch the whole organization in a new direction.

The summit includes all the organization's stakeholders—employees, customers, suppliers, and community members. It is generally a three- to four-day meeting, and can involve anything from 50 to 2,000 plus participants. Each meeting flows through the 4-D appreciative inquiry cycle of discovery, dream, design, and delivery. Each involves a combination of one-on-one interviews, small group discussions, and large processes. Each focuses on the affirmative, positive core of the organization and its potential to build upon the positive core capacities, competencies, best practices, hopes, and dreams as the organization moves forward.

An account of appreciative inquiry done with a police department of Rajasthan is available.[63]

Role Efficacy Lab

REL[64] is a short process-oriented programme to diagnose the level of role efficacy in a group of employees (generally managers) in an organization and to take steps to raise that level. We have found a 3-day REL useful for this purpose, although the lab can be of a longer duration if some other aspects are included in it. One design of a 3-day REL (about 20 hours) is given in Exhibit 5.4.

Instruments Essay on 'My Role' (EMR) is an important instrument in the REL programme. The role efficacy scale (RES) or some other structured instruments may not be as useful, as the spontaneous feelings and attitudes of the respondents are likely to filter through their conscious thinking (inhibitions and censoring) more easily in a projective device, such as the essay, rather than in a structured instrument such as the RES, to measure the respondents' perception of the role efficacy of the roles they supervise. RES may be used for this purpose. If possible, the role occupants may be asked to complete the RES beforehand, and it may then be used to compare the differences between the perceptions of the role occupants and their bosses later on in the REL.

It may be useful to administer the instruments at the very outset of the lab, so that further interventions do not affect the responses to the instruments.

Exhibit 5.4 *Role Efficacy Lab: Suggested Design*

Day 1	1.	Writing an essay on 'My Role', completion of role efficacy scale for subordinate roles, and other instruments (1 hour)
	2.	Microlab (1 hour)
	3.	About the REL (1/2 hour)
	4.	The concept of role efficacy, its aspects, and scoring method-concept session with discussion and examples (1½ hour)
	5.	Scoring one's own essays (3/4 hour)
	6.	Exchange of essays in triads, and scoring (1 hour)
	7.	Plenary session, discussing some essays (3/4 hour)
	8.	Scoring of RES (1/2 hour)
Day 2	1.	Small groups work on self and subordinates' roles to identify areas for strengthening (1/2 hour)
	2.	Plenary session, reporting and integrating (3/4 hour)
	3.	Work on increasing one's role efficacy (1 hour)
	4.	Work on increasing efficacy of subordinate roles (3/4 hour)
	5.	Force field analysis for role efficacy in the organization (small groups) (3/4 hour)
	6.	Plenary session (3/4 hour)
	7.	Work on expectations from the organization (in 3 or more small groups) (3/4 hour)
	8.	Plenary session (3/4 hour)
Day 3	1.	Consolidating recommendations and action suggestions (in 3 groups) (3/4 hour)
	2.	Plenary session for finalisation (1 hour)
	3.	Action planning for role efficacy (individual, then group work) (1 hour)
	4.	Review of action plans and collaborative plans (1 hour)
	5.	Preparation for dialogue with top management (1 hour)
	6.	Dialogue, evaluation, and closing (2 hours)

Unfreezing In the beginning some unfreezing activity such as a microlab may be useful. Most of the items in the microlab may be focused on the role. Certain items used in microlabs in some of the RELs are given below.

Some items for microlab

1. Introduce yourself to your partner in the usual manner.

2. Discuss what you enjoy most in your role.
3. Discuss what you like the least in your role.
4. Share three of your main personal strengths. Which of these are you able to use in your role and to what extent?
5. Describe aspects of your subordinates' roles that are exciting and enjoyable.
6. Describe aspects of their roles that are boring and unenjoyable.
7. Draw a figure to represent your role (a bird, an animal, a geometrical shape, a natural object, a historical figure, a mythological character, or a combination of two or more of these). Share its significance with your partner(s).
8. For small groups, prepare a picture of your roles as above and explain to the entire group.
9. For small groups, suggest three things that you would like to do to redesign your role, assuming you were free to do so. Then share these with the entire group.
10. Enumerate the main strengths of your organization that make you feel proud of being a part of it.
11. State the main contribution of your role to (i) your organization, (ii) the industry, and (c) a larger entity like the society.
12. For small groups, think of your organization 15 to 16 years hence. Prepare a non-verbal skit to represent the organization and your role in it at that point of time.

Scoring of instruments   The main purpose behind 'teaching' participants the scoring system for the EMR and RES (or other instruments) is to help understand and internalise the various aspects of role efficacy.

The more they 'search' the evidence of various dimensions of role efficacy in their own essays or in those written by their colleagues, the more their thinking will get saturated and influenced by these ideas, affecting the way they shape their own and their subordinates' roles.

Concept sessions   The concept sessions need to be short and interspersed by the working sessions. It may be useful to give some reading material to the participants, e.g., this book for reading at night, so that the next day they can use their reading to work on their diagnosis and action planning, and also in raising conceptual issues.

Small group work   A lot of group work is involved in REL. The groups may be changed from time to time. If there are a smaller number of participants, they may be divided into three groups (one each to work on role-making dimension, role-centring dimension, and role-linkage dimension). If there are a larger number of participants, 10 groups may be formed, one for each aspect of role efficacy. Similarly, groups may be formed for discussions on one's own role, subordinate roles, and suggestions (expectations) from the management. Action suggestions are discussed in the following sections. However, the groups must work out specific suggestions for their situations and generate newer ideas. Suggestions in the following sections should only be used as general guidelines.

Action planning   Each individual participant should prepare an action plan to increase his own role efficacy and that of the subordinates. These plans may be duplicated and distributed. This represents the personal commitment of each participant to himself and to the group. After individual plans are prepared, several common and collaborative action points may be developed so that a group of people may collaboratively take action to develop their role efficacy. These may also be duplicated and distributed (after all these are shared in the plenary session and generally approved by the entire group).

Dialogue with top management   The last item in the REL is aimed at (a) sharing of thoughts, and individual as well as group commitments with the top management, (b) creating an opportunity to get moral support and reinforcement from the top management, (c) generating ideas for action by the top management, (d) creating an opportunity for the top management to comment on and explain why certain expectations are unrealistic and therefore unattainable, and to announce their own action plans to do something on the other suggestions.

It is necessary to ensure that the action suggestions generated for the top management relate to the role efficacy aspects. There is a temptation for the group to use the dialogue as an opportunity to settle some other issues, which defeats the original purpose of the dialogue. It may therefore be useful to critically review what will be communicated to the top management.

The dialogue may be useful if three to five representatives of the management meet with about the same number of participants in the presence of the entire group. An opportunity may be provided for any member who has an urge to speak something, but the dialogue must be confined to the group of six to ten persons.

It is also necessary to prepare the top management for the dialogue. They should be prepared to examine the suggestions and take action on some of these. It may be useful to communicate the action taken, from time to time. The top management should feel committed to such action as much as they expect the participants to honour their own action commitments.

Follow-up   After a role efficacy lab, follow-up and reinforcement in the form of an annual 1-day conference, reviewing the experiences of attempts at role efficacy, may be helpful. In such a conference, the top management may also share what they did to increase the role efficacy of their employees. Monthly bulletins can be issued to report successful experiences in increasing role efficacy. One aspect may be specially highlighted every month (e.g., centrality, proactivity).

Counselling   Just as it is important to work on role efficacy by redesigning the role, it is important so to work on role efficacy from the point of view of a role occupant. Role efficacy may be low because the role occupant may be unable to either perceive its various aspects, or to use his own power to build those aspects in the role. The necessary counselling and help in planning action to build these aspects (by the individual), may be useful. For example, if the person perceives that linkages with other roles are weak, it may be useful to work with him on what can be done to build stronger linkages. Or, if he feels that a role does not provide opportunities to learn new things and grow, he can be helped to perceive various parts of the role that may contribute to learning new things and his growth. The purpose of such counselling is to help the individual realise what prevents him from being effective and taking necessary steps without waiting for the role to be redesigned in order to have a higher role efficacy. Such counselling may become a part of performance counselling.

Action guidelines Role efficacy can be increased by the joint effort of the role occupants, their senior managers, and the organization (the top management). A role occupant and preferably several role occupants in a group (for example, middle managers or product managers) can generate ideas for increasing the efficacy of their own roles. Similarly a supervisor can have ideas about increasing the efficacy of the roles that he supervises. The top managers can also take some steps, and ideas for such steps can be generated by groups of managers at various levels. Some ideas for increasing role efficacy by increasing each of its 10 aspects are presented in Chapter 28.

Role Contribution

An important aspect of role contribution[65] is a helping relationship 'in which at least one of the parties has the intent of promoting growth, development, maturity, improved functioning, and improved coping with life of the other'.[66] There is an emphasis on empathy and unconditional support in this definition. Helping can be responsive (the word responsive is used instead of reactive, which may have a negative connotation) or proactive. When help is given to someone who asks for it, or when one responds to the need of the other person, helping is responsive. On the other hand, when help is given because of the helper's need to give (rather than the receiver's need to receive), helping is proactive. This distinction has been clearly made in the Indian ethos.

When the receiver's need is dominant it is called *bhiksha* (whether asking or giving help), but if the need of the giver is predominant, it is called *daan* (both while giving and receiving help). This distinction is not found in other cultures, and indicates that the motive of giving help is aroused not only by other person's or group's need, but also by that of the giver.

The concepts underlying role contribution are empathy and co-operation. While role negotiation is based on the premise that taking the help of others for one's effectiveness is primarily a process of mutuality, role contribution proceeds with the basic assumption that we as individuals, among other needs, have the need to be relevant, to do something for others, and to help them. This has been called the extension motive and is suggested as an important basis of development.

Role contribution and role negotiation differ in several ways as may be seen in Exhibit 5.5.

Role contribution can be used to build cooperation and collaboration for both individuals and groups. Like role negotiation, role contribution has four main phases: unfreezing, contribution, closing, and follow-up.

Exhibit 5.5   *Comparison Between Role Negotiation and Role Contribution*

Dimensions	Role negotiation	Role contribution
Basic assumptions about people	People try to maximise their own interests; can be exploitative, untrustworthy, and competitive	One basic human need is to be relevant and do good to others. If not properly aroused and canalised, this can be subdued by self-seeking behaviour
Management of conflicts and differences	The effective alternative to conflicts is a negotiated agreement based on enforceable guarantee of mutual observance	Negotiated agreement, based on empathy and recognition of the others' power, can help in managing conflicts
Diagnosis	Focus is on the rights, power, privilege, and demands of the role occupants from each other	Focus is on the contribution and help offered to each other, and what prevents this process
Target of change	Working relationships, duties, responsibilities, authority, and accountability of role occupants	Working pressure and rewards for acting on agreement and a periodical joint review of the problems
Vulnerability	Not based on potent rewards and sanctions; unwillingness or inability to apply them, their imbalance caused by third party intervention	Insufficient working through of differences; lack of potent rewards for empathy and help; lack of periodical in-depth review; third party intervention

Unfreezing

The main purpose of the first phase is to prepare the participants for developing empathy, mutuality, and cooperation. The steps involved and the time needed are discussed below.

1. *Instruments* (1/2 hour) At the beginning of the programme all participants respond to some instruments. Two instruments can be used here: MAO-B and MAO-C.[67] MAO-B helps respondents to examine their role behaviour in terms of the functional and dysfunctional aspects of the six motives (achievement, influence, extension, control, affiliation, and dependency).

2. *Introduction* (1/2 hour) The consultant/facilitator may expound the need for mutuality for role effectiveness and the role of taking initiative in helping other role occupants to become effective. The importance of empathy is also stressed.

3. *Discussion of instruments* (2 hours) Feedback on the instruments that have been completed at the beginning is given to the participants. Details about interpreting the scores can be seen in the sources cited with them.

4. *Exercise on helping* (2 hours) A simulation exercise is useful to generate data on one's natural behaviour. 'Broken squares' (already suggested in role negotiation) is a good exercise in helping behaviour. It communicates the message that concern for others and unconditional helping not only contributes to the group effectiveness but also to the effectiveness of each member of the group.

5. *Emfeed* (1 hour) The purpose of this exercise is to develop empathy and give feedback to others (with empathy). The participants are divided into triads (groups of three persons) of mainly the role occupants having the most frequent interactions

and interface relations. Each member of the triad prepares the following five images for each of the other two members:
- Self-concept—three strengths
- Self-concept—three weaknesses
- Three main concerns
- Image of the organization (three adjective/phrases)
- Self-image (three adjectives/phrases)

The lists are then exchanged to see how much empathy exists and how close are the 'guessed' images to the images held by the person concerned. This may be followed by a discussion focusing on why one could or could not empathise, and what can be done to increase empathy.

6. *Image sharing* (1/2 hour) The process on image building and image sharing follows, as described in role negotiation: preparation of one's own image, the other's image, own image as perceived by others; sharing the images and discussing them; and building positive images of each other.

7. *Exercise on collaboration* (1 hour) Maximising your gains, as suggested in role negotiation; can be used to examine the process of inter-team competition and collaboration while working in teams.

Contribution

This is the main phase of role contribution and involves the following 10 steps:

1. *Introduction* (1 hour) The consultant/facilitator discusses the dynamics of a helping relationship, the collaborative process, and the effectiveness based on empathy and trust. The philosophy and approach of contribution to each others' role effectiveness are elaborated.

2. *Superordination* (1 hour) A short concept session on collaboration is conducted, where collaboration and helping are stimulated by shared common goals of the parties concerned, the importance of such goals for both (or all) the parties involved, and the realisation that such goals cannot be achieved by anyone party alone without the cooperation/collaboration of the others. This can be followed by group work on identification of the superordinate goals of the concerned groups. The members in the group should also discuss the importance of these goals and to what extent these inspire them. The plenary session consolidates these goals as the framework for working further. The need for mutual support in superordination is also stressed.

3. *Preparation of offers* (1 hour) Each individual/group prepares the following four lists. Not more than three groups can do the exercise at a time.
- Why I/we want to contribute to your role effectiveness
- Why I/we may not contribute to your role effectiveness
- My/our contribution to your role—list specific things that you can do to make the other group/role occupant more effective
- What can you do to help me contribute—list specific things that the other group/role occupant can do to help you make a contribution to their/his role effectiveness

4. *Exchange of offers* (1/2 hour) The lists are exchanged and the groups mark items that need clarification.
5. *Clearing up and clarification* (1 hour) Representatives of the group sit in a fish bowl design (with one empty chair in the inner group), openly discuss any difficulties or misunderstandings that they have in relation to each other (clearing up unexpressed feelings and hidden agenda), and clarify the statements made.
6. *Reciprocal contribution* (1 hour) The groups meet in their home bases and against each offer made, write an offer in exchange, either from their original list or from a new one. The emphasis is to match each offer by a complementary one (which will strengthen the other role).
7. *Discussion of offers* (1 hour) The offers made are discussed in a fish bowl design. The focus of discussion is on whether the offer made will contribute to the effectiveness of the role. Modifications may be tentatively suggested.
8. *Review in home groups* (1/2 hour) The offers discussed in the fish bowl arrangement are reviewed by each group for a consensus and commitment by all members of the groups.
9. *Agreement on offers* (1½ hours) The whole community meets to reach an agreement on the offers made and accepted.
10. *Developing pledge* (1½ hours) A small team is formed to prepare a common integrated pledge to which everyone shows commitment. Everyone signs the pledge.

Closing

The following steps are taken in the closing phase:
1. *Force field analysis* (1 hour) Mixed groups of about eight members are formed to identify positive and negative forces for successful implementation of the pledge. Positive forces are those that tend to facilitate implementation, while the negative are those that are likely to retard implementation. These are presented to the whole community and a common understanding is arrived at.
2. *Implementation details* (1/2 hour) In the light of the force field analysis, a detailed, specific, time-bound plan is prepared for implementing the pledge.
3. *Sharing with seniors* (1 hour) The whole experience, and the pledge, is shared with the top senior group for information dissemination. Senior managers may ask for some clarifications and may make some comments. This step is taken to ensure a proper understanding of the intervention at the senior level and enlisting management support in implementation.

Follow-up

As in role negotiation, the first follow-up review is done after about two months, and later on a quarterly basis for a year. New agreements are made during the follow-up review.

Positive Reinforcement

Generally, people tend to do things that are positively reinforced through appreciation, encouragement, and reward. Positive reinforcement helps in reinforcing functional aspects of behaviour. Appreciation and rewards are well-known methods of reinforcement being used by organizations.

The organization should be clear about what it would like to reinforce through rewards: performance, effort, process, credibility, team building, sincerity, etc. This needs to be clearly communicated in advance to the employees concerned. However, regardless of what the management says, people will respond to their own perception of what behaviours are rewarded. Indeed, employees should preferably be involved in such a decision.

Rewards can be classified broadly into extrinsic and intrinsic rewards. Extrinsic rewards are bonuses, paid holidays, etc. They can further be classified as monetary and non-monetary rewards. Examples of monetary rewards are performance bonuses, profit sharing, stocks, etc. Non-monetary rewards include gifts, holiday facilities, etc. Intrinsic rewards include increased responsibility, greater freedom and job discretion, more interesting and challenging work, opportunities for personal growth (not merely vertical, time-bound promotion), and diversity of activities. Since rewards are essentially symbols of recognition, non-monetary rewards are preferable.

An organizational culture is created and maintained not only by individuals but also by teams. This is true of fulfilling organizational goals as well. In fact, most organizational tasks are carried out in teams. So it is necessary to think of rewarding both individuals and teams.

As the first step in designing a reward system, an organization should achieve consensus on the values, norms, and behaviour it wants to reinforce in its members. In short, it should be clear on the kind of organizational culture it wants to create. The following are some attributes being reinforced (rewarded) by certain Indian companies.[68]

The emphasis of the new reward policy of Gujarat Gas is on rewarding the 'simply the best' employee. Its objective is to provide a sense of recognition and an achievement motivation for significant contribution. It gives 'outperform' rewards for 'outstanding performer of the year', i.e., those with performance that 'always exceeds expectations'. Gujarat Gas also rewards those involved in event management without the help of an external agency. The RPG group has a 'vacation scheme' for the best employee and also gives rewards for the 'best region' and 'best division'.

Some organizations use positive reinforcement for the following:

Loyalty When employees complete their first year with Hughes Software, they are presented with a watch. When they complete 5 years, they (and their families) are given a company-paid holiday.

Innovation Gujarat Gas gives a 'innovation helps' reward for an idea generated by an employee that has resulted in cost reduction or improved efficiency. Hughes Software holds employee polls for rewarding the 'person with the best technical solution'.

Values and behaviour Hughes Software has a formal award for adherence to company values. It also holds employee polls to reward 'the most warm and friendly person' and rewards the best sense of humour. RPG gives awards to people who have contributed to social issues, such as riot or flood relief.

Learning Infozech Software rewards personal achievement in employees. For example, employees who have cleared an examination to earn a qualification such as MCSD, MCSE, MCIP, MCDBA, CISCO certification, or Sun certification are given a cash reward at a monthly meeting. At Hughes Software, employee polls are held for rewarding 'the best teacher'. Gujarat Gas gives 'the triumph' reward to an individual employee or to a team for coming out with an in-house publication.

The main spirit of rewards is the recognition of an individual or a team. There are various ways of recognising individuals or teams. At Hughes Software, employee polls are used to pick out individuals for a reward. When the management makes the decision to reward an employee, people may fear that the management would pick its 'favourites'. Employee polls are free from this kind of bias. At NIIT, there is an annual practice of naming a conference room or office or training room after the most outstanding employee of the year. The naming is done ceremoniously: a car is sent to fetch the family, a cake is ordered, and employees assemble in that room to celebrate. The HR department also organizes a poll for choosing the best employee. Thirty names are elected from the poll results to become members of the President's Forum. At Net Across, one has to be nominated 'best employee' by one of the department members. Information about the nominee, the criteria on the basis of which the person has been nominated, the projects the nominee has undertaken, and his or her accomplishments, competency, etc., are displayed on the intranet. The best employee is finally selected after polling. No cash rewards are connected to this honour. At RPG, certificates are given to employees by their managers for small achievements and the good work that they have done.

At ICICI, recognition extends to the employees' families as well: employees' children who excel in academics or extracurricular activities are recognised through scholarships and sponsorships. At Associated Capsules and Universal Capsules, outstanding employees are chosen and asked to name an outsider who, in their opinion, has contributed to the business of the company in the last quarter. They may invite that person to the company's dinner and the chairman writes the invitation letter to such persons. This is a very innovative way of recognising external efforts through internal people.

Rewards should be given to both individuals and teams. A multidimensional reward system is likely to reduce the undue pressure on promotions from which many Indian organizations suffer. Rewards should develop employees' pride in belonging to the organization and a feeling that people are valued. They should promote teamwork and inter-team collaboration and should reinforce organizational values, especially those desirable in the unit or department concerned. Criteria of excellence in performance should be clearly determined, along with their weightages.

Exceptional organizational events (a new product launch, an export award, the crossing of a significant milestone, etc.) may be celebrated organization-wide, with small gifts (the same to all employees, from the top to the lowest level). The gift may be decided by a team of five to seven employees (or, preferably, their spouses) from different levels and locations.

At the unit or departmental level, a few 'chairman's shields' may be constituted, given each year to the units or departments being judged as the best unit with regard to the year's thrust area or other aspects to be promoted by the organization, such as, quality, culture building, teamwork, creativity, internal customer service, cost reduction, and strategic initiatives. Any of these could also become annual thrust areas or other thrust areas could be declared by the organization, unit, or department, such as export, energy saving, wastage reduction, zero defect, safety, or breakthrough in chronic problems. Survey instruments may be prepared for assessing these, or audit teams for each aspect may be set up, with their recommendations being sent to the apex team for finalisation of rewards.

Individuals and teams may also be rewarded for creativity, teamwork, team building, subordinate development, internal customer satisfaction, etc. The types of rewards may include monetary rewards, computers, family holiday plans, stock or share options, declarations in the organizational newsletter, medals, and certificates (to be given at a function by the unit or department head, or the CEO), a visit to other plants, visits abroad, etc. A person who collects, say, four or more medals may be given an additional intrinsic or extrinsic reward.

SUMMARY

There is an increasing shift towards positive thinking in psychology and organizational behaviour today. This shift indicates the long-overdue importance being given to emotional attributes, as well as to characteristics generally attributed to women. Important aspects of a positive approach are internality, self-management, optimism, trust, and collaboration (ISOTC).

Positive thinking in OB is reflected by the concepts of emotional intelligence, mindfulness, creativity, extension motivation, and role efficacy.

Several interventions with positive approach have emerged. Some of these are future search (planning with future orientation, rather than past orientation), appreciative inquiry (searching strengths, rather than weaknesses), role efficacy lab (systematic planning to make the organization effective), role contribution (helping people to make other roles more effective), and positive reinforcement (encouraging and rewarding positive behaviour).

Unfortunately, the positive aspects of OB have not been explored sufficiently. Yet these have great potential and can be leveraged for the benefit of both organizations and their members.

GLOSSARY

alignment directing interests and actions of all employees toward a company's key goals

altruism the practice of placing others before oneself

analogical thinking the transfer of an idea from one context to a new one

attribute listing identifying the key characteristics, or attributes, of the product or process and ways to change, modify, or improve each

brainstorming generating wild, even preposterous, ideas

centrality feeling important or central in a system

collaboration two or more persons working together for the attainment of a common goal that is seen as sharable

confrontation facing problems to attempt their solution

convergent thinking bringing material from a variety of sources to bear on a problem

creativity experimenting and trying out new ideas/ strategies; mental process of generating new ideas or concepts, or new associations between existing ideas or concepts

critical thinking judging the facts and seeking errors

daan or bhiksha the giving or receiving of help— when the need of the giver is predominant, it is called *daan*; when the receiver's need is dominant it is called *bhiksha*

delivery phase (AI) personal and organizational commitments and 'paths forward'

design phase (AI) recreation of the 'social and technical architecture' of an organization

discovery phase (AI) listing of affirmative topics stated in affirmative language

divergent thinking creating elaboration of ideas prompted by a stimulus

dream phase (AI) people describing their wishes and dreams for their work, their working relationships, and their organization

emotional intelligence the capacities to recognise our feelings and those of others, to motivate ourselves, and to manage emotions in ourselves and in our relationships

extension motivation the basic needs of an individual to be relevant to others, including the society

flow deep involvement in and enjoyment of the current activity; recollecting pleasant experiences

future search conference a large group planning a meeting that brings a 'whole system' into the room to work on a task-focused agenda

growth the feeling that the one occupying a role grows and learns in the role

helping relationship giving and receiving help among roles

influence the feeling that one's role can make some impact in the system

innovation the introduction of a new thing or method

inter-role linkage linkage of one's role with the other roles

lateral thinking moving from one known idea to creating new ideas

mindfulness a heightened sense of situational awareness and a conscious control over ones thoughts and behaviour relative to the situation

morphological synthesis a simple elaboration of attribute listing

positive reinforcement reinforcing functional aspects of behaviour

proactivity initiating action

role contribution an intervention based on the need to be relevant, do something for, and help others

role efficacy the potential effectiveness of a role

role efficacy lab REL is a short process-oriented programme to diagnose the level of role efficacy in a group of employees (generally managers) and to take steps to raise that level

self-restraint willingness to postpone gratification of immediate needs for long-term goals

self-role integration integration between self-concept and the role demands

serendipity discovery made by fortunate accident in the presence of sagacity (keenness of insight)

superordination linkage of one's role with a larger entity/cause

whole system a cross-section of people concerned with the activities of the organization or community undertaking the search

EXERCISES

Concept Review Questions

1. What are the main categories of positive approach in OB?

2. What are the main aspects of positive thinking in OB?
3. Describe the main process of future search conference.
4. What are the four phases of appreciative inquiry?
5. What are the main components of emotional intelligence suggested by Goleman?
6. Discuss the concepts of role efficacy and role contribution.
7. How can positive behaviour in organizations be reinforced?

Critical Thinking Exercises

1. Give an example from your experience of 'managing the self'.
2. What is the importance of optimism for effectiveness in life? Can you cite examples from your own experience (people you have known to be successful)?
3. Consider the five positive aspects of OB suggested in this chapter. Which of these are weak in Indian organizations? Take any one aspect and suggest ways of improving it.

Classroom Projects

1. The Indian cricket team was transformed during the 2002 World Cup Tournament in terms of self-confidence and performance. From what you have read, how do you think this transformation came about? What are the main features of the 'winning' Indian team? List them.
2. Are the teachers in your various courses using more positive or more negative approaches? List both sets. Which of these is more effective for your learning?

Field Projects

1. Read about two contrasting companies, one that is expanding and successful, and another that is stagnant or not progressing much. Can you identify their positive and negative approaches?
2. Interview HR personnel from the two companies. Ask them what positive and negative approaches are adopted in their companies and with what results.

Future Search: The Indian Experience*

Mahima Consultancy Services (MCS), Madurai, India, is a consultancy firm working in the area of human resources development and organization development and has been involved in HRD and OD programmes for the past several years. The following is Belinda Bennet's account of her experiences in running future search conferences with the entire workforce of a large, extremely hierarchical tire retreading company in India, while sticking closely to the model (e.g., two and a half days) and adapting it to a variety of local cultures.

OUR INITIAL YEARS

During our initial years, our main focus was on interpersonal skill training and attitudinal change. We did different programmes for different categories of people in organizations, and often ended up with enough data on what was 'wrong'—the larger organizational issues—but could not address the larger issues within the scope of our training programmes. And so we were looking for a model to create common ground for action.

The Indian Society for Applied Behavioural Science (ISABS) conducted a workshop on Total System Consulting at Jaipur in December 1995. It was facilitated by Dr Udai Pareek and Dr Uma Jain. We gained much from this workshop, and out of the few models discussed were drawn to future search.

Just before the Jaipur workshop, we had entered into a training contract with TVS Tread, a leading tire retreading company. The company's new joint managing director was very enthusiastic about the training programme. He expected training programmes to motivate shopfloor workers. His assumption was that should the attitude of the work force be changed, it would have a snowballing effect on the functioning of various other departments of the company. At the Jaipur workshop, we realised how limited this point of view was and became convinced that we needed to work with the total system.

OUR FIRST WORKSHOP FOR TVS TREAD

We had a series of discussions about the future search methodology with the joint managing director (JMD), the president, and the vice president of the company. The JMD was much convinced about the concept, and we had our first workshop for TVS Tread in March 1996.

---

*Written by Belinda Bennet, Future Search Network Homepage, issue no. 14. Reproduced with slight modification permission.

TVS Sundaram Industries Tire Service Division, known as TVS Tread, is a 38-year-old organization. At present there are 29 branches spread over six Indian states (with different regional languages). It has about 1,000 workers and 400 administrative staff. Tire retreading is a labour-intensive, low-tech industry and there are innumerable firms doing this, and the competition is heavy. As each unit at TVS Tread is a profit centre, it was decided to do 29 separate future search conferences, plus a future search conference for the central office. So far, we have done 23 future search conferences and preparatory workshops for one branch.

When the future search conferences were initiated, the company's larger issues were

- Production figures had gone down from 4,200,000 tires to 2,800,000 tires per year.
- The morale of the employees was low.
- There was discontentment about the previous salary settlement (once in 3 years).
- The employees were totally dependent on the management.
- The people in the branches perceived that the hierarchy in the organization was very rigid.
- The communication from the central office was reportedly inadequate and delayed.
- There were complaints about the quality of rubber received from the central office.
- There was no shared vision.

Of the 23 conferences held so far, all of them have been in the local regional languages—Tamil, Malayalam, Telugu, Kannada—and in Hindi and English. We had workers who could not read or write. In each of the two conferences, we had two persons who were deaf. Fifteen of the 23 conferences were done bilingually (English or a commonly spoken language, and a regional language).

For each branch we had 2 days for planning, which we called preparatory workshops. On these 2 days, we met the stakeholder groups separately in small groups, followed by a shift meeting in which all branch members participated—the shopfloor workers, sales team, administrative team, tire delivery section staff and van drivers, the branch manager, branch accountant, agents, and the customers who made up the stakeholder groups. We started each preparatory conference with a top management representative making a statement as to why a future search conference was to be done.

The situation was that many of the employees had never undergone any kind of training. Moreover, planning a future search conference and bringing the 'total system' into a room was a culture shock for many. The preparatory workshops clarified many of their queries and fears, such as 'Why is everyone to be present?' 'Why don't functional groups meet separately?' 'Why the total system?' 'Will it work?' Mixing the shopfloor staff and the management staff was seen as a threat. Many doubted whether it would succeed.

We did not move further until everyone agreed to go ahead. We also realised that having an MBA and an illiterate worker together did not give us a homogeneous cognitive group. So we told stories and utilised folklore and visual aids to get some of our points across during the preparatory workshop.

CONFERENCE SCHEDULES

The future search conference always started after lunch, and we worked for 5 hours or more. We did the time-line exercise, taking the oldest employee's years of experience in the unit as the cutoff point. This varied between 10 and 30 years. We tried the mind map exercise for two conferences and then changed our technique to having the employees bring newspaper/magazine clippings in areas related to their industry.

Clippings were pasted on posters and brought to the conference. People who contributed the articles summarised them. We had individuals present to ensure their participation as well as to destroy the myth that shopfloor workers cannot be entrusted with such activity. This was followed by the prouds and sorries exercise. The day ended here. Moving from the past to the present gave the group a feeling of movement. Hence we did the mind map and the proud and sorries exercise on the first day. On the second morning we moved into futuring and finding common ground for action.

On the afternoon of the second day, in their stakeholder groups, participants worked on how to reach the revised future. After a few trials we structured this exercise, providing a frame that encouraged participants to write down the issue, the project/activity, who would be responsible, and the time frames. Irrespective of their designation, people took up responsibilities for action. This was an overwhelming experience for the group.

On the third day, each group presented its projects and action plan in the larger group. Then each project and action plan was fine-tuned, modified, and so on. A steering committee had been established, taking volunteers from each functional team. This steering committee chaired the presentations. (Today these steering committees meet once every 2 or 3 weeks and follow up on the commitment made. In most cases the steering committee decided to work for a 1-year term and then have another group volunteer to serve on the committee.) The entire conference process was recorded by two reporters.

OUR LEARNING

Our learning can be summarised as follows:
- The future search methodology helped employees across the organization discover a common ground for action.
- Despite the rigid hierarchy of the organization, the top management's commitment to and support for the future search conference made a difference in building energy and enthusiasm about the conference and its outcomes.
- The future search conference did not cure the leadership crisis/leadership problems in the organization.

- Facilitating a future search conference in a culture that thinks fatalistically requires fine facilitation skills.
- The conference worked as a tool to level the hierarchy, which was necessary to build a common ground.
- A cultural issue in an agricultural society like India's is that the average person lives for the day and believes in fate. The participants were only comfortable looking 2 to 3 years into their future.
- The style of leadership in the branch influenced the outcome of the conference to some extent. In a few instances, soon after the conference, some managers left the service. It was clear that when self-governance was established, at the end of the conference, to steer the branch into a growth path, leaders who were too controlling or who felt threatened by the new systems (fear of sharing power) left the organization.
- The strength of the branches varied from 21 employees to 70 employees. Anonymity could not be kept in smaller branches. The methodology worked well with groups above 40.

Questions for Discussion

1. What are the main learnings from the case?
2. What factors are important for the success of the future search conference?
3. What are the limitations of the future search conference?
4. What are the limitations of people in India working on the long-term future?

NOTES AND REFERENCES

1. Luthans, Fred (2002). *Organisational Behaviour*, Chapter 9. New York: McGraw-Hill.
2. Cooperrider, D.L. and S. Srivastva (eds) (1990). *Appreciative Management and Leadership*. San Francisco: Jossey-Bass.
3. Seligman, M.E.P. (1992). *Learned Optimism*. New York: Pocket Books.
4. Csikszentmihalyi, Mihaly (1990). *Flow: The Psychology of Optimal Experience*. New York: Harper & Row.
5. Sheldon, K.M. and L. King (2001). 'Why positive psychology is necessary', *American Psychologist*, 56: 216–217; see Luthans, Fred (2002), *Organisational Behaviour*, New York: McGraw-Hill.
6. The *American Psychologist* has published two issues on positive psychology in 2000 and 2001. The *Journal of Humanistic Psychology* also published a special number in 2002 emphasising the need for positive thinking in psychology.
7. Seligman, M.E.P. (1992). *Learned Optimism*. New York: Pocket Books; Sandage S.J. and P.C. Hill (2001). 'The virtues of positive psychology: The approachment and challenges of an affirmative postmodern perspective', *Journal of the Theory of Social Behaviour*, 31(3): 241–260.
8. Pareek, Udai (1988a). 'Task analysis for human resource development', in J.W. Pfeiffer (ed.), *The 1988 Annual: Developing Human Resources*. San Diego: University Associates.
9. Pareek, Udai (1988b). 'Organisational Learning Diagnostics (OLD)', in J.W. Pfeiffer (ed.), *The 1988 Annual: Developing Human Resources*. San Diego: University Associates.
10. Pareek, Udai (1994). *Beyond Management: Essays on Institution Building and Related Topics*, 2nd edn. New Delhi: Oxford & IBH.

11. Pareek, Udai (1988a). 'Task analysis for human resource development', in J.W. Pfeiffer (ed.), *The 1988 Annual: Developing Human Resources*. San Diego: University Associates.

12. Rao, T.V. and Udai Pareek (2006). *Changing Teacher Behaviour Through Feedback*. Hyderabad: ICFAI University Press.

13. Pareek, Udai (1994). *Beyond Management: Essays on Institution Building and Related Topics*, 2nd edn. New Delhi: Oxford & IBH.

14. Khandwalla, P.N. (1984). *The Fourth Eye: Excellence Through Creativity*. Allahabad: A.H. Wheeler.

15. Luthans, Fred (2002). *Organisational Behaviour*. New York: McGraw-Hill.

16. Bandura, A. (1997). *Self-efficacy: The Exercise of Control*. New York: Freeman.

17. *Ibid.*

18. Goleman, D. (1995). *Emotional Intelligence*. New York: Bantam Books.

19. Goleman, D. (1998). *Working with Emotional Intelligence*. New York: Bantam Books.

20. Diener, E.D., E.M. Suh, and R.E. Lucas (1999). 'Subjective well-being: Three decades of progress', *Psychological Bulletin*, 125(2): 276–302.

21. Csikszentmihalyi, Mihaly (1990). *Flow: The Psychology of Optimal Experience*. New York: Harper & Row.

22. Vangen, S. and C. Huxham (2003). 'Nurturing collaborative relations: Building trust in interorganizational collaboration', *The Journal of Applied Behavioral Science*, 39(1): 5–31.

23. Rao, T.V. (1991). 'Managerial work values', in J.W. Pfeiffer (ed.), *The 1991 Annual: Developing Human Resources*, pp. 163–177. San Diego: University Associates.

24. Fryxell, G.E., R.S. Dooley, and M. Vryza (2002). 'After the ink dries: The interaction of trust and control in US-based international joint ventures', *Journal of Management Studies*, 39(6): 865–886.

25. Coffman, Curt and Gabriel Gonzalez-Molina (2002). *Follow This Path: How the World's Greatest Organizations Drive Growth by Unleashing Human Potential*. New York: Warner Business Books.

26. *Business Today*, February 2003.

27. Goleman, D. (1995). *Emotional Intelligence*. New York: Bantam Books.

28. Gardner, Howard (1983). *Frames of Mind: The Theory of Multiple Intelligences*. New York: Basic Books.

29. As quoted by Goleman, D. (1995), *Emotional Intelligence*, New York: Bantam Books.

30. Salovey, P. and J.D. Mayer (1990). 'Emotional intelligence', *Imagination, Cognition and Personality*, 9.

31. Goleman, D. (1998). *Working with Emotional Intelligence*. New York: Bantam Books.

32. Purohit, Surabhi and Sharada Nayak (2002). *Enhancing Personal Effectiveness: Training Instruments for Students, Teachers and Parents*. New Delhi: Tata McGraw-Hill.

33. Langer, Ellen (1990). *Mindfulness*. New York: Addision-Wesley.

34. Marsano, Robert J. (2003). *Classroom Management That Works*. Alexandria, VA: Association for Supervision and Curriculum Development.

35. McLaren, Carrie. 'Mindlessness in America: Ellen Langer and the social psychology of mindlessness', accessed on 4 November 2004, http://www.stayfreemagazine.org/archives/16/mindlessness.html.

36. Marzano, R., J.S. Marzano and D.G. Pickering (2003). *Classroom Management That Works* (1970) New York: Association for Supervision and Curriculum Development.

37. Ritchhart, Ron and David N. Perkins (Spring 2000). 'Life in the mindful classroom: Nurturing the disposition of mindfulness', *Journal of Social Issues*.

38. McLaren, Carrie (2004). 'Mindlessness in America: Ellen Langer and the social psychology of mindlessness' (Online). 4 November 2004, p. 3.

39. Langer Mindfulness Scale.

40. Taylor, C.W. (1988). 'Various approaches to and definitions of creativity', R.J. Sternberg (ed.), *The Nature of Creativity: Contemporary Psychological Perspectives*. West Nyack, NY: Cambridge University Press.

41. Guilford, J.P. (1967). *The Nature of Human Intelligence*. New York: McGraw-Hill.

42. de Bono, Edward (1973). *Lateral Thinking: Creativity Step by Step.* New York: Haper & Row.
43. Lateral Thinking, Wikipedia, February 2007.
44. Khandwalla, P.N. (2003). *Corporate Creativity: The Winning Edge.* New Delhi: Tata McGraw-Hill.
45. Guilford. *The Nature of Human Intelligence.*
46. Torrance, E.P. (1974). *Torrance Tests of Creative Thinking.* New York: Personnel Press.
47. Nickerson, R.S. (1999). 'Enhancing Creativity', in R.J. Sternberg (ed.) , *Handbook of Creativity.* Cambridge University Press. West Nyack: New York.
48. Robinson, Alan G. and Sam Stern (1997). *Corporate Creativity: How Innovation and Improvement Actually Happen.* San Francisco: Berrett-Koehler.
49. Amabile, Teresa (1996). *Creativity in Context.* New York: Westview Press.
50. Robinson and Stern. *Corporate Creativity.*
51. Gopalakrishnan, R. (2007). Making business sense of innovation. tata.com/tata_sons/articles/20040720_rg.htm.
52. *Ibid.*
53. Osborn, A.F. (1953). *Applied Imagination.* New York: Scribner.
54. Luecke, Richard and Ralph Katz (2003). *Managing Creativity and Innovation.* Boston, MA: Harvard Business School Press.
55. Davila, Tony, Marc J. Epstein, and Robert Shelton (2006). *Making Innovation Work: How to Manage It, Measure It, and Profit from It.* Upper Saddle River, NJ: Wharton School Publishing.
56. The OECD Oslo Manual (1995).
57. Premji's speech cited at greathumancapital.wordpress.com/tag.
58. Krishna, Geetanjali (2006). 'Sanjha Chulhas'. *Business World,* 16 October, 108–109.
59. Weisbord, M. and S. Janoff (1995). *Future Search: An Action Guide to Finding Common Ground in Organizations and Communities.* San Francisco: Berrett-Koehler.
60. Contributed by Gale S. Wood in Searchnet Group.
61. David Cooperrider and Suresh Srivastva (eds) (1990). *Appreciative Management and Leadership.* San Francisco: Jossey–Bass.
62. *Ibid.*
63. Devrajan, M.K. (2006). Appreciative Inquiry in Rajasthan Police. Manuscript.
64. Pareek, Udai (1993b). 'Assessing organisational atmosphere: MAO-A', *TMTC Journal of Management,* 2: 76–86.
65. *Ibid.*
66. Rogers, Carl (1961). *On Becoming a Person: A Therapist's View of Psychotherapy.* London: Constable.
67. MAO-B and MAO-C titles of instruments. Full form: Motivational Analysis of Organisations—Behaviour and Climate.
68. Pareek, Udai (2004) 'Reward system for nurturing talent and teams', *Indian Journal of Training and Development,* 34(1): 27–38.

The Individual

- Learning Process

- Motivational Process

- Perceptual Process

- Attributional Process: Internality and Optimism

- Personality and Personal Effectiveness

- Development of Attitudes and Values

6
Learning Process

LEARNING OBJECTIVES

After studying this chapter, you will be able to
1. Define learning as a process
2. Enumerate various learning theories and their main features
2. Explain the cycle of learning
3. Describe the learning process and its elements
4. Elaborate the role of the teacher/facilitator in learning
5. Identify the conditions for effective learning

Learning has been a favourite subject for educators, psychologists, and those interested in change in individuals and organizations. Learning is conceptualised as acquisition of new behaviour in an interactional environmental situation. Systematic studies in learning were done on animals in laboratories. Some of these early studies on animals had significant implications for the learning of human beings—children as well as adults. Learning is a vast field, and a large number of theories have been proposed. One source lists as many as 53 theories of learning.

Two aspects help us to delimit our discussion of learning theories: our interest in adult learning (and not in animal or children's learning), and the relevance of the theories to management.

WHAT IS LEARNING?

Learning has been defined in various ways and a lot of research has been done on it. For our purposes, learning may be defined as the process of acquiring, assimilating, and internalizing cognitive, motor, or behavioural inputs for their effective and varied use when required, leading to an enhanced capability for further self-monitored learning. This definition has many implications for making learning more effective:

1. The first step in learning is the acquiring of new input in terms of knowledge and understanding (cognition), some physical or motor activity, or a new behaviour (including attitudes and values). When this process is quick, learning is effective.
2. The next step is the assimilation of the new input. It should not only be acquired quickly, but should also be retained for a length of time. If the input that is acquired is short-lived in the memory, learning has not been effective.
3. Learning is not a process of collection of various inputs alone. If these inputs hang loose, independent of one another, the person merely acts as a passive

receptacle for knowledge, motor skills, or behaviour. This happens often. For example, a scientist may acquire some scientific knowledge and skills, and yet may continue to be superstitious. This is like keeping the scientific knowledge in a separate compartment. Similarly, a behavioural scientist may acquire the skill of helping people to be open, share their feelings, and collaborate, whereas his or her own behaviour may be less than understanding, habit bound, highly competitive, and threatening. Development of new technology has increased the danger of such schizophrenic living (living a divided or contradictory life in terms of knowledge and behaviour, or behaviour in different settings, without being aware of such contradictions). Effective learning is characterised by the internalisation of new inputs. New inputs are acquired from the outside environment. But after these are assimilated, they should become a part of the individual's personality, lifestyle, and psychological world. Internalisation also means that inputs get transformed according to the individual's own psychological and cognitive system and thus get integrated.

4. Once the acquired inputs are internalised, they should be available to the individual for their effective use when the need arises. If what is learnt is only 'ornamental' and not effectively used, learning cannot be said to be effective. For example, the learning of management techniques and skills should result in better management of the various activities and fields with which the person works.

5. Effective use of learning also involves creativity. Learning should have 'transfer' value. What one has learned in one field, one should be able to apply and use in another field. This is also the concept in internalisation. After one has learned management techniques, one may be required to take up some other assignment, such as administration of an agricultural project, a government department, or a political party. One should be able to use one's knowledge and skills in the new situation. This would mean being creative, making one's own contribution to what one has learnt. Thus there is continuous enrichment of knowledge and practice. Learning must contribute to this process of development of creativity, generation of new knowledge, development of new fields of application, and building of new theories and conceptual models. In fact, creativity would also imply improvement of practice with new knowledge and skills, and the development of new knowledge from improved action and practice.

6. Learning should, in addition, increase a person's capability for learning more on his or her own. This does happen in effective learning. After a child has learned to take the first few steps, its learns to walk and balance itself on its own. Similarly, initial learning in a particular field enables a person to organize further learning on his or her own. Without such self-learning, an individual's growth would remain limited and dependent on external resources.

LEARNING THEORIES

Different approaches have been proposed to explain the phenomenon of learning.

These have emerged as models or theories. We shall discuss these theories and their implications for improving the learning process.

Stimulus–Response Theories

Classical conditioning

The earliest theory of learning developed around the turn of the last century. Russian physiologist, Ivan Pavlov, experimenting on the digestive system of dogs, gave meat powder to the dogs to salivate them. He discovered a strange phenomenon after sometime. While the presence of food (the eliciting stimulus) in the animals' mouth could reliably predict the flow of saliva (the innate response), the sight of the experimenter who brought the food (who was paired with the food) soon came to elicit salivation. Pavlov termed salivation by the presence of the sight of the experimenter who brought the food (and who was paired with meat powder) as *conditioned reflex*. He distinguished *natural reflex* (salivation on meat powder) from conditioned reflex (salivation on the presence of the experimenter, who had been paired with meat powder). This research became pioneering in several ways. Pavlov's theory can also be called *stimulus generalisation theory*. When a stimulus gets associated with another neutral phenomenon, the neutral phenomenon acquires the quality of the original stimulus to get the desired response. This can be understood in a social setting. For example, a woman worker has bad experience with two consecutive male bosses. They aroused anger, anxiety, etc. in her. Because of stimulus generalisation, other men elicit same feelings in her when she encounters them. As a result, she may develop negative attitudes towards men.

Instrumental conditioning

Around the same time as Pavlov worked in Russia, E.L. Thorndike in the US was working on cats, chicks, and dogs to understand the learning process. He differed in one major way from Pavlov. Thorndike placed his animals in a 'puzzle box' from which they were required to escape, by manipulating the correct lever or pulley, in order to obtain food reward. Through the process of 'trial and error', Thorndike's animals eventually 'learned'. Since the animal's behaviours were instrumental in escaping from the box and in obtaining food, the paradigm was labelled 'instrumental conditioning'. For Thorndike response was more important for learning than the stimulus. His theory can, therefore, be called *response generalisation theory*.

Operant conditioning

Skinner[1] built on both these traditions of Pavlov (which he called Type S conditioning) and Thorndike, (which he called Type R conditioning), and became one of the most influential theorists of learning. He developed a science and technology built upon Type R or, *operant conditioning*. Skinner differed radically from learning and clinical psychologists. While many learning theorists stressed the importance of the immediately preceding stimulus, for Skinner stimulus did not occupy specific place as an independent variable. Similarly, while clinical psychologists like Freud stressed the past as an important antecedent for learning, Skinner focussed only on the present. He concentrated his studies on operants (freely emitted behaviours, which operate upon the environment, and which are, in turn, controlled by their environmental consequences, i.e., the events that follow their emission can increase or decrease their future probability of occurrence). Operants are learned behaviours, and can be distinguished from 'respondents'; a respondent is a behaviour under the control of prior eliciting stimuli and is a part of the individual's biological equipment (either at birth or as a result of maturation). The knee jerk reflex is an example of a respondent.

One key concept in operant analysis is the contingency relationship between an operant and the events that follow it. The relationship of a student's raising hand in a classroom and the teacher's attention to the student is typically a contingent act. The teacher selectively recognises the student; he is not forced to do so. Hand raising can be considered as operant, under the control of contingent events (including the teacher's response, in addition to the reaction of other students, etc.).

Reinforcement is another important element in Skinner's theory. Thousands of experiments have been conducted to find out the various factors associated with effectiveness of reinforcement. One important element is the schedule of reinforcement. 'Schedules of reinforcement have regular and profound effects on the organism's rate of responding. The importance of schedules of reinforcement cannot be overestimated. No description, account, or explanation of any operant behaviour of any organism is complete unless the schedule of reinforcement is specified.'[2] Basically, operant conditioning is a simple feedback system: If a reward or reinforcement follows the response to a stimulus, then the response becomes more probable in the future.

In operant conditioning, a schedule of reinforcement is any rule determining which responses should be followed by reinforcement under conditions where not every response is necessarily reinforced. The reason schedules were important theoretically was that different kinds of schedules induced different patterns of behaviour, and these patterns were highly orderly.

There are two types of schedules: simple and compound. Simple schedules are those involving a single rule to determine the delivery of a single type of reinforcer for making a single type of response. The simplest schedules of all barely deserve the name: they are continuous reinforcement (the reinforcement of every response) and extinction (the cessation of all reinforcement). Compound schedules combine two or more different simple schedules in some way.

Skinner achieved amazing results by his research. His pigeons were able to learn to dance and to bowl a ball in a mini-alley. The pigeons were able to work in a pharmaceutical firm as quality control 'inspectors', rejecting the defective capsules. The time taken by the pigeons was less, and the level of task accuracy was higher, compared with that of human beings. Skinner even experimented with the pigeons to accurately deliver missiles on some targets. His experiments led to the technology of operant shaping, usefully employed in attitude change.

Cognitive Theories

Stimulus-response theories have their limitations. They disregard the activities of the mind, and so cannot explain all types of learning. Even research on animals has shown that they adapt their reinforced patterns to new information. Experiments on monkeys showed that they changed their behaviour on perceiving change in the environment, without any reinforcement. Many learning theorists recognised the importance of thinking. Their theories can be called cognitive theories of learning.

Constructivist theory

Bruner[3] has been a very influential learning theorist. According to him, learning is an active process in which learners construct new ideas or concepts based upon their current/past knowledge. The learner selects and transforms information, constructs hypotheses, and makes decisions, based on a cognitive structure to do so. Cognitive structure (i.e., schema, mental models) provides meaning and organization to experiences and allows the individual to 'go beyond the information given'.

Bruner's main work was on children's cognitive learning, and he emphasised the importance of instruction and the organization of learning by the instructor. According to him a theory of instruction should address four major aspects:

1. The predisposition towards learning
2. The ways in which a body of knowledge can be structured so that it can be most readily grasped by the learner
3. The most effective sequences in which to present material
4. The nature and pacing of rewards and punishments

Good methods for structuring knowledge should result in simplifying, generating new propositions, and increasing the manipulation of information.

The main task of the instructor is to encourage students to discover principles by themselves. The instructor should engage the student in an active dialogue (Socratic learning) and translate information to be learned into a format appropriate to the learner's current state of understanding.

Piaget is another well-known learning theorist who emphasised the importance of mental models. According to him the developing child builds cognitive structures (mental 'maps', schemes, or networked concepts) for understanding and responding to physical experiences within his or her environment. This is true of adults also. Instructors must emphasise the critical role that experiences—or interactions with the surrounding environment—play in student learning.

Theory of cognitive dissonance

Festinger[4] proposed the cognitive dissonance theory, primarily applicable to learning (or change) of attitudes. According to this theory, individuals tend to seek consistency among their cognitions (i.e., knowledge, beliefs, and opinions). When there is an inconsistency between attitudes or behaviours (dissonance), something must change to eliminate the dissonance. In the case of a discrepancy between attitudes and behaviour, it is most likely that the attitude will change to accommodate the behaviour.

Two factors affect the strength of the dissonance: the number of dissonant beliefs and the importance attached to each belief. There are three ways to eliminate dissonance: (1) reduce the importance of the dissonant beliefs, (2) add more consonant beliefs that outweigh the dissonant beliefs, or (3) change the dissonant beliefs so that they are no longer inconsistent.

Dissonance occurs most often in situations where an individual must choose between two incompatible beliefs or actions. The greatest dissonance is created when the two alternatives are equally attractive. Attitude change is more likely with less incentive for changed behaviour, since it produces dissonance, resolved by shifting of attitude. (Example: students who were against police action but wrote essays supporting the same for a payment of US $1 changed their attitude in favour of police action compared with like-thinking students who were paid US $100 for the same writing task.) This is contradictory to most behavioural theories that would predict greater attitude change with increased incentive (i.e., reinforcement).

Another example: Consider someone who buys an expensive car but discovers that it is not comfortable on long drives. Dissonance exists between the beliefs that a good car has been bought and that a good car should be comfortable. Dissonance could be eliminated by deciding that it does not matter that the car is uncomfortable on long drives since the car is mainly used for short trips (thereby reducing the importance of the dissonant belief) or focusing on the cars strengths such as safety, appearance, handling (thereby adding more consonant beliefs). Getting rid of the car could also eliminate the dissonance, but this behaviour is a lot harder to achieve than changing beliefs.

Theory of lateral thinking

Edward De Bono[5] popularised lateral thinking—the generation of novel solutions to problems. Lateral thinking is based on the premise that many problems require a different perspective to solve successfully. The main principle of lateral thinking is that breaking up the elements and recombining them, perhaps randomly, in a different way can achieve a different perspective on a problem.

De Bono identifies four critical factors associated with lateral thinking:
1. Recognising dominant ideas that polarise perception of a problem
2. Searching for different ways of looking at things
3. Relaxation of rigid control of thinking
4. Use of chance to encourage other ideas

De Bono has given the following example of lateral thinking. A merchant who owes money to a moneylender agrees to settle the debt based upon the choice of two stones (one black, one white) from a moneybag. If his daughter chooses the white stone, the debt is cancelled; if she picks the black stone, the moneylender gets the merchant's daughter. However, the moneylender 'fixes' the outcome by putting two black stones in the bag. The daughter sees this and when she picks a stone out of the bag, immediately drops it onto the path full of other stones. She then points out that the stone she picked must have been the opposite colour of the one remaining in the bag. Unwilling to be unveiled as dishonest, the moneylender must agree and cancel the debt. The daughter has solved an intractable problem using lateral thinking.

Adult Learning Theories

So far, the theories we have briefly reviewed were primarily developed with experiments on animals or studies on child development and learning. Some scholars emphatically argued that adult learning had its own dynamics. Malcolm Knowles' theory of andragogy is an attempt to develop a theory specifically for adult learning. Knowles emphasizes that adults are self-directed and expect to take responsibility for decisions. Adult learning programmes must accommodate this fundamental aspect.

Andragogy makes the following assumptions about the design of learning: (1) adults need to know why they need to learn something, (2) adults need to learn experientially, (3) adults approach learning as problem solving, and (4) adults learn best when the topic is of immediate value.

In practical terms, andragogy means that instruction for adults needs to focus more on the process and less on the content being taught. Strategies such as case studies, role playing, simulations, and self-evaluation are most useful. Instructors adopt the role of a facilitator or a resource rather than a lecturer or grader.

Andragogy applies to any form of adult learning and has been used extensively in the design of organizational training programmes. The main principles of andragogy are as follows:

1. Adults need to be involved in the planning and evaluation of their instruction.
2. Experience (including mistakes) provides the basis for learning activities.
3. Adults are most interested in learning subjects that have immediate relevance to their job or personal life.
4. Adult learning is problem centered rather than content oriented.

Knowles[6] provides an example of applying andragogy principles to the design of personal computer training:

1. There is a need to explain why specific things are being taught (e.g., certain commands, functions, operations, etc.).
2. Instruction should be task oriented instead of memorisation—learning activities should be in the context of common tasks to be performed.
3. Instruction should take into account the wide range of backgrounds of learners; learning materials and activities should allow for different levels/types of previous experience with computers.
4. Since adults are self-directed, instruction should allow learners to discover things for themselves, providing guidance and help when mistakes are made.

Building on Knowles' andragogy, Cross[7] proposed the Characteristics of Adults as Learners (CAL) model in the context of her analysis of lifelong learning programmes. The model consists of two classes of variables: personal characteristics and situational characteristics. Personal characteristics include aging, life phases, and developmental stages. These three dimensions have different characteristics for lifelong learning: Aging results in the deterioration of certain sensory–motor abilities (e.g., eyesight, hearing, reaction time), while intelligence abilities (e.g., decision-making skills, reasoning, vocabulary) tend to improve. Life phases and developmental stages (e.g., marriage, job changes, and retirement) involve a series of plateaus and transitions that may or may not be directly related to age. Learning can be part-time or full-time, and this will affect the administration of learning (i.e., schedules, locations, procedures). Learning being voluntary or compulsory pertains to the self-directed, problem-centered nature of most adult learning.

The following are the main principles of CAL:

1. Adult learning programmes should capitalize on the experience of participants.
2. Adult learning programmes should adapt to the aging limitations of the participants.
3. Adults should be challenged to move to increasingly advanced stages of personal development.
4. Adults should have as much choice as possible in the availability and organization of learning programmes.

Social Learning Theories

Modelling theory

The social learning theory of Bandura emphasises the importance of observing and modelling the behaviours, attitudes, and emotional reactions of others. Bandura[8] states: 'Learning would be exceedingly laborious, not to mention hazardous, if people had to rely solely on the effects of their own actions to inform them what to do. Fortunately, most human behaviour is learned observationally through modelling: from observing others one forms an idea of how new behaviours are performed, and on later occasions this coded information serves as a guide for action' (p. 22). Social learning theory explains human behaviour in terms of continuous reciprocal interaction between cognitive, behavioural, and environmental influences. The component processes underlying observational learning are

1. Attention, including modelled events (distinctiveness, affective valence, complexity, prevalence, functional value) and observer characteristics (sensory capacities, arousal level, perceptual set, past reinforcement)
2. Retention, including symbolic coding, cognitive organization, symbolic rehearsal, motor rehearsal
3. Motor reproduction, including physical capabilities, self-observation of reproduction, accuracy of feedback
4. Motivation, including external, vicarious, and self-reinforcement

Because it encompasses attention, memory, and motivation, social learning theory spans both cognitive and behavioural frameworks. Bandura's theory improves upon the strictly behavioural interpretation of modelling. The principles of Bandura's theory can be summarized as follows:

1. Organizing and rehearsing the modelled behaviour symbolically and then enacting it overtly helps to achieve the highest level of observational learning. Coding modelled behaviour into words, labels, or images results in better retention than simply observing.

2. Individuals are more likely to adopt a modelled behaviour if it results in outcomes they value.

3. Individuals are more likely to adopt a modelled behaviour if the model is similar to the observer and has admired status and the behaviour has functional value.

The most common (and pervasive) examples of social learning situations are television commercials. Commercials suggest that drinking a certain beverage or using a particular hair shampoo will make us popular and win the admiration of attractive people. Depending upon the component processes involved (such as attention or motivation), we may model the behaviour shown in the commercial and buy the product being advertised.

Theory of social cognition

Vygotsky[9] proposed the social cognition learning model that states culture is the prime determinant of individual development. Culture (including the culture of the family environment) affects a child's learning development.

Culture makes two sorts of contributions to a child's intellectual development. First, through culture children acquire much of the content of their thinking, that is, their knowledge. Second, the surrounding culture provides children with the processes or means of their thinking, what Vygotskians call the tools of intellectual adaptation. In short, according to the social cognition learning model, culture teaches children both what to think and how to think.

Since children learn much through interaction, curricula should be designed to emphasise interaction between learners and learning tasks. With appropriate adult help, children can often perform tasks that they are incapable of completing on their own. With this in mind, scaffolding—where the adult continually adjusts the level of his or her help in response to the child's level of performance—is an effective form of teaching. Scaffolding not only produces immediate results, but also instils the skills necessary for independent problem-solving in the future.

The principles of social cognition theory are as follows:

1. Cognitive development results from a dialectical process whereby a child learns through problem-solving experiences shared with someone else, usually a parent or teacher but sometimes a sibling or peer.

2. Initially, the person interacting with child assumes most of the responsibility for guiding the problem solving, but gradually this responsibility transfers to the child.

3. Language is a primary form of interaction through which adults transmit to the child the rich body of knowledge that exists in the culture.

4. As learning progresses, the child's own language comes to serve as her primary tool of intellectual adaptation. Eventually, the child can use internal language to direct her own behaviour.

5. Internalisation refers to the process of learning—and thereby internalising—a rich body of knowledge and tools of thought that first exist outside the child. This happens primarily through language.

6. A difference exists between what the child can do on her own and what the child can do with help. Vygotskians call this difference the zone of proximal development.

7. Since much of what a child learns comes from the culture around her and much of the child's problem solving is mediated through an adult's help, it is wrong to focus on a child in isolation. Such focus does not reveal the processes by which children acquire new skills.

8. Interactions with surrounding culture and social agents, such as parents and more competent peers, contribute significantly to a child's intellectual development.

Experiential Learning Theories

Action learning theory

The theoretical framework of action learning has been widely applied to management education.[10] Action learning involves structured projects in organizations rather than traditional classroom instruction. The key elements of action learning are commitment to learning, social interaction, action plans, and assessing the results of actions.

Humanistic theory

Carl Rogers' theory of learning[11] evolved as part of the humanistic education movement. Rogers distinguished two types of learning: cognitive (meaningless) and experiential (significant). The former corresponds to academic knowledge such as learning vocabulary or multiplication tables and the latter refers to applied knowledge such as learning about engines in order to repair a car. The key to the distinction is that experiential learning addresses the needs and wants of the learner. Rogers lists the following qualities of experiential learning: personal involvement, self-initiation, evaluation by the learner, and pervasive effects on the learner.

According to Rogers, experiential learning is equivalent to personal change and growth. Rogers feels that all human beings have a natural propensity to learn; the role of the teacher is to facilitate such learning. This includes

1. Setting a positive climate for learning
2. Clarifying the purposes of the learner(s)
3. Organizing and making available learning resources
4. Balancing intellectual and emotional components of learning
5. Sharing feelings and thoughts with learners but not dominating

According to Rogers, learning is facilitated when

1. The student participates completely in the learning process and has control over its nature and direction.
2. It is primarily based upon direct confrontation with practical, social, personal, or research problems.
3. Self-evaluation is the principal method of assessing progress or success. Rogers also emphasises the importance of learning to learn and an openness to change.

The following are the principles of Roger's theory:

1. Significant learning takes place when the subject matter is relevant to the personal interests of the student.
2. Learning that is threatening to the self (e.g., new attitudes or perspectives) is more easily assimilated when external threats are at a minimum.
3. Learning proceeds faster when the threat to the self is low.
4. Self-initiated learning is the most lasting and pervasive.

Double-loop theory

Argyris[12] has proposed double-loop learning theory, which pertains to learning to change underlying values and assumptions. The focus of the theory is on solving problems that are complex and ill-structured and that change as problem solving advances.

The double-loop theory is based on a 'theory of action' perspective outlined by Argyris and Schon.[13] This perspective examines reality from the point of view of human beings as actors. Changes in values, behaviour, leadership, and helping others are all part of, and informed by, the actors' theory of action. An important aspect of the theory is the distinction between individuals' espoused theory and their 'theory-in-use' (what they actually do); bringing these two into congruence is the primary concern of double-loop learning. Interaction with others is necessary in this regard.

There are four basic steps in the 'action theory' learning process:

1. Discovery of the espoused and the theory-in-use
2. Invention of new meanings
3. Production of new actions
4. Generalisation of results

In double-loop learning, assumptions underlying current views are questioned and hypotheses about behaviour tested publicly. The end result of double-loop learning should be increased effectiveness in decision making and better acceptance of failures and mistakes.

According to it, effective problem solving about interpersonal or technical issues requires frequent public testing of theories-in-use, and double-loop learning requires learning situations in which participants can examine and experiment with their theories of action.

Here are two examples[14]: A teacher who believes that she has a class of 'stupid' students will communicate expectations such that the children behave stupidly. She confirms her theory by asking them questions and eliciting stupid answers or puts them in situations where they behave stupidly. The theory-in-use is self-fulfilling. Similarly, a manager who believes his subordinates are passive, dependent, and require authoritarian guidance rewards dependent and submissive behaviour. He tests his theory by posing challenges for employees and eliciting dependent outcomes. In order to break this congruency, the teacher or manager would need to engage in open-loop learning in which they deliberately disconfirm their theory-in-use.

Cyclic theory

Kolb[15] proposed the cycle of experiential learning of adults. The cycle has four parts (see Exhibit 6.1), one following the other, in order:

Experiencing   The learner has some concrete experience, or is helped to have experience during the training programme.

Processing   The learner reflects on and analyses the experience individually and in a group.

Generalising   The learner forms a tentative theory or a way to explain the data–abstract conceptualization based on the experience.

Applying   The learner tries the new behaviour, or uses it in the day-to-day work, followed by a new experience, and the cycle continues–active experimentation.

Exhibit 6.1   *Kolb's Learning Cycle*

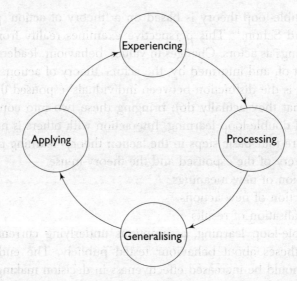

Motivation Theories

Attribution theory

Attribution theory is concerned with how individuals interpret events and how this relates to their thinking and behaviour. Heider[16] was the first to propose a psychological theory of attribution, but Weiner[17] developed a theoretical framework that has become a major research paradigm of social psychology. Attribution theory assumes that people try to determine why people do what they do, i.e., attribute causes to behaviour.

Weiner focused his attribution theory on achievement. He identified ability, effort, task difficulty, and luck as the most important factors affecting attributions for achievement. Attributions are classified along three causal dimensions: locus of control, stability, and controllability. The locus of control dimension has two poles: internal versus external locus of control. The stability dimension captures whether causes change over time or not. For instance, ability can be classified as a stable, internal cause, and effort classified as unstable and internal. Controllability contrasts causes one can control, such as skill/efficacy, from causes one cannot control, such as aptitude, mood, others' actions, and luck.

Weiner's theory has been widely applied in education, law, clinical psychology, and the mental health domain. There is a strong relationship between self-concept and achievement. Weiner states: 'Causal attributions determine affective reactions to success and failure. For example, one is not likely to experience pride in success, or feelings of competence, when receiving an "A" from a teacher who gives only that grade, or when defeating a tennis player who always loses. On the other hand, an "A" from a teacher who gives few high grades or a victory over a highly rated tennis player following a great deal of practice generates great positive affect' (p. 362).[18] Students with higher ratings of self-esteem and with higher school achievement tend to attribute success to internal, stable, uncontrollable factors such as ability, while they contribute failure to either internal, unstable, controllable factors such as effort, or external, uncontrollable factors such as task difficulty. For example, students who experience repeated failures in reading are likely to see themselves as being less competent in reading. This self-perception of reading ability reflects itself in children's expectations of success on reading tasks and reasoning of success or failure of reading. Similarly, students with learning disabilities seem less likely than non-disabled peers to attribute failure to effort, an unstable, controllable factor, and more likely to attribute failure to ability, a stable, uncontrollable factor. The principles, in summary, are

1. Attribution is a three-stage process in which (a) behaviour is observed, (b) behaviour is determined to be deliberate, and (c) behaviour is attributed to internal or external causes.
2. Achievement can be attributed to (a) effort, (b) ability, (c) level of task difficulty, or (d) luck.
3. Causal dimensions of behaviour are (a) locus of control, (b) stability, and (c) controllability.

Attribution theory has been used to explain the difference in motivation between high and low achievers. According to attribution theory, high achievers will approach rather than avoid tasks related to succeeding because they believe success is due to the high ability and effort that they are confident of. They attribute failure to bad luck or a poor exam, i.e., not their fault. Thus, failure does not affect their self-esteem, but success builds pride and confidence. On the other hand, low achievers avoid success-related activities because they tend to (a) doubt their ability and/or (b) assume success is related to luck, or to 'whom you know', or to other factors beyond their control. Thus, even when successful, it is not as rewarding to the low achiever because he/she does not feel responsible, i.e., it does not increase his/her pride and confidence.

Martin Seligman built on the attribution theory and suggested two stable factors— permanent and pervasive, relating to time and space, respectively, and two variable factors—temporary and specific. He applied the theory of attribution to the learning of helplessness. His book on learned helplessness[19] was an important contribution to the understanding of depression and helplessness. His interest switched to the positive aspects. He became interested in how people learn to be optimist or pessimist. Sequel to his earlier book, this book on learned optimism[20] was another important landmark in the learning of emotional states like optimism. More recently, he led a group of psychologists to form what is called positive psychology.

In the attribution framework, optimism is defined as attributing miseries, failures, and bad experiences to variable factors (temporary or specific). Pessimism, on the other hand, is defined as attributing miseries, failures, and bad experiences to stable (permanent or pervasive) and good experiences and success to variable (temporary or specific) causes.

A study of insurance agents showed that less optimistic agents were twice as likely to quit as more optimistic ones. The agents from the top half scores on optimism sold 20 per cent more than the less optimistic ones (from bottom half); those from the top quarter sold 50 per cent more than those from the bottom quarter. When a special force of highly optimistic agents was created, they outsold the pessimists in the regular force by 21 per cent during the first year, and 57 per cent in the second year.[21]

Regarding learning of optimism, Seligman's advice is to monitor internal dialogue. We are constantly talking to ourselves. When one finds oneself anxious or worried, one should pause for a moment and pay attention to what one is saying to oneself. We tend to have automatic responses to different situations. We need to develop awareness of those automatic responses, and then develop new, more effective ways to interpret life's events.

We should start paying attention to our internal dialogue, notice the patterns, and try to optimise our three Ps: personalisation, permanence, and pervasiveness. We should create new habits.

Seligman has suggested the ABCDE method for learning optimism (changing the attributional style, the way one explains life events, from pessimism to optimism). Seligman suggests that people record their reactions to life events and modify those reactions to be more optimistic.

Identify the *adversity* that you are experiencing or have experienced, that is, what bad event has happened to you. Identify the *beliefs* that you are using to explain that bad event, that is, what attributions do you have about the event. These beliefs might be hard to identify sometimes, because often they occur automatically. We have learned to explain the world using these beliefs so well that the explanations are automatic. Examine the *consequences* of having that belief, that is, what do you do because of the belief. Many times a pessimistic attributional (belief) style will result in quitting, or avoiding, or ending an activity, to escape the bad feelings that the individual has experienced from facing adversity.

Use *disputation* to change the beliefs that you are using to explain the adversities you are facing. Disputation involves the following:

1. Examining whether there is any evidence for the beliefs
2. Identifying alternative explanations (beliefs)
3. Understanding the implications of the beliefs (do the beliefs really justify the consequences?)
4. Identifying the usefulness of the beliefs (do they really serve some function for me, or am I better off thinking something else?)

Generally, the consequences of negative beliefs are negative things, which often involve withdrawal from the situation and decreased enthusiasm for the situation or activity. Thus, changing the beliefs often leads to an energization, such that the person feels good about what he/she is doing and looks forward to where he/she is going from here.

Motivation acquisition theory

David McClelland made seminal contribution by demonstrating that people could 'learn' motivation. His famous experiment in Kakinada, India, demonstrated that even adults in advanced age could learn new motives.[22] A 10-day programme was designed to change affiliation motivation of people from the affluent society of Kakinada to achievement motivation.

Some theoretical notions of what motive acquisition involves and how it can be effectively promoted in adults have been summarised in the form of twelve propositions. The propositions are given below[23]:

Proposition 1. The more reasons an individual has in advance to believe that he can, will, or should develop a motive, the more the educational attempts designed to develop that motive are likely to succeed.

Proposition 2. The more an individual perceives that developing a motive is consistent with the demands of reality (and reason), the more the educational attempts designed to develop that motive are likely to succeed.

Proposition 3. The more thoroughly an individual develops and clearly conceptualises the associative network defining the motive, the more likely he is to develop the motive.

Proposition 4. The more an individual can link the newly conceptualised association–action complex (or motive) to events in his everyday life, the more likely the motive complex is to influence his thoughts and actions in situations outside the training experience.

Proposition 6. The more an individual can perceive and experience the newly conceptualised motive as an improvement in the self-image, the more the motive is likely to influence his future thoughts and actions.

Proposition 7. The more an individual can perceive and experience the newly conceptualised motive as an improvement on prevailing cultural values, the more the motive is likely to influence his future thoughts and actions.

Proposition 8. The more an individual commits himself to achieving concrete goals in life, related to the newly formed motive, the more the motive is likely to influence his future thoughts and actions.

Proposition 9. The more an individual keeps a record of his progress towards achieving goals to which he is committed, the more the newly formed motive is likely to influence his future thoughts and actions.

Proposition 10. Changes in motives are more likely to occur in an interpersonal atmosphere in which the individual feels warmly but honestly supported and respected by others as a person capable of guiding and directing his own future behaviour.

Proposition 11. Changes in motives are more likely to occur when the setting dramatises the importance of self-study and lifts it out of the routine of everyday life.

Proposition 12. Changes in motives are more likely to occur and persist if the new motive is a sign of membership in a new reference group.

LEARNING STYLES

Learning or cognitive styles refer to the preferred way individual processes information. Unlike individual differences in abilities, styles describe a person's typical mode of thinking, remembering, or problem solving. Furthermore, styles are usually considered bipolar dimensions, whereas abilities are unipolar (ranging from zero to a maximum value). Having more of an ability is usually considered beneficial, while having a particular cognitive style simply denotes a tendency to behave in a certain manner. Cognitive style is usually described as a personality dimension, which influences attitudes, values, and social interaction. A number of cognitive or learning styles have been proposed and studied over the years. Some are briefly mentioned below.

Field independence vs field dependence This classification is quite well known in the literature. A field-independent person approaches the environment in an analytical way, and is able to distinguish figures as discrete from their backgrounds. On the other hand, a field-dependent person approaches the environment in a global way, and experiences events in an undifferentiated way. In addition, field-dependent individuals have a greater social orientation relative to field-independent personalities. Studies have identified number connections between this cognitive style and learning.[24] For example, field-independent individuals are likely to learn more effectively under conditions of intrinsic motivation (e.g., self-study) and are influenced less by social reinforcement.

Levelling vs sharpening Individual variations in remembering that pertain to the distinctiveness of memories and the tendency to merge similar events.

Reflection vs impulsivity Individual consistencies in the speed and adequacy with which alternative hypotheses are formed and responses made.

Serialist vs holist Serialists prefer to learn in a sequential fashion, whereas holists prefer to learn in a hierarchical manner (i.e., top-down).

4MAT Framework   Bernice McCarthy has suggested four learning styles (analytic, imaginative, common sense, and dynamic).[25]

Kolb's Styles   Kolb[26] proposes four stages in experiential learning: concrete experiences (CE), reflective observation (RO), abstract conceptualisation (AC), and active experimentation (AE). Proposing CE/AC and AE/RO dimensions as two poles, he has suggested four types of learners (divergers, assimilators, convergers, and accommodators) depending upon their position on these two dimensions. For example, an accommodator prefers concrete experiences and active experimentation (AE, CE).

Based on the cycle of experiential learning, Kolb also proposed four learning styles. *Concrete experiencers* are excited by the new activity or experience and share it with others. They generally combine experiencing and generalising parts of the cycle. *Reflecting observers* learn from objective observation, reflect on it, discuss it, and then generalise. They benefit from processing and generalising parts of the cycle. *Abstract conceptualisers* rely mainly on logic and rational analysis. They tend to generalise from their exposure to logical material. *Active experimenters* are pragmatic and rely on trying things out in their familiar situation. The applying part of the learning cycle is more appealing to them.

Theoretically, cognitive and learning styles could be used to predict what kind of instructional strategies or methods would be most effective for a given individual and learning task.

The learning styles theory is based on research demonstrating that as a result of heredity, upbringing, and current environmental demands, different individuals have a tendency to both perceive and process information differently. The different ways of doing so are generally classified as

Concrete and abstract perceivers   Concrete perceivers absorb information through direct experience, by doing, acting, sensing, and feeling. Abstract perceivers, however, take in information through analysis, observation, and thinking.

Active and reflective processors   Active processors make sense of an experience by immediately using the new information. Reflective processors make sense of an experience by reflecting on and thinking about it.

Traditional schooling tends to favour abstract perceiving and reflective processing. Other kinds of learning are not rewarded and reflected in curriculum, instruction, and assessment nearly as much.

OVERVIEW OF LEARNING PROCESS

The various elements involved in the process of learning are the training/teaching organization, the trainer/teacher, the learner, and the technology of training/learning. All these four elements are important. Each of these can be treated as a system or a sub-system.

The training/teaching organization, including the training/teaching group, can be called the endosystem. This system has its own culture and dynamics. The main function of this system is to maximize the motivation for learning by creating the culture and climate conducive to such motivation.

The system of the teaching/training technology is concerned with the mechanics of teaching/training. Methodology and aids help in the various aspects of learning. However, the main function of this system is to help assimilation and stabilisation of learning through practice and application.

The trainer/teacher is certainly an important person in this whole cycle and is the main representative of the influence system. Although other elements also produce influence, the main impact is made by the teacher/trainer through his or her behaviour, values, and competence. The way the trainer/teacher influences the learner may determine the effectiveness of learning to a great extent.

The last, but certainly the most important element in the process of learning is the learner. The learner makes use of the other systems. His or her main function is the development and effective use of processes. Process is the dynamic system of various procedures used in assimilating, internalising, using, and creating learning. This system may therefore be called the process system.

Exhibit 6.2 gives the management process of learning and the interrelationships among the four elements. As may be seen from the exhibit, the most important

Exhibit 6.2 *Learning Process*

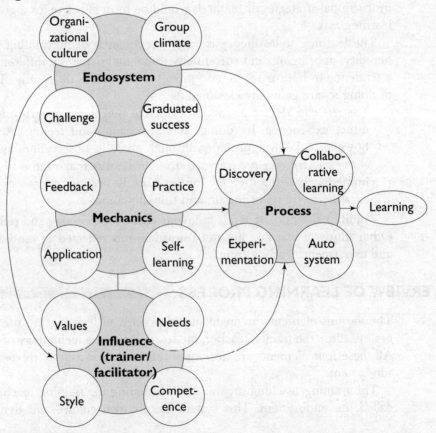

element directly contributing to effective learning is the process system. All the other three systems contribute to learning through this system. In other words, all other systems may be able to influence learning only by contributing to the development of an effective process and helping the learner to do so. As discussed later, the process system consists of discovery and experimentation by the learner, collaborative learning, and the development of a person's own small learning systems.

Another important feature of the interrelationship among the four elements is that while the three elements—the endosystem, the process, and the influence of trainer/teacher—make mutual contributions, the mechanics of learning only receives contributions from the endosystem and the trainer/teacher, while being in a mutual relationship with the process system. This means that the technology of training is not crucial in determining the effectiveness of learning. Because of the glamour of technology, it may draw more attention; but it plays a limited, though important role in making learning effective. Each element in the learning process is discussed further below.

Endosystem

The main focus of a training organization is to create the necessary motivation for learning. Various aspects of the endosystem help in creating such motivation. Some of these are discussed below.

Organizational culture

The culture of the organization is very important for learning. If the learning institute functions as a closed, authoritarian system and the trainers emphasise the value of democratic and participative methods in their class lectures, learning becomes an ineffective farce. The general atmosphere of the training institute communicates much more and with greater impact than what is taught in the classroom. It may be worthwhile for training institutes to examine whether their own culture reflects what is being taught. Sometimes the institutes do not perceive the glaring contradiction between what is stressed in teaching and what actually happens in the institute. Institutes running effective programmes on team building may themselves be working in watertight compartments of departments and sections, and individual faculty members may not even meet to plan programmes.

Moreover, the culture of the institute should encourage participation and experimentation. If the institute has a completely fixed and rigid curriculum without any possibility of change, the students or participants get a certain message. Thus a training organization may like to examine its organizational culture to see whether it encourages self-learning, participation of learners in designing the curriculum (or at least in reviewing and criticising it), feedback from learners on teaching programmes and methods, openness to different views and disagreement, and creativity (i.e., different and new ways of dealing with the same problems). If the culture is conducive to the development of such values and norms, learning is speeded up.

Non-threatening climate

Equally important is the classroom climate. Learning is faster in a non-threatening climate. If the learner fears being ridiculed by his or her peers or teachers, learning will be slow as the learner will not be able to experiment, take the risk of expressing doubts, or ask questions. Similarly, if results of the evaluation of classroom work are communicated to the organizations that have sent the participants, the participants will be very hesitant in expressing themselves and their learning will suffer. One of the main advantages of programmed learning is that a learner does not feel threatened in committing mistakes. The learner should not have apprehensions of being laughed at or considered naive and ignorant.

Various steps can be taken to create a non-threatening climate. Distance between the teachers/trainers and the learners creates some threat. Similarly, unknown groups also pose a threat. In the beginning, special programmes can be organized to create a friendly and free atmosphere. An activity called 'microlab' tries to achieve this. In the microlab, a number of activities are planned in quick succession to help the learners get a glimpse of the various ways of teaching–learning likely to be adopted in the programme. The various items are discussed in small groups, which are quickly changed so that interaction among the participants is maximised. Sometimes, the teachers/trainers also participate. This can be very helpful in creating a non-threatening climate. Microlabs also include activities addressing the individual's personal attributes—strengths, weaknesses, style, values, aspirations, etc.

The behaviour of the teachers in the classroom, of course, contributes the most to the classroom climate. If differences of opinion, difficult questions, and doubts are tolerated and appreciated, an encouraging climate may be created. Teachers may deliberately ask silent members to express their opinions. The formation of small groups to discuss topics also contributes to a climate conducive to learning.

Challenge in learning

Learning is effective and satisfying if the learner achieves something by overcoming challenges. If learning cannot provide challenge, it ceases to motivate. One way to produce challenge is to develop programmes that encourage new learning. The learner should feel that he or she is learning something new and worthwhile. Technical subjects often appeal because such challenge is provided.

Another factor that helps in producing a sense of challenge is the pressure of learning itself. The demand on the learner should be fairly high. The more demanding a programme is in terms of time and effort invested by the learner, generally speaking, the more satisfaction it produces.

Challenge can also be created by encouraging healthy competition. If healthy competition is recognised and rewarded, it may create a challenging climate. It may, however, be useful to balance competition and cooperation. Competitive exercises can also promote collaboration. This can be done, for example, by holding competitions between groups so that members collaborate to work together, but compete for the excellence of their collaborative effort with other groups. Collaboration produces mutual support and mutual reinforcement, which are favourable for effective learning. Competition produces challenge and a pressure to give the best of oneself, which is necessary for learning. Thus, a combination of both may be very helpful.

Graduated challenging successes

Nothing is more motivating than success in a difficult and challenging job. Easy success does not produce as much satisfaction. Similarly, failure to achieve a goal, however challenging it may be, does not motivate unless it is taken as only an experience to learn from and activities are replanned to attain the target next time. If programmes can be designed to provide successful experiences in a challenging job, learning can be sustained for longer, and astonishing results can be achieved. Programmed instruction is based on the principle of increasing difficulty and challenge with every success so that each time the learner gets both—a new challenge and success in overcoming the challenge. This reinforces the success and motivates the learner to proceed to a new success experience. This is illustrated by an incident in Skinner's class (Skinner is regarded as the father of the learning theory and research). One of his doctoral students was awkward at social dancing, and therefore no girl would date him steadily. An aptitude test showed that he had a very low aptitude for music. Skinner suggested an experiment. The student was first given a very simple task of discriminating various intervals and rhythms, then had to proceed to tones, notes, etc. A graduated programme was thus prepared. At the end of the 'course', not only did he find a date, but he also got married, and was hired by a newspaper as a critic of musical performances in town to boot! The secret of this miracle lies in the graduated challenging successes that were organized meticulously for the learner.

If a learner is helped to succeed on a challenging job, and subsequently the challenge increases a little bit each time, learning can become very effective. Of

The course on programmed learning seems to have transformed shy Shalini into a confident speaker.

course, this would require a great deal of work. But if this principle is applied to help individual learners use programmed learning and enough gradually increasing challenges are built into the classroom work, learning can be made more effective.

Mechanics of Learning

Learning technology plays an important role in stabilizing learning so that what has been learned is properly assimilated and becomes a part of the individual's normal behaviour. Some of its main aspects are discussed below.

Feedback

Feedback is a necessary condition for stabilising learning. If a learner does not know how much he or she has learned, the learning will be slow. However, if the learner knows how much he or she has learned, what he or she could not learn, and why, learning will be more effective.

The principle of feedback is very effectively used in programmed instruction. After the learner goes through some new information, he or she reads a question on the material learned and chooses one of the responses given there. Then the learner turns a page to find out whether the response chosen was correct. This is feedback. Suppose the learner has chosen the wrong answer. He or she is then asked to find out why that answer is wrong. This is another kind of feedback. Feedback can be built-in in various other ways. Review exercises, review sessions, short tests, etc. provide similar feedback.

It is important that feedback is given as close to the learning event as possible. It should help the learner to understand the cause of his or her success and/or failure, so that the learner can plan more systematically for future effectiveness. Feedback is important not only for cognitive learning and the learning of technical skills, but also for the learning of behavioural skills and for behavioural change. In the latter case, feedback is much more complex.

Practice

For effective learning, it is necessary that the learner is able to practise what he or she has learnt. This helps in stabilising learning. Practice may give the learner an opportunity to test whether learning has been effective, to take steps to improve, and to gain enough confidence to use this learning in future. Enough opportunities should therefore be provided for practice. This is particularly important in the case of skills—both technical and behavioural. Practice should be accompanied by feedback, so that each period of practice is followed by reinforcement of success. This helps in stabilisation of learning. For example, if a participant decides to develop the skill of listening, he or she may be helped to practice the skill several times, and some detailed data (feedback) may be provided as to whether he or she listened or failed to listen to different group members each time. Specific time periods, clearly outlined and effective methods of assessment and feedback group support, and a non-threatening climate are necessary for effective practice. Programmes of mass practice or mutual feedback on the practice of common skills can help in the practice of the skills and their use in behaviour.

Application

Learning is of no use unless it leads to action. Knowledge or skills are meant for certain purposes. Unless these are properly used, they are as good as absent. The application of learning implies the development of insight in the learner and an ability to respond to a situation effectively. Training technology can offer various ways of organizing the application of learning. It may range from applying the acquired knowledge to problems as defined in classroom situations or cases to its application in real-life situations. Application can also be aided if a demonstration can be organized. Films are a good medium for this. In a film, the use of a particular principle or a set of principles can be effectively shown. The use of a system like MbO (management by objectives) can be shown quite effectively in a film. Demonstration through an actual situation may be equally, and sometimes more, effective. After learning about MbO, if a learner is taken to a unit where MbO is practised, his or her ability to apply this knowledge in real-life situations increases.

After having seen the application, the learner may be encouraged to try it himself or herself. A simple exercise of describing situations and asking the learner to apply some part of this knowledge may be useful. A detailed case may be even better. Another step can be taken in preparing a detailed simulation, with the learner being required to work out the details. Such simulation can be either in the form of written material only or an actual organizational situation. The most lifelike way of learning application is to take up an exercise in a company or in the field. For example, after a learner has learned how to diagnose organizational culture and has seen its application in a film, he or she may be sent to an organization to apply his or her knowledge and prepare a report. This report may then be critiqued.

The various mechanics of application need to be planned in a proper sequence. It may, for example, be useful to have several graduated exercises on demonstration followed by several graduated exercises in actual application, testing the ability to apply knowledge and learn from the review of such exercises. For training in applied fields, enough emphasis should be given to application and new ways should be devised to ensure effective application and practice. Even the methodology of teaching contributes to this. The use of cases in teaching increase the probability of application of what is learned. But this alone may not be enough for effective application. In some areas, the use of simulation of entire systems may be effective not only at the application stage but even at the early stage of acquiring learning. Different systems of learning sequences can of course be worked out but the focus on application should never be lost.

Self-learning

The teaching/training technology should emphasise self-learning. The learner should develop both the motivation as well as the skills and capability for self-learning.

Learners may select some areas in which they are comparatively weak or about which they want to know more and may proceed at their own pace.

Programmed instruction is one device to encourage self-learning. An effective use of programmed instruction can result both in economy of learning and in faster learning of some kinds of material. Material which requires acquisition of information or knowledge can be better learned through programmed instruction, which can save on time spent in such learning in the classroom. More effective use of the teacher/trainer and the learning group can be made after the individual learner has acquired some knowledge and when most learners in the group are at the same level. In many organizations, training can be improved enormously if the concept of training is widened to include the use of self-instructional material. For example, a company with a large marketing operation may like to design a course on new sales tax laws. It can do this best by designing self-instructional material on the new laws. After most managers have gone through their individual 'courses', short programmes for batches can be organized to discuss doubts, implications, changes needed in marketing strategy, and so on.

Self-learning needs to be stressed as a necessary component in all learning situations. Enough time should be given to participants to read, consult the library, and select their own material for learning. Assignments requiring self-study and search for relevant material can themselves promote self-learning. Such work can be satisfying and also help in stabilizing what has been learned.

Learning Process

In learning, the process is the most important factor, which emphasises creativity. In general, the process is concerned with how learning develops, how the learner and the teacher/trainer interact, and how the learner is involved in the process. Such concerns are crucial for managing the effectiveness of learning. Some important dimensions of the learning process are discussed below.

Discovery

Learning can be more effective in the individual's personal development if he or she 'discovers' knowledge rather than 'getting' it from the teacher/trainer. Learning by discovery emphasizes the importance of the learner and expresses trust in the learner's ability to be active and creative. This has implications for technology as well as other systems—the endosystem and the influence system (the teacher/trainer). If a teacher/ trainer provides the minimum necessary guidance and encourages the learner to explore the environment, the field of knowledge, situations, and organizations and to discover various aspects himself or herself, then learning contributes to creativity. This is, of course, a challenge for training managers and trainers.

Discovery also emphasises the use of the learner's experience in learning. This is particularly true in the case of behavioural skills. Such skills cannot be learned unless the learner, through taking active part and incurring some risk, discovers for himself or herself the 'principles' of behaviour. For example, learning empathy is not possible if a person learns about it in books. The learner has to 'discover' what empathy is in a situation he or she is involved in, and where the learner takes necessary risks to get feedback and help. Laboratory training, for instance, proceeds on this assumption. This is true of all other learning as well. One may have learned about designing a control system, but the real learning comes about only when one 'discovers' it through sudden insight, which makes the cognitive learning meaningful. It is then that various ideas, techniques, and facts fall into a meaningful pattern like the pieces of a jigsaw puzzle.

Experimentation

Related to discovery is experimentation—taking an active role in trying out a new thing or taking some risk. All skills involve experimentation. If learning is to be creative and lead to creativity, experimentation is necessary. It is through experimenting that the learner understands that there are various ways of doing things and discovers alternatives that make him more effective in being able to choose from a variety of alternatives. In fact, he or she learns to create new alternatives.

Without experimentation, learning cannot help in the development of a field. If a learner merely learns how to apply some techniques as taught, he or she becomes only a technician. The learner should, instead, become an engineer, able to innovate according to the challenge.

Experimentation is very important in the learning of behavioural skills. Laboratory training and other types of behavioural training use experimentation to a great extent. When a learner is dissatisfied with his or her present level of a particular skill or behaviour, he or she will be able to develop the particular skill or learn a new skill only by experimenting with his or her behaviour in a group that provides encouragement and psychological safety. Feedback on the experimentation will reinforce the lesson and encourage the learner to practise the skill or behaviour. In all learning situations, enough opportunities should be provided to learners to experiment, to try out new ways, and to learn from such efforts.

Auto systems design

Learning should also help the learner to learn 'how to learn further'. For this purpose, the learner should be helped to develop his or her own system of self-learning. Each learner uses a particular system. While one person learns by organizing his or her thoughts using a systematic outline, another may learn through application and conceptualisation. Similarly, people develop their own ways of remembering things, preparing notes, preparing records, reference cards, and other material, referencing, etc. Learners should be encouraged to review the effectiveness of their systems and find out about other available methods so that they can finally choose their own system and develop it further.

Collaborative learning

So far learning has been discussed only from the point of view of individual learners. But learning is also a function of the entire group. Also, the group is an important resource for the individual. All learners, and certainly the trainers as well, constitute the group. Learners learn not only from the teacher/trainer but also from one another. The process of collaborative learning—mutually helping one another in learning and facilitating this process—is very significant. In real-life situations, people work most of the time in groups and influence one another to achieve results. Such situations involve learning. Collaborative learning, therefore, is a very important dimension of growth and of building the skills to help and receive help. All formal learning programmes should stress and strengthen collaborative learning. Such learning should also include the teacher/trainer. Then learning does not debase the learner as an object.

Influence: The Trainer

The teacher/trainer influences the learning situation a great deal. The trainer's values, general style of interaction, competence, and individual needs matter a great deal. His or her contribution to the learning process is most vital. The main dimensions of his influence are discussed below.

Values

The trainer's main contribution is through his or her values. Some trainers/teachers may not be aware of their values; others are. Whether one is aware of them or not, everyone has a set of values and behaves according to these. Therefore, it may be useful for teachers/trainers to examine what values they are operating with. Since the main role of the trainer/teacher is to influence the learners and their learning process, the question they should ask themselves is what their model of an ideal human being is.

Probably, two factors are important in determining one's model of an ideal human being. One is social awareness, and the other one's concept of human nature. Regarding social awareness, two extreme positions were held by Karl Marx and Max Weber, the former emphatically asserting the primacy of social reality of power held by the different classes, and the latter that of ideas and institutions. With regard to human nature, contrasting positions are represented by, on one hand, the classical Western proselytising stance (human beings are basically ignorant and need to be 'converted' to awareness, or human beings' basic animal nature is motivated by the fulfilment of physical needs) and, on the other, the Eastern faith in the goodness and godliness of humanity, with an emphasis on self-awareness (symbolised so dramatically by Mahatma Gandhi). The former position culminated in Taylorism and work systematisation and the latter in humanism, more recently represented by Freire, Maslow, Rogers, and others. Not that these people directly borrowed from Gandhi or other Eastern thinkers, but their impact did percolate. That, however, is a separate discussion.

In the teaching/learning context, Carl Rogers represents a strong trend regarding values and the model human being. His non-directive teaching emphasised 'nurturing self-direction and fulfilment' of the learners. His faith in the learner as a resource is immense. Although Bruner comes from a different tradition, his emphasis on exploration and enquiry has made a significant contribution to the theory of instruction. He emphasises that cognitive learning takes place best through enquiry, through the learner's own motivations. He emphasises also the 'autonomy of self-reward' as against outside rewards. Paulo Freire, mixing a Marxian understanding of society with humanism, has contributed the concept of 'conscientisation'—arousal of a positive self-concept in human beings, in relation to their environment and society through a liberating education that treats learners as subjects (active agents) and not objects (passive recipients).

Skinner, the best-known person in the field of learning, held a peculiar position. He emphasised the role of external conditions of the environment in human behaviour, and accordingly proposed a theory of shaping behaviour through manipulation of external conditions. He made a tremendous contribution to the technology of learning (he is considered the father of programmed instruction technology) as well. However, the Skinnerian model of humanity is a passive one, even though it is the human being who manipulates the environment in it.

It may be useful for teachers/trainers to become aware of some of these thinkers— and others in their own countries and traditions—and consciously develop their own model of humanity. If they do not exercise their conscious choice, the choice gets determined without their awareness. There is no escape.

Style

The trainer's style is very important in the learning process. However, the trainer's style will be determined to a great extent by his or her values and concept of humanity. One dimension of the trainer's style is the type of influence he or she uses. Teachers/trainers can be classified as having a 'direct influence style' or an 'indirect influence style'. Various other ways of looking at style can also be considered—how much use the trainer makes of the different training methods; what reviewing devices he or she uses; whether the trainer deals with his or her subject in isolation or builds linkages with other subjects; the trainer's degree of emphasis on theory and application respectively, etc.

The interaction process between the trainer/teacher and the learner is very important. In the words of Paulo Freire, 'it is important whether the trainer/teacher treats learners as subjects (active agents) or as objects (passive recipients) in the process of learning'.[27] This is reflected in their process of interaction. One simple and useful system of classification for the interaction process is that based on the influence of the trainer.

The trainer influences learners in various ways. The main question is how does he or she influence them? Is the trainer's influence 'liberating' or 'prescriptive'? Is his or her influence indirect or direct? Does the trainer's influence result in expressive behaviour or coping behaviour? Several thinkers have dealt with this important aspect and have raised similar questions.

Using Bales's interaction process categories, Flanders[28] developed the categories of 'direct' and 'indirect' influence behaviour for teachers in a classroom situation. Direct influence restricts the freedom of the learner, is prescriptive, and develops coping behaviour. Indirect influence increases the learner's freedom, is liberating, and develops expressive behaviour. Several studies show this to be true. The interaction analysis method gives valid, observable, and highly reliable data about these two categories of behaviour (and some other relevant data).

Direct influence behaviour by the trainer includes negative reinforcement (criticising, reprimanding, punishing), ordering and giving directions, asking specific testing questions, lecturing, defensive behaviour (justifying), expressing anger, and so on. Indirect influence behaviour includes accepting feelings, expressing feelings, accepting ideas, building on the learner's ideas, positive reinforcement (praising, encouraging), asking exploring questions, sensitivity (encouraging silent members to participate), and so on. Studies show that if indirect influence behaviour by the teacher/trainer is rewarded (feedback and satisfaction are also rewards), his or her style will change.

Teachers/trainers must therefore examine how they can use more indirect influence behaviour and encourage creativity and development of potential in learners. This would in fact mean providing minimal guidance and recognising the learners as important resources in learning. Learning then become a process of mutual influence and the teacher/trainer is as much in the learning role as the learner. The whole approach to teaching and training then changes. Much more emphasis is given to helping learners to discover, innovate, develop their own systems, and develop their capability for self-learning.

You won't believe the influence the trainer has had on Mr Gupta—looks like he took the seminar on negative reinforcement literally.

Needs

The trainer's own motivation and needs are equally important in the learning process. If the trainer has a high need recognition and acceptance, he or she may become charismatic and try to create dependence. The trainer should therefore examine what his or her motivational pattern is, and what needs this is creating and arousing in the learners.

The trainer is in a very influential role—his or her expectations will also influence the behaviour of the learners to a great extent. If the trainer's expectations are high, the learners are likely to fulfil these expectations. As has been shown by Rosenthal and Jacobson, expectations influence the style and general behaviour of teachers and they help the learners to fulfil their expectations. The experiment reported by them is too well known to require detailed reference. Briefly, some primary school children were 'selected' as potential geniuses and this was made known to their teachers, parents, and peers. In fact, they were picked out at random. But the effect of raising expectations was dramatic and the children did show marked improvement in all dimensions, including their IQ. It was the miracle of expectations at work. The high expectations of teachers changed the teachers' behaviour, which became more supportive and helped the children fulfil the psychological prophecy.

Competence

Of course, the competence of the teacher/trainer in his or her own field is very important in the learning process. A teacher/trainer commands the students' respect to a great extent through his or her competence. The trainer can be of great help to the learners in discussing creative ways of applying knowledge if he or she knows the field well—the importance of this factor cannot be overemphasised.

In sum, the effectiveness of learning can be defined in terms of learning being quick and sustained, effectively used, leading to creativity and the development of a capacity for self-learning. The following conditions are conducive to such learning:

- Authentic and open system at the training institution
- Non-threatening climate
- Challenging learning tasks
- Collaborative arrangements for mutual support of learners
- Organization of graduated experiences of challenging successes
- Mechanisms for supportive and quick feedback
- Opportunities to practise skills learned
- Opportunities to apply learning
- Opportunities for and encouragement of self-learning
- Opportunities and support for experimentation
- Emphasis on learning through discovery
- Indirect and liberating influence of the trainer through minimum guidance
- Trainer's human values and faith in humanity

- Trainer's high expectations from learners and openness to examining own needs
- Trainer's competence

The better such conditions are, the more effective the learning can become.

SUMMARY

Learning involves acquiring, assimilating, and internalising various inputs and making effective and varied use of them. The learning cycle has four parts: experiencing, processing the experience, generalising or conceptualising, and applying or experimenting, which again leads to new experience, and so on. There are four corresponding learning styles. There are four elements in the learning process: the process system (which is central), the endosystem (the culture and the climate), the training mechanics, and the facilitator/facilitation process. Effective learning will involve using these in practice.

GLOSSARY

endosystem the main overarching system

experiencing having, or helping to have, concrete experience

generalising abstract conceptualisation based on an experience, forming a tentative theory or a way to explain data

learning the process of acquiring, assimilating, and internalising cognitive, motor, or behavioural inputs for their effective and varied use when required, leading to enhanced capability of further self-monitored learning

learning cycle the phases of learning, reinforcing each other

EXERCISES

Concept Review Questions

1. Define organizational learning as a process.
2. What are the four elements in the learning cycle suggested by Kolb? Illustrate them with an example of your own learning.
3. What are the main contributions of Carl Rogers and Paulo Freire to our understanding of learning?
4. Give some suggestions on ways to accelerate and promote learning in an organization.
5. What are the main elements of the learning process?

Critical Thinking Questions

1. Applying Kolb's learning cycle, identify your own learning style. Give a few examples.
2. Critique the teaching of OB in your class. Which learning cycle is your OB instructor following while helping you to learn OB?

Classroom Projects

1. You have been learning various things. In some cases you were highly satisfied; in other cases you felt frustrated. Recall one experience when you learned a lot and retained it. What were the conditions that helped you to learn? List them. You will have 10 minutes. Then form groups of three or four.

Share your lists and develop a common list. You will have another 10 minutes for this. One member from each group will report to the whole class (10 minutes again).

2. Give three or four suggestions on what you would do as a manager to enhance the learning of new trainees reporting to you.

Field Projects

1. Interview two people you know who learn very fast. Ask them what helps them to learn so quickly.
2. Interview two students and list the factors that help in their learning and those that delay or retard their learning. Critique your reading of the chapter in the light of these findings.

Restrategising for Survival*

Associated Betty International Ltd (ABIL), owners of a leading brand of bread, commenced its operations at Calcutta in 1928. The company had its 50 per cent shares owned by Shannon, a leading multinational dairy products company, based in Canada. The other 50 per cent shares were owned by Shei Dorabji, a leading industrialist. ABIL had its four plants at metros (Chennai, Kolkata, Delhi, and Mumbai) and its corporate headquarters at Bangalore, with a turn over of 25,000 million rupees. The Delhi unit started at Rohini in 1967, and later shifted to Lawrence Road in 1975. It had 807 employees.

To improve workers' productivity, ABIL contacted the Central Board of Workers Education (CBWE) and sought its services for organizing a workers training programme. The agenda for the programme was decided with the joint consultation of Krishna Mohan, a top-level executive, and the CBWE. The choice of the trainers was made by Krishna Mohan who insisted upon lady trainers, with an intention to thwart any possible resistance to the programme. Two lady trainers were chosen for the entire training programme.

The first day of the programme saw the discussion focusing on the international issues in related areas, which were narrowed down to national and finally to regional happenings. On the third day, the management conducted the programme along with the CBWE trainers. They appraised the union leaders of the happenings in the bread industries, the options open to them, and their decision to retain the existing workers. They also assured them of non-retrenchment if necessary skills were acquired.

The union leaders, noticing the direct interaction between management and workers through training sessions, got panicky about their role in the whole process. Krishna Mohan initiated one-to-one dialogue with union leaders to establish rapport and sought help from Sardars (as the union leaders were called in the region) and ex-union leaders in removing the of the workers' fears. Forty per cent workers were covered in the training programmes within a duration of 3 months.

Outside leaders and unions were also taken into confidence. Discussions with Bhanu Pratap, a powerful union leader, resulted in a favourable response from him; he had asked the management to share reports on plant layout, market research, and manpower deployment pattern. The company agreed to provide these documents, including the confidential marketing research report. As the company proposed to

*This case was developed by Manoj M. Patwardhan, Rajesh K. Jain, Jainendra Jain, Saurabh Mukherjee (Prestige Institute of Management, Gwalior), Sujoy Bhattacharya, (The ABV-IIITM, Gwalior), Seema Bhattacharya (Gurukul Kangri University, Hardwar) in the Third National Case Writing Workshop organized by Prestige Institute of Management, Gwalior, 10–12 January 2003. Reproduced with permission.

shift three ovens out of six in phase one, all the four unions joined hands in their resistance to this change. In a meeting, the union leaders asked for a written assurance from management for no retrenchment due to this change. Krishna Mohan promptly agreed to this and also proposed to put up the signed declaration on the notice board. As a consequence of this, union leaders put forward a proposal in which they agreed to the shifting of one oven. They also agreed to the shifting of the other two ovens only after the arrival of new machinery. Meanwhile, the shipment of equipment for the new plant was on its way and it was expected in a month. The marketing department put pressure on Krishna Mohan to facilitate the shifting of the other two plants simultaneously. Krishna Mohan, however, resisted the demand of the marketing department. A month later the SwissRoll shipment arrived. The training programme continued and Krishna Mohan utilised this forum as a means of continuous communication and updating. Afterwards, the other two plants were also shifted. Krishna Mohan then made a list of 30 non-productive workers who for the last many years worked in general shifts.

These workers were asked to come in different shifts and as a consequence a lot of them came forward for settlement, as they did not want to compromise with their comfort. In 2 years, 20 people identified as troublemakers were also dismissed. This included the union leader belonging to the unrecognised union and who had earlier filed a case against the company. The later training programmes run during this period focused on positive thinking and attitude building. An interesting phenomenon emerged; the workers themselves made a hit list of nuisance creating workers and discussed the reasons for their dismissals. The long-term settlement of 3 years was due in 1998 and the other three plants had to be shifted. At this stage ABIL decided to organize the Art of Living Programme for 3 days. This programme was helpful in inculcating the positive attitude approach and in enhancing the receptivity of the workers. The management for the first time was able to achieve this settlement bilaterally. Not only did the proposal for the settlement come from the management, which the workers agreed to after some deliberations, but also the signing as well as the implementation of the agreement went hand in hand. The workers were empowered to reject the raw material, even after being approved by the quality control department. The company abolished 105 jobs and implemented a ploughback system, where the benefits achieved out of this settlement were to be distributed partly among the workers. The workers also agreed to reduce the number of holidays from 13 to 10 per year in lieu of 3 additional casual leaves. The technical and the behavioural training programme continued.

ABIL decided to introduce the 'check-off system', wherein the contribution of union was to be deducted directly from the salary of the workers and paid to their respective unions. ABIL initially asked the unions to prepare a list of their members. Around 100 workers appeared on the lists of the two rival unions. Krishna Mohan called the leaders of the unions and asked them to decide on the disputed cases. Within 7 days the issue was sorted out and the check-off system was enforced.

Once ABIL's transporters went on strike. As bread is a perishable good, Krishna Mohan was faced with closing operations in the units after a 12-hour run, due to inventory stock piling. The transport employees had deliberately chosen the main gate of ABIL as the place for strike to pressurize the management. Krishna Mohan sought the help of the union leader Bhanu Pratap, who promptly responded, called the workers, and dispersed the strikers from the main gate of ABIL, taking advantage of the larger membership of his union. Some issues like enhancement of mutual trust, upgradation of skills, job enlargement, empowerment of workers, and benchmarking needed further consolidation in the system.

Questions for Discussion

1. What road map of learning did Krishna Mohan follow for various time intervals to address the various issues?
2. What were the key success factors for ABIL?
3. Suggest an alternative mechanism approach to manage the problems.

NOTES AND REFERENCES

1. Skinner, B.F. (1957). *Verbal Learning.* New York: Appleton-Century-Crofts.
2. Reynolds, G.S. (1968). *A Primer of Operant Conditioning*, p. 60. New York: Foresman & Co.
3. Bruner, J. (1966). *Toward a Theory of Instruction.* MA: Harward University Press.
4. Festinger, I. (1957). *A Theory of Cognitive Dissonance.* Standford, CA: Stanford University Press.
5. de Bono, Edward (1973) *Lateral Thinking: Creativity Step by Step.* New York: Haper & Row.
6. Knowles, M.S. (1984). *The Modern Practice of Adult Education: Andragogy Versus Pedagogy, Appendix D.* Englewood Cliffs: Prentice Hall.
7. Cross, K.P. (1981). *Adults as Learners.* San Francisco: Jossey-Bass.
8. Bandura, A. (1977). *Social Learning Theory.* New York: General Learning Press.
9. Vygotsky, L.S. (1978). *Mind and Society: The Development of Higher Mental Processes.* Cambridge, MA: Harvard University Press.
10. Revans, R. (1980). *Action Learning: New Techniques for Management.* London: Bond & Briggs Ltd.
11. Rogers, Carl (1951). *Client-centred Therapy.* Boston: Houghton Mifflin.
12. Argyris, C. (1977). 'Double loop learning in organisations', *Harvard Business Review* (5): 16.
13. Agyris, C. and D.A. Schon (1978). *Organizational Learning: A Theory of Action Perspective.* Reading, MA: Addison-Wesley.
14. Argyris, C. (1977). 'Double loop learning in organisations'.
15. Kolb, D.A. (1984). *Experiential Learning: Experience as the Source of Learning and Development.* New Jersey: Prentice-Hall.
16. Heider, F. (1958). *The Psychology of Interpersonal Relations.* New York: Wiley.
17. Weiner, B. (1972). *Theories of Motivation: From Mechanism to Cognition.* Chicago: Markham; Weiner, B. (ed.) (1974). *Attribution Theory and Achievement Motivation.* New York: General Learning Press.
18. Weiner, Bernard (1977). *Human Motivation.* New York: Holt, Raine Hart & Winston.
19. Seligman, M.E.P. (1992). *Learned Optimism.* New York: Pocket Books.
20. *Ibid.*
21. *Ibid.*, 102.
22. McClelland, D.C. and D.C. Winter (1969). *Motivating Economic Achievement.* New York: Free Press.
23. McClelland, David C. (1965). 'Achievement motivation can be developed', *Harvard Business Review.*
24. Messick, Samuel (ed.) (1976). *Individuality in Learning.* San Francisco: Jossey-Bass.

25. McCarthy, Bernice and Dennis McCarthy (2006). *Teaching Around the 4MAT@ Cycle: Designing Instruction for Diverse Learners with Diverse Learning Styles*, published February 2006, 120 pages format pb.
26. Kolb, D.A. (1976). *Learning Style Inventory: Technical Manual.* Boston: McBer.
27. Freire, P. (1977). *Cultural Action for Freedom.* London: Penguin.
28. Flanders, N.A. (1970). *Analyzing Teacher Behavior.* Reading, NJ: Addison-Wesley.

7
Motivational Process

LEARNING OBJECTIVES

After studying this chapter, you will be able to
1. Define motivation
2. Explain the need-based theories of motivation
3. Enumerate the cognitive theories of motivation
4. Critique Herzberg's two-factor theory
5. Elaborate on the expectancy theories of motivation
6. Describe the integrated theory of motivation

In a certain unit of a plant, a supervisor reviewing the section gave the following inputs to the manager: She complimented the worker Joseph by saying that his motivation was high, that he took a great deal of interest in his work, that whenever any difficulty arose, Joseph tried various ways of solving the problem before going to someone who could help, that he was always occupied, and that he seemed to enjoy his work. On the other hand, she said of another worker, Raju, that his motivation was low, that he seemed to be sluggish, that he complained more, that he went to the supervisor with his problems, that he neglected his work, and that he was seen socialising with other workers in the canteen.

When the same workers came to work in another unit, their new supervisor had different reports to make. According to her, Raju's motivation was quite different from Joseph's. Raju had a high affiliation motivation—he enjoyed making friends and working with friends. When he was put in a small group in which most of his friends were working, his output increased and he seemed to enjoy his work. On the other hand, Joseph worked best when he was given a challenging assignment. He did not, however, get along very well with others and was basically a loner.

What can you make out about motivation from these two examples? The first supervisor uses 'motivation' as a general term meaning an individual's involvement in his or her work. The second supervisor uses it in a specific sense, meaning a particular motivation. But by examining these two meanings carefully, it can be seen that the second concept of motivation is an explanation of the general term 'work motivation'. Motivation has been used with both meanings in management literature and this has created some confusion.

Motivation essentially relates to an individual. An individual has either high or low motivation, or has one or another kind of motivation. It also refers to such basic questions as why Joseph works harder than Raju and why Raju socialises more than

Joseph. The answer to the first question is partly contained in the second question. Perhaps Raju does not work as hard as Joseph because he has a higher psychological need (motivation) for socialisation. If his job can provide Raju the opportunity to satisfy his need for socialisation, maybe he would work harder (in fact, in the example cited, the second supervisor did report this about Raju). Joseph may work hard because he has a high need for competition and draws satisfaction from meeting challenges. However, in the final analysis of employee behaviour, the question raised is why some people have a higher motivation for work (i.e., they are more involved) than others.

Motivation theories help us to understand the dynamics of motivation. There are broadly two groups of motivation theory—need theories (explaining motivation from internal factors) and cognitive theories (explaining motivation by external factors, as understood or perceived by the person concerned).

NEED THEORIES OF MOTIVATION

Several theories give importance to the basic psychological needs in explaining a person's behaviour (including his/her involvement in goal-directed behaviour).

Maslow's Needs Hierarchy

One of the earliest and most popular models of motivation was proposed by Maslow.[1] He considered several needs to explain human behaviour and proposed that these needs have a hierarchy, i.e., some needs are 'lower-order' needs as compared to other 'higher-order' needs. He also proposed that unless the need at the lower level is satisfied, the higher-order need will not be operative, and that once the lower-order need is satisfied, it will no longer motivate the person. Maslow proposed five main hierarchical levels of needs, as shown in Exhibit 7.1. Physiological needs (hunger, thirst, etc. symbolised by the need for wages and salary in the modern world) are the lowest needs in the hierarchy. Safety needs come next. These would include security of all kinds. Love needs (the need to relate closely to others) are next in the order, followed by ego needs (the need for status and recognition). The highest-order needs are those of self-actualisation or achieving one's potential.

Exhibit 7.1   *Maslow's Model of Need Hierarchy*

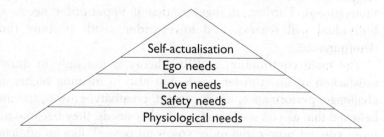

Self-actualisation
Ego needs
Love needs
Safety needs
Physiological needs

The relation of Maslow's five needs with different organizational aspects is shown in Exhibit 7.2.

Exhibit 7.2   *Need Hierarchy and Organizational Aspects*

Needs	Organizational aspects
Self-actualisation needs	Job challenge, performance, advancement, creativity, growth, training, self-image
Ego needs	Status, responsibilities, recognition
Love needs	Cohesive and supportive coworkers, teams, other work groups, supervisors, subordinates, customers, etc.
Safety needs	Work safety, job security, health insurance
Physiological needs	Work place conditions (air, water, temperature), base salary

Applied to work organizations, then, the lowest-order need would be that for a salary. Security needs would include seniority and security in the job. Love needs would include the need to belong to a friendly work group; the ego (or esteem) needs would be the needs for status and promotion. The highest is the need for self-actualisation, which is the need for achievement of things consonant with one's self-image. Maslow's theory has made a very valuable contribution in drawing attention to the lower-order needs, which may be neglected in some organizations. Yet if these needs are not satisfied, the higher-order needs may not be operative. The limitation of this theory, however, lies in that in no organization do the higher-order needs await the satisfaction of the lower-order needs. All the needs operate simultaneously.

Alderfer's ERG Theory

In a way Alderfer's ERG theory[2] is an extension of Maslow's theory. Alderfer suggested three categories of needs, rather than five: existence, relatedness, and growth. Existence needs are similar to Maslow's physiological and safety need categories. Relatedness needs involve interpersonal relationships and are comparable to aspects of Maslow's love and ego needs. Growth needs are those related to the attainment of one's potential and are associated with Maslow's self-actualisation needs.

However, Alderfer's theory differs from Maslow's in two respects. It does not suggest that lower-order needs must be satisfied before upper-order needs become motivational. Further, it suggests that if upper-order needs are not satisfied, an individual will regress, and lower-order needs become the major motivation determinants.

The main contribution of ERG theory is not only in drawing attention to the satisfaction of lower-order needs, but also in meeting higher-order needs, like job challenge, performance, advancement, creativity, growth, training, etc. Alderfer also believed that as you start satisfying higher needs, they become more intense (e.g., the more you get power, the more you want power), like an addiction.

Herzberg's Two-Factor Theory

Maslow's theory of motivation implicitly distinguishes between the need for self-actualisation as that evinced by development and growth of the individual and the other needs as making up for some deficiency. This distinction was dramatically sharpened by Herzberg,[3] whose theory of work motivation is most widely known, applied, and discussed. His theory is also called the two-factor theory of motivation, as he discusses two main classes of deficit and development needs.

Using the critical incident technique, Herzberg collected data about people's satisfaction or dissatisfaction with their jobs. The analysis of this data led him to propose two sets of needs: one set of needs caused dissatisfaction if they were not met; the other set provided positive satisfaction to people if they were met. Using his prior experience in the field of health, Herzberg proposed his two-factor theory. He classified the various needs he found into terms of what he called hygiene factors (factors which may prevent dissatisfaction) and motivators (factors which may provide satisfaction). These factors are given in Exhibit 7.3. According to Herzberg, preventing or reducing dissatisfaction in the work situation is not the same as providing positive satisfaction. These two are qualitatively different aspects of work motivation. According to him, motivation can be provided only if motivators are used in the work situation in addition to hygiene factors.

Exhibit 7.3   Herzberg's Two-Factor Model of Work Motivation

Hygiene factors	Motivators
Salary	Advancement
Working conditions	Development
Company policy	Responsibility
Supervision	Recognition
Work group	Achievement
	Work itself

However, there have been several criticisms of Herzberg's theory, mostly directed at his methodology and saying that his theory is method bound. Nevertheless, Herzberg's contribution to work motivation has been significant.

Based on their review of several Indian studies using Herzberg's methodology, Roy and Raja have tentatively concluded that the evidence regarding the two-factor theory of job satisfaction is equivocal. The Herzbergian thesis that job satisfaction and dissatisfaction represent two different continua finds support in most of the studies. On the other hand, motivators and hygiene factors have generally been found to influence both satisfaction and dissatisfaction in a mixed fashion. While intrinsic factors (e.g., job content, promotion, and growth) contribute to dissatisfaction, extrinsic factors (e.g., security, coworker relations, and friendliness of superior) contribute to satisfaction. Roy and Raja also concluded that criticisms of the Herzbergian model as being method bound and artefactual seemed to apply to the Indian context. It appears that the higher-order needs of even managers are thwarted in organizational practice. A study of a sample of Indian managers found them equally divided in terms of lower- and higher-order needs; the order of needs was related directly to the level of management and inversely to age.

Herzberg's theory of work motivation has, however, led to 'job enrichment' programmes, entailing redesigning of jobs. Job enrichment attempts to build as many motivators into the job as possible.

McClelland's Three Motives

It was Murray who originally suggested a long list of human motives or needs. Murray's work inspired a number of subsequent studies and resulted in different lists of significant motives. McClelland and his associates suggested three motives as being important—achievement, affiliation, and power. They also suggested elaborate methods of measuring them. Subsequently, they demonstrated the importance of the achievement motive to entrepreneurship and marketing, and of power motivation (among other things) to management. McClelland has attempted to develop a leadership motive pattern, in which the power motive plays an important role. Litwin and Stringer[4] used these three motives—achievement, affiliation, and power—in their study of organizational climate and found these useful for the study of organizational behaviour.

While McClelland's study of the achievement and affiliation motives showed these to be simple variables, he found the power motive to be a complex one. As he admitted during his study of the power motive, it included both an urge to control others as well as the desire to make an impact. He called these instances of personalised power and socialised power. Thus McClelland seems to suggest three different elements in the power motive: the need to control others (personalised power), the need to make an impact on others, and the need to use power for doing something for other persons and groups, like organizations (both these being socialised power).

It seems necessary to make clear distinctions among these three. Management literature gives considerable importance to the concept of 'control', i.e., keeping track of developments according to an agreed plan. This also seems to be one important need or motive. The so-called socialised dimension of power (as reflected in the use of power for the benefit of other persons and groups) seems to be a separate need or motive that is reflected in a concern for and desire to do something for others. This need is important for social development also and may be called the extension motive.

One more motive or need so far neglected, though relevant to organizational behaviour, is that of dependency. Thus far dependency was regarded as a negative force. However, Levinson pointed out the importance of dependency in the development of managers, and this need is reflected in the mentoring process to which considerable attention is being paid currently.

Thus we have six main needs or motives relevant for understanding the dynamics of people's behaviour in organizations. These are briefly defined below.

1. The achievement motive: This is characterised by a concern for excellence, a tendency to compete with standards of excellence set by others or by the self, the

setting of challenging goals for oneself, an awareness of the hurdles in the way of achieving one's goals, and persistence in trying out alternative paths to one's goal.

2. The affiliation motive: This is characterised by a concern for establishing and maintaining close personal relationships, considerable value for friendship, and a tendency to express one's emotions.

3. The influence motive: This is characterised by a concern for making an impact on others, a desire to make people do what one thinks is right, and an urge to change matters and 'develop' people.

4. The control motive: This is characterised by a concern for orderliness, a desire to stay informed, and an urge to monitor a situation and take corrective action if needed.

5. The extension motive: This is characterised by a concern for others, an interest in the superordinate goal, and a need to be relevant and useful to larger groups, including society as a whole.

6. The dependency motive: This is characterised by a concern for self-development with others' help, checking ideas or proposed actions with significant others (those more knowledgeable or having higher status, experts, close associates), a need for approval, and expectations of such an 'approval' relationship.

Expansion of Needs

Intrinsic vs extrinsic needs   A simple way to classify 'needs' is to put them in two categories: internal and external. These have also been called intrinsic and extrinsic. Intrinsic needs or motives are derived from the internal source within an individual or task (an individual's interests or the nature of the job). Extrinsic needs or motives are external, tangible, and satisfied by others (money or a regular salary).

Individuals differ in their patterns of needs. Some have higher intrinsic motivation, while others have stronger extrinsic needs. The distinction, however, is not a sharp one. Some extrinsic motives (e.g., a reward) may arouse an intrinsic need (in this case, say for recognition).

Rewards can also be classified as extrinsic and intrinsic. Extrinsic rewards (often called incentives) make a person select a particular activity or organization over others and put in extra effort and time. However, external rewards may not stimulate creativity and may, in the long run, reduce a person's 'intrinsic' motivation. On the other hand, intrinsic rewards (such as recognition and opportunities for growth) sustain and strengthen a person's intrinsic motives. However, things are not always so clear-cut. There seems to be clearer relation between negative extrinsic factors and intrinsic motivation, since punishment, threats, pressure, imposed goals, etc. reduce intrinsic motivation.

However, an individual's needs can be classified based on several different criteria. There are also several dimensions to needs. Motivation can be better managed if one has a deeper insight into the way needs operate. Considering the various dimensions can be helpful in this regard.

We have seen a jump in motivation and productivity levels among our women workers ever since we started the free crèche.

Expressed vs wanted dimension   Schutz[5] has postulated two dimensions for three interpersonal needs—inclusion (the need to socialise and interact with people), affection (the need to be close and relate personally to people), and control (the need to influence). He suggested that each of these interpersonal needs have both dimensions—the need for the person to take initiative (the 'expressed' dimension) and the need for others to take initiative (the 'wanted' dimension). For example, a high wanted need for inclusion will be shown in a person attending a party and waiting eagerly for others to come and talk to him or her. On the other hand, a person with a high expressed need for inclusion will take the initiative in meeting new people and talking to them. Based on this concept, Schutz has devised an instrument called FIRO-B to measure both dimensions of the three needs. Data from FIRO-B can be used for planning interpersonal effectiveness. Another system, called interpersonal need inventory (IPNI), measures the other-directed (what Schutz calls 'expressed') and self-directed (what Schutz calls 'wanted') dimensions of six interpersonal needs—inclusion, affiliation, extension, recognition, control, and influence.

Approach vs avoidance dimension   The approach–avoidance model was originally proposed by Atkinson.[6] This model has been used mostly with regard to achievement motivation (termed 'hope of success' or 'fear of failure'). But it can be used for other needs such as control, power, affiliation, extension, and dependency also. Any of these needs can be satisfied either by striving for the positive attainment of the goal (approach) or by reducing the possibilities of deprivation from goal attainment (avoidance). For example, say two persons A and B have equally high achievement motivation. A is high on the approach dimension (called 'hope of success') and B is high on the avoidance dimension (called 'fear of failure'). Their working behaviours would be different. While A may set more challenging goals and enjoy the (positive) stress, B may be scared of such challenges and may either set lower goals in order to avoid failure or may become so anxious as to eventually not succeed. Yet both have high achievement motivation.

A lot of research has been done on fear of failure, which (as an avoidance behaviour) has been found to be dysfunctional, although a part of the achievement motive. For example, Varga,[7] analysing data collected from Indonesia, Iran, Pakistan, and Poland, showed that 'hope of success' vs 'fear of failure' (approach vs avoidance) is the main intervening variable determining whether one benefits from achievement motivation training programmes in terms of increase in entrepreneurial activities. The approach–avoidance dimension may be significant in explaining the effects of deprivation (e.g., poverty) as well. In the case of power motivation, the approach dimension may be reflected in attempts to influence, whereas the avoidance dimension may be shown in compensatory behaviour such as collecting symbols of prestige and power (a big car, expensive furniture, etc.). In the case of extension motivation, the approach dimension may result in providing help and support to people for their development, whereas the avoidance dimension may be shown in acts of individual charity and generosity. Exhibit 7.4 briefly explains the approach and avoidance dimensions of each motive, based respectively on hope or fear of something. The behaviour of an employee can thus be analysed not only in terms of the various motives, but also on the basis of a positive aspect (approach) vs a negative aspect (avoidance), reflected as hope or fear. It is assumed that all the six motives have their legitimate place in organizations and contribute to the effectiveness of an employee.

Exhibit 7.4 *Approach and Avoidance Dimensions of Six Motives*

Motives	Approach (hope of)	Avoidance (fear of)
Achievement	Success	Failure
Affiliation	Inclusion	Exclusion
Extension	Relevance	Irrelevance
Influence	Impacting	Importance
Control	Order	Chaos
Dependency	Growth	Loneliness

An employee's effectiveness from the point of view of motivation can be defined in two ways. First, we may examine to what extent the individual has a particular motivation. Since all the six motives are relevant for an employee, if he or she is deficient in any one, overall effectiveness may suffer. Secondly, an employee's effectiveness will also depend on the extent of avoidance behaviour related to a particular motivation. Any motive, howsoever strong it may be, may be rendered ineffective by high avoidance behaviour. A high score on motive indicates potential for effectiveness, but a larger share of avoidance items in the total score may reduce one's actual effectiveness. The behavioural aspects of motivation (both approach and avoidance) can be measured with the help of a special instrument—MAO-B.

Personal vs interpersonal dimension Some needs may be fulfilled without any interpersonal context. For example, the need for achievement does not necessarily involve interpersonal interaction. Similarly, the need for creativity and curiosity may not involve interpersonal relations. But most needs are interpersonal in nature, like the needs for affiliation and power.

Individual vs social dimension Prayag Mehta[8] has proposed that achievement and power motives have both individual and social aspects. A person who has a high need for personal achievement may have great concern for his or her career and will adopt all possible means to achieve personal excellence. On the other hand, a person with a high need for social achievement would strive to work with others towards a common goal. Similarly, the personal power motive may be reflected in attempts to control others, whereas a need for social power may be found in attempts to overcome obstacles or in collective action. Mehta has reported a difference between the needs of workers and of managers in a public sector company, showing that the former are characterised more by the social dimension and the latter by the personal dimension. He has proposed a scoring system to measure these dimensions. McClelland has also made a distinction between 'personalised power' and 'socialised power'.

COGNITIVE THEORIES

Cognitive (also called process) theories of motivation focus on conscious human decision processes as an explanation of motivation. The cognitive theories are concerned with determining how individual behaviour is energised, directed, and maintained in the self-directed human cognitive processes. Cognitive theories of motivation are based on the early cognitive theories, which postulate that behaviour is the result of conscious decision-making processes.

Expectancy Theories

Expectancy means the subjective probability of an outcome. If a student feels that there are very good chances (high subjective probability) that by working hard he or she may get one of the top ranks in an examination, expectancy is said to be high. Expectancy explains the subjective probability of the effort resulting in the outcome (called the first-level outcome).

A related concept is that of instrumentality. If the first-level outcome is seen as leading to the second-level outcome, the instrumentality is said to be high. The second-level outcome is the ultimate of the two outcomes. For example, if a student preparing to enter the Indian Administrative Service feels that by working hard he or she can get good marks in the examination (first-level outcome), the expectancy is high. If the students feels that getting good marks (the first-level outcome) will help him or her in getting into the IAS (second-level outcome), the instrumentality is high.

Similarly, a manager may feel that strenuous effort on his or her part is likely to result in higher production (high expectancy) and that higher production will result in the manager getting a reward or a promotion (high instrumentality).

Work motivation is the result of a combination of high expectancy, high instrumentality, and high attraction to the second-level outcome. These may be viewed as having a multiplicative relationship to produce motivation, i.e., if any one of the three factors is zero, the resulting motivation is zero. On the other hand, an increase in each of the factors raises the level of work motivation dramatically. In other words, for high work motivation, the second-level outcome (salary, reward, or promotion) should be valued highly by the employees, there should be high instrumentality (belief that the second-level outcome will be the result of the first-level outcome, e.g., increase in production), and expectancy should be high (belief that increased effort will lead to increased production).

Vroom's theory   Vroom[9] was among the first to propose the expectancy theory of motivation and he used all the three concepts—expectancy, instrumentality, and valence (strength of the individual's preference for a particular outcome)—to explain motivation.

Vroom has used two main propositions in developing his theory of work motivation. These are (i) the valence of an outcome to a person is a monotonically increasing function of the algebraic sum of the products of the valence of all other outcomes and his conceptions of its instrumentality of the attainment of these other outcomes and (ii) the force on a person to perform an act is a monotonically increasing function of the algebraic sum of the products of the valences of all outcomes and the strength of the person's expectancy that the act will be followed by the attainment of these outcomes. In simple terms (i) a person's attraction to a particulor outcome increases with increasing expectation that all other desired outcomes can be attained by the relevant action and (ii) the motivation for a particular action increases with increasing attraction for various outcomes and increasing expectation that the action will lead to the attainment of these outcomes.

Vroom uses four main concepts in his theory of motivation: force, valence, expectancy, and instrumentality. The concept of force is basically equivalent to motivation. By valence, Vroom means the strength of the individual's preference for a particular outcome. The meaning of expectancy is more or less the same as used in other theories, i.e., the subjective probability of achieving an outcome. Instrumentality differs from expectancy in this model—expectancy relates efforts to first-level outcomes whereas instrumentality relates the first- and second-level outcomes to each other.

Hunt and Hill have explained this further thus: 'For example, assume that an individual desires promotion and feels that superior performance is a very strong factor in achieving that goal. His first-level outcomes are then superior, average, or poor performance. His second-level outcome is promotion. The first-level outcome of high performance thus acquires a positive valence by virtue of its expected relationship to the preferred second-level outcome of promotion.' Vroom also uses the multiplicative combination of expectancy and valence to explain motivation.

According to this relationship, the presence of a certain amount of both expectancy and valence is important for motivation; the value of zero in either one may result in zero motivation.

Smith and Cranny   Another theory using the expectancy hypothesis has been put forward by Smith and Cranny.[10] According to them, work motivation can be explained in terms of the interaction among three main variables—effort, satisfaction, and reward. The relationships among these variables are shown in Exhibit 7.5. As the exhibit shows, performance is influenced only by effort, but performance in turn influences both satisfaction and rewards. The significant part of this model is that all other relationships are two-way relationships.

Exhibit 7.5   *Work Motivation Model by Smith and Cranny*

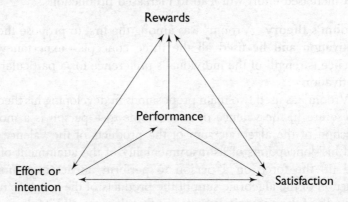

Patchen   Another model that has used the expectancy theory and is based mainly on achievement motivation is that of Patchen.[11] According to Patchen, two-level motivations are important to explain work motivation, achievement motivation at the first level and approval motivation at the second level. Patchen uses the general expectancy paradigm suggested by Atkinson. He regards work motivation as a function of achievement motivation, achievement incentive (amount of success possible in a situation), and expectancy (that effort will lead to achievement).

At the second level, Patchen uses different elements to explain the three elements in the first level. Achievement motivation has been explained in terms of expected intrinsic satisfaction, expected satisfaction in the approval that achievement will bring, and other expected satisfactions. This seems to be similar to Vroom's idea of instrumentality. If achievement motivation (first level) is seen as instrumental in getting the approval and other satisfactions such as promotion (second level), this achievement will result in job motivation. The achievement incentive has also been explained by four different elements—standards of excellence, feedback, responsibility, and difficulty of task. The difficulty of the task, the availability of resources, self-confidence, and previous experience of success build up the expectancy that effort will lead to achievement. Patchen further explains each of the second-level elements (of intrinsic satisfaction, approval motivation, and other satisfactions) in terms of other elements. His theory can be summarised as indicating that the motive to achieve is the basis for work motivation. The motive works according to the incentive value and expectancy in the situation. The motive to achieve also depends on the expected approval and other expected satisfactions a person can derive as a result of achieving a goal, and these in turn depend on certain on-the-job factors of the job and goals, and the approval motivation.

Porter and Lawler An important and comprehensive expectancy model of work motivation has been proposed by Porter and Lawler.[12] The model explains the relationship between job attitudes and job performance. The variables in the model are

1. The value of reward (attractiveness of a potential outcome of an individual's behaviour in the work situation)
2. Efforts (the energy expended to perform some task)
3. Abilities and traits of the individual
4. Role perceptions (the way in which the individual defines the job, the types of effort the individual believes are essential to effective job performance)
5. Performance (a person's accomplishments on tasks that comprise his or her job)
6. Rewards (desirable states of affairs that a person receives from either his or her own thinking or the action of others)
7. Perceived equitable rewards (the amount of rewards that a person feels is fair, given his or her performance on a task)
8. Satisfaction (the extent to which the rewards actually received meet or exceed the perceived equitable level of rewards)

Porter and Lawler have postulated relationships among these variables to explain work satisfaction and have proposed a feedback loop from work satisfaction to the value of the reward. They carried out research on the model and have made several recommendations (based on the implications of the model) for organizations.

According to Porter and Lawler, organizations should go beyond traditional 'satisfaction' and should measure the values of possible rewards and consequences, perceptions of the probability that positively valued rewards can be obtained by high levels of effort, and role participations. Besides obtaining data on job satisfaction, organizations 'should concentrate on determining how closely the levels of satisfaction are related to levels of performance'. They should also examine the operation of their reward practices and 'should consider adopting the practice of monitoring employee attitudes on a continuing basis'.

Lawler[13] has proposed another model where he has studied in detail the question of pay. According to this model, motivation (motivation to perform at a given level) is primarily determined by two variables: the subjective probability that effort will lead to performance, and a combination of beliefs about what the outcomes of accomplishing the intended level of performance will be and the valence of these outcomes. Subjective probability can vary from 1 (sure that effort will lead to intended performance) to 0 (sure that effort will not lead to intended performance), and valence can vary from 1 (very desirable) to −1 (very undesirable). Subjective probability is influenced by the subject's self-esteem and previous personal and observed experience. The model has been used to explain how pay motivates behaviour.

Cognitive Evaluation Theory

According to this theory there are two types of persons—intrinsically motivated and extrinsically motivated. Each individual evaluates a situation and responds to it according to his/her frame of reference. Intrinsically motivated individuals perform for their own achievement and satisfaction and are motivated by intrinsic motivators, like the intrinsic interest of the work, nature of job, responsibility, competence, actual performance, etc. If they perceive that they are doing some job because of the pay or the working conditions or some other extrinsic reason, they begin to lose motivation. Some others are motivated by extrinsic factors, like pay, promotion, feedback, working conditions—things that come from a person's environment, controlled by others.

According to this theory the presence of powerful extrinsic motivators can actually reduce a person's intrinsic motivation, particularly if the extrinsic motivators are perceived by the person to be controlled by people. In other words, a boss who is always dangling this reward or that stick will turn off the intrinsically motivated people.

Equity Theory

Adams' Equity Theory[14] posits that subtle and variable factors affect employees' assessment and perception of their relationship with their work and their employers. Motivation is the function of perceived equity—equity (or fair balance) of input (effort) with output (recognition), and equity of one's output with others' output of the same input. Individuals assess the equity or fairness of the outcome. Equity is individuals' beliefs that they are being treated fairly relative to their inputs and relative to the treatment of others.

Inputs typically include effort, loyalty, hard work, commitment, competence, adaptability, flexibility, tolerance, determination, enthusiasm, trust in superiors, supporting colleagues, personal sacrifice, etc. Outputs typically include financial rewards (salary, benefits, perks, etc.), recognition, reputation, responsibility, sense of achievement, praise, sense of advancement/growth, job security, etc. Managers should seek to find a fair balance between the inputs that an employee gives and the outputs received. They will feel satisfied and motivated when they perceive these to be in balance.

Reinforcement Theory

Reinforcement theory is based on Skinner's concept of shaping behaviour by controlling the consequences of the behaviour.[15] In reinforcement theory a combination of rewards and/or punishments is used to reinforce desired behaviour or extinguish unwanted behaviour.

According to the theory, individuals can choose from several responses to a given stimulus and will generally select the response that has been associated with positive outcomes in the past. Generally speaking, there are two types of reinforcements: positive and negative. Positive reinforcement results when the desired behaviour (say, performance) is followed by the valued consequence (say, reward). The specific behavioural consequence (reward, in this case) is called a reinforcer. The use of the positive reinforcer will generally result in repetition of the desired behaviour. Behaviour that results in rewarding consequences is likely to be repeated.

Negative reinforcement results when an undesirable behavioural consequence is withheld, with the effect of strengthening the probability of the behaviour being repeated. Negative reinforcement is often confused with punishment, but they are not the same. Punishment attempts to decrease the probability of specific behaviours; negative reinforcement attempts to increase desired behaviour.

Both positive and negative reinforcement have the effect of increasing the probability that a particular behaviour will be learned and repeated. An example of negative reinforcement might be a salesperson who exerts effort to increase sales in his or her sales territory (behaviour), which is followed by a decision not to reassign the salesperson to an undesirable sales route (negative reinforcer). The administration of the negative reinforcer should make it more likely that the salesperson will continue to exert the necessary effort in the future.

Applied aspect of Skinner's theory is called operant conditioning, which we have already discussed in Chapter 6. There are four types of operant conditioning: positive reinforcement, negative reinforcement, punishment, and extinction. Both positive and negative reinforcement strengthen behaviour, while both punishment and extinction weaken behaviour.

Positive reinforcement   Strengthening a behaviour. This is the process of getting a desired thing as a consequence of a behaviour. Examples: Getting a commission after making a sale; getting a bonus and a promotion after doing a good job.

Negative reinforcement   Strengthening a behaviour. This is the process of having a stressor taken away as a consequence of a behaviour. Example: Long-term sanctions are removed from countries when their human rights records improve.

Extinction   Weakening a behaviour. This is the process of not getting a desired thing following a behaviour. Example: If a person puts in extra effort, but does not get appreciation for it, he/she would stop doing it.

Punishment   Weakening a behaviour. This is the process of getting an undesirable thing punished as a consequence of a behaviour. Example: Being fined for coming late.

AN INTEGRATED THEORY

The model of work motivation proposed here combines and integrates the two main trends, the expectancy theories and the need-specific theories of motivation. It also takes into account the organizational context, which seems to be missing from many theories of work motivation. The conceptual model of this approach is summarised in Exhibit 7.6.

Exhibit 7.6   Three-level Work Motivation Model

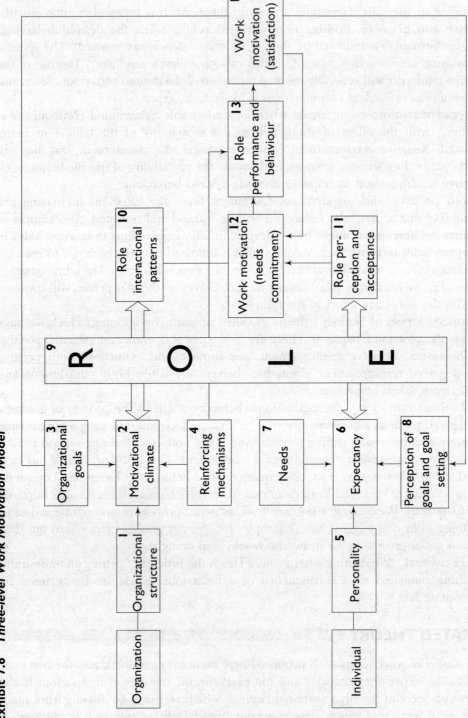

According to this model, work motivation can be conceived of at three levels. The first is the individual level, visualised in terms of the needs of the individual. Though the organization and the individual start independently of each other, the role of a person working in the organization helps in the psychological interaction between the organization and the individual and also in the integration of the individual in the organization. The second and third levels of work motivation follow the individual's interaction with the organizational environment. The three levels are as follows:

Level 1 The individual has various psychological needs (Box 7). The most important needs are those of achievement (concern for excellence), affiliation (concern for personal relationships), inclusion (concern for social interaction), power (concern for influence and control), dependency (concern for direction), and extension (concern for others).

Level 2 During the interaction of the individual with the organization through his or her role in the organization, work motivation develops in terms of changing strengths associated with his or her need patterns and commitment to working in the organization (Box 12). The original strengths of the various needs change as a result of the individual's interaction with the organization and acceptance of the organizational culture. A highly competitive organization may, for example, increase the individual's need for achievement.

Level 3 The final psychological outcome of the person's working in an organization is the satisfaction derived from both work and role. This is also an aspect of work motivation (Box 14). Work motivation at this level is defined in terms of the work itself and role satisfaction.

Since work motivation in the organization is primarily concerned with the second level (Box 12) and the third level (Box 14), it is essential to examine how these develop.

Second-level Work Motivation

Both the individual and the organizational variables contribute to the development of second-level work motivation (modified needs and commitment to work, Box 12). At the individual level, expectancy (Box 6) influences second-level work motivation. Expectancy is the subjective probability of getting rewards—approval, appreciation, promotion—through the individual's role enactment in the organization. Expectancy is influenced by three individual-level variables: the personality of the individual (Box 5), the individual's initial motivation (strengths of various needs, Box 7), and the individual's perception of the goals and goal-setting mechanisms of the organization (Box 8). For instance, if the individual's locus of control is external, expectancy is likely to be low. Similarly, a high dependency and low perception of organizational goals will produce low expectancy. Although expectancy influences both role perception and role acceptance (Box 11), it is likely to be influenced by them in its turn.

At the organizational level, the motivational climate (Box 2) influences work motivation. The motivational climate is the general culture of the organization as characterised by the dominant psychological needs. For example, an organization may have a 'power–dependency motivational climate'. In such an organization the employees' main concern may be to get to controlling positions by currying favour with the people in power and then to distribute similar largesse to others.

A combination of any two of the needs mentioned above can be used to characterise the motivational climate. The motivational climate is influenced by two factors: organizational goals (Box 3) and reinforcing mechanisms (Box 4). If the organizational goals are clear, challenging, and realistic, a climate of achievement and power motivation may develop in the organization. However, if the goals are unclear and there is no involvement of the employees in the setting of goals, a motivational climate of dependency may develop. Reinforcing mechanisms include the reward system. If politicking through election and lobbying is rewarded in a system, a power-dominated climate will prevail. Rewarding of academic excellence, however, may help develop an achievement-dominated climate.

Second-level work motivation (Box 12) is directly influenced by two factors: role interactional patterns (Box 10) and role perception and acceptance (Box 11). Each organization has a specific pattern of interaction of its various roles. For example, in one organization the pattern may be characterised by congeniality or reciprocity; in another the pattern may be more of the clique type—interactions may be high within informal groups, but may be rather low between the formal groups. The other factor, role perception and acceptance (Box 11), is also important. The degree of acceptance of a role by the individual contributes to commitment to work and reinforces certain psychological needs in the individual. This is second-level motivation.

Third-level Work Motivation

Third-level work motivation is the ultimate satisfaction an individual derives from his or her work (Box 14). This is influenced by the individual's role performance and behaviour (Box 13); the more effective the role performance is, the higher will be the work motivation (role satisfaction). Role performance is in turn influenced by second-level work motivation—the modified need pattern of the individual and his or her commitment to the work. It is also influenced by reinforcing mechanisms (Box 4).

In the model there are two feedback loops—a and b. Third-level work motivation influences both the organizational goals (loop a) as well as the perception of goals and individual goal-setting (loop b). Work satisfaction contributes to the setting up of challenging goals and a positive perception of such organizational goals. Work satisfaction also influences second-level work motivation. Similarly, role interactional patterns influence the motivational climate, role perception and acceptance, and expectancy.

To summarise, the model proposes three levels of work motivation, starting with the strength of patterns of need of an individual (level 1), leading to the modification in this pattern after he or she has worked in the organization for a time, and the level of the individual's commitment to work (level 2), resulting in work satisfaction (level

3). This development of work motivation is set in the organizational context, in which role plays a very significant part.

To illustrate how this process operates in an individual, let us take the example of Mohan, a young, energetic student. After acquiring a degree in engineering, Mohan joined a management training institute and successfully completed 2 years of education there. He then got a good job in an engineering firm. As a student, he used to love company, and derived great satisfaction from being with friends. He was proud to have some very close and sincere friends. At the institute, he put in the least effort required to pass the courses. Though he was quite intelligent, he was never excited about getting a good rank in class. Yet he was the spirit of the dorms: people liked him and he liked to be with people. The profile of his motivation when he joined the organization: high need for being with people, medium need for occupying an important position, and medium to low need for competition (first level of motivation).

After he joined the organization, he experienced considerable work pressure, which he did not like. The people in the company were basically congenial, but kept a distance from Mohan. Although there were some social get-togethers in the evenings, there was hardly any time to get to know people personally and close friendships between employees was not encouraged. This was rather frustrating for Mohan. In his job, he tried hard to complete his assignments. On several occasions, his boss complimented Mohan on his creative ideas and his good work. These compliments meant a lot to Mohan and he wished to come up to the boss's expectations. At the end of the first year, Mohan was given a raise, which (his boss told him) was given only to a very few employees, in recognition of their excellent work. Mohan now spent even more time on his work. When alone at home, his mind was full of problems he had to solve. After 3 years in the company, his motivational profile changed. He now had a high need for achieving excellence and competing for a reward, a medium to high need for assuming a significant position of influence, and a medium to low need for being with people (second level of motivation).

Did you know Mohan turned down the big offer from our rival firm? He believes he has found nirvana *at work right here.*

With success and a boss who recognised his work to encourage him, Mohan's involvement in his work became very high. He enjoyed his work in this organization and would not accept any other offers, even at a higher salary (third level of motivation).

In this model of work motivation, the individual's needs assume a great deal of importance. In fact, the terms motivation and need are interchangeable. We can say that a person has high power motivation or that he has a high need for power. All people have various psychological needs. Some of these psychological needs are more relevant to work, some less. Motivation and psychological needs have been examined by various researchers for understanding and managing motivation better.

SUMMARY

The term 'motivation' is used in two senses: general commitment to work and the specific psychological needs of an individual. The terms 'needs' and 'motives' are used interchangeably.

There are mainly two groups of theories of motivation: need theories and cognitive theories. Among need theories, the hierarchy of needs (Maslow), the two-factor theory (Herzberg), and McClelland's three needs (achievement, power, and affiliation needs) are well known. Other needs proposed are control, extension, and dependence. Several dimensions of needs have been proposed: intrinsic–extrinsic, personal–interpersonal, individual–social, expressed–wanted, approach–avoidance.

The main cognitive theories of motivation are expectancy theories (Vroom, Smith and Cranny, Patchen, Porter and Lawler), cognitive evaluation theory, equity theory, and reinforcement theory. Expectancy theories are more elaborate, explaining motivation (commitment) as being a result of the subjective probability of the outcome of effort. An integrated theory of motivation has been suggested in the chapter.

GLOSSARY

achievement motive concern for excellence, competition with standards of excellence set by others or self, setting of challenging goals for oneself, awareness of hurdles in the way of achieving one's goals, and persistence in trying out alternative paths to one's goal

affiliation motive concern for establishing and maintaining close personal relationships, value for friendship, a tendency to express emotions

approach striving for the positive attainment of the goal

avoidance reducing the possibility of deprivation of goal attainment

control motive concern for orderliness, a desire to be kept informed, and an urge to monitor and take corrective action when needed

dependency motive concern for self-development with others' help; checking ideas, proposed actions, etc. with significant others (those more knowledgeable or of higher status, experts, close associates) for their approval; expectations of such an 'approval' relationship

extension motive concern for others, interest in the superordinate goal, desire to be relevant and useful to larger groups, including the society as a whole

expectancy subjective probability of getting an outcome

extrinsic needs needs or motives that are external, tangible, and satisfied by others (e.g., money, salary)

hygiene factors factors that may prevent dissatisfaction

influence motive concern with making an impact on others, a desire to make people do what one thinks is right, and an urge to change matters and (develop) people

inclusion need need to be a part of a dyad or a group

instrumentality relating the first- and second-level outcomes to each other

intrinsic needs needs or motives that derive from an internal source in an individual or the task

job satisfaction satisfaction with the job or work a person undertakes in an organization

motivation the process that makes a person pursue a goal with intensity

motivators factors that may provide satisfaction

need hierarchy hierarchy of psychological needs

self-actualisation becoming what one is capable of becoming

personalised power the need to control others

socialised power the need to make an impact on others, and the need to use power for doing something for other persons and groups (such as organizations)

valence the strength of an individual's preference

EXERCISES

Concept Review Questions

1. What is motivation? In which two senses is the term used?
2. What is the main contribution of Maslow's theory of need hierarchy?
3. Explain Herzberg's two-factor theory of motivation and its significance.
4. What is the expectancy theory of motivation?
5. List the approach and avoidance dimensions of three major motives.

Critical Thinking Questions

1. What is the basic concept in the expectancy theories of motivation? Which expectancy theory do you see as most relevant in the Indian context and why?
2. There is a general complaint about the 'low motivation' of students in ordinary colleges and universities, contrasted with the 'high motivation' of students in well-known management institutes. Analyse the dynamics of student motivation, applying the integrated theory of motivation.

Classroom Projects

1. Interview one of your friends and find out his or her dominant needs (motives). Are these reflected in his or her behaviour in the classroom? Explore with your friend what he or she looks for in a job.
2. Respond to the enclosed instrument and score your responses as suggested.

What do you look for in a job?

Different people look for different things when deciding to take up a job. There is no right or wrong answer. Rank the 14 factors given below in terms of their priority to you. Put 1 against the item that is most important to you, 2 against the second most important item, and so on. Place 14 against the factor with lowest priority to you. Do not leave any item unanswered and use each number (from 1 to 14) only once.

1. Job security _____
2. Adequate salary _____
3. Fringe benefits (perks, etc.) _____
4. Opportunities for promotion _____

5. Comfortable working conditions   _____
6. Interesting work   _____
7. Sound company policies and practices   _____
8. Respect and recognition   _____
9. Responsibility and independence   _____
10. Doing something worthwhile   _____
11. Considerate and sympathetic supervisor   _____
12. Technically competent supervisor   _____
13. Restricted hours of work   _____
14. Pay according to ability and competence   _____

Scoring

Go back to your responses to the above instrument. Add the ranks given to items 4, 6, 8, 9, 10, 12, and 14. This is your score for intrinsic motivation. Add the ranks given to items 1, 2, 3, 5, 7, 11, and 13. This is your score for extrinsic motivation. The lower the score, the stronger is the need. Which is higher in your case, intrinsic or extrinsic motivation? Think of ways to raise the level of your intrinsic motivation.

Field Projects

1. Interview two students to find out why they study hard (what is their main motivation). Which theory is most relevant to explain their motives?
2. Interview two executives to learn what satisfies/thrills them in their jobs, and with what aspects they are dissatisfied. Critique Herzberg's theory in the light of their responses.

Achieving Innovative Excellence at IERT*

In the early fifties, a few years after independence, Pandit Jawahar Lal Nehru, the first prime minister of independent India, delivered an inspiring speech at Allahabad. In his speech, Pandit Nehru emphasised the need for technical personnel to build a strong and self-reliant India. The speech inspired the founding fathers of IERT, a group of eminent citizens of Allahabad, to do something in this direction and they decided to start a school of civil engineering under the aegis of Ishwar Saran Ashram. Some of the members of the first managing committee were Mr Shankar Saran, retired high court judge (chairman); Mr Kunwar Balbir Singh, retired chief engineer (member); Mr K.P. Modwel, retired chief engineer, railways (member); and Mr Vishwa Mitra, leading high court advocate (secretary).

With the blessings of this dedicated team, the institute started as a civil engineering school in 1955. Mr Ramesh Chandra, a retired chief engineer, became the first honorary principal of the school. Until 1962 the school did not get any grants and it also did not accept any donations. It ran on the fees received from the students. Therefore, to meet the costs during the initial years, the number of students used to be high.

In the year 1962 the school was renamed as Allahabad Polytechnic and it was approved as grants-in-aid polytechnic by the state government of Uttar Pradesh, India. At the same time its diplomas were recognised by the UP Board of Technical Education. This brought in some restrictions and the number of students reduced to 200 from the earlier 450. The committee recommended that the polytechnic should continue as a private grants-in-aid polytechnic. This was important because a number of other polytechnics that were also started during mid-fifties were either closed down or were taken over by the government.

The change in the status of the school also led to a change in the structure of the managing committee with eight nominees of the government. In 1963, the first principal retired and Mr R.N. Kapoor, who was a faculty member in the polytechnic, took over as the principal.

The polytechnic stared part-time diploma courses in 1966 and further expanded its activities, and the number of students on its rolls also started increasing. In the year 1985–86, it had 1,748 students on its rolls in various full-time courses and 950 in various part-time courses.

In the year 1981, because of its expansion and multifarious activities, the polytechnic

---

*Prepared by Rajen K. Gupta and Satish K. Kalra. Reproduced as abridged and slightly edited version with permission.

was renamed as the Institute of Engineering and Rural Technology and was given the status of an autonomous institution, with freedom to design and conduct their own programmes, as well as hold their own exams and award their own diplomas. The diplomas continue to be recognised by the UP Board of Technical Education as well as the Government of India.

It is one of the most sought after polytechnics in the country and it attracts around 18,000 applicants for 600 seats in various engineering diploma courses. Recently, it has also started a number of non-engineering diploma courses.

MAJOR ACHIEVEMENTS

Course Variety

It started in 1955 as a civil engineering school, but over the years it has developed technical diploma courses in 15 areas of specialisation. Besides these engineering courses, the institute has developed many non-engineering diploma courses in the areas of management, rural technology, and management of rural development. Some of these are diploma in commercial practice, physiotherapy, personnel management, postgraduate diploma in rural development and management, advance diploma course in rural technology development and management, etc.

Technical Hospital

In the year 1970 it was the first polytechnic in the country to set up a training-cum-production centre on the model of medical education in a teaching hospital. Its additional director refers to it as a 'technical hospital'. Within a short period it grew manifold and diversified its activities. This centre provides a real situation for practical learning of technicians and their teachers. It helps students in developing the attitude of self-employment. The centre has two divisions—manufacturing and commercial. The manufacturing division is the biggest one and has the following major subdivisions:

(i) The Apoly Designs Division comprises (a) wooden furniture unit, (b) steel furniture unit, and (c) knockdown furniture (export quality) unit. It manufactures all varieties of furniture for official, industrial, and domestic use.

(ii) The Apoly Plastic Processing Division manufactures a wide range of consumer and industrial plastic products.

(iii) The Apoly Sewing Machine Division assembles low-cost sewing machines for rural masses.

(iv) The Apoly Farm Equipment Divisions manufactures a number of farm equipments.

(v) The Apoly Fabricators Division undertakes installation of bio-gas plants and windmills all over the country.

(vi) The Apoly Cottage Industry Division manufactures various types of consumer goods like soap, chalks, candlesticks, etc.

(vii) The Rural Industrial Equipment Division manufactures equipments like power ghani, handmade paper, mill equipment, etc.

Besides these, IERT also has the Architectural Design—the Drafting Division and the Printing Press Division. It has a showroom in the heart of the city. According to one of the senior respondents of this study, the annual turnover of production from this centre is around 40–50 lakh rupees and it employees over 100 workers. It caters to the needs of the defence, the railways, the Indian telephone industry, etc., and it has even exported its material to the Netherlands.

Curriculum Development Centre (CDC)

It is the only polytechnic-level institute in the country to have a curriculum development centre. There are four other similar centres in Technical Teachers Training Institutes (TTTIs). This connotes a special recognition for IERT, as TTTIs have a higher status because they train teachers for polytechnics.

Some of the activities undertaken by the centre are (i) framing, reframing, and revising curriculum—not only for U.P., but for other states in the country and also for other countries like Bhutan, Iraq, etc.; (ii) developing many new courses in the management discipline and also some useful courses for village training centres; (iii) sending new useful proposals, schemes, and reports to the Directorate of Technical Education for the improvement of technical education; (iv) producing of text books; (v) organizing workshops, conferences, and short-term in-service training programmes; (vi) developing audio-visual aids; (vii) examining reforms on the basis of some studies. The centre suggested some reforms in conducting examinations to the Board of Technical Education, which implemented these reforms in the examinations conducted by it.

Centre for Development of Rural Technology (CDRT)

In the year 1981, the institute became the first polytechnic-level institute to have a government recognised and supported centre for the development of rural technology. Some of the major achievements of the centre are (i) development of various renewable energy devices for utilisation of solar energy, wind energy, biomass energy, etc., and development of some domestic appliances/technologies for village households and agricultural implements, such as smokeless cook stove, box solar cooker, improved hand-chakki, cattle-feed trough, thermo-siphon water heater, portable community solar cooker, winnowing fan, etc.; (ii) information dissemination through its various pamphlets and *Rural Technology Journal*; (iii) establishment of rural energy centres; (iv) human resources development (HRD), which is accorded high priority in CDRT's developmental efforts.

A large number of personnel and development workers from various technical institutions, voluntary organizations, and government bodies of India as well as from abroad have attended IERT programmes in the areas of appropriate technology and renewable sources of energy. Some of the important programmes conducted in the recent past are—appropriate technology orientation programme for a group of school teachers from Birmingham, UK (1979); National Seminar on Rural Technology on behalf of Ministry of Rural Development, Government of India (1981); Regional Training Programme on appropriate technology for south and central Asian countries, sponsored by UNESCO (1983); state-level workshop on transfer of technology to rural areas conducted at the request of states of Himachal Pradesh (1983) and Karnataka (1984) in their respective capitals; appropriate technology orientation programme for senior officers of Science Policy Centre, Government of Iran (1984); National Seminar on Decentralised Energy Planning for Rural Development, sponsored by the Council for Scientific and Industrial Research (CSIR) and the Department of Non-conventional Energy Sources, Government of India (1985); etc. Using this as a model, the Government of India has set up about a dozen more such centres in other polytechnics. These other centres were established with the active help of IERT. The institute has also been entrusted with responsibility of guiding and coordinating the activities of all CDRTs in the country.

Community Development Cell (CDC)

In 1976, the polytechnic established a community development cell (CDC) and promoted a voluntary organization named the Allahabad Rural Development Society to integrate its technological extension programme with the overall development of rural areas. Under the aegis of this cell, the institute operates and supports various growth centres, *mahila mandals* (women's club), *balwadis* (education-cum-play centres for children), training-cum-production centres, primary and junior high schools, adult education centres, rural marketing centres, medical centres, etc. in various villages in and around Allahabad. According to the institute, the objective of all these types of centres is to help the rural community to be self-reliant through the process of social awakening in rural societies.

National Wind Energy Research and Development Centre

In 1981, the National Wind Energy Research and Development Centre was started at the institute by the Department of Non-conventional Energy Sources, Government of India. In this case also, the work on windmill technology was being developed in the institute since 1978.

The centre is engaged in twofold activities. A demonstration programme of windmill pumps, developed in collaboration with tool foundation of the Netherlands, has been organized and over 300 windmill pumps have been installed all over India during 1981–82. All these windmill pumps have been produced in this centre. The centre also undertakes research and development work in this area.

In July 1987, the activities of the centre got recognition and the centre was declared as one of the regional wind energy testing stations of the country. So far the centre has designed over 700 windmills and aerogenerators on orders from the government and other agencies.

Moving in New Directions

Around 1985, the institute started a 1-year diploma course in hotel management. To run this course effectively it has entered into an agreement with a private party to provide its technical and managerial expertise to run a restaurant in a commercial area of Allahabad. The restaurant serves as an agency for providing practical training to the diploma students and also earns royalty for the institute. The interior design of the restaurant as well as the design and fabrication of its furniture is done by the institute.

The above achievements establish the innovativeness of the institute. Therefore, it would be worthwhile to see how the institution could achieve such an innovative culture.

CREATING THE CULTURE

IERT has been able to create an effective culture. It would be interesting to see how such a culture was created, what processes helped in building up such a culture, and what contextual factors, leadership aspects, etc. led to the development of such culture.

Institute's Saga

The organization has been able to successfully develop a sense of history. Everybody took pride in talking about the history of the institute and never got tired of elaborating event after event. It seems to us that this sense of history was itself a force contributing to the continuing impetus of the institute.

This pervading sense of history revealed some common linkages that most members of the institute found meaningful, symbolically as well as operationally. Symbolically, it reflected the mission and philosophy of developing Indian society through technology—and this being the mission and philosophy, the institute was able to unite its members around certain core values. For example, the institute has a norm that no class should be cancelled at any point of time and no student should be absent from any class without a genuine reason. Symbolically, this got reflected in the way everybody talked about it, and, operationally, it got reflected in their daily 'morning meetings'. We attended one of the morning meetings as observers. It resembled a typical daily production meeting of industrial organizations, which is held for taking stock of the situation and scheduling the day's activities.

While taking about the history and philosophy of the institute, the respondents also said that the institute's philosophy is not only to pass on bookish knowledge, but also to produce good practitioners. For this they even create opportunities for its staff as well as students. The first event, as retold by everybody, illustrates this philosophy. When the Public Works Department delayed the construction of its buildings in the early sixties, the institute threw a challenge to the government that as an engineering institution, it would do this task better. The government, after some hesitation, made an exception. The staff and students worked day and night to prove themselves. Not only the buildings, but even the furniture and the folders were made by them.

There are several examples of commitment to the philosophy and mission of the institute practically by everybody.

Leadership

The missionary leadership during the initial years of the institute helped in sustaining the culture of the institute. In the case of IERT, the missionary leadership was complemented by sacrificing leadership of Ramesh Chandra. His successor, R.N. Kapoor, provided dynamic leadership to the institute and encouraged his staff to innovate, assuring them of his support. The first event in this direction was the construction of the building in 1965 and this was the start of the story of success. His philosophy and practice seemed to be of institution building. He institutionalised this culture.

We found the leadership down the line to be simultaneously demanding, supportive, and enabling. Paradoxical as it may sound, everyone experiences freedom to work and innovate. While most other educational institutes feel constrained in terms of funds, the leadership at this institute considers it a challenge to provide whatever support is required to do any useful activity. The institute's leadership has been successful in taking away the unnecessary fears of committing mistakes, which inspires the staff to continuously improve and innovate in their activities. The only thing the leadership does not tolerate is acting against the values and interests of the institute.

Culture of Innovation

The achievements of the institute indicate that the institute has an innovative culture. The Training-cum-Production Centre, on the lines of a hospital attached to a medical college, is a good example. For curriculum development, each department first holds an internal workshop for curriculum development. Then a college-level workshop is organized, where outside experts are invited. This process itself encourages the generation of innovative ideas and climate. The other way to encourage innovation is that the faculty is encouraged to write. Further, IERT has tried to attract best people in the field by using innovative recruitment procedures. Structuring of the organization and its various system allows for the growth and development of innovative ideas. The institute has tried to knit its vision in its structures. One important point about innovative welfare measures is that the institute also provides a caring culture. The contributions of the institutes' own employees in some of the welfare measures during initial years of the institute speaks of the commitment of its employees to the institute, its philosophy, its mission, and its cause.

Questions for Discussion

1. What practices promoted motivation (commitment) for people working in IERT?
2. How was good performance rewarded to motivate people?
3. What main lessons do we learn from the workings of IERT?

REFERENCES

1. Maslow, A. (1954). *Motivation and Personality*. New York: Harper.
2. Alderfer, C. (1972). *Existence, Relatedness, and Growth*. New York: Free Press.

 3. Herzberg, F. (1966). *Work and the Nature of Work.* Cleveland: World Publishing.
 4. McClelland, D.C. (1965). 'Achievement motivation can be developed', *Harvard Business Review,* 43(6): 6–23.
 5. Schutz, W.C. (1958). *FIRO: A Three Dimensional Theory of Interpersonal Behavior.* New York: Holt, Raine Hart & Winston.
 6. Atkinson, J.W. and N.T. Feather (1974). *A Theory of Achievement Motivation.* New York: Krieger Publications.
 7. Varga, K. (1977). 'Who benefits from motivation achievement training?' *Vikalpa,* 2(3): 187–200.
 8. Mehta, Prayag (1994). *Social Achievement Needs, Values and Work Organization.* New Delhi: Concept.
 9. Vroom, V.H. (1964). *Work and Motivation.* New York: John Wiley.
10. Smith, P.C. and C.J. Cranny (1968). *Psychology of Men at Work. Annual Review of Psychology,* 19: 467–490.
11. Patchen, M. (1970). *Participation, Achievement and Involvement on the Job.* Englewood Cliffs, NJ: Prentice Hall.
12. Porter, L.W. and E.E. Lawler (1968). *Managerial Attitudes and Performance.* Homewood, IL: Dorsey Press.
13. Lawler, E.E. (1981). 'Substitutes for hierarchy', *Organisational Dynamics* (Summer).
14. Hunt, James G., Richard N. Osborn, and John R. Schermerhorn, Jr. (2000). *Organizational Behavior.* New York: John Wiley.
15. Skinner, B.F. (1957). *Verbal Learning.* New York: Appleton-Century-Crofts.

8
Perceptual Process

Different people often see the same phenomenon differently. For example, in the case of an industrial strike, a manager may perceive the immediate cause of the strike to be trivial while the workers may see it as very serious. Similarly, an incident on the shop floor may be interpreted by the supervisor as an indication of workers' carelessness, whereas the workers may see it as being caused by the supervisor's high-handed attitude. When people exchange their roles, they begin to see things differently. When a worker is promoted to the post of supervisor, his or her perception of the shop floor often changes. In order to understand the significance of this phenomenon and to understand why people see the same situation differently, one needs to look at the several processes involved in perception.

Perception is the source of one's knowledge of the world. One wants to know the world and the surrounding environment. Knowledge is power. Without knowledge one cannot act effectively. Perception is the main source of such knowledge. Perception can be defined as the process of receiving, selecting, organizing, interpreting, checking, and reacting to sensory stimuli or data. This definition contains several aspects or processes of perception. Each process is examined below.

PROCESS OF RECEIVING STIMULI

The first process of perception is the reception of stimuli or data from various sources. Most data is received through the five sense organs. One sees things, hears them, smells or tastes things, or touches them, and hence learns about the various aspects of things. For example, while taking a round of the shop floor, a supervisor may become aware of some trouble from smelling something strange and may then draw the attention of a worker to something burning due to a small electrical fire. Most of the time, workers perceive several things relevant to their jobs through touch. Similarly, our visual and auditory senses are used in seeing and listening to things continuously.

THE PROCESS OF SELECTING STIMULI ▨▨▨▨▨▨▨▨▨▨▨▨▨▨▨▨

After receiving the stimuli or data, only some are selected for our attention. It is not possible to pay attention to all the stimuli received. In order to prevent attention being unnecessarily diverted, stimuli are screened and selected for further processing. Two sets of factors govern the selection of stimuli: internal and external.

External Factors Influencing Selection

Several studies have been conducted on the factors which influence selection of stimuli. Most of these studies concern the visual perception of objects. However, these factors are equally applicable to the perception of people and situations. Some factors found important in the selection of stimuli are:

Intensity   Generally, stimuli which are higher in intensity are perceived more readily than those which are low in intensity. Advertisements make good use of this factor. For example, at night, brighter lights are more noticeable than dim lights. Therefore, advertisements which are displayed in brighter light attract more attention.

Similarly, during a strike, workers attract the attention of managers by shouting slogans. Such slogans, in contrast to silent demonstrations, help the agitators gain the attention of their target audience.

Size   Generally, larger objects attract more attention, because they are perceived faster. Many companies use this factor by packaging products to make them look larger. Similarly, larger advertisements are perceived more easily than smaller ones.

Contrast   Usually, things which differ from the familiar attract attention quickly. If one is familiar with a particular sound, a sudden change in it attracts attention. Similarly, a worker who is very different from other workers stands out. Many people, knowingly or unknowingly, do strange things to attract attention. Unusual behaviour attracts attention because of the principle of contrast. Training managers utilize this factor by organizing training programmes away from the workplace (usually in quieter places, in which contrast with the workplace may be maximized).

Movement   Things which are in motion attract more attention than those which are stationary. Most advertisements displayed at night use this principle by creating the illusion of movement through a clever arrangement of lights. Short advertisement films in cinema halls or on television also make use of this principle.

Repetition   Usually things which are repetitive attract attention. Some advertisers use this factor to their advantage: from time to time, the same advertisement is displayed even though the product may not be on the market at that moment. Such repetition keeps the product in the popular eye and people perceive it better than products which do not appear frequently in the media. Frequent repetition may, however, result in semantic satiation, so that the stimuli loses perceptive significance. Repetition catches attention only as long as it is used prudently.

Familiarity   Things which are familiar attract attention, particularly when they are not expected in a particular context. For example, in a foreign country where there are not many people of one's own nationality, one's attention is caught by a familiar face from his country. Similarly, in an organization, people notice those from the same background more, as well as pay more attention to them, than people from a different background.

Novelty   This factor may seem contradictory to the factor of familiarity. However, things which are new also attract attention. When one is inured to a familiar context, novelty attracts attention. For example, a worker notices a strange or new sound in a machine immediately, taking it as a clue that something may be wrong with it. Similarly, while driving a car, the driver may suddenly become aware of a strange sound from the engine, which is striking to someone familiar with the sounds normally expected from the various parts of the car.

Internal Factors Influencing Selection

In selecting various phenomena for attention, the internal factors are as important as the external. These factors relate to one's self.

Psychological need   An individual's psychological needs influence his perception. Sometimes even things which do not exist are 'seen' because of a psychological need. For example, a thirsty person may keep 'seeing' water: such mirages are common in the desert. When people are deprived of a particular need, they perceive the concerned objects more frequently. In one experiment, people who had been kept hungry for some time were shown some pictures and asked to write down what they saw. Most of them reported perceiving more food items. In an organization, a person who has a high need for establishing good relationships with others may quickly identify those who are friendly and may be attracted to such people. Similarly, a person who has a high need to control people may be attracted to those who respond to such a need by being docile and may therefore selectively notice such people.

Background   One's background also influences one's selection of objects. People from a particular background look for people from a similar background. For example, a person educated in a management training institute may attend more to a person who has been through a similar education.

Experience   Similar to background is the factor of experience. Experience prepares a person to look for people, objects, and phenomena similar to his or her earlier personal experiences. A person who has had a bad experience while working with a certain type of people may select these people for a particular kind of perception. For example, a person who has had a bad experience with people speaking a particular language may perceive people speaking that language unfavourably, even in different surroundings. The same holds true for pleasant experiences. For example, those who have had a long experience of working in marketing may be attracted to people with some salesmanship ability.

Personality   Personality also influences perception. An introvert may be attracted to people either similar to or quite dissimilar to him or her. Various factors in the personality influence selection in perception. General attitudes and beliefs also influence perception. People with a certain attitude towards female colleagues or those speaking a particular language are likely to perceive various minor things about members of these groups which may otherwise go unnoticed. Generally, things which conform to our individual beliefs and attitudes attract attention. This phenomenon will be discussed later.

Self-acceptance   Self-acceptance is an important characteristic which influences perception. Some studies have shown that those who have high self-acceptance perceive things more accurately than those with low self-acceptance. The implication of this finding is that the accuracy of perception can be increased by helping people accept themselves more.

PROCESS OF ORGANIZING STIMULI

After the data or stimuli have been received, these are organized in some form. In order to make sense of the data received, it is necessary to organize them. This follows the principle of economy. There are three main dimensions to the organization of stimuli.

Grouping

The various stimuli received are grouped together using several factors. Some of these are:

Similarity   Stimuli which are similar are put together. All workers, for example, are perceived in the same category by managers and, similarly, all managers are perceived as one category by workers. Again, all financial and accounting people are grouped into one category. Further, people who belong to a particular category are perceived in a similar way. Such groupings help in economizing perception: the advantage of grouping people into categories is that similar terms can be used for members of a category rather than perceiving each member independently.

Proximity   Objects which are close to each other are also grouped together. People or things which are in the same place would thus be grouped together. This is often reflected in people's reference to a person belonging to a particular organization or hailing from a certain place.

Closure   There is a tendency in all of us to complete incomplete things. When perceiving the three lines shown in Exhibit 8.1, the tendency is to perceive these not as three separate lines but as a triangle. The reason for such a perception is that the entire configuration is perceived as a whole and the gaps which may otherwise prevent one from seeing the 'entirety' of the configuration are closed in our perception of it. This tendency to create a complete configuration is common because things are perceived as wholes rather than as parts. This tendency is reflected in our perception of things that do not exist but are created in order to complete a particular phenomenon which otherwise seems incomplete. For example, when looking at a person one may find several characteristics which indicate that the person is lazy and irresponsible. However, one may assume several other things without checking whether the person behaves differently on those matters from the way an irresponsible or lazy person would behave. This tendency to see things in a complete form may even make a person perceive characteristics that do not exist or prevent the perception of several contradictory characteristics.

Exhibit 8.1   *Closure Phenomenon*

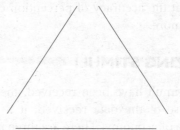

Figure–ground

Another principle of organization of stimuli is called figure–ground. It is one of the most interesting and basic processes in perception. In perceiving stimuli or phenomena, the tendency is to keep certain phenomena in focus and other stimuli or phenomena in the background. For example, during a lecture, the various stimuli received by people attending are grouped into two. Certain stimuli are not in the focus of people's attention: for example, the chirping of birds outside, certain noises made by people walking outside, a conversation going on outside the room, the noise of the fan, etc. All these become the background and not much attention is paid to them.

What remains in focus is what the lecturer is saying. The stimuli are thus organized into two groups, figure (what the speaker is saying) and ground (background stimuli, which are not in the focus of attention).

Thus perception may change if certain stimuli are changed from figure to ground. For example, a student who is listening to a particular lecture may suddenly hear a familiar voice and although the conversation outside the room may be faint, may listen to that conversation with enough attention to make it the figure at that time and what the lecturer is saying may become the ground for that moment. When a particular

Continue daydreaming and you will become an optical illusion in this company.

phenomenon or stimulus becomes the figure, it is in the focus of immediate attention; those stimuli which are the ground do not hold our immediate attention. No attention may be paid, for example, even to loud conversation next door when one is discussing something very important and is totally engrossed in one's own conversation. The ground hardly distracts if the figure is held in sharp focus.

Perceptual Constancy

There is a tendency to stabilise perceptions so that contextual changes do not affect them. Once an individual's height is perceived as a certain number of feet, it is continued to be so perceived even when he or she is standing at a distance and may therefore appear to be physically smaller. The perceptual world is thus ordered according to the principle of constancy. In our perception of the three-dimensional world, this factor of constancy plays an important role.

In the organizational context, perceptual constancy may help a manager perceive similar problems from the same perspective, even if the context changes. Constancy helps in accuracy of perception in this case. While several contextual factors may influence perceptions (sometimes producing illusions), perceptual constancy helps to put perceptions in a particular order and to recreate this order each time similar stimuli or data are received.

THE PROCESS OF INTERPRETING

After the data have been received and organized, the perceiver interprets the data in various ways. Perception is said to have taken place only after the data are interpreted. Indeed, perception is essentially giving meaning to the various data received and interpreted. Various factors contribute to this interpretation of data; and these are discussed below.

Perceptual Set

Previously held beliefs pertinent to the perception can influence individual perception. These general opinions or attitudes a person has, constitute the perceptual set.

For example, a manager may have developed a general belief that workers are lazy, shirk work, and want to get all the advantages from an organization without giving their best to it. In such a case, he or she already has a mental or perceptual set. His or her subsequent perceptions will be influenced by this set. When he or she meets a group of workers, this manager will tend to interpret their behaviour according to this mental set. Another manager—having different beliefs, attitudes, and opinions—may have a different interpretation of the same phenomenon.

In one study, when people were prepared to meet a 'warm' person, not only did they form a favourable opinion of the person but also behaved differently with her. The role of expectations (the so-called 'Pygmalion effect') can thus be explained by the concept of the perceptual set.

Some studies made in organizations indicate how the mental set operates: People having different individual opinions about various groups of people tend to form similar individual opinions when they meet new people based on these, without checking whether their opinions or attitudes were accurate in the first instance.

Stereotyping

When people form opinions about a particular class of objects or persons and act according to such opinions, it is called stereotyping. The word 'stereotype' has been used to indicate a generally favourable or unfavourable opinion a person holds for a particular group of people. For example, managers perceive a manager as being more honest than a worker, just as a worker perceives another worker as being more honest than a manager. Stereotyping is necessary for economy of perception. But stereotypes also lead to prejudices about various groups of people, which influence perception and interpretation of data.

The Halo Effect

The halo effect is similar to stereotyping. While in stereotyping the person forms an opinion or develops an attitude towards a group of people or objects, in the halo effect the person develops an opinion or attitude towards a single person or object. If someone has a favourable attitude towards a person, his or her subsequent perceptions of the same person are influenced by this attitude. For example, if a manager has a good impression about a particular subordinate (a positive halo effect), mistakes made by the latter may be condoned or the interpretation may give the latter the benefit of doubt. When similar mistakes are made by another person about whom the manager has an unfavourable opinion (negative halo effect), those mistakes may be perceptually exaggerated as irresponsible behaviour. Further, as a result of the halo effect, the manager may tend to interpret even feedback information received according to the preconceived impression. For example, irrespective of the available information, the manager may tend to overrate one person and underrate another. Our interpretation of data and partial data (about which very few cues are available), therefore, is influenced by already held impressions.

Perceptual Defense

Perceptual defense is used by the perceiver to deal with conflicting messages and data. If the data a person receives threaten beliefs already held, the recipient uses perceptual defense to deal with this phenomenon. For example, if a manager gets data from a union on strike, showing that it is taking positive steps in the direction of resolving conflicts or is doing something useful for the organization, the manager may find such data in conflict with a preconceived opinion that the union is by and large negative in its approach.

One way to deal with conflicting data is not to perceive or accept such data and to group them as unacceptable information. This may be done by adopting mechanisms to defend the positions already held. Such defense mechanisms could include

- Denial of the information or data received (e.g., the manager may deny the data and simply say that workers can never be loyal to the organization and therefore any information received about their good intention is incorrect).
- Some modification of the data received (e.g., a statement such as: 'While the workers may be showing pro-organization behaviour at this stage, by and large their intentions are negative and therefore cannot be trusted only on the basis of one incident.'
- Justification for holding on to one's own belief (such as saying, 'The workers may be showing pro-organizational behaviour, but this is a trick and this is one of the ways of deceiving the management, and therefore their behaviour cannot be taken seriously and they cannot be trusted.' Such mechanisms of dealing with data may help a person to avoid changing or modifying own values, attitudes, and beliefs in relation to a particular phenomenon. It may be useful for organizations to be aware of such instances of perceptual defense so as to recognize them when such defenses occur and find ways in which such defense can be counteracted and perception improved.

One defense mechanism worth mentioning is projection. Sometimes people tend to interpret information and data received from other people in the light of their own behaviour or inclination. When a person sees his or her own characteristics in others, it is called projection. For example, a person who is strong and authoritarian tends to interpret others' behaviour in the same way. Studies have shown that people who know themselves better have more accurate ways of perceiving and interpreting data received from others. Those who do not know themselves very well tend to use their own characteristics in interpreting data. Thus, a short-tempered man tends to see others as short-tempered. Projection is more frequent in cases of negative perception, although it also occurs with positive perceptions.

Contextual Factors

Several contextual dimensions influence the interpretation of stimuli or perceptual data. The following factors are worth considering:

Interpersonal context The relationship between the perceiver and others present in a given situation influences interpretation of the cues received. Studies have shown that when an interpersonal relationship is congenial, people perceive others as being similar to themselves. When the interpersonal relationship is not congenial, people tend to perceive others as being dissimilar. The implications are clear: if people can be helped to develop better interpersonal relationships in an organization, their perception of others as similar to themselves will increase, and, as a result, the grouping of their perceptions will be more conducive to the objectives of the organization.

Other person's background Familiar people and strangers have different influences on an individual's perceptions. For example, it has been shown in one study that facts and information given by strangers have higher credibility. People tended to perceive such information more favourably than when the same information was given by familiar people. When givers of information are unknown people or when information is unexpectedly received from those whose ability to provide information is uncertain, their credibility increases.

Organizational context   Several studies show that the climate of an organization or a department has great significance for the perception of various phenomena by people working in that organization or department. If the climate is congenial, the perceptions are likely to be more favourable. One study showed that in friendly and congenial climates, the perception of people's goal-related behaviour was much more accurate although the perception of purely personal behaviour was less accurate. In organizations with a liberal and congenial climate, people's perception of organizational goals is likely to be similar and more accurate, as a result of which the efforts to achieve these goals are likely to be more concerted.

The client found my proposal brash, careless, and impulsive. And I thought I was energetic, proactive, and competitive.

A special aspect of the organizational context is the reference group. The group to which a person belongs or wishes to belong influences his or her perception. Studies have shown that people categorise various perceptions according to their feelings about the group to which they belong. In one study, it was found that managers generally paid more attention to situations and phenomena pertaining to the group to which they belonged or thought they belonged rather than to factors and phenomena occurring in other groups or other parts of the organization. This is an interesting aspect of perception. In order to increase a manager's interest in the affairs of the entire organization, it may therefore be necessary to help him or her become a member of various groups. Thus if the manager is made a member of inter-departmental working groups, his or her interest in and attention to things happening in the other departments also increases. If the manager remains confined to his or her own department, his or her perception of the organization as a whole and of other departments is limited.

PROCESS OF CHECKING

After data have been received and interpreted, the perceiver takes steps to check whether his or her interpretations are right or wrong. The process of checking may be so fast that the person is not even aware of it. Such checking may be done occasionally in order to confirm whether the interpretations or perceptions are reinforced by new data. Alternatively, data or impressions may be checked by asking other people about their perceptions. This is by way of feedback about one's own perceptions. For example, a manager who has perceived a certain characteristic in a subordinate on a few occasions may check with other managers who worked with that subordinate previously to find out whether this perception is endorsed by them. The manager may also use another method of checking which is more useful but difficult to adopt: He or she may check certain things with the person in question directly. For example, if the manager finds an employee disturbed or annoyed, instead of waiting for the employee to take the initiative in conveying his or her feelings, the manager may check with the employee whether the latter feels disturbed, or offended, or annoyed. By encouraging such feedback from the source of the communication itself, the perceiver may slowly increase the accuracy of his or her perceptions.

PROCESS OF REACTING

The last phase of the perceptual process is that of acting upon what has been perceived. This is usually when people do something in reaction to their perceptions. For example, a person may act on the basis of the favourable or unfavourable perceptions he or she has formed. The cycle of perception is not complete unless it leads to some action. The action may be covert or overt. Covert action implies the formation of opinions or attitudes, and overt action is a definite action in response to the perception.

One phenomenon which has attracted attention with regard to covert action is 'impression formation'. Impression formation refers to the way a perceiver forms an impression about an object or a person on the basis of characteristics he or she perceives or data he or she receives from various sources. A manager has to form impressions most of the time, being required to make quick judgements. While interviewing people, for example, a manager has to form a quick opinion of the interviewees to take a decision. The more accurate a manager is in forming a realistic impression, the more effective he or she is likely to be.

One author has described four limitations in the formation of accurate impressions:

Surroundings An impression is likely to be affected by the type of situation or surroundings in which the impression is made, rather than by the person who makes the impression. For example, if someone is seen in an undesirable surrounding, the impression formed about that person is likely to be low. Similarly, if one sees another person in a posh environment frequented exclusively by people of high status, one's impression of that person is likely to be more favourable, being based on the latter's apparent affluence.

Generalisations Although impressions may be based on limited cues or data, sweeping generalizations may be made from the same. This usually happens when a person already has some stereotypes and mental sets.

Situational limitations A situation may not provide adequate opportunity for a person to show the behaviours critical to the formation of a certain impression. For example, in an interview, the interviewee may not be able to show how much commitment he or she is capable of having towards goals.

Preconceived notions An impression may be determined by the prejudices or individual reactions of the perceiver. The mental set, stereotypes, and halo effect, in particular, may influence a person's perception.

In order to increase the accuracy of impression formation, it may be useful to be aware of the various factors which influence interpretation of data. It may also be useful for a person to check from time to time the impressions he or she has formed and to reflect on the accuracy of these perceptions as well as question why the accuracy may be less than desired.

SUMMARY

Perception is the process of receiving, selecting, organizing, interpreting, checking, and reacting to sensory stimuli or data. Both external and internal factors influence perception. While intensity, size, contrast, movement, etc., influence selection of stimuli, closure and figure–ground help in grouping the various stimuli received. The perceptual set, stereotyping, and the halo effect show the application of these to social phenomena, while perceptual defense and impression formation are important in organizational life. However, perception is considered complete as a process only when it has been checked and a reaction is elicited as a result of the perception.

GLOSSARY

closure a tendency to complete incomplete things

figure certain phenomena kept in focus

ground background stimuli which are not in the focus of attention

halo effect forming a fixed opinion or attitude towards a single person or object

impression formation forming an impression about an object or a person on the basis of the characteristics one perceives or the data one receives from various sources

perception the process of receiving, selecting, organizing, interpreting, checking, and reacting to sensory stimuli or data

perceptual constancy stabilised perceptions not affected by contextual changes

perceptual defense   adopting defense mechanisms to deal with data in order to defend the positions already held

perceptual set   previously held beliefs influencing the perceiver's perception

stereotyping   forming opinions about a particular class of objects or persons and acting according to such opinions

EXERCISES

Concept Review Questions

1. What is perception? What are the main elements in the perceptual process?
2. What is closure in perception? Give an example.
3. What is the importance of figure–ground in perception?
4. How are impressions formed? Give one example from your experience in the classroom.

Classroom Projects

1. Interview two friends and explore with them their perception of a teacher. How do you explain these perceptions in light of what you have just read?
2. Analyse the controversy over globalization. How do you explain the two contrasting views voiced by the advocates and adversaries of globalization?

Field Projects

1. Interview two managers and two workers in a company to find out their views on downsizing. Explain the difference in views using the theory of perception.
2. Find out about stereotypical images of people from a particular background (for instance, students from rural areas). How are such stereotypes formed? Discuss how these can be broken for better social and interpersonal understanding.

McDonald's 'Beef Fries' Controversy*

CONTROVERSY ERUPTS

In May 2001, a class action lawsuit was filed against the world's largest fast-food chain McDonald's, in Seattle, US. The lawsuit alleged that the company had, for over a decade, duped vegetarian customers into eating French fries that contained beef extracts. The lawsuit followed a spate of media reports detailing how the French fries served at McDonald's were falsely promoted as being '100 per cent vegetarian.'

Although McDonald's initially declined to comment on the issue, the company issued a 'conditional apology', admitting to using beef flavouring in the fries. The furore over the matter seemed to be settling down, when to McDonald's horror, some of its restaurants in India were vandalised. Activists of Hindu fundamentalist groups—the Shiv Sena, the Vishwa Hindu Parishad (VHP), and the Bajrang Dal—staged a demonstration in front of the McDonald's head office in Delhi, protesting the alleged use of beef flavouring. They submitted a memorandum to the prime minister, demanding the closure of all McDonald's outlets in the country.

Activists also staged protests in front of McDonald's restaurants in south Mumbai and Thane. Mobs ransacked the outlet at Thane, broke the glass panes, and smeared the McDonald's mascot Ronald with cow dung. About 30 people were arrested and later let off on bail. Company officials estimated the loss to the outlet at 2 million rupees.

Officials at McDonald's India quickly announced that the vegetarian products served in India did not have any non-vegetarian content. However, despite this reassurance, the anti-McDonald's wave refused to die down.

Meanwhile, more cases were being filed against McDonald's—this time in California (US) and Canada. It seemed certain that the company would have to shell out millions of dollars to settle the class action lawsuit representing the 1 million US-based Hindus and 15 million other vegetarians.

BACKGROUND NOTE

McDonald's was started as a drive-in restaurant by two brothers, Richard and Maurice McDonald, in California, in the year 1937. The business, which was generating US $ 200,000 per annum in the 1940s, got a further boost with the emergence of a revolutionary new concept called 'self-service'. The brothers designed their kitchen for mass production with assembly line procedures.

---

*This case was written by A. Mukund, ICFAI Center for Management Research (ICMR). Reproduced with slight modification with the permission of ICFAI Center for Management Research (ICMR), Hyderabad.

Prices were kept low. Speed, service, and cleanliness became the critical success factors of the business. By mid-1950s, the restaurant's revenues reached US $350,000. As word of their success spread, franchisees started showing interest. However, the franchising system failed because the McDonald brothers observed very transparent business practices. As a consequence, they encouraged imitators who copied their business practices and emerged as competitors. The franchisees also did not maintain the same standards for cleanliness, customer service, and product uniformity.

At this point, Ray Kroc, an exclusive distributor for milkshake machines expressed interest in the McDonald brothers' business. Kroc finalised a deal with the McDonald brothers in 1954. He established a franchising company, the McDonald System Inc., and appointed franchisees. In 1961 he bought out the McDonald brothers' share for 2.7 million US dollars, and changed the name of the company to McDonald's Corporation. In 1965, McDonald's went public.

By the end of the 1960s, Kroc had established over 400 franchising outlets. McDonald's began leasing/buying potential store sites and then subleased them to franchisees initially at a 20 per cent markup and later at a 40 per cent markup. To execute this, Kroc set up the Franchise Realty Corporation. The real estate operations improved McDonald's profitability. By the end of the 1970s, McDonald's had over 5,000 restaurants with sales exceeding 3 billion US dollars.

However, in the early 1990s, McDonald's was facing problems due to changing customer preferences and increasing competition. Customers were becoming increasingly health conscious and they wanted to avoid red meat and fried food. They also preferred to eat at other fast food joints that offered discounts. During this time, McDonald's also faced increased competition from supermarkets, convenience stores, mom-and-dad delicacies, gas stations, and other outlets selling repeatable packaged food. McDonald's added only 195 restaurants during 1991–92.

In 1993, McDonald's finalised an arrangement for setting up restaurants inside Wal-Mart retail stores. The company also opened restaurants in gas stations owned by Amoco and Chevron. In 1996, McDonald's entered into a 10-year agreement worth 1 billion US dollars with Disney. McDonald's agreed to promote Disney through its restaurants and opened restaurants in Disney's theme parks. In 1998, McDonald's took a minority stake in Chipotle Mexican Grill—an 18-restaurant chain in the US. In October 1996, McDonald's opened its first restaurant in India.

By 1998, McDonald's was operating 25,000 restaurants in 116 countries, serving more than 15 billion customers annually. During the same year, the company recorded sales of 36 billion US dollars, and a net income of 1.5 billion US dollars. McDonald's overseas restaurants accounted for nearly 60 per cent of its total sales. Franchisees owned and operated 80 per cent of McDonald's restaurants across the globe. However, much to the company's chagrin, in 1998, a survey in the US revealed that customers rated McDonald's menu as one of the worst-tasting ever.

Undeterred by these developments, the company continued with its expansion plans and by 2001, it had 30,093 restaurants all over the world with sales of 24 billion US dollars. By mid-2001, the company had 28 outlets in India, spread across New Delhi, Bombay, Pune, Jaipur, and on the Delhi–Agra highway.

TROUBLED HISTORY

McDonald's has had a long history of lawsuits being filed against it. It had been frequently accused of resorting to unfair and unethical business practices—16 October is even observed as a 'World anti-McDonald's day'. In the late 1990s, the company had to settle over 700 incidents of scalding coffee burns. Reportedly, McDonald's kept the coffee at 185°F—approximately 20°F hotter than the standard temperature at other restaurants—which could cause third-degree burns in just 2–7 seconds. An 81-year-old woman suffered third-degree burns on her lower body that required skin grafts and hospitalisation for a week. After McDonald's dismissed her request for compensation for medical bills, she filed a lawsuit against the company.

A McDonald's quality assurance manager testified in the case that the company was aware of the risk of serving dangerously hot coffee, but it had no plans to lower the temperature or to post a warning on the coffee cups about the possibility of severe burns. In 1994, the court declared McDonald's guilty of serving 'unreasonably dangerous' hot coffee. The court awarded punitive damages of 2.7 million US dollars, which was later lowered to 480,000 US dollars.

The company also had to settle multi-million dollar lawsuits in many other cases, such as the one filed by a woman who was permanently scarred by an extremely hot pickle slice in a hamburger and a customer who found the crushed head of a rat inside his hamburger. There were a host of other allegations against the company (refer Exhibit I for some notable allegations).

Exhibit I *Allegations Against McDonald's*

Nutrition—McDonald's high-fat, low-fibre food can cause diseases such as cancer, heart problems, obesity, and diabetes, which are responsible for about 75 per cent of premature deaths in the West. McDonald's refuted the allegation saying that scientific evidence has never been conclusive and that its food can be a valuable part of a balanced diet. The company also argued that it had the right to sell junk food just like chocolate or ice-cream manufacturers did. However, critics claimed that the company should at least refrain from advertising the products as nutritious, sponsoring sports events, and opening outlets in hospitals.

Environment—McDonald's has been accused of destroying tropical forests to facilitate cattle ranching. Although the company claimed that the one million tons of packaging it used was recyclable, it still was accused of causing environmental pollution due to the litter generated.

Advertising—McDonald's annual ad spend of over 2 billion dollars was criticised for exerting a negative influence on children and exploiting them. Through its collectable toys, Ronald the clown, TV advertisements, and promotional schemes in schools, it has an extremely strong hold on children.

Employment—Though McDonald's has generated millions of jobs worldwide, it is accused of offering low wages and forcing local food outlets out of business. Charges of discrimination, curtailing workers' rights, understaffing, few breaks, illegal hours, poor safety conditions, crushing unionisation attempts, kitchens flooded with sewage, and selling contaminated food were also levelled against the company.

Animals—As the world's largest user of meat, McDonald's slaughters hundreds of thousands of cows, chickens, lambs, and other animals per year.

Expansion—By opening restaurants in developing countries, McDonald's is creating a globalized system in which wealth is drained out of local economies into the hands of a very few rich elite. This results in self-sufficient and sustainable farming being replaced by cash crops and agribusiness under control of multinationals.

Free speech—McDonald's uses its clout to influence the media, and legal powers to intimidate people into not speaking out against it. Many media organizations that voiced strong opinions on the above issues have been sued by the company.

Source: ICMR

Most of these allegations were made way back in the early 1980s in a movement spearheaded by two London Greenpeace activists—Helen Steel and Dave Morris. They started their protests by distributing leaflets containing allegations against the company. Soon, the issue snowballed into a bitter £1,000,000 (approx. 1,929,656 US dollars) courtroom battle against the activists.

The company was severely criticised for hiring detective agencies to break into the activist group. According to an analyst, 'The company had employed at least seven undercover agents to spy on Greenpeace. During some London Greenpeace meetings, about half the people in attendance were corporate spies. One spy broke into the London Greenpeace office, took photographs, and stole documents. Another had a 6-month affair with a member of London Greenpeace while informing on his activities.'

Steel and Morris were later found, by a British court, to have libelled McDonald's. However, the company was also found guilty of endangering the health of its customers and paying workers unreasonably low wages. The case, chronicled completely at www.mcspotlight.org, has become a classic example of a corporate giant's struggle to uphold its image amid allegations of unethical practices.

In the light of the company's chequered history of legal problems, the French fries controversy seemed 'run-of-the-mill'. However, when McDonald's issued a conditional apology, the matter acquired serious undertones. This was because it was one of the very few instances where the company seemed to have publicly acknowledged any kind of wrong-doing.

THE BEEF FRIES CONTROVERSY

With an overwhelming majority of the people in the West being non-vegetarian, products often contain hidden animal-based ingredients. Incidents of vegetarians finding non-vegetarian food items in their food abound throughout the world. Whether a person has chosen to be a vegetarian for religious, health, ethical, or philosophical reasons, it is not easy to get vegetarian food in public restaurants. Well-established restaurants tend to do away with vegetarian food from their menu, leaving the vegetarians with the choice to either try to eat what is offered or to avoid.

The French fries controversy began in 2000, when a Hindu Jain software engineer Hitesh Shah, based in the US, happened to read a news article, which mentioned that the French fries at McDonald's contained beef. Shah sent an e-mail to McDonald's customer service department, asking whether the French fries contained beef or not and if they did, why this was not mentioned in the ingredient list. Shah soon got a reply from Megan Magee, the company's Home Office Customer Satisfaction Department.

The reply stated: 'Thank you for taking time to contact McDonald's with your questions regarding the ingredients in our French fries. For flavor enhancement, McDonald's French fry suppliers use a miniscule amount of beef flavoring as an ingredient in the raw product. The reason beef is not listed as an ingredient is because McDonald's voluntarily (restaurants are not required to list ingredients) follow the 'Code of Federal Regulations' (required for packaged goods) for labeling its products. As such, like food labels you would read on packaged goods, the ingredients in 'natural flavors' are not broken down. Again, we are sorry if this has caused any confusion.'

A popular Indian–American newspaper *West India* carried Shah's story. The news created widespread outrage among Hindus and vegetarians in the US. In May 2001, Harish Bharti, a US-based Indian attorney filed the class action lawsuit against McDonald's.

McDonald's immediately released a statement saying it never claimed the fries sold in the US were vegetarian. A spokesperson said that though the fries were cooked in pure vegetable oil, the company never explicitly stated that the fries were appropriate for vegetarians and that the customers were always told that the flavour came partly from beef. He added that it was upto the customer to ask about the flavour and its source. This enraged the vegetarian customers further. Bharti said, 'Not only did they deceive millions of people who may not want to have any beef extraction in their food for religious, ethical, and health reasons, now McDonald's is suggesting that these people are at fault, that they are stupid. This adds insult to injury.'

Interestingly enough, McDonald's statement that it never claimed its French fries were vegetarian was proved completely wrong after Bharti found a 1993 letter sent by the company's corporate headquarters to a consumer in response to an inquiry about vegetarian menu items. The letter clearly bundled the fries along with garden salads, whole grain cereals, and English muffins as a completely vegetarian item.

The letter stated: 'At McDonald's, we are always reviewing our menu, developing new products and looking for ways to satisfy the diverse tastes of our customers. We feel it is important to offer a variety of menu items that can be enjoyed and fit into any well-balanced diet. With that in mind, we presently serve several items that vegetarians can enjoy at McDonald's—garden salads, French fries and hash browns (cooked in 100 per cent vegetable oil), hotcakes, scrambled eggs, whole grain cereals and English muffins to name a few.' Further, it was reported that many McDonald's employees repeatedly told customers that there was absolutely no meat product in the fries.

The whole controversy rested on a decision McDonald's had taken in 1990 regarding the way French fries were prepared. Prior to 1990, the company made the fries using tallow. However, to address the increasing customer concern about cholesterol control, McDonald's declared that it would use only pure vegetable oil to make the fries in the future. However, after the decision to change from tallow to pure vegetable oil, the company realised that it could have difficulty in retaining customers who were accustomed to beef flavoured fries.

According to Eric Scholsser, author of the best-selling book *Fast Food Nation: The Dark Side of the All-American Meal*, 'For decades, McDonald's cooked its French fries in a mixture of about 7 per cent cottonseed oil and 93 per cent beef tallow. The mix gave the fries their unique flavour.' This unique flavour was lost when tallow was replaced by vegetable oil. To address this issue, McDonald's decided to add the 'natural flavour', i.e., the beef extract, which was added to the water while the potatoes were being partially cooked.

The 'beef fries' controversy attained greater dimensions in India, as 85 per cent of the country's population was vegetarian. Non-vegetarians also usually did not consume beef because Hindus consider cows to be holy and sacred. Eating beef is thus a sacrilege. A US-based Hindu plaintiff in one of the lawsuits said, 'I feel sick in the morning every day, like I want to vomit. Now it is always there in my mind that I have done this sin.'

Experts commented that the issue was not of adding beef extract to a supposedly vegetarian food item—it was more to do with the moral and ethical responsibility of a company to be honest about the products and services it offered. According to James Pizzirusso, founder of the Vegetarian Legal Action Network at George Washington University, 'Corporates need to pay attention to consumers who avoid certain food products for religious or health reasons, or because they have allergies. They say they are complying with the law in terms of disclosing their ingredients, but they should go beyond the law.'

While it was true that McDonald's complied with the Federal Food and Drug Administration (FDA) guidelines by classifying beef extract as 'natural flavour', critics claimed that the company was trying to 'play with words' to brush off the allegations. This prompted analysts to remark that a large part of the blame was with the weak guidelines stipulated by the FDA. The guidelines did not require the companies or the restaurants buying these flavours to disclose the ingredients in their additives as long as they were generally regarded as safe. Analysts added that as long as the FDA did not make the guidelines more specific, companies could legally get away with serving dishes containing animal-based products.

Meanwhile in June 2001, another class action lawsuit was filed in the District Court in Travis County, Austin, Texas, on behalf of all Hindus in Texas, alleging that Hindu moral and religious principles had been violated by their unintentional consumption of French fries that were flavoured with beef. As public outrage intensified, McDonald's released its conditional apology on its website, admitting that the recipe for the fries used 'a miniscule trace of beef flavoring, not tallow'.

McDonald's said that it issued an apology only to provide more details about its products to customers. A company spokesperson said, 'Customers responded to the news about the lawsuit. In the end, we are responding to those customers. We took a fresh look at how we could help customers get more information about natural flavours.'

Unsatisfied by the apology, Bharti said, 'Apology is good for the soul if it comes from the heart. It is not an unconditional apology. Why do they go around using words like "if there was any confusion" in their apology?' Further, news reports quoting company sources said that the apology did not mean McDonald's was admitting to claims that it misled million of customers by adding beef extract to its fries. Bharti said that the legal battle would continue and that McDonald's would have to issue an unconditional apology and pay a substantial amount of money. By this time, two more lawsuits were filed in Illinois and New Jersey, taking the total number cases of five.

THE AFTERMATH

The courtroom battle had entered the eleventh month when McDonald's announced that it would issue a new apology and pay 10 million US dollars to vegetarians and religious groups in a proposed settlement of all the lawsuits in March 2002. Around 60 per cent of this payment went to vegetarian organizations and the rest to various groups devoted to Hindus and Sikhs, children's nutrition and assistance, and kosher dietary practices.

The company also decided to pay 4,000 US dollars each to the 12 plaintiffs in the five lawsuits and post a new and more detailed apology on the company website and in various other publications. McDonald's also decided to convene an advisory board to advise on vegetarian matters.

In April 2002, McDonald's planned to insert advertisements in newspapers apologising for its mistakes: 'We acknowledge that, upon our switch to vegetable oil in the early 1990s for the purpose of reducing cholesterol, mistakes were made in communicating to the public and customers about the ingredients in our French fries and hash browns. Those mistakes included instances in which French fries and hash browns sold at US restaurants were improperly identified as vegetarian. We regret we did not provide these customers with complete information, and we sincerely apologize for any hardship that these miscommunications have caused among Hindus, vegetarians and others.'

Unhappy with the monetary compensation the company was offering, Bharti said, 'Wish I could do better in terms of money. But our focus was to change the fast food industry, and this is a big victory for consumers in this country because we have brought this giant to this.'

Though 10 million US dollars was definitely a pittance for the 24-billion-dollar McDonald's, what remained to be seen was whether the case would set a precedent and make corporates throughout the world more aware and responsible towards their customers or not.

What Happened in India

In May 2001, managing directors of McDonald's India—Vikram Bakshi of Delhi's Connaught Plaza Restaurants and Amit Jatia of Mumbai's Hardcastle Restaurants— said at a press conference, 'We are open to any kind of investigation by the authorities, from the state or central governments. We categorically state that the French fries and other vegetarian products that we serve in India do not contain any beef or animal extracts and flavouring of whatsoever kind.'

Bakshi said that the company had developed a special menu for Indian customers, taking into consideration Indian culture and religious sentiments. McDonald's officials circulated official statements by McCain Foods India Pvt. Ltd and Lamb Weston, suppliers of French fries to McDonald's India, stating that the fries were par-fried in pure vegetable oil, without any beef tallow or any fat ingredient of animal origin.

People were, however, sceptical of the company's assurance because it had made similar false promises in the US as well. Their fears came true when it was revealed that Lamb Weston's supplies had been rejected after they failed to meet standards set by McDonald's. McCain Foods was still in the process of growing the appropriate potatoes and needed another 2 years to begin supply. The French fries were being sourced from the US.

However, tests conducted on the French fries and the cooking medium by Brihanmumbai Municipal Corporation (BMC) and the Food and Drug Administration (FDA) confirmed the fries contained no animal fat.

Exhibit II *McDonald's Social Responsibility Statement*

The McDonald's brand lives and grows where it counts the most—in the hearts of customers worldwide. We, in turn, hold our customers close to our heart, striving to do the right thing and giving back to the communities where we do business. At McDonald's, social responsibility is a part of our heritage and we are committed to building on it worldwide; some of our efforts to do so are described here.

Ronald McDonald House Charities—McDonald's supports one of the world's premier philanthropic organizations, Ronald McDonald House Charities (RMHC). RMHC provides comfort and care to children and their families by awarding grants to organizations through chapters in 31 countries and supporting more than 200 Ronald McDonald Houses in 19 countries.

Environmental Leadership—We take action around the world to develop innovative solutions to local environmental challenges. Ten years ago, we began a groundbreaking alliance with the Environmental Defense Fund (EDF) to reduce, reuse and recycle. Since then we eliminated 150,000 tons of packaging, purchased more than $3 billion of recycled products and recycled more than one million tons of corrugated cardboard in the US. We continue to set new waste reduction goals and are focusing on reducing energy usage in our restaurants. In Switzerland, we annually avoid 420,000 kilometers of trucking and, in turn, the use of 132,000 liters of diesel fuel by shipping restaurant supplies via rail. In Latin America, we have partnered with Conservation International to create and implement a sustainable agriculture program to protect the rainforests in Costa Rica and Panama. In Australia, we have committed to meet that country's Greenhouse Challenge to reduce greenhouse emissions.

Diversity—We believe a global team of talented, diverse employees, franchisees and suppliers is key to the company's ongoing success. We work to create and maintain an inclusive environment and expand the range of opportunities, thereby enabling all our people to reach their highest potential and generate the most value for McDonald's and the best experience for customers. McDonald's also provides opportunities for women and minorities to become franchisees and suppliers and offers a wide range of support to help them build their businesses. These efforts have paid off: Today, more than 30 per cent of McDonald's franchisees are women and minorities, and in 1999, we purchased about $3 billion worth of goods and services from women and minority suppliers.

Employment—Being a good corporate citizen begins with the way we treat our people. We are focused on developing people at every level, starting in our restaurants. We invest in training and development programs that encourage personal growth and higher levels of performance. These efforts help us attract and retain quality people and motivate superior performance.

Education—As one of the largest employers of youth, education is a key priority. So the company, our franchisees and RMHC proudly provide about $5 million in educational assistance through a variety of scholarship programs. We also honor teachers' dedication and commitment to education with the McDonald's Education Award.

Safety/quality—We are committed to ensuring safety and quality in every country where we do business. Accordingly, we set strict quality specifications for our products and work with suppliers worldwide to see that they are met. This includes ongoing testing in labs and on-site inspection of supplier facilities. Restaurant managers worldwide are extensively trained in safe handling and preparation of our food. Also, we continually review, modify and upgrade the equipment at Play Places and Play Lands to provide a safe play environment. Our quality control efforts also encompass animal welfare. Notably, we are working with a leading animal welfare expert in the US to implement an auditing process with our meat suppliers to ensure the safe and humane treatment of animals.

Questions for Discussion

1. Analyse the various allegations levelled against McDonald's before the French fries controversy. What perceptual processes contributed to so much hostility and criticism despite McDonald's being the number one fast-food chain in the world?

2. Discuss the French fries controversy and critically comment on the company's stand that it had never claimed the fries were vegetarian. Do you think the company handled the controversy effectively from the point of management of rumour?

3. Discuss the steps taken by McDonald's to play down the French fries controversy and critically comment whether the company will be able to come out of this unscathed.

9
Attributional Process: Internality and Optimism

LEARNING OBJECTIVES

After studying this chapter, you will be able to
1. Explain the significance of internality for personal effectiveness
2. Discuss various ways of developing internality
3. Define optimism and pessimism in attributional terms
4. Describe how rumination affects individuals and how flow can be achieved

How is the individual related to his or her environment, especially the social environment? Does the individual shape the environment or is it the other way round? Who or what determines individual or collective destinies? By and large, people have two contrasting attitudes to this question. Some believe that one cannot predict, much less 'cause', most of what happens, as it is all predetermined or destined; others believe that one can both predict and largely 'cause' events significant to oneself.

The questions relating to prediction and causation of social and personal matters have intrigued philosophers, politicians, and psychologists alike. People have used various terms for the causality of social and personal matters. The most popular term, 'locus of control', was suggested by Rotter in the early 1960s.[1] A large body of research has been done on the locus of control. The concept of locus of control refers to the perception of contingencies between action and outcomes—to what extent an action produces an outcome. Those who have a high perception of such contingencies (i.e., believe their actions produce the outcomes) are said to be 'internals' (have an internal locus of control) and those who have low perceptions of contingencies (who believe that the outcomes are not produced by their actions) are said to be 'externals' (have an external locus of control).

A relevant concept in this context is that of the causal attribution, as defined by Weiner.[2] He added another dimension to the locus of control, that of stability–variability. According to him, both internal and external causes can be either stable or variable, thus giving four categories of factors to which outcomes can be attributed. This is shown in Exhibit 9.1.

Exhibit 9.1 *Perceived Determinants of Outcomes*

Internality–Externality

	Internal	External
Stable	Ability	Task difficulty
Variable	Effort	Luck

(row dimension labelled: Stability–Variability)

Internal causes are either stable, so that they do not change easily (e.g., ability), or variable, so that they can vary or change (e.g., effort). Similarly, external causes are either stable (e.g., difficulty of a task) or variable (e.g., luck or chance).

Weiner has further proposed that the interaction between the locus of control and stability has a significance for the attribution of positive outcomes (success) and negative outcomes (failure). Based on several investigations, Weiner has proposed that persistence in an activity will result if

(a) Success is attributed to an internal variable factor, say, effort, because if people perceive that their effort (which they can vary) has resulted in the desired outcome, they will find more pleasure in increasing their efforts in that activity

(b) Failure is attributed to variable factors (both internal, i.e., effort, and external, i.e., luck or chance). If people perceive that their failure is due to factors that can change, such as luck, or factors that can be changed, like effort, they retain the hope of getting results by putting in more effort. However, if people attribute their failure to stable factors such as ability or difficulty of the task, they are likely to give up their efforts, because on the one hand, their abilities cannot change easily and on the other, the level of difficulty remains a constant hindrance. Therefore, there seems to be no sense in persisting in the activity.

Weiner's concept has wider implications. However, research on these aspects of causal attributions has just begun, and more significant results are likely to be reported in the near future.

INTERNALITY–EXTERNALITY

Internality is a general orientation based on the belief that a person causes most phenomena experienced himself or herself, or at least can influence them. The nature of such a belief can range from paranoid delusions or manias (exaggerated belief in one's capability to cause or influence all phenomena) to self-determination. In order to gain a comprehensive understanding of internality, it may be useful to look at various dimensions.

A person perceives a contingency either as an individual or as a member of a group. Both perceptions belong to internality. These aspects—personal and group—are combined with the stability–variability dimension suggested by Weiner. One may thus have four dimensions of internality: personal–stable, personal–variable, group–stable, and group–variable.

Similarly, externality can be seen in two dimensions—human and non-human. An outcome may be attributed either to human factors (the social system or 'other people') or to non-human factors (fate or luck). Combining these with the stability–variability dimension, one has four externality dimensions: human–stable, human–variable, non-human–stable, and non-human–variable. Exhibit 9.2 gives these dimensions. It also shows the four internality-oriented and four externality-oriented determinants of outcome. It further suggests what the resultant mode of behaviour is likely to be for each factor. These are only speculations at this stage and need to be verified by research. The implications of the various determinants and the time perspective of the locus of control have been discussed in detail elsewhere.[3]

Exhibit 9.2 *Internality–Externality Factors and Behavioural Modes*

Locus and attribution	Determinant	Resultant mode
	Internality with stability	
Personal–stable	Ability	Supermanship
Personal–variable	Effort	Self-determination
Group–stable	Race/caste	Super-racism
Group–variable	Group effort	Social determination
	Externality with stability	
Human–stable	Social system	Role playing
Human–variable	Others	Compliance
Non-human–stable	Fate	Fatalism
Non-human–variable	Luck/chance	Probabilism

Internal Determinants of Outcomes

Achievement or failure to achieve an outcome may be attributed to the four factors shown in Exhibit 9.2, which influence the behaviour of an individual.

Ability If a person attributes positive outcomes to his or her ability (personal–stable factor), the person may come to believe that he or she has greater ability than most others and may behave like an extraordinary person, a 'superman'. Such a

Honey, I was just presented with this new toy! My optimism paid off—I stuck around when times were lean and now my confidence in my abilities has been justified.

person is likely to dominate others and to become authoritarian, seeing it as his or her natural right to determine things not only for himself or herself but for others also. This personal–stable factor may include other aspects, such as self-righteousness. Those who impose their own values on others may exhibit a high degree of this tendency.

Effort Effort is a personal–variable factor. Attribution of outcome to personal effort may result in perseverance in a task and self-deterministic behaviour mode, i.e, the individual may like to take his or her own decisions with regard to matters affecting him or her.

Race or caste Attribution of outcomes to the group to which one belongs is likely to exaggerate the group's value to the individual. It may also result in super-racial feelings.

A similar process operates in attempts at group conversion, such as religious conversions. A self-righteous attitude in the members of a group may inspire them to take on to themselves the task of converting others to their own views or way of life, as they feel that their group is a superior one.

Group effort As in the case of the individual–variable factor, the group–variable factor may lead to social determination of social matters. Collective actions belong to this category. People feel that they may be able to alter conditions through their collective action.

External Determinants of Outcomes

Outcomes may be attributed to external factors either related to other persons and society or to non-human agencies. Thus there are four determinants in this group:

Social system Some people may attribute outcomes to the social system, be it a political system, a work organization, or a social system such as the caste system. Such people perceive individuals merely as roles in a system. In a family system, for example, they may see their main responsibility as satisfying their role obligations. Their main mode of behaviour is to honestly live the role. They refuse to question any pressures the system may impose on them.

Others This external human–variable factor comprises 'other people' who are not a part of the stable system, but who are in a temporary relation with the individual. Leaders in various fields may be included in this category. Teachers and researchers may also be included here. Attributing an outcome to such persons may result in their importance to the individual being exaggerated. The individual may then comply with whatever is being demanded or suggested by them. Many findings on compliant behaviour and conformity may be explained by this factor.

Fate If people attribute outcomes to fate, they are likely to be resigned to whatever may happen, since they believe that neither they nor others can affect anything. Several experiments are cited later to show how such fatalism operates.

Luck or chance While fate is an external–stable factor, luck or chance is an external–variable factor. People attributing outcomes to luck or chance believe in the probability of change and may be hopeful and optimistic. They may look for a more opportune time for a given activity and also make other efforts in the hope that they may be lucky the next time.

Internality and Time Perspective

Another dimension that deserves attention in relation to internality–externality is time. The past and future dimensions seem to be particularly significant in this connection. To what do people attribute their past experiences? To what do people attribute or what do they expect from their possible future? These two dimensions of time (past and future) need not be similarly perceived. Combining the internality–externality dimensions, one gets four attributional modes, as shown in Exhibit 9.3.

Exhibit 9.3 *Internality–Externality Approaches*

	Past internality	Past externality
Future externality	Authoritarianism	Fatalism
Future internality	Religiosity	Activism

Authoritarianism Authoritarianism produces guilt in people for being responsible for the past (which is usually unsatisfactory) and consequently a lack of self-confidence. At the same time, it provides a way out by projecting a strong image of an external authority, a saviour, who can be expected to change the situation. Thus attribution of the past to internal factors and the future to external factors produces a combination of dissatisfaction and dependence, so that ultimately hope is produced.

Fatalism In fatalism, people attribute both the past (what has happened) and the future (what will happen) to external factors, thus creating a state of helplessness.

Religiosity Religiosity is the opposite of fatalism. Generally, religion instils a sense of internality—positive correlations between internality and religiosity have been reported. Religions usually suggest that people themselves are responsible for their fate and can themselves change it (of course, through religious ways). Emphasis on attribution of the past to internality again builds a sense of guilt and then a future-oriented internality helps people to become self-directed for action, leading to a search for religious or spiritual solutions. At the same time, religion also subtly develops people's dependency on it.

Activism The radical activist approach is quite different from the above—it externalises people's guilt. It helps people to attribute their past miseries and sufferings to external factors ('the previous corrupt government', 'the social system', 'the dominant class or race', etc.). Simultaneously, it develops a sense of internality among people— a belief that they can change their destiny themselves by taking systematic action. Such an approach has very successfully activated people for action.

Costs of Externality and Internality

Cost of externality   Internality is not only a major human weapon in mastering the material and non-material phenomena, it is also an appropriate mode of meaningful living for the individual. The cost of extreme externality is quite high. Loss of hope (a perception that outcomes or consequences cannot be influenced) has been reported to lead not only to depression but also suicide.[4]

Certain experiments on animals have dramatically brought out the high cost of extreme externality. Richter, while studying the endurance of swimming rats, accidentally discovered that some rats whose whiskers had been trimmed swam below the surface for some time, then suddenly stopped and died. Their deaths were intriguing because the autopsy showed that the deaths were not due to drowning. Further investigations showed that some rats died the same way even without the trimming of whiskers (all these were wild rats), whereas another group (of laboratory rats) did not die even after their whiskers had been trimmed. Richter concluded that the death was due to the handling of the wild rats, who—during the process of handling—experienced that escape was not possible and developed high 'externality'. So when they were placed in a jar of water, they swam for some time, but then gave up any hope of escape and died. Subsequently, wild rats were immersed in water and quickly removed. These rats quickly learnt that the situation was not actually hopeless and so became aggressive enough to try to free themselves or escape. These showed no signs of giving up hope in the water either.

The cost of externality is very high to the individuals and to the society. People can enjoy life and attain self-actualisation if they believe they are the determinants of their destiny. A society that creates a meaningful sense of instrumentality to personal and social outcomes in individuals and in groups can extract more creative contributions from its members and can attain new heights of civilisation. The cost of externality can be seen in feudal society in particular. Fortunately, human beings are ingenious in creating ways of developing internality even within the worst circumstances. But sometimes the price may be too high for any society to afford.

Cost of internality   While internality plays an important role in human development and meaningful living, it has its own cost. Internals who perceive personal–stable factors (lack of ability) or even personal–variable factors (lack of effort) as responsible for their failure may become self-punitive. In contrast, attribution of failure or negative conditions of life to external factors may help people cope with such adverse experiences more effectively and lead them to perceive the social reality in the proper perspective, fight injustice, and rectify the situation. Internality also produces stress, as a typical internal person is psychologically more aroused, resulting in physiological stress.

CONSEQUENCE OF INTERNALITY

A large body of research on the locus of control exists and is currently being added to, so that it is difficult to summarise the results in terms of clear conclusions.

Lefcourt has provided a good summary of several studies in this area.[5] However, some generalisation can be made on the basis of the results reported.

Some studies have thrown light on the role of internality in learning. Among other things, learning involves awareness of the situation and its context, curiosity, eagerness to obtain information, and processing of the information available. These aspects appear to be related to internality. Internals have been reported to be more sensitive to new information than externals. They make more observations and are more likely to attend to cues that could help resolve uncertainties. They appear to be consistently better than externals on both intentional and incidental learning. This relationship of internality to various aspects of learning seems to make sense. An internal, in order to influence an outcome, would want more information and would have to process the available information faster. An internal's control over events could also increase as a result of learning new tasks.

There is also evidence of the close relationship between the locus of control and academic achievement.

Some studies have shown a high positive correlation between internality and perseverance. Persistence is shown by time spent on work, continued involvement in difficult and complex tasks, and willingness to defer gratification. Lefcourt has summarised the research on the relationship between internality and deferred gratification well. Involvement with long-term goals requires deferring of immediate gratification. Persistence in effort requires undivided attention, which is not possible unless the temptation of gratification of immediate needs is resisted. An internal is more sure of the effort leading to a favourable outcome and can rely on his or her understanding and predictability. An external, in the absence of such predictability and fearing that any unforeseen external factors may affect the outcome, may find it more attractive to get immediate gratification rather than wait for the outcome of a distant goal.

Internality has been found to be an important characteristic of persons with high achievement motivation as well. One characteristic behaviour reported of high nAch people (people with high achievement motivation) is moderate or calculated risk-taking. An interesting finding indicates that internality plays an important role with regard to achievement motivation and a preference for moderate risk. The correlation between the latter two variables is significant and positive among internals but almost zero among externals.

Increased importance is being given to the process of valuing—the process of gaining an awareness of one's values, willingness to declare those values in public, and adherence to the values and to related behaviour in spite of external pressures. This is the process of developing ethical norms and using those norms even in a period of crisis. This is also called inner-directedness—being directed by one's own standards (internal values) rather than merely conforming to external expectations, norms, or pressures. Internality seems to be the cornerstone of such a process. Some studies have also indicated a significant relationship between internality and morality (resistance to temptation, helping others, and low Machiavellianism). Various studies indicate that internality plays an important role in the development of standards for judging one's behaviour (internalisation of values and morality). Both personal autonomy and responsibility are involved in the process of valuing, which is necessary for the development of a healthy and proactive society.

Some interesting findings have also been reported on the relationship between internality and mental health. Neurotic and psychotic symptoms are negatively related to behaviours that have been found among internals: delayed gratification and a heightened sense of time. Psychopathological conditions such as schizophrenia and depression have been found to be associated with an external locus of control. Using normal subjects, externals have been shown to be more defensive (rationalisation of one's behaviour). Some findings on the relationship between forgetting and internality have been interpreted as the readiness of externals to recall negative information, which provides access to defensiveness, rather than using forgetting as a mechanism to deal with a situation. A relationship between externality and depression has been reported as well. Lefcourt has summarised several studies on the relationship between the locus of control and anxiety and has concluded that the evidence counterindicates the seemingly sensible assumption that negative affect-states such as depression and anxiety should be more common among those who are likely to hold themselves responsible for their successes and failures.

The analysis of the findings showed that two types of anxiety were being investigated—facilitating anxiety (which is motivating in nature) and debilitating anxiety (which blocks the person from proceeding towards a goal). Internals showed more of the former and externals more of the latter. These findings raise the main issue of coping styles. Internals and externals seem to use two different patterns of coping with stress. While the former use a coping mechanism to persist with the problem (confronting or approach style), the latter use a more defensive behaviour (escape or avoidance style).

One study has reported interesting relationships between internality and externality and some organizational behaviours—internals had higher job satisfaction and were more satisfied with a participatory management style; externals were more satisfied with directive style. Internals believed that working hard was more likely to lead to good performance and that good performance was more likely to lead to other rewards. They had more control over how they spent time on the job than did externals. Another interesting finding was that while internal supervisors saw persuasive power bases as more effective, externals found coercive power more effective. Internals saw rewards, respect, and expertise as the most effective ways to influence their subordinates, while externals saw coercion and their formal position as more effective tools.

DEVELOPING INTERNALITY

Internality is not an innate characteristic. People acquire it. Therefore, it can also be developed. Some evidence is available about the development of internality from a variety of sources: work with children, clinical work with mental patients, and experiments in producing change in people. An understanding of the process of developing internality also helps in the search for interventions that can be used to increase internality in people. The following main groups of such interventions are suggested, for which special training programmes can be planned.

Self-awareness   A variety of programmes attempt to increase an individual's self-awareness. In process or encounter groups (like T-groups), individuals are helped to confront themselves, understand their basic stance in life, and experiment with new behaviour. Transaction analysis (TA) can be used to help a person understand his or her existential (life) position and life script so that he or she can take new decisions in life. In TA language, internality is the 'OK' position and externality is the 'Not-OK' position.

Motivation development   McClelland and Winter have contributed a new approach to changing people's basic attitudes towards risk-taking and responsibility.[6] The approach consists in bringing about change in the motives of people (what McClelland called 'affectively toned associative network') by helping them to analyse their imagery for the 'associated network' and then to learn to change the imagery. The following techniques are used: setting up the network, conceptualising the network, tying the network to as many cases as possible in everyday life, and working out the relation of the network to superordinate associative clusters, such as the self-concept.

Internality can be increased through achievement motivation training, which essentially focuses on helping an individual analyse his or her dominant imagery style and saturate it with new content—a concern for excellence, and an understanding of the role of personal responsibility in determining outcomes. The training is directly related to internality. McClelland and Winter have described this training in detail.[7]

Valuing and assertion   One of the schools of the Gestalt group of training (humanistic psychology group) offers programmes in value clarification and assertion (as opposed to either aggression or submission). Several exercises have been evolved for such training. The main approach is to help the individual understand his or her current mode and learn how this can be changed to a more aware and assertive one. Exercises have been prepared for developing an assertive belief system, cognitive restructuring procedures, behaviour rehearsal procedures, modelling procedures, and assessment procedures.

Reinterpretation   Individuals develop a cognitive world around themselves. They each have their own theories and interpret various actions and behaviours (own and others') according to these theories. They may thus interpret their refusal to conform or typical annoying behaviour as assertive. If individuals can be helped to analyse their conceptual systems, and reinterpret their own and others' actions, they may be able to see that while they interpreted some of their own actions as assertive, they were merely reactive—the individual was not 'the origin' but merely a 'pawn'.

In one technique of reinterpretation, children are helped to state how they would act and then are helped to change externality modes in the statement of action to internality modes. Such intervention may help a person internalise the meaning of internality and see how it operates in action.

Success experience   If individuals are helped to succeed in controlling outcomes, they will develop as internals. This requires a sustained programme of setting challenging goals and achieving them. For example, graduated challenging goals can be prepared for children and they can be helped to achieve one at a time, going from one goal to the next. Independence training, much talked about in child-rearing practices, is one example of such intervention. The individual needs to be given responsibility and challenging tasks. This is likely to increase internality.

Supportive demands   If people get enough warmth and support to help them make an effort and succeed, and then enough demand is put on them to cope with tasks and their consequences by themselves (providing support when required), people develop high internality. This can be programmed both for individuals and groups. It can also be achieved through simulation, as a training intervention.

Social awareness   All activist programmes are based on increasing the social awareness of individuals. Knowledge is power and an individual feels much more capable of dealing with problems once he or she understands them. The programme of conscientisation, for example, increases the internality of people who have very low self-regard to begin with.

Collective actions   Collaboration for action helps people increase each other's internality. Collectivity develops a new sense of power. Collaboration helps in developing internality when there is mutual support, the outcomes are success experiences, and outcomes are reinforced through appreciation. Effective programmes can help in developing internality in both children and adults.

OPTIMISM

Another important variable for effectiveness in all aspects of life is optimism. Seligman[8] has popularised the key role of optimism in several aspects of life, including health (see Chapter 10). He narrates the story of a paediatric nurse, Madelon Visintainer, who did pioneering experiments on rats in 1978. She experimented on three groups of rats: (1) mild escapable shock was given to the first group (optimist rats), (2) mild inescapable shock to the second group (pessimist rats), and (3) no shock was given to the third group (control group). A few days before the experiment, she planted a few cells of sarcoma on each rat's flank. The tumour is lethal if it grows and is not rejected by the animal's immune defences. Visintainer had planted a specific number of sarcoma cells so that 50 per cent of the rats would reject the tumour and live. Within a month, 50 per cent died in the third group ('control'), 70 per cent rejected it in the first group ('optimist'), and only 27 per cent rejected it in the second group ('pessimist').[9] This proved the role of control and optimism in fighting cancer. Interestingly, a rat's childhood experience of mastery made the difference. Most of the rats who had been trained in mastery rejected the tumour, whereas the most helpless ones died.[10]

In another study, George Valliant studied 200 men between 39 and 44 years of age and followed up their lives. Their health at 60 years was found to be strongly related to their optimism at 25 years.[11]

Optimism and Health

How does optimism promote better health? Optimism seems to improve the functioning of the immune system by preventing helplessness. We have two types of cells in our immune system. T-cells recognise specific invaders, greatly multiply, and kill the invaders (such as virus, bacteria, tumour) while natural killer (NK) cells kill anything foreign. The brain and immune system are connected through hormones. When depressed, neurotran-smitters—especially catecholamines—become depleted and the level of another class of chemicals called endorphins goes up. The immune system detects their presence and turns itself down. As a result, T-cells do not multiply rapidly when they come across specific invaders.

Optimism has been reported to help people cope with stress and reduce the risk of illness.[12] Optimists use more problem-focused coping, seek social support, and see the positive aspects of a situation.[13] Optimism was also found to be an important predictor of recovery from surgery in coronary artery bypass patients.[14] Optimism has been reported to be associated with faster recovery and better adjustments in the post-surgery period in general too.[15]

Seligman, building on the works of Rotter[16] (on the locus of control) and Weiner[17] (on the causal attribution), used the time and space dimension to suggest two types of stable factors (permanent and universal) and two types of variable factors (temporary and specific). He defined optimism in two ways: attributing success or good events to permanent and universal factors and attributing failure or misfortunes to temporary or specific factors. He developed a 4-item (pairs) instrument for measuring optimism, pessimism, and the internal locus of control.

Scheier and Carver developed a 12-item yes–no instrument (the life orientation test, or LOT) to measure optimism.[18] Four items in this are filler items, four are positive, and four negative (which are reversed to score optimism). LOT has been used in a large number of investigations since.

The attribution of success and failure (Asufa) inventory[19] measures several aspects of the locus of control and optimism. It analyses the factors to which respondents attribute success and failure.

In one study, women diagnosed with breast cancer were given the LOT. They were interviewed the day before their surgery, and then again 7 days, 10 days, and 3 months following surgery.[20] At the time of the surgery, women who scored higher on optimism reviewed the situation in a positive light and accepted its reality. Women who scored higher on pessimism denied the reality of the situation and reported giving up or feeling that the surgery was hopeless.

In these women undergoing surgery, optimism was associated with a positive mood and the ability to maintain a sense of humour, while pessimism was associated with reports of emotional distress, denial, and disengagement.

These studies also demonstrated that acceptance of reality is important. Those who accepted the reality prior to the surgery did not show serious distress after the surgery.

In other cases studying surgery candidates, optimists and pessimists differed from the beginning. Even before the surgery, the pessimists reported higher levels of hostility and depression than the optimists. After the surgery, they were reported to be less happy and less relieved than the optimists, who seemed to be less focused on the negative experiences associated with surgery. After the surgery, the optimists sought information that would help them in the recovery process. They got up and began walking around their rooms after surgery, in contrast to the pessimists. Six months after surgery, the optimists had returned to vigorous exercise, showed better adaptation to the surgery, and appeared to return to their normal lives at a more rapid pace.

Optimism seems to be an important variable in various aspects of life. Seligman has fascinatingly discussed how it is important in political leadership. Success in the presidential and senate elections in the US were predicted on the basis of scores on pessimism and rumination.[21] Rumination is defined as a tendency to recall miserable experiences and failure, mull over them, and constantly think about them, and their causes. Those who had high scores on 'pessrum' (the combination of pessimism and rumination) failed to win the elections. Seligman has given enough evidence to show how optimism is important in sports, school achievement, and in work.[22]

A study of insurance agents showed that less optimistic agents were twice as likely to quit as more optimistic ones. The agents with the top half scores on optimism sold 20 per cent more than the less optimistic ones (from the bottom half); those from the top quarter sold 50 per cent more than those from the bottom quarter. When a special force of highly optimistic agents was created, they outsold the pessimists in the regular force by 21 per cent during the first year and 57 per cent in the second year.[23]

In the attributional framework, optimism is defined as attributing miseries, failures, and bad experiences to variable factors (temporary or specific). Pessimism, on the other hand, is defined as attributing miseries, failures, and bad experiences to stable (permanent or pervasive) and good experiences and success to variable (temporary or specific) causes.

It is encouraging that medium-sized business in India is very high in optimism. Grant Thornton—one of the six global accountancy firms who conduct International Business Owners Survey (IBOS)—have reported the highest optimism in the world in the Indian mid-size business for the third time in a row.

Conducted in countries around the world, the survey shows a marked shift in the mood of medium-sized businesses across the world. The most optimistic business owners of all are in India, with an optimism–pessimism balance of +93, while in

China, surveyed by IBOS for the first time, the confidence score was a balance of +77. 'India's business owners continue to thrive and remain very optimistic ... the growing reliance on the private sector and trade liberalisation ... is proving fruitful for medium-sized enterprises ...' Grant Thornton India's partner and director, Vishesh Chandiok, said in a release. In contrast, the confidence of business owners in the US, regarding the economy, has dropped by nearly half from an optimism–pessimism balance of +62 to +32 in one year. Japan (–14) has the second most pessimistic business owners.[24]

HOPE: WILL-POWER AND WAY-POWER

Another related concept is that of hope. Hope has been recognised as a part of emotional intelligence. 'Having hope means that one will not give in to anxiety'.[25] It is an integral element of optimism, and Seligman defines it as 'finding temporary and specific causes for misfortune is the art of hope'. However, Snyder[26] suggests two aspects of hope—an individual's determination that goals can be achieved (called agency or will power) and also his or her belief that effective plans can be formulated to achieve the goals (called pathways or way power). Snyder has prepared a short scale to measure these two aspects of hope. It has been found that persons with hope perform better in human service professions. Snyder has also distinguished between hope as a trait (general orientation) and as a state (situation specific). This has promising implications for personal and organizational effectiveness.

Snyder has suggested a checklist for increasing both will power and way power. The edited list for agency or will power is given below:

Do

- Tell yourself that you have chosen the goal, so it is your job to go after it.
- Learn to talk to yourself in positive voices (e.g., 'I can do this').
- Anticipate roadblocks that may happen.
- Think of problems as challenges that arouse you.
- Recall your previous successful pursuits of goals, particularly when you are in a jam.
- Be able to laugh at yourself, especially if you encounter some impediment in the pursuit of your goal.
- Find a substitute goal when the original goal is blocked.
- Enjoy the process of getting to your goals and do not focus only on the final attainment.

Don't

- Allow yourself to be surprised repeatedly by roadblocks that appear in your life.
- Try to squelch any internal putdowns because even silent repetition will only make them stronger.
- Get impatient if your 'willful' thinking does not increase quickly.
- Panic when you run into a roadblock.
- Conclude that things never will change, especially if you are down.

- Engage in self-pity when faced with adversity.
- Take yourself seriously all the time.
- Stick to a blocked goal when it is well and truly blocked.
- Constantly ask 'How am I doing?' in order to evaluate your progress towards a goal.

Here is the list for pathways or way power:

Do
- Break a long-range goal into steps or sub-goals.
- Begin your pursuit of a distant goal by concentrating on the first sub-goal.
- Practise taking different routes to your goals and select the best one.
- In your mind, rehearse what you will need to do to attain your goal.
- Mentally rehearse scripts for what you would do when you encounter a blockage.
- Conclude that you did not use a workable strategy when you do not reach a goal rather than blaming yourself.
- If you need a new skill to reach your goal, learn it.
- Cultivate two-way friendships where you can give and get advice.
- Be willing to ask for help when you do not know how to get to a desired goal.

Don't
- Think you can reach your big goals 'all at once'.
- Be too hurried in producing routes to your goals.
- Rush to select the best or first route to your goal.
- Get obsessed with the idea of finding the one perfect route to your goal.
- Stop thinking about alternate strategies when the chosen one does not work.
- Conclude you are lacking in talent or are 'no good' when an initial strategy fails.
- Be caught off guard when one approach does not work.
- Get into friendships where you are praised for not coming up with solutions to your problems.
- View asking for help as a sign of weakness.

RUMINATION AND FLOW

When we sit and daydream, recalling all our miseries, misfortunes, failures, or bad experiences with people, it is called rumination. Sitting in groups and talking about past miseries or current disappointments is also rumination. We almost always relive the same experiences when we indulge in such recollections. On the other hand, when we recollect our good experiences, enjoy such recollection, or are involved in a highly absorbing activity, it is called flow.

Worrying about matters is also rumination. Rumination is dysfunctional and damaging. It makes the situation worse, particularly when one is under pressure. Often it is better to put off thinking in order to do our best. We can learn to control not only what we think but when we think.

Women are twice as likely to suffer depression than men because they tend to think about problems in ways that amplify depression. Men tend to act rather than reflect, but women tend to contemplate their depression, mulling it over and over, trying to analyse it to determine its source. When asked to state what they actually did when they were depressed, the majority of women subjects said that they tried to analyse their mood or the cause behind it whereas most men said they did something they enjoyed.

Psychologists call this process of obsessive analysis rumination, the usual meaning of the word being 'chewing the cud'. Ruminant animals such as cattle, sheep, and goats chew cud, which is regurgitated, partially digested food—not a very appealing image of what people who ruminate do with their thoughts, but an exceedingly apt one! Rumination combined with a pessimistic explanatory style leads to severe depression.

People who mull over bad events are called ruminators. A ruminator can be either an optimist or a pessimist. Optimistic ruminators are action oriented. They rarely talk to themselves and when they do, it is not about how bad things are. The belief structure of pessimistic ruminators is pessimistic and they repeatedly tell themselves how bad things are. There is a positive relationship between pessimism and rumination, both of them leading to depression. If a person believes that he or she is helpless in some situation and that the cause of the situation is permanent, pervasive, and personal, the consequences can include depression.

The more a person ruminates, more the feeling of helplessness arises. And more the feeling of helplessness, the more depressed the person is. That is why ruminators keep thinking about how bad things are.

People who do not ruminate tend to avoid depression even if they are pessimists. Similarly, optimists who ruminate also avoid depression. Avoiding either rumination or pessimism helps relieve depression. Avoiding both helps the most.

Susan Noalen Hocksama of Standford University is the originator of the rumination theory.[27] Mihaly Csikszentmihalyi proposed the concept of 'flow' as deep involvement in positive activity and thought and the joy one gets in the recollection of good and positive experiences or in activities demanding high involvement.[28] According to Csikszentmihalyi, flow exists in the present and it is possible to flow while engaged in any activity. Daniel Goleman suggests five steps in achieving flow.[29] These are

1. Fit difficulty to skill (match the difficulty of a challenge and a person's ability to meet it).
2. Focus attention (focusing attention to allow the merging of awareness and activity).
3. Forget time (the ability to focus on the moment, on the here and now).
4. Relax and wake up (alert mind and relaxed body).
5. Train for flow (e.g., dance, meditation, some Eastern martial arts, music, etc.).

Thus flow means involvement in positive thinking, recalling pleasant experiences, pleasant daydreams, and involvement in activities that one enjoys.

SUMMARY

Locus of control (who or what controls most of the things happening to an individual—the individual, other people, or external forces) is an important concept in relation to personal effectiveness. Internals (who believe they are responsible for most of the significant happenings in their lives) have been found to be more effective, being high achievers, resisting temptation, helping others, internalising values, and having high energy.

An attributional framework (to what one attributes one's success and/or failure) can be used to define optimism as attributing misfortunes or failures to variable factors (internal and external) and pessimism as attributing bad experiences and failure to stable and success to variable factors (internal and external).

Optimism is very important for all aspects of life, including organizations. The related concepts of hope (both will power and way power), rumination (indulging in recollecting all bad experiences), and flow (achieving joy in any activity undertaken) are also important for personal effectiveness and success. These can be developed.

GLOSSARY

internality the belief that one 'causes', or at least can influence, most of the phenomena one experiences

agency (will power) the individual's determination that goals can be achieved

external locus of control belief that outcomes are not produced by one's actions

flow recollecting good experiences, enjoying such recollection, or being involved in a highly absorbing activity

hope finding temporary and specific causes for misfortune

internal a person with internal locus of control

locus of control the perception of the contingencies between action and outcome (to what extent an action produces an outcome)

optimism attributing miseries, failures, and bad experiences to variable factors (temporary or specific)

pathway (way power) belief that effective plans can be formulated to achieve goals

pessimism attributing miseries, failures, and bad experiences to stable (permanent or pervasive) and good experiences and success to variable (temporary or specific) causes

rumination a tendency to recall, mull over, and constantly think about miserable experiences and failures

stable that which does not change easily

variable that which can vary or change (e.g., effort)

EXERCISES

Concept Review Questions

1. What is the importance of internality? Give examples from the experiences of people whom you know.
2. How can the level of internality be raised?
3. What are optimism and pessimism in attributional terms? Do you find any relevance of this concept among your friends?
4. What is Snyder's concept of hope? How can hope be developed, both in terms of will power and way power?
5. What is rumination? How is it related to effectiveness?

Critical Thinking Question

1. Given below are some statements that show how people experience their lives. There are no right or wrong answers. Read each statement and indicate on the left-hand side of each statement the extent to which you feel that way, using the following key for your responses:

Key

Write 4 if you strongly feel this way
Write 3 if you generally feel this way
Write 2 if you feel somewhat this way (and somewhat not)
Write 1 if you feel slightly this way
Write 0 if you hardly or never feel this way

1. The course of my career largely depends on me.
2. The people who are important control most matters in my life.
3. One's career, to a great extent, is a matter of chance.
4. Successful completion of assignments is mainly because of my detailed planning and hard work.
5. The success of one's plans, to a large extent, is a matter of luck.
6. Senior people's preferences determine who would be rewarded in an organization.
7. My experience is that most things in the organization are beyond one's control.
8. Generally, I determine what happens to me in the organization.
9. My ideas get accepted if I make them fit in with the desires of my seniors.

Scoring

Calculate your scores on three aspects of the locus of control as follows:
Total of items 1 + 4 + 8 gives you a score on internality.
Total of items 2 + 6 + 9 gives you a score on significant others.
Total of items 3 + 5 + 7 gives you a score on chance.

(a) If your score on internality is 6 or below, prepare a plan to increase it. If your score on significant others is either below 3 or above 9, you may plan to raise or lower it. If your score on chance is 6 or above, prepare a plan to reduce it.

(b) What is generally responsible for a student's failure—lack of talent or laziness? What do these two attitudes signify in the attributional framework?

(c) Collect a few proverbs that reflect internality and some that reflect externality.

Classroom Projects

1. In groups of two or three, analyse the phenomenon of the increase in the number of student visits to temples, mosques, or churches as examinations draw close. What does such behaviour show?
2. In groups of two or three, list examples of internality and externality in your classmates' behaviour and statements.

Field Projects

1. Interview two people on what they usually think about when they are alone: do they ruminate more or enjoy flow?
2. Interview someone in your family to find out how much will power and how much way power the person has. Write down the indicators of will power and way power you find from the interview.

National Dairy Development Board*

In early 1999, the United Nation's Food and Agriculture Organization (FAO) declared India as the world's largest producer of milk. According to FAO's Global Food Outlook Report, milk production in India crossed 74 million tonnes (mts) by March 1999, while milk production in the US, the second largest producer, was 71 mts.

This was truly a moment of glory for India, which, less than four decades earlier, had been a milk-deficit country. According to analysts, India's transformation into a milk-surplus country was largely due to the collective initiative undertaken by various government and semi-government bodies to promote milk production and animal husbandry. In 1970, Operation Flood was launched by the National Dairy Development Board (NDDB), an institution constituted as a body corporate in 1965.

Declared as an institution of national importance by an Act of Parliament, in 1965, NDDB was established with the objective of replicating the 'Anand Model' of dairy development. This model was first implemented in the Kheda (formerly called Kaira) district of the northwestern state of Gujarat. It was built around institutions (cooperative societies) that were owned and managed by rural milk producers who wished to market their produce collectively. The basic philosophy of the Anand Model was the scientific and professional management of a vertically integrated structure that created a direct link between milk producers and ultimate consumers.

The model owed its success to the vision, foresight, and leadership of Dr Verghese Kurien, the architect of Operation Flood. The initiative was aimed at ending India's milk deficit and at using cooperatives as a catalyst to transform India into a leading milk producer. Operation Flood went on to become a successful rural development project that made dairying a core economic activity in the country. By the late 1990s, Operation Flood had over 10 million farmer members from across 70,000 villages in its cooperative network.

Helping other emerging countries establish cooperatives in the dairy industry was one of the elements of the three-pronged strategic plan outlined by Amrita Patel, who took over as chairman of NDDB in 1999 (after Kurien's 33-year stint). In addition to aiming at capitalising the success of cooperative-run diaries, the plan also involved transforming India into a major milk exporter and extending the cooperative model to other domestic agricultural products.

However, in 2001, basic differences between Kurien and Patel led to a major conflict. This case covers the period upto the the end of the last century.

* This case was written by A. Neela Radhika, under the direction of A. Mukund, ICFAI Center for Management Research (ICMR). Slightly abridged and modified version reproduced with the permission of ICFAI Center for Management Research (ICMR), Hyderabad, India.

BACKGROUND NOTE

The earliest attempts at modernising dairy development in India can be traced back to the early 1940s. During this period, private dairies with reasonably modern processing facilities emerged in major cities such as Mumbai, Kolkata, Delhi, and Chennai, and in some large townships. As these dairies received their milk supplies through middlemen, who bought milk from milk producers on their behalf, they were not concerned with improving milch animal varieties. The dairies and the middlemen stood between the milk producers and the ultimate consumers, leading to the exploitation of both. While the middlemen paid the producers inadequately, the dairies exploited the end customers by charging high prices.

With the country's economy gradually moving from an agrarian to an industrialised environment, the population shift to urban areas picked up momentum. This, coupled with the fact that almost the entire milch population of India was located in the rural areas, resulted in the urban areas facing an acute shortage of milk.

Polsons, a private dairy at Anand, a small town in the Kheda district, was one of the first dairy farms that entered into a milk supply contract with the government. This contract was signed under the Bombay Milk Scheme (BMS) 1945, a programme aimed at providing a regular supply of milk to the city of Bombay. Polsons procured milk from producers through traders, processed it, and then sent it to Bombay (425 km from Anand). As Bombay was a good market for milk, Polsons reaped high profits, but paid the milk producers at Anand very poorly. In the mid-1940s, the discontented milk producers asked for their proportionate share in the trade margins of Polsons. When Polsons refused, the milk producers went on strike and refused to supply milk to it. It was at this point that the dairy cooperative movement in India began to take shape.

A deputation of these milk producers approached Sardar Vallabhai Patel, one of the stalwarts of India's independence movement. Sardar Patel advised them to set up a cooperative society of their own and to process and market their produce themselves. The milk producers decided to set up a dairy cooperative society in every village of the Kheda district and to form a union to handle their activities. This resulted in the formation of the Kaira District Cooperative Milk Producers' Union Ltd (KDCMPUL) in 1946. Under the chairmanship of Tribhuvandas Patel, the union began supplying milk directly to Bombay under the BMS (Bombay Milk Scheme).

The union began on a modest note, with only two village dairy cooperatives under it, supplying less than 250 litres of milk per day. But the business proved highly profitable and the profits made by the cooperatives were redistributed to the members. The dairy cooperative movement soon gained momentum, resulting in the establishment of many village dairy cooperatives in the Kheda district. The KDCMPUL expanded its milk processing capacities as the milk collection activity increased. The union soon realised the need for professional management and support to look after its expanding operations. It also realised that its role should not be restricted to just acting as a collection and selling agent for the milk producers.

There was a need to provide a variety of support services to help the milk producers continue selling an adequate quantity of milk and to avoid disasters such as death of their cattle. A majority of milk producers owned only one or two milch animals and milk was a major source of income for them. The death of cattle either from illness or malnutrition would, therefore, have disastrous consequences for them. So, the union began offering many new services such veterinary care, education on better cattle feeding, supply of balanced cattle feed, and facilities for artificial insemination of cattle. All these services were provided to members at affordable prices.

Ever since its inception, the union had been trying to acquire monopoly rights for sale of milk to the BMS. It finally succeeded in 1952, when the government cancelled Polson's contract and gave it to the union. In winter though, the union found itself facing a surplus of milk, as the production of milk was high. To put the excess milk to use, it decided to produce milk products with a higher shelf life, such as butter, ghee (clarified butter), milk powder, and baby food.

In 1955, the KDCMPUL changed its name to Anand Milk Union Limited (Amul). In the same year, Amul set up a new dairy plant at Anand for producing milk products. These products were sold under the brand name Amul, which soon became a major success. Amul's success attracted the interest of milk producers from neighbouring districts as well, and they sought its help to organize dairy cooperatives. By the late 1950s, the dairy cooperative movement had spread to all the major districts in Gujarat. The dairying pattern established by these cooperatives across Gujarat with Anand as the base soon became popular as the Anand Model (see Exhibit I for salient features of the Anand Model).

Exhibit I *Salient Features of Anand Model*

- Ensure that each co-operative has the right blend of policy makers, milk producers (who comprise the board of management), and professionals, with each group appreciating its role and limitations.
- Provide the rural milk producers the best of the technology and harness its fruit for betterment.
- Provide a support system to the milk producers without disturbing their agro-economic systems.
- Plough back the profits by optimal use of human resources, material, and machines in the rural sector for the common good and betterment of the member producers.
- Ensure that the interests of small producer members remain the priority even when the cooperatives grow in scale with time.

ANAND MODEL

The Anand Model was structured around three 'tiers'—the primary village dairy cooperatives, the district milk producers' union, and the state cooperative dairy federation.

The village dairy cooperatives were voluntary associations of milk producers that marketed their milk collectively. Membership to the cooperative was open to any person who owned cattle and was willing to supply surplus milk to the cooperative society. Every village cooperative was governed by a management committee of nine members elected by the members themselves at an annual general meeting. The management committee was responsible for framing the plans and policies that governed the day-to-day affairs of the cooperative. The profits/losses were divided among the members in proportion to their investment in the society.

This is how the milk collection system functioned: The villagers gathered twice (morning and evening) at specified times at the village cooperative centres, where they received a uniform price based on their milk's quality and quantity. The milk was tested on the spot for fat content, and the price decided. The milk thus collected was sent to Anand in milk vans/trucks. The morning milk was paid for in the evening and the evening milk was paid for next morning. Milk collection, testing, and payment were done by paid staff from the same village. The staff members were appointed by the management committee and their salaries depended on the earnings of the cooperative. This way, the cooperatives generated substantial local employment in the rural areas.

The village dairy cooperatives were affiliated to the district milk producers' union. The union processed the milk that it procured from the village dairy cooperatives. The processing was generally done at the union's own processing plants. These unions were governed by a board of directors elected by the chairpersons of the village cooperatives and representatives (chairpersons) of affiliated village cooperative societies.

The 17-member board was headed by a managing director. The board was responsible for framing appropriate policies and for management of operations such as collection and transportation of milk from village cooperatives, ensuring regular and timely payment to the village cooperatives, offering technical support to milk producers to enhance milk production and processing, and marketing milk and milk products. Other functions included long-term and strategic planning, communicating with members, overall control of village cooperatives, and representing the union on legislative and regulatory forums.

The union also had a team of professionals and staff to look after services such as emergency veterinary health care, supply of balanced cattle feed and breeding services, artificial insemination services, and the provision of improved varieties of fodder seeds. According to reports, the union encouraged milk producers to enhance production by promising to buy the entire quantity of milk produced by them, irrespective of the season. This meant that even during winter (when milk production was at its peak), the cooperatives bought the entire milk from the producers. To make this financially feasible, the unions installed milk drying equipment. Surplus milk could, therefore, be dried and used in the lean season. In winter, the cooperatives paid 80 per cent of the lean season price to milk producers as against 50 per cent paid by the traditional milk traders. All district milk producer unions joined together to form an apex state cooperative dairy federation. The primary responsibilities of this federation were to coordinate the operations of the unions, provide a platform for sharing common benefits to avoid competition among them, and market milk and milk products outside the state.

By the mid-1960s, the Anand Model had evolved into a successful, organized dairy development model. By 1965, Amul had 110,000 members. From just 250 litres in 1946, it was collecting 65,905 tonnes of milk and processing over 500,000 litres of milk every day. Amul's wide product portfolio (comprising milk, baby food, cheese, ghee, butter, whole milk and skimmed milk powders, condensed milk, etc.) generated sales of around 92.2 million rupees in 1965.

According to analysts, the success of the Anand Model did not lie in the extensive use of modern dairying techniques or technology or its product extension or marketing strategies. It was due more to its unique ability to bring in substantial socioeconomical changes in the dairy industry by organizing the rural producers.

FORMATION OF NDDB

While Amul laid the foundation for a systematic approach to dairy development in India, through the early 1950s, the government also began its efforts to modernise the dairy industry. As a part of this, it made modernisation of the industry a priority under the first five-year plan of India in 1951. Under this, the government set itself the goal of providing hygienic milk to the growing urban population.

To achieve this goal, the government encouraged establishment of dairy cooperative societies and also organized 'milk schemes' in all major cities across the country. It also implemented the Intensive Cattle Development Project (ICDP), which focused on artificial insemination and veterinary services, and the Small Farmer Development Agencies (SFDA), which offered cattle farmers (milk producers) financial aid to enhance milk production. In 1959, the government introduced the Delhi Milk Scheme to cater to the milk requirements of the national capital, Delhi. Under this scheme, government milk plants collected milk at chilling centres through middlemen. It then pasteurised the milk and marketed it through specially set up booths across the city. Various state governments introduced similar schemes during the 1960s. Apart from this, the state governments tried out different strategies such as building milk processing plants in cities, organizing milk schemes, and setting up cattle colonies in urban areas.

However, many of these government projects failed to organize rural milk procurement and selling activities economically. This was largely because these projects depended on contractors and middlemen. The contractors took advantage of the perishable nature and relative scarcity of milk and exploited the government-run dairy plants. The high prices charged by the middlemen forced these plants to go in for imported milk powder, which was much cheaper.

As the use of milk powder increased, the demand for fresh milk started to decline. Consequently, rural milk producers saw little reason to increase production, and this led to a rise in the dependency on imports. Apart from this, the establishment of cattle colonies in the urban areas also adversely affected dairy development in rural areas. Providing financial aid to milk producers to purchase milch animals did not work as expected as many of those who took loans did not use them for the purpose.

Even those who did buy cattle did not bring the milk to the cooperatives, but sold it directly to middlemen. This not only led to a large amount of investments being written off, but also marred the credibility of the dairy cooperative movement (the government provided these loans through cooperatives who were supposed to recover the amount through milk money).

By the mid-1960s, many of the dairy development schemes of the government had been branded as dismal failures (handling less than one million litres of milk per day). Interestingly, at the same time, the government was importing more than 60,000 tons of milk powder annually. It became necessary to ration the milk supply in the urban areas; according to analysts, the situation was nothing short of a milk famine. The greatest concern to analysts at that point was that the dumping of cheap imports was working against the interests of indigenous milk producers.

It was at this juncture (in October 1964) that Lal Bahadur Shastri, the then prime minister of India, came to the Kheda district to inaugurate the country's largest modern cattle feed plant. Impressed by the socioeconomic changes brought about in the region because of the Anand Model, he soon set in motion the effort to establish a national organization to replicate it across the country (see Exhibit II for the socioeconomic benefits reaped by the Kheda district).

Exhibit II *Socioeconomic Benefits Reaped by Kheda District by Implementing Anand Model*

According to many independent studies by various institutions and individuals, around 48 per cent of the income of rural households in Kheda district was derived from dairying. So, the implementation of the Anand Model had an immense effect on the district's socioeconomic scenario. The major socio-economic benefits were as follows—

Cooperative members became aware of their rights and the process of electing the right persons for the right job by conducting annual elections for selection of management committee and its chairman. Social inequalities were eliminated with different ethnic and social groups coming together voluntarily twice a day at milk collection centres for a common cause. Cooperation among them was encouraged for mutual betterment.

The members became increasingly aware of various modern dairy technologies as village cooperative workers gave them live exposure to such technologies. These technologies were simplified to enable milk producers to adopt them, resulting in increased milk production rates.

Employment opportunities were generated for the people in more than 900 village cooperatives. This helped reduce the exodus of people from the rural areas to the cities.

Women's participation in cooperatives increased. This contributed to their household economy and to an increase in the standard of living of their families. Indirectly, it resulted in an increased percentage of children going to school in the villages.

This led to the establishment of the National Diary Development Board (NDDB) in 1965. The NDDB was headquartered at Anand, and was headed by Kurien, the then general manager of the KDCMPUL. The NDDB was initially registered as a society under the Societies Act 1860. The general superintendence, direction, management, and control of NDDB's operations vested with the board of directors headed by the chairman, who was appointed by the government.

NDDB faced many obstacles initially due to limited financial resources and a lack of support from various government departments. Even by the end of the 1960s, very little progress had been achieved in terms of rolling out the Anand Model across India. According to reports, between 1951 and 1970, the government invested 11.4 billion rupees on various animal husbandry and dairy development schemes, many of which flopped badly.

At the same time, the accumulating dairy commodity surplus in Europe emerged as a major potential threat to the dairy industry in India. Industry observers felt that it would not be long before Europe began dumping its surplus on milk-deficit countries like India. Already, a large quantity of milk products was being imported. Analysts said that if the European milk surplus was dumped in India, it would signal the end of dairy development movement in the country.

However, Kurien saw the situation in Europe as a major opportunity to generate the financial resources necessary for achieving NDDB's objective. His idea was to seek food aid from European countries and generate the finance necessary for the development of dairy cooperatives through the sale of those milk commodities (in India). Thus, what had been a serious threat was converted into an asset as the Operation Flood programme was conceptualised.

OPERATION FLOOD

In 1970, the government approved the Operation Flood programme proposed by Kurien. However, as per the statutes under which NDDB was registered, it was not authorised to handle government funds. To overcome this hurdle, the government established the Indian Dairy Corporation (IDC), a public sector company. IDC was made responsible for receiving donated commodities (for Operation Flood), for undertaking quality tests, for looking after storage and transfer of those commodities to dairy plants for sale, and then for receiving the sale proceeds. In effect, IDC operated as a finance and promotion entity, while NDDB functioned as a technical support entity to the Operation Flood programme.

Operation Flood aimed to create a 'flood of milk' across the country, to augment rural incomes and to empower milk producers so that they would become self-dependent and earn profits from marketing their produce (see Exhibit III for the programme's objectives). The programme mainly aimed at replicating the Anand Model across India by establishing dairy co-operatives in villages and making modern dairy development technology available to all the milk producers.

Exhibit III *Major Objectives of Operation Flood*

- To enable each city's liquid milk scheme to capture a commendable share of its market.
- To identify the needs of consumers and milk producers, and help fulfil those needs to reduce the cost of milk for the consumers and increase the share of milk price obtained by producers.
- To facilitate a long-term investment in dairying and cattle development.
- To ensure availability of efficient personnel to manage and control every facet of the programme.

In 1970, in a small departure from the Anand Model, NDDB added another tier to the model, the National Co-operative Dairy Federation of India (NCDFI). The NCDFI was the apex body of all the state dairy federations. Its major functions were to provide basic institutional framework for better coordination and control and to help the state federations establish a stronger cooperative milk marketing system in India. Another major function of the NCDFI was to manage the activities of the National Milk Grid, which it established to coordinate the supply of milk from the surplus-producing areas to urban markets that were facing a scarcity.

The Operation Flood programme was divided into three phases. Phase I was launched in 1970 and ended in 1978. Under this phase, NDDB, with the assistance of the World Food Program (WFP), obtained food aid (in the form of 126,000 mts of skimmed milk powder and 42,000 mts of butter oil), from the European Economic Community (EEC) countries (see Exhibit IV for Phase I targets).

Exhibit IV *Operation Flood Phase I—Targets*

- Establishing/organazing village dairy cooperatives with required physical and institutional infrastructure to ensure efficient production and procurement of milk.
- Creating union-owned and union-managed modern production, processing, and marketing facilities.
- Setting up dairies in major metros such as Mumbai, Kolkata, Delhi, and Chennai.
- Linking these major metros with 18 potential milk-sheds in the country and ensuring that these 18 potential milk sheds captured commanding share in these milk markets.

The funds generated through the sale of these commodities were used to build 27 rural milk sheds across 10 states and to establish dairies in rural areas and the four major metros in India. As a result, milk production increased by 60 per cent (from 20 mts in 1970 to over 32 mts in 1978). The sale of milk in major urban milk centres rose by 140 per cent. In 1974, NDDB introduced the Mother Dairy Project in Delhi as part of its initiatives to encourage milk consumption in urban areas by effective marketing of milk and milk products.

The success of Phase I encouraged the government to decide in favour of continuing Operation Flood on a larger scale. Operation Flood Phase II (1981–85) was aimed at building a National Milk Grid, linking 136 rural milk sheds with urban milk centres across 22 states and union territories in the country. This phase was implemented with a World Bank credit of 150 million US dollars and food aid from ECC (216,584 mts of skimmed milk powder, 62,402 mts of butter oil, and 16,577 mts of butter). By 1985, a self-sustaining system of 43,000 village cooperatives was established, taking the number of milk producers in them to over 4.25 million.

Between 1985 and 1987, NDDB invested over 2.81 billion rupees in Operation Flood. In 1987, the organization underwent a structural change when it was merged with the IDC (registered under the Companies Act 1956, by NDDB Act 1987). The resulting corporate body retained the name NDDB. According to reports, the objective of the merger was to avoid duplication of activities between the IDC and NDDB.

The government approved Operation Flood Phase III in 1987; once again NDDB sought the help of external sources such as the EEC and the World Bank. The funds released for Phase III (1987–96) included a 365-million-dollar credit from the World Bank, 75,000 mts of milk powder, 25,000 mts butter/butter oil from EEC, and 2.08 billion rupees from NDDB's own resources.

Phase III aimed at consolidating the gains of the earlier two phases that were linked to over 290 urban milk markets with a population of over 15 million. It focused on enabling the unions and state federations to achieve financial self-sustainability. Another aim was to adopt the salient features of the Anand Model, such as substantial expansion of dairy processing and marketing facilities, extended milk procurement infrastructure, increased promotion of milk production enhancement activities, and promotion of professional management at dairy institutions.

NDDB realised that to increase milk production in India, the milch animal breeds had to be upgraded and cross-bred with other improved varieties. Therefore, it focused on intensive R&D activities in animal husbandry. By the late 1990s, it had achieved significant progress in three major areas: artificial insemination and quantitative genetic techniques, biotechnology and genetics engineering, and embryo transfer and embryo micro-manipulation techniques. These developments resulted in the evolution of genetically improved varieties of milch animals. To encourage embryo transfers, NDDB established an embryo transfer lab at Sabarmati Ashram Gaushala, Ahmedabad. The embryo transfers and artificial insemination techniques were reported to have resulted in rapid multiplication of superior variety milch cattle in India.

NDDB also focused on improving animal feed quality, wherein the nutritional quality of the normal cattle feed was enhanced. The organization also provided a variety of vaccines and veterinary formulations through its subsidiary, Indian Immuniologicals Ltd (IIL) as part of its veterinary health care programmes.

NDDB made the movement of milk over long distances possible by using over 140 insulated rail milk tankers, each with a capacity of 40,000 litres. This enabled the National Milk Grid to efficiently perform its function of balancing regional fluctuations of milk across India. For balancing seasonal fluctuations of milk supply, large milk powder storage facilities were established. As part of its aim to encourage women to participate in the cooperative movement, NDDB, in cooperation with some NGOs, established over 6,000 women-only cooperatives across India. Through such women empowerment initiatives, NDDB aimed at indirect benefits, such as an increased percentage of children attending schools on account of increased family income. This, in turn, was expected to increase the demand for education in Indian villages.

Buoyed by the success of Operation Flood, the government brought many primary commodities such as edible oil, fruits, and vegetables under the ambit of NDDB. The government also extended the cooperative movement to tree plantation and salt farming (see Exhibit V for NDDB's cooperative initiatives in other industry sectors).

Exhibit V *Co-operative Initiatives of NDDB in Other Industry Sectors*

Edible oils and oil seeds NDDB launched the Restructuring Edible Oil and Oilseeds Production and Marketing (REOOPM) Project in 1979. This was aimed at encouraging farmers to join farmer-owned oilseeds growers' cooperative societies and at increasing farmers' investments in the oilseeds sector. By the late 1990s, there were over 900,000 farmer members in over 5,500 oilseed growers cooperatives affiliated to 18 unions across states such as Andhra Pradesh, Karnataka, Tamil Nadu, Orissa, Madhya Pradesh, Maharashtra, and Rajasthan. Facilities with a capacity to crush 3,735 tpd (tonnes per day) of oilseeds, extract 2,180 tpd of oil cake, and refine 778 tpd edible oil were established. Storage facilities that could handle up to 190,000 mts of oilseeds and 296,000 mts of oil were also built. To reduce uncertainties such as unexpected climatic fluctuations, NDDB promoted multi-oilseed cropping system by introducing non-traditional oilseed crops to farmers.

The government appointed NDDB as the Market Intervention Agency (MIA) for oilseeds and edible oil in 1989. The major responsibility of the MIA was to ensure that imported oil was not used against indigenous farmers, and to help farmers achieve self-sufficiency by ensuring them of good remuneration for their produce and by helping them to enhance oilseeds productivity. In order to establish a direct link between the producers and consumers, NDDB decided to enter the consumer pack market and launched the Dhara brand of refined rapeseed and groundnut oil. Soon, Dhara became the market leader in the branded edible oils segment, largely due to its superior quality and tamper-proof packing.

Forestry At the request of the National Wasteland Development Board (NWDB), NDDB launched a pilot project on Tree Growers' Co-operatives in 1986 across various states in India including Andhra Pradesh, Gujarat, Karnataka, Orissa, and Rajasthan. The primary objective of this project was to create self-sustaining institutions to restore the productivity in wastelands and marginally productive lands by planting fuel wood and fodder trees to fulfil local needs. This project was implemented by the National Tree Growers' Co-Operative Federation Ltd (NTGCF) between 1986 and 1987. A similar project was implemented in Uttar Pradesh in 1992–93.

Salt farming In 1987, NDDB established 'The Sabarmati Salt Farmers' Society', thus initiating the cooperative movement in the salt industry. This was aimed at reducing the dependence of salt farmers on middlemen and helping them receive a better price for their produce. Through the cooperative movement, NDDB also aimed at improving the quality of life of salt farmers, who till then had been highly exploited by traders. Towards this end, many developmental programmes such as education, medical and health care programmes were initiated.

Fruits and vegetables NDDB entered the fruits and vegetables market in 1988, when it launched its Fruit and Vegetable Project in Delhi. The project was aimed at creating a direct link between fruit and vegetable growers and consumers and was designed to handle up to 120,000 mts of fruits and vegetables annually in Delhi. By the late 1990s, NDDB had set up more than 200 specially designed modern retail outlets with a capacity of handling 1,600 kg of fruit and vegetables per day. These outlets also marketed other cooperative products such as butter, oil, cheese, and chocolates. Apart from fresh vegetables and fruits, NDDB also offered frozen vegetables (carrot, peas, cauliflower, etc.) under the Safal brand name at these outlets.

Operation Flood 'Floods' India

According to reports, by the end of 1995, approximately 20 billion rupees was invested under the three phases of Operation Flood. NDDB was reported to have earned an incremental return of over 400 billion rupees on this investment. By this time, India's milk production had increased to over 60 mts from 20 mts in 1970; the per capita availability of milk, which had declined to 107 grams per day between 1951 and 1970, increased to over 187 grams per day despite the rapid growth in population during this period.

The import of dairy commodities was negligible as compared to the total dairy throughput in India. The rural milk processing capacity was 19.4 million litres per day. Also, facilities to market over 7.2 million litres of milk per day were operational in the urban areas. Factors such as an assured market, increased income, readily available services (artificial insemination, balanced cattle feed, veterinary health care, etc.) continued to contribute to increased milk production.

By the end of Phase III, NDDB succeeded in establishing a network of multi-tier producers' cooperatives (in various industrial sectors). Care was taken to see that these bodies were democratic in structure, that they were professionally managed, and that they aimed at economic growth through social justice. According to analysts, placing technology and professional management in the hands of village cooperatives was a major reason for the improved quality of life of millions of farmers in India. They said that the cooperative model proved that true development was possible only when the instruments of development were put in the hands of the people, at whom these development programmes were aimed.

By the late 1990s, NDDB had become a financially self-sustainable body and had decided to self-finance future dairy development projects to fulfil the objectives of the Operation Flood programme. In the late 1990s, Operation Flood involved more than 10.1 million members and supplied an average of 13,659 mts of milk every day via more than 81,000 cooperative societies. These societies sent this milk to over 170 unions for processing and marketing it both as milk and as milk products.

By the late 1990s, there were over 13,377 artificial insemination centres and 787 mobile veterinary clinics across India run by NDDB. Milk and milk products such as cheese, butter, milk powder, baby food, condensed milk, and ghee were marketed across 1000 cities and towns in India by village cooperatives and the annual revenue of diary cooperatives exceeded 80 billion rupees. According to analysts, by the early twenty-first century, Operation Flood had become one of the largest and most successful rural employment programmes in the world.

Many analysts saw NDDB as a unique model of organization, innovation and development, human resource management, and cooperative development. The programme had created employment opportunities for thousands of people. Commenting on the socioeconomic changes brought about by Operation Flood, a World Bank report said: 'Operation Flood had clear benefits for the poor and women. Indirectly, it has expanded the number of children attending school because of the high income elasticity of demand for education in Indian villages.'

Analysts credited Amul's success to its commitment to the cooperative system, professional management, and the efficient and committed top management. In the early twenty-first century, Amul had nearly an 80 per cent share in the dairy market in India and its annual turnover was over 23 billion rupees (2002). Though a few brands such as Vijaya (Andhra Pradesh), Verka (Punjab), Saras (Rajasthan), Nandini (Karnataka), and Milma (Kerala) met with success, their popularity was limited to their respective regions; they could not achieve national popularity/success like Amul. However, even in the early twenty-first century, the milk market in India was dominated by the un-organized sector with 80 per cent of the market share. The organized sector was represented by three major sectors—cooperatives, private players, and the government. Thanks to the Operation Flood programme, the cooperative sector dominated the organized milk market in India in terms of milk handling, installed processing capacities, and marketing infrastructure. However, it was closely followed by the private sector, which has been constantly strengthening its presence in the market since 1991, when the government opened up the milk market for private players as part of its liberalisation policy.

The government had the least and a nearly negligible share in the organized milk market in India. In 1999, while the cooperative sector had a 49 per cent share of the total milk processing capacity in the organized milk market, the private and government sectors held 45 per cent and 6 per cent shares, respectively. With the unorganized milk market dominating the Indian milk market and with the private players posing a threat to the business of the cooperatives, through the late 1990s, NDDB intensified its efforts to spread and strengthen the dairy cooperative movement in India.

BUILDING ON SUCCESS

Since the late 1990s, NDDB has primarily focused on building on the success of Operation Flood. Its major objectives have been to increase milk and milk product exports, to spread the cooperative movement to other domestic agricultural products, and to help other developing countries replicate the success of the dairy development programme in their own countries. So, the organization has been providing extensive support to all cooperative unions in India to help them perform successfully. It has also been dovetailing its activities with those of other government agencies for dairy and agro development. NDDB has been assisting the unions in recruiting and training personnel and offering technical support in the design and selection of dairy equipment and construction of dairy plants.

In 2000, NDDB announced a 10-year plan—Perspective 2010—aimed at strengthening the cooperative movement in the dairy sector. The major objectives of Perspective 2010 were to increase milk procurement by cooperatives from 5.75 mts in 2000 to 17.8 mts by 2010, increase the number of dairy cooperative societies from 84,289 in 2000 to 1,29,480, and to increase membership in dairy cooperatives from 10.62 million in 2000 to 15.62 million by 2010. The plan also aimed at increasing the amount of milk marketed from 4.7 mts in 2000 to 14 mts by 2010.

Under Perspective 2010, NDDB identified four thrust areas that included strengthening the cooperative framework, quality and plant management, productivity enhancement and national information network (in 2003, 34 projects worth 2.9 billion rupees were under execution under these four categories and another 150 projects were in the pipeline). Analysts felt that though the goals set under Perspective 2010 were challenging, they might not be difficult for NDDB to achieve, thanks to its partnership with various federations and unions.

In 2000, NDDB established a new company, Mother Dairy Fruit and Vegetable Ltd (MDFL), by merging Mother Dairy (Delhi), and the Fruit and Vegetable Project (Delhi). This was done with the aim of efficiently marketing and distributing milk, milk products, and horticulture produce. While milk and milk products were marketed under the Mother Dairy brand name, fruits, vegetables, and related products were marketed under the Safal brand name.

Questions for Discussion

1. What role did NDDB play in developing an internal locus of control among the milk producers of the area?
2. How did NDDB turn the external locus of control (dependence on imported milk powder from advanced countries) into the internal locus of control (a sense of self-reliance and mastery over milk resources)?
3. What is the extent of the influence of NDDB in organizing farmers cooperative societies for collection and sale of milk?
4. To what other area did NDDB extend help to the village producers to shape their own destiny?

NOTES AND REFERENCES

1. Rotter, J.B. (1966). 'Generalised expectancies for internal versus external control of reinforcement', *Psychological Monograph*, 1: 1–28.
2. Weiner, Bernard (1977). *Human Motivation*. New York: Holt, Rinehart, and Winston.
3. Pareek, Udai (1988a). 'Task analysis for human resource development', in J.W. Pfeiffer (ed.), *The 1988 Annual: Developing Human Resources*. San Diego: University Associates; Pareek, Udai (1988b). Organisational Learning Diagnostics (OLD), in J.W. Pfeiffer (ed.), *The 1988 Annual: Developing Human Resources*. San Diego: University Associates.
4. Lefcourt, H.M. (1976). *Locus of Control*. Hillasdale, NJ: Lawrence Erlbaum.
5. *Ibid.*
6. McClelland, D.C. and D.C. Winter (1969). *Motivating Economic Achievement*. New York: Free Press.
7. McClelland, David C. (1965). 'Achievement motivation can be developed', *Harvard Business Review*, 23(1): 6–25.
8. Seligman, M.E.P. (1992). *Learned Optimism*. New York: Pocket Books.
9. Visintainer, M.A., J.R. Volpicelli, and M.E.P. Seligman (1982). 'Tumor rejection in rats after inescapable or escapable electric shock', *Science*, 216: 437–439.
10. Seligman, M. and M. Visintainer (1985), 'Tumor rejection and early experience by uncontrollable shock in the rat', in F.R. Brush (ed.) *Affect, Conditioning and Cognition: Essays on the Determinants of Behavior*, pp. 203–210. Hillsdale, NJ: Erlbaum.
11. Peterson, C., M.E.P. Seligman, and G.E. Vaillant (1988). 'Pessimistic explanatory style is a risk factor for physical illness: A thirty-five-year longitudinal study', *Journal of Personality and Social Psychology*, 55, 23–27.

12. Scheier, M.F., J.K. Weintraub, and C.S. Carver (1986). 'Coping with stress: Divergent strategies of optimists and pessimists', *Journal of Personality and Social Psychology*, 57, 1024–40; Scheier, M.F. and C.S. Carver (1985). 'Optimism, coping, and health: Assessment and implications of generalized outcome expectancies', *Health Psychology*, 4: 219–47.

13. Scheier, M.F., J.K. Weintraub, and C.S. Carver (1986). 'Coping with stress: Divergent strategies of optimists and pessimists', *Journal of Personality and Social Psychology*, 51: 1257–64.

14. Scheier, M.F., K.A. Matthews, J. Owens, C.J. Magovern, R.C. Lefebvre, R.A. Abbott, and C.S. Carver (1989). 'Dispositional optimism and recovery from coronary artery bypass surgery: The beneficial effects on physical and psychological well-being', *Journal of Personality and Social Psychology*, 57: 1024–1264.

15. Fitzgerald, T.E., H. Tennen, G. Affleck, and G.S. Pransky (1993). 'The relative importance of dispositional optimism and control appraisals in quality of life after coronary artery bypass surgery', *Journal of Behavioural Medicine*, 16: 25–43; Scheier. 'Dispositional optimism'.

16. Rotter. 'Generalised expectancies for internal versus external control of reinforcement'.

17. Weiner, B. (ed.) (1974). *Attribution Theory and Achievement Motivation.* New York: General Learning Press.

18. Scheier, M.F. and C.S. Carver (1985). 'Optimism, coping, and health: Assessment and implications of generalized outcome expectancies', *Health Psychology*, 4: 219–247.

19. Pareek, U. (2002). *Training instruments for HRD & OD.* New Delhi: Tata McGraw-Hill.

20. Spiegel, D. (1993). 'Psychological intervention in cancer', *Journal of National Cancer Institute*, 85(15): 1198–1205.

21. Seligman. *Learned Optimism*, Chapter 11.

22. *Ibid.*, Chapter 8 and 9.

23. *Ibid.*, 102–104.

24. Thornton, Grant (2006). International Business Owners Survey.

25. Goleman, D. (1995). *Emotional Intelligence.* New York: Bantam Books.

26. Snyder, C.R. (1994). *The Psychology of Hope: You Can Get There from Here.* New York: Free Press; Snyder, C.R. (2000). *Handbook of Hope.* San Diego, CA: Academic Press.

27. Susan Noalen Hoeksema (2000). 'The role of rumination in depressive disorders and mixed anxiety/depression symptoms', *Journal of Abnormal Psychology*, 109: 504–511.

28. Csikszentmihalyi, Mahaly (1976). *Beyond Boredom and Anxiety.* New Delhi: Jossey-Bass.

29. Flow and mindfulness: An instructional cassette. Consumer Service Division, New York.

10
Personality and Personal Effectiveness

LEARNING OBJECTIVES

After studying this chapter, you will be able to
1. Elaborate pschometric theories of personality
2. Enumerate psychodynamic theories of personality, and their main features
3. Distinguish between Type A and Type B personalities and between enlarging and enfolding lifestyles
4. Relate Holland's personality types to occupational groups
5. Discuss the three-dimensional model of personal effectiveness
6. Enumerate theories of emotion

The term personality is used in several senses. When people say 'she has a good personality', they probably refer to the person's physical appearance. When someone says that X should have a more dynamic personality, what is meant is the desired behaviour of X and so on. There is no agreement even among psychologists about the definition of 'personality'. For Carl Rogers, 'personality is an organized, consistent pattern of perception of the 'I', around which the individual interacts and has experiences.' Psychologists have attempted to describe personality in terms of standard 'traits'. Some have attempted to search for patterns to suggest 'types' of personality. Several theories have been proposed to understand, measure, and develop personality.

PSYCHOMETRIC THEORIES OF PERSONALITY

In a way, psychometric theories of personality are trait theories. A trait is a characteristic way in which an individual perceives, feels, believes, or acts. When we casually describe someone, we are likely to use trait terms, like introvert, nervous person, depressed, obsessive, intelligent.

Hans Eysenck

Hans Eysenck was the first psychologist to attempt standardisation of traits. He gave long lists of adjectives to hundreds of thousands of people and factor analysed the data to identify the key traits. Based on the results, he developed a test called the Eysenck Personality Questionnaire (EPQ).[1]

He treated the traits as dimensions, each as a continuum. He identified three basic traits: extraversion–introversion (low score for introversion, high score for extraversion), neuroticism (low score for emotional stability, high score for neurotic tendency), and psychoticism (low score for normality, high score for psychotic tendency).

R.B. Cattell

Cattell, a champion of the factor analysis methodology, believed that there are three major sources of data for personality traits: L-Data (actual records of a person's behaviour; Cattell gathered the majority of L-Data from ratings given by peers); Q-Data (self-ratings of behaviour); and T-Data (responses to objective tests).

Cattell isolated 171 traits. Finding this list too large, he extracted the following 16 primary traits through factor analysis and prepared an instrument called 16 P-F.[2]

Through factor analysis, Cattell identified what he referred to as surface and source traits. Surface traits represent clusters of correlated variables, and source traits represent the underlying structure of the personality. Cattell considered source traits much more important in understanding personality than surface traits.[3] The identified source traits became the primary basis for the 16 P-F Model.

The 16 Personality Factor Model measures personality based upon the 16 source traits shown below.

1. Warmth: Outgoing vs reserved
2. Reasoning: More intelligent vs less intelligent
3. Emotional stability: Emotionally stable vs unstable
4. Dominance: Assertive vs humble
5. Liveliness: Happy-go-lucky vs sober
6. Rule-consciousness: Conscientious vs expedient
7. Social boldness: Venturesome vs timid
8. Sensitivity: Tough-minded vs sensitive
9. Vigilance: Suspicious vs trusting
10. Abstractedness: Imaginative vs practical
11. Privateness: Shrewd vs forthright
12. Apprehension: Apprehensive vs self-assured
13. Openness to change: Experimental vs conservative
14. Self-reliance: Self-sufficient vs group dependent
15. Perfectionism: Controlled vs casual
16. Tension: Relaxed vs tense

Big Five

With further factor analysis, five basic factors were extracted.[4] This is called the five-factor theory of personality, more popularly called the 'Big Five'. Extensive research has shown that these five basic dimensions underlie all others and cover most of the significant variations in personality. The Big Five are

- Extraversion (refers to one's comfort level with relationships; individual is talkative, assertive, sociable, and outgoing)
- Agreeableness (refers to one's inclination to defer to others; individual is good-natured, cooperative, warm, caring, and trusting)

- Conscientiousness (refers to one's reliability regarding responsibility; individual is self-disciplined, hardworking, organized, dependable, and persistent)
- Emotional stability (refers to one's ability to withstand stress; individual is calm, happy, and secure)
- Openness to experience (refers to one's range of interests and fascination with novelty; individual is creative, curious, intellectual, imaginative, and artistically sensitive)

PSYCHODYNAMIC THEORIES

While psychometric theories use factor analysis and statistical analysis, psychodynamic theories emphasise psychological processes and use conceptual models based on clinical experience. Significant contributions have been made by these theories. We shall briefly discuss the major ones here.

Sigmund Freud

Sigmund Freud has made tremendous impact in psychology. His theory is quite complex and covers many dimensions. We shall briefly review his concepts of the structure of psyche, stages of development, and defence mechanisms.

Structure of psyche   Freud proposed the concept of the structure of psyche in terms of Id, Ego, and Superego. According to Freud, we are born with Id. The Id is an important part of our personality because it allows us to get our basic needs met when we are newborns. Freud believed that the Id is based on the pleasure principle. In other words, the Id wants whatever feels good at the time, with no consideration for the reality of the situation. When a child is hungry, the Id wants food, and therefore the child cries. The Id does not care about reality, about the needs of anyone else, only its own satisfaction.

Over the next 3 years, as the child interacts more and more with the world, the second part of the personality, the ego, begins to develop. The ego is based on the reality principle. It meets the needs of the Id, while taking into consideration the reality of the situation.

By the age of five, the Superego develops. The Superego is our moral part, and develops with the influence of and sanctions by role models and other significant persons.

According to Freud, the Ego is the strongest in a healthy person, and does the balancing act, satisfying the needs of the Id, and not weakening the Superego. If the Id gets too strong, impulses and self-gratification take over the person's life. If the Superego becomes too strong, the person would be driven by rigid morals, would be judgmental and unbending.

Freud also proposed a topographic model of the psyche, in terms of three layers: unconscious, conscious, and subconscious. He believed that most of what drives us is buried in our unconscious, and continues to impact us dramatically. Everything we are aware of is stored in our conscious, which is only a small part of our psyche.

The final part is the preconscious or subconscious. We can access it if prompted, but it is not in our active consciousness.

Stages of psychosexual development

Freud's Stages of Psychosexual Development are important for personality development. Their successful completion is likely to result in a healthy personality, and their failure may lead to an unhealthy personality. During each stage, an unsuccessful completion means that a child becomes fixated on that particular erogenous zone and either over- or under-indulges once he or she becomes an adult. There are four stages of development. We briefly discuss below these stages. Later, in another chapter, we shall discuss implication of these stages for leadership development.

Oral stage   (birth to 18 months) During the oral stage, the child is focused on oral pleasures (sucking). Too much or too little gratification can result in an Oral Fixation or Oral Personality, which is evidenced by a preoccupation with oral activities. This type of personality may have a stronger tendency to smoke, drink alcohol, overeat, or bite his or her nails. Personality-wise, these individuals may become overly dependent upon others, gullible, and perpetual followers. On the other hand, they may also fight these urges and develop pessimism and aggression towards others.

Anal stage   (18 months to 3 years) The child's focus of pleasure in this stage is on eliminating and retaining faeces. Through society's pressure, mainly via parents, the child has to learn to control anal stimulation. In terms of personality, after effects of an anal fixation during this stage can result in an obsession with cleanliness, perfection, and control (anal retentive). On the opposite end of the spectrum, they may become messy and disorganized (anal expulsive).

Phallic stage   (3 years to 6 years) The pleasure zone switches to the genitals. Freud believed that during this stage boys develop unconscious sexual desires for their mothers. Because of this, they become rivals with their fathers and see their fathers as competition for their mothers' affection. Boys also develop a fear of their fathers' punishment for these feelings, such as the fear of being castrated by them. This group of feelings is known as Oedipus Complex (after the Greek story of Oedipus, who accidentally killed his father and married his mother).

Later it was added that girls go through a similar situation, developing unconscious sexual attraction to their fathers. It has been termed the Electra Complex by more recent psychoanalysts.

According to Freud, out of fear of castration, and due to the strong competition of his father, a boy eventually decides to identify with the father rather than fight him. By identifying with his father, the boy develops masculine characteristics and identifies himself as a male, and represses his sexual feelings towards his mother. A fixation at this stage could result in sexual deviancies (both overindulging and avoidance) and weak or confused sexual identity according to psychoanalysts.

Genital stage   (puberty onwards) The final stage of psychosexual development begins at the start of puberty when sexual urges are once again awakened. Through the lessons learned during the previous stages, adolescents direct their sexual urges onto opposite sex. This is the final stage of maturation.

Psychological types   Freud's four phases of psycho-sexual development (oral, anal, phallic, and genital) can be used to describe four types of personality (Freud, in fact, used these terms): erotic (dependent), obsessive (orderly), narcissistic (independent), and detached (interdependent). Freud elaborated on only the first three types. The various traits of these types are summarised in Exhibit 10.1.[5]

Exhibit 10.1   *Freudian Personality Types*

Stage	Personality stage of psycho-sexual development	Type
1	Erotic (oral)	Optimistic, manipulative, cocky, gullible
2	Obsessive (anal)	Stingy, stubborn, orderly, meticulous
3	Narcissistic (phallic)	Vain, brash, courageous, stylish
4	Detached (genital)	Democratic, building systems, linking with others, situation specific

Stewart, based on McClelland's theory of power (using Freud's framework), developed a scoring system to measure what she called psycho-social maturity. A scoring manual for these four stages (better called types) has been published.[6]

Ego defence mechanisms

As we have stated, the Ego does a balancing act of satisfying both the Id and the Superego. The Ego has some tools it can use in its balancing function, tools that help to defend the Ego. These are called ego defence mechanisms or defences. These are shown in Exhibit 10.2.[7]

Exhibit 10.2   *Main Defence Mechanisms*

Defences with description	Examples
Denial arguing against an anxiety provoking stimuli by stating it does not exist	Denying that your physician's diagnosis of cancer is correct and seeking a second opinion
Displacement taking out impulses on a less threatening target	Slamming a door instead of hitting at the person; yelling at your spouse after an argument with your boss
Intellectualisation avoiding unacceptable emotions by focusing on the intellectual aspects	Focusing on the details of a funeral as opposed to the sadness and grief
Projection placing unacceptable impulses in yourself onto someone else	When losing an argument, you state 'You're just stupid'; homophobia
Rationalisation supplying a logical or rational reason as opposed to the real reason	Stating that you were fired because you didn't kiss up the boss, when the real reason was your poor performance

(Contd)

Exhibit 10.2 (Contd)

Defences with description	Examples
Reaction formation taking the opposite belief because the true belief causes anxiety	Having a bias against a particular race or culture and then embracing that race or culture to the extreme
Regression returning to a previous stage of development	Sitting in a corner and crying after hearing bad news; throwing a temper tantrum when you do not get your way
Repression pulling into the unconscious	Forgetting sexual abuse from your childhood due to the trauma and anxiety
Sublimation acting out unacceptable impulses in a socially acceptable way	Chanelalising your aggressive impulses toward a career as a boxer; becoming a surgeon because of your desire to cut; lifting weights to release 'pent up' energy
Suppression pushing into the unconscious	Trying to forget something that causes you anxiety

Source: Cramer, P. (1991) *The Development of Defence Mechanisms*, New York: Springer-Verlag.

Ego defences are not necessarily unhealthy as you can see by the examples above. The lack of these defences or the inability to use them can often lead to problems in life. However, we sometimes employ the defences at the wrong time or overuse them, which can be equally dysfunctional.

Alfred Adler

Some of Freud's associates had differences with him, and propounded their own theories. Alfred Adler was the first one. For Adler, the main driving force for human beings is *striving for superiority*. According to Adler everyone has a sense of inferiority. According to him, the feeling of inferiority makes people overcome it by their accomplishments. However, excessive feeling of inferiority can also have the opposite effect. Without the needed successes, one can develop an inferiority complex.

Adler identified two parental styles that are likely to cause problems in adulthood: pampering and neglect. Overprotecting a child, giving him too much attention, and sheltering him from the negative realities of life will make him ill-equipped to deal with these realities, may cause him to doubt his own abilities or decision-making skills, and may result in his seeking out others to replace the safety he once enjoyed as a child.

On the other extreme is what Adler called neglect. A neglected child is one who is not protected at all from the world and is forced to face life's struggles alone. This child may grow up to fear the world, have a strong sense of mistrust for others, and may have a difficult time forming intimate relationships.

The best approach, according to this theory, is to protect children from the evils of the world but not shelter children from them. In more practical terms, it means allowing them to hear or see the negative aspects of the world while still feeling the safety of parental influence. In other words, do not immediately go to the school principal if your child is getting bullied, but rather teach your child how to respond or take care of herself at school.

Adler believed that the order in which one is born affects one's personality. First-born children get excessive attention and pampering by their parents, until the little brother or sister arrives. Suddenly they are no longer the centre of attention. They are left feeling inferior. The firstborn children often have the greatest number of problems as they get older. Middle-born children have a high need for superiority and are often able to seek it out such as through healthy competition.

The youngest child, like the first-born, may be more likely to experience personality problems later in life. The child grows up knowing that he has the least amount of power in the whole family. He also gets pampered and protected more than any other child did. This could leave him with a sense that he cannot take on the world alone and will always be inferior to others.

Carl Jung and MBTI

Jung broke away from Freud, and had some basic differences. Jung believed that there were fears, behaviours, and thoughts that children and adults exhibit that are remarkably similar across time and culture. He believed that this was more than coincidence and represented what he called the *collective unconscious*. Jung described many archetypes in his writings—three of which have received a lot of attention and thought: the animus/anima, the shadow, and the self. The animus is the masculine side of the female and the anima is the feminine side of the male. We all have an unconscious opposite gender hidden within us and the role of this archetype is to guide us towards the perfect mate.

The shadow is basically the unconscious negative or dark side of our personality. In Judeo-Christian writings, according to Jung, the shadow archetype is called the Devil. Finally, the self-archetype is the unifying part of all of us that finds balance in our lives. Working with the ego (which is partly in our personal unconscious), it helps us manage the other archetypes and helps us feel complete.[8]

Carl Jung is most known for the theory behind the well-known instrument MBTI. Based on his basic elements of human psyche, a mother–daughter team developed a 100-item instrument, popularly called MBTI (Myers-Briggs type indicator).[9] MBTI is the most widely used instrument for personality analysis. Sixteen personality types are generated by the instrument (a person can be of any one type). These 16 types are based on a combination of four basic elements of psyche (see Exhibit 10.3).

Exhibit 10.3 *Four Jungian Aspects of MBTI Framework*

Aspects	Characteristics
Source of energy Extroversion (E)	Outgoing; speaks, then thinks. Relates more easily to the outer world of people and things than to the inner world of ideas.
Introversion (I)	Reflective; thinks, then speaks. Relates more easily to the inner world of ideas than to the outer world of people.

(Contd)

Exhibit 10.3 (*Contd*)

Aspects	Characteristics
Collecting information	
Sensing (S)	Practical, concrete. Would work with known facts than look for possibilities and relationships.
Intuiting (N)	Theoretical, abstract. Would look for possibilities and relationships than work with known facts.
Decision making	
Thinking (T)	Analytical (head). Relies more on interpersonal analysis and logic than on personal values.
Feeling (F)	Subjective (heart). Relies more on personal values than on impersonal analysis and logic.
Understanding the world	
Judging (J)	Structured, organized. Likes a planned and orderly way of life rather than a flexible, spontaneous way.
Perceiving (P)	Flexible, spontaneous. Likes a flexible, spontaneous way rather than a planned and orderly way of life.

Combining these four aspects, we get the following sixteen types of personality (Exhibit 10.4). Each type has its own dynamics. A detailed description is available in the MBTI literature.

Exhibit 10.4   *Combination of Four Jungian Aspects for 16 Personality Types*

ISTJ	ESTJ	INTJ	ENTJ
ISTP	ESTP	INTP	ENTP
ISFJ	ESFJ	INFJ	ENFJ
ISFP	ESFP	INFP	ENFP

Research has shown that most managers are of the ESTJ type. Landrum has given profiles of 13 contemporary business executives and all were NTs (intuitive thinkers).

Erik Erikson

Erikson's two major contributions to psychodynamic thought include a reappraisal of the ego and an extended view of the developmental stages.

He saw the ego as a positive driving force in human development and personality. As such, he believed the ego's main job was to establish and maintain a sense of identity. A person with a strong sense of identity is one who knows where he is in life and has a sense of uniqueness while also having a sense of belonging and wholeness. According to Erikson, an identity crisis is a situation when a person lacks direction, feels unproductive, and does not feel a strong sense of identity. He believed that we all have identity crises at one time or the other in our lives and that these crises do not necessarily represent a negative; rather they can be a driving force towards positive resolution.

Erikson's stages of psychosocial development

Erikson postulated the following eight stages. Failure to successfully complete a stage can result in a reduced ability to complete further stages and therefore a more unhealthy personality and sense of self.

Trust vs mistrust   From birth to age one, children begin to learn the ability to trust others, based upon the consistency of their caregiver(s). If trust develops successfully, the child gains confidence and security in the world around him and is able to feel secure even when threatened.

Autonomy vs shame and doubt   Between the ages of one and three, children begin to assert their independence, by walking away from their mother, picking which toy to play with, and making choices about what they like to wear, eat, etc. If children in this stage are encouraged and supported in their increased independence, they become more confident and secure in their own ability to survive in the world. If children are criticised, overly controlled, or not given the opportunity to assert themselves, they begin to feel inadequate in their ability to survive, and may then become overly dependent upon others, lack self-esteem, and feel a sense of shame or doubt in their own abilities.

Initiative vs guilt   Around age three and continuing to age six, children assert themselves more frequently. They begin to plan activities, make up games, and initiate activities with others. If given this opportunity, children develop a sense of initiative, and feel secure in their ability to lead others and make decisions. Conversely, if this tendency is squelched, either through criticism or control, children develop a sense of guilt. They may feel like a nuisance to others and will therefore remain followers, lacking in self-initiative.

Industry vs inferiority   From age 6 to puberty, children begin to develop a sense of pride in their accomplishments. They initiate projects, see them through to completion, and feel good about what they have achieved. During this time, teachers play an increased role in the child's development. If children are encouraged and reinforced for their initiative, they begin to feel industrious and feel confident in their ability to achieve goals. If this initiative is not encouraged, if it is restricted by parents or teacher, then the child begins to feel inferior, doubting his own abilities and therefore may not reach his potential.

Identity vs role confusion   Adolescence, the transition from childhood to adulthood, is most important. Children become more independent, and begin to look at the future in terms of career, relationships, families, housing, etc. During this period, they explore possibilities and begin to form their own identity based upon the outcome of their explorations. This sense of who they are can be hindered, which results in a sense of confusion ('I don't know what I want to be when I grow up') about themselves and their role in the world.

Intimacy vs isolation Occurring in young adulthood, we begin to share ourselves more intimately with others. We explore relationships leading towards long-term commitments with someone other than a family member. Successful completion can lead to comfortable relationships and a sense of commitment, safety, and care within a relationship. Avoiding intimacy, fearing commitment and relationships can lead to isolation, loneliness, and sometimes depression.

Generativity vs stagnation During middle adulthood, we establish our careers, settle down within a relationship, begin our own families and develop a sense of being a part of the bigger picture. We give back to society through raising our children, being productive at work, and becoming involved in community activities and organizations. By failing to achieve these objectives, we become stagnant and feel unproductive.

Ego integrity vs despair As we grow older and become senior citizens, we tend to slow down our productivity, and explore life as a retired person. It is during this time that we contemplate our accomplishments and are able to develop integrity if we see ourselves as leading a successful life. If we see our lives as unproductive, feel guilt about our pasts, or feel that we did not accomplish our life goals, we become dissatisfied with life and develop despair, often leading to depression and hopelessness.

Transactional Analysis

One of the popular theories of personality and human development is transactional analysis (TA), originated by Eric Berne.[10] Departing from classical psychoanalysis, Berne used simple day-to-day language to explain the dynamics of personality and its application for human development. His theory has the following components:

1. *Structural analysis*, proposing the main structure of a personality in terms of three ego states.
2. *Interaction analysis*, explaining the dynamics of interpersonal communication in terms of transactions between ego states of A and B.
3. *Life-position analysis*, suggesting the four positions individuals adopt in their transaction with the outside world.
4. *Games analysis*, discussing ulterior transactions leading to a pay-off.
5. *Script analysis*, detailing of specific life dramas that people compulsively play out.

For our purposes, two of the above are especially relevant—structural analysis and life-position analysis. However, we shall briefly explain the other aspects of TA also.

Structural analysis

Structural analysis deals with the structure of the personality. A personality consists of three ego states. Berne defined an ego state as 'a consistent pattern of feeling and experience directly related to a corresponding consistent pattern of behaviour'.[11] He used everyday language for his concepts. He called the three ego states Parent, Adult, and Child.

The Parent ego-state is 'a set of feelings, attitudes and behaviour patterns which resemble those of the parental figure'.[12] The Adult ego-state is 'an autonomous set of feelings, attitudes and behaviour patterns which are adapted to the current reality'. And the Child ego-state is 'a set of feelings, attitudes and behaviour patterns which are relics of the individual's own childhood'.

There are two main Parental functions—nurturing and, what Berne called, controlling. Nurturing is done by providing needed support. Controlling behaviour (of others) is done through prescriptions (instructing in detail what should be done and how) and sanctions (punishing that behaviour which the Parent disapproves of). The main focus of the Parent seems to be on values and norms.

The Adult ego-state has the function of collecting and processing information in the present. It responds to reality. The Adult works like a computer, without any values or emotions.

The Child ego-state has several aspects. These were named Natural Child (curious, fun-loving), Rebellious Child (revolting against authority), and Adapted Child (the ego-state under the influence of the Parent). All these relate to emotions.

Interaction analysis

A transaction is the act of communication or interaction between two people. A transaction starts with a stimulus and ends with a response to the stimulus. Since each individual involved in the transaction has three ego-states, the transactions are between the various ego-states.

When A sends a message, B receives it; B then responds and this response is received by A. This is one transaction. A person can send a prescriptive or admonishing message (from what is called the Parent ego-state), an information message (from the Adult), or a feeling message (from the Child). Any of these messages may be sent to (and received by) one of the three ego-states of the other person (Parent, Adult, or Child). If the response is by the same ego-state as the one that received the message, it is called a complementary or parallel transaction. Such transactions are very satisfying. These are shown in Exhibit 10.5.

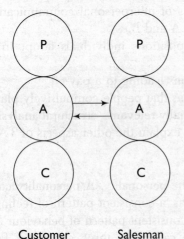

Customer   Salesman

Customer: What is the price of the watch?
Salesman: Rs 400.

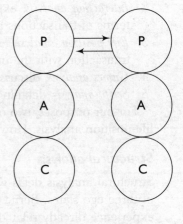

Boss   Subordinate

Boss: Our values are getting eroded.
Subordinate: I agree with you. We are deteriorating every day.

Exhibit 10.5   *Complementary Transactions* (Contd)

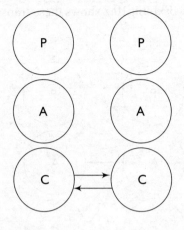

Subordinate   Boss

Subordinate: Would you like to go to the
                  magic show? I have two tickets.
Boss: Sure, let's go.

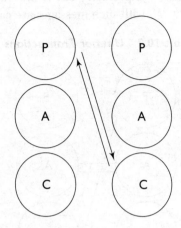

Boss   Subordinate

Boss: You are late again.
Subordinate: I am sorry, sir.

The response, however, may not originate from the ego-state that has received the message. Then it is a *crossed transaction*. Exhibit 10.6 gives examples of crossed transactions.

Exhibit 10.6   *Crossed Transactions*

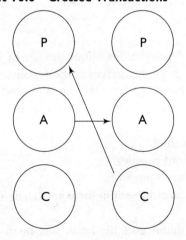

Boss: Is the report ready?
Subordinate: Do you think I have no
                  other work to do?

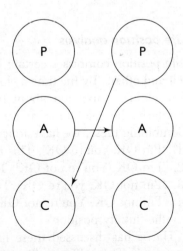

Subordinate: I want to discuss the resources that
                  I need to complete the assignment.
Boss: You are always complaining.

The message sent may not be a simple one. To use TA terminology, a message sent may have two targets (ego states). There may be an overt message (open and expressed), but it may also contain a covert message (a hidden one). Transactions with such messages are called *ulterior transactions*. Exhibit 10.7 shows these transactions.

Exhibit 10.7 *Ulterior Transactions*

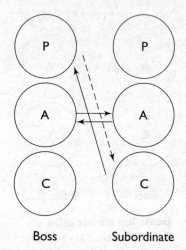

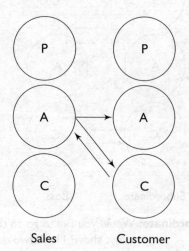

Boss: What is the date today?
Overt message (A ⟶ A) asking date
Covert message (P ⟶ C) You are late again!
Subordinate: Sir, I shall definitely send the
report tomorrow. (C ⟶ P)

Salesperson: This shirt is rather expensive, especially
tailored for exclusive tastes.
Overt message (A ⟶ A) giving information.
Covert message (A ⟶ C) It is beyond your
capacity to buy.
Customer: I shall buy it. (C ⟶ A)

Life position analysis

Life position comprises certain deeply ingrained convictions about the worth of the self and others. By the time a child is ready for school, he arrives at these convictions. The child's conviction about himself may either be 'I'm OK' or 'I'm not OK'. Similarly, he may look at others and think: 'You're OK' or 'You're not OK'. Combining these, we have four life positions:

1. 'I'm OK, you're OK'. This is the healthy position.
2. 'I'm OK, You're not OK'. This is the paranoid position.
3. 'I'm not OK, you're OK'. This is the depressive position.
4. 'I'm not OK, You're not OK'. This is the schizoid position, or what Berne called the 'futility position'.

Harris has discussed these life positions in detail and his book has been quite popular.[13] These life positions can be used to understand one's style of working with others. Style is a consistent and stable way of interacting with others. The four general interactional or transactional styles can be depicted as shown in Exhibit 10.8.

Exhibit 10.8 *General Transactional Styles in the Four Life Positions*

	I'm not OK	I'm OK
You're not OK	**A** Avoidant/averse	**B** Bossing
You're OK	**D** Diffident	**C** Competent Confident/creative

Games analysis

A game is 'a series of ulterior transactions with a gimmick, leading to a well-defined pay-off'. A gimmick is a 'snare' or 'a concealed motivation'. Games analysis occupies a very important position in TA theory and therapy. Berne's well-known book describes more than 30 games people habitually play, such as 'kick me', 'Yes ... but'.[14] Later Berne introduced another element in his theory of games, summed up in the following formula that contains the six phases of a game[15]:

$$C + G = R \rightarrow S \rightarrow X \rightarrow P$$

According to this, Con plus Gimmick is equal to Response, which leads to Switch, which leads to Crossup, ending in Pay-off. 'The initiator of the game begins by issuing her Con. This is an ulterior invitation to the other person to join her in playing the game. The second person then reveals his Gimmick, a weakness or need, which makes him respond to the Con. Following this Response, the first player suddenly shifts her ground, making the Switch. Both players then feel a moment of confusion, the Crossup ('X'). Immediately afterwards, they both collect a Pay-off of bad feelings.'[16]

Berne himself gave this illustration of a brief game: '... a patient asked: 'Do you think I'll get better, doctor?' And the sentimental therapist replied 'Of course you will.' At that point the patient revealed her ulterior motive in asking the question. Instead of saying 'Thank you,' as in a straight transaction, she pulled the switch with, 'What makes you think you know everything?'[17] This reply crossed the therapist up and threw him off balance for a moment, which is what the patient wanted to do. Then the game ended—the patient feeling elated at having conned the therapist, and the therapist feeling frustrated; and those were the payoffs.

'This game followed the formula precisely. The Con was the original question, and the Gimmick was the therapist's sentimentality. When the Con hooked into the Gimmick, he responded in the way she expected. Then she pulled the Switch, causing a Crossup, after which each collected a Payoff.'

Script analysis

According to Berne, every person decides in early childhood how he or she will live and will die, and this plan is called the script. Script analysis is a sophisticated and complex part of TA. Steiner has done extensive work on script analysis and his book on the subject is well known.[18] Although Berne suggested seven elements in the script apparatus, the following four have been generally accepted:

Pay-off or curse This is the way the parents tell the children to end their life. Verbal or non-verbal parental messages to children may be 'drop dead' or 'long life', etc. According to Berne, the script pay-off will not take effect unless it is accepted by the children.

Injunctions or stoppers An injunction is an unfair negative command from the parent. For example, 'Get lost' or 'Don't be smart'. These are accepted by the child if these are accompanied by punishment for violating them and are repeated several times. Berne used the term 'stopper' to convey the quality by which an injunction may stop a person in his or her tracks whenever it is replayed later in life.

Counterscript While script pay-offs and injunctions are given to the child in his early years (up to about 6 years), counterscript messages are communicated in later childhood. Such messages are in the form of slogans, proverbs, etc. For example, 'work hard', 'save money', and 'be good'. These determine the person's style, while the script pay-off determines his or her destiny, according to Berne.

Programme or pattern Programme is what the parent teaches the child to do in order to live out the script. Modelling is the most frequent way of communicating the programme. These are known as process script types. Berne suggested six types as follows.[19]

Never The person with this script follows the motto: 'I never get what I most want.' He is like the Greek hero Tantalus, who was condemned to spend eternity in sight of food and water but never to eat or drink again.

Always This is exemplified by Arachne, who challenged the goddess Minerva to a contest in needlework and was unwise enough to win. As a punishment she was changed into a spider, condemned to spin her web for ever and ever. The person with this script adopted it in response to a message from his or her parents: 'If that's what you want to do, then you can just spend the rest of your life doing it.'

Until 'I've spent some time with the bad.' This is typified by Jason, who could not become a king until he had performed a set of tasks.

After This is the converse of Until. Its pattern is: 'I can get the good now, but I'll pay for it by getting the bad tomorrow.' The mythical correspondence is with Damocles, who feasted while a sword hung above his head suspended by a single horsehair.

Over and Over (now called *Almost*) We see this pattern in the myth of Sisyphus. He was condemned to spend eternity rolling a heavy rock to the top a hill. Each time he almost made it, the rock would slip from his grasp and roll all the way back down again.

Open-ended Berne called this the 'pie in the sky' scenario. In this pattern, the person comes to a specific point in his or her life, then finds he or she has carried out all the parental directives in his or her script and does not know what to do next. The associated myth is that of Philemon and Baucis, who were transformed into laurel trees to stand motionless beside each other for all time.

Though the process script patterns may have suggested themselves to Berne on the basis of Greek myths, the evidence for their existence lies in empirical observation. This evidence gives clear support for the existence of these script patterns in reality. These script patterns apply cross-culturally and appear not to be dependent on age, gender, education, or other features of personal background.

LIFESTYLE APPROACH

From the point of view of broad lifestyles, two types of personalities have been identified—Type A and Type B. Type As work under continuous time pressure, enjoy working against deadlines, and in fact create deadlines for themselves. As a result, they generally suffer from hypertension. Type Bs are relaxed and enjoy leisure. A contrasting picture of the two types is shown in Exhibit 10.9.

Exhibit 10.9 *Characteristics of Type A and Type B Personality*

Type A	Type B
Are impatient with the rate of work	Never feel urgency and are patient
Move and eat rapidly	Are relaxed, eat in a leisurely fashion, and enjoy themselves
Want to measure everything	Do not display their achievements
Do several things simultaneously	Play for fun rather than to prove themselves

Another framework of managerial lifestyles suggests two types. Based on an in-depth and longitudinal study of successful (showing fast upward movement) and less successful executives in a well-known organization, a number of factors associated with career and role successes and failures were identified.[20] Two distinct patterns emerged from grouping these. The one associated with career/job success was called the *enlarging style,* while the other, associated with less career/job success, was called the *enfolding style.*

The enlarging lifestyle is oriented towards the goals of innovation, change, and growth. The enlarger moves away from tradition and places emphasis on adaptation, self-development, and the extension of influence outward into the spheres of work and community. Such an individual looks for responsibility on the job and is also likely to seek and achieve a position of influence in organizations. Self-development activities are stressed. Thus, enlargers are likely not only to read, attend the theatre, and keep up with current events, they might also take courses in physical fitness and respond to promptings regarding health foods. At the same time, their early ties to parents and formal religious practices weaken. The established 'enlarger' finds that his or her values have changed so dramatically that he or she no longer enjoys the company of childhood friends. Except for a certain nostalgia when visiting parents and relatives, the enlarger is not satisfied with the ties of yesterday. A complete commitment to religion is similarly less meaningful, particularly since an enlarger makes every effort to see alternative points of view and to lend himself or herself to new experiences of all varieties. This does not mean that he or she breaks off from the religious group entirely, but it can happen.

The enfolding lifestyle is oriented to the goals of tradition, stability, and inward strength. Rather than pitching strength outwards, the enfolder seeks to cultivate and consolidate that which invites attention within his or her familiar sphere. The enfolder is not a member of social or community organizations. When this individual does enter into such activities, he or she rarely seeks an active role. Such an individual values parental ties and, if possible, seeks to continue an active relationship with childhood friends. The enfolder may find it quite upsetting to leave his or her hometown even if the move portends job advancement. In a new place, he or she is likely to experience considerable difficulty feeling at home. This is not a person likely to attend night college or to study on his or her own time unless assured that such efforts will bring direct rewards at work. He or she may begin a self-improvement programme, but the enfolder's heart is seldom in it. The enfolder likes to settle into a job and see it through to a full conclusion, getting great satisfaction from a job well done. He or she is not awed by fads. This individual forms a close attachment to a small circle of friends and most of his or her socialisation is restricted to relatives. Status considerations sometimes embarrass an enfolder, who values informality and sincerity in human affairs. Bray et al. describe an enfolder as follows: 'It seems that he has been reluctant to take transfers in the past, especially during times of family stress when his wife was near delivery in a pregnancy (they now have four children), when his father was about to have an operation, and so forth. The couple have had to move four times in the past eight years, and even though they were distantly removed from their parents on only one of these occasions, neither he nor his wife have been happy with the company's seeming policy of uprooting its managers every few years. Peers and superiors have told him in the past that his attitude is not conducive to upward mobility on the job, but he had not been able to see their point at the time. It seemed to him that it was in the company's interest to keep their employees happy' (p. 109). Further, 'he values a rich family life, loves to play with his children and seems to be a perfect husband and father ... He likes to grow things and apparently has quite a green thumb ... He has thought about leaving the Bell system to enter his own business, but he lacks capital and has some doubts about whether the move would be worth the risk .... In many ways he believes himself to be a success in life, in view of his happy home life, good health and satisfying work (for he does like the actual work that he does). One could not consider this man to be unhappy, except in the sense that he feels somewhat embarrassed about his lack of advancement' (pp. 110–111).

PERSONALITY–JOB FIT THEORY

Holland has proposed a 'personality–job fit' theory of personality.[21] This theory makes a case for job-specific personality types. He has suggested six personality types and has prepared an instrument containing 160 occupational titles. Based on respondents' preferences, their personality profiles are prepared. Exhibit 10.10 gives the six groups of occupations and the related personality types.

Exhibit 10.10   Holland's Personality Types for Occupational Groups

Occupational groups	Preferred mode	Personality types
Mechanics, operators, assembly line workers, farmers	Physical, requiring strength and coordination	Realistic
Biologists, economists, mathematicians, news reporters	Thinking, understanding, and organizing	Investigative
Teachers, social workers, counsellors, clinical psychologists	Helping and developing people	Social
Accountants, managers, bank workers, clerks	Precise, orderly, rule regulated	Conventional
Lawyers, real estate agents, PROs, small entrepreneurs	Verbal, impacting people	Enterprising
Painters, musicians, interior decorators, writers	Imaginative, emotional, ambiguous	Artistic

PERSONAL EFFECTIVENESS

While personality measurement helps us to see a consistent pattern in a person's orientation, individuals with different types of personalities can be equally effective. What are the aspects of personal effectiveness? One precondition for personal effectiveness is better self-awareness. But only understanding oneself does not make a person effective. One simple model for self-awareness that is widely used is the Johari Window, developed by Luft and Ingham.[22] In this model, there are two main dimensions for understanding the self—those aspects of a person's behaviour and style that are known to him or her (self) and those aspects of behaviour that are known to those with whom he or she interacts (others). A combination of these two dimensions reveals four areas of knowledge about the self (Exhibit 10.11).

Exhibit 10.11   Johari Window

	Known to self	Not known to self
Known to others	A — Arena	B — Blind
Not known to others	C — Closed	D — Dark

The upper left-hand square is the arena or the public self—that part of an individual's behaviour known both to himself or herself and to those with whom the individual interacts. The arena includes information such as name, age, physical appearance, and familial or organizational affiliations.

The blind area contains those aspects of the person's behaviour and style that others know, but the person himself or herself does not know. A person may have mannerisms of which he or she is unaware but which are perceived by others as funny, annoying, or pleasing. For example, an individual might be surprised to hear that her method of asking questions annoys others, who interpret it as cross-examination rather than curiosity or a request for information.

The closed area involves that which is known to the person but not revealed to others—things in this area are secret. For example, a subordinate may be annoyed if a supervisor does not ask him or her to sit down during a meeting but will remain standing without letting the supervisor know of this annoyance. The supervisor may think that the subordinate does not mind standing and accept the behaviour as part of their hierarchical relationship. Most of us have many such feelings in our closed areas that we are unwilling to reveal to the persons concerned.

The fourth area is dark, inaccessible to both the self and others. Some psychologists believe that this is a very large area indeed and that certain circumstances (e.g., an accident), a particular stage of one's life, or special techniques such as psychoanalysis or psychodynamics may suddenly reveal to a person some of the hidden aspects of the self. Since the dark area cannot be consciously controlled or changed, this discussion will be limited to the arena, the blind, and the closed areas.

In the Johari Window model, the size of the arena or open space is critical for personal effectiveness. The arena increases in proportion to the decrease in the blind and the closed areas.

Openness

Openness is critical for personal effectiveness. It has two aspects—self-disclosure (sharing with others what they do not seem to know about one-self) and use of feedback (being open to what others say on aspects that one may not be aware of). In addition, perceptiveness or sensitivity to others' feelings and to non-verbal cues is also important. Let us look at these three aspects.

Self-disclosure The extent to which one shares ideas, feelings, experiences, impressions, perceptions, and various other personal data with others shows one's degree of openness, which is an important quality and contributes a great deal to a person's effectiveness.

Openness in combination with perceptiveness and communication makes a person much more effective. But openness alone is often misunderstood as 'sharing everything with everyone'. Pfeiffer and Jones have used the term 'Carolesque openness' to describe openness without an accompanying sensitivity to others in the situation.[23] The word was coined from Carol's behaviour in the movie *Bob & Carol & Ted & Alice*. Carol, recently 'turned on' by a weekend growth centre experience, pours out her feelings in a way that embarrasses her dinner companions and confronts a waiter with 'feeling data'. Although such behaviour may indicate that the person is 'in touch' with his or her own feelings, it also indicates that he or she is out of touch with the feelings of others.

Pfeiffer and Jones suggest that destructive openness can result from an inordinate value being placed upon 'telling it like it is, from insensitivity to the recipients of the communication, or from a desire to be punitive'. They suggest what they call strategic openness as an alternative, that is, 'determining how much open data flow the system can stand, and then giving it about a ten per cent boost'.

Openness can be characterised as effective, firstly, if the person sees that sharing what he or she wants to share is appropriate. Inappropriate sharing does not contribute to effective openness. For example, a typical task group is usually an inappropriate place for a person to share marital problems. Secondly, openness can be characterised as effective if the person is aware of what his or her openness is likely to do to others. Those who practice openness by calling others names or pouring out all their feelings are unlikely to be effective. For example, a supervisor who takes out his or her anger on a subordinate without taking into consideration that person's ability to process and use the data generated will not be effective. The supervisor would be better advised to listen to the subordinate and share his or her concerns in a manner that will help the subordinate use the data received.

Receiving feedback   Feedback on those aspects of a person about which others are aware but the person is not, may be positive or negative. Generally, there is no problem with a positive feedback.

Congratulations! You have all emerged as achievers at this year's adventure camp. Now translate your experience in the workplace.

Negative feedback, however, creates a dissonance with the self-image and may be threatening to the ego. When one receives negative feedback (e.g., if one is criticised or blamed), one generally tends to use defensive behaviour to deal with the feedback.

Exhibit 10.12 summarises the various defensive (and its alternative, confronting) behaviours to deal with negative feedback. These are discussed further in Chapter 17.

Exhibit 10.12 *Defensive and Confronting Behaviour in Dealing with Feedback*

Defensive behaviour	Confronting behaviour
Denial	Owning up
Rationalisation	Self-analysis
Projection	Empathy
Displacement	Exploration
Quick acceptance	Data collection
Withdrawal	Expressing feelings
Aggression	Help seeking
Humour	Concern
Competition with authority	Listening
Cynicism	Positive critical attitude
Intellectualisation	Sharing of concern
Generalisation	Experimenting
Pairing	Relating to the group
Results in a conflicted self	*Results in an integrated self*

Defensive behaviour in dealing with threatening feedback is like using pain-killing drugs to deal with pain—it merely reduces one's awareness of the pain. Defensive behaviour may create an illusion of having dealt with the situation, but does not change the situation or behaviour. For example, if a subordinate receives negative feedback from a superior officer saying that his or her motivation in the past year has been low, the former may feel threatened. He or she may then reduce the threat by projecting his or her own anger on to the superior officer and saying that the feedback is prejudiced. This may satisfy the subordinate so that he or she does not feel threatened any more. However, this changes neither the situation (the superior officer will continue to feel that the subordinate has low motivation) nor the behaviour of the subordinate (who will continue to feel that the superior officer is prejudiced and therefore he or she need not change his or her behaviour).

Defensive behaviour is not helpful; although it may reduce anxiety, the conflict within the self is not resolved. Excessive use of defensive behaviour is likely to result in a conflicted self. On the other hand, if confronting behaviour is used, the conflict is reduced, and continued use of such behaviour results in an integrated self.

The intention is not to suggest here that defensive behaviour is universally bad. Nor is it suggested that defensive behaviour should never be used. In many situations, defensive behaviour may be functional. However, if the main purpose of feedback is to develop mutuality and if both people involved are interested in a relationship of trust and openness, the more defensive behaviour is used, the less effective it will be. The individual receiving feedback should examine his or her defensive behaviour and prepare a plan (preferably with the help of one or more persons) for reducing it and moving towards the corresponding confronting behaviour as indicated in Exhibit 10.10.

Perceptiveness

The ability to pick up verbal and non-verbal cues from others indicates perceptiveness. However, like openness, this dimension must be combined with the other two dimensions for effectiveness. A person who is not open may receive many cues and much feedback from others at first, but may soon be seen as manipulative and generally unavailable. Perceptiveness and openness reinforce each other and, if used effectively, are likely to increase personal effectiveness.

Like openness, perceptiveness can be used appropriately or inappropriately. If a person is too conscious of others' feelings, he or she may inhibit interaction. Similarly, a person who is too conscious of his or her own limitations will tend not to take risks. Effective perceptiveness can be increased by checking others' reactions to what is said. A person who does not do this (in other words, if a person who is not open) may become excessively concerned about the cues received.

Combining the three aspects of personal effectiveness, we get eight categories, ranging from effective to ineffective. These are shown in Exhibit 10.13. Instruments have been developed to measure effectiveness as well.[24]

Exhibit 10.13 *Categories of Personal Effectiveness*

S. No.	Category	Self-disclosure	Openness to feedback	Perceptiveness
1.	Effective	High	High	High
2.	Insensitive	High	High	Low
3.	Egocentric	High	Low	Low
4.	Dogmatic	High	Low	High
5.	Secretive	Low	High	High
6.	Task obsessed	Low	High	Low
7.	Lonely-empathic	Low	Low	High
8.	Ineffective	Low	Low	Low

Developing Personal Effectiveness

Personal effectiveness must be viewed across three dimensions—openness, perceptiveness, and communication—all significant to interpersonal relationships. By becoming more open, a person reduces his or her closed area; the blind area is reduced by increasing perceptiveness. Communication can be improved in various ways as discussed in Chapter 17. These three dimensions, however, do not function in isolation, but interact with each other. In order to increase effectiveness, it is necessary to work on a combination of all three.

Personal effectiveness can be increased by moving towards appropriate perceptiveness and openness. Organizational consultants and trainers, while working on the processes leading to increased effectiveness, will find it useful to emphasise the role of both openness and perceptiveness as contributing factors to effectiveness. Movement in these directions is possible, however, only through a greater emphasis on communication. People must learn to take risks in giving feedback to others and to use in an appropriate manner the feedback they receive. Only in this way can personal effectiveness be truly increased.

Process trainers may emphasise the concept of effectiveness in their groups in terms of a balance between openness and perceptiveness. In T-groups, more emphasis may be given to the latter to correct the imbalance.

EMOTIONS

With increased emphasis on human processes in organizations, emotions and feelings have gained considerable importance. Emotion is a neural impulse that moves an organism to action. There are four related terms (affect, emotion, feeling, and mood) that need to be diffentiated from each other. Affect is a general term that covers emotions, feelings, and moods. Emotions have been differentiated from mood based on structural differences, such as the specificity of the targets (e.g., emotions are specific and intense and are a reaction to a particular event, whereas moods are diffused and unfocused.[25] Another interesting distinction has been stated thus: 'Feelings are personal and *biographical*, emotions are *social*, and affects are *prepersonal*.'[26]

Emotions have three components: cognitive component, physiological component, and conative or expressive component. Cognitive component includes the conscious experience of emotions, and the way we 'label' our emotions.

Physiological component includes emotional arousal. Different emotions have different arousals. For example, fear, anger, and sadness increase heart rate; anger raises blood pressure; embarrassment is shown in blushing. However, many emotions do not have a unique physiological signature; the same physiological activation occurs for many emotions. For example, fear, joy, anger, sadness, and shame are accompanied by faster heart rate. Expressive component includes body language (gaze, gestures, posture, and walk), and paralanguage (intonation, faked smile vs genuine smile, etc.).

Primary and Secondary Emotions

It is useful to understand the concept of primary and secondary emotions. Plutchik has elaborated the distinction.[27] Primary emotions are those that we feel first, as a first response to a situation. Thus, if we are threatened, we may feel fear. When we hear of a death, we may feel sadness. They are our instinctive responses. Typical primary emotions include fear, anger, sadness, and happiness (although these can also be felt as secondary emotions). The problem sometimes with primary emotions is that they disappear as fast as they appear.

Secondary emotions appear after primary emotions. They may be caused directly by them—for example, where the fear of a threat turns to anger that fuels the body for a fight reaction. They may also come from more complex chains of thought.

The secondary emotions give a picture of the person's mental processing of the primary emotion.

Plutchik's psycho-evolutionary theory of basic emotions has 10 postulates.[28]

1. The concept of emotion is applicable to all evolutionary levels and applies to animals as well as to humans.
2. Emotions have an evolutionary history and have evolved various forms of expression in different species.
3. Emotions served an adaptive role in helping organisms deal with key survival issues posed by the environment.
4. Despite different forms of expression of emotions in different species, there are certain common elements, or prototype patterns, that can be identified.
5. There is a small number of basic, primary, or prototype emotions.
6. All other emotions are mixed or derivative states; that is, they occur as combinations, mixtures, or compounds of the primary emotions.
7. Primary emotions are hypothethical constructs or idealised states whose properties and characteristics can only be inferred from various kinds of evidence.
8. Primary emotions can be conceptualised in terms of pairs of polar opposites.
9. All emotions vary in their degree of similarity to one another.
10. Each emotion can exist in varying degrees of intensity or levels of arousal.

Theories of Emotion

Theories of emotion explain the relation between stimulus, physiological arousal, and emotion. Do we feel an emotion because we have a physiological change, or we have a physiological change because we feel an emotion? For example, I am breathing hard because I feel afraid (Stimulus → Conscious feeling → Autonomic arousal), or I feel afraid because I realise I am breathing hard (Stimulus → Autonomic arousal → Conscious feeling). These theories of emotion differ depending on the relationship of physiological change and cognitive interpretation of emotion. What causes the emotion in each theory?

James-Lange theory This is the oldest theory. It was proposed in 1884 and combined the ideas of William James and Danish physiologist Carl Lange, who largely independently arrived at the same conclusion. We have experiences, and as a result, our autonomic nervous system creates physiological events such as muscular tension, heart rate increases, perspiration, dryness of the mouth, etc. This theory proposes that emotions happen *as a result* of these, rather than being the cause of them. William James described it thus:

> My theory ... is that the bodily changes follow directly the perception of the exciting fact, and that our feeling of the same changes as they occur is the emotion. Common sense says, we lose our fortune, are sorry and weep; we meet a bear, are frightened and run; we are insulted by a rival, and angry and strike. The hypothesis here to be defended says that this order of sequence is incorrect ... and that the more rational statement is that we feel sorry because we cry, angry because we strike, afraid because we tremble ... Without the

bodily states following on the perception, the latter would be purely cognitive in form, pale, colorless, destitute of emotional warmth. We might then see the bear, and judge it best to run, receive the insult and deem it right to strike, but we should not actually feel afraid or angry.[29]

Lange particularly added that vasomotor changes *are* the emotions.

Although it is an old theory, it has significant implications for management of emotions. And in a way, it is the basis of behaviour modification approach. For example, if we want to make a person more democratic, we must help him to consult others when taking decisions; after sometime the person may begin to enjoy consulting others. Goleman has given an example of 'managing' anger by changing behaviour.[30]

Cannon-Bard theory   This theory is also quite old. According to this theory people feel emotions first, and then act upon them. These actions include changes in muscular tension, perspiration, etc. I see a tiger, I am afraid, I begin to perspire. The Cannon-Bard Theory of Emotion is based on the premise that one is only able to react to a specific stimulus after experiencing an emotion. Therefore, if one is afraid of heights and is travelling to the top of a skyscraper, one is likely to experience the emotion of fear. Subsequently, the perception of this emotion (fear) influences the person's reaction to the stimulus (heights). The theory proposed that one is able to react to a stimulus only after experiencing the related emotion.

Two-Factor theory   This theory has been proposed by Schachter and Singer.[31] According to this theory the first step is to experience physiological arousal. We then try to find a label to explain our feelings, usually by looking at what we are doing and what else is happening at the time of the arousal. Thus we experience feelings and then decide what they mean. For example, when we are feeling unwell, we often will deduce the illness from the symptoms.

Experiencing and Expressing Feelings

Experiencing and expressing feelings are integral parts of life. Healthy emotional life requires us to learn how to experience emotion and how to express feelings. The first step is to accept and value feelings. Often, there is a strong relationship between the events in one's life and one's feelings—for example, to feel sadness in response to loss, or to feel happiness in response to something desirable. Feelings may also be related to past events or even to expectations of the future. Rather than ignore or exaggerate the feelings, it is helpful to be able to take the feelings as they are, accept them, think about them, and learn from them. It may be useful to reflect on the following kinds of questions:

- What is this feeling?
- What is this feeling telling me about this situation?
- Why has this feeling come up right now?

We have options about how to express the feelings we experience. Often we limit the range of our expressive options by erroneously believing that there are only two options: either directly expressing them to someone else (e.g., in a personal confrontation), or 'swallowing' the feelings and keeping them to ourselves. In actuality, there are many ways to respond to feelings. First, we should consider what our options are. For example, if a close friend is planning to move away, we may feel very sad about that. We have several options. For example, we can tell him/her how much we will miss him/her. Also, we can make a special effort to spend more time with him/her. On the other hand, we can avoid him/her by staying busy. The latter choice may allow us to postpone or avoid painful feelings at the time, but they do not provide the opportunity for closure with the friend. Here are some useful questions to consider when deciding how to respond to our feelings[32]:

- Does the intensity of my feelings match the situation?
- Do I have several feelings that I need to pay attention to?
- What are my options for expressing my feelings?
- What are the consequences of each option for me?
- What are the consequences of each option for others?
- What result am I hoping for?
- What do I want to do?
- What if I do nothing?

Emotional Intelligence

We have already briefly discussed emotional intelligence in Chapter 5. It has become a very popular topic. Emotional intelligence has its roots in the concept of social intelligence, first identified by E.L. Thorndike in 1920. Psychologists have been uncovering other intelligences for some time now, and grouping them mainly into three clusters: abstract intelligence (the ability to understand and manipulate with verbal and mathematic symbols), concrete intelligence (the ability to understand and manipulate with objects), and social intelligence (the ability to understand and relate to people).[33] Thorndike defined social intelligence as 'the ability to understand and manage men and women, boys and girls—to act wisely in human relations'.[34] And Gardner includes interpersonal and intrapersonal intelligences in his theory of multiple intelligences. These two intelligences comprise social intelligence. He defines them as follows[35]:

Interpersonal intelligence is the ability to understand other people: what motivates them, how they work, how to work cooperatively with them. Successful salespeople, politicians, teachers, clinicians, and religious leaders are all likely to be individuals with high degrees of interpersonal intelligence. Intrapersonal intelligence is a correlative ability, turned inward. It is a capacity to form an accurate, veridical model of oneself and to be able to use that model to operate effectively in life.

Emotional intelligence, on the other hand, 'is a type of social intelligence that involves the ability to monitor one's own and others' emotions, to discriminate among them, and to use the information to guide one's thinking and actions'.[36] According to Salovey and Mayer, emotional intelligence subsumes Gardner's interpersonal and intrapersonal intelligences, and involves abilities that may be categorised into five domains[37]:

- Self-awareness (observing yourself and recognising a feeling as it happens)
- Managing emotions (handling feelings so that they are appropriate; realising what is behind a feeling; finding ways to handle fears and anxieties, anger, and sadness)
- Motivating oneself (channeling emotions in the service of a goal; emotional self-control—(delaying gratification and stifling impulses)
- Empathy (sensitivity to others' feelings and concerns and taking their perspective; appreciating the differences in how people feel about things)
- Handling relationships (managing emotions in others; social competence and social skills)

Social scientists are just beginning to uncover the relationship of emotional intelligence to other phenomena, e.g., leadership,[38] group performance,[39] individual performance, interpersonal/social exchange, managing change, and conducting performance evaluations.[40] And according to Goleman, 'Emotional intelligence, the skills that help people harmonize, should become increasingly valued as a workplace asset in the years to come.'[41]

SUMMARY

Personality is the organized and consistent pattern of perception of the 'I'. There are different approaches to understanding and measuring personality. Psychometric theories identify basic traits to explain different personalities. 16 P-F and the Big Five are well known in this regard. While the Freudian approach uses the four stages of psycho-sexual development, the Jungian approach has led to the wide use of the MBTI instrument. Erikson's stages of development have important implications. Another popular theory is that of Transactional Analysis, with wide implications for action. Two personality types (Type A and Type B) are measured from tense and relaxed lifestyles. Similarly, the enlarging lifestyle (more achievement oriented) has been contrasted with enfolding lifestyle (more relaxed and relationship oriented). The former has been found to be significant in people's career growth. Another theory has linked six personality types to six categories of occupational groups.

A simpler approach to understanding personal effectiveness is given by the popular model of the Johari Window. However, a third dimension (perceptiveness) has been added to the two suggested by the Johari Window (self-disclosure and openness to feedback) to give eight types of personal effectiveness, which can be measured and enhanced.

Emotions and feelings are an important part of our life. The theories of emotion deal with the question of causality: does behaviour follow emotion, or does emotion follow behaviour? We need to learn how to experience and express feelings.

GLOSSARY

adult ego-state an autonomous set of feelings, attitudes, and behaviour patterns that are adapted to the current reality

affect a general term to cover emotions, feeling, and mood

agreeableness one's inclination to defer to others; being good-natured, cooperative, warm, caring, trusting

child ego-state a set of feelings, attitudes, and behaviour patterns that are relics of the individual's own childhood

conscientiousness one's reliability regarding responsibility; being self-disciplined, hard-working, organized, dependable, persistent

emotion a specific and intense reaction to a referent

emotional stability ability to withstand stress; being calm, happy, secure

enfolding lifestyle oriented to the goals of tradition, stability, and inward strength

enlarging lifestyle oriented towards the goals of innovation, change, and growth

extraversion being outgoing; speaking and then thinking; relating more easily to the outer world of people and things than to the inner world of ideas

feeling subjectivity; heart; relying more on personal values than on impersonal analysis and logic

game a series of ulterior transactions with a gimmick, leading to a well-defined pay-off. A gimmick is a 'snare' or a 'concealed motivation'

injunction an unfair negative command from the parent

introversion being reflective; thinking and then speaking; relating more easily to the inner world of ideas than to the outer world of people

intuiting theoretical, abstract, looking for possibilities and relationships rather than working with known facts

judging structured, organized, liking a planned and orderly way of life rather than a flexible, spontaneous way

mood diffused and unfocused feeling

parent ego-state a set of feelings, attitudes, and behaviour patterns that resemble those of the parental figure

perceiving flexible, spontaneous; liking a flexible, spontaneous way rather than a planned and orderly way of life

perceptiveness ability to pick up verbal and non-verbal cues from others

personality organized, consistent pattern of perception of 'I', around which one interacts and has experiences

sensing practical, concrete; working with known facts rather than look for possibilities and relationships

thinking analytical; relying more on interpersonal analysis and logic than on personal values

Type A personality working under continuous time pressure, enjoying working against deadlines

Type B personality relaxed and enjoying leisure

EXERCISES

Concept Review Questions

1. Recount the factors in the Big Five theory of personality.
2. Describe the four aspects of the Jungian theory as reflected in the MBTI.
3. What are the main differences in the theories and Erikson and Freudian?
4. What are crossed and ulterior transactions? Give one example of each.
5. How is the concept of a script useful in understanding a person's life?
6. What is the lifestyle of high-flyers—enlarging or enfolding? Type A or Type B? Why?
7. How can personal effectiveness be increased?
8. Discuss the theories of emotion and their implications.

Critical Thinking Questions

1. Read each statement given below and indicate on the blank space at its left how far it is true of your behaviour, using the following key:

Key

Write 4 if it is most characteristic of you, or if you always or most often behave or feel this way.

Write 3 if it is fairly true of you, or you quite often behave or feel this way.

Write 2 if it is somewhat true in your case.

Write 1 if it is not usually true of you, or if you only occasionally feel or behave this way.

Write 0 if it is not at all characteristic of you, or you seldom feel or behave this way.

_____ 1. I find it difficult to be frank with people unless I know them very well.

_____ 2. I listen carefully to others' opinions about my behaviour.

_____ 3. Generally, I hesitate to express my feelings to others.

_____ 4. On hindsight, I regret it if I said something tactlessly.

_____ 5. I deliberately observe how a person will take what I am going to tell him and communicate to him or her accordingly.

_____ 6. If someone criticises me, I hear him or her at that time but do not bother myself about it later.

_____ 7. I fail to pick up cues about others' feelings and reactions when I am involved in an argument or a conversation.

_____ 8. I enjoy talking with others about my personal concerns.

_____ 9. I value what people have to say about my style of communication, behaviour, etc.

Scoring

Reverse your responses for items 1, 3, 4, 6, and 7 (0 becomes 4 and 4 becomes 0; 1 becomes 3 and 3 becomes 1; 2 remains unchanged). Now calculate the three aspects of your personal effectiveness by adding the scores on the three items for each. The score will range between 0 and 12. A score above 6 is high and one below 6 is low. Reflect on your scores and consider what you can do to increase your interpersonal effectiveness.

Self-disclosure $(1 + 3 + 8) =$ ☐

Use of feedback $(2 + 6 + 9) =$ ☐

Perceptiveness $(4 + 5 + 7) =$ ☐

2. After reading the description of enlarging and enfolding lifestyles, assess your own lifestyle. What are its implications?

3. Which of Holland's six personality types is closest to your own self-assessment? Does it match the profession you hope to take up?

Classroom Projects

1. Form dyads (two-member groups) of individuals who know each other quite well. Using your understanding of the MBTI types, guess your own and your partner's types. Exchange your perceptions and discuss on what basis you formed the impressions.

2. In the same pairs, discuss what your lifestyle is—enlarging or enfolding. How is it related to the MBTI type you guessed about yourself?

Field Projects

1. Interview two persons to find out their types (Type A or Type B) and also their lifestyles (enlarging or enfolding). Is there any relationship between the two?

2. Interview one successful executive to find out his or her lifestyle. Is it enlarging or enfolding? What did you learn from the interview?

NOTES AND REFERENCES

1. Eysenck, H.J. and S.B.J. Eysenck (1969). *Personality Structure and Measurement.* London: Routledge.
2. Cattell, R.B. (1946). *Description and Measurement of Personality.* New York: World.
3. Block, J. (1995). 'A contrarian view of the five-factor approach to personality description', *Psychological Bulletin*, 117: 187–215.
4. Hall, C.S. and G. Lindzey. (1957). *Theories of Personality.* New York: Wiley.
5. Maddi, S.R. (2000). *Personality Theories: A Comparative Analysis.* Prospective Heights, IL: Waveland Press.
6. Rao, T.V. (1991). 'Managerial work values', in J.W. Pfeiffer (ed.), *The 1991 Annual: Developing Human Resources*, pp. 163–177. San Diego: University Associates.
7. AllPsych Online, 2004, allpsych.com/psychology101/defenses.html.
8. Jung, C.G. (1967). *The Development of Personality* (1991 ed.). London: Routledge.
9. Myers, I. Briggs (1980). *Gifts Differing: Understanding Personality Type.* New York: Davies-Black Publishing.
10. Berne, Eric (1961). *Transactional Analysis in Psychotherapy.* New York: Grove Press.
11. Berne, E. (1966). *Principles of Group Treatment*, p. 364. New York: Oxford University Press Inc.
12. Berne, Eric (1961). *Transactional Analysis in Psychotherapy*, p. 66. New York: Grove Press.
13. Harris, T. (1967). *I'm OK-You're OK.* New York: Grove Press.
14. Berne, E. (1972). *What Do You Say After You Say Hello? The Psychology of Human Destiny.* New York: Grove Press.
15. *Ibid.*
16. *Ibid.*, 24.
17. Stewart, Ian (1992). *Eric Berne*, p. 40. New Delhi: Sage.
18. Steiner, C. (1974). *Scripts People Live.* New York: Grove Press.
19. Stewart. *Eric Berne*, p. 57.
20. Bray, D.W., R.J. Campbell, and D.I. Grant (1974). *Formative Years in Business: A Long Term AT&T Study of Managerial Lives.* New York: John Wiley.
21. Spokane A.R. and Holland J.L. (1995). 'The self-directed search: A family of self-guided career interventions', *Journal of Career Assessment*, 3(4): 373–390.
22. Luft, Joseph (1973). *On Human Interaction.* New York: Mayfield Pub Co.
23. Pfeiffer, J.W. and J.E. Jones (1972). 'Openness, collusion and feedback', in J.W. Pfeiffer and J.E. Jones (eds), *The 1972 Annual Handbook for Group Facilitators.* La Jolla, CA: University Associates.
24. Pareek, Udai (2002). *Training Instruments in HRD & OD*, 2nd edn, Chapter 7. New Delhi: Tata McGraw Hill.
25. Cornelius, R.R. (1995). *The Science of Emotion.* New York: Prentice Hall.
26. Shouse, Eric (2005). 'Feeling, Emotion, Affect', *M/C Journal*, 8(6): 3–7.
27. Plutchick R. (1980). *Emotion: A Psycho Evolutionary Synthesis.* New York: Harper & Row.
28. Cannon, W.B. (1927). 'The James-Lange theory of emotions', *American Journal of Psychology*, 39: 115–124.
29. *Ibid.*
30. Goleman, D. (1995). *Emotional Intelligence.* New York: Bantam Books; Goleman, D. (1998). *Working with Emotional Intelligence.* New York: Bantam Books.
31. Schachter, S. (1959). *The Psychology of Affiliation.* Stanford, CA: Stanford University Press.

32. Experiencing and expressing emotions, self-help brochure of the Counseling Center at the University of Illinois, http://www.couns.uiuc.edu/brochures/Emotions.htm.

33. Ruisel, I. (1992). 'Social intelligence: Conception and methodological problem', *Studia Psychologia*, 34(4–5): 281–296.

34. Thorndike, E.L. (1920). 'Intelligence and its use', *Harper's Magazine*, 140–228.

35. Gardner, Howard (1983). *Frames of Mind: The Theory of Multiple Intelligences*. New York: Basic Books.

36. Mayer, J.D. and P. Salovy (1993). 'The intelligence of emotional intelligence', *Intelligence*, 17: 433–442.

37. Salovey, P. and J.D. Mayer (1990). 'Emotional intelligence', *Imagination, Cognition and Personality*, 9.

38. Ashforth, B.E. and R.H. Humphrey (1955). 'Emotion in the workplace: A reappraisal', *Human Relations*, 48(2): 97–125.

39. Williams, W.M. and R.J. Sternberg (1988). 'Group intelligence: Why some groups are better than others', *Intelligence*, 12, 351–377.

40. Goleman, D. (1995). *Emotional Intelligence*. New York: Bantam Books.

41. *Ibid.*, 160.

11
Development of Attitudes and Values

There are three related terms—beliefs, attitudes, and values. Clarity about their meanings helps us to use them for personal and organizational effectiveness.

Beliefs are primarily cognitive in nature.

Attitudes are essentially affective (emotional) in nature. Attitudes have referents (the objects for which there are feelings). For example, when I say that I like my organization, I am expressing an attitude (positive) towards my organization. Attitudes are about liking (favourable) or not liking (unfavourable) certain aspects of the referent. We shall discuss these in more detail later in this chapter.

Values are judgmental in nature. They are about preference. When we say that certain aspects of an object or situation are desirable, we express a value: some things are more desirable than others, so that we have a hierarchy of values. We shall discuss values too in more detail later in this chapter.

WHAT IS ATTITUDE?

The term 'attitude' is being used quite frequently nowadays in describing people's behaviour. There are two main senses in which it is used. One is in general terms, meaning the positive or negative orientation of a person. For example, when it is said that Mala has a positive attitude or that Geeta has a negative attitude, what is probably meant is that Mala's general orientation towards most things is positive whereas Geeta's general orientation is negative. However, this is not a correct usage of the term 'attitude'. Attitude always has a referent, i.e., an object towards which positive or negative orientation is implied. Attitude is always 'towards' something. For example, you may say that Mohan has a positive attitude towards his organization.

Although attitudes are generally affective (or emotional) in nature, they also have a cognitive (information or knowledge) element and a conative (action) element, in terms of acting or behaving on the basis of that feeling. For example, my exposure to my job gives me enough knowledge about it. Then I develop a feeling for it (I like it or I do not like it). Finally, I act on the feeling—stay on in my job or quit it. So generally attitudes lead to behaviour.

Attitude can also be defined as a multiplicative function of beliefs and values. A belief is an association between two cognitive elements. For example, if a person believes that not spacing out one's children (having children without enough gap between their births) is injurious to the mother's health, he or she is combining two concepts—family planning and maternal health. If the person has a high value for the mother's health, then his or her attitude towards contraception is likely to be positive. However, if the above belief is not strong or the value placed on the mother's health is low, the attitude towards contraception may be negative. If either the strength of the belief or the value of maternal health is zero, the attitude will be one of complete indifference, so that this person is not likely to use a contraceptive.

Similarly, a particular region, religion, or caste may be one cognitive element. The other element may be 'reliable', 'honest', or 'talkative'. When we connect these elements, we have a belief that persons of a certain category behave in a particular way.

Beliefs may be formed through direct behaviour and experience or by exposure to information (people we know and respect, books, journals, films, TV, etc.).

In fact, attitude scales can be prepared by combining statements of beliefs and values.

WORK ATTITUDES

In relation to organizations, the general meaning of attitude is applied to work. Work attitudes are reflected in job satisfaction and in organizational commitment.

Job Satisfaction

Job satisfaction includes various aspects—the nature of the job itself, the compensation a person gets by working on the job, growth opportunities, opportunities for career advancement, the organizational climate, the behaviour of the supervisor and coworkers, and so on.

When we measure work attitudes in the form of job satisfaction, we cover several of these aspects. Several parts of Chapters 7, 12, and 13 are relevant in this regard. Job satisfaction can be increased by increasing role efficacy (Chapter 12), by understanding a person's needs and making sure that these needs are met in the work assigned to the person (Chapter 7), and developing various ways of involving the person in the work itself by redesigning the job profile, etc. (Chapter 13).

Job satisfaction leads to improved performance and retention of personnel in the organization. Recruitment policies, placement practices, development schemes, etc. contribute to job satisfaction.

Organizational Commitment

Organizational commitment is another aspect of work attitudes. While job satisfaction is primarily concerned with the job or the work a person undertakes in an organization, commitment shows the relationship between the individual and the organization. The stronger such a relationship is, the higher the organizational commitment will be. It has been suggested that organizational commitment is a critical aspect of work attitude.[1] Organizational commitment indicates a person's feelings with regard to continuing his or her association with the organization, acceptance of the values and goals of the organization, and willingness to help the organization achieve such goals and values.

There are three dimensions of organizational commitment[2]—affective commitment, i.e., a person's emotional attachment to and identification with the organization; continuous commitment, based on the benefits the person sees in continuing with the organization; and normative commitment, i.e., the willingness of the person to continue with the organization because it is commonly considered a good thing to stay on. This model has been tested and has been found to be applicable to non-western cultures also.

Organizational commitment can be enhanced by clarifying the mission and values of the organization, involving people in the development of organizational goals, ensuring equitable treatment without discrimination, developing a collective sense of the organization, and investing in people's growth and advancement.

Attitudes have also been studied in relation to specific aspects of the work situation. For example, employee's attitudes can be studied before new practices are introduced. Banks in India undertook an attitude survey of employees towards new technology such as computers. Attitude surveys can be made with regard to structural aspects (e.g., the 'divisionalisation' of a company), technological aspects (e.g., acquiring a new technology), or process aspects (e.g., introducing a new appraisal system.) There is an advantage in surveying attitudes before introducing change in an organization—action can then be taken to ensure smooth introduction of the change.

ATTITUDE CHANGE

As already stated, attitudes have three components—cognitive (knowledge and understanding), affective (feelings), and conative (action). Attitude change covers all three aspects. Several theories have been proposed for attitude change.

Reinforcement Theory

Hovland et al. propounded one of the first major theories of attitude change, developed in the framework of Hull's learning theory, and oriented towards the effects of persuasive communication.[3] According to this theory, changes in opinions can result in attitude change, depending on the presence or absence of rewards. The learning of new attitudes is not different in nature than any other verbal or motor skill, except that opinions relate to a single proposition, whereas other skills involve a series of propositions. The acceptance of a new opinion (and hence attitude formation) is dependent upon the incentives that are offered in the communication.

Balance Theory

Heider developed a balance theory of attitude change that was influenced by Gestalt principles.[4] In Heider's theory, when beliefs are unbalanced, stress is created and there is pressure to change attitudes. The two main factors affecting balance are the sentiment (e.g., liking, approving, admiring) and unity (e.g., similarity, proximity, membership) qualities of beliefs. Balance exists if the sentiment or unity between beliefs about events or people are equally positive or negative; imbalance occurs when they are dissimilar in nature.

Cognitive Consistency Theory

Abelson and others developed theories of cognitive consistency.[5] Cognitive consistency suggests that people will try and maintain consistency among their beliefs and make changes (i.e., accept or reject ideas) when this does not occur. For example, if a college student who wants to live in a co-ed dormitory and also wants to get good grades is presented with the fact that students who live in co-ed dorms get poor grades, the student will either reject this proposition or change his attitudes about co-ed dorms or good grades.

Cognitive Dissonance Theory

Festinger's theory of cognitive dissonance[6] is one of the best-known and most researched frameworks pertaining to attitude change. According to this theory, attitude change is caused by conflict among beliefs. A number of factors determine the strength of the dissonance and hence how much effort is required to change attitudes. By manipulating these factors, attitude change can be facilitated or inhibited.

The effect of incentives or rewards on attitude change has also been studied. Incentive theorists and dissonance theorists take two contrasting positions on this. Some studies have reported a change in attitude, when some reward was associated with it, suggesting that the higher the incentive, the greater the change in attitude is likely to be. On the other hand, some studies (dissonance theory) have shown that the amount of resultant internalisation (i.e., change in the direction of the advocated position) will increase as the amount of positive incentive for covert compliance decreases.

A subject induced to lie for a $20 payment ended up believing the lie less than a group of subjects who told the same lie for a $1 payment.[7]

This effect extended even to smaller incentives—the less monetary incentive the person was given for a lie, the more he or she believed it.[8] The explanation is provided by the theory of cognitive dissonance. The person agreeing to comply with the message finds a dissonance between the action and his or her original belief. However, when given a large incentive, the person can justify the change in belief or behaviour in terms of having done it for money. But when the amount is small, he or she cannot justify the new belief or behaviour in this way, which then reduces the dissonance by shifting the person's own attitude. This is the 'insufficient justification' hypothesis.

The two approaches (dissonance vs incentive) can be reconciled. Research findings show that there is dissonance in a person's commitment to a new view if there is no justification (or insufficient or inactive justification) for behaving differently. However, a larger incentive will make the person carry out the commitment in action. The implication of this finding is that intrinsic motivation or change cannot be achieved by high extrinsic incentives; intrinsic motivation or attitude change would require intrinsic rewards (recognition, support, more responsibility, etc.) and not higher extrinsic incentives. Compliance to a change can, however, be increased with extrinsic motivation.

Comprehensive Theory

One of the most thorough treatments of attitude and attitude change is that by McGuire.[9] He has suggested five aspects of attitude change: attention, comprehension, yielding, retention, and action. These take one through the various stages from paying attention to an object to accepting its influence and acting according to the changed attitude. McGuire has also suggested a matrix of attitudinal change, one axis comprising the five modes (or stages) of attitude change and the other axis comprising the five communication processes—source, message, channel, receiver, and destination (see Exhibit 11.1).

We shall briefly discuss each of these communication processes in relation to attitude changes.

Exhibit 11.1 *McGuire's Matrix of Attitudinal Change*

Aspects of attitude change	Communication process				
	Source	Message	Channel	Receiver	Destination
Attention					
Comprehension					
Yielding					
Retention					
Action					

Source

The source of communication has great influence on the first three phases of attitude change—attention, comprehension, and yielding. Kelman suggested three main characteristics of the source in relation to attitude change—credibility, attractiveness, and power.[10] Credibility, according to Kelman, helps in the internalisation of the message; attractiveness helps in the identification of the recipient with the source of the message; and power results in compliance.

Three factors contribute to the attractiveness of the source: similarity of the receiver and the source, familiarity of the source, and the recipient's liking for the source. The more similar the source of influence is to the receiver, the greater the likelihood of accepting the new attitude. Similarly, a familiar source is likely to influence attitude change more. Liking for the source adds to its attractiveness and has also been found to influence change of attitudes. The various advertisements on TV make use of these factors. For example, well-known actors or players, who are generally liked by people, are used for sending messages encouraging people to buy certain products. This is likely to not only get people's attention and increase their awareness of the message, but may also change their feelings towards the products.

The power of a source can be of three kinds. A source can have the power of sanction, i.e., control of the means and ends. In other words, a source that has control over both reward and punishment is likely to induce individuals to conform to his or her message. Conformity generally means public acquiescence (i.e., accepting the influence of and behaving accordingly before others) and not necessarily private commitment. The second kind of power concerns compliance. This kind of power is less direct and is reflected in such a concern being communicated to the person whose attitude is being changed. It is likely to lead to a more private commitment for attitude change. The third form of power is the source's potential for scrutiny, i.e., the ability of the source to monitor compliance, checking whether the individuals on whom influence is exercised are behaving according to the programme.

A large number of studies on the adoption of innovations (new drugs or practices) by doctors and farmers have focussed on this aspect. The questions that are relevant in this connection are who exerts influence, how the influence is exercised, and so on. For example, studies on the source of communication and its relationship with the adoption of new practices in agriculture have shown that the status of a person (the source) in a village community has considerable influence on such attitudinal changes (acceptance and adoption of a new drug or a new seed, for example).

Message

Four types of messages have generally been studied in relation to attitude change: suggestions, conformity, persuasion, and indoctrination. Suggestion is a repetitive presentation of a message to a person. TV advertisements are repeated to get the attention and increase the understanding of viewers. Conformity refers to feedback given on the discrepancy between a person's behaviour and the norms, which are themselves suggested in the message. For example, some advertisements on TV ask whether viewers are using a particular product that is also being used by members of a reference group (such as beautiful young women or well-known actors). For example, when women with long flowing hair are depicted and the viewer is asked whether he or she is using a particular shampoo or hair oil that is being used by these beautiful models, the message emphasises the discrepancy between the viewer's behaviour and the norms or desirable behaviour shown on the screen (the models'). Persuasion is a little more active and gives reasons for the acceptance of a particular message. It appeals in different ways. Explicit appeals are less likely to influence than subtle appeals. Also, appeals can be either rational or emotional. Rational appeals are more likely to influence people than emotional appeals.

Studies on messages producing fear or offering positive reinforcement have found that fear does not produce adequate change of attitude; reinforcement or reward has more influence on attitudes. Thus, messages are more likely to be accepted when pleasant experiences are associated with their delivery. This tendency is utilised by several organizations when introducing a new product. For example, several banks invite people to five-star hotels for dinner and introduce their new products over cocktails or a pleasant dinner. People are likely to be more positively inclined towards these products in such an atmosphere.

Experiments have also been carried out on the exercising of influence during the process of communication. The use of humour is particularly effective in influencing attitude. The results are not conclusive, but the findings are that humour facilitates reception of messages.

Channel

There are certain variables related to the channel through which a persuasive message is communicated. We may consider four such variables: direct experience, interpersonal communication, group discussion, and mass media.

Regarding direct contact with the object of the message, the receiver's initial attitude is important—those who have a favourable or an unfavourable attitude towards the object are likely to become more favourable or unfavourable, respectively. However, there is evidence that long contact generally produces a favourable attitude. This is because long contact produces familiarity and, as discussed while speaking of the source, familiarity influences attitudes. The dramatic story of attitudinal (and behavioural) change from utter dislike to extreme liking discussed in Chapter 20 illustrates the effect of long contact.

As far as interpersonal communication is concerned, research shows that the spoken word has more persuasive impact than the written word. In the spoken message, the source of communication also becomes an added factor in persuasion.

Extensive research has been done on the impact of mass media. Some findings have already been discussed above in talking of the message. Research on the dissemination of innovations has suggested that mass media have a great impact on attention, comprehension, and yielding. On the other hand, face-to-face contact with opinion leaders often results in action (behavioural change) as well.

Receiver

Receivers have been found to differ with regard to acceptance of a persuasive message and resultant behaviour. Some basic personality differences have been identified in this regard. It has been suggested that people are different in terms of traits such as suggestibility,[11] conformity,[12] and persuability.[13]

Advocates of non-directive therapy have recommended active participation by the receiver in the development of a programme of change. It is argued that receivers develop a sense of ownership during participation and are then more likely to shift their attitudes in the positive direction.

Destination

Here the concern is with variables dealing with the target or destination of attitude change: the duration of change (short-term vs long-term), the 'delayed action' effect, and the immunising effect (developing resistance against subsequent counter messages).

The general finding is that an attitude change induced by 'typical persuasive communication' has a half-life of about 6 months. The implication of this is that repetitive reinforcement may help in stabilising the change in attitudes.

In some cases the impact of a persuasive message is seen only some time after the target's exposure to it. Hovland et al. proposed a 'discounting cue' hypothesis to explain delayed action.[14] According to this explanation, if a persuasive message is presented along with a discounting cue (unfavourable conditions such as an uncomfortable place or unfamiliar sources), the discounting cue attenuates the initial impact; but as time passes, the cue is forgotten or dissociated from the message and the desired attitude change is manifested at a later date.

The immunisation effect (resisting a counter message) is produced in many ways. One approach is called anchoring. Each individual is an integrated person who tries to maintain a coherent set of beliefs and values. Anchoring involves linking the message with the individual's core values. Advertisements try to do this by linking a message about a product with a core value, say, child welfare. According to the preference theory, anchoring is achieved by linking the message with respected individuals or valued groups to which the individual wants to belong (the reference group). In a certain TV ad, for example, a particular brand of *zarda* (a kind of tobacco product) is linked with a violent show of fighting off an abductor. It is assumed that, generally, users of zarda value courage and physical strength and fantasise about playing Tarzan or Superman.

The inoculation approach to immunisation involves pre-exposure to a weakened form of possible counter messages. 'It has been demonstrated that pre-exposure to weakened forms of counter arguments (typically involving a mention and then refutation of these arguments) is more effective in conferring resistance to strong subsequent attacks than is prior presentation of supportive arguments.'[15]

WHAT ARE VALUES?

'A value is a conception, explicit or implicit, distinctive of an individual or characteristic of a group, of the desirable which influences the selection from available modes, means, and ends of action.'[16] In this definition, they emphasise the affective (desirable), cognitive (conception), and conative (selection) elements as essential to the concept of value.

Values represent basic conviction that a specific mode of conduct or end state of existence is personally or socially preferable to an opposite or converse mode of conduct or end state of existence.[17]

Once a value is internalised, it becomes a standard for guiding action or a criterion for selection of an action.[18] Although values are internal to the individual, they are basically social products. They are generally acceptable to the society as a whole or a section of the society as preferred 'modes of conduct' or 'end states'.

Chakraborty has defined values as 'the manner in which an individual tends to make judgements or choices, both about goals and means, at different stages of one's life, in different facets of it, as are deemed to lead to the well being and happiness of oneself and society'.[19]

Values are functions of preferences. Values essentially characterise a collective. Members of a collective generally accept its values. We may thus have societal values, organizational values, and individual values.

SOCIETAL VALUES

We shall take up four main Western conceptual frameworks of societal values and then see the values of the Indian society. Values do not operate singly. Several values interact with each other and value systems or value orientations are formed. Most conceptual frameworks propose such systems.

Kluckhohn–Strodtbeck Framework

Kluckhohn and Strodtbeck singled out five crucial problems common to all human groups[20]:

- Human–nature orientation, dealing with the character of innate human nature
- Man–nature orientation, dealing with the relation of man to nature
- Time orientation, dealing with the temporal focus of human life
- Activity orientation, dealing with the modality of human activity
- Relational orientation, dealing with the modality of a human being's relationship to others

Human–nature orientation   This mainly delves into ethical values, which fall in a conservatism–liberalism continuum. Values such as purification of the mind, respect for individuals, containment of greed, self-restraint, integrity, detachment, compassion, etc. come under this category.

Man–nature orientation   This is represented by the fatalism–scientism dimension—does nature control human beings or do humans control nature? Fatalism can be defined as a belief that human situations and acts are predetermined by some supernatural power and can never be, or is little, influenced by individual volition. On the other hand, scientism can be defined as a belief that human situations are the result of natural and/or social forces, which can be understood and changed by human volition or human action.

Time orientation   This is reflected in past orientation, present orientation, or future orientation.

Activity orientation Conservatism–liberalism mainly represents the human nature dimension and also the activity dimension in part. Conservatism can be defined as a positive attitude towards traditional institutions and practices and a maintaining of the status quo, producing a tendency to resist change. Likewise, liberalism can be defined as a positive attitude towards the search for new ways and new ideas and a modification or change in the status quo.

Levinson was the first to use the term 'liberalism–conservatism dimension'.[21] Conservatism is marked by a preference for the past; dislike for social change; holding vested interests; preserving the status quo of existing institutions, practices, and customs; supporting traditional and religious creeds; looking to authority for guidance; viewing social problems as a result of individual incompetence and immorality.

Liberalism implies the opposite trends. The main characteristics of liberalism are a spirit of adventure; a quest for new ideas; the modification of old ways; a fearless and critical search for new ways of life; favouring rational social experimentation; a critical assessment of old religious traditions; viewing social problems as symptoms of the underlying social structure.

Relational orientation This is reflected in the authoritarianism–non-authoritarianism dimension. A profusion of both intensive and extensive studies has been reported on this dimension. The classic work of Adorno et al.[22] and the vast body of literature succeeding it[23] demonstrate that the concept of the authoritarian personality is a very important one, sustaining the interest of social scientists.

While there is a general agreement on authoritarianism constituting one extreme, no fully satisfactory term for the opposite extreme is available. Eysenck[24] presented an authoritarian–democratic continuum, but he also used Ferguson's term 'humanitarianism',[25] depicting the pole opposed to the authoritarianism concept of Adorno et al.[26]

Authoritarianism can be defined as a positive attitude towards accepting an idealised person or institution for setting tasks, prescribing procedures, or judging results without permitting others to share in the decision-making process. Non-authoritarianism, likewise, can be defined as a positive attitude towards accepting the decision-making process as a shared responsibility and an understanding and tolerance of variations in thinking and behaviour.

Some salient features of authoritarianism can be extracted from past research. These are

- A craving for unquestioning obedience and subordination
- Servile acceptance of a superior authority
- Scorn for weakness
- Rigidity
- Rejection of the out-group
- Conventionality
- Intolerance for ambiguity
- Cynicism

Rokeach Framework

According to Rokeach, values serve not only as standards and plans but also as existence. According to him, value systems are composed of rank-ordered sets of values that fall into two general categories of terminal and instrumental values.[27] While terminal values reflect the desired end states of existence, instrumental values guide the choice of behaviour in reaching these end states. Rokeach further differentiates terminal and instrumental values into two subcategories each of self-centred and other-centred. He differentiates also between social and personal terminal values, and moral (e.g., helping, forgiving, honesty) and competence (e.g., logical, independent) instrumental values. Taking their cue from him, Musser and Orke have proposed a 2 × 2 value system matrix, giving four types: effective crusader (high social–high competence), virtuous advocate (high social–high moral), independent (high personal–high competence), and honourable egoist (high personal–high moral).[28]

Values help an individual to conduct himself or herself effectively while interacting with other individuals and groups or confronting situations. According to Rokeach, values serve the following functions[29]:

- They predispose us to favour one particular position or religious ideology over another.
- They lead us to take a particular position on social issues.
- They guide our presentation of the self to others and help us to evaluate and judge or praise and blame others and us.
- They help us to ascertain whether we are as moral and as competent as others are.
- They lead us to persuade and influence others by suggesting to us that beliefs, attitudes, values, and actions of others need to be influenced or changed.
- They tell us how to rationalise in the psychoanalytic sense, beliefs, attitudes, and actions that would otherwise be personally and socially unacceptable.

Hofstede Framework

We have already discussed the Hofstede framework in Chapter 3. Hofstede studied cultural values across 50 countries.[30] He suggested four dimensions of culture: power distance (how power is distributed), uncertainty avoidance (how societies respond to unknown forte), individualism–collectivism (how the individual is related to the group of which he or she is a member), and masculinity–femininity (the dominant gender-based value systems). Hofstede found different patterns in different societies. Indian society can be characterised as being oriented towards centralised decision making, high tolerance for ambiguity, collectivism rather than individualism, and a strong tendency to show off and give importance to material things (masculinity).

Chakraborty Framework

Chakraborty[31] is a strong advocate of the Vedic values of Indian society. He has suggested that understanding Indian values is possible only by examining the traditional religio-philosophical repertoire of knowledge. According to Chakraborty, the values of Indians are anchored in the transcendental aspect of human existence.[32] He has suggested that the following values are salient to the Indian sociocultural ethos: respect for individuals; cooperation and trust; purification of the mind; top quality products and services; work as worship; containment of greed; ethical–moral boundaries; self-discipline and restraint; need to give, and renunciation and detachment.

Values in Indian Society

Several studies have been conducted on the values of the Indian society. According to Prakash, two sets of values appear in the organizational context.[33] On one hand, there are values that characterise those sociocultural systems in which economic relationships are submerged in social relationships. On the other hand, there are values that generally characterise modern industrial societies, in which relationships of members of organizations with each other and with the organization are contractual. In the latter case, relationships are less strong and serve relatively differentiated functions. The Indian society can be characterised by the following cultural components and the dominant values:

Karta The *karta* is one of the earliest and strongest socialisation experiences of the Indian child. It is the nurturing, caring, dependable, sacrificing yet demanding, authoritative, and strict dimension of the father figure, which an Indian learns to value and look for in life.

Relationships From an early age, Indians are exposed to warm and close personal relationships with parents, grandparents, siblings, and others. Thus Indian families are extended families and an Indian child also experiences an extended childhood. Individuals come to the workplace with a strong need to relate with others. Values like empathy, intimacy, togetherness, concern for one another, mutual understanding, and respect are shown in the workplace.[34]

Proximity to power The powerlessness and dependency experienced in childhood and adolescence in India results in people placing a high value on the power source as well as a need to be close to the power source. The power source is thus idealised and invested with heroic dimensions in terms of capacity and action.

Security The *kutumb* (family) system of the early parent–child relationship of dependence produces a preference for security rather than venturing out, for comfort rather than risk.

Simple living and high thinking This value is reflected in the reverence given to saints and their simplicity of personal lifestyle and richness of inner life. Mahatma Gandhi as a role model is a dramatic illustration of this cultural imperative in recent times, being able to unify and organize the diverse masses. Living by ideals is thus the value that is most cherished by Indian people in general. They desire these values in their leaders, although they themselves may not necessarily practise them.

Survival Indians have immense faith in luck and fate and also in past *karma* (actions or deeds). They believe that these factors govern their destinies. Therefore, there is a tendency to undervalue the power of human endeavour to change one's destiny in the present life. Consequently, Indians tend to be satisfied and contented with whatever they get rather than making an effort to get more.

ORGANIZATIONAL VALUES AND WORK VALUES

Organizations have certain core values. Core values are the deeply ingrained principles that guide a company's actions and practices; they serve as its cultural cornerstone. According to Collins and Porras, core values are inherent and sacrosanct and so cannot be compromised either for convenience or for short-term economic gain.[35] Four types of organizational values have been proposed[36]:
(a) Power, elitism, and reward
(b) Effectiveness, efficiency, and economy
(c) Fairness, teamwork, and law and order
(d) Defence, competitiveness, and opportunism

Peters and Waterman identified several values related to performance and excellence in the marketplace.[37] Their findings indicated that excellent firms possess a distinct and identifiable set of organizational values that include beliefs about superior quality and service, being the best, innovation, the importance of people as individuals, the importance of detail in execution, the importance of informality to enhance communication, and the importance of profit orientation and goal accomplishment.

Work Values

Work values may be defined as the conceptions of what is 'preferable' from among 'the alternative modes of conduct or end-states' with respect to one's work. In other words, these are individually held conceptions of what is desirable with respect to the individual's work activity. Work values are expected to be an integral part of the nation's ethos; as such, they need to be internalised by members of the society through socialisation, via various institutional channels, so that they become an aspect of individual personalities.[38]

In relation to work, Allport and Vernon identified six types of values: (1) theoretical, i.e., discovery of truth through a critical and rational approach, (2) economic, i.e., emphasis on the useful and practical, (3) aesthetic, i.e., emphasis on form and harmony, (4) social, i.e., love of people, (5) political, i.e., acquisition of power and influence, and (6) religious, i.e., unity of experience and understanding of the cosmos as a whole.[39] People in different occupations place different importance on the six value types.

T.V. Rao[40] has studied work values in terms of the satisfaction one experiences in a job or career. It depends partly on the extent to which the job or career one chooses has elements one 'values'. According to him, a career anchor represents a person's self-image of what he or she excels in, wants, and values. Although a person can have only one career anchor, the categories can be arranged in a hierarchy according to what the person would be willing to give up if forced to choose between two anchors.

Rao has proposed the following framework of work values and has developed an instrument to measure them. The instrument is likely to help an individual select the appropriate work or career, where one will be able to give one's best.

- *Creativity and challenge* the scope to do new things, and challenges to the employees' potential and ability
- *Economic* the satisfaction of financial needs
- *Independence* the freedom to take one's own decisions and not being answerable for all of one's activities
- *Service* the opportunity to serve others
- *Work conditions* the conditions that would facilitate productivity, e.g., work station, computers, water coolers, phone, air coolers, etc.
- *Status* a good designation and the associated prestige, status, authority, and power to influence others
- *Coworkers* the availability of good colleagues who help the person enjoy a good relationship with them
- *Security* the assurance of job continuity
- *Academic* the work relationship to research and academics

Managerial Values

Various studies have reported the values held by managers. Using the personal values questionnaire (PVQ) of England, one study found that managers were equally distributed in the materialistic, pragmatic, and mixed categories.[41] It was also found that pragmatic managers had comparatively shorter service records and spent less time in each job situation. The study also indicated that the goals of the organization (efficiency, growth, and productivity) and the groups of people (customers, employees, subordinates, etc.) were given high priority by managers.

While defining managerial values, Indian executives cited work ethics, commitment, self-motivation, integrity, hard work, character, etc. Respondents indicated integrity, trust, achievement, motivation, truthfulness, humility, and contentment. The study found that stability, skill, creativity, achievement, and flexibility were the five dominant personal traits for a manager. The five most important goals of a typical Indian manager, as reported in the study, were customer satisfaction, achievement of departmental/organizational goals within a scheduled time frame, employee motivation, and career progress.

On the basis of a meta-analysis of various studies,[42] Upadhyay concluded that Indian managers are status and power oriented; evaluate their status by the size of their office, the quality and size of their office table, chairs, furnishings, and perks, etc.; believe that maintaining distance from subordinates is a safer route to managing them effectively than mixing with them; regard decision making as their prerogative and consultation or joint decision making as means of eroding their authority; tend to take credit for work done themselves rather than share it with individual members of the team; show indifference towards bringing about improvement in the work environment as they move up the hierarchy, etc.

Posing three questions on their five most important values to about hundred managers (the five most important values they held, values they wanted people to practise but did not practise themselves, and the values being practised in organizations) found the following responses most frequent (Exhibit 11.1).[43]

Exhibit 11.1   *Five Most Important Values for Indian Managers*

Value held	Rank	Held by %	Wanted values in others (%)
Honesty and truthfulness	1	47	34
Dedication	2	31	30
Concern and respect for others	3	25	28
Family duty and responsibility	4	23	16
Sincerity	5	22	14

DEVELOPING VALUES

Values can be developed in individuals and organizations—not by sermons or lectures on values, but by role modelling and open examination of the values practised as against values espoused or desired. There is always a gap between exposed or desired and practised values. An index of value congruence can be given by the gap between these two—the less the gap, the more the value congruence in the organization.

Value Clarification

One intervention, value clarification, has been suggested for development of values in organizations.[44] The following descriptions of value clarification have been taken from Jain[45].

A typical value clarification workshop (with about 15–20 people) has these steps:
- Participants are asked to identify their five most important values without being given any input.
- They select the five most important values from an instrument that lists 27 values.
- They also participate in a 'value auction'[46] in which they bid for and buy certain items. The items relating to values concerning work, living, personal growth, and society. They have a specified budget available, which they can use in any way they like. Two joint biddings are also allowed in the auction.
- After the auction and some conceptual input being given on the subject of values, the participants once again list their final understanding of their own values.

- In addition to individual value clarification exercises, there are several group decision-making events in which the participants are first asked to take their decisions individually and are then divided into groups. The groups are given the task of taking decisions based on value criteria.
- After the group decisions, each group presents the criteria used for their decisions and the other groups identify the values upheld by these decisions. In various in-house workshops, too, participants are divided into groups to identify the values desirable for their organization to function effectively in the current environment.
- Exercises like Princess, Cave Rescue, Psychic Power, Discovery, Who to Retain are also used.[47]

Long experience of value clarification workshops has revealed people's feelings of frustration, helplessness, powerlessness, and disappointment. It is often believed that people cannot practise the values that they want to because of constraints in work organizations. The following reasons were identified for such feelings.[48]

- Lack of awareness about one's own values and practice
- Choices and decisions based on habits, fears, and expectations of others rather than own values
- Differing standards for self and others
- Tendency to avoid pain/loss rather than actively seek meaning and well-being
- People making choices based on values different from others feeling they are 'alone'
- People wanting others to change the system while their own choices support the status quo
- Blindness to group processes and larger entities
- People holding incompatible values, often with materialistic and self-serving values taking priority
- End values not supported by process values and skills
- Unquestioned pursuit of materialistic goals without balancing spiritual goals/values

Jain also found the following changes were encouraged through value clarification workshops:

- Clarity of values
- Awareness of the priority of one's values
- Courage and willingness to pay the price
- Setting goals in congruence with values
- Awareness of the larger picture
- Leadership in clarifying values and role modelling
- Understanding and respecting other people's values
- Recognising the current reality and working for the ideal

SUMMARY

Attitudes are affective (emotional) in nature. They are about liking (favourable) or not liking (unfavourable) an aspect of the object. Attitudes, therefore, have referents.

Values are judgmental in nature, being about preference. Work attitudes are reflected in job satisfaction and in organizational commitment. Job satisfaction leads to improved performance. While job satisfaction is related to the work or the job, commitment shows the relationship between the individual and the organization. Although attitudes are affective (emotional) in nature, they also have cognitive (knowledge) and conative (action) elements.

Attitudes change and can be changed by an external agency. There are five styles or aspects of attitude change: attention, comprehension, yielding, retention, and action. Five aspects of the communication process influence attitude change: source, message, channel, receiver, and destination.

Several value dimensions have been proposed. Kluckhohn and Strodtbeck proposed fatalism, scientism, time orientation, conservatism–liberalism, and authoritarianism. Rokeach distinguished between terminal (desired states of being) and instrumental values (choice of behaviour in reaching end states). Hofstede has suggested four sets of values: power distance (how power is distributed), uncertainty avoidance, individualism–collectivism, and masculinity–feminity. Chakraborty and others have suggested some Indian values.

Values can be developed. Uma Jain has suggested certain exercises for value clarification and developing organizational values.

GLOSSARY

attitude   liking (favourable) or not liking (unfavourable) something or someone

authoritarianism   a positive attitude towards accepting an idealised person or institution for setting tasks, prescribing procedures, or judging results without permitting others to share in the decision-making process

belief   notion of a causal relationship between two concepts

conservatism   a positive attitude towards traditional institutions and practices and towards the maintaining of the status quo, producing a tendency to resist change

ethics   concerns about right and wrong behaviour

fatalism   belief that human situations and acts are predetermined by some supernatural power and cannot be, or are very little, influenced by individual volition

instrumental values   choices of behaviour in reaching end states

karta   the nurturing, caring, dependable, sacrificing yet demanding, authoritative, and strict dimension of the father figure

liberalism   a positive attitude towards the search for new ways and new ideas and towards modification of or change in the status quo

terminal values   desired end states of existence

values   preference of some states over others

EXERCISES

Concept Review Questions
1. What is attitude and what is value? How are attitudes, values, and beliefs related to each other?
2. How can job satisfaction and organizational commitment be increased?
3. What are the different levels of attitude change?

4. Enumerate the various communication processes in relation to attitude change.
5. List a few generalisations about the change of attitude (how can attitudes be changed?).
6. What is the importance of values in organizations? Discuss the role of ethics and different dimensions of ethics in organizations.
7. What is value clarification? How does it help in developing values?

Critical Thinking Questions

1. Beliefs and values

A. Read the statements given below and indicate your agreement or disagreement with each by using the following key:

Key A

Write 0 if you completely disagree with it.
Write 1 if you disagree with it.
Write 2 if you are undecided.
Write 3 if you agree with it.
Write 4 if you strongly agree with it.

_____ 1. You can achieve your goal if you pursue it and do not give it up despite all difficulties.
_____ 2. You may be able to shape things according to your ideas if you work on a task until it is finished.
_____ 3. A challenge can be met if you work out the details of what you want to do, including how to go about doing it.

B. Now read each item given below and indicate, in the space given on its left, how much you value it. Use a number to indicate your preference, according to the following key:

Key B

Write 0 if you do not have any value for it at all.
Write 1 if you value it a little.
Write 2 if you have some value for it.
Write 3 if you value it highly.
Write 4 if you value it very highly.

_____ 1. Earning profit
_____ 2. Determining or shaping things according to one's own ideas
_____ 3. Achievement in life

Scoring

Statements in part A are beliefs, and in part B are values. Multiply your responses to the statements as follows:

A1 _____ ×			B3 _____ = _____
A2 _____ ×			B2 _____ = _____
A3 _____ ×			B1 _____ = _____
Total			_____

The grand total will range from 0 to 16. This is the score for your attitude towards achievement. A total below 6 is low, 6 to 10 is medium, and above 10 is high.

2. Sanctioning a loan

(This exercise will be done in groups of five.)

You are a member of a team of consultants appointed by a bank to scrutinise applications for loans submitted by entrepreneurs. Every applicant is expected to submit an application giving details of his or her background along with the signatures of two guarantors and a project plan for the project to be undertaken. The project plan is scrutinised by a group of technical consultants appointed by the bank. After obtaining the recommendations of technical experts and verifying some of the critical information supplied by the applicant, the details are presented to a committee of five members, who make the final decision about the entrepreneurs to be financed. You are a member of this committee. Enclosed are summaries of the applications of six different candidates. This year, your committee has already decided to finance a number of entrepreneurs. You are now left with only 250,00 million rupees in the kitty to finance any one entrepreneur. Go through the profiles of the candidates and rank them in order of preference, where 1 indicates your most preferred candidate and 6 indicates the least preferred. Also note down the reason why you want to finance that candidate. You have 10 minutes to give your individual ranks.

Record your individual preferences below:

If I have complete freedom to make the decision on behalf of this bank, I would prefer to finance the candidates in the following order:		
Rank No.	Name of the candidate	Reason/observation
1		
2		
3		
4		
5		

After you have individually given your ranks, please discuss these with your group. Your groups will have 20 minutes to discuss and assign final ranks, with reasons, for the rankings.

Rank No.	Name of the candidate	Reason/observation
1		
2		
3		
4		
5		

Now your team will select only *one* candidate. Give justifications for your choice.

Summary background of loan applicants

Janardhan Nagar   Age 50 years. A very active politician having high-level political contacts. Known to have provided employment for a number of people in his area through his contacts. Has held some important positions in the past. It is rumoured that he may become the president of the ruling party in the state. He has no technical background. His son is completing his studies in chemical engineering in the US. The project deals with the setting up of a factory to manufacture some chemicals that are currently being imported. The money required from the bank is about 230,000 million rupees. The estimated annual turnover if the plant comes into existence is 150,000 million rupees. The technical experts find it difficult to comment on the proposal as they do not have a complete knowledge of the chemicals for which the plant has been prepared. However, with the knowledge they have, they feel that the proposal appears to be sound. Marketing is guaranteed and several concessions may be available as the products manufactured will be import substitutes. However, there is danger of the factory causing pollution of the drinking water in that area and causing health hazards. The preventive measures for the health hazards require expensive equipment, which would increase the costs by another 70,000 million rupees. The applicant stated in an interview that he might be able to buy this equipment 4 or 5 years after the plant is commissioned, by which time he would have made sufficient profits. The experts feel that this period would do some damage to the neighbouring areas. Mr Nagar is known to be a close friend of the chairman of the bank and he is on the board of two other banks.

Kailash Pande   Age 40 years. Doctorate in automobile engineering from the US. Has worked with a reputed automobile manufacturing company in the USA for 15 years. Wants to settle down in India. His project is the setting up of a scooter manufacturing industry. The total cost estimated is 200,000,000 million rupees. He is sure of being able to provide the working capital on his own. The project proposes to import some parts and manufacture only the body and a few other parts. He is willing to raise some money from other sources. He wants as much as the bank can give. The technical experts rate his project as an excellent one with a very high possibility of success. This is the only project that has supplied all the details for a thorough assessment by the technical experts. All papers have been found to be in order. There are other partners who are willing to join in this venture.

Vatasala Purushotham   Age 38 years. B.Sc. in home science. Has been working in a small industry service institute and has been in charge of a women's self-employment programme. She is known to have been running the programme well for the last 5 years. She has recently taught the knitting of sweaters on an imported machine to a number of unemployed women. She wants to set up a cooperative of women for knitting sweaters for export. She wants to set up this cooperative with 200 unemployed women as members. Each machine costs Rs 10,000. The estimated cost of a building and other materials is about 70,000 million rupees. The members of the cooperative will provide the working capital. The total requirement from the bank is 180,000 million rupees. The technical experts rate this scheme as somewhat feasible, but they have some doubts about the marketability of the products. Profits, however, are not likely to be of a high order in this project.

Shivachandra Dube   Medical graduate. His wife is also a medical graduate. Both of them are prominent social workers. They have established several community hospitals. In his social work pursuits, Dube could not make any money for himself. Dube now wants to settle down in a metropolitan city and earn his living. He wants to set up a hospital that serves both rich and poor. The investment estimated for this hospital is 250,000 million rupees, as it will have an operation theatre and a clinical laboratory. He expects to earn about 100,000 million rupees a years as consultation fee. He wishes to charge only those who can pay. His projects are assessed by technical experts as somewhat ambitious, as the Dube couple also has a service motive. There are also high risks involved as it is rumoured that another group of doctors plans to set up a polyclinic in that area. Dube's area is known for treating allergies and the incidence of allergies is quite high in that city, particularly in the slums.

Pratibha Desai   Age 37 years. Science graduate, with an MBA from a reputed management training institute. Comes from a family of business persons. Her father is chairman of a reputed engineering company. She has been working as a manager in an advertising company. She has now decided to set up her own advertising agency. She has enough contacts and has already lined up some contracts. She is planning to take a building on hire for her offices. However, she has to buy equipment for a laboratory and other materials. The estimated total costs for her project are 500,000 million rupees. She is willing to raise about 300,000 million rupees on her own from partners. She has applied for a loan of 200,000 million rupees. Technical experts rate the project as sound and having a high potential, as the world of advertising is developing fast.

Classroom Project
List three values held in high regard by your family. Are these practised? If not, why not? What is the effect? Exchange information and discuss your reflections with another friend.

Field Projects
1. Interview two managers to find out their three most important values. Also discuss whether their organization gives them opportunities to practise those values.
2. Interview a manager from an organization. Find out which one value, according to him, has helped the organization acquire its unique identity. Which two values would he like the organization to practise?

Om Prakash at Cross Roads*

In 2003, Om Prakash (popularly known as OP), a 40-year-old IFS (Indian Forest Services) officer, was deputed as the Regional Employees' Provident Fund Commissioner (PFC) of the state of Bihar and stationed at Patna—a challenging post, since this particular department was well known for its corruption and delays in repayment of the employees' share of provident fund.

OP hailed from western UP and his upbringing had been in a feudal family in which autocracy was the norm. At the age of 10, OP went to a boarding school at Agra, where he acquired knowledge in the areas of science and humanities. During his schooling, he developed interest in understanding the relationship between science and technology. This understanding brought about a change in his mindset—being open to reason rather than guided by traditions. Prior to this, his mindset had been like that of a typical Indian who believes that whatever has to happen will happen.

During his 15-year tenure as an IFS officer, OP had handled many assignments in different parts of Bihar. The exposure helped him understand the complexities involved in interpersonal relationships, since he had to interact with people from diverse backgrounds and varied experiences. The zeal to understand the people around him led him to different levels of belief patterns that were deeply rooted in the Indian culture. His quest for knowledge also made him read books on Islam, Christianity, and other religions. He started believing that truth is the ultimate.

On taking over as the PFC, OP noticed that some people in the department had been around for quite a long period—this despite the fact that there were well-defined rules for transfer, wherein an employee could stay in a particular posting maximum for 3 years. This rule was flexible in extreme cases such as ill health or family problems. OP felt that long stays in a posting was one of the reasons for corruption taking strong roots in the department—it facilitated the vicious circle of corruption to expand and survive.

In keeping with the transfer policy of the department, he prepared a list of employees who were due for transfer, and then acted upon it. But before the transfer orders were issued, OP, a firm believer in human justice, thoroughly examined applications requesting him to waive transfer on the grounds of poor health or family problems. He scanned through the applications for reconsideration. While doing so, he came across an application requesting a waiver on the premise that the applicant

*This case has been developed by Santosh Dhar, Akhilesh Misra, Vinit S. Chauhan, Manisha Singhai (Prestige Institute of Management and Research, Indore), and Gazal Rai (Prestige Institute of Management, Dewas) in the Twelfth National Case Writing Workshop held at Prestige Institute of Management and Research, Indore, and sponsored by Association of Indian Management Schools (AIMS) on April 23–25, 2004.

was the only son of a widow suffering from serious ailments and frequent hospitalisations. OP decided to investigate the truth through informal means—he got another employee to collect all available information about the applicant. On enquiry, it was found that the applicant was not staying with his mother and, in fact, was not on talking terms with her. To confirm the truth, OP himself talked to the applicant's mother on phone, without disclosing his own identity.

Next, OP called the applicant and confronted him with the truth. Now asked whether he would still like to stay back, the applicant straightaway refused and opted to take the transfer—in the past four occasions he had managed to stay back on false grounds.

But this was just the beginning of OP's troubles with posting and transfer issues. One morning, he got a phone call from the labour minister asking him to transfer a recruitee from Sasaram to Ara town. Now OP was in a dilemma. If he would approve the transfer, there would be no end to such requests from politicians. Succumbing to political pressures would prick his conscience—it would be unjust to deserving candidates, besides setting a precedent, as manipulators would create havoc in the system. However, if he refused to oblige the politician, he would have to prepare himself to face the consequences, since he knew that there was no place for rules or logic in politics. Therefore, he decided to avoid a direct confrontation with the minister.

The matter demanded tactful handling of the situation, wherein the minister himself would withdraw the request. OP called for the file of the recruitee and found that he was not eligible for the post he had been selected to and had been given a back-door entry by the labour minister. He also came to know through one of his informers that the recruitee had a schedule caste certificate. OP got a complaint registered that the schedule caste certificate of the recruitee was fake, although this was not true. The recruitee had a genuine schedule caste certificate. OP then informed the minister about the complaint lodged against the recruitee. As anticipated, the minister, fearing the negative publicity that the episode would generate, decided to detach himself from the matter and asked OP not to enforce the transfer orders. OP felt that through this tactic he had been able to resolve the issue—by drawing a bigger line in comparison to the lines drawn by others.

OP believed that if he was accessible to the public, he could deliver better results in less time. He installed a direct phone line through which anybody from any part of the state could contact him. This telephone number was displayed at various locations throughout the state to make the public aware that the PFC was accessible to them. He got many phone calls from the employees and subscribers. This gave him an overview of the organization right from his office.

One day, through one such phone call, a delay in the release of a part of the PF contribution was brought to his notice. A subscriber had applied under the Tatkal scheme, wherein disbursement of money was to be done within 24 hours, for the hospitalisation of his father. Ten days had elapsed, and the money had not been released. OP enquired into the matter and came to know that the LDC (lower division clerk) had already passed the file on time but it had been retained by the accountant. OP had the accountant suspended with immediate effect.

The accountant wanted to meet OP. OP readily agreed, since he believed in listening to others' viewpoint and saw this meeting as an opportunity to correct himself and alleviate conflict. OP had inquired about the accountant and found that no such incident had occurred in the past. That evening, the accountant along with his wife, father, and four daughters came to the office and started pleading. Looking at the man's past records, OP decided to let him go with a warning and decided to keep a track of his movements. He was quite satisfied with the feedback he got, and with his decision, as the accountant was doing well with the job.

In another incident, a complaint of bribery was lodged against an LDC, appointed through the sports quota 6 months earlier. He was demanding Rs 2,000 from Mehta to forward his file. A trap was laid down to catch the LDC red-handed. Currency notes signed by OP were handed over by Mehta to the LDC and, at the same time, their conversation was also tape-recorded by Mehta. On the basis of the evidence so generated, OP decided not only to dismiss the LDC from his services, but also debarred him from applying to other government services. OP justified this stern action on the ground that he could foresee a corrupt employee in the LDC, since the offence was too grave for a new recruit. Moreover, investigations had revealed that even his father had been dismissed from government services for the same reason.

OP was softhearted and believed in participatory administration. But over the years, he started feeling that soft corrective measures could not always help to set the system right; rather, at times, punitive and coercive measures become imperative. To rid the system of inefficient people, within 1 year he dismissed 12 employees and punished another 25 senior employees by demoting them and even stopping their increments. Surprisingly, in spite of such stern actions, the union did not interfere. OP, from time to time, would convey to his staff that if they would not perform well, they would have to face the consequences of privatisation, which was likely to happen during the coming years as it had happened in the insurance sector. The Provident Fund Organization had introduced a reward and recognition system—out-of-turn promotion, and financial rewards of Rs 500–5,000 awarded to workers who met deadlines. Attitude and conduct were also taken into consideration while evaluating the performance of the employee. OP involved his employees in intellectual activities like thinking promotion and logical thinking and the like. They were also given lectures on politics and science, and on religion—to inculcate beliefs such as to respect ones work, not the hierarchy, and to respect one-self before respecting others.

OP believed that transparency, honesty, and sincerity in a leader can pave the way to a system devoid of corruption. Yet, he was not sure how far he would be able to remove the rot from the system.

Questions for Discussion
1. Identify and discuss OP's value system.
2. How far do you think OP has been ethical in his decisions? Discuss.
3. Justify actions of OP against the accountant and the LDC.
4. While handling the labour minister, OP has shown escapist tendency. Discuss.

NOTES AND REFERENCES

1. Anti-Deformation League (1998). *How to Combat Bias and Hate Crimes: An ADL Blueprint for Action*, p. 6. Washington: ADL.
2. Meyer, J.P. and N.J. Allen (1991). 'A three-component conceptualisation of organisational commitment', *Human Resource Management Review*, 1: 61–89.
3. Hovland, C.I., I.L. Janis, and H.H. Kalley (1953). *Communication and Persuasion*. New Haven: Yale University Press.
4. Heider, F. (1958). *The Psychology of Interpersonal Relations*. New York: Wiley.
5. Abelson, R.P. (1968). 'Psychological implication', in R.P. Abelson, E. Aronson, W.J. McGuire, T.M. Newcomb, M.J. Rosenberg, and P.H. Tannenbaum (eds), *Theories of Cognitive Consistency: A Source Book*, pp. 112–139. Skokie, IL: Rand Mcnally.
6. Festinger, I. (1957). *A Theory of Cognitive Dissonance*. Standford, CA: Stanford University Press.
7. Festinger, L. and J.M. Carlsmith (1959). 'Cognitive consequences of forced compliance', *Journal of Abnormal and Social Psychology*, 58: 203–211.
8. Brehm, J. and A.R. Cohen (1962). *Explorations in Cognitive Dissonance*. New York: Wiley.
9. McGuire, W.J. (1969). 'The nature of attitudes and attitude change', in G. Lindzey and E. Aronson (ed.). *The Handbook of Social Psychology. Volume Three*, pp. 136–314. New York: Addison-Wesley.
10. Kelman, H.C. (1950). 'Effects of success and failure on suggestibility in the auto-kinetic situation', *Journal of Abnormal and Social Psychology*, 45: 267–285.
11. Eysenck, H.J. and W.D. Furneaux (1945). 'Primary and secondary suggestibility: An experimental and statistical study', *Journal of Experimental Psychology*, 35: 485–503.
12. Beloff, H. (1958). 'Two forms of social conformity: Acquiescence and conventionality', *Journal of Abnormal and Social Psychology*, 56: 99–104.
13. Janis, I.L. (1954). 'Personality correlates of susceptibility to persuasion', *Journal of Abnormal and Social Psychology*, 51: 663–667.
14. Hovland, C.I., I.L. Janis, and H.H. Kalley (1953). *Communication and Persuasion*. New Haven: Yale University Press.
15. McGuire, W.J. (1969). 'The nature of attitudes and attitude change', in G. Lindzey and E. Aronson (ed.), *The Handbook of Social Psychology*, Volume Three, pp. 136–314. New York: Addison-Wesley.
16. Kluckhohn, C. et. al (1951). 'Values and value-orientations in the theory of action', in T. Parsons and E.A. Shils (eds), *Toward a General Theory of Action*. Cambridge, MA: Harvard Univ. Press.
17. Rokeach, Milton (1973). *The Nature of Human Values*. New York: Free Press.
18. Ramachandran, S. (2003). 'A study of congruence between individual values and perceived organisational values and its impact on commitment to the organisation'. Doctoral thesis, AHRD-XLRI.
19. Chakraborty, S.K. (1987). *Managerial Effectiveness and Quality of Work Life: Indian Insight*. Delhi: Tata McGraw-Hill.
20. Kluckhohn, F. and F.L. Strodtbeck (1961). *Variations in Value Orientation*. Evanston, IL: Rowe Peterson.
21. O'Neill, W.M. and D.J. Levinson (1954). 'A factorial exploration of authoritarianism and some of its ideological correlates', *Journal of Personality*, 22: 449–463.
22. Adorno, T.W., E. Frenkel-Brunswik, J. Levinson, and R.N. Sanford (1950). *The Authoritarian Personality*. New York: Wiley.
23. Titus, H.E. and E.P. Hollander (1957). 'The California F scale in psychological research: 1950–1955', *Psychological Bulletin*, 54: 47–64; Christie and M. Jahoda (1954). *Studies in the Scope and Methods of the Authoritarian Personality*. New York: Free Press; Christie, R. and P. Cooge (1958). 'A guide to published literature relating to the authoritarian personality through 1956', *Format of Psychology*, 45: 171–199.
24. Eysenck, H.J. (1979). *The Psychology of Politics*. Routledge, London.
25. *Ibid.*, 378

26. Adorno, et al. *The Authoritarian Personality*. New York: Wiley.
27. Rokeach, Milton (1973). *The Nature of Human Values*, pp. 13–14. New York: Free Press.
28. Musser, S.J. and E.A. Orke (1992). 'Ethical value system: A typology', *Journal of Applied Behavioural Science*, 28(3): 348–362.
29. Rokeach, Milton (1973). *The Nature of Human Values*, p. 13. New York: Free Press.
30. Hofstede, G. (1980). *Culture's Consequences: International Difference in Work-Related Values*. Beverly Hills: Sage.
31. Chakraborty, S.K. (1991). *Management by Values*. Oxford: Oxford Publishing Company.
32. *Ibid.*
33. Prakash, A. (1982). 'A study of organizational socialisation of industrial workers', unpublished doctoral dissertation, University of Allahabad.
34. Ramachandran. 'Study of congruence'.
35. Collins, J.C. and J.I. Porras (1997). *Built to Last*. New York: Harper.
36. Woodcock, M. and F. Dave (1989). *Clarifying Organisational Values*, pp. 10–15. Englewood Cliffs, NJ: Prentice Hall.
37. Peters, T.J. and R.H. Waterman (1982). *In Search of Excellence: Lessons from America's Best-Run Companies*. New York: Warner Books.
38. Amsa, P. and V.B. Punekar (1985). 'A value-based conceptual model of commitment to work: An empirical validation', *Indian Journal of Industrial Relations*, 21(1): 16–23.
39. Allport, G.W., P.E. Vernon, and G. Lindzey (1960). *Study of Values*, 3rd ed. Boston: Houghton Mifflin.
40. Rao, T.V. (1991). 'Managerial work values', in J.W. Pfeiffer (ed.), *The 1991 Annual: Developing Human Resources*, pp. 163–177. San Diego: University Associates.
41. Roy, S. and S.K. Dhawan (1984) reported in Mehta, C. (2005), 'Value orientation of HRD professionals in India', *Journal of Human Values*, 11: 103–115.
42. Upadhyay, D.P. (1985). 'Value, people and organization', *Indian Management*, 24(12): 31–34.
43. Jain, Uma (2002). 'Value erosion in organizations and society: Diagnosis and change through value clarification interventions', in Udai Pareek, Aahad M. Osma-Gani, S. Ramanarayan, and T.V. Rao (eds), *Human Resource Development in Asia: Trends and Challenges*, pp. 297–308. New Delhi: Oxford & IBH.
44. Kirschenbaum, Howard (1977). *Advanced Value Clarification*. San Diego, CA: Pfeiffer & Co.
45. Jain, Uma (2002). 'Value erosion in organizations and society: Diagnosis and change through value clarification interventions', in Udai Pareek, Aahad M. Osma-Gani, S. Ramanarayan, and T.V. Rao (2002) (eds), *Human Resource Development in Asia: Trends and Challenges*, pp. 297–308. New Delhi: Oxford & IBH.
46. Kirschenbaum. *Advanced Value Clarification*.
47. For details of these exercises, see Kirschenbaun, *Advanced Value Clarification*.
48. Jain, Uma (2002). 'Value erosion in organizations and society: Diagnosis and change through value clarification interventions', in Udai Pareek, *Human Resource Development in Asia*.

The Role

- Roles and Role Effectiveness

- Managing Work Motivation

- Coping with Frustration, Stress, and Burnout

- Decisional Process

- Managerial Roles, Functions, and Styles

12
Roles and Role Effectiveness

In any social system, such as a family, club, religious community, or work organization, individuals have certain obligations towards the system, which in turn gives each one of them a defined place in the system. This scheme of mutual obligations can be called a role and the individual's place in the system a position or an office.

For example, when one joins a new club, one is admitted as a 'member' (this is an office or a position). One's position as a member is defined in terms of placement in the hierarchy and the privileges one will enjoy. One also agrees to abide by certain rules, participate in certain activities when required, volunteer for certain tasks, etc. The other members of the club expect all this from the individual and the individual also expects to do the needful. All these expectations and one's own response to them comprise the 'role'. Briefly then, an individual occupies a hierarchical position in a system, along with the ensuing powers and privileges, and also performs certain functions in response to his or her own and the other members' expectations. In this case, the former is the office (or position) and the latter the role.

ROLE VS OFFICE

A role is the place one occupies in a social system as defined by the functions one performs in response to the expectations of the 'significant' members of a social system and one's own expectations from that position or office.

'Role' and 'office' (or position), though two sides of the same coin, are nevertheless two separate concepts. According to Katz and Kahn,[1] 'Office is essentially a relational concept, defining each position in terms of its relationships to others and to the system as a whole.' While 'office' is a relational and power-related concept, 'role' is an 'obligational' concept. An office is concerned with the hierarchical position and privileges while a role is concerned with the obligations of the position. Exhibit 12.1 distinguishes between these two concepts. While an office is a point in the social

Exhibit 12.1   *Office (or Position) and Role*

Office/position	Role
Is based on power relations	Is based on mutuality
Has related privileges	Has related obligations
Is usually hierarchical	Is non-hierarchical
Is created by others	Is created by others and the role occupant
Is part of the structure	Is part of the dynamics
Is evaluative	Is descriptive

structure defining the office-holder's power, a role is the integrated set of behaviours expected from a person occupying that office.

An organization can be represented according to its offices or its roles. Exhibits 12.2 and 12.3 represent a part of an organization in these two different ways.

An office becomes a role when it is actually defined and determined by the expectations of other office-holders (as reflected in the way an office is discharged by the concerned office-holder). Each role has its own system, consisting of the occupant

Exhibit 12.2   *Organization as a Structure of Offices/Positions*

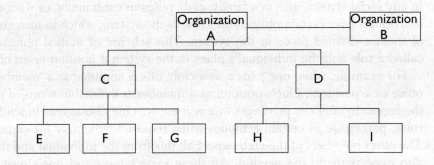

Exhibit 12.3   *Organization as a System of Roles*

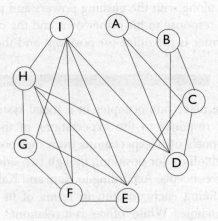

of the role and those who have a direct relationship with him or her, and thereby certain expectations from the role. Using the currently accepted terminology suggested by Katz and Kahn, we will term the 'significant' others having expectations from a role as 'role senders'. They 'send' expectations to the role. The role occupant also has expectations from the role—in that sense, the role occupant is also a role sender.

Let us take an example. In a family, the father has both a position (office) and a role. The father's position defines his authority in the family. In some societies, he is the final decision-maker for the family and the other members abide by his decisions. There are certain expectations from the father that define his role—in his position as the head of the family system, his role is to maintain and protect the family. In a traditional Indian family, the father would also be expected to earn and provide for the family. While the position gives him some privileges, the role places certain obligations on him.

A role is not defined without the expectations of the role senders, including those of the role occupant. The position of a personnel manager may be created in an organization, but his or her role will be defined by the expectations (stated or unstated) that different persons have from the personnel manager and the expectations that he or she in turn has from the role. In this sense, the role gets defined in each system by the specific role senders, including the role occupant.

However, a question can be raised here: If the role is defined in each case by the role senders, how can we talk about a role in general, for example, 'the father's role'? Strictly speaking, 'a role in general' does not make much sense. However, in a larger social system, expectations from a role are generally shared across society, so that similar roles in its sub-systems (e.g., the 'family' in 'Indian society') have common elements. These are generalised so that we can talk about the role of the Indian mother or the role of a chairman in a public sector concern, etc.

Confusion sometimes arises because the word 'role' has two different connotations. At times it denotes the position a person holds in an organization along with the expectations from that position (e.g., the role of a teacher, a police officer), but sometimes it describes only the expected behaviour or activities (e.g., a teacher's role as a disciplinarian or an evaluator, task and maintenance roles). For the sake of convenience, we shall here use the word 'role' only for a position a person holds in a system (organization) as defined by the expectations various 'significant' persons (including the role occupant) have from that person. We will use the term 'function' to indicate a set of interrelated expectations from a role. For example, developing a sales force and facilitating customer contact are the functions of a sales manager's role.

A similar distinction needs to be made between several work-related terms, in fact: office, role, job, function, task, etc. Although there are no universally accepted definitions, 'work' is generally a wider term, whereas 'office', 'role', and 'job' are ways of organizing work or dividing responsibilities. 'Functions' are sub-units of a role. A function can be further subdivided into 'tasks'. Exhibit 12.4 provides the definitions of these terms and Exhibit 12.5 shows their conceptual hierarchy.

Exhibit 12.4   *Work-related Terms*

- *Work* is a wider concept, linking a person with his or her tools and with others performing a similar activity.
- An *office* or a *position* is a specific point in an organizational structure, defining the power of the person occupying it.
- A *role* is the set of obligations generated by 'significant' others and the individual occupying an office.
- A *job* is a specific requirement to produce a product or achieve an objective.
- A *function* is a group of expected behaviours from a role.
- A *task* is a specific activity that is part of a function, often bound by time.

Exhibit 12.5   *Hierarchy of Some Work-related Terms*

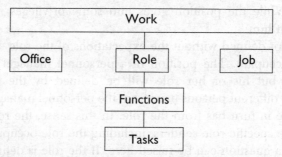

For example, an individual X may occupy the office of manager at Branch Y of a bank. As a part of this office, X reports to the regional manager. Similarly, a large number of persons in turn report to X. X's role is to develop Branch Y by getting a successively larger market share of deposits and advances. One of the functions under this role is to increase deposits. One task that X performs as a part of this function is to undertake a survey of potential depositors and another is to contact the prestigious or 'big' depositors personally.

The concept of roles is vital for the integration of individuals with an organization. The individual and the organization come together through a role. As shown in Exhibit 12.6, the organization has its own structure and goals. Similarly, the individual has his or her own personality and needs (motivations). These interact with each other and to some extent get integrated into a role.

The role is also a central concept in work motivation. It is only through a role that the individual and an organization interact with each other (as shown in Exhibit 12.7).

Exhibit 12.6   *Role as Integrating Point of Organization and Individual*

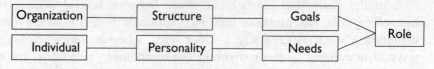

Exhibit 12.7 *Role as Region of Individual–Organization Interaction*

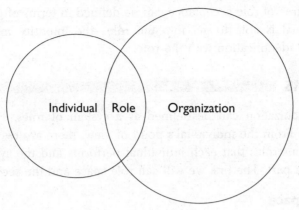

THE ROLE AND THE INDIVIDUAL

When a person becomes a member of a social system, he or she 'receives' certain expectations from other members and responds to these, at the same time projecting his or her own expectations on to the role. Either one of these attitudes (responding to others' expectations and projecting one's own expectations on to one's role) may dominate.

One may react very positively and with great satisfaction to others' expectations and fulfil them to the best of one's abilities. Such a 'reactive' (responsive) approach will help the individual take on the role effectively. In contrast, another individual may use the expectations he or she has from the role—what Kahn and Quinn[2] call reflexive role expectations—to develop a role behaviour. This is a 'proactive' approach to role performance. Some authors have contrasted these two approaches, calling the first 'role taking' and the second 'role making'.

Katz and Kahn have proposed the concept of a 'role episode' to explain the process of role taking. Role taking involves both role sending (by the 'significant' others) and role receiving (by the role occupant). The role occupant and the role senders constantly interact and the processes of role sending and role receiving together influence the role behaviour of the individual. The role senders have expectations on the basis of their perception of the role occupant's behaviour. The role occupant, in turn, acts on the basis of his or her perception of the role. However, a person's role behaviour also influences the expectations of the role senders. Thus a role episode has a feedback loop. Katz and Kahn have further elaborated this concept to include the interaction between role senders and the role occupant as well as interpersonal and personality factors.

The other aspect of role taking is concerned with the identification of the self with the role. If the role expectations are congruent with the self-concept, there is role acceptance. However, if the expectations conflict with the self-concept, it may result in what we call self–role distance. Even when there is no evident self–role distance the degree of role acceptance can be defined in terms of the intensity with which an individual is able to get into the role—the intensity may vary from casual to a morbid identification with the role.

ROLE SYSTEMS

An organization can be defined as a system of roles. However, a role is itself a system. From the individual's point of view, there are two role systems—the system of various roles that each individual performs and the system of roles of that each role is a part. The first we will call role space and the second a role set.

Role Space

Each individual occupies and plays several roles. A person X is a daughter, a mother, a salesperson, a member of a club, a member of a voluntary organization, and so on. All these roles constitute the role space of X. At the centre of the role space is the self. As the concept of the role is central to the organization, so the concept of the self is central to the several roles of a person. The term 'self' refers to the interpretations a person makes about the referent 'I'. It is a cognitive structure that evolves from past experience with other persons and objects. The self can be defined as the experience of an identity, arising from a person's interactions with external reality—things, persons, and systems.

A person performs various roles that are centred around the self. These roles are at varying distances from the self (and from each other). These various relationships define the role space. Role space, then, is a dynamic interrelationship between the self and the various roles an individual occupies and also among these roles.

The distance between a role and the self indicates the extent to which the role is integrated with the self. When we do not enjoy a particular role or do not get involved in it, there is a distance between the self and the role. We shall again use the term self–role distance to denote this. Similarly, there may be a distance between two roles that a person occupies. For example, the role of 'club member' may be distant from the role of 'husband'. This we will term inter-role distance or inter-role conflict.

The role space map of an individual can be drawn by locating the self in the centre and the various roles at varying distances from the self. Exhibit 12.8 presents the role space of a person A who is a personnel manager in a company. The numbers 9 to 1 for the various circles represent distances from the self—1 denoting the least distance and 9 the most. The various roles of A are located in the four quadrants according to their contexts (i.e., family, organization, profession, and recreation). Of course, more segments of role space can be added in the diagram.

Exhibit 12.8 *Role Space Map of A*

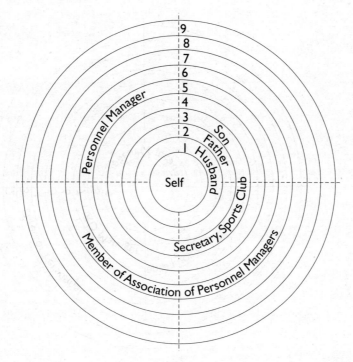

Role Set

The individual's role in the organization is defined by the expectations of other significant roles and those of the individual himself or herself. The role set is a pattern of interrelationships between a particular role and the other roles in the system.

The role set map for an individual can also be prepared on the same lines as those suggested for preparing a role space map. In a role set map, the occupant's role will be in the centre and all the other roles in the system can be located at various points on the map. Using a circular model, the roles can be located in concentric circles marked 9 to 1 (9 indicating the roles closest to the occupant's role, and 1 indicating those that are the most distant). We will use the term inter-role distance to indicate the distance between the occupant's role and other roles. A smaller distance indicates higher role linkages (which is the reverse of inter-role distance). Role linkage is an important concept in role satisfaction and role conflict. Exhibit 12.9 gives the role set map of a person A.

Role sets are the sub-systems in an organizational system. In Exhibit 12.3, nine role sets for the roles of offices A, B, C, D, E, F, G, H, and I are indicated.

In conclusion, a role is a very useful concept in understanding the dynamics of integration of an individual with a social system. It also helps in understanding the problems that arise in this individual–organization interaction and integration. The concept of the role goes beyond the individual employee and indicates a need to

Exhibit 12.9   Role Set Map of A

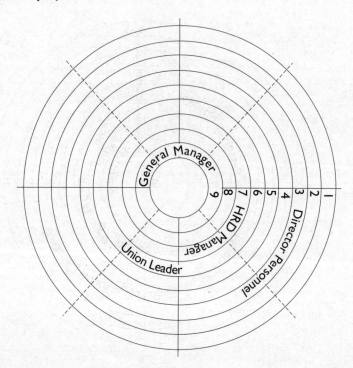

involve other significant persons in defining role requirements. A focus on roles can be useful in planning organizational effectiveness.

ROLE EFFICACY

The performance of a person working in an organization depends on his or her own potential effectiveness as a person, technical competence, managerial experience, etc., as well as the way the role that the person performs in the organization is designed. It is the integration of the two (the person and the role) that ensures a person's effectiveness in the organization. Unless the person has the requisite knowledge, technical competence, and skills required for a role, he or she cannot be effective. Equally important is how the role that the individual occupies is designed. If the role does not allow the individual to use his or her competence, so that he or she constantly feels frustrated in the role, the individual's effectiveness is likely to be low. The integration of the person and the role comes about when the role is able to fulfil the needs of the individual and when the individual is able to contribute to the evolution of the role. The more we move from role taking (responding to the expectations

Dinesh seems to have taken the citation for 'Best Integrated Employee' too seriously—now he's trying to 'integrate' his bedroll into his work!

of various other persons) to role making (taking initiative in designing the role more creatively, so that the various expectations from others as well as those of the role occupant are integrated), the more the role is likely to be effective.

The effectiveness of a role occupant in an organization, therefore, depends on the individual's own potential effectiveness, the potential effectiveness of the role, and the organizational climate. These potential effectivenesses can be called efficacy. Personal efficacy would mean the potential effectiveness of a person in both personal and interpersonal situations. Role efficacy then means the potential effectiveness of an individual occupying a particular role in an organization.

Role efficacy can thus be seen as the psychological factor underlying role effectiveness. In short, role efficacy is potential role effectiveness.

Role efficacy has several aspects. The more these aspects are present in a role, the higher the efficacy of that role is likely to be. These aspects can be classified into three groups or dimensions.

One dimension of role efficacy is role making as contrasted with role taking. The first is an active attitude towards the role (to define and make the role as one likes), whereas the second is a passive attitude (mainly responding to others' expectations).

The aspects in the second dimension are concerned with increasing the power of the role, making it more important. This can be called 'role centring', which can be contrasted with 'role entering' (accepting the role as given and reconciling oneself to its present importance or unimportance).

The third dimension is called 'role linking' (extending the relationship of the role with other roles and groups) as contrasted with 'role shrinking' (making the role narrower, more confined to work-related expectations).

Role Making

Self–role integration   Every person has certain strengths—experience, technical training, special skills—some unique contribution he or she may be able to make. The more the role provides opportunities for the use of its occupant's such special strengths, the higher the efficacy is likely to be. This is called self–role integration.

The self of the person and the role get integrated through the possibility of a person's use of his or her special strengths in the role. Say a person is promoted to a responsible position in a certain organization and this is seen as a convertible reward, so that the person is happy to get this well-deserved promotion. However, he or she soon discovers that, in this new position, he or she is no longer able to use his or her special skills of training, counselling, and organizational diagnosis. In spite of this person working very hard in the new role, his or her efficacy is not as high as it was in the previous role. Later, when the role is redesigned to enable this person to use his or her skills better, the individual's efficacy goes up. All of us want that our special strengths are used in a role so that it is possible for us to demonstrate how effective we can be. Integration contributes to such high role efficacy. On the other hand, if there is distance between the self and the role, role efficacy is likely to be low.

Proactivity   A person who occupies a role responds to various expectations people in the organization have from that role. This certainly gives the person satisfaction and it also satisfies others in the organization. However, if he or she is also to take initiative in starting a new activity, the person's efficacy will be higher. Reactive behaviour (responding to the expectations of others) helps a person to be effective to a certain extent, but proactivity (taking the initiative rather than only responding to others' expectations) contributes much more to efficacy. If a person feels that he or she would like to take initiative but has no opportunity to do so in the role he or she occupies in the organization, the person's efficacy will be low.

Creativity   It is not only initiative that is important for efficacy. Opportunities to try new and unconventional ways of solving problems or to be creative are equally important.

In a certain department in a state government, people performing certain clerical roles met as a part of a reorganization experiment to discuss how each individual could experiment with a system of cutting down delays in processing papers. The results were amazing. Not only did the satisfaction levels of the people in that department go up, the delays were considerably reduced and some innovative systems emerged. Certainly these were discussed further and modified, but this opportunity the people got to be creative and try out innovative ideas increased their role efficacy, so that their performance became markedly better than their own previous performance and that of other departments in the same secretariat.

If a person perceives that he or she has to perform only routine tasks, it does not help the person to achieve high role efficacy. Also, if he or she feels that the role does not allow any time or opportunity to be creative, the person's efficacy will be low.

Conformation   In general, if people in an organization avoid problems or shift them to other people, their role efficacy is low. The tendency to confront problems and find relevant solutions contributes to efficacy. When people facing interpersonal problems sit down, talk about these problems, and search out solutions, their efficacy is likely to be higher compared with situations in which they either deny such problems or refer these to their senior officers.

Role Centering

Centrality   If a person occupying a particular role in the organization generally feels that the role he or she occupies is central to the organization, his or her role efficacy is likely to be high. Everyone working in an organization wants to feel that his or her role is important. If people occupying various roles feel that their roles are peripheral, that is, they are not very important, their potential effectiveness will be low.

This is true not only of people at higher levels in the organization, but also people at the lowest level.

In a certain large hospital, the Class IV employees (sweepers and ward attendants) had very high motivation when they first joined the hospital. Coming from nearby villages, they would bring their friends and relatives to proudly show them the place they were working in. However, within a few months, they began to neglect their work, sat around gossiping in groups, and not caring about the cleanliness of the ward. They were rated as being very low in their effectiveness. An investigation of the problem showed that within a few months of their joining the hospital, their perception about the importance of their role changed, so that they felt their role was not important at all.

In contrast with this, in another hospital, the guard was trained to screen the requests of visitors who wanted to have an exception made to the rules regarding visiting hours. She used her discretion in making or not making exceptions in such cases and referred a case to the nurses or doctors only when she needed clarification and guidance. Interviews with Class IV employees in this hospital showed that they perceived their roles as quite important.

One obvious clue to the low motivation of the former set of employees and higher motivation of the latter was the perceived importance of their roles.

Influence   A related concept is that of influence or power. The more influence a person is able to exercise in a role, the higher the role efficacy is likely to be. One factor that may make roles in the public sector or civil service more efficacious is the opportunity to influence a larger section of society. On the other hand, if a person feels that he or she has no power in the role he or she occupies in the organization, the person is likely to have low efficacy.

Personal growth   One factor that contributes effectively to role efficacy is the perception that the role provides the individual with an opportunity to grow and develop. There are several examples of people leaving one role and becoming very effective in another, primarily because they felt that they had more opportunities to grow in the latter.

The head of a certain training institute accepted the position after taking a big financial cut in salary mainly because she felt that she had nothing more to learn in the previous role but had opportunities to grow further in the new one. Examples of executives of companies going for faculty roles in management training institutes also indicate the importance of this factor of self-development for role efficacy.

If a person feels that he or she is stagnating in a role and does not get any opportunity to grow, he or she is likely to have low role efficacy. In many institutes of higher learning, the roles of the staff suffer from low efficacy. The main factor contributing to this is the lack of opportunity for them to systematically grow in their roles. Institutes that are able to plan the growth of such people in their roles are able to have higher efficacy and a great deal of contribution from them.

Role Linking

Inter-role linkage   Linkage of one's role with other roles in the organization increases efficacy. If there is a joint effort in understanding problems, finding solutions, etc., the efficacy of the various roles involved is likely to be high. Of course, the assumption is that people know how to work effectively. Similarly, if a person is a member of a task group set up for a specific purpose, his or her efficacy (other factors being common) is likely to be high. The feeling of isolation in a role (that a person works without any linkage to other roles) reduces role efficacy.

Helping relationship   In addition to inter-role linkages, the opportunity for people to receive and give help also increases role efficacy. If people performing a particular role feel that they can get help from another source in the organization whenever they need, they are likely to have higher role efficacy. On the other hand, if there is a feeling that either no help is given when asked for or that the respondents are hostile, role efficacy will be low. Helping relationships must feature both qualities—people feeling free to ask for help and expecting that help will be available when it is needed as well as people's willingness to give help and respond to the needs of others.

Superordination   A role may have linkages with systems, groups, and entities beyond the organization. When a person performing a particular role feels that what he or she does as a part of the role is likely to be of value to a larger group, the efficacy is likely to be high.

Roles that give opportunities to role occupants to work for superordinate goals have very high role efficacy. Superordinate goals are those serving large groups and those that cannot be achieved without some collaborative effort. One major motivation for people at the top to move to public sector undertakings is the opportunity to work for larger goals that are likely to help larger sections of the society. Many people have voluntarily accepted cuts in their salaries to move from the private sector to the top level of the public sector, mainly because their new roles would give them an opportunity to serve larger interests.

Roles in which people feel that what they are doing is helpful to the organization in which they work also results in some role efficacy. But if a person feels that he or she does not get an opportunity to be of help to a larger group, his or her role efficacy is likely to be low.

Regarding the personal profile of role efficacy, research has shown that people with high role efficacy seem to rely on their own strengths to cope with problems, are active and interact with people and the environment, and persist in solving problems mostly by themselves and sometimes by taking the help of other people. They show positive approach behaviour and feel satisfied with life and with their jobs and roles in their organizations. Such is the profile of an effective manager.

Regarding organizational aspects, a participative climate in which employees find high job satisfaction contributes to role efficacy. It seems that a climate promoting a concern for excellence, the use of available expertise, and a concern for the larger issues also contributes to role efficacy. On the other hand, a climate characterised by control and affiliation seems to lower employees' role efficacy, according to Sayeed and Pareek.[3]

INCREASING ROLE EFFICACY

One can plan to increase the efficacy of one's own role as well as those of one's subordinates. Some practical suggestions, based on actual practices in some organizations, are given below for supervisors who wish to increase the role efficacy of their subordinates:

Self–role Integration

1. Work with subordinates to redesign their roles so that their strengths can be utilised.
2. Recommend moving a 'misfit' to a job that can use his or her assets.

Proactivity

1. Minimise supervision of subordinates, and encourage them to ask for your help when they need it.
2. Reward initiative in subordinates.
3. Listen to subordinates, respect their views, and use these wherever possible.
4. Arrange for subordinates to visit other organizations.

Creativity

1. Encourage your subordinates to come up with ideas to solve problems.
2. Create a climate that encourages people to generate ideas without fear of being criticised.
3. Appreciate and use new ideas given by subordinates.
4. Encourage and reward suggestions to solve problems.

Confrontation

1. Take subordinates into confidence while confronting a problem.
2. Support the action taken by a subordinate if it is within the rules and procedures.
3. Appoint a task group for a problematic decision.
4. Use a subordinate's failure as useful experience—help him or her to learn from it.
5. Encourage subordinates to bring problems forward.
6. Anticipate problems together.
7. Encourage subordinates to solve problems themselves and then report to you.
8. Follow the 'buck stops here' dictum.

Centrality

1. Communicate the importance of roles (their critical contributions) to their incumbents.
2. Communicate the importance of the roles as perceived by others.
3. Give enough freedom to each subordinate to set his or her own objectives and decide on ways of achieving them.
4. Give increasingly difficult and challenging responsibilities.

Influence

1. Delegate authority.
2. Give relevant details of decisions made.
3. Send good ideas from subordinates to higher management.
4. Give feedback to subordinates on their suggestions.
5. Be willing to accept mistakes.

Growth

1. Appreciate your subordinates' work.
2. Do not snub employees for their shortcomings, instead cooperate with them to overcome these.
3. Delegate increasingly difficult and challenging tasks to them.

Inter-role Linkage

1. Encourage subordinates to seek and render cooperation from and to other departments.
2. Encourage employees to solve problems by working with their peers (and not refer the problems to you unless they need your intervention).

Helping

1. Encourage subordinates to respond to requests from other departments.
2. Encourage them to seek help from peers in other departments.
3. Seek the help of your subordinates in areas where they can contribute.
4. Encourage your subordinates to come to you for help and respond to them positively.

Superordination

1. Help subordinates to understand and appreciate the contributions of their role to the society.
2. Help subordinates link (and see the linkage of) the objectives of their roles to organizational objectives.
3. Encourage them to include in their roles whatever may be useful to a larger section of people.
4. Encourage teamwork.
5. Remain accessible to subordinates.

SUMMARY

A role is a position a person occupies in a system as determined by his or her own expectations as well as those of people who interact face to face with the person. Contrasted with position (or office), which is hierarchical, the role is obligational.

While a job is defined by significant outsiders, a role is defined by members of the role set, which is a constellation of people interacting with the role occupant (who occupies the central place in the role set).

A role space is the map of a person's various roles, with the person himself or herself in the centre.

A role integrates an individual with the system and can be used to increase the motivation of all role-holders. This can be done by increasing role efficacy, which is the potential effectiveness of the role and has 10 aspects under three categories: role centring, role making, and role linking. Ways of increasing role efficacy have been suggested.

GLOSSARY

inter-role distance conflicts between two roles an individual occupies

intra-role conflict incompatibility between one's expectations (functions) from one's own role

role making defining the role according to one's own strengths and taking steps to make the role more challenging

role set a system of relationships between a role and other related roles in a social system

role taking seeking clarification from various sources and defining one's role in the light of such clarifications

role space the dynamic interrelationship both between the self and the various roles an individual occupies and among these roles themselves

self–role integration occupying a role that is close to one's self-concept

EXERCISES

Concept Review Questions

1. What is a role? How is it different from a job and from an organizational position?
2. What are role space and role set? What is at the centre of a role space and of a role set?
3. What are the principles of and procedures for job enrichment?
4. What is work re-structuring? How is it done?
5. What is the meaning of 'humanisation' of work? What other terms are used for such a process?
6. What is role efficacy? Enumerate its 10 aspects.
7. Draw your own role space map. Examine the distances of each role from your self.
8. What promotes role efficacy?

Classroom Projects

1. Prepare an organizational structure for your institute and a role set map for your teacher.
2. Ask a person to write an essay on his or her role in any system. Analyse the essay in terms of the 10 aspects of role efficacy, checking whether each of these is present in the essay or not.

Field Projects

1. Take the role of a helper (peon) at your institution and develop a plan for increasing his or her role efficacy.
2. Interview two people in any organization to find out which aspects of their role efficacy are weak. Give two suggestions for strengthening them.

Career Comes First, but at What Cost?*

As the Indian Airlines plane circled and climbed eastward out of Mumbai airport, Sanjay Ramaswamy began to unwind from the gruelling 2 days spent in the board meeting at the corporate office, Mumbai. In the relative silence of the first-class cabin, with no immediate pressures for another 2 hours, his thoughts drifted to his recent past, both personal and professional.

Sanjay was born into a family of modest means, in Chennai, Tamil Nadu. Academics came naturally to him and, luckily, he was focused in choosing his career from an early age. Sanjay had always been fascinated by his father's drive and potential and his strategic approach to his business. He looked up to his father as a great man—he had made it as a bright and successful entrepreneur, even without the backing of a formal education.

His father had started out in his career in his early twenties as a salesman selling soft toys. Sanjay, like his father, was drawn to the profession instinctively. He realised this during his first stint at selling raffle tickets for a school event. But he did not want to start his career as a peddler. He wanted more. An MBA degree from a good institute and a job as a management trainee at a reputed FMCG (fast moving consumer goods) company in Bangalore gave his career the right start.

When Sanjay first relocated to Mumbai, he was 26, single, and his time was completely his own. He enjoyed the odd timings and the frequent travelling. Marketing in FMCG is an intense business, but he relished the time advantage he had over other colleagues. If he needed to work at the office late, or if he had to take home a pile of papers to read or to prepare for a meeting the next day, he had no problems. In fact, it all seemed like so much fun. He was reporting to the marketing manager and was responsible for new product launches and brand management. He was also in charge of market planning at various national and local levels. He had intensive exposure in all areas of marketing, including media and e-commerce. He loved his job.

A year later, Sanjay met Neetu at a party. Neetu was a software engineer in a fast-growing IT organization. She was intelligent and soft spoken and they had a lot in common. They spent weekends visiting art shows and watching plays, going on long drives and walking along the beach. Neetu's career was very important to her and Sanjay admired her commitment to her work. They soon became inseparable and were married within 6 months of their meeting. Neetu and Sanjay were happy with

---

*This case study originally appeared in *Human Capital*, volume 9, issue no. 9, along with analysis of the case by two experts, one of them Prasenjit Bhattacharya, vice president, Consulting Services, Grow Talent Co. Ltd. Reproduced with permission from HR Information Services. More information on www.humancapitalonline.com.

their lifestyle and they were scoring equally well in their respective careers. As the years passed by, and with the coming of children, the commitment on both the fronts—family and career—doubled. Life, however, was still good.

After receiving consistent glowing performance appraisals for 5 years as a marketing manager in charge for brand management, Sanjay was transferred to a front-line managerial position at Kolkata. Although the transfer was only a lateral move on paper, it enabled him to move into the company's main-line of business where there were more opportunities for growth. Neetu decided to stay in Mumbai, since she was leading a critical project. It was a strange feeling—living apart though married. But then, it was only a matter of 8 months, they reasoned. Time would fly. And it did.

Within his 8 months tenure in Kolkata, Sanjay's outstanding performance was recognised and rewarded—Sanjay was promoted as a senior manager back to the Mumbai head office. The profile included an international assignment for 2 years.

Initially, Sanjay was happy about the offer. The profile was appealing—he would handle development of new global brands. But there was a catch—the offer needed him to be relocated internationally—for 2 years.

Neetu was away on an official trip to the US and was scheduled back only after 2 weeks. He needed to have a discussion with her in detail before he made a decision. Two years was a long time. Would she move with him? What about her job and the children's future? Neetu's commitment to the job and her developmental drive to shape her career had increased. He was not sure how they would handle this relocation dilemma. The children were very young. Arjun was three and Tarini just one. It would be unfair on Neetu to juggle her job and the home single-handedly for such a long time. And it was equally unfair to expect her to give up her job and move with him. What would they do? He decided it should be her call. He would simply leave the choice to her. Neetu had a tough decision to make. Many sleepless nights and dozens of tense arguments later, she announced that she would take a sabbatical for 2 years and relocate with him to California. She took a career break and joined Sanjay. Maybe the change would do her good, she convinced herself. But things did not turn out for the best. The shift from a career woman to a housewife did not suit Neetu. She became very frightened and concerned about her identity and security. There were frequent fights and disagreements at home. Neetu was cut off from the corporate world that gave her her professional identity. She felt that she had lost her sense of purpose and self-esteem. Sanjay saw her in pain, but he could not help her out. He could understand her anger, frustration, resentfulness, and boredom at simply being a trailing spouse. There was now a real breach between them. There were days when they even went to the extent of thinking about a separation. Fortunately it did not happen.

Sanjay could understand Neetu's feelings. She was experiencing a sense of discomfort with an unfamiliar lifestyle, a loss of continuity in her career progression, and a loss of network with people who had been central to her professional life. On the one hand, he needed to build his career and excel in his chosen field. On the other, he was pressurised by a need to fulfil the expectations and duties accompanying parenthood and nurturing the family. He felt torn between his career and the family. He felt he was letting Neetu down as a husband and life partner. He felt pulled in so many directions.

He was now finding it virtually impossible to keep up with the promises, deadlines, and targets crucial to his role. Being in charge of the global brand development of a reputed FMCG sector, he had major responsibilities and accountabilities, managing an exciting portfolio of globally recognised brands, and positioning a group of products bought by millions every day. He wondered whether he should feel excited at the possibilities of vertical advancement in his career or cry 'No more'. Each additional responsibility was adding a new burden to his personal life. Was this what he had wanted for himself?

Would the quality of their life have been better if he had remained single? After marriage and children, his priorities had changed. The responsibilities at work were rising with each passing month. His timings were getting more and more irregular, work days extended into late nights, and he was hardly ever home before dinner time. He had even started scheduling frequent breakfast meetings and left home before Neetu was up. He met the children only on Sundays, that is, when he was in town. He could barely remember the last time when he and Neetu had spent a peaceful hour together. They were growing apart day by day. He had no idea how she spent her day or who her friends were. She was irritable and uncommunicative and constantly complained about how sick she was of shopping, cooking, and cleaning. They had nothing in common anymore. They would argue about inconsequential things. His work was costing him their relationship!

Last week, when Arjun tripped in the backyard and grazed his knee, he had cried incessantly and refused to calm down in spite of Sanjay offering him his favourite ice cream. It was only when Neetu picked him up that he had stopped crying. Sanjay was afraid that Arjun and Tarini would grow up isolated from him. Would he become 'the man they saw once in 7–10 days'?

Neetu was almost like a single parent. She missed the simple joys of life, like whole family outings, and sharing happy and no-so-happy moments with Sanjay. He was hardly ever there when she needed him the most—like the time when Arjun was fighting bullies at school, or when they had had that burglary scare—nor to share happy moments like when Tarini said her first words. He had stopped noticing changes in his family and household. He was always so stressed out that she did not feel like burdening him more with her own troubles. But she was human too—she needed someone to talk to. And much as she tried not to, she would find herself pouring out her woes to him—the little irritants, the small nuisances—they were all symptoms of her problem. She was bored to death and hated not being able to pursue her career.

Neetu's 2-year sabbatical would end in a couple of months, but seeing Sanjay's crazy schedule, she could not imagine her career taking off. Leaving the children at a creche or with a babysitter could be an option, but a couple of years later. Tarini was too young right now. Neetu cringed at the thought of wasting away another 2–3 years of her life. Her only consolation was that the children needed her at this time, and she was doing this all for them.

As the plane touched the ground, Sanjay found himself in an increasingly frustrated mood, thinking about the discussion with his new CEO at the board meeting. The CEO was a tough boss and had his priorities clearly chalked out. He was a man in a hurry. He was also the type of person who felt it was his right as a CEO to push everybody to match his pace. His constant agenda was 'Let's do it yesterday.'

Sanjay recalled the CEO's words: 'We are coming out of a stage where we were not profitable enough. We need to expand our business globally. Our competitive environment is changing, and our customers are demanding a different set of requirements from us. There is no alternative but to change. This may lead to excessive workload, extended duration of work, schedule conflicts, and deadlines. I hope you are prepared for more travel. This is a critical phase for our globalization.'

Sanjay was reminded of a saying that he had read somewhere: 'Ask yourself what you would like to have on your tombstone, how you want to be remembered.' As a corporate professional, he felt he would like to be remembered for the contributions that he had made to his field, but in all reality that was a short-term phenomenon. In his quest for career success, he felt guilty that he was neglecting his family. But then, what about his and Neetu's dream of bringing up the children with the best education, facilities, and support? How would that be possible without establishing a proper career? How could he balance his attention between his career and his family?

Questions for Discussion
1. Draw a map of Sanjay's role-space, and indicate the distance between his major roles?
2. What kind of role conflict was Sanjay experiencing?
3. How widespread is the work–family balance conflict today?
4. What can Sanjay do to deal with this role stress?
5. How can role negotiation be used to manage the stress?
6. What can the organization do to help employees manage their stress?

Analysis

After discussing the case study with the help of questions given above, you may read the following analysis given by an expert. This will help you to gain more insights into the subject.

At the institute that I head in India, we do a yearly survey in over hundred organizations to understand if they can be called a Great Place to Work@. Our partners in 24 countries across the world do a similar survey every year. The results of this survey form the basis for the *Fortune* magazine's 100 Best Employer issue, and similar issues in business magazines across the world (including *Business World* in India). In this survey we ask employees to respond to a specific statement, 'People are encouraged to balance their work life and their personal life.' The answers are revealing.

In 2004, when we did our survey and identified the Top 25 Great Places to Work@ in India, only 67 per cent of the employees even in these great work places felt that their organizations encourage them to balance their work life and personal life. This is among the three lowest scores in the 57-statement survey and a full 10 per cent lower than the average score of the 100 Best Employers in US, indicating that work–life balance issues are particularly evident in the Indian context even among the best employers.

At that time, writing in a business magazine I had commented, 'As the Indian economy opens up, today's generation of Indians are pushing themselves to make the most of opportunities. Working hours are getting longer, stress and fatigue are now common—much like what US went through in the 1950s, Japan and Germany went through in the 1960s and 1970s, and the Asian Tigers more recently. Very often, people tend to mix their personal and professional lives. Think of the number of times that you've invited business partners home, taken official telephone calls at home, and spent hours downloading e-mail on your laptop. In the days to come, work–life balance issues could well become an important differentiator for a Great Place to Work.'

In my conversations with industry leaders many argued passionately that if India is to be an economic superpower in our lifetime, work–life balance cannot be allowed to come in the way.

Indeed like the American, Japanese, and Koreans in the past, one generation will have to make a big sacrifice, and that generation is ours. We are making history and a GDP growth rate in excess of 8 per cent and a per capita income of 3,000 US dollars (from around 300 US dollars, currently) will not happen by constantly harping on work–life balance.

We were eagerly awaiting the results of the 2005 survey to see if work–life balance issues continue to be a lower priority in the Great Places to Work@ in India. We were in for a surprise.

Ten per cent more employees were agreeing with the statement, 'People are encouraged to balance their work life and their personal life.' This is the single highest jump in employee perception for any statement in the survey. This shows that at least among the best employers there is a growing emphasis on work–life balance issues of employees. And there are number of ways in which some of the best workplaces are encouraging employees like Sanjay to meet the seemingly conflicting requirements of the organization, himself, and his family. We shall talk about some of these in a while.

Why has work–family balance become a critical issue today? Work–family balance has become critical today for a variety of reasons. Increased competition and expectations of customers mean that employees have to work not only smarter, but harder and longer as well. Opportunities for many Indian organizations are of a global scale, and growth is largely a factor of how much one can deliver. Opportunities of a global scale have not only fuelled ambitions of organizations, but aspirations of their employees as well. Today, an employee can aspire to grow faster and achieve more in the corporate rate race than ever before. Not many have the time to pause and ponder over the old adage that winning the rat race presupposes that you are a rat.

Though a recent CII survey shows there are only 6 per cent women in the organized workforce, their numbers are growing, particularly in new sectors like BPOs (where the women employment is often 50 per cent or higher). Anecdotal evidence suggests that more women are seeking financial independence and a career—in short, an identity of their own, beyond that of their father's or husband's. This has significant implications for a traditionally patriarchal society like ours. How can society, organizations, and individuals collaborate to increase the chances of both men and women realising their aspirations? What will be the impact of more and more dual-career couples on future generations? This case represents an interesting opportunity to look at some of these issues.

What is Sanjay's situation today? Sanjay is highly ambitious and has developed a self-image where his identity is inextricably linked to his job and success at work. These are also qualities that attracted him to his wife Neetu. If one were to forget gender stereotypes for a while, Sanjay is very much like Neetu. For a moment if we are to imagine that Sanjay is the wife and Neetu the husband, we can visualise Sanjay reacting exactly in the way Neetu is reacting.

So why did Neetu agree to take a 2-year sabbatical and accompany Sanjay to California? I believe to a large extent the answer to that is not just in Neetu's personality but also in societal expectations. A patriarchal society encourages women to accept (a) gender-based stereotypes, (b) denial of equal self-expression, (c) sacrifice for family, and (d) a belief that these are just. Sometime back, I was visiting a new project being commissioned by a well-known organization in a rural hinterland of India. I was pleasantly surprised to know that more than 30 per cent of the engineers were women. In the evening, I participated in a focus group discussion with a group of women engineers. Almost all of them expressed a need for creating a distinct identity for themselves in their professional career. This was similar to the response I get from similar groups of men. What was different was almost all women considered marriage as an equally important decision compared to their job, and a majority of them gave marriage as the primary reason for switching jobs.

Regardless of what prompted Neetu to relocate with her husband to California, there is no evidence in the case to lead us to believe that Neetu and Sanjay were adequately prepared for the change in environment, lifestyle, and related issues. There is enough anecdotal evidence to suggest that the transition to a society where one does not have the family and social support that one has in India is not smooth, even for single-career couples. A free and frank discussion between Sanjay, Neetu, and Sanjay's organization before the relocation might have obviated some of the issues Sanjay is grappling with now.

Sanjay is dealing with three obvious conflicts. The first is the conflict between his and his wife's career ambition. In both the cases, their self-image seems to be linked to their career. The second conflict is between his roles as a manager, which is largely defined by the organization's expectation from him, and as a husband and a father, which is defined by expectations of his family. The biggest conflict could be not clarifying his own expectations of himself and thereby prioritising what he needs to do.

For Sanjay, the consequence of not dealing with his conflicts could be high, not only in relation to his family (where they have contemplated separation), but also in his job. In a recent address Dr Mashelkar gives the example of Sachin Tendulkar to illustrate how family support is important to reach and stay at the top. In a recent article in *Harvard Business Review*, 'Overloaded circuits—why smart people under perform', Edward M. Hallowell gives examples of people suffering from attention deficit trait (ADT), a disorder that causes inability to deal with challenges at work. Sanjay can become a statistic in executive burnout if he does not deal with his current conflicts effectively.

What Can Sanjay Do?

In my opinion the starting point is understanding the way we look at work–family balance issues. Many of us raised on Western concepts of balance look at the various roles we play as distinct, and therefore try to meet the expectations of each of these roles—expectations that might conflict.

An alternate way of looking at self and roles is what has been written in some of our sources of ancient wisdom, among others, Patanjali's *Yoga Sutra* that looks at various roles not in isolation. In this frame, the various roles we play are not distinct, but each one builds on the other, starting with the self. The starting point is defining the priority between different roles and establishing balance in each preceding role. Life is an opportunity to play different roles with the ultimate aim of realising one's vision by being of greatest service to maximum others. This model presupposes that to play a higher role you must have achieved balance in the previous role by negotiating expectations from that role or even eliminating that role if required (e.g., most clergies do not have to play family roles).

As a first step, Sanjay has to define a vision for himself, not in narrow terms by being limited to one role alone. A vision to be inspiring and energising needs to capture the meaning of one's existence based on one's interpretation of such meaning. This vision would reflect the deeply held values of the individual. Viktor E. Frank in his bestseller *Man's Search for Meaning* says, 'Man is a being whose main concern consists in fulfilling a meaning and in actualising values, rather than in the mere gratification and satisfaction of drives and instincts.' Arriving at a personal vision is a creative process that involves deep introspection and reflection. When we look at all the incidents and events that influence us in our life, we will notice that there are some common values that drive us and shape our reaction to life's situations. Sanjay needs to ask himself the question, 'If I had no constraint of time or money, what would I be doing for the rest of my life? Why would I be doing it?' For most of us, the answer to the first question may not necessarily be what we are doing now. This does not mean we have to leave everything we are doing and chart a new course from next day. The second question is very helpful in understanding what drives us—what are our values. Rather than waiting for that ideal day and time when we have no constraints, we need to ask ourselves, 'What do I need to do differently from today to live my values?'

In answering the question of what is one's vision and values, one also arrives at the prioritisation of various roles. Very often one realises that the family and the workplace offer maximum opportunity to practise the value one holds dearly. In some cases one might find that a role that is taking a lot of time is actually not important from the point of one's vision and values.

For Sanjay and Neetu it will be worthwhile to have a heart-to-heart chat to re-establish how important their marriage and their family are to them. When one partner in a marriage starts complaining about the other partner not spending enough time, very often the issue is their relationship itself and not just time. To ensure that this discussion does not become an exercise in blaming each other, Sanjay (or Neetu) should take the lead and start by genuinely talking about all the things that attracted them to each other, and things that made their marriage work so far. This process, called appreciative inquiry, is about discovering what works in a situation rather than what does not. Very often we get so engrossed with day-to-day irritants that we lose sight of what is working well. If Sanjay and Neetu are able to do this, there is hope in this marriage.

The next step is to understand each other's aspirations. It is important for Sanjay to understand Neetu's aspirations and talk about his. It is normal to be confused about what one really wants to do unless one has spent some time thinking about what his or her vision is. Most likely each person may come up with a list of things they would want to do or things they would not want to do. This is also the time to clarify expectations one has from the other, including unstated expectations. This is the tough part of making the relationship work. Hopefully, before they come to this part, Sanjay and Neetu would have already figured out why they need to make the relationship work.

I know of a married woman who got a dream offer in another city. She had a dialogue with her husband, similar to what's suggested above, and the couple came to the conclusion that this time the husband would shift cities (which meant a change of job for him). However, next time if the husband would get a good opportunity, the wife would reciprocate. This did happen 8 years later, and though the wife did not get an appropriate opportunity (commensurate to her career stage) in the new city, she perceived the whole situation to be a fair deal in light of their previous agreement. For both, their marriage was very important.

In another case, the husband assumed that as long as he was earning significantly more than his wife, she would follow him wherever his work took him. Unfortunately, by the time he could verbalise this assumption the marriage had already soured and the wife blamed him and the constant changes of cities for her inability to earn as much as him.

Apart from the partner in a family, it is important to take one's children into confidence. When I changed jobs from line HR to consulting, I remember spending time with my 7-year son explaining to him what this means—constant travel, time away from home, etc. I also explained the reason why I want to do this. We talked about it and finally came to a conclusion—we will try it for 5 years. I will try and spend all Sundays at home, we will not compromise on our vacation time, and my son will do his studies regularly, even when I am not at home.

I recommend that Sanjay and his family arrive at norms that are acceptable to all family members. Sanjay and Neetu should, for example, explore what will happen if Neetu gets a similar career break later. Would Sanjay accompany her, the same way she did? Norms ensure that family members perceive there is mutual respect and equality.

Some of these norms might mean that Sanjay and Neetu look for newer options. Neetu may like to look at part-time options to work or upgrade her skills. Sanjay may need to negotiate with his organization and boss about aspects like not travelling or working on weekends.

I have taken the self, the spouse, and the family first on the assumption that they (and therefore the roles Sanjay plays vis-à-vis them) are the priority. The same process that Sanjay uses for his wife and family can be used with his boss to attempt a better work–life balance.

What Can Organizations Do to Promote Better Work–Family Balance?

Organizations, particularly those who want to build their employer brands (and therefore attract better talent), are taking proactive steps to address this issue. Crèche and playground facility for employee's children has been introduced by some organizations (Texas Instruments, Honeywell, etc). This is a big help, particularly for women. In the US, where 62 per cent of adult women participate in the workforce, 54 per cent of children use daycare facilities. In India, daycare facilities are almost non-existent and very few organizations provide crèches.

Organizations are now providing professional relocation services, which includes advance information about socio-economic conditions in the new city/country. Many organizations encourage the spouse to go in advance of the actual transfer to get a first-hand feel about the city, including aspects like housing and schools, etc.

Employee assistance programmes is a global multi-billion-dollar industry, which uses specialised service providers to help organizations address issues of work–life balance, among other things. Some of these service providers are now available in India. Organizations like Texas Instruments have introduced counselling services for employees, a practice that was limited earlier to manufacturing organizations tackling absenteeism and alcoholism in blue-collared employees.

Organizations in India are one step ahead in involving families in a number of informal ways, apart from formal occasions like annual days and family days. Similarly, flexible timings are a norm in the IT industry.

Sabbaticals, paternity leave, flexitime, concierge services are a norm in most companies that make it to the Great Places to Work@ list. Sasken, for example, has a hibernation leave, which is a paid leave of 8 weeks for 2 years of service, recognising the intense work that most employees have to put in.

However, not enough is being done. The medical implications of stress due to work–family issues is one reason why we need to focus on this area. A study published some time back in the *Journal of the American Medical Association* estimated that the cost of lost productivity to only one disorder—major depression—is over 31 billion US dollars annually.

There is enough evidence to suggest that governments, organizations, and the society should start taking the issue of work–family balance seriously, particularly if we want to attract and retain talented women in the workforce. Compared to 46 per cent women managers in the US, in India it is a dismal 4 per cent.[4] It is an irony that while India has the largest number of young people, most organizations are seriously short of talent. One major reason is girls who do equally well (if not better) as boys in schools do not make it to the workforce, let alone management levels.

In a way this case is as much about Neetu realising her potential, as it is about Sanjay gaining his work–family balance.

REFERENCES

1. Katz, D. and R.L. Kahn (1978). *The Social Psychology of Organisations.* New York: Wiley.
2. Kahn, R.L. and R.P. Quinn (1970). 'Role Stress: A Framework for Analysis', in A. McClean (ed.) *Mental Health and Work Organisations,* pp. 50–115. Chicago: Rand McNally.
3. Sayeed, O.B. and Udai Pareek (eds) (2000). *Actualising Managerial Roles.* New Delhi: Tata McGraw-Hill.
4. Guha Thakurta, Paranjoy. 'India's health-care paradox', *Business Line* (The Hindu Group), Tuesday, 21 September 2004.

13
Managing Work Motivation

LEARNING OBJECTIVES

After studying this chapter, you will be able to
1. Analyse the main motivational problems in Indian organizations
2. Describe steps for job enrichment
3. Identify the factors that make job enrichment programmes successful
4. Discuss various approaches to humanisation of work
5. List different ways of improving motivation at the levels of the individual, the role, and the organization

In Chapter 6, various approaches to work motivation were discussed. These have certain implications for increasing work motivation in organizations. In this chapter, the findings from Indian studies are briefly reviewed, the means of understanding and measuring motivation are discussed, and methods of increasing motivation are proposed.

THE ASIAN PERSPECTIVE

Several studies have been reported about the motivation of Indian workers and managers. It is difficult to summarise these studies, as different methods have been used in collecting and analysing data. However, most of the studies tried to answer the question of what motivates a worker or a manager in an Indian organization. In most cases, respondents rank-ordered some factors or rated them for their importance. A review of about 50 published studies has indicated that while workers generally give importance to wages, security, and working conditions, supervisors and managers give more importance to advancement, responsibility, and the work itself.

However, several studies show the opposite results also. It would therefore be worthwhile to analyse the studies in greater depth. A clue was provided when it was found that security and income were rated as the most important factors by the least satisfied workers whereas these were given fifth and seventh ranks by the most satisfied workers.[1] This finding is consistent with Herzberg's two-factor theory of motivation. Thus, more systematic studies are needed in this area.

A comprehensive review of studies on the motivation of supervisors and managers in India indicated the following tentative trends[2]:
- Promotion is the most important incentive and also the most important source of dissatisfaction for supervisors and middle-level managers.

- Recognition is the most important factor in terms of both satisfaction and dissatisfaction.
- Among factors contributing only to dissatisfaction, the most frequently mentioned factors are lack of adequate organizational policy and administration, lack of technically competent and sympathetic supervision, unfriendliness of superiors, and lack of opportunities for growth.
- Job factors causing satisfaction and dissatisfaction in managers and supervisors differ from those cited by the rank and file. For example, salary and job security emerge as the two most important factors for job satisfaction among the latter, whereas for the former these consistently sink towards the bottom of the hierarchy. Occupational level thus appears to influence perception of needs.
- No clear evidence is available differentiating managers and supervisors in terms of their sources of satisfaction and dissatisfaction. They do, however, differ in terms of their perception of needs. First-line supervisors value income, promotion, job security, and working conditions the most. Middle-level managers value advancement, type of work, and earnings. Higher-level managers, on the other hand, value most the feeling of worthwhile accomplishment, recognition for good work done, and authority to make decisions. This shows the shift from job context factors to job content factors, or from the lower-order needs to the higher-order needs.
- Managers in private and public industry are not found to differ with regard to job satisfaction. They are similarly influenced by the motivators. However, motivators and hygiene factors contribute to satisfaction and dissatisfaction differently: while for public sector managers, motivators contribute more towards satisfaction, for private sectors executives, the absence of these contribute more to dissatisfaction.
- There is no evidence linking job satisfaction to outcome variables such as job involvement and performance.
- Neither personal variables (e.g., education, level of income) nor organizational variables (e.g., blue-collar vs white-collar work, tall vs flat organizational structure) have been found to have a significant influence on motivation.

MOTIVATING THROUGH WORK

The traditional approach to organizational effectiveness was based on the combined use of managerial authority, reward/punishment, and training. The assumptions were that people work best under pressure from the top, that they work mainly for money, and that they can become effective if they are given the knowledge and skills required for the job. However, with the growing complexity of organizations and society of late, these assumptions are being questioned. It has become clear that internal pressure (motivation) is more important than external pressure and that people develop more through what they 'experience' in their organizations and jobs than through formal training. And therefore the job has come to assume more importance, alongside the organization.

Job Enrichment: Early Attempts

People had become dissatisfied with the traditional approach to jobs. With industrialisation and the advent of scientific methods of production, there came a tendency to break up the job into tasks and assign a specific task to each person. The use of assembly line technology led to fragmentation of work until each individual was given a very specific and simple task. It was hoped that from doing a particular task continuously and having sole responsibility for it, the individual would become more efficient at it and thereby increase his or her output in a given period of time.

With simpler technology, this proved to be true. However, apologists for this approach were wrong in believing it to be universally applicable. There were several disadvantages to such a division of work. First, the individual lost control over the work as a whole as also the sense of identity that he or she had while influencing it or creating something in its entirety. Second, it became monotonous for the person to perform the same job over and over again. Third, there was no sense of achievement or learning due to the repetitive nature of work. It was later realised that this process had in fact a dehumanising effect, reducing people to mere machines. The detrimental consequences of the dehumanisation of work became evident with the shift in emphasis to motivation and people's participation in decision making.

Herzberg was among the first to pay attention to this issue.[3] Based on his experience at medical school, he made a distinction between two kinds of factors in relation to the work people did. He distinguished between factors that reduced their dissatisfaction and those that contributed towards positive satisfaction. He thus also made a qualitative distinction between satisfaction and dissatisfaction.

According to Herzberg, lack of dissatisfaction does not necessarily result in satisfaction. The problem before an organization is to reduce dissatisfaction on the one hand and to provide increasing satisfaction to its employees on the other. He used the term 'hygienes' for the factors that cause dissatisfaction and 'motivators' for those that contribute towards people's satisfaction at work.

Under the hygienes, he listed administrative policies, quality of supervision, the employee–supervisor relationship, working conditions, salary, relationships with peers and subordinates, status, security, etc. According to Herzberg, getting these factors right (hygiene management) would reduce dissatisfaction. Otherwise people would remain dissatisfied (just as people get sick in the absence of proper physiological hygiene). On the other hand, this would not necessarily lead to an increased level of satisfaction (just as people do not necessarily become healthy by living in hygienic conditions). To provide positive satisfaction to people, Herzberg highlighted the necessity of attending to a qualitatively different set of factors (motivators). These are the sense of achievement a person gets from the job, recognition for work done, the nature of the work, the amount of responsibility the individual shares, possibilities for advancement or promotion, and opportunities to learn new things and grow.

The main distinction that Herzberg made between hygienes and motivators was that hygienes were not directly related to work, so he called them 'job context factors', while motivators were directly related to work, so he called them 'job content factors'. In other words, Herzberg proposed the need to look at the work itself and analyse the factors that would make it a satisfying experience. According to him, motivators contribute towards people's satisfaction (and development) in their jobs. Herzberg's major contribution included not only the theory of work motivation but also several organizational practices designed on the basis of this theory.

Herzberg's theory, which is called the 'two-factor theory of motivation', led to a practical programme of using a job as a major medium for developing people and changing organizational practices. The practical side of intervening in an organization was called job enrichment. Herzberg also called this 'vertical loading of the job' to indicate the need for providing more motivators in work. The process of enrichment is the process of providing valuable 'things' to a person (valuable from the person's point of view). If an employee's job is extended so that he or she has to do more work, then it is not vertical loading but what Herzberg called 'horizontal loading'. Vertical loading is an attempt to provide more and more motivators in a job. Several experiments have been carried out on job enrichment. A programme of job enrichment is conducted according to certain general principles.

Herzberg suggested that a job should be taken up for detailed analysis in order to find out the level of motivators present in it and then steps should be taken to enrich the job. Such steps would make the job more satisfying to the individual and contribute towards his or her development. Herzberg suggested certain principles (see Exhibit 13.1) and procedures[4] (see Exhibit 13.2) for job enrichment.

Exhibit 13.1 *Principles of Job Enrichment*

- Remove some controls while retaining accountability.
- Increase the accountability of individuals to their work.
- Give each person a complete natural unit of work—a module, division, area, etc.
- Grant additional authority to an employee in his or her work—in other words, job freedom.
- Make periodic reports directly available to the worker rather than to the supervisor.
- Introduce new and more difficult tasks compared to those handled previously.
- Assign specific steps or tasks to specific people, enabling them to become experts in these.

Exhibit 13.2 *Job Enrichment Procedure*

- Select appropriate jobs for the job enrichment programme. The job should have possibilities for improvement, yet it should be such that
  - There is evidence of people's involvement and motivation.
  - Improvement of hygiene factors become costly.
  - Other changes that have been tried out have not made much difference to the levels of motivation.
  - There is a general belief that a programme of motivation will make a difference.
- Start the job enrichment programme with a belief that changes made in the jobs will produce good results.
- Brainstorm a list of changes that can be made in a job for its enrichment.
- Review the list and eliminate those suggestions that involve hygienes.
- Review the list again to remove those suggestions that are too general and do not give any specific ideas.

Exhibit 13.2 (*Contd*)

- Review the list again and remove those suggestions that are only concerned with additional work and that do not fall in the category of motivators.
- Avoid direct participation by the job-holders. Any ideas they may have can be given to others and may be reviewed in advance. Moreover, they should not directly participate in the final programme of job enrichment.
- Start with a small controlled experiment rather than introducing the programme throughout the organization. This would mean that the results of this experimental group can be compared with the results from control groups to see how much difference is made by the job enrichment programme.
- Be prepared for initial setbacks in terms of lower productivity and other teething troubles. Any change is bound to cause some problems in the beginning and may result in the lowering of productivity for a short while.
- Also be prepared for an initial negative reaction from supervisory staff as well as for their anxiety and hostility towards the experiment. It is difficult to change supervisory attitudes, as any change where new supervisory practices are required produces some anxiety about the redundancy of the supervisory role (which is partly true), resulting in a negative attitude. Supervisors take time to adopt new and different practices.

Several experiments have been reported from various parts of the world to indicate how job enrichment helps in improving motivational levels among employees and contributes towards their development. Job enrichment uses jobs as the main medium of developing competence and the ability of employees to share higher responsibilities. A job enrichment programme for one job has repercussions for other jobs also. Once the programme succeeds in relation to one job, it will help redefine other jobs, particularly those of the immediate supervisor in addition to some other peer roles.

Six job enrichment studies done at the Imperial Chemical Industry (ICI) used control groups, keeping hygienes constant.[5] The studies were kept confidential (to avoid the 'Hawthorne effect'). The steps followed in the procedure are shown in Exhibit 13.3. The results, in terms of sales, efficiency, output, budget, control, quality of work, and job satisfaction, showed marked improvements on account of the job enrichment programmes.[6]

From Enrichment to Humanisation

Though job enrichment programmes became quite popular, in due course of time it was evident that job enrichment took a limited view of the job and treated it in

Exhibit 13.3 *Steps in Job Enrichment Study*

- Discussion with the division directors and senior managers
- Discussion with the departmental heads and their senior staff
- Meeting with all the managers (not immediate supervisors) for a brainstorming session
- Screening ideas to eliminate hygienes
- Finalising suggestions
- Deciding measurement criteria
- Gradual introduction of changes

isolation. Job enrichment programmes also ran into problems. After reviewing scores of job enrichment programmes and interviewing hundreds of managers and workers, Hackman suggested what goes wrong in job enrichment programmes, resulting in their failure. Exhibits 13.4 and 13.5 contain his suggestions for successful job enrichment programmes along with the various issues involved.[7]

Since Herzberg's work on job enrichment, a great deal of interest has been aroused about interventions in jobs and work. The emerging emphasis on human values added new dimensions to this interest and several related concepts have been proposed.

The concept of job design was proposed in the mid-1950s. It was originally defined as 'the organization (or structuring) of a job to satisfy the technical–organizational requirements of the work to be accomplished and the human

Exhibit 13.4 *What Goes Wrong in Job Enrichment Programmes*

- Rarely are the problems in the work system diagnosed before jobs are redesigned.
- Sometimes the work itself is not actually changed.
- Even when the work itself is substantially changed, anticipated gains are sometimes diminished or reversed because of unexpected effects on the surrounding work system.
- Rarely are the work redesign projects systematically evaluated.
- The managers, consulting staff members, and union officers do not obtain appropriate education on the theory, strategy, and tactics of work design.
- Traditional bureaucratic practice creeps into work redesign activities.

Exhibit 13.5 *Characteristics of Successful Job Enrichment Programmes*

Key individuals responsible for the work redesign project attack the especially difficult problems right from the beginning.
Issues
- Guidelines regarding the nature and extent of commitment of the management and union leaders and the circumstances under which to terminate the project have to be provided.
- The criteria by which the project will ultimately be evaluated and how the evaluation will be made must be laid down.
- The management makes sure that the diagnosis of the changes needed in target jobs, based on some articulated theory of work redesign, is conducted much before implementation.
  Issues o Can the jobs under consideration be changed in a meaningful manner?
      o Are the employees reasonably ready for change and are they capable of handling their new duties?
      o Is the management itself ready to handle the extra burden and challenges that will be created by the change?
      o How are supervisors, related peer groups, and clients likely to be affected by the change?
- The management ensures that specific changes are explicitly based on diagnosis and are publicly discussed.
- The people responsible for the project prepare contingency plans to deal with both the problems and the opportunities that emerge from work redesigning activities.
- Those responsible for the project are prepared to evaluate the project continuously throughout its life.

Exhibit 13.6   *Some Concerns in Job Design*

- Putting together tasks that constitute 'meaningful' units of activity for the workers
- Providing a sequence of tasks or operations (for organization of work) that makes for a 'meaningful' relationship between jobs
- Putting together tasks that would include each of the four types of work activity inherent in productive work, namely, production (processing), auxiliary work (supply, tooling), preparatory work (set-up), and control (inspection)
- Dividing the product into units (parts, components, documents) that are 'meaningful' entities to the workers
- Arranging facilities and communications so that the feedback on all aspects of performance and production needs takes place automatically and constantly
- Providing 'meaningful' measures of performance to individuals
- Providing 'meaningful' incentives or rewards

requirements of the person performing the work'. Job design was done through the following three activities: specifying the content of the individual task, specifying the method of performing each task (including the use of machinery, tools, and any special technique), and combining individual tasks with specific jobs. Some concerns on job design are listed in Exhibit 13.6.[8]

An extension of the idea of job design (and job redesign) was work reorganization. 'Work' connotes a broader concept than a job. Work restructuring was influenced by several developments: socio-technical system studies, emphasis on the quality of working life, and concern for the worker as a person. These are all interrelated. Experiments in Europe, particularly those in Sweden, indicated the effectiveness of restructuring work groups—what are now called 'autonomous work groups'.

Work restructuring or work redesigning emphasised the use of responsibility, autonomy, adaptability, variety, and participation. The concept of autonomy is central to the concept of work reorganization. According to Davis and Trist, 'By autonomy we mean that the content, structure and organization of jobs is such that individuals or groups performing those jobs can plan, regulate and control their own work worlds.' According to them, autonomy implies the need for multiple skills and self-regulation, in both individuals and groups. 'Under the principle of self-regulation only the critical interventions, desired outcomes and organizational maintenance requirements needed to be specified by those managing, leaving the remainder to those doing.' Under self-regulation, the individuals in a group accept responsibility to complete the product or service; decide on output quality, quantity, and rate; organize their work; set their own goals; evaluate their own performance; and plan the necessary modifications in the work system. Some criteria for autonomy have been suggested (see Exhibit 13.7).[9] The socio-technical systems approach has been effectively used in redesigning work groups and the other related parts of an organization.

Exhibit 13.7 *Criteria for Autonomy*

- The group can influence the formulation of its goals, including (a) the qualitative aspects and (b) the quantitative aspects.
- Provided that established goals governing relationships to the superordinate system are satisfied, the group can govern its own performance by deciding
   - Where to work
   - When to work
   - Which other activities to engage in
- The group makes the necessary decisions in connection with the choice of a production method.
- The group makes its own internal distribution of the task.
- The group decides on its own membership.
- The group makes its own decisions with respect to two crucial matters of leadership:
   - Whether it wants to have a leader with respect to internal questions, and if it does, who this leader will be
   - Whether it wants a leader for the purpose of regulating boundary conditions, and if it does, who this leader will be
- The group members decide how the work operations will be performed.

Exhibit 13.8 *Characteristics of Open Work Systems*

- The primary task of a manager is to control the boundary conditions of his or her unit.
- The goals of an open system can be understood only as special forms of interdependence between the system and its environment.
- The goal state has the characteristics of a steady state, which requires (a) constancy of direction and (b) a tolerable rate of progress.
- A steady state can be achieved only through leadership and commitment.
- The basis of regulating open systems is self-regulation.
- As individuals have open system properties, the enterprise must allow its members a sufficient measure of autonomy.

An organization and its sub-systems are regarded as open socio-technical systems (open to input-through-output changes with the environment). The concept of open systems is relevant for work redesigning (for characteristics of open work systems, see Exhibit 13.8).[10]

The relationship between a person and his or her work is a basic element of social life. Drastic changes in this relationship can constitute a revolution. It has been suggested that so far there have been two such revolutions—the first with the advent of machine power (replacing people with machines in the nineteenth century) and the second with the information explosion through computers. The third revolution is taking place now—that of the humanisation of work.

The terms 'humanisation of work', 'industrial democracy', 'quality of working life', and 'participative work' are interchangeably used to define the same concept, the core of the concept being the value of treating the worker as a human being, improving his or her work environment, and emphasising his or her involvement in work-related decisions.

Based on a review done in India, De has suggested seven stages in the dynamics of development of new forms of work organization: hostile reluctance, guarded commitment, indifference, intergroup dynamics, positive interest, interest, and interlinkage with other experimental groups and organizations. He has also discussed the characteristics of each of these stages and has summarised nine case studies in India.

MANAGING MOTIVATION

The integrated theory of work motivation can be used for planning interventions in an organization. The basic implication of the model is that work motivation can be developed in the organizational context. The interaction between the individual and the organization contributes to the development of work motivation. This interaction takes place through the role. By implication, the roles people occupy in the organization may form convenient units for working on problems of motivation. An analysis of the role and its contribution to the development of work motivation in the organization may be useful to planning intervention strategies.

The most important variables at the organizational level are the motivational climate of the organization and its role-interactional patterns. The management of an organization should ask itself about the prevalent motivational climate. In order to understand the type of climate, it may be necessary to pay attention to the reinforcing mechanisms and the process of goal-setting in the organization. For example, does the organization use the system of rewarding good performance or does it use the system of punishing bad performance? A positive or negative reinforcing mechanism will determine to a great extent the motivational climate in the organization. Another relevant question asks what is being rewarded or punished. If achievement is rewarded in one organization, the climate will be conducive to efficiency, whereas in an organization where dependency and conformity are rewarded, the climate will be more power oriented and will encourage the formation of cliques.

Similarly, attention should be paid to the strategies of goal-setting. How and at what level are goals set? Are goals set by people at the top and communicated downward for achievement, or do people who have to achieve these goals participate in the process of goal-setting?

Another important variable is the interactional pattern of various roles. The psychological distance between various roles will determine to a great extent how the roles interact and collaborate with each other. These both influence and are influenced by the organizational climate.

As the model has proposed, work motivation can be thought of at three levels.

It is necessary for an organization to understand the needs of the employees, how they perceive the goal-setting process in the organization, and what their expectancy about being rewarded for good work is. If most of the employees perceive that reward does not depend on performance in an organization, their motivation will be low. The organization then needs to raise their expectancy and examine why expectancy is low.

The second level of work motivation is the commitment employees have to the organization and the modified patterns of their needs as a result of their work in the organization. An organization that is able to increase achievement and power motivation among its employees will have more committed employees.

The third level of motivation is the satisfaction employees derive from working in the organization. The model suggests that this kind of work satisfaction, which is the basis of people's commitment to the organization, can come about if attention is paid to both—organizational factors and the understanding of individual employees. However, the model suggests that the starting point for this two-pronged approach is the role. Diagnostic details for several variables proposed in the model can be used to determine at what point the intervention would be most effective for organizational development.

There is no standard answer to the question of how to increase work motivation, especially of those who seem to lose interest and initiative. Each situation in an organization requires special treatment. However, a knowledge and understanding of motivation does provide some general guidelines for action programmes. Motivation results from the interaction of the individual with the organization through a role. So all the three elements are important for planning the management of motivation— the organization, the role (the job), and the individual. Based on the discussion about work motivation in this chapter and in Chapter 7, some propositions and related suggestions are put forward.

The Organization

Organizational climate

A profile of the organizational climate can be prepared by indicating motivations that seem to dominate the climate and therefore are being generated in the organization.

It may be useful to have periodical diagnostic studies of the organizational climate. The profiles thus prepared can be used as an important intervention for several groups, to discuss whether they are satisfied with that profile, and, if not, what can be done to bring about change. This can be used as one of the initial interventions.

Reinforcement

The systems in an organization reinforce some motivations more than others. While designing systems or making changes in them, it may be worthwhile to discuss what motivations they will reinforce. This may help in designing systems for reinforcing motivations relevant to organizational effectiveness—achievement, power, extension. For example, an information control system that provides relevant information to the person who has to take decisions will reinforce power motivation; a promotion system that objectively rewards high performance will reinforce achievement motivation. Similarly, a system requiring people from various departments or sections or levels to meet and discuss and come to a decision will reinforce extension motivation (collaboration).

Communication

Open communication in an organization tends to increase work motivation. Open communication includes communication of policies, difficulties, and problems from the top to the various levels concerned and communication of help required from below to the top. It also includes supportive feedback from the boss about performance. Such open communication is likely to increase the general satisfaction of employees, contributing to higher work motivation.

Hygiene factors

Deficit needs (hygiene), if not attended to, are likely to affect work motivation. Attention needs to be paid to hygiene factors such as salary, security, company policy, working conditions, and the general atmosphere in the department/units. If these are unsatisfactory, the necessary work to raise the level of motivation cannot be done. Hence these factors need to be analysed and the necessary improvements need to be made in them.

The Role or the Job
Role efficacy

Role efficacy contributes to work motivation. It is the potential effectiveness of a person in his or her role. Several factors contribute to role efficacy, for example, the individual's feeling of his or her role being central in the organization, self–role integration, possibilities for the individual to take initiative and be creative, linkage of the role with other roles in the organization, helping relationships in the organization, opportunities to influence and to work on larger goals beneficial to others, opportunities for growth, and so on. It may be useful to measure the efficacy of several roles in the organization and take steps to raise it in each case.

Recognition

Norms for the recognition of competence promote work motivation. In an organization, competence and good work should be recognised. If people perceive that there is such recognition, the level of motivation rises. Managers may like to examine whether contributions by employees are recognised. Such recognition should be genuine and given only when an individual deserves it.

Challenge

Work motivation is correlated to the challenge the job provides to the individual. Challenge is one of the factors Herzberg has suggested as motivators. If a job does not provide enough challenge to the individual, his or her motivation will be low. If there seems to be lack of challenge, it may be useful to examine the job content and do something to build more challenge in the job, perhaps by delegating more responsibility or expanding the scope of the job.

Decision making

Opportunities to influence decisions increase work motivation. Every individual should feel that he or she is able to influence some decision in the job. This is possible when there is some autonomy and freedom to the individual who is also able to perceive it. Even a helper or a gardener feels motivated if he is given a specific responsibility, is given freedom to operate, and is held responsible for the results. Enough autonomy with adequate support, and a demand for responsibility combine to increase motivation. Each job may be examined to see how such autonomy and responsibility can be increased.

Growth opportunities

Work motivation is directly related to perception of opportunities for development and growth in the job. If people feel that what they do in their jobs helps them to learn new things and contributes to their development, their motivation will be high. Each job should be analysed from this point of view. When individuals reach a stage where they feel that they are only repeating themselves, the possibilities of job rotation to help them learn new jobs may be explored. Of course, this principle has some limitations and every job cannot provide a learning opportunity for everyone at all times.

Goals of wider relevance

The perception that a person is contributing to a larger goal increases motivation. The importance of the job should be communicated to the employee and he or she may be helped to see how the job is useful for the section/department and for the organization, for a larger section of the community, the entire profession, society, or for the nation. An employee's perception of the context of the job in terms of its contribution to a larger goal contributes to his work motivation.

The Individual

Changing patterns

An individual's motivational pattern can be changed. Like the organization, an individual also has motivational patterns. Some needs are stronger in him or her than others. Experiments and experience have shown that it is possible to raise the level of specific needs in an individual. For example, if an individual has low achievement motivation and if this is of concern because he or she wants to raise his or her level of achievement, this can be done. It may be useful to provide opportunities to individuals to first get a picture of their motivational profile and then to attend special programmes to help them raise the level of a specific psychological need in which they may be interested. Some agencies are organizing such motivation development laboratories. One design for such programmes is available.[11] Further advances, of course, have been made in the field. McClelland and Burnham proposed another design in 1976.[12] McClelland has also given evidence of the application of what can be called 'motivational technology' to several fields such as education, industry, health, and development.[13]

Performance and effort

Performance directly contributes to work satisfaction and is a direct result of effort, and not vice versa. In order to increase work motivation, stress should be laid on increasing employees' effort for good performance. It is wrong to expect higher performance directly from general satisfaction. Unless rewards are related to efforts, the resulting satisfaction will not lead to high performance.

Success experiences

An individual's work motivation and ability to achieve increase with success in gradually more challenging tasks. If an individual is helped to experience success in achieving goals that gradually become more challenging, his or her motivation and capability for higher achievement increases. It may be useful to plan goals for an individual in a graduated series of challenges.

Salary and Reward System

Reinforcement

Generally, the behaviour that is rewarded is reinforced. An organization should analyse what behaviour gets rewarded in the organization. Not only is the formal reward system important, the informal system plays an equally significant role. For example, if those who can get close to the boss seem to get rewarded (by way of a salary increase or promotion), the dependency motivation will be reinforced in the organization—a tendency to expect solutions of problems from above (senior managers). It may be useful to examine people's perceptions of such formal and informal reward systems from time to time and take corrective measures.

Promotions

Promotions based on merit and competence create a climate of high work motivation. It is extremely important that the organization pays attention to its promotion policies. If it is perceived that promotions are given on the basis of personal considerations and not on the basis of competence, potential for higher responsibility, or merit, the general climate in the organization will reduce work motivation. In such a climate, motivation to do good work is low and people try to find the bases on which promotions are made so as to work towards those criteria (smart appearance, good personal relations, being good golf players, or whatever).

Challenge

Promotion motivates only when the new job to which a person is promoted provides greater challenge. Some companies make the mistake of thinking that promotion per se may motivate people. If after a promotion the person continues to do what he or she was doing before and does not have any new responsibilities, his or her motivation will go down after some time. In one public sector company, several competent and bright young people who had been given quick promotions felt highly satisfied for some time, but after the initial euphoria of being promoted wore off, they felt dissatisfied because the new jobs were not more challenging than the previous ones. New responsibilities and challenges should be built into new jobs if promotion is to be used as a motivator. Otherwise, people feel cheated because they have been given more salary and higher designations without the accompanying responsibility and challenge.

Approach vs avoidance

Generally, positive reinforcement builds the approach dimensions of motivation and negative reinforcement promotes the avoidance aspect. The role of reward and punishment is very crucial in work motivation. Reward would include recognition, appreciation, salary increase, non-financial rewards, promotion, etc. These are called positive reinforces. Punishment, in a wider sense, includes criticism, admonishment, holding back salary increments, demotion, termination of employment, etc. This is negative reinforcement. These reinforce the tendency to avoid certain behaviours. It is a better policy to use rewards than to use punishment. In employee feedback, for example, appreciation of good performance should precede criticism of poor performance. Those who get more positive reinforcement take more initiative and responsibility and those who get more negative reinforcement tend to avoid opportunities with possibilities of failure and thus tend to avoid challenging tasks. Certainly, competence should be rewarded so that people may realise that competence does not go unnoticed.

SUMMARY

Employees' motivation (commitment to their work and organization) can be developed through their work. Herzberg did pioneering work in developing a methodology of job enrichment (by increasing motivators in the jobs concerned). Further work on the humanisation of work led to interventions such as work redesigning, the open system approach, industrial democracy, and quality of working life. Motivation development requires interventions at all levels: the organization (including the reward system), the role or the job, and the individual.

GLOSSARY

autonomy providing scope for individuals or groups performing jobs to plan, regulate, and control their own work worlds

horizontal loading providing more motivators in work

hygiene the factor(s) that causes dissatisfaction

motivator the factor(s) that contributes towards people's satisfaction at work

open socio-technical system an organization and its sub-systems open to input-through-output changes with the environment

vertical loading providing more routine work

EXERCISES

Concept Review Questions

1. What contributes to dissatisfaction and what contributes to satisfaction among managers in India/Asia?
2. Summarise the main trends discovered through motivation studies of Indian managers.
3. What are the principles and procedures of job enrichment?
4. What usually goes wrong with job enrichment?
5. What is the concept of humanisation of work?
6. How can an organization raise the motivational level of its employees?

Critical Thinking Questions

1. How will you undertake job enrichment for the clerk in your institution?
2. Why do some students have low motivation for studies? Find out by interviewing one or two students and exploring the reasons for their commitment to studies.
3. How can teachers in schools develop children's motivation for reading?
4. Analyse your own motivation in different areas. Why is it high in some and low in others?

Classroom Projects

1. Read about the reward systems used in some companies. What effect do the systems have on employee motivation? Why?
2. Develop recommendations for your institution to raise the level of motivation of the students.

Field Projects

1. Interview two workers and two managers to identify the factors contributing to their dissatisfaction and satisfaction. Relate your findings to Herzberg's theory.
2. Interview one employee in any organization and develop a plan of work redesigning (work humanisation) for him or her.

Thomrich-Wooge Private Limited*

CASE STUDY

THE ORGANIZATION

Thomson and Richards, two technocrats from Holland, both in their late thirties, came as consultants to Calcutta with a French company on a project assignment in 1940. They were quite impressed with the Indian culture and decided to settle down in India. On completion of the project, they started their own company Thomrich Pvt. Ltd, which manufactured agricultural equipments. Encouraged by the performance of the company, they ventured into the manufacturing of fertiliser equipments in 1944, under the same banner. Their entrepreneurial skills and success prompted them to diversify their business into manufacturing of lubricants in 1951 and electrical gadgets for industrial use in the year 1970. In 1992, Thomrich Pvt. Ltd entered into the tractor segment and established its plant at Gwalior, in the state of Madhya Pradesh. It was entering this segment when another company, KCP, had already established its reputation as the sole reliable brand. Unaffected by the competition, Thomrich started its own brand of tractors and after 3 years it started manufacturing cultivators too.

So far Thomrich had a smooth sailing. But with liberalisation and globalization in the 1990s, Thomrich did not remain untouched by the surmounting pressures of MNCs venturing into the Indian market. This made the company sell one of its profit-making divisions, i.e., the fertilizer equipments unit, to a leading Indian business house, to concentrate on its core competency areas. To add to its woes, the rumours of Elegators, the world's number one tractor manufacturer, foraying into the Indian market gave it sleepless nights. Being proactive, the company decided to enter in a collaborative venture with Wooge of France, the world's number two tractor manufacturer, and rechristened itself as Thomrich-Wooge Pvt. Ltd. In the year 2002, it improvised the then existing model in terms of efficiency by reducing its cycle-time, thereby becoming number one in the country. The company considered this product its flagship, although the product had not been able to take the place of KCP Tractors, despite improvisation in its efficiency.

The company was purely technocratic in nature with an annual turnover of 100,000 million rupees, with Thomrich-Wooge Pvt. Ltd contributing 1,250 million rupees to it. The Gwalior unit had a total strength of 308 employees, which included 94 executives and supervisors, and the rest workmen. All the executives were engineering

* This case was developed by Santosh Dhar, Akhilesh K. Misra (Prestige Institute of Management and Research, Indore), Aney Alex (Institute of Management Studies, DAVV, Indore), and Praveen Saxena (Govindram Sekseria Institute of Management and Research, Indore) in the Thirteenth Case Writing Workshop organized by Prestige Institute of Management and Research, Indore, and sponsored by Association of Indian Management Schools (AIMS), 03–05 December 2004.

graduates with 50 per cent of them locals. The workmen were ITI (Industrial Training Institutes) qualified with 60 per cent of them employed as welders, 10 per cent as mechanics, and 30 per cent as fitters. About 40 per cent of the workmen were from Maharashtra and the rest from Madhya Pradesh. K. Vaswani, a 54-year-old technocrat, headed the Gwalior unit as chief executive. Vaswani had previously been with the company from 1972 to 1993 and had left to join an MNC as chief executive. Seeing new developments in the company, he rejoined Thomrich-Wooge Pvt. Ltd in June 2004. Vaswani perpetuated the employee-friendly culture in the organization. He regularly held meetings with employees, irrespective of their levels, and also made frequent visits to the shop floor to have face-to-face interactions with the workmen.

HR PROCESSES

The company recruited in two phases. The corporate office at Calcutta, through campus selection, recruited the engineering graduates, and the certificate and diploma holders were recruited independently at the unit level. The company did not encourage inter-unit transfers, although there were a few need-based transfers to facilitate the employees' and company's operations. The company had the policy of recruiting graduate engineers at entry level and nurturing and grooming them for higher positions. As a result, only Thomrichians occupied all the top positions in all the units of the organization.

Although the top management acknowledged and appreciated verbally the performance of workers from time to time, the company had a fixed wage/salary structure across all the units in India (allowances, however, varied from place to place). The company had a firm belief that employees would always put their best efforts if facilitated with good quality of work-life and, therefore, did not have provision for monetary incentives. It also believed that incentive schemes would hamper the quality of the products by compelling employees to pay more attention to quantity rather than quality—lured by incentives, employees would somehow try to sell the products without due consideration to customer needs. The company felt that monetary incentives can motivate an employee to a certain extent, but beyond that level it would fail to have any impact on employee efficiency; rather it would raise employee expectations, and unfulfilled expectations would lower the morale of the employee.

The company had a performance appraisal system based on management by objectives (MBO). The top management would set the goals and communicate them to the CE, who in turn would pass them down to the HODs (heads of departments). The HODs would be given sufficient time to speculate on the feasibility of the goals, and once the feasibility was decided, the goals would be frozen and communicated to the employees. Every quarter, the superiors would discuss the performance with the employees and pass on the ratings to the HR department. The expert committee consisting of 4–5 members from various functional departments evaluated these ratings. These members knew all the employees who were being evaluated, and they re-rated them to reduce the inter-rater bias. The ratings of the committee would be final and would be communicated to the respective superiors, and discussed with the concerned employees. The superiors would also counsel the subordinates in order to redress their grievances, if any. Decisions regarding promotions and rewards would be made annually, which would be based on quarterly performance appraisals.

The company had a two-tier system of training—one at the plant level and the other at the corporate level. It had its own management development centre at Darjeeling, where most of the training programmes were conducted for managers, incorporating prayers and yoga too. The company did not have a separate budget for training—training was need based. Each employee was required to undergo at least 15 days of training each year. Since, multiskilling was practised within assembly lines, the employees were exposed to both technical as well as behavioural training. Most of the trainers engaged by the company were outsiders. All the training programmes were thoroughly evaluated every quarter by taking feedback from the immediate superior of the employee. The company would administer psychometric measures once in 3 years to appraise the potential of employees for various functional areas. Once a particular competence or aptitude was identified in an employee, he or she would be groomed in that particular area by a mentor.

The company had a recognised trade union, which was earlier affiliated to the Bharatiya Mazdoor Sangh (BMS), but was now enjoying an independent status. The union would place a charter of demand before the management once in 4 years, which would be followed by harmonious negotiations between the two. As the management involved the workmen even in the market survey of the products, the union also discussed quality issues with the management. The company's employment policies radiated a single principle—that the company believed in people and that they were the most valuable assets for it. Employees had the freedom to see any superior any time without prior appointment. The company boasted of open communication system, total transparency, no-status barrier, security, and sense of professionalism among the employees—which were reflected in the company not witnessing any strike or major indiscipline since its inception.

The company had also introduced 'Prayaas', an HR-initiative, as a proactive measure to have a competitive edge in the dynamic scenario. Prayaas involved organization development interventions like cross-functional team, large-scale integration, kaizen (continuous improvement), etc. All the employees in three- to five-member groups were asked to suggest changes for the betterment of the unit. Solutions and action plans were also invited from the employees, and the consolidated suggestions were implemented, which resulted in the introduction of suggestion schemes, wastage utilisation, and recycling of packaging material. Some of the brilliant ideas of the employees were suitably recognised and widely circulated through in-house journals in all the units of Thomrich.

CHALLENGES

Since 2002, the company had seen 12 per cent executive turnover, which was earlier just 3 per cent. This drew the attention of the top management, who were confident of high degree of employee loyalty and believed that the employees were emotionally attached to the unit. At this juncture, the HR head, S. Abraham anticipated trouble, as he feared that the turnover rate might increase in the wake of globalization and liberalization, with more and more MNCs offering lucrative packages and challenging assignments to the executives. These firms were recruiting people at all levels, which made the employees feel that there was slow growth prospect at their unit. Moreover, employees had also become more risk taking and their varied expertise encouraged them to experiment in new segments, namely IT, banking, and BPOs. Though the MNCs had 15–18 hours of working, the changing orientation of employees made them feel that they were handsomely compensated.

Abraham apprehended further deterioration due to the influence of dollar packages, which was unaffordable for Thomrich-Wooge Pvt. Ltd. The market conditions were already tight—with too many competitors, prices slashing down, customers becoming more demanding and choosy—making the inputs scarce for the unit. Abraham was considering the options of overcoming the exodus of executives by increasing the efficiency with lesser input—for which the company would have to minimise its task force. This strategy would tarnish its employee-friendly image. The other option was to increase the profits by exploring new markets. The Indian market by now was already flooded with many players, leaving the international market as the only option, which was equally a hard nut to crack. Abraham felt trapped in a highly volatile situation, where he fumbled for a speedy and pragmatic remedy.

Questions for Discussion

1. What are the motivational principles underlying the HR policies of the company?
2. Analyse 'Prayaas' from the point of view of managing motivation of the people.
3. What new challenges is the company facing in relation to employees' motivation?
4. Suggest any changes you would like to make to raise the motivational level of the employees?

NOTES AND REFERENCES

1. Kalanidhi, M.S. (1972). 'A study of job satisfaction among draughts-women', *Manas*, 19(2): 73–82.
2. Roy, S.K., G.A. Raja, and A.S. Menon (eds) (1977). *Motivational and Organizational Effectiveness*, pp. 104–135. New Delhi: Sri Ram Centre of Industrial Relations.
3. Herzberg, F. (1966). *Work and the Nature of Work*. Cleveland: World Publishing.
4. Herzberg, F. (1968). 'How do you motivate employees?' *Harvard Business Review*, 46(1).
5. Paul, W.J. and K.B. Robertson (1970). *Job Enrichment and Employee Motivation*. London: Gower Press.
6. *Ibid.*
7. Hackman, J.R. (1975). 'Is job enrichment just a fad?', *Harvard Business Review*, 53(5): 129–138.
8. Davis, L.E. and C. Taylor (eds) (1975). *The Quality of Working Life*, 2 vols. New York: Free Press.
9. J. Gulowsen in Davis, L.E. and C. Taylor (eds) (1979). *Design of Jobs*. Santa Monica: Good Year.
10. P.H. Engelstad in Davis, L.E. and C. Taylor (eds) (1979). *Design of Jobs*. Santa Monica: Good Year.
11. McClelland, D.C. and D.C. Winter (1969). *Motivating Economic Achievement*. New York: Free Press.
12. McClelland, D.C. and D.H. Burnham (1976). 'Power is the great motivatior', *Harvard Business Review*, 54(2): 100–10.
13. McClelland, D.C. and D.C. Winter (1969). *Motivating Economic Achievement*. New York: Free Press.

14
Coping with Frustration, Stress, and Burnout

LEARNING OBJECTIVES

After studying this chapter, you will be able to
1. Understand the concepts of frustration, stress, and burnout
2. Explain the dynamics of frustration and stress
3. Elaborate different role stresses
4. Define the phenomenon of burnout
5. Distinguish between functional and dysfunctional strategies of coping with role stress

An employee has worked very hard and expects to be rewarded for this work. He or she does not get any reward, not even appreciation. He or she feels frustrated.

Another employee has been promised a very exciting assignment but his or her work continues to be routine and dull. The employee feels disappointed.

A salesperson visits a corporate customer who has promised to buy the product. But the customer refuses the product. The salesperson is frustrated.

We can cite many such examples of frustration and disappointment. Every day, we face situations that frustrate us.

WHAT IS FRUSTRATION?

Frustration is the blocking or slowing down of a goal-directed activity. Human behaviour is purposive and goal directed. We undertake a series of activities to achieve a goal. A goal may be immediate or short term (e.g., seeing a movie) or distant and long term (e.g., becoming a physician).

Movement towards a goal is not easy. Hurdles may appear between the starting point and the end state (goal). For example, a person wanting to go to a movie may be called upon by a parent or a spouse to do something else at that time. A student studying hard to enter medical school may face problems of insufficient funds, inadequate preparation in an important subject, etc. This may produce a sense of deprivation in the individual. And this in turn may result in frustration. Frustration, then, is the resultant feeling caused by a sense of privation (lack of something), deprivation (blocking of or interference with a goal), or conflict in relation to goal-directed activities.

Frustration can thus be caused by three categories of factors: privation, deprivation, and conflict. If a person experiences the lack of something relevant to a desired goal, he or she may feel frustrated. For example, take the case of a student who is working hard to get into a medical school, but does not have adequate financial resources. He or she will feel frustrated because he or she cannot pursue the goal.

Similarly, frustration is caused if goal-directed activities are blocked or interfered with. For example, an employee preparing for a career-advancing examination may fall ill and be forced to take a long rest. He or she may then feel frustrated.

Frustration can also be caused by conflicts between two goals: equally attractive goals (approach–approach conflict) or equally unattractive goals (avoidance–avoidance conflict). An employee's conflict between taking up a high-paying assignment in a foreign country where he or she cannot take his or her family along and remaining at home with the family in a poorly paid job is an example of approach–approach conflict.

An employee asked to choose between a lucrative assignment in a far-off place and giving up his or her chances of advancement by continuing in his or her own hometown will face an avoidance–avoidance conflict (choosing between two equally undesirable end states).

When a goal is very attractive and at the same time has certain negative aspects, it produces an approach–avoidance conflict. A person getting an attractive offer of employment from a rather unpleasant country may feel conflicted about accepting the offer.

Dynamics of Frustration

What causes frustration? Let us take the example of Anna who felt frustrated because she had worked hard and been promised a higher position by her boss but found she did not get the position when the announcements were made. How frustrated did she feel?

Several factors contribute to frustration. All of these are goal-related factors. These are shown in the following formula:

$$F = fL \times V \times O + I + P$$

where F denotes frustration, f the function, L denotes the expectation to achieve the goal, V the valence (attractiveness of the goal), O the opportunity to achieve the goal in the near future (low), I the investment of effort and other inputs in the achievement of the goal, and P is the public knowledge of the expected achievement.

In this formula, three variables have a multiplicative function—they enhance frustration faster. If one of them is zero, the resulting frustration will be zero. In the example given above, if Anna had no expectation of being promoted (her goal), she would have experienced very little (or no) frustration even if she was not promoted. Similarly, if the goal (getting promoted) was not seen as attractive or valuable, there would be little frustration. The more attractive the goal, the more the frustration caused by the obstacle in achieving the goal. In the same way, if Anna saw another possibility of getting a promotion very soon (say, in the next year), the frustration caused by not being promoted would not be much. The more opportunities one has for achieving the goal in the near future, the less is the frustration caused by deprivation of the goal at a given time.

The other two elements (effort invested and publicity of expected reward) have an additive function. They add to the frustration, but not in the same proportion as the multiplicative facts. The more effort one has invested in the process of achieving a goal, the higher is the frustration on deprivation of the goal. For example, Anna's frustration would be high because she worked very hard for the promotion. Similarly, the more others know about the possible achievement of a goal by a person, the higher the frustration is if he or she does not reach the goal. For example, if more people knew that Anna was likely to get promoted, she would feel more frustrated compared with a situation in which no one knew that she was likely to be rewarded.

Circularity of Frustration

When a person is frustrated or disappointed, he or she may react in a particular way that starts off a cycle—a cycle of frustration or a cycle of hope. The frustration cycle is as follows: adaptive deterioration, isolation, distorted perception, defensive behaviour. The hope cycle is the opposite: realistic analysis, exploration, insight, problem solving. This is shown in Exhibit 14.1.

Disappointment may cause loss of flexibility and what may be called 'adaptive deterioration'. A person may be preoccupied with disappointment, leading to neglect of work and signs of general deterioration in the standard of performance. A disappointed employee may thus neglect his work, may cause delays, may make errors, etc. The frustrated person may be annoyed with himself or herself for such deterioration, but will continue in such a state. Often, others will not approve of such

Exhibit 14.1 *Frustration and Hope Cycles*

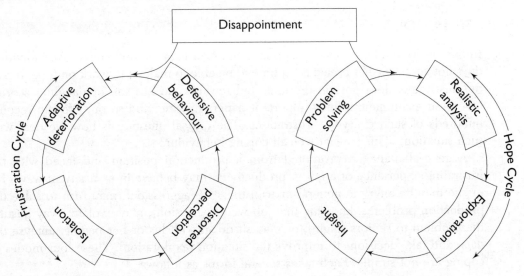

behaviour. The person then feels and becomes isolated and tries to cope with the situation as well as he or she can. However, isolation often leads to exaggeration and a distorted perception of the situation. A frustrated employee may see his or her boss as being in 'collusion' with others in creating the disappointment. He or she is likely to see himself or herself as a victim, misinterpreting normal happenings as a part of the frustration-producing events. In response to such distorted perceptions, the frustrated person is likely to show behaviour that will help him or her escape or defend himself or herself against anxiety as well as maintain and even enhance self-esteem by absolving the self of any responsibility in this deteriorating frustration cycle.

These behaviours use what are called 'defense mechanisms' (mechanisms that defend against anxiety) and the behaviours can be called defensive behaviour. This does not solve the problem but helps to reduce anxiety. The frustrated person may deny that he or she is disappointed or may see 'designs' by several people jealous of his or her ability or popularity persecuting him or her, and so on. In the next section, we shall discuss defense mechanisms in greater detail. Defensive behaviour often justifies and reinforces adaptive deterioration, thus completing the frustration cycle.

The cycle of hope is the opposite of this. A disappointed individual, instead of being overwhelmed by disappointment and losing interest in work, analyses the situation with greater objectivity, understands what has caused what, where things went wrong, etc. This is likely to lead to exploration of the situation with others, collection of information, and discovery of facts. With comprehensive information, the person is likely to get a better insight into the situation, leading to action that can deal with the situation. This is problem-solving behaviour. Problem-solving behaviour reinforces realistic analysis, completing the cycle of hope.

Both the cycles of frustration and hope, like all such continuous cycles, are self-perpetuating. As the cycle advances, it gets stronger, and is likely to repeat itself.

COPING BEHAVIOUR

In our everyday life, we face disappointment or frustration quite often. An individual does not get his or her breakfast in time to be able to make it to work on time, misses the bus home, does not get the expected rewards, finds a son or daughter scoring low in an examination, finds important papers missing, and so on. We can recount hundreds of such everyday frustrations. The critical question is how we deal with such situations. This is what we call coping behaviour.

A general manager, promoted from a production position and faced with the frustrating experience of a fall in productivity, may behave in a variety of ways. He or she may be angry in general or with the staff (aggression); may rush to solve the production problems, knowing that job well (regression); may explain away (justify) the problem to seniors (flight); or may sit down with his or her people, analyse the data, and take decisions to improve the situation (exploration). These four modes of coping are not simple. Each takes several forms as follows.

Aggression

Aggression is the most common and most frequent reaction to frustration. It may take any one of the forms given below:

General aggression General irritation, restlessness, and violent/destructive expressions of aggression (kicking, knocking, breaking things, etc.) are the general forms of aggression.

Target-directed aggression Anger, blaming others, and hostility expressed towards people seen as causing disappointment (such as anger towards the boss or subordinate)—whether expressed in person or in absentia—are quite common.

Self-directed aggression Sometimes the frustrated person may blame himself or herself for the situation. This is self-directed aggression.

Displaced aggression When aggression is directed to a person(s) other than the people seen as causing disappointment, it is called displaced aggression. A manager may express anger or resentment to a subordinate because he cannot express anger towards his or her boss.

Displaced aggression may find three types of targets: someone who is similar to the source of frustration (anger with a female boss being expressed towards all women employees), someone who is dissimilar, if the aggression cannot be expressed against the frustrating person (e.g., anger towards the father will not be expressed towards elderly persons but towards younger ones), or a new 'weak' target (anger is often thus expressed towards a spouse, subordinate, or minority group).

Regression

Regression is characterised by primitive or previously used modes of behaviour. Under emotional pressure, a person may revert to earlier behavioural modes that make him or her feel more secure. Regression may take three forms:

Retrogression An individual reverts to old behaviour. In the example cited above, a general manager (promoted from the position of production manager) may behave like a production manager and straighten out production problems under the emotional pressure of frustration.

Primitivation Sometimes an individual does something he or she did not do in the past but which nevertheless shows primitive or immature behaviour. An employee may thus behave like a recalcitrant adolescent when tense or frustrated.

Stereotype Frustration may make a person lose all flexibility and revert to fixated, receptive behaviour. A manager feeling frustrated may deal with a situation in a known way, repeating the same behaviour even if it is seen as dysfunctional. This is best demonstrated in a gambler's behaviour in a series of moves in which he or she loses. The person may thus repeat an approach (gambling) and lose everything he or she has.

Flight

One reaction to frustration is flight or escape from the frustrating situation. This may take several forms:

Apathy A manager may not pay any attention to the frustrating situation and may neglect it.

Withdrawal A frustrated employee in an organization may leave it or avoid attending meetings. In a conflict situation, one party may thus withdraw from the situation.

Denial A person may deny feeling any frustration. In order to escape the pain of frustration, one may repress the feeling of pain and deny experiencing any frustration in the situation.

Fantasy One way to escape unpleasant feelings is to daydream pleasant things and create fantasies of doing something one cannot do in real life.

Rationalisation Even if one acknowledges frustration, one can explain it away, giving a 'reason' for it. An employee failing to get a coveted reward may see the reward as not worthwhile (sour grapes) or may justify not getting the reward on some other basis.

Exploration

All the three behavioural modes mentioned above are dysfunctional. They may reduce anxiety and tension in an individual but do not help in solving a problem. The exploration mode, however, is a problem-solving mode. An individual explores the issues with others, takes steps to analyse the situation, and prepares alternative strategies of action. Exploration may take the following forms:

Alternative generation A frustrated individual may search for alternative avenues. An employee excelling in another area rather than pursuing one in which he or she has failed several times shows a special mode that is called 'compensation'.

Self-action All explorations are action oriented. A frustrated person may search for solutions, working alone.

Action by others An employee may alternatively expect others to solve the problem or request others for help.

Joint action Often, a better coping mode is joint exploration, collaborating with others in analysing the problem, and working out alternative action plans.

Managing Frustration

Managers are frequently required to deal with the frustration of their subordinates. The following sequential steps are suggested for effective management of employee frustration.

Listen to the feelings of the staff   This first step is taken by the manager through trying to understand the feelings and views of the frustrated subordinate(s). This may be done by asking the subordinate(s) to state their problems, their feelings, and their perceptions. Instead of being defensive if subordinates express negative impressions, the manager will do well to patiently listen to them. One test of listening, and a desirable behaviour assuring subordinates that the manager listens to them, is to restate their points of view, feelings, and perceptions at the end of the session before taking the next step.

Share own feelings of disappointment   If a manager is able to level with subordinates, he or she may be able to reach out to them. In most situations causing frustration to subordinates, the manager is also experiencing disappointment. If a subordinate is not rewarded, the manager is also disappointed. It may help in building rapport with the subordinates if the manager shares his or her own disappointment. This should not be done as a gimmick but only if he or she has some feelings he or she needs to share.

Share feelings of guilt (if any)   Sometimes the manager may partly contribute to the disappointment of the subordinates. He or she may build high expectations and subordinates may feel frustrated because the expectations are not met. Or he or she may promise something to an employee who does not eventually get it. In such situations, a manager's usual tendency is to explain the reasons for the disappointment. Before any explanation is given, however, the manager may share any feelings of guilt for arousing expectations, etc.

Help the employees to own up to their feelings   The manager's modelling behaviour in sharing feelings and owning up feelings of guilt may help the subordinates own up their own feelings of disappointment, anger, etc. This may help in taking the next constructive steps.

Help the staff to accept and confront reality   The first step in constructive action is to acknowledge the reality and be ready to deal with it. Airing their feelings may help the employee–manager team to move forward and not to get fixated on feelings. The new situation as it exists may be clearly stated, understood, and accepted as a reality.

Help the staff assess damage caused by frustration   Frustration causes some damage in terms of physical effects (sleeplessness, tension, loss of appetite), social effects (effect on personal relationships, reduced social contact, lack of enjoyment in family life), effects on work (neglect of work, errors, fall in quality, absenteeism), etc. It may be useful to help the staff reflect on and assess the damage frustration is causing them. Even if the work in the organization suffers, the main damage is done to the frustrated employee. The employees need to understand and realise this.

Develop alternatives to solve the problem   The final step is to involve the frustrated employees in generating alternatives to the problem and in taking constructive steps. While subordinates generate the alternatives, the manager may suggest some possibilities. Often, the subordinates—being too close to the frustrating situation—are not able to think of creative alternatives. The manager can then generate such possibilities with them.

In short, frustration is an everyday life experience. It may be useful to understand the nature of frustration, its cyclic dynamics, what causes it, how people cope with frustration, and with what consequences. Such an understanding can help managers to manage frustration more effectively.

STRESS

Modern life is full of stress. As organizations become more complex, the potential for and the amount of stress increases. Urbanisation, industrialisation, and the increase in scales of operations are causing increasing stresses. These are the inevitable consequences of socio-economic complexity. People feel stressed as they can no longer have complete control over what happens in their life. The telephone goes out of order, the power is shut off, the water supply is disrupted, an expected promotion is denied, a son or a daughter does not do well in school, prices of essential commodities increase disproportionately to the income, and so on and so forth—and we feel frustrated and then stressed out.

There is no escape from stress in modern life. Hence we need to find ways of using stress in a productive way, reducing dysfunctional stress, and dealing effectively with it.

Several terms have been used synonymously with stress. Four terms are in related literature: stress, strain, conflict, and pressure. The word 'strain' has been used to denote the effect of stress on the individual. 'Pressure' has been used in the same sense. The word 'conflict' usually denotes incompatibility between two variables: goals, means, ideas, etc. The term 'stress' has been used to denote a stimulus (or cause) like an out-of-order telephone; the response (physiological, behavioural, or cognitive changes) to such a cause, for example, heightened blood pressure, quickened breathing, stamping of the foot, perceiving the telephone department as incompetent, etc.; or the resultant state of the organism, for example, indifference, effort to get the telephone repaired, etc.

In order to avoid confusion, we shall use the term 'stressor' for the stimuli that produce stress; the term 'stress' for the affective (emotional) part of the experience of incongruence; the term 'symptoms' for physiological, behavioural, and conceptual responses or changes; and the term 'coping' for behaviour to deal with the emotional component of the experience of incongruence (i.e., stress).

There does not seem to be much value in making a finer distinction among the various terms used, such as stress, strain, or pressure. The general term 'stress' will be used here to refer to all such terms and concepts.

Not only is stress inevitable in complex modern life, it is also necessary for human progress. It is similar to the optimum stress needed in a musical instrument to produce good music—loose wires (less stress) may result in screeching. A distinction has been made between productive or functional stress (stress related to creative works, entrepreneurial activities, Olympic competitions, etc.) and dysfunctional stress (the stress of boredom, unmanageable conflicts, overwork, etc.). The former has been called *eustress* and the latter *dis-stress*.

Life Stress

Stress is produced by several happenings in life. In general, every transition or change produces stress. People in newer states of life experience such stress of transition more. Young adults between 20 and 30 years of age have been found to report twice as many stressful events compared to older subjects. Stress disorders have been found to be more prevalent among the urban population than the rural population and greater in the higher educational categories.

To study general life stress, respondents are given a list of several life events and they are required to check each event for the amount of stress it produces. Generally, in developing countries, events that threaten the basic biological needs are ranked higher for stress than events that create sociocultural conflicts. In one study involving executives, the events producing stress were (in order) pressure to work harder, major festivals, change in the health of a family member, change in work responsibility, arguing with a spouse, loud noise, and finally several changes, for example, in living conditions, habits, recreation, and work hours.

Such life events stress scales also provide information about the respondent's total stress score and how harmful it could be.

Role Stress: Role–Space Conflicts

We have already discussed in Chapter 12 the concept of a role as a position a person occupies in a system as defined or determined by the expectations of the significant members of the social system and his or her own expectations from the position he or she occupies in the social system.

You will recall that role space (the dynamic relationship among various roles the individual occupies and his or her self) has three main variables: the self, the role in question, and other roles the individual occupies. Any conflicts within this field are referred to as role–space conflicts or stress. These conflicts may be the following:

Self–role distance   This stress arises out of the conflict between the self-concept and one's expectations from the role as perceived by the role occupant. If a person occupies a role that he or she subsequently finds is conflicting with his or her self-concept, the person feels stress. For example, an introvert, who is fond of studying and writing rather them socialising may find considerable self–role distance if he or she accepts the role of a salesperson in an organization, and comes to realise that the expectations from the role would include his or her meeting people and being social. Such conflicts are fairly common although they may not be severe.

Intra-role conflict Since the individual learns to develop expectations as a result of socialisation and identification with significant others, it is quite likely that he or she may see some incompatibility among the various expectations (functions) from his or her own role. For example, a professor may see an incompatibility between the expectations of teaching students and of doing research. These may not be inherently conflicting but the individual may perceive these as incompatible.

Role stagnation The individual grows in the role he or she occupies in an organization. He or she expects to learn new things, take up challenging tasks, prepare for higher responsibilities, etc. When the role does not provide such opportunities, the individual experiences role stagnation. This becomes an acute problem especially when the individual has occupied the role for the long time and keeps performing the same routine functions.

Inter-role distance The individual occupies more than one role. There may be conflicts among the roles he or she occupies. For example, an executive often faces a conflict between the organizational role of an executive and the familial roles of a spouse and a parent. The demands from a wife and children to share his or her time may be incompatible with the organizational demands on the individual to spend time on organizational problems. Such inter-role conflicts are quite frequent in modern society as the individual is increasingly occupying multiple roles in various organizations and groups.

Role Stress: Role-set Conflicts

The other field that is important for the individual's role is his role-set. A role set has been conceived of as a system of relationship between the role and other related roles in a social system. A role set consists of persons like boss, colleagues, subordinates, and clients, who have different expectations from the role the individual occupies. The conflicts that arise as a result of incompatibility among these expectations of the significant other roles and the individual himself are referred to as role-set conflicts. These conflicts are as follows:

Role ambiguity When the individual is not clear about the various expectations people have from his or her role, he or she faces the conflict called role ambiguity. Role ambiguity may be due to lack of information available to the role occupant or due to the individual's lack of understanding of the cues available. Role ambiguity may be in relation to activities, responsibilities, priorities, norms, or general expectations. Generally, role ambiguity is experienced by people occupying roles newly created in the organization, roles in organizations undergoing change, or process roles (with less clear and concrete activities).

Role expectation conflict When there are conflicting expectations or demands from different role senders (people having expectations from the role), the role occupant may experience this stress. There may be conflicting expectations from the boss, subordinates, peers, or clients.

Role overload   When the role occupant feels that there are too many expectations from the significant role senders in the role set, he or she experiences role overload. Role overload has been measured by asking questions about people's feelings on whether they could possibly finish work given to them during a modified workday and whether they felt that the amount of work they did might interfere with how well it was done. Most executive role occupants experience role overload. Role overload is more likely to occur in the absence of a mechanism of role integration, in the absence of power ceded to role occupants, in situations where there are large variations in expected output, and in instances when delegation does not result in more time as expected.

Role erosion   When a role occupant feels that some functions that he or she would like to perform are being performed by some other role, the stress felt is called role erosion. Role erosion is the subjective feeling of an individual that some important role expectations he or she has from the role are shared by other roles in the role set. Role erosion is likely to be experienced in an organization that is redefining roles and creating new roles. In several organizations that redefined their structure, the stress of role erosion was inevitably felt. In the State Bank of India, the role of general manager was split into two roles, those of GM (Operations) and GM (Planning). The role occupants of both these new roles experienced role erosion and felt that their roles had become less important compared to the old role.

Resource inadequacy   Resource inadequacy stress is experienced when the resources required by the role occupant to perform the role effectively— information, people, material, finance, and facilities—are not available.

Personal inadequacy   When a role occupant feels that he or she is not prepared (does not have the required competencies) to undertake a role effectively, he or she may experience this kind of stress. The individual may feel he or she does not have enough knowledge, skills, or training, or has not had time to prepare for the role assigned to him or her. People who are assigned new roles without enough preparation or orientation are likely to experience such stress.

Role isolation   In a role set, a role occupant may feel that certain roles are psychologically closer to him or her, while other roles are at a distance. The main criteria governing this perception of distance are frequency and ease of interaction. When linkages are strong, role isolation will be low. In the absence of strong linkages, role isolation may be high. Role isolation can, therefore, be measured in terms of existing and desired linkages. The gap between desired and actual linkages will indicate the amount of role isolation.

BURNOUT

Stress is like electric power. It can make a bulb light up and provide brilliant illumination. However, if the voltage is higher than what the bulb can take, it can burn the bulb out. The phenomenon of burnout is a harmful effect of stress resulting in loss of effectiveness. Burnout can be defined as the end result of stress experienced but not properly coped with, resulting in the symptoms of exhaustion, irritation, ineffectiveness, inaction, discounting of the self and others, and health problems (hypertension, ulcers, and heart ailments). The opposite phenomenon of 'glow-up' occurs when stress is properly channelled, resulting in a feeling of challenge, high job satisfaction, creativity, effectiveness, and better adjustment to work and life.

Generally, roles requiring continuous work with people (teacher, trainer, salesperson, and personnel care roles) experience burnout more than roles requiring less contact with people. Highly routine and mechanical roles also produce burnout. The amount of stress experienced ('dis-stress', experienced as a source of irritation) also contributes to burnout.

Some personality factors have been found to contribute to burnout as well. The personality orientation called Type A has been found to be associated with burnout (this is discussed in Chapter 10). More recent research has shown that two specific elements in Type A personality contribute to burnout: cynicism (low interpersonal trust) and a sense of loneliness. Other personality factors contributing to burnout are externality (a feeling that the person does not have control over what happens and that external forces, chance, or fate determine things), low self-esteem, rigidity, alienation, and Machiavellism (manipulative orientation). One study has shown that stress tolerance is higher in individuals with greater impulse control (voluntary delay of gratification of physical and physiological needs) or self-control.

Several factors contribute to burnout: stress being very low or very high, discomfiting kinds of stress (called 'dis-stress'), a stress-prone personality, an alienating role or job, hostile relationships, a stress-absorbing lifestyle, an avoidance-oriented role style, use of dysfunctional coping modes or styles, and a hostile organizational climate. The opposites of these contribute to the phenomenon of glow-up.

How do we prevent burnout? How do we convert the energy leading to burnout into one that may help us glow up? Factors contributing to burnout and glow-up as well as some conversion strategies are shown in Exhibit 14.2. This shows that development of inner-directedness (self-obligating orientation) achieves the optimum level of stress—one factor contributing to glow-up. For each contributing factor, a conversion strategy has been suggested. Most of these are self-explanatory. For changing one's lifestyle, the use of transactional analysis has been suggested: understanding the life script and then terminating it (de-scripting) through new decisions (see Chapter 10). Some special interventions may be needed for effective use of these conversion strategies.

COPING WITH STRESS

When individuals experience stress, they adopt ways of dealing with it. An individual cannot remain in a continual state of tension. Therefore, even if a deliberate and conscious strategy is not utilised to deal with the stress, some strategy is adopted. We call this coping. The word 'coping' has been used mainly in two senses: in the

Exhibit 14.2   *Executive Glow-up and Burnout: Contributing Factors and Conversion Strategies*

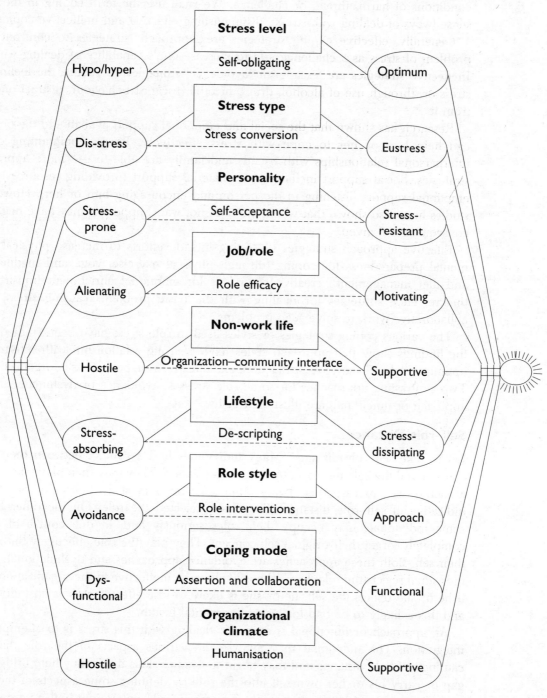

Note: Dotted lines show conversion strategies

general sense of 'ways of dealing with stress' and the sense of an effort to 'master' conditions of harm, threat, or challenge. We shall use the term coping in the first sense (ways of dealing with stress), distinguishing effective and ineffective coping.

Generally, effective coping strategies are 'approach' strategies to confront the problem of stress as a challenge and to increase one's capability of dealing with it. Ineffective strategies are 'escape' or 'avoidance' strategies, to reduce the feeling of stress or, through use of alcohol, drugs, or other escapist behaviour, distract oneself from it.

Research has shown that the social and emotional support available to the person can help him or her to cope with stress effectively. People maintaining close interpersonal relationships with friends and family are able to use more approach strategies. Social support includes both material support (providing resources) and emotional support (listening to the person and encouraging him or her). However, studies have also shown that when one does not want support, it may have negative consequences if given.

Effective approach strategies of coping include efforts to increase physical and mental preparedness for coping (through physical exercise, yoga and meditation, and diet management), creative diversions for emotional enrichment (music, art, theatre, etc.), strategies for dealing with the basic problems causing stress, and collaborative work to solve such problems.

The various coping strategies or styles used in role stress have been studied and the findings show that approach styles have a strong relationship with internality, optimism, role efficacy, job satisfaction, and effective role behaviour in organizations. Two contrasting approaches for some role stresses (avoidance or dysfunctional and approach or functional) are illustrated below.

Self–role Distance

Let us take self–role distance. Many individuals find a conflict between their self-concept and the role they occupy in an organization. They may then play that role in a routine way to earn their living—they take no interest in their role and this is indicative of self–role distance. They have rejected the role. On the other hand, some individuals may occupy their roles seriously and, in due course of time, completely forget their original self-concept. They play the role effectively but reject their self. Both these approaches are avoidance approaches and dysfunctional. If an individual rejects the role, he or she is likely to be ineffective in the organization. Yet if he or she rejects the self, he or she is likely to lose effectiveness as an individual and this is likely to be bad for his or her mental health.

An approach or functional strategy for dealing with this stress is to attempt role integration. The individual may analyse the various aspects of the role that are causing self–role distance and may begin to acquire skills if this may help bridge the gap or carry his or her own self into the role by defining some aspects of the role according to his or her own strengths. In other words, an attempt both to grow into the role and make the role grow to use the special capabilities of the person would result in role integration, so that the individual gets the satisfaction of occupying a role that is nearer to his or her self-concept. Such integration is not easy to achieve but with systematic effort, it is also not very difficult.

Role Expectation Conflict

Similar is the case of role expectation conflict. When the various expectations from the role one occupies conflict with one another, role stress may develop. One way to deal with this stress is to eliminate those expectations from the role that are likely to conflict with other expectations. This is the process of role shrinkage. Role shrinkage is the action of pruning the role in such a way that some expectations can be given up. Role shrinkage may help to avoid the problem but it is a dysfunctional approach since the advantage of a larger role is lost.

Instead of role shrinkage, if role linkages are established with other roles and the problem is solved by devising new ways of achieving the conflicting expectations, the individual can experience both the process of growth as well as satisfaction.

For example, a professor who is experiencing conflict between three expectations from the role—those of teaching students, doing research, and consulting with organizations—may find the stress is essentially that of personal inadequacy. He or she may not have enough skills for doing research. Because of the lack of related skills, he or she may take recourse to role shrinkage. However, one way to deal with this problem is to develop role linkages with other colleagues who are good at research and work out an arrangement whereby research is not neglected. A better way of resolving the problems may be to find ways of doing things in a more non-traditional and productive way.

Role Stagnation

Role stagnation is a common stress in organizations when individuals get into new roles as a result of their advancement in the organization or as a result of taking over more challenging roles. In such cases, there may be a feeling of apprehension because the role is new and may require skills that the role occupant may not have. In such a situation, the usual way is to continue to play the previous role about which the individual is sure and has been doing successfully. Many people, even after advancement to top positions, continue to play the role of lower-level managers. A workshop supervisor, for example, may in due course become a general manager and may still continue to play the role of workshop supervisor, with consequent frustrations to the new supervisor and to others who expect him or her to devote time to more productive aspects of the new role.

In an organization, after several self-searching sessions, it became clear to many at the senior management level that their tendency to undertake close supervision was really a tendency to continue to play old roles. This is especially likely if the new role requires more skills to be developed. For example, planning roles and the role of scanning the environment require altogether different skills. In the absence of such skills, the usual tendency is to fall back on the old, tried-out roles. This is role fixation and is an avoidance strategy.

It is necessary for an individual to grow out of a role from time to time. As a child grows into an adolescent, and then an adult, it is similarly important for people to grow out of their old roles into new ones and face up to the challenge. A functional way to resolve this conflict is by role transition. Role transition is the process by which a previous role, howsoever successful and satisfying it may have been, is given up for a new and more developed role. Role transition is helped by various processes, including anticipatory socialisation, role clarity, substitute gratification, and transition procedures. In order to make role transition more effective, it is necessary to have anticipatory socialisation, that is, preparation for the taking of the new role. This would also include delegation of responsibility and functions to people below one's own role so that one can be free to experiment. One can take help in such experimentation from others.

Inter-role Distance

In inter-role distance, an individual may experience stress due to conflict between two or more roles occupied. The usual approach to deal with this problem is to either partition the roles clearly, so that a person is a spouse or parent when at home and an executive when in the office, or to employ role elimination, that is, accepting one role at the cost of the other role. In the latter case, the individual takes recourse to rationalisation. For example, an executive who neglects his or her family at home, and in this process ignores the roles of spouse and parent, rationalises the process by thinking that he or she makes a unique contribution to the company and therefore can afford to neglect family life, or say that he or she earns enough for the family who should pay the price by missing him or her as a spouse and as a parent. Such rationalisations are part of the process of role elimination. These are avoidance strategies.

A more functional approach to the problem is role negotiation. The process of role negotiation is one of establishing mutuality of roles and getting the necessary help to play all the roles more effectively and giving help in turn to other roles. For example, an executive who is not able to find time for the family may sit down and negotiate with his or her spouse and children how best he or she can spend time with them meaningfully within the given constraints.

One executive in the largest nationalised bank in India solved this problem by discussing the situation with his family and working out an arrangement whereby he would give the whole of every Sunday to his family and would avoid accepting invitations to dine out unless both the wife and the husband were invited. This negotiation was highly satisfying because neither role had to be sacrificed or eliminated.

Role Ambiguity

For role ambiguity, the usual approach is to make the roles clearer by putting various things down on paper. This is role prescription. The various expectations are thus defined more clearly. Or the individual may remove the ambiguity by fitting into the role as described in some expectations. This is the process of role taking. Both are avoidance strategies.

An approach strategy may be to seek clarification from various sources and to define the role in the light of such clarifications. In contrast with role taking, a more creative way is to define the role according to one's own strengths and to take steps to make the role more challenging. This is the process of role making.

Role Overload

To deal with the stress of role overload, that is, a feeling of too many expectations from several sources, the role occupant usually prepares a list of all the functions in terms of priorities. He or she gives top priority to those functions that are most important. This kind of prioritisation may help put things in order of importance. However, the problem may be that the functions with which a person is less familiar and less comfortable may tend to be pushed lower down the priority list and be neglected. Those functions that a person is able to perform without any effort get top priority. Since those that are at the lower level of priority always tend to remain neglected, this approach may be dysfunctional. This is an avoidance strategy.

A more functional approach may be to redefine the role and see which aspects of the role may be delegated to other persons who may be helped and developed to take on these functions. This may help the other individuals to grow as well. This may be called role slimming. The role does not lose its vitality in the process of delegating some functions; in fact, the vitality increases with decrease in obesity.

Role Isolation

In role isolation (when there is tension and distance between two roles in an organization), the usual tendency is for each role occupant to play his or her role most efficiently and avoid interactions. The role occupant confines himself or herself to his or her own role. This may be called role-boundness. Each occupant voluntarily agrees to be bound by the role. This strategy avoids possible conflicts. We thus find individual executives and managers who are highly efficient in their own roles but who do not take corporate responsibility and whose linkages with other roles are very weak. The individual withdraws in a kind of isolation of efficiency. He or she gets satisfaction out of playing the individual role effectively and efficiently but does not contribute as much as he or she could have done to the overall functioning of the organization. This is likely to be dysfunctional as it does not help the individual play his or her role in the larger interests of the organization. A better method is the approach strategy of role negotiation.

Role Erosion

In role erosion, an individual feels that some important functions that he or she would prefer to perform are being performed by other roles. The usual reaction in such a situation is to fight for the rights of the role and to insist on a clarification of roles. The solution is often sought in making structural clarifications. However, this is not likely to be functional and helpful since the basic conflict is avoided and it continues.

Exhibit 14.3 *Coping Strategies for Role Stresses*

Role stresses	Dysfunctional strategies	Functional strategies
Self–role distance	Role rejection, self-rejection	Role integration
Inter-role distance	Role partition, role elimination	Role negotiation
Role stagnation	Role fixation	Role transition
Role isolation	Role-boundness	Role linkage
Role ambiguity	Role prescription	Role clarification
Role expectation conflict	Role taking	Role making
Role overload	Role reduction	Role slimming
Role erosion	Role visibility	Role development/enrichment
Resource inadequacy	Role atrophy	Resource generation
Personal inadequacy	Role shrinkage	Role linkage

An approach strategy may be that of role enrichment. Like job enrichment, the concept of role enrichment suggests vertical loading of the role. Role enrichment can be done by analysing the role systematically and helping individuals see the various strengths in their roles and the various challenges the roles contain, which might not have been apparent to the individuals when performing them. Significant role-set members can help to make a role more challenging and satisfying to the role occupant.

Exhibit 14.3 summarises the functional and dysfunctional strategies for the 10 role stresses.

Thus, effective management of stress involves directing stress for productive purposes, preparing role occupants to understand the nature of stress, helping role occupants to understand their strengths and usual styles, and equipping them to develop approach strategies for coping with stress. The next chapter deals with one systematic approach to make roles more effective and to develop approach competence to deal with some dimensions of role stress.

SUMMARY

Frustration is the blocking or slowing down of goal-directed activity. The two most important elements in the dynamics of frustration, having a multiplicative relationship, are attractiveness of the goal and expectations of achieving it. Coping with frustration through aggression, regression, or flight (withdrawal) is dysfunctional. Exploration is an effective way of coping.

Stress is a natural phenomenon of a complex life. Besides life stresses, role stresses are important in organizational life. Ten different types of role stresses have been identified. Burnout is the result of stress not properly coped with. Burnout is characterised by emotional exhaustion, depersonalisation and a reduced sense of accomplishment. Effective coping with stress and prevention of burnout require changing dysfunctional modes of coping to functional ones.

GLOSSARY

burnout the end result of stress experienced but not properly coped with, including the symptoms of exhaustion, irritation, ineffectiveness, inaction, discounting of the self and others, and health problems (hypertension, ulcers, and heart ailments)

conflict incompatibility between two variables

coping ways of dealing with stress

coping behaviour dealing with situations of privation, deprivation, frustration, and stress

deprivation blocking of or interfering with goal-directed activities

frustration the resultant feeling caused by a sense of privation, deprivation, or conflict in relation to the goal-directed activities

glow-up feeling of challenge, high job satisfaction, creativity, effectiveness, and better adjustment to work and life

primitivisation showing primitive or less mature behaviour

privation experiencing lack of something relevant to a desired goal

regression using primitive or previously used modes of behaviour

resource inadequacy feeling that the resources required by the role occupant to perform the role effectively are not available

retrogression reverting to one's old behaviour

role ambiguity lack of clarity about the various expectations people have from one's role

role erosion feeling that some functions that the role occupant would like to perform are being performed by other roles

role expectation conflict conflict between expectations or demands by different role senders

role fixation continuing to play the previous role

role isolation the gap between the desired and actual linkages with other roles

role overload feeling that there are too many expectations by significant role senders

role partition partitioning one's role clearly so that a person is a spouse or parent when at home and an executive when at work so as to avoid role elimination, that is, accepting one role at the cost of other roles

role prescription making roles clearer by putting various things down on paper; fitting into the role as described in some expectations

role shrinkage pruning a role in such a way that some expectations can be given up if role linkages are established with other roles

role slimming redefining the role to explore which functions of the role can be delegated to other roles who may be helped and developed to perform these functions

role stagnation feeling that the role does not provide opportunities of growth

role transition the process by which a previous role, howsoever successful and satisfying it may have been, is given up for a new and more developed role

self–role distance conflict between the self-concept and the expectations from the role as perceived by the role occupant

stress experience of incongruence

stressor stimulus that produces stress

symptoms physiological, behavioural, and conceptual responses or changes

EXERCISES

Concept Review Questions
1. Explain the dynamics of frustration.
2. What are the dysfunctional and functional ways of managing frustration?
3. What are the different role stresses? Give examples of two of them.
4. What are the burnout and glow-up phenomena? How can we prevent burnout?
5. Enumerate both the functional and the dysfunctional ways of coping with stress.

Critical Thinking Questions

1. Explain the process and dynamics of frustration in a student who is not able to get admission to the course of choice.
2. Give examples of role overload and role erosion in the case of students similar to yourself. What is an effective way of coping with these stresses?
3. Identify any one frustration you have experienced and explain its impact on you using the dynamics of frustration you have read about in this chapter.
4. What are students' main role stresses? How do they usually cope with them? Suggest better coping strategies.
5. Do you know a case of burnout? How do you explain it?

Classroom Projects

1. You perform different roles in your life. For example, you have some family roles at home (you are a son or a daughter, etc.) and you may have a work role in an organization. You may have roles in other systems such as a club, social work organization, professional body, or political party. Read the three statements given below and check how often you have the feeling expressed in the statement. Use the following key to respond.

   Key

   Write 0 if you never or scarcely feel this way.

   Write 1 if you occasionally feel this way.

   Write 2 if you sometimes feel this way.

   Write 3 if you frequently feel this way.

   Write 4 if you almost always feel this way.

   1. I am not able to do many things for which I have a great liking.
   2. My role in the family conflicts with my work role.
   3. I do not have enough knowledge/skills needed to do justice to my roles.

   Scoring

   The three statements show (1) self–role distance, (2) inter-role distance, and (3) role inadequacy. If your score is 6 or above, you should be concerned. Prepare a plan to cope with the situation effectively.

2. Two cartoon strips are given here, each featuring two people. In each picture, one person is saying something. Guess what the other person would say in response and write it in the blank space.

   After reading the various strategies of coping with stress, analyse your responses to the two cartoons. Are you satisfied with these coping strategies? Think of more functional (approach) strategies to deal with the situation.

Field Projects

1. Interview an employee in your institution or an organization to find out his or her main stresses and how he or she copes with them.
2. Find two people who share their experiences in managing frustration effectively. What helped them in coping?

Role Negotiation at Bokaro Steel Plant*

At Bokaro Steel Plant, the main objective of role negotiation between the Personnel and Finance departments was to understand each other's role in the area of employee services (payment of salaries and other items), redressal of grievances, giving error-free service, eliminating hardships, treating employees as human beings, and image building of the departments along with an improvement in the services rendered by them to the employees. A total of 32 persons participated in the exercise, 8 from Personnel, 19 from Finance and Accounting, and 5 from EDP. A total of 11 hours were spent on the exercise, spread over 2 days. The schedule is given in Exhibit I.

Exhibit I *Brief Outline of the Schedule*

Day 1	
14:00 – 15.00	Microlab
15:00 – 16.30	Image building
16:30 – 17.15	Image sharing and clarifications (fishbowl)
17:15 – 17.30	Empathy building (positive images)
Day 2	
09:30 – 10.15	Expectations in home group
10:45 – 11.00	Exchange of expectations and clarification
11:00 – 12.00	Discussion in home groups
12:00 – 13.00	Role negotiations—Round 1 (fishbowl)
13:30 – 14.00	Discussion in home groups
14:00 – 14.30	Role negotiation—Round 2 (fishbowl)
14:30 – 15.15	Consolidation by a joint team and listing joint recommendations
15:30 – 16.15	Signing of agreement and preparation for dialogue (plenary)
16.15 – 17.15	Dialogue with the top management

UNFREEZING

Role negotiation has three phases: unfreezing, role negotiating, and dialoguing with top management. Unfreezing exercises consist of microlab, image building, and image sharing. The purpose of these exercises is to bring the prejudices out in the open, leading to a mutual empathy through positive images of each other.

The exercise started with a microlab in which the executives from different departments worked in small groups that changed every few minutes, and they

---

*Slightly edited note prepared by P.S. Dwivedi and Asit Pal, published in *Making Organisational Roles Effective* by Udai Pareek, Tata McGraw Hill, New Delhi, pp. 220–227. Reproduced with permission.

shared pleasant and unpleasant experiences with each other, as also their own strengths and weaknesses. This was followed by sharing of perception about their own department, the other department, and what they felt was the other's perception about their own department. They exchanged images and had an opportunity to seek clarification on the images in a fishbowl design. This was followed by an empathy-building exercise through sharing of strengths and positive images about the other group. The images generated in the exercise appear in Exhibit II.

Exhibit II *Images Generated Through Empathy building Exercise*
Images of the Personnel Department

Own image	Image by finance	Personnel's guess of image by finance/EDP
Helpful	Poor record keeping	Wrong pay fixation with subsequent corrigendum
Service oriented	Good team work	Poor record keeping
Humane	Problem-solving attitude	Inconsistency in application of rules
Effective communicators	Projecting good image at the cost of others	Ad hoc decisions
Change agents/catalysts	Wrong pay fixation with subsequent corrigendum	Shifting of blame
Accountable	Partiality (inconsistency)	Blame personnel department for all problems
Adaptable	Shifting of blame	Bureaucratic approach
Easily accessible	Bureaucratic approach	Projecting good image at the cost of others
More involved in production by creating conducive environment (proactive IR)	Ad hoc decisions	Good team work
Actively solve problems	For all problems, blame others	Problem-solving attitude

Images of Finance and EDP Department

Own image	Image by personnel	Finance/EDP guess of image by personnel
Timely	Prompt in payment of certain items	Reasonable
Punctual	Good finance management and effective cost control	Logical
Effective	Rule oriented, lacking human touch	Timely
Sincere	Less accessible (distance location)	Ambiguous
Honest	Low initiative on communication with employees and other departments	Tactful

(Contd)

Exhibit II (*Contd*)

Cooperative	Lack of problem-solving approach	Erroneous
Open	More centralised functioning	Inefficient
Communicative	No involvement in plant problems	Boastful
Understanding	Subordinate-oriented approach	Cooperative
Helping	Lack of coordination with sister departments, isolated	Responsible

Positive Images

Strengths of finance (by personnel)	Strengths of personnel (by finance/EDP)
Effective cost control	Team spirit
Strong budgetary control	Tactful
Promptness in making payment	Human approach
Good team spirit	Motivating force
Good system of timely job rotation	Cooperation

Role negotiation started with working out in home groups on what the other group could do to make their (the home group's) roles effective. Lists were prepared to demand three things from the other group(s): what they should continue to do, stop (or reduce), and start (or increase) doing, to help the home group members to become more effective in their role performance. Such expectations were exchanged and clarifications were sought and given to help understand their meaning and purpose. The expectations of the two groups appear in Exhibit III.

Exhibit III   Summary of Expectations

(A) EXPECTATIONS OF PERSONNEL FROM FINANCE AND EDP

I. Continue

1. Time schedules prescribed for various payments
2. Enquiry counters at the shop floor
3. Prompt response to final settlement cell
4. Prompt payment of travel and conveyance allowance
5. Disbursement of salary and PF at shop floor
6. Time-keeping system
7. Preparation of computerised statements of income tax, PF, absenteeism rate, leave ledgers, and final settlement sheets

II. Stop/reduce

1. Time for giving pay clearance in final settlement cases
2. Insisting on individual orders
3. Asking for pay slips in support of claims
4. Discrimination in making payments
5. Late arrival of the payment staff at payment counters
6. Raising superficial objections regarding eligibility for payment in compensation cases (under Workmen's Compensation Act)

Exhibit III (*Contd*)

III. Start/increase

1. Functioning of pay accounts section at shop floor
2. Cash payment to employees not having bank account
3. Communication with concerned personnel executives for minor clarifications
4. Time bound replies to all queries
5. Notifying their standard operating practices to personnel executives
6. Simplification of rules and procedures for disbursement of medical and other advances
7. Simplification of final settlement requirement to reduce delays and hardships to employees/dependents

(B) EXPECTATIONS OF FINANCE/EDP FROM PERSONNEL

I. Continue

1. Issuing orders regarding appointment, promotion, transfer, and separations
2. Certifying claims of employees regarding LTC/LLTC
3. Certifying claims for payment of PF/gratuity/leave salary, etc.
4. Maintaining good personal relations and coordination
5. Issuing service certificates to superannuating employees
6. Working of final settlement cell

II. Stop/reduce

1. Issuing pay fixation orders time and again for the same employee with multiple corrigenda and comments: 'This supersedes all previous orders'. Reference numbers of previous orders should be given.
2. Issuing cumbersome pay fixation orders. Orders should be complete in all respects. Avoid issuing vague orders.
3. Delay in enquiry proceedings regarding suspended employees finalising their payment cases.
4. Issuing orders containing employees of different departments/grades in one order. Avoid '-do-' indication against basic pay fixation/scales of pay.
5. Delay in replying representations.
6. Delay in sending DA rate orders.
7. Sending incomplete claim files for PF/gratuity payment.
8. Delay in processing cases for final settlement.
9. Issuing piecemeal transfer orders. Transfer orders issued in a month should be given on a particular date every month.

III. Start/increase

1. Thorough checking of file by finance representative in Finance Section Cell before sending to the PF section, to avoid unnecessary delay
2. Total completion of PF/gratuity nominations including that of new entrants. Similar action for group insurance and family benefit scheme within given time frame
3. Sending final settlement file of separating employees 15 days before retirement and other cases within 7 days of issuing of separation order
4. Issuing fixation orders along with promotion/appointments/completion of training of employees
5. Issuing modification orders along with copy of earlier orders

ROLE NEGOTIATION

View points were considered in the home groups and role negotiation was conducted in a fishbowl design, in which negotiations were conducted on acceptance of each others' expectations. Finally in the second round of role negotiation, agreements were evolved on most of the points. One team consolidated and integrated the points on which there was unanimous agreement, and which could be implemented jointly by both the groups without any external help. These agreements appear in Exhibit IV.

The groups agreed to implement these with immediate effect. Another joint team consolidated points that were not within their competence and needed the approval and support of the top management. This also included simplification of rules and procedures. The list of agreed points appears in Exhibit V, and the list of recommendations discussed with the top management appears in Exhibit VI.

Exhibit IV   *Final Contract*

The Personnel–Finance interface group unanimously agreed to the following:

1. Insistence on individual office orders regarding pay fixation, etc. will be avoided, but wherever more than one department's employees are detailed in a single-office order, sufficient copies will be supplied for ensuring prompt action.
2. While entertaining pay-related grievances of the employees, there will be no insistence on the employees submitting their pay slips along with their enquiry/grievances, if their cases are less than 2 years old.
3. For better interaction and role appreciation, Finance and Personnel groups will meet at least once a month on a regular basis.
4. In cases where any clarification is desired with reference to any specific office order, the same will be immediately communicated to the concerned issuing authority either on phone or in writing so as to minimise delay.
5. Correspondence received will be replied to immediately after ascertaining facts.
6. As far as it is practical, not more than one office order will be issued to an individual on the same issue. However in cases requiring re-fixation of pay, etc., reference of the earlier office orders relevant to the issue will be specifically mentioned.
7. A campaign will be undertaken for ensuring 100 per cent coverage for filing PF/gratuity nomination by the end of May.
8. All office orders regarding transfer, etc. may be sent to the Personnel and Administration (P&A) department once a month in accordance with a specified schedule to be worked out later.
9. Error-free payment system will be ensured.

Exhibit V   *Consensus on Simplification of Rules*

List of agreed points on simplification of rules/procedures, system improvement, and decentralisation
1. Payment of medical advances
2. Final settlement through single window clearance system
3. Decentralisation of the pay accounts section
4. Decentralisation of the OD section

Exhibit V (*Contd*)

5. Payment of compensation in case of fatal accidents under Workmen's Compensation Act. No financial concurrence required.
6. Automatic payment/enhancement release of increments/LTE/incentives, etc.
7. Direct payment of arrears of incentive, LTE, HRA, etc.

Exhibit VI *Dialogue with Top Management*

The final contract was shared and the recommendations were discussed with the top management. Regarding all points of Exhibit V, it was agreed to simplify rules and procedures to reduce delays and hardship to the employees.

A task force comprising five members was constituted (two from Personnel, two from Finance, and one from EDP) to work out the details for improvement in each area and submit the action plan. It was decided to review the results of the role negotiation exercise after 2 months.

DIALOGUING WITH TOP MANAGEMENT

At the end, a dialogue was held with the top management, consisting of the MD, ED (P&A), OCM (Pers), and OCM (P). The top team promised their full support in the implementation of the commitments and recommendations. Further, a task force was constituted with five executes—two from Personnel, two from F&A, and one from EDP—to ensure implementation within 15 days. It was decided to review the implementation after 2 months, and report.

Questions for Discussion

1. What are the main steps in role negotiation?
2. Was the final contract able to deal with problems between the personal and finance departments?
3. What is the advantage of the dialogue of top management in role negotiation exercises?

15
Decisional Process

LEARNING OBJECTIVES

After studying this chapter, you will be able to
1. Explain the rationality model of decision making
2. Critically review the rationality model and its limitations, and cite alternative models and their characteristics
3. Enumerate the various individual decision making styles and their appropriateness
4. Discuss the process of consensus building
5. Identify facilitating and hindering forces in consensus building
6. Formulate a strategy of consensus building for a group

Managers make decisions all the time. In fact, all of us are making decisions in most matters most of the time. For example, a student makes a decision about the course of study he or she would like to pursue, the college/institute to which he or she would like to go for further study, or the company he or she would like to join provided he or she has some choices. So decision making can be defined as choosing between alternatives.

Although the definition of decision making is simple, the process of decision making is quite complex. There have been several explanations of the process.

DECISION-MAKING MODELS

Rationality Models

Economics and financial disciplines emphasised the complete rationality of decision making based on known alternatives, which can be evaluated on the basis of calculation of pay-off and known, consistent patterns of preference. The aim was to get the maximum profit, equalising managerial cost and managerial revenue.

Recent models of rational decision making include activity-based costing (ABC), which determines costs according to what is paid for different tasks performed by employees (not according to expenditure categories such as salary). This method provides much more accurate information on costs. Other rational methods are economic value added (EVA) and market value added (MVA). Under EVA, the true cost of all capital is determined and the total cost of capital is subtracted from the post-tax operating profit. MVA is the difference between the market value and the invested capital, a positive difference showing the wealth created by the company.

Bounded Rationality and Heuristics Models

In the rational choice models, an individual or a group maximises profits by examining all the alternatives on the basis of all the information. However, in practice this is unrealistic. An individual or a group searches for a solution that is both satisfactory and sufficient, and Simon used the term 'satisfice' for this.[1] Although it is a rationality model, the rationality is bounded and the individual or group extracts the essential features of a problem without capturing all of its complexity. Decision-makers, according to this model, identify obvious alternatives and choose one which is acceptable. The bounded rationality model does not discuss how the choice will be influenced.

Another step forward was taken by cognitive decision theorists, who suggested that decision-makers rely on heuristics (shortcuts to judgements). Several heuristics are used for decision making: availability (tendency to base judgement on available information), representativeness (tendency to base judgement on matching against a pre-existing category), anchoring (basing judgement on the initial value or anchor and then adjusting it if necessary). All these are shortcuts to judgements.

Embedded Models

Alternatives to the rationality or bounded rationality models are the psychological and culturally embedded models. These models emphasise the role of values, emotions, intuition, and habits for individual decision making and are socially, culturally, and politically embedded for organizational decision making.

Individual Decision making

According to the rationality and bounded rationality models, decisions are made to maximise self-interest. According to Etziomi, most decisions are based not on rationality but on emotional involvement and value commitment.[2] Etziomi's concept of the normative–affective factor, driven by values and emotions, is an ideal type. According to him, values and emotions are not additional factors but are essential in explaining decision making. According to him, the normative–affective basis provides the dynamic quality choice. Frank has also demonstrated that feelings and emotions are apparently the proximate causes of most behaviours.[3]

Mansbridge considers love and duty (altruistic motives) as important bases for decision making.[4] She used the Prisoner's Dilemma game to study decision-making processes and found that several solutions required one or more of the interaction partners to make someone else's good their own or to be committed to a course of action requiring cooperation. Mansbridge points out, however, that these decisions cannot usually be sustained independently by the action of others. Empathetic and moral commitments are socially embedded, that is, they can be undermined by the self-interested behaviour of others.

Flam demonstrates the emotional components of decision making and holds that emotional motives help to explain voluntary collective action that the normative and rational self cannot explain.[5] She has drawn out the implications of her theory for corporate actors by proposing three things: (1) corporate actors are emotion-motivated emotion managers who construct emotions in organizations, (2) feeling rules regulate and emotions accompany corporate interactions, and (3) corporate actors experience proscribed and prescribed emotional outbursts. According to her, not only do internal feeling rules regulate organizational behaviour, inter-organizational feeling rules also regulate organizations within a culture.

Based on his classical study of various types of crimes, Katz proposes that the need to transcend, to be recognised, admired, and feared (which can be called power motive) is the basis of decision making.[6] Although Katz recognised the correlation between low socio-economic status and crime, he argues that this relationship is not causal. Zey takes Katz's proposition ahead by showing that securities frauds and white-collar crimes (which according to Zey 'are of far greater magnitude than those committed by the low class') are embedded in the political elite, who are able to influence the state to alter the regulatory parameters 'so that their illicit acts do not fit the statutes'.[7]

Habit has also been given the central place in decision making.[8] It is the least explored aspect and its relationship with emotions, values, and rationality needs to be studied.

Organizational Decision Making

The models of Etziomi, Mansbridge, Flam, and others discussed in the previous section demonstrate decision making is socially, culturally, and politically embedded. It is necessary to explain the transition from micro-level decision making (at the individual level) to macro-level decision making (at the organizational level).

March and Shapira differentiate between the individual choice theory and the organizational decision-making theory[9]: 'Organizational decisions are no more made by individuals than the choices of individuals are made by the hands that sign the papers.' They point out five main areas demonstrating how the rationality model fails to explain the reality:

1. Most organizations in reality make decisions and then collect information to validate the decisions.
2. Most organizations copy what others do instead of applying a rational decision making process to organizational change.
3. In reality, means are only loosely coupled to ends and loosely coupled to one another, unlike the means–end relation concept in the rationality model.
4. Rationality choice theories are unconcerned with the possibility of uncertainty about preferences.
5. Myths, symbols, and rituals are important in decision making but not recognised by the rationality models.

Based on a study of decision making in publishing companies, Powel shows that organizational decision making is embedded in 'a history of previous associations, and guided by norms of reciprocity'. Instead of profit, 'prestige is frequently the currency of exchange'.[10]

Fligstein has developed a political/institutional embedded theory, proposing that organizational decisions are shaped by power blocks as well as by the struggle for power.[11] According to him, the motives of managers of large groups in the economy of a country are motivated by the control of competition through the creation of cartels.

It has been demonstrated that organizational decision making is politically embedded, by pointing out the role of electoral politics and the legal system in the complex phenomenon of organizational decision making.[12]

In conclusion, decision making, both at the individual and organizational levels, is influenced by rational as well as psychological, social, cultural, and political factors. Each case of decision making is unique and requires a multi-disciplinary approach to understand and analyse it.

DECISION-MAKING STYLES

Decisions are made by individuals either in personal matters, or in their roles concerning groups or organizations. Leadership is an important group/organization role. We shall review some decision making styles in both the contexts.

Decision-making Styles of Leaders

Leaders in groups and organizations have the responsibility of making decisions. Leaders differ in their decision making styles, according to their process orientation. The styles can be seen on the centralisation–decentralisation continuum. The following styles may be used by leaders.

Autocratic or directive style The leader defines the problem, diagnoses the problem, generates, evaluates, and chooses among alternative solutions.

Autocratic with group information input The leader defines the problem. Although the leader diagnoses the cause of the problem, the leader may use the group as an information source in obtaining data to determine cause. Using his or her list of potential solutions, the leader may once again obtain data from the group in evaluation of these alternatives and make a choice among them.

Autocratic with group's review and feedback The leader defines the problem, diagnoses its causes, and selects a solution. The leader then presents his or her plan to the group for understanding, review, and feedback.

Individual consultative style The leader defines the problem, and shares his/her definition with individual members of the work group. The leader solicits ideas regarding problem causes and potential solutions. The leader may also use these individuals' expertise in evaluation of alternative solutions. Once this information is obtained, the leader makes the choice of which alternative solution to implement.

Group consultative style Same as the previous one, except the leader shares his or her definition of the problem with the group as a whole.

Group decision style   Leader shares his or her definition of the problem with the work group. The group then proceeds to diagnose the causes of the problem. Following diagnoses, the group generates, evaluates, and chooses among solutions.

Participative style   The group as a whole proceeds through the entire decision making process. The group defines the problem and performs all other functions as a group. The role of the leader is that of process facilitator.

Leaderless team   The group has no formal leader, but rather is assembled as a leaderless team. If no substitute for task leadership, or process leadership, is present, a process leader often emerges. This person may change from problem to problem. The group generates its own problem definition, performs its own diagnoses, generates alternatives, and chooses among alternatives.

Individual Decision-making Styles

Individual decision-making styles reflect the individual's orientations. According to Myres, a person's decision-making style depends to a significant degree on his/her cognitive style. In terms of MBTI categories (already discussed in Chapter 10), she claimed that a person's decision-making style is based largely on the person's score on the four dimensions. For example, someone who scored near the thinking, extroversion, sensing, and judgement ends of the dimensions would tend to have a logical, analytical, objective, critical, and empirical decision making style.

The following six decision-making styles represent a good range. There is no best style, although some styles like procrastination may be dysfunctional. Different situations may require different approaches or styles. While defining the styles, their appropriateness is also mentioned.

Deep deliberation

In this style the person spends large (possibly excessive) amounts of time and attention, weighing out all possible options before deciding on one. Agonising over a decision requires that a person place great time and importance on the decision.

Deep deliberation is likely to be an appropriate way to handle the decision over an issue that has great importance to or has serious consequences for a person. People often agonise over their career choices, serious relationship issues, or problems with family. It may be appropriate to use this style of decision making when a decision could have long-term effects on oneself or could seriously affect others dear to oneself.

This style is not appropriate for matters that have little importance or consequence, and when one feels it might be best to act impulsively to solve the problem. Everyday decisions such as what meals to eat or what social activities to participate in should not become time consuming situations requiring deep deliberation.

Impulsive decision

In this style a decision is based on one's first reaction. Impulsive decision-makers spend little to no time considering their options. They simply react to the circumstances in front of them.

Impulsive decisions may be appropriate in social situations. Depending on one's definition of fun or enjoyment, one might like to act impulsively (but responsibly) with friends. For example, an unexpected day trip to the beach might be an unplanned, spontaneous decision that would be considered impulsive.

Impulsive decisions are also intuitive decisions. Situations of emergency or crisis often require people to use an impulsive decision making style to handle the situation. For example, jumping in a lake to save a drowning person would be an impulsive decision. There is no time for thinking over and weighing all possible options in many emergency situations. Impulsive decision making is inappropriate when there are major life decisions to be made. Career choices, academic choices, family issues, and relationship issues should generally not be situations during which a person acts impulsively. It is also important to be aware of other people's feelings and not to act impulsively by saying or doing something that may hurt someone unnecessarily.

Escape

In this style a decision is avoided, usually giving a false answer to temporarily solve a situation, thus escaping from making a decision.

It is rarely a good choice to use this style of decision making. But, it can be an appropriate method of decision making if one is put in an uncomfortable or dangerous situation. For example, one student shared his experience of being offered drugs. He was out with people who were not his steady group of friends and they began using drugs and offered them to this student. The student was embarrassed to simply "say no". He did not want the pressure of explaining why he did not want to share. So, the student simply responded, "I have a cold and I'm on medication, so I can't." Uncomfortable situations such as these can often be a good time to utilise the escape method of decision making.

It is inappropriate to escape a decision that is inevitable. If one has done something one does not want to face, this is not a good style to choose. Escape would be an inappropriate decision if one has to face reality and is attempting to avoid it—for example, if a student has failed and does not repeat the course, he is trying to escape the inevitable.

Compliance

In this style the person allows someone else to take the decision. As opposed to taking responsibility/ownership for the decision, compliant people allow others to make decisions for them.

Compliance may be appropriate when making decisions in areas in which the person does not have enough information. If a person does not feel comfortable enough to make a decision on his own, it may be a good idea to consult someone who is more knowledgeable or has expertise in a certain area. Relationships and family situations that are not of great importance may also be good situations to use compliance. Allowing others the option to make choices could be a very effective way to increase the strength of a relationship.

It is not appropriate to use compliance as a way of avoiding responsibility for actions or decisions. Compliance should not be used for important life decisions. For example, it is not appropriate to let parents decide what courses one should take up for study.

Safe playing

In this style the person chooses the option that has the least amount of risk. Safe playing is normally the option that would be most socially acceptable, the 'norm', and would allow a person comfort rather than risk.

Safe playing is normally the best option when there is a dangerous risk involved in the decision to be made. For example, if one is considering experimenting with a drug that is known to be very harmful or possibly fatal, the best thing to do is to 'play it safe' and abstain from using the drug.

It is best to choose safe options in situations where the consequences may be too difficult for one to handle. For example, if a married person cannot handle the responsibility of having a child, the best thing to do would be to practice safe sex or abstain from sex.

Safe playing can become a negative experience if a person always chooses to play it safe. Often, the most rewarding experiences and opportunities come from situations that require taking a risk—for example, a student leaving his/her hometown to pursue a career, to reach a goal or dream.

Procrastination

In this style the decision is simply delayed. Procrastinators refuse to actually make a decision. Often, they delay so long that the options that were once available to them become unavailable. For example, a student who is considering joining a good university but fails to send her applications by the required deadlines would be considered a procrastinator. By not sending the applications, the options that may have been available to her no longer exist.

Procrastination is generally not a good style of decision making. While there are few situations that would best be handled by procrastinating, it is possible that a person may procrastinate or delay a decision because he or she has chosen to wait until he or she is more ready to make the decision. For example, if a student is unsure of what to major in, it may be to her benefit to wait a term or two. This would allow her the time to learn more about herself, become more mature, and then make a decision when she feels more capable of making one.

Procrastination is not an effective decision style for any decision that has urgency or a timeline. It is not effective to continually delay a decision that will inevitably have to be made. For example, a student who delays registering for classes until registration closes has lost many options for scheduling and has lost the convenience of having registered early. Delaying decisions generally makes the ultimate decision more difficult.

CONSENSUS BUILDING

The classical decision making theory assumed rationality and certainty in the process of decision making. Herbert Simon had proposed a theory of the decision making process with three phases, which was later confirmed by Mintzberg through research and reformulated[13] as: identification (recognising a problem and diagnosing it), development (searching or designing a solution), and selection (arriving at a solution by the judgement of the decision-maker, logical analysis of the alternatives, or bargaining among decision-makers and others involved). The following four steps are generally followed.

Identifying the problem Analysis of the current situation and the gap between the desired and the existing state helps to define what the individual or the group is working for. For example, in the game Desert Survival, the analysis of the situation (hot burning sun, long distance in the desert) may help to see the problem in terms of survival and being located by the rescuing team.

Identifying alternative strategies There may be several ways of solving a problem. In Desert Survival, for example, there are three strategies to solve the problem: locomotion (moving towards the base camp), survival, and being located by the search team.

Prioritising the strategies Each strategy is evaluated for its effectiveness in solving the problem and priorities are determined for each strategy. For example, if the group discusses the conditions in the Desert Survival exercise, they will conclude that walking (locomotion) has very low priority because the individuals may get lost in different directions, may get exhausted, and may not be seen when the rescue team arrives—the team would search around the spot at which contact with them was lost. Being rescued is the top priority and the rescue team is bound to start a search. Priorities are made on the basis of certain criteria.

Selecting and detailing a strategy Once the priorities are clear, the best alternative strategy is selected and details of the selected strategy are worked out. For example, in Desert Survival, if it is clear that being located is the best strategy, the group works out the details of how to facilitate the rescuing party's attempt to locate the team.

While the above steps help in decision making, consensus building is important in group decisions. Each individual member has his or her own understanding and rationale. Unless these are shared and there is a general agreement, the quality of the decision is likely to suffer.

Decision making involves making a choice from available or generated alternatives. When a decision is made by a group meeting face to face (a task group, a committee, or a departmental team), every member is a potential contributor to the process of decision making, which involves understanding the problem or the issue, breaking it down into meaningful components that indicate the real problems on which decisions are required, formulating a general strategy in terms of a sequence of action steps, generating alternatives, providing and pooling required information, generating favourable and unfavourable points for each alternative, coming to a shared understanding, making a final choice, and getting the commitment of all members to the choice made. The main advantage of a group is that it has more resources than a single individual has and, as the saying goes, no one of us is as bright as all of us.

In the process of decision making, the group may range between two extremes. At the one extreme may be the main concern of getting one's own point of view accepted. At this extreme, members are mainly concerned about whose views will be accepted. Instead of being concerned with the problem on which a decision is to be made, they are more concerned about the personal influence they can wield and use various methods of testing the strength and power different members have. At the other extreme is the focus on making a good decision, generating resources in the group, and pooling and using the resources. The decision making process can be nearer to any of these two points on the continuum.

Broadly, then, decision making in a group can be either by the process of division or by the process of consensus. In the process of division, the strength of various members is tested and the group gets divided. In the process of consensus, the strength of various members is pooled and brought to bear on the best possible decision.

Consensus does not necessarily mean unanimity. It means a sharing of differences, listening to each other, accepting the final choice in spite of the differences that may still exist. As a result of consensus, all members of the group do not come to the same conclusion. The differences may continue. However, members have an opportunity to express such differences, discuss the rationale behind the different points of view, and have the satisfaction that other members of the group listened to them and that they in turn listened to the logic put forward by the other members. At the end of such a discussion, the members come to a conclusion that one optimum solution is to be selected. This helps them accept one solution out of several alternatives even though some of them may not agree with that alternative completely. The commitment of the members to the implementation of the solution is thus assured.

Factors Hindering Consensus

The following factors come in the way of a decision by consensus in groups:

Domination by a few Where there is a tendency among some members to dominate a group and influence the decision, consensus is difficult to reach.

Withdrawal The natural result of domination by a few is withdrawal by several other members when they do not see an opportunity to express themselves freely and influence the process of decision making.

Tendency to make a quick decision   When members of the group rush to make decisions very fast, the possibility of consensus decreases. Consensus requires patience and the members' inclination to pay attention to the opinions of others. This process takes time.

Testing strengths   In the process of decision making, when some ways are used to test strengths and take decisions according to the strength of argument, the group splits. Instead of moving towards consensus there is a tendency to move towards division in the group. Voting is one way of testing strengths, usually used in a group to find the majority and minority of opinion. Voting does not help the group to move towards consensus. It only divides the group into majority and minority, and the members in the minority usually fail to commit themselves to the decision that is taken by the majority.

Avoiding confrontation   When members of a group avoid confronting differences and make the choice by avoiding discussion, the possibility of consensus decreases. One way to avoid confrontation is to use third-party intervention or decide by chance (such as flipping a coin).

Trading or compromising   Sometimes people, in order to get their suggestion or point of view accepted, trade their point of view with others so that they come to an agreement that the suggestion given by one member will be accepted in exchange for another suggestion given by another member. This kind of trading or compromising reduces the possibility of consensus.

Factors Facilitating Consensus

In contrast with the factors discussed above, there are other factors that help in moving towards a consensus. Some of these are

Concern for others   The basis of consensus is the respect and concern people have for others. This also helps them to look for expertise and resources available in various members.

Listening   A consequence of respect and concern for others is that people listen carefully to what others say rather than being obsessed with their own ideas about a problem.

Identifying and using resources   People in the group realise that each member is a special resource. In order to make a good decision, it is necessary that all the resources are utilised. The group takes active steps to find out what the dimensions of the problem are and whether anyone in the group seems to have the necessary resources on the various dimensions. It is recognised that different members have different skills. Without unnecessary formal discussions on the matter, an effective group begins to use these skills in order to perform its task effectively.

Discussing underlying assumptions and logic When people discuss not only their own suggestions and ideas, but also the reason for which they are proposing these and the underlying rationale of these suggestions and ideas, movement towards a common understanding becomes easier and the group is able to move towards consensus.

Testing consensus and disagreements Consensus is helped when, after substantial discussion, the members of the group test whether there are still some disagreements and such disagreements are allowed to be expressed and discussed. If, however, agreements are not discussed and are avoided or are not voiced, it would be difficult to develop consensus. From time to time, the group may stop and see whether enough consensus exists about what is to be decided.

Process orientation The group that spends some time on the process is able to develop consensus faster. Instead of being concerned only with the task, the group is also concerned about the way the people are feeling, whether some people have withdrawn as a result of a heated exchange of words, the number of people speaking and the number remaining silent, the speed at which the group has been progressing with the decision making, etc. Such matters, when discussed from time to time, will help to move towards consensus faster.

CONSENSUS COMPETENCIES

Three categories of skills may help members to move towards consensus. These skills relate to problem solving, task facilitating, and group building.

Problem solving

In decision making, the main focus is on solving certain specific problems. The process of decision making is essentially similar to that of problem solving—identifying the specific issues, prioritising the various dimensions or elements, diagnosing the situation, generating alternative ideas and possible solutions, comparing the pay-offs of the alternatives, selecting one alternative for action, implementing the plan, evaluating the plan of action, and replanning the next phase. Several problem-solving skills useful for the decision making process are discussed below:

Deciding priorities A group can achieve consensus faster if the members are clear about and can reach an agreement on priorities. Most of the time, disagreements among members continue and they do not reach a consensus because different members have different priorities in mind. In solving problems, clarity about the priorities is important. If people spend enough time in a group discussing what priorities should be considered and come to some agreement on the priorities, decisions can be taken much faster. Some discussion on priorities may also help in bringing out the basic differences in the assumptions people have. Such clarity helps in understanding the different points of view about priorities and eventually helps in arriving at a consensus.

Analysing the problem at several levels A problem on which a decision is made may appear to be a simple one but it may have several dimensions. For example, in taking a decision on the location of a facility centre in a community, analyses of the factors at various levels may be needed—state, district, and local levels. Similarly, analyses of problems from the point of view of different communities may become important. It may be useful to spend some time understanding these dimensions and clarifying critical aspects before going on to the main problem on which the decision is to be taken.

Generating alternatives Collective decisions are better when a number of alternative solutions are generated and a decision is taken to adopt one alternative after comparing the pay-offs of the several alternatives. If a decision is taken by hastily adopting one apparently good solution, many people who may have been able to contribute better strategies will not have an opportunity to do so. The main advantage of several persons meeting in a group is that they may be able to generate a number of ideas. This may not only help in considering the merits of several solutions but may also help in evolving a better solution than the best suggested in a group by combining the good features of several. This is how synergy is achieved through group work.

Discussing the consequences of each alternative After several alternative solutions are proposed, both positive and negative pay-offs of each case need to be thoroughly discussed. Each alternative may have some advantages and disadvantages. It is useful to consider the advantages and disadvantages in terms of the possible consequences of implementing a particular idea. During such a discussion, new suggestions may be offered to increase the positive pay-off of a potential alternative and to reduce its negative pay-off. When the possible consequences of an alternative are discussed, even people who may have originally suggested the alternative may see it from a different angle and may be convinced that the suggested alternative may not have as many advantages as another. This helps people to give up their own ideas and accept an idea proposed by somebody else.

Developing criteria for decision making In order to narrow down the range of discussion and focus more sharply on the critical dimensions of a problem, it may be useful to discuss and agree on the main criteria that will be used for taking decisions on a particular problem. For example, in locating a facility centre in a community, it may be decided that the location should enable the underprivileged and weaker sections of the community to use it, that it should be accessible to most people in the area, and so on. Once such criteria are evolved and agreed upon, consensus on the decision may become easier. In the Desert Survival and Moon Landing games, the teams that spend time discussing criteria like survival, locomotion, communication, etc. develop consensus much faster and make better decisions.

Reviewing   A healthy group spends some time after the decision has been taken to review it and ensures that significant points have not been left out. Such a review gives an opportunity to those people who may still have some doubts about some aspects of the decision to reflect on them. Sometimes such doubts save the group from making decisions for which they may have had to pay heavily otherwise. It may be useful for a group, therefore, to leave some time at the end of the meeting to look back and thoroughly examine whatever decisions have been taken.

Task Facilitating

In addition to the problem-solving skills, several other skills are involved in working effectively on the task of decision making:

Initiative   Unless people take initiative in discussions, not enough ideas can be generated. Initiative may be evinced in various aspects of the contribution of a member to the group—expressing opinions, giving information, asking questions, raising doubts, pointing out critical dimensions of a problem, etc. People in a group take the necessary initiative if the other members encourage such acts and use the ideas generated.

Information seeking   A specific initiative that helps in working on the task effectively is asking for and collecting more information from various members in the group. When a member expresses his or her opinion in the group, other members may ask for more information. In this process, new dimensions are pointed out and the group is able to examine the problem in depth.

Giving information   Every member in the group has to provide the necessary or relevant information he or she may have. Unless people volunteer to give the information they have, consensus cannot emerge. Giving information serves two main purposes. First, all relevant information that may have some bearing on the decision to be taken gets communicated. The pool of information helps members explore the various dimensions of the issues, the various alternatives, and their pay-offs. Second, when information is provided, the involvement of members increases. Members who provide the necessary information and share what they know about the different dimensions of the problem have a higher commitment to the decisions that are taken later. This helps in evolving consensus.

Summarising   When discussions on a problem are long-drawn and people get involved in arguing their points of view, an important function to help the group to move forward is to summarise what has been discussed, where differences continue to exist, where agreements are emerging, and what issues need to be discussed further. Such a summary of what has gone on and what remains to be discussed is very useful for the proper planning of discussions. A summary also helps in clearing up the points on which consensus has emerged and the points on which further discussion is needed. Without such a summary even though consensus may emerge on some points, these may be brought back up later in the discussion and a great deal of time wasted. Summarising also helps in making it clear that the consensus is evolving and that, while there may be differences, there are areas of clear agreement.

Expressing opinions   Taking initiative in the form of giving information is different from expressing one's opinion about a problem. Expressing an opinion involves more risk taking. The more people clearly and openly express their opinions, the faster is the movement towards consensus. When a person gives his or her opinion about a particular point expressed by another member, he or she is providing information that may be relevant to the problem under discussion. In the absence of such opinions, the pros and cons of the various alternatives being discussed cannot come out. Members should be encouraged to express their opinions in the group.

The expression of an opinion also has a cathartic value. When a person expresses an opinion, he or she feels much better about the group and his or her commitment both to the group and to the decisions being taken increases.

Synthesising   When different points of view are expressed in the group, sometimes there are common areas on which some agreement may be possible. An opinion or idea given may contain some good points. Similarly, other opinions or ideas may contain other elements worth considering. It may be possible to put these together and evolve a fresh point or idea that contains the strengths of various ideas or opinions expressed. This is the synthesising function. The skill of seeing things common to the various opinions expressed and bringing them out in the form of a new idea that contains the strengths of the different points of view or opinions is needed for developing consensus. The attitude of synthesising may indicate that people are aware that various strengths exist and different ideas or points of view expressed contain elements that are worth noticing. The synthesising of different points of view or ideas also increases the tendency to listen more carefully to others and look for more such common elements in the various opinions and ideas expressed.

Focusing on strategies   The decision to be taken by a group may involve acting on certain aspects of the problem. A good way of planning action is to focus on the basic approaches or strategies to be adopted. By raising questions about a comprehensive strategy, the discussion may be taken beyond a single narrow dimension to which attention is being paid at a particular time. The questions are then posed in a wider context. Strategy planning helps in making action more relevant; it also helps to relate an action to several other elements that may be neglected if attention is focused only on the specific action rather than on the total approach. Thus strategy is an important context for action planning.

Time keeping   Most problem-solving groups spend so much time on a few dimensions that hardly any time is available towards the end and the group then rushes into taking a decision. One important function or skill of an effective group is that of keeping time. A member may either remind the group how much time has been spent on different dimensions or some kind of time budgeting may be done in advance with someone reviewing from time to time whether the group is progressing according to the time schedule agreed on. Many members perform this function very well. Such members may remind the group that only so much time is left and only so little has been done. This helps in not only performing a task more effectively but also helps coax people into agreeing on various dimensions and moving systematically according to the agenda.

Group building

There are many other skills that help the group to function well. The skills so far considered are those that relate to the particular task. Group-building skills may not directly help in working on the task but they have great value in facilitating work on the task by helping the group to function as an effective group. Some of these skills are explained as follows:

Listening   Effective group work requires the skill of listening. Listening does not mean merely hearing what other people are saying. Listening means the involvement of a person in what is going on in the group, eagerness to know what other people are contributing, giving importance to the opinions and ideas of other people, and indicating that such ideas or opinions are being received. Listening is possible only when a person is interested in what is being discussed and accords value to the opinions of other people. By carefully and deliberately listening to what people say in the group, a member may increase his or her respect for others as also his or her skill of learning from various ideas and points of view expressed. Listening involves paying attention and giving clear cues of interest and eagerness. Sitting back and closing one's eyes while another person is speaking may give cues of indifference and non-listening even though the person may be listening carefully to what is being said.

Expressing and responding to feelings   Often feelings are neglected in 'task groups'. People do not pay much attention to either their own feelings or to the feelings of others even when they have some impression of how others may be feeling. Without attending to feelings, consensus may not be possible. By expressing his or her own feelings, a member legitimises the expression of feelings and indicates his or her confidence in the group. Only when a member has enough confidence in the group can he or she freely express his or her feelings. Moreover, expression of feelings will also encourage others to express such feelings. In addition to expressing feelings, it may also be useful to respond to the feelings being expressed. For example, if someone is upset with a particular expression, it may be useful to bring the matter out by restating the fact and making it clear that the opinion was expressed without any intention to hurt anyone's feelings. Expression of and responding to feelings may help the group to work as a cohesive and effective group.

Gatekeeping   In a group, when people are eager to express their opinions, many people may speak simultaneously. The more involved the members in a group are in a discussion, the greater is the problem of ensuring that people listen to each other and wait their turn to express their opinions. Everyone wants to express his or her opinion. As a result, there is such a rush to speak that communication may get blocked. This is like people blocking a gate in their eagerness to rush out of a room. It is necessary to keep the gate open so that people can go in and out easily, without any problems. This function in a group is called gatekeeping. A member may find several people speaking simultaneously and may point out that he or she would like to listen to one at a time. This function may be performed by the chairperson or any other member. Such a function is helpful in establishing norms of listening to each other, patiently waiting for one's turn to express an opinion, and observing some order in the discussion.

Supporting   One skill that helps in increasing people's commitment in a group and eventually evolving consensus is that of supporting. When a person expresses an opinion or a point of view and is supported by another member in the group, his or her commitment to the group increases. Supporting presupposes that people respect one another and are eager to see each other's strengths. This increases mutual support and builds a general climate of acceptance in the group, in which people look for the positive aspects of opinions or ideas expressed by others.

Building on others' ideas   People have a tendency to offer an idea and then try and prove that the idea is an entirely new one. The skill which helps in building an effective group is that of expressing one's opinions and relating them to what somebody else has already said in the group. This would mean that the contributions of other members are recognised and those are used as bases for the further building up of ideas. In an effective group, this is continuously done. In a less effective group, members claim originality and credit for the various ideas they express and make efforts to prove that similar ideas by somebody else were quite different. The skill of building on others' ideas is difficult but necessary for building a stronger group.

Encouraging silent members   In every group, there are some people who are not very active and wait for their turn to participate in discussions. If other members are very active and participate more effectively, those who are silent may continue to remain silent. Eventually, the group may find it has some members who hardly participate or contribute. A group cannot get ideas from such members. Yet many a time such ideas may have been very useful. Furthermore, the silent members eventually lose interest and their commitment to the group and its decisions decreases. It is useful to encourage such members by emphasising from time to time the need of hearing the opinions of those who have not spoken so far in the group.

Process reviewing   In relation to problem-solving skills, reviewing was pointed out as an important skill. Similarly, in relation to the functioning of the group, process reviewing is important. Process reviewing means reviewing various dimensions of the functioning of the group, including how parts of the group work. For example, at some stage in the functioning of the group, the chairperson or some other member may point out and review that so far only two or three members have spoken, that only one member has taken up most of the group's time, that there were conflicts which were not resolved, or that the climate has been more hostile and people are attacking each other, etc. By reviewing from time to time how the group has functioned, the group may be able to pay attention to those dimensions on which some work needs to be done before the group can continue to work on the task before it. In such a review, both positive and negative aspects may be pointed out. Process reviewing helps all the more if the group agrees in the beginning on the various processes to be followed and then examines how these were functioning.

Two things need to be said in relation to the various skills that have been proposed here. The first dimension relates to the leadership function. The various skills that have been proposed as problem-solving skills, task-facilitating skills, and group-building skills are usually the functions of a leader.

The leader may be appointed or elected. It is usually expected that this leader will help group members to move more effectively on the task, will pay attention to the various dimensions in solving problems, and will also attend to the effective functioning of the group.

This concept, however, does not necessarily help to make the group more effective. Leadership of this kind has to be widely shared in the group. The more different members are able to perform these functions, the better it is for the group. In the first place, one individual does not have the ability to perform all these functions well. He or she probably does not have all the skills enumerated above. Therefore, he or she may need help from other members. Second, when members share the leadership function or the various skills stated above, they are also accepting the group as their own. Their commitment to the group increases. This helps people to recognise that the success or failure of the group is of concern for the entire group, in fact, for each member in the group.

A mature group is one in which it is difficult to find out who the leader is. In other words, in a mature group, different members perform different leadership functions as required by the group and the 'leader' facilitates such shared leadership. This is possible when people perform these functions according to the skills they have.

The second dimension relates to the evolution of a group. The functioning of a group will be much more effective if, in the early stages of its life, the group is able to pay attention to both the problem-solving and group-building skills. If these functions are attended to in the beginning, the group will have enough time later to proceed faster with the task and will not need to pay as much attention to the process dimensions. This is shown in Exhibit 15.1. As may be seen from the exhibit, if attention is paid to the problem-solving and group-building functions towards the beginning of the group's life, the group can thereafter use all its energy and time on the task dimensions. If attention is not paid to these functions in the beginning of the group's life, these will come up in a hidden form from time to time and are likely to block the effective functioning of the group. It would therefore be useful for the leader to ensure that these functions are properly attended to.

Exhibit 15.1   *Focus on Three Types of Functions During the Life of a Group*

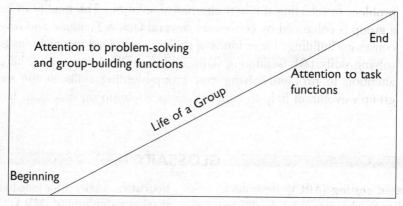

While the group may attend to the various functions and use the skills of a member as desired, on many occasions the group may not have as much time at its disposal as it would like. If a decision is to be made under time pressure, some consensus may be evolved for a few members to work with the ideas generated by the various members in the group—the group must then divide the task and have enough trust in members to take decisions. In other words, there is no single ideal way for the working of a group. The only comment that can be made in relation to a decision by consensus in a group is that the members should be as completely involved as possible and there should be emphasis on learning from one another and accepting the different points of view expressed.

A decision by consensus creates synergy in the group. When members listen to one another, use the resources represented by one another, and arrive at a decision to which they are committed in spite of their differences of opinion, the decision made may be even better than the one taken by the most capable person in the group alone. The group is, in a way, able to produce even more than the total sum of the resources represented. This is the concept of synergy. The group can move towards synergy by taking steps to continuously build the group as a team and identify and use various available resources.

SUMMARY

Decision making involves making a choice from among two or more available alternatives. Several approaches have been proposed to explain how individual or organizational decisions are made and how they should be made.

Rationalist models propose that choices maximise the outcome and self-interest. This approach has limitations.

Other models propose emphasising the roles of individual needs, emotions, habits, and values.

Organizational decisions are also socially, culturally, and politically embedded and these factors influence decision making.

The process of decision making involves a number of steps, from defining the problem to selecting the best alternative solution. The quality of decision making in a group is enhanced by consensus. Several factors facilitate and several others hinder consensus building. Three kinds of skills are involved in consensus building: problem-solving skills, task-facilitating skills, and group-building skills. Shared leadership and attention to problem-solving and group-building skills in the early stages of the group's evolution help to concentrate its attention on task skills later.

GLOSSARY

activity-based costing (ABC) determining costs according to what is paid for the different tasks performed by employees

consensus sharing of differences, listening to each other, and accepting the final choice in spite of the differences that may still exist

decision making choosing between alternatives

economic value added (EVA) determining the true cost of all capital; the total cost of capital is subtracted from post-tax operating profit

heuristics shortcuts for judgements

market value added (MVA) difference between the market value and the invested capital, the positive difference showing the wealth created by the company

political/institutional embedded theory organizational decisions are shaped by power blocks as well as by a struggle for power

satisfice solution that is both satisfactory and sufficient

EXERCISES

Concept Review Questions

1. What is decision making? What are the steps in decision making?
2. What are the main features of the rationality models of decision making? What are their limitations?
3. How do the bounded rationality and embedded models correct the limitations of the rationalist models?
4. What are the facilitating and hindering factors in consensus building?
5. Distinguish between problem-solving, task-facilitating, and group building skills.
6. How can consensus be made effective?

Critical Thinking Questions

1. Give an example of rationalist decision making from your past experiences.
2. How did you take the decision of joining your present institution/organization? Which model of decision making fits your case?
3. Read a recent decision taken by a company and trace its decisional process (steps followed).

Classroom Projects

1. Discuss, in groups of two or three, two decisions recently taken in the class. Critique the process (what was done well and what was lacking).
2. Observe a group meeting of your class. Analyse the process in the light of what you have read on consensus building.

Field Projects

1. Interview two people from an organization and write down the process followed in taking some decision in that organization.
2. Observe a decision being taken in your family. Are the consensus-building processes followed? To what extent? With what results? Prepare a note on the decision making process in your family.

Sales Targets at KNB Bank*

It was the first meeting that was being convened by Raj Malhotra, the new branch manager of the Tirupur branch of KNB Bank, a growing private sector bank. In comparison to other branches, the Tirupur branch had performed badly ever since its inception 7 years ago, and Malhotra, being young and enthusiastic, was determined to bring about a dramatic improvement in its performance.

The meeting was the first such in the history of the branch, as it involved the participation of all the employees of the branch not just to welcome their new manager, but also to make certain crucial decisions that would result in enhancing the branch's performance. The assistant manager, Abhiram Krishna, had made all the arrangements for the meeting that commenced with Malhotra thanking everyone present for the warm welcome he was given on taking charge. After a brief mention of the various posts and responsibilities he had held till then in his career, Malhotra described the bank's foray into the insurance sector and pointed out the additional responsibility that every employee of the bank had to make this diversification a success. Malhotra then emphasised the targets that had to be achieved by the branch for that financial year, both in its regular products as well as in insurance.

With the opening up of the insurance sector in India, a majority of the private sector banks began to show keen interest in entering the sector by forming joint ventures with established insurance companies. KNB Bank too entered into a joint venture with Secure Insurance Services, a UK-based insurance company, to sell life insurance products to Indian customers. All the branch offices of KNB Bank were instructed by the corporate office to promote the sales of insurance products along with the regular bank products such as loans, fixed deposits, safety bonds, credit cards, and various types of accounts.

Malhotra invited suggestions from all employees to improve the branch's performance and achieve the annual target for that year. However, there was very little participation from the employees despite Malhotra making repeated requests to them to fearlessly voice their opinions. Having received no substantial inputs from his subordinates, Malhotra presented his plan of action to them.

Of the various measures put forth by Malhotra to enhance sales, there was enforcement of sales targets even for employees dealing with routine banking operations such as cash transactions, generation of demand drafts, opening of new

*This case was written by M. Aarathy and B. Madhubala under the direction of C. Sridevi, ICFAI Center for Management Research (ICMR). Reproduced with slight modification with the permission of ICFAI Center for Management Research (ICMR), Hyderabad, India.

accounts, and handling of customer queries. Although this was unacceptable to the employees, none of them voiced their objection even when Malhotra asked for their opinion. The meeting concluded after a few more strategies to develop the branch sales were discussed.

The next day, one of the senior employees, Anand Trivedi, approached Krishna, with a document in hand. Krishna, who was busy preparing the monthly reports for the bank, glanced up, and seeing the document in Trivedi's hand, asked what it was about. Trivedi replied that it was a representation from the employees. Krishna immediately stopped what he was doing and reached for the document. In their representation, the employees requested the management not to impose sales targets on them. They justified their protest by stating that it would be extremely stressful for them to concentrate both on processing routine transactions and on enhancing sales of the bank's products and services. They claimed that of late the number of transactions had increased tremendously.

Krishna was visibly irritated after he read the representation and asked Trivedi why the employees had not opposed the decision during the meeting itself. Trivedi replied that while the meeting was in progress, each employee had thought that he would be the only one to oppose it and had hesitated to voice his opposition for fear of antagonizing the management. It was only after the meeting was over and the employees could discuss the matter with each other that they realized that everyone was equally opposed to the decision. Krishna assured Trivedi that although it was not possible for him to promise anything, he would certainly make all efforts possible to make the management reconsider the action plan.

Questions for Discussion

1. Raj Malhotra encouraged employee participation in the decision-making process of his branch. Discuss the possible benefits of employee participation in decision-making.
2. Malhotra attempted to develop consensus but failed. Which processes impeded consensus building?
3. What could Malhotra do to build consensus leading to commitment for action?

REFERENCES

1. Simon, Herbert (1957). *Administrative Behaviour*. New York: Macmillan.
2. Etziomi, A. (1988). *The Moral Dimension: Toward a New Economics*. New York: Free Press.
3. Frank, R.H. (1988). *Passions Within Reason: The Strategic Role of the Emotions*. New York: Norton.
4. Mansbridge, J.J. (1990). *Beyond Self-interest*. Chicago: Chicago University Press.
5. Flam, H. (1990). 'Emotional man', *International Sociology*, 5(1): 39–56.
6. Katz, Jack (1988). *Seduction of Crime*. New York: Basic Books.
7. Zey, Mary (ed.) (1992). *Decision Making: Alternatives to Rational Choice Models*. London: Sage.
8. Canic, C. (1987). 'The matter of habit', *American Journal of Sociology*, 91: 481–510.
9. March, J.G. and Zur Shapira (1982). 'Behaviour decision theory and organizational decision theory', in R.U. Gerado and D.N. Braunstein (eds), *Decision Making: An Inter-disciplinary Enquiry*, pp. 92–115. New York: PWS-Kent Publishing Co.

10. Powel, W.W. (1985). *Getting into Print: The Decision Making Process in Scholarly Publishing*. Chicago: University of Chicago Press.
11. Fligstein, N. (1996). 'Market as Politics: A Political-Cultural Approach to Market Institutions', *American Sociological Review*, 61(4): 651–673.
12. Katz, Jack (1988). *Seduction of Crime*. New York: Basic Books; Zey, Mary (ed.) (1992). *Decision Making: Alternatives to Rational Choice Models*. London: Sage; Burk, J. (1988). *Values in the Market Place*. Berlin: Walter de Gruyter.
13. Mintzberg H. (1990). 'Strategy formation: Schools of thought', in J.W. Frederickson (ed.), *Perspectives on Strategic Management*. New York: Harper Business.

16
Managerial Roles, Functions, and Styles

LEARNING OBJECTIVES

After studying this chapter, you will be able to
1. Distinguish between roles and functions
2. Enumerate the various managerial roles and functions
3. Identify the main aspects of transactional analysis relevant to managerial styles
4. Discuss interpersonal styles in the interactional framework of ego states and life positions
5. Suggest ways of increasing operating effectiveness of styles

MANAGERIAL ROLES

Management is the process of getting activities completed efficiently and effectively with and through other people. The manager takes responsibility for this process by performing certain roles and functions.

We have already discussed the concept of role in Chapter 12. Role is a cluster of functions expected to be performed by the persons occupying a particular position in the system. Those who have expectations from the focal role, as we have seen in that chapter, are called role senders. Functions are the main clusters of activities that are carried out by the role occupant. Competencies are the special characteristics the role occupant should have to be effective in the role. Finally, style is the quasi-stable way of performing the functions by a role occupant.

The manager occupies a significant position in the organization. Those working with him (seniors, peers, and subordinates) expect the manager to perform certain functions. Henry Mintzberg was the first person to use and elaborate the term 'managerial roles'. By 'role' he understood 'a set of certain behavioural rules associated with a concrete organization or post'.[1] Mintzberg has identified 10 roles common to the work of all managers. The 10 roles are divided into three groups: interpersonal, informational, and decisional. Exhibit 16.1 gives details about these managerial roles.[2]

Interpersonal Roles

The three interpersonal roles are primarily concerned with interpersonal relationships. In the figurehead role, the manager represents the organization in all matters. While

Exhibit 16.1 *Managerial Roles*

Interpersonal Roles

Role	Description	Identifiable activities
Figurehead	The symbolic head who is required to perform a number of routine social or legal duties	Ceremony, status requests, and solicitations
Leader	Responsible for motivating and activating subordinates as well as for staffing, training, and associated duties	Virtually all managerial activities involving subordinates
Liaison	Maintains a self-developed network of outsiders and contacts who provide favours and information	Acknowledgments of mail, external board work, and other activities involving outsiders

Informational Roles

Role	Description	Identifiable activities
Monitor	Seeks and receives wide variety of special and current information to develop a thorough understanding of the organization and the environment so as to be the nerve centre of internal and external information of the organization	Handling mail and contracts concerned with receiving information, including periodical news and observational tours
Disseminator	Transmits information received from outsiders and subordinates to organization members, some of it being factual, some involving interpretation and integration of diverse value positions of organizational influencers	Forwarding mail into organization for informational purposes, verbal contracts involving information flow to subordinates, such as review sessions and instant communication
Spokesperson	Transmits information to outsiders about organization plans, policies, actions, and results and serves as an expert about the organization's industry	Board meetings, handling mail and contracts involving the transmission of information to outsiders

Decisional Roles

Role	Description	Identifiable activities
Entrepreneur	Searches internally and externally for opportunities, initiates improvement projects to bring about change, and supervises the design of certain projects	Strategy and review sessions involving initiation or design of improvement projects
Disturbance handler	Responsible for corrective action when the organization faces important, unexpected disturbances	Strategy and review sessions involving disturbances and crises
Resource allocation	Responsible for the allocation of resources, thereby making or approving all significant decisions	Scheduling, requesting authorisation, budgeting activities, and programming subordinates' work
Negotiator	Responsible for representing the organization at major negotiations	Negotiation

the top-level managers represent the company in the outer world, the supervisors interface between the higher management and the work group, by representing one to the other.

In the leader role the manager ensures motivation and growth of the employees. While the top managers give vision and inspire through examples, the supervisors meet the psychological needs of the employees and reward them for their good work.

In the liaison role, the manager interacts with peers and people outside the organization. While the top-level managers act like a window, using the liaison role to get significant information and lobby for the organization, the supervisors use it to maintain the routine flow of work.

Informational Roles

The three informational roles are primarily concerned with the information aspects of managerial work. In the monitor role, the manager uses information to keep track of the progress towards the goals of the organization. While the managers at the top level collect important information for the entire organization, the supervisors does so for their units/departments.

In the role of a disseminator, the manager transmits information to the concerned persons in the organization. While the managers at the top level get and transmit more information from outside, the supervisors collect information relevant for their units/departments, and disseminate it among their people.

In the role of spokesperson, the manager disseminates the organization's information into its environment. While the managers at the top level function as industry experts, the supervisors are seen as unit/departmental experts.

Decisional Roles

Informational roles equip the managers well for decision making. There are four decisional roles. In the entrepreneur role, the managers at the top level look for opportunities internally and externally, and initiate change; the supervisors design the details of the projects.

In the disturbance handler role, the manager deals with threats to the organization. While the managers at the top level are alert to important, unexpected disturbances and take necessary corrective action, supervisors alert the top managers of new developments, and support them in coping with such developments.

In the resource allocator role, the manager wisely decides who needs when and how much to work for achieving the goals. While the managers at the top level are concerned with allocation of resources among the units/departments, the supervisors are involved in optimum utilisation of available resources.

In the negotiator role, the manager negotiates on behalf of the organization. While the managers at the top level negotiate with significant external agencies about resources and marketing support, as well as with their units/departments about productivity, supervisors do the same with their top management (for resources and support) and their people for results.

Exhibit 16.2　*Time Spent on the Managerial Roles and Effectiveness Levels*

ACTIVITY	Percentage of time		
	Average managers	**Successful managers**	**Effective managers**
Traditional management	32	13	19
Communication	29	28	44
HR management	20	11	26
Networking	19	48	11

In all these roles the managers at the top level focus on the total organization and the environment, and take a long-term view, while supervisors are more focused internally and have a short-term view.

A number of studies have tested Mintzberg's theory and the evidence generally supports Mintzberg's roles. However, it has been found that the roles change depending on the hierarchical position of the manager, and especially the distinction as to whether they manage people to complete tasks, or set the direction for task completion. For example, the roles of disseminator, liaison, figure-head, negotiator, and spokesperson are practised more at higher levels than at lower-level management.

After studying 450 managers, Luthans and his colleagues defined four managerial roles[3]:

- Traditional management—decision making, planning, and controlling
- Communication—exchanging routine information and processing paperwork
- Human resource management—motivating, disciplining, managing conflict, staffing, and training
- Networking—socialising, politicising, and interacting with outsiders

Then they studied the percentage of time spent by each category of manager on the managerial roles. These are shown in Exhibit 16.2.

MANAGERIAL FUNCTIONS

As noted earlier, managerial roles are the clusters of functions that the role occupant (manager) is expected to perform by the role senders (subordinates, senior people, colleagues, and self). Similarly, managerial functions are the cluster of activities that a manager performs to fulfil the main obligations (roles).

Henry Fayol was the first to propose the concept of managerial functions. Fayol has been described as the father of modern operational management theory. He suggested that management should be viewed as a process, and argued that 'to manage means to forecast and plan, to organize and give orders, to coordinate and control'.[4]

Fayol was one of the most influential contributors to the modern concepts of management. He proposed the following five primary functions of management:

- Planning—projecting the future and preparing action plans
- Organizing—designing the structure of the organization
- Commanding—maintaining activity among the employees
- Coordinating—unifying and harmonising activities and efforts
- Controlling—seeing that everything occurs in conformity with policies and practices

Many of today's management texts[5] have reduced the five functions to four, as shown below:

- Planning—deciding what needs to happen in the future (today, next week, next month, next year, over the next 5 years, etc.) and generating plans for action
- Organizing—making optimum use of the resources required to enable the successful carrying out of plans
- Leading/motivating—getting others to play an effective part in achieving plans
- Controlling/monitoring—checking progress against plans, which may need modification based on feedback

There are several differences in roles and functions. While roles are more relational, functions go beyond interpersonal relations. In roles the manager interfaces with several other role occupants. The roles involve expectations of others and require managers to respond to those expectations. On the other hand, the functions like planning, decision making, etc. may not necessarily involve working with others, and several managerial functions can be performed without communication with people.

Functions also may cut across several roles. In that sense functions represent broader characteristics. For example, the function of motivating is involved in several roles like leader role, resource allocator, etc.

It has been suggested that while the roles answer the question 'how to be interfaced with other people to reach our goals?', the functions answer the question 'what do you do to accomplish our goals?'

Managerial Competencies

The managers need to have some competencies (skills, attitudes, orientation, knowledge, etc.) to perform various functions expected of them. Katz was the first to suggest three groups of competencies required for management: conceptual competencies, human competencies, and technical competencies. Katz called them skills. We shall use the term competency, as it has been currently accepted. According to Katz, while all managers need competencies, their importance is related to the level of management. This is shown in the exhibit, originally suggested by Katz (Exhibit 16.3).[6] This shows that while senior management needs conceptual competencies, management at the lower level need more technical competencies.

Exhibit 16.3 *Katz Model of Managerial Competencies*

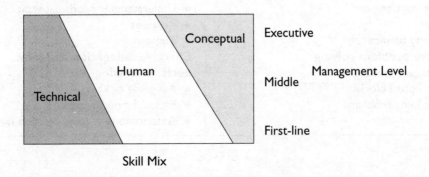

Skill Mix

Technical competencies require knowledge of a particular technology and proficiency in the use of the techniques. Managers need to have knowledge of techniques as well as skills of using it.

Human competencies involve working effectively with people, getting their co-operation and commitment. These also involve inspiring people and helping them to recognise and use their strengths.

Conceptual competencies involve working with ideas. In order to have insight into a problem, managers need to have an understanding of the ideas, their relationships, and different patterns of the combination of ideas (generally called theory).

As already stated, the importance of the three categories of competencies is related with the level of management. Lowest level of management deals with techniques and specific work to be done. So, technical competencies are more important for them. For middle-level managers, human competencies are more important, because they need to inspire people and get their commitment to achieve the organizational goals. The managers at top level require conceptual competencies, to think of different ways of formulating problems, searching alternative solutions. They also work for the future development of the organization. All these require conceptual strength.

Competencies differ from personality traits (e.g., hardiness), motives (e.g., power need), roles (e.g., supervisor), and functions (e.g., planning). Competencies are the requirements for effectiveness of a role. Competencies include knowledge, skills, attitudes, etc. A managerial competency involves a sequential pattern of behaviours performed in order to achieve a desired outcome.[7]

Based on a study of a sample of about 400 managers, Whetten and Cameron identified competencies of effective managers. After comparing their results with other well-known authors on management competencies, they summarised characteristics of effective management, which are shown in Exhibit 16.4.[8]

Exhibit 16.4   *Characteristics of Effective Managers*

Self-awareness	**Establishing supportive**
• Personality	• Listening
• Values	• Empathising
• Needs	• Counselling
• Cognitive style	**Improving employee performance/**
Managing personal stress	**motivating others**
• Time management	• Understanding needs/expectations
• Goals	• Rewards
• Activity balance	• Timing
Creative problem solving	**Effective delegation and joint**
• Divergent thinking	**decision making**
• Conceptual blocks	• Assigning tasks
• Redefining problems	• Evaluating performance
	• Autonomous vs joint decision making

(Contd)

Exhibit 16.4 (*Contd*)

Gaining power and influence	Improving group decision making
<ul><li>Sources of power</li><li>Converting power to influence</li><li>Beneficial use, not abuse, of power</li></ul>**Managing conflict**<ul><li>Sources of conflict</li><li>Assertiveness and sensitivity</li><li>Handling criticism</li></ul>	<ul><li>Chairing meetings</li><li>Avoiding pitfalls of bad meetings</li><li>Making effective presentations</li></ul>

TRANSACTIONAL MANAGERIAL STYLES

Managers continuously interact with other persons, mainly their seniors, colleagues, and juniors. One relevant framework to understand their interactional styles is that of transactional analysis (TA), which we have already discussed in Chapter 10. Two aspects of TA are relevant for understanding the managerial styles—ego states and life positions.

To recall, while interacting with others we operate from the sub-ego states of the three ego states. The three ego states can be understood as three functions. There are two main parental functions—nurturing and controlling (we shall use the term regulating). Nurturing is done by providing needed support. Controlling or regulating behaviour (of others) is done through prescriptions and sanctions. We may call these sub-functions. The main focus of the Parent seems to be on values and norms.

As discussed in Chapter 10, the Adult ego state has the function of collecting and processing information in the present. It responds to reality. The Adult works like a computer, without any values or emotions. We can call this a task function.

The Child ego state has several aspects, all relating to emotions. We shall take the liberty of using different terms with slightly different meanings—creativity, confrontation, and adaptation. We shall take these up later.

All the three ego states (and their sub-states) are important for a person. If any one of them is weak, we call it 'underdeveloped'. Numerically speaking, the three ego states should be about 33 per cent each; the same is true of the three Child sub-ego states with respect to their composition of the child. The two Parent sub-ego states should be about 50 per cent each of the full Parent. Norms for underdevelopment have been worked out and it has been suggested that a percentage ratio of 20 or below (for the three ego states or three Child sub-ego states) and 30 or below (for the two Parent sub-ego states) show underdevelopment. Other criteria for underdevelopment have also been suggested.[9]

As discussed in Chapter 10, we operate from four life positions ('I'm OK, you're OK'; 'I'm OK, you're not OK'; 'I'm not OK, you're OK'; and 'I'm not OK, you're not OK'). These life positions can be used to understand one's style of working with others. Style is a consistent and stable way of interacting with others. The four general interactional or transactional styles can be depicted as shown in Exhibit 16.5.

Exhibit 16.5   *General Transactional Styles in the Four Life Positions*

I'm not OK, I'm OK

You're not OK	**A** Avoidant/averse	**B** Bossing
You're OK	**C** Diffident	**D** Competent Confident/creative

The four life positions are combined with the three ego states. All the three ego states and their dimensions (sub-ego states) are important and perform distinct functions. Their effectiveness, however, depends to a large extent on the basic life position an individual takes. Thus, combining the four life positions and six ego state dimensions, we get the 24 different transactional styles shown in Exhibit 16.6.

Avoidant (I'm not OK, You're not OK)

In this life position, the person has respect neither for himself or herself, nor for others. It seems meaningless to the person to do anything worthwhile. The following styles are likely to be shown with the dominance of various ego states:

Traditional   (Regulating Parent) The role of the Regulating Parent is to establish norms and regulations of behaviour, disapprove of any deviation from the norms, and ensure that such norms are followed. In the traditional style, a manager will have faith neither in himself or herself, nor in subordinates with regard to proper

Exhibit 16.6   *Transactional Styles Elaborated*

Ego states		Life positions			
		A I'm not OK You're not OK	**B** I'm OK You're not OK	**C** I'm OK You're OK	**D** I'm not OK You're OK
Parent	Regulating Nurturing	Traditional Overindulgent	Prescriptive Patronising	Normative Supportive	Indifferent Ingratiating
Adult	Adaptive	Cynical	Task-obsessive	Problem solving	Overwhelming
Child	Reactive Creative Adaptive	Withdrawn Sulking Humorous	Aggressive Bohemian Complaining	Confronting Innovative Resilient	Intropunitive Satirical Dependent

behaviour. The easiest way to deal with this person, therefore, would be to follow the rules and regulations and the procedures laid down.

A trainer shows this style by doing what he or she has learnt as a participant. A consultant may be interested in norms and standards of behaviour only to the extent to which these are directly relevant to his or her tasks and may follow well-established practices at work.

Overindulgent (Nurturing Parent) The Nurturing Parent is interested in protecting and providing support to others. Not being sure how to provide such support, nor trusting others to demand such support, the general style becomes overindulgent. A manager, a consultant, or a trainer with this style may show more consideration towards others than necessary.

Cynical (Adult) The Adult ego state is concerned with tasks. The attitude of the avoidant style in the Adult is one of lack of faith and concern with work. This produces a cynical attitude. A manager, consultant, or trainer using this style is likely to indicate this attitude by remarks indicating that nothing significant can ever be done.

Sulking (Adaptive Child) The Adaptive Child accepts the norms of others and enjoys approval and conformity. However, if the person has 'not-OK' feelings both for himself or herself and others, this person does not share his or her feelings with others and proceeds to sulk. A manager, consultant, or trainer of this style may adapt to a situation by keeping feelings of dissatisfaction private. This is a dysfunctional adaptation, growing out of a need for safety.

Withdrawn (Reactive Child) In a not-OK–not-OK position, a child feeling angry tends to show anger (or aggressiveness) by withdrawal behaviour. A manager may become disinterested and uninvolved; a consultant may break off the consulting relationship with a client; a trainer may lose interest in his or her profession.

Humorous (Creative Child) The creativity of a child in an influencing role in the not-OK–not-OK position is likely to result in ill-timed humour. Humour may help to avoid the immediate problems, but this is different from genuine humour, which is used occasionally to enliven difficult situations. A manager, consultant, or trainer in this style may try to show imaginativeness by using humour all the time, which then reduces the seriousness of a situation until it seems ludicrous.

Bossing (I'm OK, You're not OK)

Generally a person in this life position takes a holier-than-thou attitude. This is reflected in an attitude of superiority. The various styles in this position are as follows:

Prescriptive (Regulating Parent) Such a manager has the opportunity to establish proper norms for subordinates and to ensure that these are followed; a consultant indicates to clients what he or she thinks they should do and is unhappy when they do not act according to the instructions; a trainer regards his or her main role as one of laying down detailed rules and regulations for learners and ensuring that these are properly followed. Such people are also overcritical of others.

Patronising   (Nurturing Parent) In this style, nurturance and support are provided by almost imposing oneself on others. The manager provides support and makes it obvious that he or she is doing the subordinate a favour as the latter is not capable of taking care of himself or herself. A consultant with this style treats the client like a child and shows him or her favour by giving advice and support. This style is particularly obvious in a trainer, who may show favour to remind learners that he or she is taking care of them as they are more or less helpless.

Task obsessive   (Adult) The manager, consultant, or trainer in this style is primarily concerned with tasks and is so obsessed with the work to be done that he or she overlooks various other things. In task obsessiveness, the individual takes responsibility for completing the tasks himself or herself and involves others in secondary roles only.

Complaining   (Adaptive Child) This person tries to adapt and seeks safety, but feels that he or she does not have the situations he or she deserves. This is reflected in complaining behaviour. A manager finds fault with the organization and with other managers and employees; a trainer is unhappy but only expresses general complaints; a consultant points out various external factors responsible for slow progress.

Aggressive   (Reactive Child) A person with this style is likely to show aggressiveness through infighting, making heavy demands, fighting, or going back to the same issues and never allowing these to be settled. The result of all such behaviour is that he or she gets alienated. People do not take such a person seriously for long.

Bohemian   (Creative Child) Such a person does not seem able to sustain a single idea and is obsessed with finding new ideas all the time. He or she overwhelms subordinates, clients, or colleagues with the new ideas he or she gets.

Competent (I'm OK, You're OK)

People with this life position are creative, confident of themselves, and competent. They have respect for themselves as well as for others. The following six styles may be shown in this position:

Normative   (Regulating Parent) This manager, consultant, or trainer is concerned with setting appropriate norms but involves subordinates, clients, or learners both in evolving these norms and in deciding how such norms will be followed.

Supportive   (Nurturing Parent) A person with this style provides the necessary support needed by others with whom he or she interacts. Support is provided only if such support is either solicited or needed.

Problem solving (Adult) This person's concern is to solve the problem by working himself or herself and involving others in it as well. This is different from being obsessed with the task. It is ironical that excessive concern with tasks may sometimes come in the way of a solution to a problem.

Resilient (Adaptive Child) This style is characterised by functional adaptation. The person assesses the situation and adapts to suit it. This is effective contingency behaviour. A manager is quick to assess the situation and quicker to change his or her approach if needed. A trainer or consultant gives up the well-prepared plans of teaching or intervention if the situation demands a different approach.

Confronting (Reactive Child) Aggressiveness is characteristic of this style. However, aggressiveness becomes functional when the person does not give up but perseveres and is content only when the problem is solved. This is confrontation of the problem. A distinction needs to be made between pseudo-confrontation (expression of aggression to people) and real confrontation (reflected in concern with the problem). Even when an issue has to be explored with a person, in effective confrontation the focus remains on the particular issue or problem and the other person is not a target.

Innovative (Creative Child) A person with this style is not satisfied with the available solutions but continuously searches for new ways of solving a problem or new methods to be used. However, the person is also interested in stabilising such an innovation before going on to new ones.

Diffident (I'm not OK, You're OK)

The general attitude in this style is to depreciate oneself. As the person does not have much trust in his or her own ability, he or she may not be assertive. This may be shown in various ways. The following six styles may be found in this position:

Indifferent (Regulating Parent) A person with this style leaves following the norms to the discretion of others and does not care to see how well the norms are understood. Most of the time, such a person manages to overlook whether the norms are being followed. He or she does not have enough trust in his or her ability to help people develop proper norms and follow them. Such a trainer may take no notice of serious deviations in the session. A manager may ignore the issue of the propriety of his or her subordinates' behaviour.

Ingratiating (Nurturing Parent) In this style, the effort is to try to please or placate others. A manager may do certain things to keep subordinates in good humour, thinking that this will help him or her to get work done by them. A trainer may get too personal, inviting students for social occasions at home and visiting them in their homes. A consultant may go out of his or her way to do more than the client may want.

Overwhelmed (Adult) Such a person is always concerned with the task but remains confused and feels that he or she has too much work to do. He or she never gets out of this task-orientation and constantly feels overworked and overburdened.

Dependent (Adaptive Child) The need for safety may be reflected in overdependence on others. A dependent manager may go blindly by what subordinates tell him or her to do or may seek approval for all actions from the boss. A trainer with this style follows the norms strictly and, in case change is needed, asks the head of the institution or group for approval. A dependent consultant is guided primarily by the client's wishes and understanding.

Intropunitive (Reactive Child) A person with this style takes out aggression on himself or herself. Such a person is angry with himself or herself for not doing certain things and blames his or her own lack of ability, skills, or courage for ineffectiveness. Intropunitive people suffer from self-pity.

Satirical (Creative Child) This style takes a more pungent form. The person shows his critical attitude, but escapes confrontation by using satire.

The 24 styles shown in Exhibit 16.6 may be too many for most analyses. Following James,[10] it may be more useful to combine the two basic life positions (OK and not-OK) with the six ego-state dimensions giving 12 interactional or transactional styles. These are given in Exhibit 16.7. It may be noted that the terms 'OK', 'approach', and 'functional' are treated as synonymous. Similarly, the terms 'not-OK', 'avoidance', and 'dysfunctional' are used interchangeably.

A transactional styles inventory (TSI) has been designed to measure these styles. The TSI is available for managers, consultants, counsellors, trainers, teachers, students, nurses, journalists, parents of children in three age groups, etc.[11] These styles are briefly described below:

Rescuing style Such a style develops a dependency relationship in which the manager, trainer, or consultant perceives his or her main role as that of rescuing subordinates, learners, or clients. The latter are seen as incapable of taking care of themselves. Another characteristic of this style is that support is provided conditionally, contingent upon the deference of client to consultant, subordinate to manager, or

Exhibit 16.7 *Twelve Interactional or Transactional Styles*

Functions	Ego states	Styles in two life positions	
		Avoidance/not OK/ dysfunctional	Approach/OK/ functional
Nurturing	Nurturing Parent	Rescuing	Supportive
Regulating	Regulating Parent	Prescriptive	Normative
Task management	Adult	Task-obsessive	Problem solving
Adapting	Adaptive Child	Sulking	Resilient
Creating	Creative Child	Bohemian	Innovative
Confronting	Reactive Child	Aggressive	Assertive

learner to trainer. In this style, the general attitude is of the superiority of the manager, consultant, or trainer, and these people offer their support in problem solving. However, such support constantly reminds others of their dependence on their 'rescuer'. Such a style does not help people to become independent enough to act by themselves.

Supportive style   In this style, support is provided when needed. James[12] uses the term 'supportive coaches' for managers with this style. They encourage their subordinates, cheer them on, and provide the necessary conditions for their continuous improvement. Consultants with this style show patience in learning about the problems of their clients, and empathise with them. The same is true of trainers. Managers with this style motivate their employees. They listen to them with sympathy and empathy. They take care of their subordinates.

Prescriptive style   People with this style are critical of others' behaviour. They develop rules and regulations and impose these on others. Managers with this style make quick judgments and insist that certain norms for which they have respect should also be followed by their subordinates. For example, a manager who does not smoke may dislike a subordinate because the latter smokes. A consultant is more inclined to give advice and prescribe solutions to the client rather than helping the client to work out alternative solutions for a problem.

Normative style   In this style, managers are interested in developing proper norms for behaviour for their subordinates and helping their subordinates to understand how some norms are more important than others. A consultant with this style not only helps the client to develop ways of approaching a problem but also raises questions about relevant values. Such a consultant emphasises the development of a general approach to the problem. A trainer with this style influences learners through the modelling of behaviour, that is, by behaving the way he or she would like them to behave. He or she also raises questions about the appropriateness of some aspects of behaviour and work.

Task-obsessive style   Managers, consultants, or trainers with this style are more concerned with the task in hand. Matters not directly related to the task are ignored. Such people are not concerned with feelings and in fact fail to recognise them since they do not seem related to the task. These people function like computers. The consultant focuses his or her attention solely on the task, ignoring any 'non-task' information. The trainer is insensitive to the emotional needs, personal problems, and apprehensions of learners.

Problem-solving style   In this style, a manager is concerned about solving problems but does not see the problems as being merely confined to the task. For such a person, problems have various dimensions. The focus of this manager, consultant, or trainer is on dealing with and finding solutions to problems. In the process, he or she takes the help of and involves subordinates, clients, and students.

Sulking style A manager, consultant, or trainer with this style keeps negative feelings to himself or herself and finds it difficult to share them. Such a person avoids meeting people if he or she has not been able to fulfil his or her part of the contract. Instead of confronting problems, a person with this style avoids them and feels bad about situations but does not express himself or herself.

Resilient style In this style, a person shows creative adaptability—learning from others, accepting from others ideas that appeal to him or her, and changing his or her approach when such a change is needed.

Bohemian style In this style, the Creative Child is active. A manager, consultant, or trainer in this style has lots of ideas and is impatient with current practices. He or she is less concerned about the working out of the new ideas and is mainly concerned with the ideas themselves. Such people are nonconformists and enjoy experimenting with new approaches mainly for fun. They rarely allow an idea or a practice to stabilise. They go from one to the other continuously. James calls such managers 'scatterbrains'.[13]

Innovative style People with this style are enthusiastic about new approaches and carry others along with them. However, they pay enough attention to nurturing an idea so that it results in concrete action and gets internalised into the system. Such people are innovators.

Aggressive style People with this style are fighters. James calls them 'punks'. Managers, consultants, or trainers with this style direct their aggression towards others. They may fight for their subordinates, clients, trainees, or their ideas and suggestions. They hope that this will help them achieve results. Their aggressiveness, however, often makes people ignore them and not take them seriously.

Assertive style In this style, as already discussed, a person is concerned with the exploration of a problem. Perseverance is the main characteristic. James has used the term 'partners' for such managers. They confront the organization to get things done for their subordinates. The same is true of trainers who confront the institution on behalf of learners. People with this style are more concerned about confronting problems rather than confronting other people for the sake of confrontation. A consultant with this style confronts various sources on behalf of the client and also confronts the client as necessary, which helps the latter to openly explore the relationship. Such people are frank and open but, equally, perceptive and sensitive. They respect others' feelings.

A person may show behaviours relating to several of the styles described above. However, he or she would use one style more frequently than others. We may thus get a style profile of a person in an interactional or transactional role. We call this the person's transactional styles profile.

An operating effectiveness quotient (OEQ) for each function (and sub-function) can be worked out by comparing scores on the OK aspect with those on the not-OK aspect. If TSI is used, tables are given to read off the OEQ scores for any TSI instrument.[14]

SUMMARY

Managers take several roles. These can be clustered into three categories: interpersonal, informational, and decisional. They perform several functions in relation to these roles, the main being planning, organizing, leading/motivating, and controlling/ monitoring. Managers need to have necessary competencies to perform these roles. Three groups of competencies have been suggested: technical, managerial, and conceptual. The importance of these competencies varies according to the level of management. While lower managers need to have more technical competency, middle managers require managerial competencies, and higher managers primarily must have conceptual competencies.

Managers' effectiveness also depends on their styles. Transactional analysis is a comprehensive framework to understand and modify personality, styles, and behaviour. Its concepts of ego states and of transactions between persons and life positions are useful for analysing interpersonal styles. The concept of games and scripts is useful in understanding the dynamics of dysfunctional exchanges and lifestyles of individuals. Combining the three ego states with OK and not-OK positions, we get six functional and six dysfunctional interpersonal or transactional styles. These have been described and instruments formulated for measuring them.

GLOSSARY

aggressive style showing aggression towards others

assertive style persistently exploring a problem

bohemian style less concern with the working out of new ideas and more concern with the ideas themselves

ego state a consistent pattern of feeling and experience directly related to a corresponding consistent pattern of behaviour

innovative style paying enough attention to nurturing an idea so that it results in concrete action and gets internalised into the system

normative style developing proper norms of behaviour for employees and helping them understand how some norms are more important than others

prescriptive style being critical of others' behaviour, developing rules and regulations, and imposing them on others

rescuing style seeing 'others' as incapable of taking care of themselves and providing support conditionally, contingent upon deference

resilient style creative adaptability, i.e., learning from others, accepting others' ideas that appeal to one, and changing one's approach when such a change is needed

sulking style keeping negative feelings to oneself, finding it difficult to share such feelings, and avoiding meeting people if one has not been able to fulfil one's part of the contract

supportive style providing support when needed

EXERCISES

Concept Review Questions

1. Describe the three clusters of managerial roles proposed by Mintzberg.
2. How do managerial roles differ from managerial functions?
3. What are the main managerial competencies at the three management levels?
4. What are the three ego states? What functions do they represent?
5. What are the four life positions? What general styles can be derived from their combination?

Critical Thinking Questions

1. Assume that you are a manager. Read each statement below and write your response (how often you will behave this way) in the space to the left, according to the key.

   Key
   Write 1 if you rarely or never behave this way.
   Write 2 if you occasionally behave this way.
   Write 3 if you sometimes behave this way.
   Write 4 if you often behave this way.
   Write 5 if you almost always behave this way.

_____	1	I would assure my people of my availability to them.
_____	2	I would delay doing things that I do not like.
_____	3	I would help my people to see the ethical dimensions of some of our actions.
_____	4	I would communicate strong feelings and resentment to my colleagues and seniors without caring whether this will affect my relationship with them.
_____	5	I would collect all the information needed to solve various problems.
_____	6	I would overwhelm my colleagues with new ideas.
_____	7	I would respect and follow organizational traditions that seem to give the organization its identity.
_____	8	I would provide my people with the solutions to their problems.
_____	9	I would zealously argue my point of view in organizational meetings.
_____	10	I would admonish my people for not acting according to my instructions.
_____	11	I would try out new things.
_____	12	I would collect information and data even when these are not immediately needed or used.
_____	13	I would help my people to become aware of some of their own strengths.
_____	14	I would not express my negative feelings during unpleasant meetings but would continue to be bothered by them.
_____	15	I would raise questions with my people about what should or should not be done.
_____	16	I would champion my people's cause even at the cost of organizational effectiveness.
_____	17	I would think out several alternative solutions to problems before adopting one for action.
_____	18	I would try out new ideas or methods without waiting to consolidate the previous ones.
_____	19	I would accept others' suggestions that appeal to me.
_____	20	I would instruct my people in detail about work problems and their solutions.
_____	21	I would express my feelings and reactions frankly in meetings with seniors and colleagues.

_____ 22   I would clearly prescribe standards of behaviour to be followed in my work unit.

_____ 23   I would try out new ways and see each problem as a challenge.

_____ 24   I would work primarily on organizational tasks, overlooking the feelings of people.

Scoring

Total your responses for the following items and write down the totals in the given space.

	Pn	Pr	A	Cc	Cr	Ca
(a)	1+13 ____	3+15 ____	5+17 ____	11+23 ____	9+21 ____	7+19 ____
(b)	8+20 ____	10+22 ____	12+24 ____	6+18 ____	4+16 ____	2+14 ____

Difference
in totals
(a minus b)   ____   ____   ____   ____   ____   ____

Find the difference for each pair (a minus b), keeping the algebraic sign. The totals in each case will range between 8 and —8. The positive scores show an OK position and the negative scores show a not-OK position. Reflect on your scores.

2. Which of your transactional functions is dysfunctional? List a few actions you would take to increase your functionality.

What Should Vora Do?*

The Navjivan Institute of Financial Management (NIFM) was started with a view to develop financial management skills of managers and administrators in various sectors. The institute conducts regular short-term and long-term programmes for different categories of managers from industry, government, voluntary agencies, cooperatives, and other agencies. Famous among its programme is the 1-month programme on Management of Finance Function in Government. For this programme senior officers in the government from various sectors (health, education, railways, posts and telegraphs, agriculture, industry, power, etc.) who are involved in managing the finance function are invited. Mr Vora, a faculty member of the NIFM, was in charge of this programme. In early 1980, Vora was asked to reply to a letter received from an IAS officer posted as the chief executive of an industrial finance corporation, Mr Advani, stating that he was interested in attending a management development programme conducted by NIFM and enquiring whether there was one in the immediate future.

Vora wrote to Advani mentioning the 1-month programme but at the same time saying that this was more for specialists in finance and Advani may find it too long and a bit unrelated. Vora suggested to Advani that if there was any other programme for finance corporations he would write to him. Vora also enclosed a copy of the programme brochure of the 1-month programme to Advani for information.

A few weeks later Vora received the nomination of Advani for the 1-month programme on Management Finance Function in Government. Vora did not refuse nomination although he felt a little uncomfortable to have a senior officer like Advani in the programme. Since there were nominations from a few other IAS officers (not as senior as Advani), Vora felt that Advani may be able to adjust.

A few days before the programme began there was a telegram from Mr Advani's office to Vora informing him that Advani would be arriving the day before the programme, and transport must be arranged to receive him at the airport. A day later there was a telephone call from local financial corporation enquiring whether a car had been arranged to receive Advani. Vora replied that he was trying to arrange one, although the NIFM normally did not arrange transportation for participants attending their programmes due to logistics problems. Ultimately, for that programme, Vora provided transport facilities to all participants who intimated to him their arrival schedule.

---

*Prepared by T.V. Rao, and published in *Behavioural Processes in Organizations*, by Udai Pareek, T.V. Rao, and D.M. Pestonjee, New Delhi: Oxford & IBH, 1981. Reproduced with permission.

Advani was brought to the trainees' hostel, which is a very well-equipped hostel of the NIFM. It has air-conditioned double rooms with attached baths. The programmes run by the NIFM for government officers are normally subsidised and the participants are required to share rooms in the hostel. On arrival at the NIFM hostel, Advani wanted a single room. When he was informed about the norm of the institution and extra costs involved, he did not insist on getting a single room.

There were 25 participants attending the programme, drawn from different government departments. None was, except for Advani, from a finance corporation. Some were as senior as Advani, although only one had the same status in government—from a batch senior to Advani and of equal status in a state department. Every Saturday was scheduled as a review day, when the participants and faculty reviewed the programme, its progress, and problems.

On the first day during the inaugural session, while inaugurating the training programme, the principal of NIFM said that the participants would find a number of programmes and professional activities of interest on the campus. He suggested that there was going to be a conference of chiefs of banks in the campus after 3 days, and a series of Peter Drucker's films would be screened by a local management association during the weekend, and so on. The principal advised that the participants may be on the lookout for such programmes and expressed that Vora being a benevolent coordinator would be able to provide a number of such opportunities for them to learn.

The seating for the programme was in alphabetical order. Advani was, therefore, required to sit in the front row. But on the first day, he dragged his chair back and arranged it in the fourth row. The first three rows were filled with participants and he was the only one in the fourth row. However, there were few empty chairs in the fourth row. Some of the faculty of NIFM used to join some classes and sit in the fourth row. During the first day in the session on organizational behaviour the topic of discussion was 'personal effectiveness'. During the discussion the instructor talked about the need for finance managers to understand how their own personality is likely to influence their financial management skills. The instructor then introduced the concept of Johari Window and discussed the same briefly. After the class was over, Advani met Vora and said that he had attended a programme in one of the Indian Institutes of Management and was already aware of the concept of the Johari Window. He said that this concept should have been discussed in more detail in the class. The instructor had not done justice to it.

On the second day, Vora saw Advani writing letters while the lecture was going on. The second day evening, Advani approached Vora with the request that he was interested in attending the conference of the bank chiefs starting the next day at the campus. He said that since he was heading a financial institution, discussions of the conference were likely to be of more interest to him.

Vora approached the coordinator of the conference of the chiefs of banks and requested that all the participants of the management programme be permitted to attend whenever they had time. Since the management programme was only in the morning, the participants could attend the conference in the afternoons. The conference coordinator told Vora that apart from the 50 persons participating in the deliberations, a number of faculty of the institute were sitting as observers, and that the conference room could not accommodate more. Vora then requested that at least one participant of the management programme be invited. The conference coordinator readily accepted this and gave all the background material along with an invitation for Advani. That evening Vora went to the hostel, gave the papers to Advani and said that this opportunity has been given exclusively only to Advani and that after the 2-day conference he may return to the programme.

The next morning other participants of the management programme noticed Advani's absence in the class and made some guesses about it. The day after, Vora saw a crowd of participants outside the classroom, surrounding the instructor who was to take the session that morning. The instructor said: 'Mr Vora, they want to attend the Chief of Banks Conference. They feel that this is an important conference and may benefit them a lot. I do not mind leaving them for the conference if they feel it is so important. However, I think you should take a decision.' To this Vora replied, 'While I agree that the conference is likely to be useful, it will disturb the class schedule. I will find it difficult to contact the other instructors and rearrange their sessions. Therefore, I suggest that the class continues as planned.' On hearing this, some of the participants grumbled. One them said to his friend loudly: 'It is all right, *yaar*. If Vora sahib says we must attend the class, we must.' Another participant remarked, 'But how is Mr Advani attending the conference?' The participants went inside the classroom without further protest, but a few more negative and sarcastic comments were made.

Vora entered the classroom and said: 'I understand that some of you are interested in attending the conference. I am aware that the conference is likely to be of some interest to you. Knowing your interest I already approached the coordinator of the conference, so that you could attend the conference in the afternoons. However, the coordinator told me that there were no seats to sit in the conference room. In a 30-seat room there are already 50 participants. I myself went to the conference room yesterday afternoon and finding no place had to come out. I hope you would understand the situation and appreciate the difficulty. May I also point out that we give top priority to this programme. Conferences of this kind keep going on. We prefer not to disturb our programmes unless we find that such conferences are extremely useful. For your information, the next instructor Mr Raghvan, who is going to take your class from 10:30 is addressing the participants of the conference from 9:30 to 10:30 a.m. and is walking straight from the conference to your classroom. You can see the amount of importance we attach to the class. I hope you will appreciate our orientations.' After having said this Vora also sat through the class.

The next day the conference was over and Advani returned to the class. On returning to the class he took his usual position in the fourth row. He continued to write letters and read some other notes, participating occasionally. Vora observed that whenever Advani made a comment or raised an issue with the instructor, others would laugh or whisper among themselves. This, however, did not happen with other participants. Meanwhile, other instructors had expressed to Vora their doubts of Advani learning anything from the programme.

Vora felt that Advani should mix with the other participants. So, in the morning he would come early and keep Advani's chair in the first row. But when the class was about to start, Advani would pull his chair again back to the fourth row. Vora had all extra chairs in the fourth row removed. In spite of removing the extra chairs, Advani used to pull his chair and make a row for himself.

On the sixth day there was a review session of the programme. The entire faculty who taught in the first week was present. During the session Advani suggested the following: 'We are all senior government officers. We come from different departments. We all know how to manage the finance function. However, we do not know how each person is managing the finance function in his own department. We also do not know much about the problems of other departments. Since we have the afternoons free, I suggest that we take one department everyday, where one or two participants belonging to that department present details about that department, about the finance function, about the problems, and about how they have been managing the finance function in their department. In this way we can learn a lot from each other also. This will also give the instructors of this institute an opportunity to know something about different departments.'

In response to the suggestion a few of the faculty whispered 'Very good, it is a damn good suggestion.' Vora immediately responded to this suggestion by saying 'I am very happy to note this suggestion coming from you. I was myself thinking of something like this. I think it is an excellent idea. Can we have some opinions on this?' A few of the participants said that it was a good idea. Some participants kept quiet. Vora felt that all the participants had agreed to this idea. He then asked the participants to volunteer and work out a schedule on who was going to speak on which date. After some debate a tentative schedule was worked out. The participants suggested that Advani should begin the series by presenting information about his own organization. Advani readily agreed to initiate this programme on the first day of the next week.

Advani's session was scheduled after the lunch break. After the last session of the morning, some of the participants met Vora and made the following comments: 'Sir, we do not want to attend this afternoon session of Mr Advani. Some of us feel there is no point in attending the class of a person who himself does not listen to what the instructors say.' Vora tried to persuade them.

Advani's lecture was attended by 15 of the 24 participants. The session was also attended by a few of the faculty. Some of the faculty remarked that Advani made an excellent presentation. A few of the participants said that the session was quite informative. A few other participants said that they have not learnt much from the session. Those participants who felt they did not learn anything also commented that they did not believe in the utility of this kind of sessions anyway.

Vora felt a little upset that some of the participants did not come for the session. When he mentioned this to one of his colleagues, the colleague remarked, 'It is your fault. In the first place why did you allow Mr Advani to attend the bankers' conference?' To this Vora replied, 'You know, years ago I attended a course on educational psychology. In this course I was told that I must keep the needs of each individual in mind and design my instruction in such a way that people learn at their own pace. I was told that the needs of the learner should be kept in mind and the learner does not learn unless an interest is generated. I felt that as an instructor it is my duty to provide the right kind of learning climate to my participants. I had also learned that a good instructor is one who takes into consideration the individual differences and needs. So is it my mistake to use the little psychology I have learnt?' What should Vora do?

Questions for Discussion

1. What is Vora's dominant managerial style?
2. Based on the data in the case, prepare an ego-gram of Vora's three ego states and sub-states to indicate that which seems to be under-developed?
3. What problems did Vora face in using his style without combining it with other effective styles?
4. Suggest ways in which Vora could effectively use his style?

NOTES AND REFERENCES

1. Mintzberg, H. (1973). *The Nature of Managerial Work*, p. 36. New York: Harper & Row.
2. *Ibid.*
3. Luthans, Fred, R.M. Hedgetts, and S. Rosenkrantz (1988). *Real Managers*. Cambridge, MA: Ballinger.
4. Foyal, H.(1949). *General and Industrial Administration*, p. 71. London: Sir Isaac Pitman & Sons Ltd.
5. Daft, R.L. (2005). *The Leadership Experience*. Mason. OH: South-Western.
6. Katz, D. and R.L. Kahn (1966). *The Social Psychology of Organization*. New York : John Wiley.
7. Boyatzis, R.E. (2001). *The Competent Manager*. New York: Wiley.
8. Cameron, Kim S. and David A. Whetten (1983). *Organisational Effectiveness: A Comparison of Multiple Models*. New York: Academic Press.
9. Pareek, Udai (2002). *Effective Organizations: Beyond Management to Institution Building*, pp. 333–334. New Delhi: Oxford & IBH.
10. James, Muriel (1975). *The OK Boss*. Reading, MA: Addison Wesley.
11. Pareek. *Effective Organizations*.
12. Muriel. *The OK Boss*.
13. *Ibid.*
14. Pareek. *Effective Organizations*.

The Team

- Interpersonal Communication

- Effective Teams

- Conflict Management

- Developing Collaboration

- Leadership Theories and Styles

- Developing Leadership for Tomorrow

17
Interpersonal Communication

LEARNING OBJECTIVES

After studying this chapter, you will be able to
1. Define communication as a process
2. Discuss different types of interpersonal transactions
3. Explain the significance of fidelity of communication and how to prevent communication distortion
4. Enumerate the steps to be taken by the giver and also by the receiver of interpersonal feedback to make it more effective
5. Identify defensive behaviours and suggest ways of promoting confronting behaviour

Interpersonal communication is the basis of most interactions in organizations. People in organizations interact with others within their own groups, across groups, and across levels. The effectiveness of these communications may contribute a great deal to the smooth functioning of organizations.

Interpersonal communication can be defined as the process of sharing goal-oriented messages between two or more sources through a medium or media.

COMMUNICATION PROCESS

Communication is a process. It consists of several units. The basic unit of communication can be called a communication act. This can be defined as the transmission, through medium or media, of a goal-oriented message from a source to, and its reception by, a target.

The various elements in this definition are (a) the source, (b) the target, (c) the message transmitted, (d) the message received, (e) the goal of the message, and (f) the medium.

Source

The source of communication contributes to its effectiveness. A lot of research has been done on source credibility. A particular source may be more credible than others and communication from such a source may produce more effective results. For some messages, a senior manager may be a more credible source; for other types of messages, a union leader may have higher credibility. There are different credibility levels of various sources for different categories of messages.

Studies have been done on key communicators—the most effective sources o communication. Key communicators in villages, who influence adoption of improvec agricultural practices, etc. were found to have higher social preferences, greatei contacts with agents of change, better communication skills, and higher adoptior behaviour compared with 'low' communicators.

Target

If the target of communication is receptive, communication is more likely to be effective. It may, therefore, be useful to assess a target's readiness and receptivity and to take the necessary action to ensure a minimum level of these before sending the message. In terms of readiness, the communication should meet the target's needs. Receptivity may be determined by the target's perception of the source, the target's needs, and the target's view of the instrumentality of the communication (whether the act of communication will satisfy his or her felt needs).

Message

The message may be one of three types: some information, a feeling, or a request for action. Communication of ideas and knowledge is communication of information. Communication of concerns, reactions, pleasant or unpleasant feelings, attitudes, and likes and dislikes relates to the second category of messages (feelings). In addition to those two types of messages, a message may relate to orders or requests to do certain things. Some good work has been done on transactional analysis of messages, which has been discussed in Chapter 10.

In the definition of communication, a distinction is made between the transmitted message and the received message. The received message (the interpretation) may not be the same as the transmitted message. For example, a message of feelings may be transmitted by an employee when he or she narrates an experience to the boss, but the latter may receive only the information message and not the feeling message. Similarly, a boss may transmit a message of positive feelings, but the subordinate may receive a message of negative feelings (he or she may receive a message of sarcasm when the boss may actually be expressing appreciation). There is no guarantee that the transmitted and received messages will be the same. In many cases, these turn out to be different and this distortion causes problems. Such distortion can be measured, as shown in Exhibit 17.1.

Exhibit 17.1   *Distortion Angle of Communication*

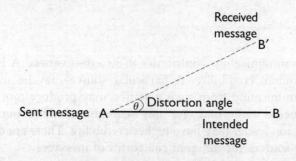

Medium

The media used in communication can be classified in several ways. For instance, media may be verbal or non-verbal. Non-verbal communication is as important as—and, in some cases, even more important than—verbal communication. Non-verbal communication includes such a variety of behaviour that these cannot be enumerated.

Even silence may be eloquent and may communicate a message. In terms of attitudes and values, non-verbal communication is much more influential. Studies have shown that one of the most effective ways of developing social skills and attitudes is modelling—living the values and attitudes you want others to practice. People learn more from what they experience than from what they hear. In an organization, the orally delivered messages of a general manager about the importance of technical people may have no effect if the manager himself or herself does not have respect for them and often overrules their recommendations on the basis of their analysis of technical data.

A verbal medium can either be a written or oral one and either in a face-to-face or distance situation. Letters and telephones are, for instance, distance media.

COMMUNICATION EFFECTIVENESS

There has been a great impact of technology on communication. It is estimated that about 50 per cent of the interpersonal messages in an organization are exchanged over the telephone. With the introduction of cellular (mobile) phones, the telephone has become the most frequently used medium of communication.

It is followed by e-mail, which accounts for almost 40 per cent of all acts of communication. Besides that, faxes and 'snail mail' (including airmail, surface mail, and courier) are the main written media of communication.

The impact of the Internet can be felt in both the content and form of communication. The search for information has become so easy that an individual can collect relevant information on almost any subject and can even download readymade material for PowerPoint presentations. As a result, people are spending more time on the computer, cutting down face-to-face interactions. The use of computers has also influenced the language: new terms and abbreviations are being added at a fast pace.

In face-to-face communication, non-verbal communication or body language also plays an important part. Besides modelling (behaving as one would like others to behave), the use of tone, volume, and pitch, eye contact, undistracted attention, 'non-fluencies' (saying 'ah', 'oh', etc. to show interest and inviting the person to continue), smile, etc. are equally important. Behaviour speaks louder than words. How a person delivers a message (its non-verbal aspects) and receives a message (non-verbal responses during exchange of communication) influence the quality and effect of communication. Attention should be paid to these aspects also.

The effectiveness of communication can be examined in terms of certain criteria. Communication can be said to be effective if (a) the message received is very close to the message sent, (b) the act of communication involves the minimum encoding of a message, (c) the non-verbal messages are congruent with the verbal messages, (d) the message elicits the desired response, and (e) the communication results in building trust between the source and the target. These criteria are briefly discussed below.

Fidelity of Communication

The absence of distortion in a message is called fidelity. An effective person gets the message across to others with the minimum of possible misunderstanding. If the gap between what a person wants to communicate and what the other person understands is large, the effectiveness of the person who is sending the communication is low. For example, if a supervisor intends to communicate his or her confidence in an employee by not oversupervising but the employee instead receives the message that the supervisor is disinterested, then the supervisor has low effectiveness.

The definition of communication emphasises the 'sent' message and the 'received' message as two distinct elements. They may be the same or they may differ. The extent to which they differ will indicate the distortion in communication. The concept of 'distortion angle' is shown in Exhibit 17.1. The line AB indicates the sent message, A being the message sent and B being the received message intended. However, AB shows the message actually received, B being the message received. The angle BAB is the angle of distortion.

Many factors contribute to the distortion of communication. The source of communication (the one who sends the message) has his or her own background—values, motivation, style, etc. The message is filtered through these before it is transmitted. For example, its decoding may be influenced by some of these background factors. The words he or she chooses to use in encoding the message may produce a particular effect. On the other hand, the target (the one who receives the message) also has his or her psychological filters, through which the message passes before its final interpretation. Distortion can occur either during the encoding or during the decoding process.

The problem of communication fidelity can be solved by taking some remedial steps. Distortion can be reduced by helping the people involved (the source or sender of a message as well as the target or receiver of the message) to understand each others' filters (background factors) and to become aware of their own. One good technique to reduce distortion is to ask the target to encode the received message (put it in his or her own words) and check back with the source whether the message received (as decoded by the target) is the one he or she sent. Such an exercise may help in understanding the factors causing distortion and enable the taking of steps to eliminate or minimise them.

Economy

In an effective communication, a minimum of energy, time, symbols, and cues are used to encode a message, without losing its fidelity and impact. In an organization, attention needs to be paid to this factor as people are engaged in several tasks and have very little time to spend on dealing with elaborate messages. When messages are couched in a large number of symbols (words, pages, or other coded forms), the person receiving the message may have lower motivation to decode the message. In organizations, emphasis is thus to be on making communication short, clear, and focused.

In many cases, the message is not clear, well defined, or well encoded. A message may either be inadequately encoded (not being fully explanatory) or the communication may be ambiguous (have double meaning). Again, checking back with the target may help in reducing ambiguity. Also, sufficient time should be spent on encoding the message properly.

Congruence

Effective communication integrates both verbal and non-verbal cues. If a verbal message conflicts with the speaker's non-verbal cues, the speaker's effectiveness will be low. For example, if a supervisor tells a subordinate that he or she is pleased with the latter, but frowns while doing so, he or she is giving a conflicting message and it is not likely to be effective.

Feedback is a useful mechanism to develop congruence in communication. It is discussed in detail later in this chapter.

Influence

The most important criterion of effectiveness is the influence that the communicator is able to exercise over the receiver of the communication. Influence does not mean control; it means that the communicator achieves the result he or she intended. If he or she wanted an empathic response and achieved that as a result of the interaction, he or she has successfully influenced the other person. If a supervisor sends a message of trust and confidence to a subordinate and helps the subordinate develop autonomy and the ability to take initiative, the supervisor has succeeded in influencing the subordinate.

Relationship building

One of the goals of interpersonal communication is to build a trusting relationship between the source and the target. Such a relationship facilitates future communication between the two. Effective communication contributes to the building of trust and a better interpersonal relationship between the source(s) and the target(s).

One factor that contributes to influencing and building of trust is the credibility of the source. If the source from which the message emanates has low credibility, the communication may not be effective. For example, if an important communication is sent by a middle manager, it may not be taken as seriously as it would if it came from a higher level that commands more respect. It may be useful to examine what level will provide the designed amount of credibility for a particular message to be acceptable enough to produce the desired effect. In most cases, this is carefully examined in organizations.

USING FEEDBACK

Feedback is a very effective mechanism for improving communication. Several approaches to giving and receiving feedback are discussed below.

In most organizational situations, individuals interact with other individuals: two people working together on a job, the boss talking to the subordinate about how well the latter has been doing or where he or she has not fared well, the subordinate discussing with the boss how things can be improved, and so on.

Individuals also communicate to each other their impressions of various things. Such interactions can be the basis of effectiveness at work. If better solutions are evolved as a result of such interaction and decisions are implemented in earnest, it may contribute both to the effectiveness of the organization and to the effectiveness of managers and teams working on various goals and tasks.

When people work together and interact, they need to communicate to one another their feelings, impressions, and views on various matters.

When such feelings and perceptions communicated to a person are regarding his or her own behaviour, style of working, etc., it is called feedback. In simple terms, feedback is the communication of feelings and perceptions by one individual to another individual about the latter's behaviour and style of working. Such interpersonal feedback is involved in everyday life in various situations. The boss sits with a subordinate and counsels him or her on the latter's performance. This includes sharing perceptions about the latter's achievements, strengths, and areas in which there is scope for improvement. Such opinions about styles and behaviour are expressed so that the information may be used to make the necessary changes as well as to emphasise positive behaviour.

A subordinate may also do the same. If the boss pulled him or her up in the presence of others, he or she may go and tell the boss how bad he or she felt about this. This may help the boss to improve his or her way of communicating.

Functions of Feedback

Interpersonal feedback involves at least two persons, the one who gives feedback and the one who receives it. Feedback thus has two perspectives. The functions of feedback can be considered from these two perspectives. Although the main purpose of feedback is to help a person increase his or her personal and interpersonal effectiveness, the functions can be considered in relation to giving and receiving feedback.

The main function of giving feedback is to provide data about a person's style of behaviour and its effect on others. Such data can be verified by the individual concerned by either collecting more data from other sources or by checking some aspects of the feedback with others.

Feedback also provides several alternatives to the individual, out of which he or she can choose one or two to experiment with.

Interpersonal feedback contributes towards the improvement of communication between the two people involved in giving and receiving feedback through the establishment of a culture of openness and interpersonal trust. Continuous feedback will help in establishing a norm of being open. Eventually, effective communication of feedback will help in increasing the autonomy of the individual who receives feedback if such feedback does not give any prescriptions but helps the individual, through offering information, to discover more ways of increasing his or her effectiveness.

Similarly, receiving feedback fulfils several purposes. Primarily, the individual (recipient) must process the behavioural data he or she has received from others (the perceptions and feelings people have communicated to him or her about the effect of the individual's behaviour on them). This helps the individual to have a better awareness of his or her own self and behaviour. Getting information about how his or her behaviour is perceived and what impact it makes on others increases the individual's sensitivity, that is, his or her ability to pick up cues from the environment to indicate what perceptions and feelings people have about his or her behaviour. Such sensitivity is very useful. It encourages the individual to experiment with new behaviour to find out ways of increasing personal and interpersonal effectiveness. Effective use of feedback helps in building and integrating the self. A person who receives feedback is encouraged to give feedback to others in turn. Thus the process encourages both openness and mutuality.

The functions of feedback, both giving and receiving it, are summarised in Exhibit 17.2. This assumes that feedback is given and received with openness and sensitivity. A balance of these two is necessary for effectiveness. The dynamics of openness and sensitivity as a part of self-awareness, contributing to personal and interpersonal effectiveness, have been discussed in Chapter 10.

Process of Interpersonal Feedback

The process of interpersonal feedback is a transactional process, the transaction being between two individuals as a unit. In a group, such transactions take place in

Exhibit 17.2   *Functions of Feedback*

Giving feedback	Receiving feedback
• Provides verifiable data about behaviour	• Helps in processing behavioural data
• Encourages collecting data from several sources	• Increases self-awareness
• Suggests alternatives to be considered	• Increases sensitivity to cues
• Improves interpersonal communication	• Encourages experimentation with new behaviour
• Establishes culture of openness	• Helps in building an integrated self
• Promotes interpersonal trust	• Encourages openness
• Facilitates autonomy	• Develops mutuality

several pairs of individuals. Such transactions are fairly complex. In this sense, feedback is not merely the communication of an impression by A to B, but it is the establishing of an understanding and a trusting relationship between two individuals.

In order to understand this, the process of a feedback episode is examined in detail. You will recall that a feedback episode is an act of communicating information by an individual A to another individual B about how the former sees the latter. The process of a feedback episode is diagrammatically shown in Exhibit 17.3. The various parts of the process are discussed below.

Psychological make-up of individuals The logical and chronological beginning of a feedback episode is with A's perception of B's behaviour (as shown in boxes 10a, 10b, and 11 of Exhibit 17.3). But the psychological backgrounds of both A and B function as intervening variables of which one should be aware of in the beginning. Both individuals have their own needs, value systems, and personality. Thus the two individuals (the one who is giving and the one who is receiving feedback) will behave in entirely different ways. In addition to their needs and psychological background, they may have typical relationship patterns (box 11). They may either like each other or may hate each other. They may have either accepting or non-accepting relationships with other people in general. These factors are important in influencing the various aspects of a feedback episode.

A's perception of B's behaviour In an incident where A and B are both involved and where B has shown a certain behaviour, A interprets this behaviour in a certain way (boxes 1 and 2). A receives the stimuli of B's behaviour. For example, he or she listens to what B has said and observes how B said it. Receiving both the verbal and non-verbal stimuli (box 1), A assigns meaning to them (box 2). The way A perceives or interprets the stimuli received from B depends to a great extent on A's own psychological make-up as well as A's relationship with B.

A's communication of the perception to B Individual A communicates his or her perception to B and this is what is usually called feedback (box 3). Communication may either be verbal (box 3a) or non-verbal (box 3b). Usually verbal communication will be more open. If A is clear about what he or she wants to communicate and has no hesitation in communicating it, A will usually communicate verbally. However, more messages may be communicated through non-verbal cues. If A does not feel free to communicate with B, he or she may still succeed in communicating this resentment by unsmiling interaction: with a frown knitting his or her forehead (of which A may not be conscious) or an indifferent attitude, for instance. These non-verbal cues are, in many cases, much more significant than the verbally delivered messages.

Often, the non-verbal cues are just the opposite of what is communicated verbally. For example, A may tell B that he or she is enjoying the conversation and the points being raised but may look at the clock frequently, thus giving a non-verbal signal of being fed up without being aware of it. Such contradictory verbal and non-verbal

Exhibit 17.3 Process of a Feedback Episode

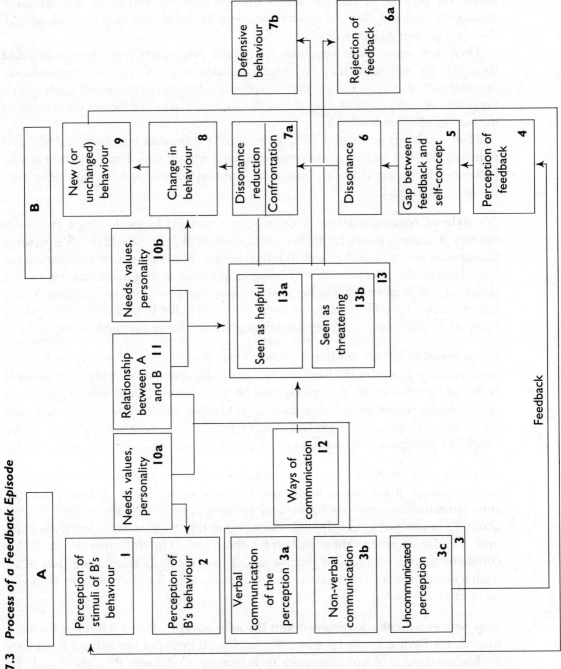

messages may distort the message and interfere with the effectiveness of feedback. Often, the non-verbal cues are much stronger than the verbal, so that the latter message is loud and clear. In other cases, the non-verbal cues may be weak enough that they are not picked up by B.

There are many emotions, however, which remain entirely uncommunicated (box 3c). An individual may feel highly agitated and yet may not communicate resentment or anger either in verbally or through non-verbal cues. Such uncommunicated emotions may distort the communication further as these come in the way of effective feedback.

Thus, as shown in Exhibit 17.3, a message is communicated both verbally and non-verbally, with some portion remaining uncommunicated. This process is greatly influenced by an individual's personal background and his or her relationship with the other individual.

A's style of communication   One important variable in the feedback episode is the way A communicates his or her perceptions to B (box 12). Again, A's personal background and relationship with B influence this. Many aspects of communication contribute to the effectiveness of feedback. Whether A communicates his or her judgment and, therefore, his or her criticism and disapproval of B or whether A only communicates how he or she has been affected by B's behaviour would make a tremendous difference to the feedback being either effective or ineffective.

B's perception of A's feedback   After A has given feedback, usually verbally, B receives it and perceives the feedback in a particular way (box 4). Either B may see it as A had intended or B's perception may be quite different from what A wanted to communicate. These perceptions do not get clarified unless they are checked with the source (A) and one important part of feedback is the checking back of the recipient's perceptions of messages.

B's perception of A's style of communication   Along with his or her perception of the message, B also reacts to the way the message is sent by A (box 13). If the communication is more descriptive and personal (providing data on how A feels about B's behaviour) or is helpful in encouraging B to try new behaviours, the latter may see the communication as helpful (box 13a). On the other hand, if A's communication is accusing or judgmental, B may see it as threatening (box 13b). Such a perception is a crucial factor in determining what B will do with the feedback he or she receives.

Gap between feedback received and B's self-concept   When B receives feedback from A, the feedback may be quite close to what B thinks of himself or herself (box 5). For example, if A communicates to B that he or she sees B as emotional, B's reaction to this feedback will depend to some extent on whether B perceives himself or herself as emotional or not. Thus, the feedback may either confirm or contradict B's self-concept.

Dissonance caused If the feedback received from A confirms what B thinks of himself or herself, it may reinforce B's behaviour (box 6). If, however, the feedback received from A contradicts what B thinks of himself or herself, it may cause dissonance. Dissonance has been found to be an important factor in determining whether feedback produces change or is rejected. If the feedback is seen as threatening and it produces dissonance, it is more likely to be rejected (box 6a).

Dissonance reduction The feedback is not, however, rejected outright (box 7). The dissonance has to be reduced, because an individual cannot live in a state of dissonance for long. Dissonance may either be reduced by confrontation or through defensive behaviour. If B sees the feedback as helpful, he or she may explore the issues further with A and, as a result of such exploration, may do something about these issues. This is confrontation (box 7a). However, if B sees the feedback as threatening, he or she may use all the defence mechanisms available to him or her to deal with the feedback (box 7b) before deciding whether to reject it.

Change in B's behaviour Depending on B's personality and background and whether the feedback received is seen as helpful, B may take the decision to try out new behaviour and change a part of his or her typical behaviour (box 8). Such experiments may prove satisfactory, in which case it will be integrated into B's personality. Change in behaviour as a result of feedback will, therefore, depend on how feedback is given by A and whether it is seen as helpful by B.

B's behaviour after feedback As indicated in the foregoing analyses, B may either continue his or her old behaviour if the feedback has been rejected, perhaps even using certain defence mechanisms to deal with it, or (if he or she finds the feedback useful and A has taken care to make it usable by B) may initiate a change in his or her behaviour and show new behavioural traits (box 9).

This new behaviour starts a new cycle of communication: A observes the post-feedback behaviour and a new episode starts, beginning with A's perception of B's behaviour. This cyclic process is indicated in the figure by an arrow going from box 9 to box 1.

The feedback episode thus consists of A's perception of B, influenced by A's background, needs, values, etc.; A's communication of his or her perception to B; B's perception of A's feedback as helpful or threatening; B's dealing with the feedback (by confronting it, by rejecting it, or using defence mechanisms); and B's undergoing some change. As already stated, the transaction is much more complex than depicted here. But this paradigm does show the basic elements in such a transaction.

Giving Effective Feedback

Feedback is an interpersonal transaction in which two people are involved. The effectiveness of this transaction will, therefore, depend on the behaviour and response of both the persons—the feedback provider and the feedback receiver. The person giving feedback can do several things to ensure the effectiveness of feedback. Some characteristics of effective feedback, that is, what a person genuinely interested in helping another person usually does, are discussed below.

Descriptive and non-evaluative feedback The person A who gives feedback should describe what he or she sees happening rather than passing judgment on it. The description can note the effect of B's behaviour on A ('Your remarks made me angry'), make a factual statement ('In the last 10 minutes, you repeated the same statement four times'), or state the effect of B's behaviour on others as A observed it. Such descriptive feedback may provide enough data for B to think about his or her behaviour and take some decisions.

On the other hand, feedback could be evaluative in several ways. A may pass a judgment ('Your behaviour was not proper'), may criticise or categorise B's behaviour ('You suffer from an inferiority complex'), or may give advice ('You should be bolder'). Such evaluative feedback does not help a person. Descriptive feedback is helpful in making a person more autonomous in taking decisions about what he or she would like to do.

Feedback focused on the behaviour and not the person The feedback is to help a person think about his or her behaviour and take a decision to change it. Feedback implicating the person—'You are sharp' or 'You are dumb'—is not helpful because it takes the form of evaluative feedback and the person does not know what he or she can do about it. When feedback is about the person's behaviour—'What you said and the way you said it has upset me'—the receiver is in a position to decide what can be done about that behaviour.

Data-based, specific feedback, not impressionistic Effective feedback gives specific information to an individual about his or her behaviour and provides data in the form of observations, feelings that the behaviour has evoked, and various other facts observed. This helps the person. However, if feedback is general and merely based on impressions, it tends to be more judgmental.

Even if it is non-judgmental, it may not help a person to prepare a strategy for changing his or her behaviour: for example, telling a person 'You must not interrupt' sounds like an unreasonable injunction. On the other hand, if a person is told 'You interrupted A, B, and C without allowing them to complete what they were saying,' the recipient has concrete data that he or she can use to think about his or her insensitivity and can take steps to avoid it in future.

Feedback reinforcing new positive behaviour Effective feedback helps a person to decide which style of behaviour he or she should continue to use and which to change. When a person is experimenting with new behaviour, positive feedback is likely to reinforce effective behaviour and stabilise it as a part of his or her personality. In this sense, positive feedback is very helpful.

Criticism or negative feedback does not help. It only increases the chances of a person becoming defensive. However, positive feedback has to be genuine and specific. If, for example, a person gets the feedback that he or she usually does not participate much in meetings, he or she may make special efforts to speak up subsequently. Positive feedback such as 'I liked your idea', 'I liked your taking initiative', etc. may encourage him or her to take more steps in that direction.

Suggestive, not prescriptive feedback   In many cases, the person giving feedback may suggest alternative ways of improving. For example, when the feedback indicates that B is not able to confront people in a group, others members may make suggestions to help him or her improve—'Speak out as soon as you feel bad about something', 'You can work out an arrangement where one or two members in the group act as your alter ego, so that they say what they think your feelings are at that time and later you can take these up for further exploration.' Such suggestions, however, should be in the form of alternative ways open to B for increasing his or her confrontational ability. Feedback given in a prescriptive form—that is, telling B exactly what the person should do without offering choices—does not help the person and may only make him or her dependent on solutions from external sources. Also, such advice is ineffective since the person himself or herself is not involved in the decision taken.

Continuous feedback   Usually, effective feedback does not stop with one act of feedback. It establishes a relationship of openness. The relationship is a continuing one, usually resulting in continuous feedback. Moreover, repeated feedback is likely to produce better results. Repeated feedback may reinforce what was initially communicated and may give an opportunity to the subject to discuss the feedback.

Personal feedback   Effective feedback indicates the involvement of the person who is given the feedback in the process. If the person giving feedback provides evidence from his or her own experience and gives data about how he or she perceived or was affected by the other person's behaviour, this is more helpful. If the person can provide other information and data in addition to making his or her own feelings and perceptions known to the other person, the outcome will be much more effective. If, however, only objective feedback is given without the person sharing his or her own perceptions and feelings, the relationship of mutuality is not established and the feedback is not effective enough.

Need-based and solicited feedback   Feedback that is solicited by a person is more effective than that which is given without such a need. In the former situation, the motivation to listen carefully to and use such feedback is high.

The main responsibility for the use of feedback is of course with the person receiving feedback. If he or she is on the defensive (does not genuinely accept the feedback and only justifies his actions), the feedback may not serve much purpose. The person giving feedback should assess the needs of the person for whom it is meant. If, for example, a person needs more understanding and empathy, it may be better to give more positive feedback first and afterwards he or she may be helped to see in which aspects he or she can improve. Feedback without sensitivity on the part of the person imparting it may become ineffective.

Feedback intended to help   The basic motivation of the person who is giving feedback is important. If his or her motivation is to be critical, negative, or merely to convince the other person about the accuracy of his or her own perception, the feedback will not be effective. If, however, the feedback is genuinely intended to help the other person, this aspect itself will influence the way feedback is given and it is then likely to be helpful.

Feedback focused on modifiable behaviour   The purpose of feedback is to help the other person to do something about his or her behaviour and to increase its effectiveness. This is possible when the feedback focuses on an aspect of behaviour about which a person can do something. For example, feedback given to a person about his or her stammering may not be useful because it would only reinforce the person's negative self-image, yet he or she cannot do anything about the stammering in the normal course of things.

Feedback that satisfies the needs of both parties   Feedback is a mutual transaction. For a transaction to be effective, it should satisfy the needs of both parties. The need of the individual who is giving the feedback may be to help, to influence the other person, and to establish a better relationship. These needs should be satisfied and the person should be conscious of these needs so as to use them for building mutuality. If the person giving feedback has a high need for recognition, and, therefore, the feedback given by him is motivated by this need, he may at some stage share this, once he becomes aware of such a need. Feedback based on the needs of both persons helps in building mutuality. And when the persons involved in feedback are able to share their awareness of such needs, the relationship of mutuality will be more effective.

Checked and verified feedback   While giving feedback, the person communicates one set of perceptions. Unless these are checked with the perceptions of the various other persons involved, feedback may not serve its purpose. Feedback can be effective if an attempt is made both by the giver and the receiver to check it with other people in the group.

Well-timed feedback   Feedback should be well timed. Timing implies several things. First, feedback should be given immediately after the relevant event. The advantages of immediate feedback are that the recipient then has higher motivation to reflect on the event and can examine the event without distraction.

Second, accurate timing also means that the recipient should be in a position to receive feedback and use it. For example, in a group situation, negative feedback can be effective only after a minimum level of trust has been established among the group members. In timing feedback, the main criterion used should be whether it is likely to evoke defensiveness. In circumstances where feedback is likely to be perceived as an attack or criticism, it may not be helpful.

Feedback that contributes to mutuality and group building   Feedback should be instrumental in building relationships of openness, trust, and spontaneity. If it does not contribute to such mutuality, it cannot be said to be effective. Effective feedback not only contributes to mutuality, but helps in building the group through the development of interpersonal effectiveness.

In this sense, feedback goes beyond the mutuality of two persons and contributes to the growth and development of the entire group. This function of feedback to do this should be examined from time to time so that people involved in the feedback process may be able to take decisions and monitor the feedback mechanism for the achievement of this goal.

Receiving Feedback

The effectiveness of feedback depends as much on how it is received and used as it does on how it is given. As discussed with regard to the process of a feedback episode, if feedback contradicts self-image or expectations, it causes dissonance. When an expectation is contradicted, psychological tension is caused.

Experimental evidence is available of subjects receiving discrepant outcomes being more tense and more uncertain about the permanence of the outcome. Dissonance may result either in a change of behaviour or in a perception of conflict and threat, which may lead to defensive behaviour. Broadly speaking, the person receiving feedback may use either defensive behaviour or confronting behaviour to reduce dissonance. Exhibit 17.4 summarises the two sets of behaviour, defensive and confronting.

When an individual feels threatened by the feedback he or she receives (e.g., if the individual is criticised, blamed, or given what he or she considers negative feedback that he or she does not agree with), the individual may build some defense around himself or herself so as to protect himself or herself from the threat.

Exhibit 17.4   *Defensive and Confronting Behaviour in Dealing with Feedback*

Defensive behaviour	Confronting behaviour
Denial	Owning up
Rationalisation	Self-analysis
Projection	Empathy
Displacement	Exploration
Quick acceptance	Data collection
Withdrawal	Expressing feelings
Aggression towards authority	Seeking help
Humour	Concern
Competition with authority	Listening
Cynicism	Positive critical attitude
Intellectualisation	Sharing concerns
Generalisation	Experimenting
Pairing	Relating to the group
Results in a conflicted self	Results in an integrated self

The concept of defense mechanisms was proposed by Freud. He studied severa defence mechanisms people used in psychoneuroses.

The use of defensive behaviour to deal with threatening feedback is like using pain-killing drugs to deal with pain: they reduce our awareness of the pain; but do not deal with the cause. The same is true of defensive behaviour. Defensive behaviour may create the illusion of having dealt with the situation but does not change the situation or behaviour. The conflict in the self is not resolved. Excessive use of defensive behaviour is likely to result in a 'conflicted self'. On the other hand, confronting behaviour will result in an 'integrated self'.

It is not the author's intention to suggest here that defensive behaviour is bad in all situations. Nor is it suggested that no defensive behaviour should be used. Some amount of defensive behaviour is used by everyone at some point of time and it is not possible to do away with it completely. In many situations, defensive behaviour may be functional. However, if the main purpose of feedback is to develop mutuality and if both the individuals involved in giving and receiving feedback are interested in a relationship of trust and openness, it must be noted that the more defensive behaviour is used, the less effective the feedback will be. In order to make feedback effective, an attempt should be made to move away from defensive behaviour towards confronting behaviour. The individual receiving feedback should examine what defensive behaviour he or she uses more often and should prepare a plan (preferably taking the help of others) for reducing this behaviour and moving towards the corresponding confronting behaviour as indicated in Exhibit 17.4. These pairs of defensive and confronting behaviour are discussed in detail below:

Denial vs owning up   If a person receives negative feedback that threatens him or her, the first tendency is to deny it. Denial will certainly reduce the anxiety because the person may convince himself or herself that what was said was wrong and not worth bothering about it. But this does not help the individual to change nor the situation to improve. The corresponding confronting behaviour in such a situation would be owning up to the subject of the feedback even if it is disturbing.

Owning up a certain behaviour is difficult and indicates a high level of behaviour contributing to interpersonal competence. Owning up does not mean readily accepting the feedback. As we will see later, quick acceptance is also a defensive behaviour. Owning up means being open to accepting one's limitations after examining and collecting the necessary data from various sources so that one may then be able to do something about it. Owning up indicates the respect the person has for himself or herself, and only highly self-respecting people are prepared to own up to behaviour that may be seen as their limitations or weaknesses.

Rationalisation vs self-analysis   The usual reaction to negative feedback is to explain away one's own behaviour. For example, if an employee receives the feedback that his or her motivation is low, he or she may find a reason to explain this low motivation, thereby absolving himself or herself of the responsibility for the low motivation. This is the process of rationalisation. The employee may, for example, ascribe it to physical ill health, problems in the family, and so on. Not that there may not be genuine reasons for low motivation, but quickly offering reasons or justification for a particular behaviour prevents a person from owning up to that behaviour and being responsible for it. Rationalisation, therefore, does not help.

Instead, if the person does some self-analysis and finds out why this kind of behaviour has been picked up or what is the meaning of the feedback in relation to what he or she usually does, he or she may get some ideas of improving the behaviour.

Projection vs empathy In most cases, negative feedback causes anxiety and resentment in the recipient. If the source from which the feedback is received is not trustworthy and it is difficult for the individual receiving feedback to openly explore the issues with the former, he or she is likely to feel resentful and angry. Yet a person cannot be angry without any cause; otherwise it will create dissonance and conflict. In order to reduce this conflict and to justify the resentment, the person receiving feedback may project his or her feeling of resentment on to the person giving the feedback. Then on, the recipient may see the source of the feedback as angry, biased, etc. This is the process of projection.

In projection, the person projects his or her own feelings about the other person on to the latter. Projection is a defensive behaviour and may help reduce anxiety. But, like other defensive behaviours, it does not help deal with the root cause.

Instead of getting angry and projecting resentment on to the other person, it may be useful for the recipient to empathise with the other person, try to see his or her point of view, and understand why such negative feedback has been given.

Displacement vs exploration Another well-known defensive behaviour is that of displacement. For example, if an individual cannot express anger or resentment to the person who has given feedback because the latter is in a powerful position, he or she expresses anger towards somebody else who is weaker. A manager who becomes much more strict with his or her own subordinates after getting negative feedback from his or her boss is an example of this.

Displacement is usually used in situations in which the person giving feedback is in a stronger position and the person receiving feedback cannot easily express resentment towards him or her. A more helpful behaviour may be to explore with the person who has given the feedback where and how the behaviour in question was seen. Discussing these details may help get more evidence and also dispel some of the misgivings of the feedback provider.

Quick acceptance vs data collection Quickly accepting feedback is one form of rejecting the feedback! The best way to kill an idea is to feed it on sweet words. When a person accepts feedback without much reflection, he or she wants to escape the possibility of exploring the offending behaviour and doing something about it. Instead of quickly accepting the feedback, it may be better to collect data on the different aspects of the feedback both from the person giving it and from other sources. This may help in increasing interpersonal effectiveness as well.

Withdrawal vs expression of feelings   When a person feels helpless and finds himself or herself in a position where it is difficult to express resentment, the person often reacts by losing interest in work, cutting out interaction with the person giving feedback, and generally showing signs of withdrawal. Such withdrawal behaviour may not be helpful and may, in fact, lead to a deterioration of the situation.

The confronting behaviour that may be helpful in such a case is expressing the feeling of being hurt to the person giving the feedback. It is a difficult thing to do; but if the recipient tries to express these feelings in a matter-of-fact way, communicating that certain things hurt him or her, he or she may find it increasingly easy to continue to do this in the future.

Aggression vs seeking help   Another form of defensive behaviour is the expression of aggression towards the person who has given the feedback. After receiving feedback from a person who is seen as hierarchically lower or less powerful, the person receiving feedback may shout at the source or express aggression in various other forms. This may be easy to do but does not solve the problem.

Instead of showing aggression, if the person receiving the feedback seeks the help of those giving the feedback in learning more about the particular behaviour and in planning ways of dealing with it, the feedback is likely to be used for changing the person's behaviour for the better.

Humour vs concern   In some cases, humour is employed as a way of dealing with feedback. Humour is a great quality. However, when it is used to cover up something and reduce anxiety caused by dissonance, it does not help and becomes dysfunctional. Instead, the person should show concern. This concern will help him or her explore possibilities of improving his or her behaviour.

Competition with the authority vs listening   In a T-group situation, a member who receives negative feedback is likely to deal with it by competing with the trainer (the symbol of authority) by, for example, proposing alternate theories to challenge the trainer or suggesting different ways of interpretation. This may be highly satisfying. However, it is dysfunctional. The member would benefit more if he or she listens to what has been said.

Cynicism vs positive, critical attitude   Negative feedback can be brushed aside by a cynical attitude, for example, assuming that most people say things that do not deserve consideration and that things are pretty bad in general. On the other hand, a positive critical attitude helps a person examine what feedback is given and sort out those parts that seem to make sense and reject others. Such an attitude is helpful.

Intellectualisation vs sharing concern   In a T-group, or other group situations, negative feedback is ignored by a process of intellectualisation, spinning theories to explain matters when the real need is to share the concern with others and take their help in dealing with the problems.

Generalisation vs experimentation One form of defensive behaviour to deal with negative feedback is to generalise what has been said. If a person, for example, receives the feedback that he or she used words suggesting that he or she was scolding someone and that his tone was authoritarian, the individual receiving such feedback may say that this is true in general about people who have been brought up in an Indian culture and in an Indian family. Such generalisations do not help.

Instead, if the individual experiments with different kinds of behaviour to see whether he or she can change the behaviour in spite of its being culturally influenced, he or she may be better benefited.

Pairing vs relating to the group In a T-group or other group, a person receiving feedback has the tendency to pair with another person (or other people) in the group who seems to have received such negative feedback as well, and is feeling threatened. This 'being together' may comfort people under such 'attacks'.

The confronting and helpful behaviour in such a situation is to relate to the entire group by exploring options with several members of the group and taking their help instead of pairing with one or a few. This may help further exploration and experimentation.

The use of confronting behaviour may help a person build relationships for getting further helpful feedback. The way a person receives and uses feedback will, to some extent, also influence the way people give helpful feedback. The person may plan to test various ideas and experiment on a limited basis and then seek further feedback to know whether these ways of improving are seen as effective. This may set up a cycle of self-improvement and increase the individual's interpersonal effectiveness.

If feedback is given in the spirit of helping the other person in building a relationship of trust and openness and if it is received in a spirit of learning from the situation to increase interpersonal effectiveness and to contribute to a relationship of trust and openness, feedback can be an effective instrument in building linkages of mutuality between people. If, however, feedback is not promptly or properly given or received, it may contribute to the disruption of relationships and undermine the development of the group. Feedback, therefore, is a powerful instrument and should be used effectively. It depends on the person who is giving it and the person who is receiving it that this instrument can be used for forging bonds of mutuality.

SUMMARY

Communication is the process of sharing goal-oriented messages between two or more sources through a medium or media. The various elements in communication are the source, the target, the transmitted message, the received message, the goal of the message, and the medium. Several factors contribute to effectiveness of communication: fidelity, economy, congruence, relationship building, and giving and using feedback.

Feedback is the most important element, requiring special attention. Both givers and receivers of feedback are important in improving communication.

GLOSSARY

communication act transmission, through medium or media, of a goal-oriented message from a source to and its reception by a target

confronting relating to the group by exploring issues with several members of the group and taking their help

congruence assonance between verbal and non-verbal cues

cynicism an attitude that most people say things not deserving consideration and that, in general, things are pretty bad

defensive behaviour when the individual feels threatened by the feedback he or she receives (e.g., if criticised, blamed or given what he or she may consider negative feedback that he or she does not agree with), the individual may build some defence around himself or herself to protect himself or herself from the threat

displacement expressing negative feelings to a soft target (a weaker person than onself) if one cannot express one's anger or resentment to the person who has given feedback because the latter is in a powerful position

distortion the extent to which the sent message and the received message differ

economy a minimum of energy, time, symbols, and cues used to encode a message, without losing its fidelity and impact

feedback communication of feelings and perceptions to a person regarding his or her behaviour, style of working, etc.

fidelity the distortion-free quality of a message

influence the communicator achieving the intended result

intellectualisation spinning theories in explaining matters when the real need may be to share one's concerns and take others' help in dealing with the problems one may be facing

interpersonal communication the process of sharing goal-oriented messages between two or more sources through a medium or media

non-fluencies expressions ('ah', 'oh', etc.) to show interest and invite the other person to continue to share

pairing to pair with another person (or other persons) in a group who also seems to have received negative feedback and is feeling threatened

projection projecting one's feelings about the other person on to the latter

rationalisation finding reasons to explain one's behaviour

transaction one part of the message exchanged between two persons

withdrawal losing interest in work; cutting out interaction with the person who is giving feedback

EXERCISES

Concept Review Questions

1. Explain the different elements of communication.
2. What is fidelity of communication? What factors contribute to distortion of communication?
3. When is communication congruent?
4. What are defensive behaviours? How can the giver of feedback help in reducing the receiver's defensive behaviour?

Critical Thinking Questions

1. Give an example of distortion in communication. Suggest ways of reducing it.
2. List suggestions for teachers to make their feedback to students more effective.
3. List suggestions for students to effectively use the feedback they receive.
4. What precautions will you take when you become a manager to make your feedback effective?

Classroom Project

1. Form small groups of three or four members. Each person thinks of one person whom he or she has known as an effective communicator. He or she also thinks of another person who is not effective in his or her communication. Without naming them, each member shares why he or she thought one was an effective and another an ineffective communicator. The group then summarises characteristics of effective communication and one person reports to the whole class. About 20 minutes are allotted for small group discussion and about 10 minutes for reporting to the class.

Field Projects

1. Interview two persons in an organization. List the factors that helped them (and those that did not) in benefiting from their last performance appraisal meetings with their superiors.
2. Interview two persons in an organization to list suggestions for reducing distortion in communication.

Mobilising Support Through Communication*

The new general manager (GM) of a Malaysian carpet company was faced with the challenge of turning around the firm, which was rapidly going downhill. He had to influence his own head office, senior executives, workers, bankers, dealers, and others to support the change till the firm turned the corner. But the workers were in no mood to wait and decided to go on strike demanding higher wages and bonus. A senior executive, who wanted to cut the new GM to size, was provoking them surreptitiously. One day, as the workers were planning to leave for the day, the GM decided—at the spur of the moment—to talk to them. He said, 'I understand that you are planning to go on strike and hold demonstrations. When you squat outside the factory gate tomorrow, there will be people from the press who will come and photograph you. Your pictures will appear in the newspapers. They will ask you questions and blow up the issue. But our bankers will also read about our problems. They already think that ours is a dying company and when you go on strike, they will reject our proposal for funds. If that happens, the company will close down. Of course, you will continue to hold demonstrations, but now no press people will come to take your photographs and write what you say. I have another job at the head office and so I will lose very little, but I am not so sure if all of you can find another job when the company closes down.'

The response of the workers to the GM's impromptu address was electric; the GM had established contact with the group. The GM looked directly into the eyes of a worker who was listening intently, and asked him, 'Tell me, do you want to go on strike tomorrow?' The worker avoided his eyes, but the GM persisted, 'You cannot avoid my question. It is far too important for the company's future and yours. Do you want to go on strike?' For a while, there was silence. Then, slowly, the worker said, 'No'. The GM moved to another person and repeated his question. Again the answer was no. The third person, fourth person, and soon ripples of a new sentiment were being generated. Towards the end of the address, the crisis had been averted. The GM quickly followed up with initiatives to strengthen employee communication and involvement to build on the positive sentiment that had come about.

The GM followed a different approach with the bankers. He met them regularly and frequently, each time with some good news about the company. He used his contacts to get certain purchase orders released, even if the deliveries were required later. Every time there was a big order, he told the bankers that it was only the tip of the iceberg, and there was more to follow. In the GM's words, 'No accounts were

---

*Reproduced with permission from *Change Management* (Box 4.4; p. 161) by V. Nilakant and S. Ramnarayan, published by Response Books, 2006.

presented to the bankers unless we put lipstick and mascara and made them look as pretty and healthy as possible. Finally, the banks relented and accepted the financial restructuring package we had proposed. That helped the company turn around in a remarkably short time.'

Questions for Discussion

1. How did the GM distinguish between the two target groups to make his communication effective?
2. What main factors contribute to making communication effective for mobilising support?
3. What is the main advantage of direct face-to-face communication, as against communication through circulars or memos?

18
Effective Teams

Most of the work in organizations is done in teams. Even though individuals are important, their effectiveness depends, to a large extent, on the teams of which they are members. In modern organizations, individuals are required to work in different types of teams. In fact, new organizations can be described as being composed of teams.

What is a team? A team consists of individuals. However, a collection of individuals in one place may be only a crowd. When individuals come together for certain tasks, then we have the formation of a group. The main function of a group is to exchange task-related information and discuss task-related issues. Accountability in a group remains individual. Each individual brings his or her own competencies as well as information relevant to the task. Thus the group can be defined as a collection of individuals working in face-to-face relationships to share information and resources for a task to be achieved.

The team is qualitatively different from the group in several ways. The team functions almost like an individual. In other words, the team is accountable for results and collective responsibility is taken. There is mutuality and complementarity among the members of the team. The most important characteristic of a team is that it creates synergy, that is, the performance of the team is better than the collective performance of the individual members. A team can thus be defined as a group of individuals working in a face-to-face relationship for a common goal, having collective accountability for the outcome of its effort. Exhibit 18.1 shows the difference between groups and teams.

As already stated, a team has several characteristics: members are inter-dependent; it has a common goal or goals; each member's contribution is as important as any other member's contribution; there is congruence between achievement of individual goals and that of the team goal.

Exhibit 18.1   *Difference Between Work Groups and Teams*

	Work groups	Teams
Propose	Same as organization	Specific
Work products	Individual	Collective
Process	Discuss, decide, delegate	Discuss, decide, do
Leadership	A single leader	Shared
Meetings	Efficient	Open, problem solving
Accountability	Individual	Individual and mutual
Evaluation	Indirect (e.g., financial)	Direct (collective work product)

Adapted from Katzenback and Smith, 1993.

The importance of teams was first realised from the results of the famous Hawthorne studies in the 1930s. However, it was McGregor who gave special attention to teams in the 1960s. Likert, during the same period, focussed attention on teams as important elements in the humanisation of organizations.[1]

TEAM DEVELOPMENT

Teams take time to develop. A team is not formed merely by declaring some individuals a team. A lot of research has been done on group formation and development and different theories of group development have been suggested.[2] Tuckman, summarising the various theories, suggested five stages of group development: forming, storming, norming, performing, and adjourning.[3] This model has been widely accepted. Kormanski and Mozenter integrated the various theories and suggested the following stages of team development.[4] These stages are sequential (each stage is followed by the next one). Each stage has a task outcome and a relationship outcome, as shown in Exhibit 18.2.

Exhibit 18.2 *Model of Team Building*

Stage	Theme	Task outcome	Relationship outcome
One	Awareness	Commitment	Acceptance
Two	Conflict	Clarification	Belonging
Three	Cooperation	Involvement	Support
Four	Productivity	Achievement	Pride
Five	Separation	Recognition	Satisfaction

Awareness   At this stage, individuals get to know each other. By knowing the goals of the team, they commit themselves to the goals. The members get to know each other and agree to work together for a goal about which they have enough knowledge.

Conflict   At the first stage (awareness), the members learn the team goals and agree to work together; but this is at the surface. At the second stage, they search deeper and begin to ask questions. As a result, matters are clarified. They also fight with each other and, in this process, resolve any hostilities they may have, resulting in a feeling of belonging in the group.

Cooperation In the third stage, the members accept ownership of the team goals and get involved with those goals. Having resolved their feelings, they also begin to support each other.

Productivity This is the stage for the actual achievement of goals/outcomes. Team members achieving objectives feel proud of their achievement.

Separation Having accomplished their goals or desired outcomes, some task-specific teams may decide to accept dissolution of the team. Sometimes, a time-bound project comes to a close. The excellent work done by members is recognised and team members experience a high sense of satisfaction from working with each other. This is the stage of closure of the team or closure of one task on which the team was working.

TEAM ROLES

Since team members are accountable for results and function in a cohesive way, enough attention needs to be given to the formation of teams. Synergy is produced when individual members in a team supplement and support each other. Researching the question why some teams are more effective than others, some scholars have studied how the teams should be created to achieve the desired synergy.

Belbin[5] did pioneering work in this regard. He proposed the term 'team roles' for process roles that team members play in addition to their functional roles (quality control, financial sanctions, etc.). Belbin identified eight team roles:

Chairman/coordinator Such a person is stable, dominant, an extrovert, and preoccupied with objectives. This is a person of character and discipline. He or she quantifies objectives, establishes priorities, sums them up, and comes to firm conclusions.

Shaper Such a person is anxious, dominant, and an extrovert. This individual is outgoing, full of energy, and easily frustrated. He or she gives shape to the team's effort, pushes for decisions, and is sometimes abrasive.

Plant Such a person has a very high IQ and is an introvert. He or she scatters the seeds of ideas for others to nourish and is more concerned with basic issues. He or she is of the 'Yes ... but' type, raising issues that may make some members uncomfortable. He or she can easily withdraw and so requires sensitive handling.

Monitor/evaluator Such a person is also an introvert with a high IQ, very serious, critical, given to unbiased analysis, and perhaps seen as a destroyer of ideas. He or she lacks warmth, but is rarely wrong.

Company worker Such a person is stable, controlled, and a practical organizer. He or she is adaptable. His or her greatest asset is that people ask him or her where the team is in relation to issues being discussed.

Resource investigator Such a person is a dominant, friendly, relaxed extrovert, probably the most popular member of the team. He or she brings outside resources and keeps in touch with reality.

Team worker Such a person is a stable, sensitive extrovert, concerned with people and their needs. He or she is loyal to the team and avoids confrontation.

Completor/finisher Such a person is anxious, an introvert, and ill-at-ease until all the details are worked out. He or she follows through on decisions taken, but is fussy about the details.

Belbin has also developed instruments to identify these team roles. The results have been used in selection, placement, formation of teams, diagnosis of teams, and improving of team effectiveness. In India, the RPG Group used Belbin's approach with success.

Margerison and McCann (1990) have identified key potential team roles for different team members.[6] One member can play more than one team role. The members play these roles according to their preferences and skills. The team can also identify people with the relevant skills and encourage them to take on the roles that fit. The nine team roles they suggested are as follows:

Creator Initiates creative ideas

Promoter Champions ideas after they are initiated

Assessor Offers insightful analysis of options

Organizer Provides structure

Producer Provides direction and follow-through

Controller Examines details and enforces rules

Maintainer Fights external battles

Adviser Encourages the search for more information

Linker Coordinates and integrates

Pradip Khandwalla, who has done pioneering studies on the turnaround of organizations, concludes that 'the Great Person model of turnaround maker has to be replaced by the growing Great Team model of turnaround facilitation'.[7] The following caselet illustrates how teams can be used in turning around an organization.

Turnaround Through Teams

Lakhanpal National Limited is a Japanese joint venture operating in India, producing and marketing the well-known Novino batteries. In 1990, the company launched the Human 21 campaign of innovation to 'double performance' by 1993. The campaign was designed by Matsushita Electric, one of the owners of Lakhanpal. A company brochure described Human 21 as a campaign to use all the potential energies within the staff in a visible and pronounced manner so that the company could be fully ready to meet the challenges of the twenty-first century. Each department or section undertook to double the performance in its work area by 1993.

Seventy-two sub-themes were identified and teams were formed to pursue each one of these. Some of the sub-themes were the formulation of a system for improving the health of the employees; reduction of the rejection of good cells by 50 per cent;

reduction of the parts section manpower by 50 per cent; reduction of falling of battery jackets on the floor by 50 per cent; achievement of zero ageing of a particular type of battery; cutting of water consumption by 50 per cent; reduction of total inventory level by 50 per cent; doubling of computer utilisation; reduction of the import of spares by half; halving of electrical breakdown time loss; increase of output of a battery by 70 per cent without increase in manpower; improvement in working area and working conditions 'two-fold'; reduction of telephone expenses by 50 per cent; beautification of the reception area; lifetime employment and career development plans for employees; doubling of sales to institutions and doubling of sales volume in various states; preparation of consolidated sales reports by the 5th of each month instead of the 10th; having the annual general meeting of the company within 3 months of year end instead of six; reducing the manual workload in preparing accounts by 50 per cent through computerisation; preparing costing data within 20 days of the quarter ending instead of 40; implementing systematic job rotation; doubling the productivity of every manufacturing section; and reducing electrical machinery breakdowns by 50 per cent through better plant maintenance.

Notice the large range of areas where drastic improvement was sought. Notice also the mundane, down-to-earth nature of the teams themselves: production, loading of finished goods, maintenance, preparation of accounts and reports, wastage, etc., not image, goodwill, professionalisation, morale, technological excellence, marketing excellence, or other such abstract areas of management. The strategy was to achieve large improvements through team effort in various specific areas of operations. The strategy also seemed to be one of forcing innovation by overloading. It is obvious that without innovation in every tangible area of operation, doubling performance in 3 years would be an empty slogan.

TEAM EFFECTIVENESS

McGregor and Likert, who drew attention to the importance of teams in the 1960s, listed a large number of characteristics of effective work-groups or teams. Dyer[8] summarised 11 characteristics of an effective work team as suggested by McGregor and 24 characteristics of an effective work-group as suggested by Likert. Exhibit 18.3 lists the 10 main characteristics of effective teams, covering suggestions given by both McGregor and Likert. The numbers in the exhibit refer to the serial number of the suggestions by Dyer.

Several types of teams function in an organization. The most common are the teams composed of individuals who are assigned a particular task to be completed in a given time. These are natural teams of which the organization is composed. These may be departmental teams or teams set up especially to complete some tasks. Special teams that are constituted to work on certain assignments to be completed within a time period are called task forces. Continuing groups, or those that are set up for a particular period of time to deal with certain issues, are generally called committees. Special teams may also be constituted to complete a particular task, for example, project teams. Attention needs to be given to make all such teams effective in accomplishing their goals.

Exhibit 18.3 *Characteristics of Effective Work Teams*

Characteristics	McGregor	Likert
Commitment and inspiring goals		8, 12, 13
Role clarity	3, 9	23
Self-disclosure (including confrontation)	5, 7, 8, 11	17
Openness to feedback	4	18, 19
Competence		1
Creativity with constructive confrontation		15, 16
Collaboration/support/trust	1	2, 4, 9, 14
Congruence between individual and group goals		3, 5, 6, 7, 11
Supportive leadership		10, 24
Management of power	2, 6, 10	20, 21, 22

In addition to discrete work teams and other teams in the organization, attention also needs to be paid to the working of two or more teams together. These may be cross-functional, inter-departmental, or inter-level teams. Interteam functioning is increasing in most organizations.

Team effectiveness can be considered from several angles. To use the Johari Window concept (see Chapter 9), an effective team is one in which people give their opinions and comments without hesitation, listen to others, and examine others' opinions, comments, and feedback irrespective of hierarchy, and are sensitive to the needs of others (perceptiveness). An instrument measuring effectiveness from this point of view is available.[9]

Team effectiveness can also be understood in terms of team functioning and team empowerment. There are three main characteristics of team functioning: cohesion (among members of the team), confrontation, that is, solving problems as they arise rather than shying away from them, and collaboration, that is, working together and giving to and receiving help from each other. The four main characteristics of team empowerment are clarity of roles for different members of the team, autonomy of the team, support provided to the team in terms of resources, and accountability of the team for achieving the goals to which a commitment has been made. The author[10] has developed an instrument to measure team effectiveness using this concept.

Team building

The process of making teams effective is called team building. There are several approaches to team building, depending on the kind of conceptual framework we use. Some of the approaches are as follows:

Johari Window approach According to this approach, team building involves helping individuals to take risks and frankly express their opinions and reactions, helping them to accept feedback from others with enough opportunities to explore the issues raised further, and increasing their sensitivity to and perceptiveness of others' needs and orientations. This can be done by developing a team profile based on individual members' responses to an instrument e.g., the instrument suggested by the author.[11]

Role negotiation approach   Team building can be done by using role negotiation.[12] Members of the team share each others' images, then list expectations of what they would like the others in the group to continue to do, stop doing, or reduce, and then decide which effective things to start or increase doing to make the group more effective. Based on such expectations, negotiation between two teams can be used to develop more and more collaboration.

A similar concept, using the Indian cultural context, has been proposed as role contribution. Details about role negotiation and role contributions can be seen elsewhere.[13] Role negotiation has also been summarised in Chapter 26 in this volume.

Team roles approach   As already mentioned, Belbin suggested eight 'team roles' that people take (chairman/coordinator, shaper, plant, monitor/evaluator, company worker, resource investigator, team worker, completor/finisher). Team building can be done by setting up effective teams and developing teams.[14]

Behaviour modification approach   Team building can also be done by helping people to become more effective in their individual orientations. Collaboration depends on the individual's orientation styles and attitudes. According to this approach, some instruments[15] are used to help individuals examine their styles and orientation and then increase their own effectiveness by modifying their behaviour. This is seen as an important way to enhance individuals' potential for collaboration and team building. Using the concept of power, as already suggested, an instrument[16] can be used to help team members examine their bases of power and plan to increase their persuasive power.

Simulation approach   Team building can be attempted by creating artificial teams in which people have an opportunity to experiment and learn from their behaviour in a less threatening context. Various games or exercises are used for this purpose, like Broken Squares, Hollow Square, Win as Much as You Can, Maximising Your Gains[17] for the use of such games in team building.) After people participate in such games, they also discuss how similar dynamics operate in their home situations and how they can use their lessons from the simulations to make their own teams effective.

Action research approach   In this approach, team building is done through several steps that are generally taken in action research or organization development. Dyer used this approach in his elaborate discussion of team building through five stages: data strengthening, data analysis, action planning, implementation, and evaluation.[18] In this approach, diagnosis is done on the basis of questionnaires, interviews, or observations.

Appreciative inquiry approach In this approach, there is more emphasis on the positive aspects, including inspiring future dreams and appreciating positive qualities in each other. Appreciative inquiry[19] has become quite popular as a method of increasing collaboration among people for building strong teams. We have already discussed this approach in Chapter 4.

Combining the above approaches, the following steps are suggested for team-building:

Projection into future The team may prepare a common vision of its desirable future. Members, individually or in small groups, may prepare a picture of their team as they see it in the next 5 or 7 years. A specific future scenario will help to inspire individuals to move towards it. The future is a better diagnostic device than an analysis of the past.

Linkage with individual goals The visions of the team's future should be linked with the individuals' aspirations and goals. Individuals may discuss in small groups how their own aspirations and goals in life can be achieved through the ideal of the team's future developed by the group.

Forcefield analysis The team may identify the forces that are positive and are helping the team to move towards the desirable future and the forces that are likely to hinder its progress towards that future. Such analysis is helpful in selecting the next step.

Strengthening positive forces The team may explore ways of reinforcing the positive aspects that can help the team achieve its desirable future. They can take each positive force and work out plans to strengthen it further.

Reducing negative forces The team can take up all the restraining or inhibiting forces and can plan specific action steps to reduce, if not eliminate, them.

Monitoring After decisions are taken to work on strengthening positive forces and reducing negative forces, a plan can be prepared to monitor the action being taken. The responsibility of monitoring can be taken up by one or two members and the team may meet from time to time to review the progress.

Whatever approaches are adopted for team building, emphasis should be laid on understanding team effectiveness and taking steps to increase it. Similar steps can be taken for building interteam collaboration. Dyer also discusses ways of dealing with intra-team and interteam conflicts. Team members have the responsibility of making their teams effective.[20] Kormanski and Mozenter have suggested the following characteristics—in a sequential pattern, alternating between task and relationship behaviours[21]—of team members contributing to team effectiveness.

Members of effective teams
- Understand and are committed to group goals
- Are friendly, concerned, and interested in others

- Acknowledge and confront conflict openly
- Listen to others with understanding
- Include others in the decision-making process
- Recognise and respect individual differences
- Contribute ideas and solutions
- Value the ideas and contributions of others
- Recognise and reward team efforts
- Encourage and appreciate comments about team performance

SUMMARY

Most of the work in organizations is done in teams. A team is a group of individuals working in a face-to-face relationship for a common goal. Team development passes through several phases: awareness, conflict, cooperation, productivity, and separation. Different members of the team play various roles to make the team stronger.

Various factors contribute to effectiveness of teams: inspiring goals, goal clarity, confronting problems, openness to feedback, competence, trust, supportive leadership, and management of power to ensure its equitable distribution.

Several approaches are used to build teams, including role negotiation, behaviour modification through simulation exercises, and action research (such as appreciative inquiry). Forcefield analysis can be used to identify supportive and hindering factors for team building and then action can be planned to reduce/eliminate hindering forces and to strenghten supportive forces.

GLOSSARY

group   a collection of individuals working in a face-to-face relationship to share information and resources for a task to be achieved

team   a group of individuals working in a face-to-face relationship for a common goal, having collective accountability for the outcome of its efforts

team building   the process of making teams effective

team roles   process roles that team members play

trust   belief that there is a high probability that the power of the concerned party or individual will not be used in a malevolent way

EXERCISES

Concept Review Questions

1. What is the difference between a group and a team?
2. What are the stages of team formation?
3. Enumerate some team roles and describe their characteristics.
4. How do you measure team effectiveness?
5. How can we make a team more effective?

Critical Thinking Questions

Think of a team of which you are a part. Rate your team/group on the following items:

Key

Write 4 if this is highly characteristic of the group and/or this always happens.

Write 3 if this is fairly characteristic of the group and/or this frequently happens.

Write 2 if this is slightly characteristic of this group and/or this happens sometimes.

Write 1 if this is hardly true about this group and/or this happens occasionally.

Write 0 if this is not at all true about the group and/or it almost never happens.

_____ 1. The goals of this team are well defined.

_____ 2. Members of this team generally feel that their concerns and views are ignored by the other members.

_____ 3. The team has enough freedom to decide on its way of working.

_____ 4. Members generally avoid discussing the problems facing the team.

_____ 5. The team is given adequate resources to carry out its functions.

_____ 6. Members do not volunteer to help others and to take responsibility.

_____ 7. The sense of responsibility and accountability is high among the team members.

Scoring

First reverse scores of items 2, 4, and 6 (4 becomes 0 and 0 becomes 4; 3 becomes 1 and 1 becomes 3; 2 remains unchanged). Then write down the ratings against the seven items in the table below. Add the ratings under two aspects of team functioning and team effectiveness.

Team functioning		Team empowerment	
Items	**Score**	**Items**	**Score**
2. Cohesion	_____	1. Task clarity	_____
4. Confrontation	_____	3. Autonomy	_____
6. Collaboration	_____	5. Support	_____
		7. Accountability	_____
Total	_____	Total	_____

The total score of team functioning will range from 0 to 12. If your score is 7 or below, regard it as low. The total score on team empowerment ranges from 6 to 16. Any score below 9 may be regarded as low. Reflect on your scores and write down a few suggestions for increasing the effectiveness of your team.

Classroom Projects

1. In small groups of two or three, identify one team in your institution or organization that you know fairly well (preferably a member of that team). Trace the process and various stages of its formation. How close is your account of the process to the stages suggested in this chapter?

2. Analyse in small groups of 2 or 3 the evolution of the *Lagaan* cricket team. (Lagaan is a Hindi film.) Share your findings in the total class.

Field Projects

1. Interview the members of any team you know in an organization to find out how different members take on different roles.

2. Discuss with two members of a work team the factors that help in making the team effective and those that hinder its effectiveness.

Turnaround Through Teamwork[*]

BACKGROUND

Bank of Baroda (BoB) ranked among the first four nationalised banks in branch network, deposits, advances, and profits. It distinguished itself in banking innovations and advancements. BoB's branches in the Madhya Pradesh state were classified under the MP zone in 1994. The MP zone was the smallest of the 14 zones of the bank in branch network, business size, and profits. It had 82 branches distributed in the two regions of Bhopal and Raipur.

Not many medium and large industrial units existed in the zone. Banking business was predominantly lending to the farm sector and small industries, trading, and raising deposits from the public and from government and semi-government corporations.

The State Bank of India and the Central Bank of India, which was the lead bank in MP, enjoyed premium position in MP. BoB operated in only one leading district in the zone.

The bank had two workmen unions—the All India Bank of Baroda Employees Federation and the All India Bank of Baroda Employees Coordination Committee. In 1973, the bank recognised the All India Bank of Baroda Employees Federation as the sole collective bargaining agent of workmen. The bank also signed a settlement with the All India Bank of Baroda Employees Coordination Committee. The management consulted the coordination committee on all-India issues but reached agreement only with the recognised union. The coordination committee thus mainly represented its members on local issues and disputes.

The arrangement worked well at the corporate level. At zonal, regional, and branch levels, both the unions operated as full-fledged representative bodies because down the line, both were concerned with local issues.

The recognised union was affiliated to the National Congress of Bank Employees. Let us call it Union I. The coordination committee was affiliated to the All India Bank Employees' Association (AIBEA), a constituent of the All India Trade Union Congress (AITUC). Let us call it Union II. As regards the officers, the All India Bank of Baroda Officers Association, formed in September 1964, recognised by the bank, was affiliated to the Indian National Bank Officers Congress (INBOC), banking wing of the Indian National Trade Union Congress (INTUC). Both the unions and the association were active in the MP zone. The usual rivalry between the unions existed.

---

[*]Written by K.K. Verma, currently director, Academy of Human Resource Development, Ahmedabad. Reproduced abridged version with permission.

They tried to attract each other's members and to outbid the other in resolving grievances.

Trigger

Early in August 1995, a new zonal manager took charge of the MP zone. This was to be his first hard-core banking assignment—till recently he had been in human resources development.

The bank's MP zone productivity and profitability was much below the bank's all-India average. The business per employee (deposits + advances) in MP in 1995 was 5.77 million rupees against the bank's all-India 8.17 million rupees. While the zonal cost of deposits at 7.13 per cent was comparable with that of the bank's overall 7.31 per cent, the yield on advances was 9.93 per cent against 13.15 per cent. Profit to average business was extremely low at 1.49 per cent against the bank's overall 2.13 per cent. Although the zone had performed better in the year ending March 1995, its performance declined in subsequent months. In July 1995, its deposits stood at 4659.7 million rupees against 4888.7 million rupees as of March 1995, and advances were stagnant at 2,890 million rupees against 2,854 million rupees in March 1995.

Within 15 days of taking charge, the new zonal manager wrote to the branch managers. He pointed out the bright economic growth potentials of the state and the bank's excellent business opportunities. He encouraged the staff to discover their 'tremendous hidden abilities' and to participate in the growth of MP through the bank's achievements. He shared his immediate concerns—half-yearly business targets, mobilising low-cost deposits, reducing cost, and improving health of advances; stressed the need for tackling these concerns; and assured the necessary support/guidance from his office.

He also shared his assessment about the potentials of the staff. He observed, 'People in the zone are sincere and dedicated. They are quite hard working, positive in their approach, and have tremendous hidden abilities. They could be conspicuous winners.'

The zonal manager shared his optimism that the zone's productivity and profitability would go up steeply if the employees and management took up the challenge. He concluded indicating his sense of urgency and open-door policy for people to write to him or meet him.

The letter was received positively and set the tone for better management–employee relations. Some employees took the initiative to discuss the issues concerning the zone and referred to the letter.

The management–union interaction also began on a positive note. The union leaders, as a ritual, greeted the new chief with flowers and offered their co-operation. The two unions and the association leaders expressed that 'we have a culture of cooperation', or 'we shall offer co-operation', or 'we always co-operate'.

The zonal manager and the personnel head of the zone urged them to translate words into actions for better business results and exciting experience at the workplace. Both pointed out that if the unions/association collaborated, the zone's potential could be realised. They directed the discussion to arouse their emotional belonging to the MP state.

The general secretary of the association enquired whether the management had a definite proposal. The Union I leader reminded him of how the union fostered a culture of co-operation in the past. The discussions moved towards initiating action steps.

CORPORATE AGENDA

In August 1995, the Reserve Bank of India fixed deadlines for all banks for clearing housekeeping arrears and prescribed grave penalties for non-compliance. BoB was in a serious housekeeping situation.

BoB's corporate office advised the zones to hold meetings with unions/association on regular basis up to March 1996 for clearing the arrears and reconciliation of pending accounts. Consequently, a joint meeting was called on 20 September 1995. This was the first occasion in MP that the two unions and the association sat together with the management representatives to discuss a business-related issue.

Initiative for Larger Agenda

The zonal committee of the bank included the two regional managers and senior executives of the zone. The committee discussed whether collaboration of the unions/association be sought for business development as the zone's business was below the previous year's levels (see March and July 1995 business figures quoted earlier). The personnel and planning heads were enthusiastic about the proposal. They argued that if the unions/association could collaborate in housekeeping, they could as well participate in business development. The regional managers and the credit head supported the idea but were not keen. They apprehended resistance from the unions and cautioned lest the agenda of housekeeping also suffered. Finally, it was decided to test the response of the unions/association in the meeting convened for the housekeeping agenda.

In the meeting, the zonal manager expressed his faith in the philosophy of participation and complimented the corporate office and the apex level unions/association for their initiatives. He hoped that the two unions/association would participate vigorously in bringing housekeeping under control.

All facts and figures relating to the zone's housekeeping and reconciliation of accounts, along with business targets for 1995–96 and actual performance levels reached so far were placed before members in the meeting held on 20 September 1995. The presentation stressed that a larger framework involving business performance of the zone was provided for a general feedback on performance.

Leaders of the unions/association appreciated the zonal manager's faith in participative management. They were happy for being approached for solving the housekeeping problems. They tried to understand the data. They confessed that they were under the wrong impression that the zone was doing well. All the leaders made several suggestions.

The Union I leader emphasised that reconciliation involved hard work for which arrangements should be made. 'Housekeeping is like the central nervous system of a bank and must be completed without leaving arrears behind' observed the association chief. The management representatives urged upon the leaders of the unions to communicate to their members about how far they were concerned about the commitments they were making. (The word 'commitment' was used in regard to their willingness for endeavour.)

Unions' Suggestions and Action Plan

The suggestions from the unions included the following:

- The bank should inform periodically the housekeeping position to the branch staff.
- Focus should be on improving customer service.
- The bank should dispose off the pending staff grievances.

Their suggestions were accepted. The suggestion on customer service was highly appreciated, as there was tremendous room for improvement. The action plan evolved included that the large branches should hold similar management-unions-association meetings at their end. One union suggested that large branches should identify officers and clerks who had aptitude for housekeeping and reconciliation work for assigning responsibility accordingly. It pointed out that the mundane housekeeping work required desk-oriented workers. It was also decided to set deadlines for completion of work.

A draft circular on action plan was informally cleared by the three leaders. Mentioning the intense interactions with the unions/association that led to the action programme, the circular urged the branch managers to take similar measures at their end. The circular accelerated the interaction in many branches, and conducive atmosphere started unfolding in the zone.

The leaders of the unions/association visited several branches and discussed the subject in very cordial atmosphere. A few branch managers reported that the leaders made courtesy calls on them and informally discussed housekeeping issues. In a few branches, the union representatives briefed their members about the importance of the housekeeping programme. A participative atmosphere started developing in the zone.

MANAGING PASSIVE PARTICIPATION

BoB managers were accustomed to command and control. Many of them, therefore, were not comfortable with the idea of the union participation in business matters, and their participation, even of some senior managers including the regional managers, was passive. The leaders of the unions/association preferred not to react to such managers. The zonal manager preferred not to persuade them. His assumption was that the process the passive managers were going through in this activity itself would promote the trust in joint activity. However, countervailing forces were the planning department and, to some extent, the personnel department. They thought that the new process would enlarge the performance base in the zone and solve many problems like housekeeping arrears and employee grievances.

The second meeting on 30 October moved the process of collaboration unexpectedly fast. The branch managers of 18 most potential branches and the chiefs of the unions/association had been invited. This meeting burst the bubble of passivity as the determination with which the invited branch managers demanded discipline and genuine co-operation from the unions/association set the tone to shed off apprehensions and to decide on concrete steps.

The housekeeping position and business performance for the half-year ending September 1995 were discussed.

The performance for September 1995 was dismal. Although the zone's profit growth was satisfactory, all present at the meeting expressed that the half-year performance was bad and lopsided. The performance of the 18 branches represented in this meeting was also not satisfactory.

Causes of Poor Performance

The following causes were identified for unsatisfactory performance:

1. Staff were confined to deskwork rather than doing aggressive marketing. Walk-in business gave negligible growth.
2. Branch managers were not holding group meetings on business development and housekeeping.
3. Staff involvement was not as per the expectation of the branch managers. A vast majority of staff felt that it was the branch manager's responsibility to mobilise deposits, improve recovery, manage non-productive assets (NPA), housekeeping, etc.
4. Competition was mounting, particularly in big cities like Indore. Private banks like IDBI posed a big threat.
5. The practice of sitting late and working hard was given up. Neither the officers nor the staff stayed back to complete work.
6. The tight market conditions affected the growth of the entire banking industry. Money supply had slowed down, so had industrial growth, deposit growth, and the lending support.
7. Due to complacency, the chief manager-level branches failed to set the trend expected of them.
8. The branch managers were unable to channelise staff co-operation effectively. Guidance was needed from the higher echelons in the zone.
9. The branch premises were not neat and clean. Broken furniture was left lying here and there.
10. Customer service needed improvement.

Both the union/association leaders and the branch managers identified these as the most important causes. It was analysed that these causes had varied effects on performance and that only the joint working of management and unions/association could have a positive impact. It was decided to formulate a strategy to overcome the weaknesses as soon as possible.

Confrontation Strengthened Cooperation

The unions/association offered unequivocal co-operation. The general secretary of the association cited his circular issued to officers. The general secretary of Union II referred to his recent circular issued after the first joint discussions on 20 September 1995.

One chief manager questioned all the three leaders about the co-operation they were talking about. He asked them to visit his branch and find for themselves the number of accounts opened by the staff under the staff incentive scheme of the bank. Because he had been a union leader two decades ago, when he made such scathing remarks, many other branch managers talked in the same vein. The association's general secretary replied that late sitting should not be expected regularly as many urban branches were computerised. While some managers felt that the situation was going out of control, the chief manager vehemently repeated: 'Sky is the limit as regards co-operation in business development.' 'Sky is the limit' became the slogan for the day. It finally clinched a consensus that the chiefs of the unions/association would visit the branches.

A short-term strategy was evolved for a joint visit to the six branches of Indore. Over the past few years, the bank was losing its market share in Indore, the financial capital of MP. It was felt that the turnaround of branches in Indore would have a multiplier effect on the zone's business. Chief managers headed four of the city's six branches. It was decided that the joint team would visit other important branches also during the financial year. The regional manager of Raipur hoped that the team would visit Indore branches early so that it could visit his region's branches thereafter.

The confrontation affected the regional managers and others who were passive. They saw the gates of co-operation opening up and greater clarity and direction of collaboration emerging. Apprehension that the unions would not respond favourably to business issues began clearing.

JOINT DECLARATION

Since the response of the unions, the association, and managers was evidently becoming positive, the zonal manager raised the issue of jointly signed letters, suggested earlier at the 20 September meeting. This time the leaders of the unions/association agreed to sign the letters along with the zonal manager. It was agreed that such letters be sent not only to the branch managers, but also to all employees. The first joint declaration letter was released the same day, i.e., on 30 October 1995.

Objectives for Branch Intervention

As a matter of BoB's culture and as a democratic right, representatives of the unions/ association met the branch management as per a laid-down procedure called 'structured meetings' to discuss staff grievances. It was, therefore, discussed and clarified right from the beginning to the unions/association that the joint intervention was not a grievance redressal activity. It was spelt out, though without any formal agreement, that the joint forum stood for tackling housekeeping arrears, reconciliation of accounts, and business development. The objective was to build the focus jointly on various business aspects so that the zone's vibrancy and synergy would improve. The branch intervention was specifically aimed at the zonal-level chiefs of unions/association and regional managers to facilitate branch staff and branch managers to sit together regularly to deliberate upon business growth problems by analysing performance gaps and initiate actions to involve more and more staff in the business development process.

MEGA GET-TOGETHER

Besides the formal joint forum meetings, the regional managers and union/association leaders began informally interacting. For the branch interventions in Indore (which had been discussed in the 30 October meeting), they decided to increase the awareness among the staff before starting the visits. They organized a mega get-together in November in Indore and invited the staff of all the Indore branches.

Over 200 staff gathered one evening. Union/association leaders and the regional manager talked of teamwork, togetherness, and joint business actions. The causes of poor business performance were spelt out. Extracts from the minutes of the joint forum meeting about intervention in Indore branches were read out. The regional managers and union/association leaders appealed for taking up the staff incentive scheme actively and clearing the backlog of housekeeping and reconciliation.

Many officers and clerks applauded the idea of joint activity in business areas. However, there was one stray case of a clerk expressing displeasure over his union exhorting employees for canvassing business. His union leader explained to him the challenge of the time right on the spot. It appeared that the joint declaration letter of 30 October 1995 was largely well perceived.

Message of Joint Declaration

These letters were bilingual (Hindi and English), were signed by the zonal manager and the chiefs of the unions/association, and were given to each staff member—messenger to manager. The first letter referred to the decision to issue circulars jointly, to the unsatisfactory half-yearly performance, and to the concerns on which the management, unions, and association were agreed upon. It advocated group-oriented endeavour and urged the branch manager and the staff for making 'conscious effort in creating team spirit and each staff should respond to these efforts'.

The subsequent letters focussed on the need for strategic planning, admitted performance problems, and pointed out the need to popularise staff incentive schemes for deposit mobilisation, announced for the first time that the chiefs of the unions/association and the regional manager would jointly visit Indore branches to 'help out branches at Indore in accelerating their efforts in the areas of concern'.

The letters highlighted customer service as the mechanism for survival and the bank's goal as fulfilment of the customer's expectation by all, promising that the management would facilitate self-development through training; thanked all staff for high performance, acknowledging gains of joint effort, and highlighting the learning of new concept of managing through employees' involvement in work. Management exhorted the staff to sustain the achieving trend.

Impact on Work Processes

Joint declaration messages had deep impact on the managers and members of the unions/association. Rank and file read the joint messages with great interest and enthusiasm. Receptivity to the messages came about due to the joint nature of the effort.

The general secretaries of the unions/association went from branch to branch. Other office-bearers also joined the visits. The process encouraged the staff towards greater care of customers and business. They used their contacts and neighbourhood and family relations for new accounts. Even peons and messengers went for loan recovery from small borrowers.

Inter-union rivalry began waning. In banks there had often been an intense war of circulars; each union claimed benefits it obtained for its members; and each union criticised the branch managers of favouritism towards rivals and discrimination against its own members. But now, all such complaints, fights, and noises were on the wane. Unproductive overt outbursts and attacks and claims of victories were conspicuous by absence.

The two unions started agreeing with each other on business issues. An interesting case was the transfer of a clerk who was a member of Union I. He had requested the management, through the proper channel, for a transfer to Bhopal from Khandwa branch. His widowed mother was undergoing treatment for a broken hip. Normally such transfers were done in BoB strictly on the applicant's seniority. The clerk was well-connected with a few ministers and bureaucrats in the government. The regional manager wanted the clerk to be transferred to Bhopal so that his contacts could be tapped for business development. The transfer proposal was informally put up to the two union leaders strictly as a good business proposition. Transferring the clerk meant bypassing six other applicants who belonged to Union II. The general secretary of Union II asked the other general secretary of Union I about his views on the transfer. The general secretary of Union I asked him what he would tell his members when they complained of being bypassed by this applicant. He replied, 'Had the management unilaterally effected the transfer, we would have at the most protested. Now at least we have been consulted and that is what we can tell our members.' This pro-business reaction by the two unions was a total change in the attitude and thinking of the union leaders.

Impact on Business Performance

Involving employees in defining business issues, contributing to decisions, strengthening communication about those issues, and promoting team spirit resulted in higher business growth and profits. The deposit growth of the zone was substantially better than the growth rate recorded by the bank; the performance of the zone in subsequent years was further improved. The growth in deposits of branches headed by chief managers, which had been declining or stagnant in previous years, was very much satisfactory after a long time, recording 17.29 per cent growth. A laggard zone catching up with the bank's growth rate within a year was excellent performance. In subsequent years, advances in growth rate were stable and substantial. Profitability and productivity ratios also improved. Profit was 142.9 million rupees, a rise of 38.4 million rupees over the previous year. The business per employee rose from 5.77 million rupees per employee to 6.44 million rupees per employee. The per employee incremental business rise in the zone in 1995–96 was by 0.67 million rupees, while for the bank as a whole it was by 0.52 million rupees. The balancing of books improved. Only one branch was in arrears for the 3-months category. In short, there was remarkable all-round business growth during 1995–96 in the MP zone. The same growth rates were maintained or improved upon in subsequent years.

FEEDBACK FROM OUTSIDE

What was going on in the MP zone of BoB came to the notice of the corporate management and the apex-level unions/association. In a letter to the zonal manager, the chairman and managing director of the bank appreciated the support extended by the unions/association. The all-India general secretary, officers association, in his letter of 29 November 1995 to the zonal manager, said: 'It is indeed a commendable initiative taken by you to enthuse involvement of all staff members at grass-roots level.' He suggested that regional managers should encourage branch managers and should have sustained communication with them and the staff members down the line. The all-India general secretary of Union I, who was also workman-director, expressed his views in a business development meeting with the local branch managers and the union representatives from the MP zone. In this meeting of 27 January 1996, he stated that the involvement of his union in business matters was a non-conventional union role. He expressed his confidence that 'the members are quite competent to achieve the corporate goals of our bank if they are given opportunities to work in this direction.' He exhorted that 'managers can freely discuss with his members and mutual/voluntary targets can be fixed for the staff members particularly for deposit mobilisation and NPA recovery.' The interest that the general secretary showed removed the apprehensions aired by some union members about participation in business development. The general secretary of Union II invited the zonal manager and some local branch managers to the foundation day celebrations of the union on 20 April 1996. Several people expressed solidarity with the working class, the union objectives, and the union mission. The general secretary referred to the joint forum of BoB and how a collaborative culture was developing. His remarks attracted some discussion. It was heartening that such business-oriented ideas came from a union leader who once upon a time was a fundamentalist. Probably, this was the outcome of the joint forum.

PROBLEM SOLVING

But all was not smooth. After three successful branch interventions at the Indore branches, Union II created a commotion at a meeting, alleging that a large number of employee grievances were pending at the branch and the chief manager was doing nothing about them. An emergency grievance redressal meeting between Union II and the branch manager guided by the zonal chief of personnel was held, and all the pending issues were solved. (There were no pending grievances of Union I at this branch.) This episode delayed branch meetings in Indore by 10 days. The branch resumed the joint meeting after the grievances were redressed. The Indore branches actively organized staff meetings, and consequently accelerated the collaboration climate in other branches. The discussions were healthy and productive, and a daily schedule was worked out for the staff and officers to go out for canvassing business.

The participative process continued and become more intense. The financial year had come to a close. Employee participation had contributed to excellent results in the zone, and the employees and the unions/association deserved felicitations. Amid this backdrop, a letter from the general secretary of Union I was received, in which he proposed to disassociate from the joint meetings to be held in future and requested to be invited for such meetings separately because of 'being the recognised union of this esteemed bank'. Either the members of the Union I had not liked the general secretary exhorting them to be disciplined, punctual, do whole day's work, and do extra work beyond the departmental work, or Union I wanted special attention and status in the joint forum. Both the possible causes were discussed with the general secretaries of the Union II/association. There was a consensus that without Union I, the forum would collapse.

A deputation comprising the zonal manager and the joint forum members went to the Union I office. It enquired into the cause for the withdrawal and persuaded the general secretary of Union I to open up and give an assessment of the working of the joint forum. The general secretary of Union I expressed satisfaction with the working of the forum and said that the results were encouraging and desirable. He agreed that the number of staff promoted to higher posts during the current year was more than that of the previous years due to the better performance and image of the zone. The deputation pleaded with the general secretary for over 3 hours. They argued that for the sake of progress of the MP zone and for the prosperity and happiness of the staff of the zone they should work together. They implored that if the forum failed and the zone suffered, the blame would lie on the general secretary of the recognised union and no one else. Thus, the general secretary of Union I was not only under heavy pressure from the deputation, but also from his own colleagues, who were nodding and signalling to him to be considerate. He said that the reason for the withdrawal was non-attendance of the grievances of his staff members, and his members criticising him for the same. The zonal manager promised that redressing grievances would be given top priority and that he would organise seminars for his branch managers to sharpen their skills for quicker disposal of grievances. Finally, the general secretary of Union I withdrew his letter and agreed to attend the joint forum meetings. It was decided that the next joint forum meeting would include a small function to celebrate the excellent performance of the zone for the year 1995–96.

MOVING ON

The general secretary of Union I invited the zonal manager for dinner the same evening at a restaurant. Some of his union colleagues also attended.

As it happened, in a few days thereafter, the zonal manager was transferred to the corporate office in Mumbai. The new zonal manager said at a widely attended function that he too believed in participative management and promised to carry forward his predecessor's effort. He focussed his efforts on the same objectives.

Questions for Discussion

1. What triggered the need for team-building intervention?
2. Which factors helped in team building? What was the role of the management behaviour, and the behaviour of the unions and their leaders?
3. What causes setback to collaboration and team building?
4. How was the setback managed in this case?
5. What were the outcomes of team work?

NOTES AND REFERENCES

1. Likert, R. (1961). *New Patterns of Management.* New York: McGraw-Hill.
2. Bennis, W. and H. Shepherd (1956). 'A theory of group development', *Human Relations,* 9:415–437; Bion, W.R. (1961). *Experiences in Groups.* London: Tavistock Publications; Gibb, J.R. (1964). 'Climate for trust formation', in L.P. Bradford, J.R. Gibb, and K.D. Benne (eds), *T-Group Theory and Laboratory Methods.* New York: John Wiley & Sons; Schutz, W.C. (1958). *FIRO: A Three Dimensional Theory of Interpersonal Behavior.* New York: Holt, Raine Hart & Winston; Tuckman, Bruce W. and Mary Ann C. Jensen (1977). 'Stages of small group development revisited', *Group and Organizational Studies,* 2: 419–427.
3. Tuckman, Bruce W. and Mary Ann C. Jensen (1977). 'Stages of small group development revisited', *Group and Organizational Studies,* 2, 419–427.
4. Kormanski, C.L. and A. Mozenter (1987). 'A new model of team building: A new technology of today and tomorrow'. The Annual Conferences: Developing Human Resources. La Jolla, CA: University Associates.
5. Belbin, R.M. (1981). *Management Teams: Why They Succeed or Fail.* London: Butterworth Heinemann.
6. Margerison, Charles and D. McCann (1990). *Team Management.* Chelford, NY: Management Books.
7. Khandwalla, P.N. (1992). *Excellent Corporate Turnaround.* New Delhi: Sage; Khandwalla, P.N. (1992). *Organisational Design for Excellence.* New Delhi: Tata McGraw-Hill.
8. Dyer, William G., W. Gibb Dyer, Jr., Jeffrey H. Dyer, Edgar H. Schein (2005). *Team Building: Proven Strategies for Improving Team Performance.* San Fracisco: Jossey-Bass.
9. Pareek, U. (2002). *Training instruments for HRD & OD,* Chapter 84. New Delhi: Tata McGraw-Hill.
10. *Ibid.,* Chapter 83.

11. *Ibid.*, Chapter 84.
12. Harrison, Roger (1976). 'Role Negotiation: A Tough-Minded Approach to Team Development', *Social Technology of Organization Development.* La Jolla, CA: University Associates.
13. Pareek, Udai (1993b). 'Assessing organisational atmosphere: MAO-A', *TMTC Journal of Management,* 2: 76–86.
14. Pareek, Udai (1993). *Making Organisational Roles Effective.* New Delhi: Tata McGraw-Hill.
15. Pareek, Udai (2002). *Effective Organizations: Beyond Management to Institution Building,* Chapter 36. New Delhi: Oxford & IBH.
16. Pareek, U. (2002). *Training instruments for HRD & OD,* Chapter 29. New Delhi: Tata McGraw-Hill.
17. Rao, V. and Udai Pareek (2006). *Changing Teacher Behaviour Through Feedback.* Hyderabad, India: ICFAI University Press.
18. Dyer, William G., W. Gibb Dyer, Jr., Jeffrey H. Dyer, Edgar H. Schein (2005). *Team Building: Proven Strategies for Improving Team Performance.* San Fracisco: Jossey-Bass.
19. Cooperrider, D.L. and D. Whitney (1999). 'Appreciative inquiry: Collaborating for change', in P. Holman and T. Devane (eds), *The Change Handbook.* San Francisco: Berrett-Koehler.
20. Dyer, et al. *Team Building.*
21. Kormanski, C.and Monzenter, A. (1987). 'A new model of teambuilding: A technology for today and tomorrow'. *The 1987 Annual: Developing Human Resources.* San Diego: University Associates.

19
Conflict Management

LEARNING OBJECTIVES

After studying this chapter, you will be able to
1. Distinguish between functional and dysfunctional conflict
2. Identify sources of conflict
3. Understand the avoidance and approach styles of conflict management
4. Discuss the dysfunctionality of avoidance styles
5. Detail the processes and steps in negotiation as a mode of conflict management

Conflicts are experienced every day by both individuals and groups. Conflict is the perception and/or feeling by one party, individual, or group that the 'other' party is hindering the first party from achieving a goal. Conflicts can be between two or more individuals (interpersonal), between teams or groups (intergroup), or between organizations (inter-organizational). In all these conflicts, the same process is involved: one party wants to achieve a goal (the goal may be to get an idea accepted, to complete a task, to have a close relationship, to serve a cause, or to control resources) and the 'other' party is seen as hindering the first from achieving that goal.

Why does conflict arise? Is conflict always dysfunctional? How can conflicts be prevented? How can conflicts be managed? These are some aspects which will be explored in this chapter.

SOURCES OF CONFLICT

There are several sources of conflict. However, these sources depend on the mode (mindset) of the parties involved in a situation—conflict-escalation mode or conflict-avoidance/resolution mode. Their mutual understanding, trust, and openness determine the mode. The mode influences their perception, which may cause conflict. For example, a difference in the goals of two individuals in a group is a potential source of conflict. One member's goal may be to turn out the maximum number of a product; the goal of the other member may be to ensure quality of the product. Under the conflict-escalation mode, this difference in goals may be seen as conflicting (the person with the goal of quality may see faster production as conflicting with quality and vice versa). Under the conflict-prevention-cum-resolution mode, the different goals may be seen as complementary: the person with quality as his or her goal may see his or her colleague's goal of quantity as useful to ensuring the quality

Exhibit 19.1 *Potential Sources of Conflict and Orientations*

Potential source of conflict	Conflict-escalation mode		Conflict-prevention/resolution mode	
	Perception	Resultant orientation	Perception	Resultant orientation
Concern with self	Narrow (own)	Short-term perspective	Broader	Long-term perspective
Different goals	Conflicting	Individualistic	Complementary	Superordination
Resources	Limited	Fighting	Expandable	Sharing
Power	Limited	Lack of trust	Shareable	Trust
Ideologies	Conflicting	Stereotyping	Varied	Understanding
Varied norms	Undesirable	Intolerance	Useful	Tolerance
Relationship	Dependent	Dominance/ submission	Interdependent	Empathy and cooperation

of the product and vice versa. Exhibit 19.1 shows the seven main sources of interpersonal and intergroup conflicts, possible perceptions of these sources, and the resultant orientation under the conflict-escalation and conflict-prevention-cum-resolution modes.[1]

Members are likely to experience conflict in a group if their main concern is their own interests. They engage in conflict if they have a narrow perspective resulting in a focus on short-term gains. It is ironical that such a narrow perspective may serve their interests only for some time. For example, people in a community wanting to get sufficient water may use high-power boosters if they see that getting sufficient water (when the supply is limited) will conflict with other members also getting water. The group is likely to remain in conflict unless members can broaden their perceptions by working for what Sherif and Sherif called 'superordinate goals'.[2] Superordinate goals are those which are critical for all individuals in a group but cannot be achieved by any one person alone. When they take a long-term view and realise that the interests of all can be served when they work together, they will not be in conflict but search for a solution together.

Often intra- or intergroup conflicts arise from difficulties over the sharing of available resources. Group members perceive the resources as limited and tend to fight over who will receive what. However, if people are able to perceive their resources as expandable, the energy of the members may be spent on efforts to share (and expand) them. Even if resources are not expandable, they can at least be perceived as shareable.

Power, like other resources, is often perceived as limited. For example, in a group, the 'chair' position may be very important and the person who holds it may exercise most of the power and may think that if he or she shares it with others, he or she will be left with less power. Such a view is likely to lead to lack of trust among members, so that conflict results. If the position of chair can be seen as shareable, this can lead to trust among members and can increase everyone's power (ability to make an impact).

If ideologies conflict in a group, stereotyping may result, so that people act out their 'parts' rather than cooperating for the good of the whole. If members of the group can accept that ideologies can be varied and that people can work together in spite of differences, understanding may ensue. Thus, in some families, political or religious ideologies of spouses are different, yet they live harmoniously.

Many groups work towards uniform norms or standards of behaviour, but expectations of uniformity may lead to intolerance of differences. If group members realise early in the life of a group that there are always diverse norms, and that in due course of time some shared norms will evolve, they can learn tolerance and keep differences from causing conflicts that can affect achievement of the group's goals.

One other basic problem, especially in intercultural groups, is the dynamics of hierarchical relationships. Some people are comfortable in dependent roles, while others fight to attain positions of authority. The expectation that others should be dependent often results in conflicts and stereotyped relationships. If relationships are perceived as interdependent (that A depends on B for some things and B depends on A for some other things), people are more likely to have empathy for others and to cooperate for the achievement of a common goal.

This is dramatically brought out in out-bound training. The whole group (from the chairperson to employees at the lowest level, such as helpers) is given the task of, say, climbing a hill. While doing the task, the chairperson, a lean person but not physically strong, may realise that the young, well-built, and strong helper can help him or her to climb a part of the hill. The helper then becomes a resource to the chairperson in the task of climbing.

To summarise, if people in a group perceive their own concerns to be of higher priority, want their own goals met at all costs, fight over available resources, distrust those in power, stereotype those with conflicting ideologies, refuse to tolerate varied norms, and attempt to dominate the group, conflicts will surely escalate. On the other hand, conflict will not arise if group members attempt to see differences as opportunities to prevent or resolve conflicts, consider the broader group concerns, realise that goals can be complementary, subordinate their own goals to team goals, share resources, trust those in power, share the functions of leadership, attempt to understand separate ideologies, tolerate varied norms, and cooperate with and have empathy for others. Conflicts cannot be resolved unless people are willing to take a position that involves some risk.

TYPES OF CONFLICT

Deutsch has suggested five types of basic issues underlying conflicts[3]: control over resources, preferences and nuisances, values, beliefs, and the nature of the relationship between parties. He has suggested the following six types of conflicts involving these issues:

Veridical conflict This type of conflict exists objectively and is perceived accurately. For example, a newly created department B may demand the use of spaces being occupied at present by department A.

Contingent conflict Here the existence of the conflict is dependent upon readily rearranged circumstances, but this is not recognised by the conflicting parties. For example, for the new department B, space can be created by converting vacant and unused space into usable space, but this is not being done.

Displaced conflict Here, the parties in conflict are, so to speak, arguing about the wrong things. For example, the conflict between two departments over the transfer of a person may cover up the real conflict of getting priority from the top management. The former is the manifest and the latter the underlying conflict.

Misattributed conflict In this type, the conflict is between the wrong parties, and, as a consequence, usually over the wrong issues. For example, the inefficiency of a department may be attributed to the individual representing the department even if the individual may be very efficient personally.

Latent conflict This is, in effect, a conflict that should be occurring but is not. For example, the conflict between an exploitative management and workers may not be felt and expressed until the workers are made aware, through political education, of their rights.

False conflict This is the occurrence of conflict when there is no objective basis for it. For example, department A may have a conflict with department B because the former perceives that its share of resources is being usurped by the latter although this may not be true. In a climate of suspicion, false conflicts multiply, based on and fanned by rumours.

ARE CONFLICTS DYSFUNCTIONAL?

Generally, conflicts drain energy from individuals and the team, creating problems in the achievement of organizational goals. However, conflicts are not necessarily dysfunctional. In the next chapter, we shall discuss functional and dysfunctional aspects of conflict (symbolised by Comp+ and Comp–), as well as functional and dysfunctional aspects of collaboration (symbolised as Coop+ and Coop–). For example, competition between two individuals for raising the group's productivity or achieving sales targets is a kind of conflict, but is useful in developing pride, internal performance standards, and an urge to excel.

Some organizations adopt strategies of conflict stimulation, creating functional conflicts leading to improved performance by individuals and groups.[4] So far, most organizations have preferred anti-conflict cultures. 'Such anticonflict cultures may have been tolerable in the past but not in today's fiercely competitive global economy. Those organizations that don't encourage and support dissent may find their survival

Nothing like a good game of tug of war to dissipate feelings of conflict in a fun-filled, harmless way!

threatened.'[5] Robbins has given examples of how some organizations encourage their people to dissent, challenge the system, and generate new ideas.[6]

Hewlett-Packard rewards dissenters and people who continue to have new ideas, even when those ideas are rejected by the management. Herman Miller Inc., an office furniture manufacturer, has a formal system in which employees evaluate and criticise their bosses. Such a formal system encourages dissent and lets subordinates question their bosses with impunity. When a major decision on a merger, acquisition, etc. is taken in Anheuser-Busch, it often assigns teams to make the case for each side of the question. This process frequently results in decisions and alternatives that previously hadn't been considered.

One common ingredient in organizations that successfully create functional conflict is that they reward dissent and punish conflict avoiders. The president of Innovis Interactive Technologies, for instance, fired a top executive who refused to dissent. His explanation: 'He was the ultimate yes-man. In this organization, I can't afford to pay someone to hear my own opinion.'[7]

CONFLICT MANAGEMENT

In the management of conflicts, the styles of those involved in a conflict (either as individuals or as groups, especially group leaders) play a critical role. Some styles may promote a search for solutions whereas others may lead to a deadlock. Conflict management styles are related to the theory or approach used to understand conflicts.

Several approaches to conflict management have been proposed. Two of these are quite well known: one by Likert and Likert[8] and the other by Blake et al.[9] Using the famous grid model of Blake and Mouton, which has proposed five styles of conflict management, showing different degrees of concern for two dimensions, personal goals and the relationship: 1, 1 (low concern for both); 9, 1 (high concern for personal goals and low concern for the relationship); 1, 9 (low concern for personal goals and high concern for the relationship); 9, 9 (high concern for both); and 5, 5 (moderate concern for both).

Pruitt makes a distinction between pressure tactics and exchange-oriented tactics.[10] He has suggested the following exchange-oriented tactics:

1. Make a small unilateral concession together with the clear communication that no further concession will be forthcoming until the adversary concedes. This sometimes starts a sequence of alternating concessions.
2. Propose an exchange of concessions. This is an obvious approach but often involves considerable risk because it is tantamount to making a unilateral concession.
3. Informally signal and show willingness to make a later concession if the adversary makes one now.
4. Seek a private, informal conference with the adversary or his or her representative in which it may be possible to talk more freely and frankly about compromise than in formal negotiation meetings.
5. Propose an exchange of concessions through an intermediary whose statements can be disowned if the adversary is disinterested in the proposal.
6. Propose that a mediator be brought in to help find a mutually acceptable exchange of concessions.

Pruitt has further suggested two ways of resolving differences: bargaining and norm-following. These imply two types of conflict management styles. In bargaining, 'each party endeavours to coerce or lure its adversary into making maximum concessions while conceding as little as possible.'[11] In norm-following, 'both parties attempt to locate and follow rules that are appropriate to the issue in question'.[12] He suggests three kinds of rules in norm-following: content-specific rules, equity rules, and mutual responsiveness ('in which each party makes concessions to the extent that the other party demonstrates its needs for these concessions').

Take the example of conflict between a trade union and the management. The conflict is generally managed through bargaining, both the union and the management attempting to get the best deal while conceding the least to the other party. If the norm-following approach is used, both parties sit down and identify three problem areas: the quality of the product, the differential allowance of overtime in two shifts, and the wage increase. After discussion, they agree that the payment for zero-defect pieces of equipment will be at a particular rate (content-specific rule), that the same rate will be used for overtime irrespective of whether it is the day or night shift (equity rule), and that the wages of those workers will be raised who acquire new skills and pass a trade test after attending part-time classes (mutual responsiveness rule).

The mode of conflict is primarily determined by the perceptions of conflicting parties. As Blake et al. suggest, if conflict is seen as inevitable and a solution is not possible, a situation of helplessness may lead either to a resignation to fate or to a power struggle. However, the outcome will depend mainly upon the perception of the out-group (the 'other' group, as contrasted with 'our' group).

There are two main dimensions to the perception of an out-group. It may be perceived as always opposed to the interests of the in-group and as being belligerent (in which case, in a certain sense the conflict is seen as inevitable) or it may be

Exhibit 19.2   *Conflict Management Styles*

Mode	Perception of Out-group	Style
Avoidance	• Unreasonable • Opposed to our interests and belligerent	Resignation
Avoidance	• Open to reason • Opposed to our interests and belligerent	Withdrawal
Avoidance	• Unreasonable • Having own interests, but interested in peace	Appeasement
Avoidance	• Open to reason • Having own interests, but interested in peace	Defusion
Approach	• Unreasonable • Opposed to our interests and belligerent	Confrontation
Approach	• Open to reason • Opposed to our interests and belligerent	Arbitration
Approach	• Unreasonable • Having own interests, but interested in peace	Compromise
Approach	• Open to reason • Having own interests, but interested in peace	Negotiation

perceived as having its own interests but also as being interested in peace (then the conflict will be perceived as a fact of life but not as inevitable). Similarly, the out-group may be perceived as unreasonable (resulting in lack of hope of any solution) or as open to reason (with a resultant hope of a solution to the problem). The general orientation of a group may be an avoidance orientation or an approach orientation. The avoidance approach dimension is significant in determining the effectiveness of managerial behaviour. Avoidance is characterised by a tendency to deny, rationalise, or avoid the problem; to displace anger or aggression; or to use emotional appeals. The approach orientation is characterised by making efforts to find a solution by one's own efforts or with the help of others. This comes close to what Blake et al. call active–passive mode.

Combining the two aspects, perception of the out-group and the avoidance–approach dimension, we get eight styles or modes of conflict management. These are shown in Exhibit 19.2.

Avoidance Modes

Avoidance modes (or styles) of conflict management aim at avoiding or postponing conflicts in a variety of ways. There are four main avoidance styles:

Resignation   The extreme avoidance mode is fatalistic regarding conflicts, with a sense of helplessness. Conflict is seen as a part of reality, arising out of the unreasonable stand of an out-group, usually seen as hostile.

Another form of resignation is to ignore the conflict. This may even take the form of denying the unpleasant situation in the hope that the conflict will get resolved by itself in due course. Many industries are resigned to recurring conflicts with trade unions and do not attempt to resolve them, hoping that solutions may emerge after a new industrial relations bill is passed by parliament. Or a husband and wife having differences may not sit down to resolve them, taking these to be part of life and, each hoping that the other will 'understand' some day.

Withdrawal Another form of avoidance is to get away from a conflict situation. This may take several forms. The attempt to get away from the conflict may be because the out-group is being seen as belligerent but still open to reason.

One way to get away from conflicts is to avoid situations of potential conflict. This may be done by not leaving any opportunities for the two groups to work together.

A second way may be to withdraw from a conflict when it takes place. The withdrawal may be from the situation or from the relationship with the out-group. For example, when two potential product groups are involved in getting a market share and find themselves in conflict with each other, one may decide to withdraw from marketing that product or may like to withdraw from collaborative work with the out-group.

Physical separation may be a third way to withdraw. This would include using a separate location and separation of all other hitherto common arrangements. When two people in a department fight all the time, the management may decide to transfer one of them to another section, thus ending the conflict by withdrawing one party from the scene of conflict.

A fourth form of withdrawal may be to define the boundaries of interaction with the out-group and make arrangements to limit these.

Some people may use withdrawal as their typical style. For example, whenever there is a difference of opinion between a husband and a wife, leading to an argument, instead of sorting out their differences, one of them may stop arguing and keep quiet (psychological withdrawal) or may leave the house for some time (physical withdrawal). This may be a habitual style for them.

Defusion The main objective of the defusion mode of conflict resolution is to buy time for dealing with a conflict. It may take several forms. When people feel that several emotional issues are involved in a conflict and that emotions are running too strong, they may decide to let the participants 'cool down' before taking up the real issues for resolution. Emotional overtones can be defused in several ways.

One way to defuse strong emotions in a conflict is to hope that, with the passage of time, the emotions will settle down and the groups will be ready to deal with the real issues. A good example of the defusion strategy was the management of conflict in Andhra Pradesh between the Telengana and Andhra regions. When every political party was in favour of a separate statehood for Telengana, the prime minister allowed time to defuse the conflict. Later, the issues were discussed more calmly and solutions were worked out.

Another form of defusion is to appeal to the good sense of both groups, to the sentiment that both are part of a larger group and have common interests, interdependence, mutuality, etc. Such appeals may help to defuse a conflict fraught with emotions.

A third way to defuse a situation is to develop a temporary arrangement of interaction through a third group. This is like creating a buffer to absorb the excess of emotions.

Appeasement   The main objective of appeasement is to buy temporary peace. When a group in conflict with an out-group finds the conflict embarrassing and disturbing, it may agree to some of the demands of the out-group not because it is convinced about them but because it wants to postpone the conflict. It therefore provides some concessions in the hope that the out-group will be satisfied and the conflict will be over.

Appeasement has the same dynamics as payment in a case of blackmail. The out-group gets the message that the group is weak and incapable of confronting issues. As a result of appeasement, not only does the conflict remain unresolved but the demands of the out-group increase, its posturing gets stiffer, and the situation deteriorates further.

Approach Modes

Approach modes (or styles) may take more aggressive or understanding forms by using positive steps to confront conflicts and find solutions. There are four approach modes or styles (see Exhibit 19.2):

Confrontation   When the in-group perceives the out-group to be both opposed to its interests and unreasonable, the mode of confrontation may be adopted. Confrontation is fighting out an issue to get a solution in one's favour. It is often adopted by management or trade unions. It may lead to what Blake et al. call the 'win–lose trap'. They have suggested 10 elements that contribute to this trap:
- The win–lose orientation (hope of a larger share in the gain)
- Closing ranks and increasing cohesion
- Leadership consideration
- Positional contrast (enhancing one's own position and downplaying the adversary's position)
- Attack and counter-attack
- Negative stereotypes concerning the adversary
- Perception of a representative personality
- Intellectual distortions
- Minimising of commonalities and heightening of differences
- Comprehension of one's own proposal being greater than the understanding of the competitor's proposal

The confrontation mode involves coercion and is likely to fail to reach a solution. In a laboratory study of negotiation, it was found that heavy reliance on pressure tactics while bargaining resulted in failure to reach an agreement. Thibaut and Kelley mention three problems associated with pressure tactics: (a) the cost of surveillance over the other party's behaviour when threats are employed, (b) the loss of power that sometimes results from the use of threats, punishments, and rewards, and (c) the unpleasantness of having to capitulate when the other party is unknown.[13]

Long strikes by trade unions is a good example of confrontation. Neither the union nor the management are prepared to negotiate and each try to show their greater strength—the union by striking, which affects production, and the management by trying to employ casual hands to cope with the strike. The confrontation may lead to losses on both sides—loss of wages for the workers and loss of production for the management. If a newly appointed representative of the management decides to put further pressure and continues to confront the union, the latter—not knowing the management's representative—may become more bitter if they have to give in and break the strike.

Compromise   If the out-group is seen as being interested in peace (and hence as reasonable), an attempt may be made to seek a compromise. This is the process of sharing in the gain without resolving the conflict. This may be done by bargaining. Compromise is often used in conflicts between managements and unions. If the management is interested in fulfilling certain export orders, they may agree to increase incentives for a particular period and the union may agree to work for longer hours for that time.

Arbitration   If the out-group is perceived as being belligerent and not interested in peace, and yet not totally unreasonable, arbitration by a third party may be sought to assess the situation objectively and give an 'award' acceptable to both groups. Usually, the conflict remains unresolved—it is only postponed for a time. In many management–union conflicts, arbitration by the labour commissioner is sought.

Negotiation   The most satisfactory solution can emerge only when both groups jointly confront the problem and explore alternative solutions. This mode is called negotiation. It will be discussed in greater detail later in this chapter.

Filley, like Blake et al., calls the functional method of conflict resolution a problem-solving method.[14] According to him, problem-solving methods evoke intellectual intensity rather than emotional intensity or power.

He suggests that the following changes in conditions facilitate movement from power-oriented methods to problem-solving methods. These steps also apply to the discussion of negotiation later in this chapter.

Perceptual tactics

- Identifying the problem in terms of goals rather than solutions
- Identifying the existence of mutually beneficial solutions
- Changing the focus of attention from the other party to the problem
- Identifying the costs of not resolving the problem
- Identifying the costs of self-sacrifice or domination

Affective tactics

- Establishing of positive feelings by each party about themselves and others through clinical or fact-finding methods

- Minimising feelings of anger, threat, or defensiveness by depersonalising the problem and using a neutral language

Situational tactics

- Reducing time pressure
- Providing neutral spatial arrangements
- Increasing proximity and interaction of the parties
- Equalising and ignoring power differences

Processual tactics

- Clarifying communication
- Stating issues in specific rather than general terms
- Defining the problem jointly by the parties
- Making the feedback descriptive
- Separating the process stages of problem identification, solution, generalisation, and evaluation
- Redefining problem statements in terms of needs rather than solutions
- Accepting the process rules of prescribing, forcing, acquiescing, or avoiding behaviour

Walton and McKersie have used the term 'integrative bargaining' for these tactics,[15] which comes closer to what is referred to here as negotiation. In integrative bargaining, new and better options are generated. They have suggested the following approaches for negotiators in order to increase the likelihood that new and better options will be developed:

- State your position in terms of a problem to be solved rather than a solution to be accepted by the adversary.
- Retain your flexibility by not becoming committed to a fixed position.
- Make every effort to understand your adversary's viewpoint.
- Present to your adversary an accurate picture of your own needs and motives so that the other party can think up options that satisfy the needs of both parties.

Negotiation: Towards Conflict Resolution

The negotiation mode of conflict resolution is the most mature of the approach style modes. Negotiation is possible only when the out-group is perceived both as interested in peace and as reasonable. Negotiation involves continuous interaction and dialogue between the groups in order to find a solution with maximum advantages to both. Through negotiation, mutual interests are met and the most satisfactory solution is determined. Negotiation for managing a conflict involves a number of steps. These steps are presented below in a sequence, but this need not be followed strictly.

Unfreezing   Two groups in conflict may be 'frozen' into a stereotypical relationship. Unless the expectations and patterns of the relationship are unfrozen, movements towards negotiation may be impossible. To thaw out the atmosphere, group members can generate images they have of each other and of members of the other group. The ensuing discussion may provide an opportunity for members of both groups to say things that they otherwise would not. Alternatively, members of both groups can be mixed up in order to form new groups to discuss various issues. In this way, people may increase their understanding of each other's perspectives.

Being open Group members may be 'closed' with each other and may need to develop norms of voicing different points of view or alternatives without fear of repercussions. Openness is usually most difficult when the conflict involves critical issues and the atmosphere is emotionally charged, but openness is even more vital at such times.

Learning empathy Group members may see only their own points of view, but can gain empathy for others by sharing their main concerns, apprehensions, or goals. Such sharing may help people to gain new insight into themselves and others.

Searching for common themes Groups involved in a conflict may be helped to search for common goals or other areas of overlap by listing their expectations, apprehensions, perceptions, goals, and so on.

Generating alternatives Once the groups are aware of each other's perspectives, they can generate alternatives for resolving some of the issues. If both groups participate in generating alternatives, they are likely to feel mutually responsible for finding a solution.

Responding to alternatives After alternatives have been generated, members of both groups should study and respond to them. Every effort should be made to see issues in a positive, problem-solving way. Outright rejection of alternatives should be avoided. All proposed alternatives should be discussed by the whole group for clarification and for sharing of concerns.

Searching for a solution A number of alternatives may be explored in depth by small groups made up of members from both negotiating groups. The small groups can reach a consensus on a solution and then report to the larger group. Because points of view from both parties are represented in the new groups, these groups are likely to come up with some innovative possibilities.

Breaking the deadlock Sometimes the conflicting groups may be so emotionally involved that they cannot move towards a solution by themselves. In such cases, a third party who is both objective and experienced in dealing with this type of problem may be brought in.

Committing to the solution within the group After solutions are generated by the smaller 'mixed' groups, these new groups can debate and consider these solutions and commit to some of these. Openness among group members will help genuine commitment. All doubts must be resolved or must be put aside at this point.

Committing the whole group The last phase of conflict resolution is for both negotiating groups to jointly accept a solution and to make a public commitment to implement it. Group members may share the mechanisms they plan to use for following up on the commitments made. Arrangements can also be made at this point for a joint review of any remaining issues at a later time.

Resolving conflict through negotiation involves a continuous effort on everyone's part to build a climate of openness and non-defensiveness. The success of negotiation depends on the efforts made by members of both groups to develop their own group skills. The process of negotiation itself contributes to the development of the group. The process is difficult, but extremely worthwhile.

CONFLICT PREVENTION

Preventing conflict is also a proactive approach (taking action in advance to deal with a few potential causes of conflict). Prevention means anticipating potential causes of conflict and taking quick action to turn them into positive forces for better understanding and cooperation. Two main strategies for prevention of conflicts are suggested.

Everyone concerned in a common task must be involved in order to reduce breeding grounds for conflict. Whenever problems arise, everyone must be involved in finding alternative solutions. Such participation and the resultant sense of shared responsibility for a solution helps prevent conflicts.

The solution reached through participative decision making may be more acceptable and pragmatic than one imposed from above. Representative groups from various levels of an organization can be formed for dealing with grievances, work norms and deviations from them, procedures for employee assessment, performance criteria, etc. before these issues arise in the guise of problems in order to prevent unhealthy conflict.

An emphasis on collaboration and team building also helps to change the potential causes of conflicts into positive cooperation factors. The main emphases of collaboration are on identifying common goals, recognising each other's strengths, and planning strategies for achieving these goals by working together. Team building and interventions for collaboration are discussed in Chapters 18 and 20, respectively.

SUMMARY

Conflicts are a part of life. In fact, some conflicts are useful (functional), contributing to growth and development. Conflicts occur when the concerns are narrow, different goals are seen as conflicting, resources and power are perceived as limited, differences in values and norms are regarded as undesirable, and some individuals or groups are dependent on others. Conflicts can be prevented through the participatory mode of management. There are eight styles of conflict management under two broad categories (four avoidance or dysfunctional, and four approach or functional modes or styles). Negotiation is the most functional mode. Several steps involved in negotiation are described.

GLOSSARY

appeasement providing some concessions in the hope that the out-group will be satisfied and the conflict will be over

arbitration a third party giving an 'award' acceptable to both groups

conflict the perception and/or feeling by one party (individual or group) that the other party is hindering the first party from achieving

confrontation fighting out an issue to get a solution in one's favour

defusion buying time for dealing with a conflict

displaced conflict parties in conflict arguing about the wrong things

false conflict conflict when there is no objective basis for it

latent conflict conflict that should be occurring but is not

misattributed conflict conflict between the wrong parties and, as a consequence, usually over the wrong issues

negotiation continuous interaction and dialogue between groups in order to find a solution with maximum advantages to both

withdrawal getting away from a conflict

EXERCISES

Concept Review Questions

1. Can conflicts be functional or useful? Give an example.
2. What are the sources of conflict and how do these operate under the conflict-escalation and conflict-resolution modes?
3. List the approach and avoidance modes (or styles) of conflict management.
4. How does our perception of the out-group determine which approach or avoidance modes we use?
5. What are the various steps in the process of negotiation?

Critical Thinking Questions

1. What approach do you follow in managing conflicts? We give below eight approaches. Rank them in terms of your own preferences. Give rank 1 to the statement that best describes your approach or style; 2 to the statement that is the next best description of your style or approach, and so on. Thus, the statement that is least true of your style will get a rank of 8.

   (a) Dialogue with the conflicting party on the underlying problem and jointly search for a mutually acceptable solution.
   (b) Work out your best solution for the conflict and fight for its acceptance for implementation.
   (c) In the spirit of give and take, accept some demands made by the other party in exchange for their meeting some of your own.
   (d) Use the help of a third party for arbitration.
   (e) Allow some time to pass, hoping that things will cool down and thus help to solve the problem.
   (f) Provide small concessions to the opposite party.
   (g) Avoid situations that are likely to lead to conflicts.
   (h) Do nothing about the conflict because such attempts usually do not help.

   Scoring

   Go back to the ranks you gave to the eight approaches to conflict management. As you will realise these approaches are

   (a) Negotiation (b) Confrontation (c) Compromise (d) Arbitration
   (e) Defusion   (f) Appeasement   (g) Withdrawal   (h) Resignation

As you see, the first four (a to d) represent the approach mode and the last four (f to h) the avoidance mode. Add your ranks for avoidance and approach strategies. Which total is lower? (The lower the number, the higher is your preference.) What is your rank on the first approach (a)? This is negotiation. How can you strengthen this mode?

2. What style of conflict management do you usually use? Write down the pay-off for that style (both favourable points and points of dysfunctionality).
3. Are you satisfied with your style? If not, what can you do to develop a more functional strategy of managing a conflict?
4. Try out the new strategy (preferably negotiation) next time you are involved in a conflict situation.

Classroom Projects

1. Identify some conflicts you have observed in your group. What was the source of these conflicts? How were these managed? With what consequences?
2. In small groups of two or three, discuss what you will do as a manager to help the concerned parties use the negotiation strategy for conflict management. Develop an action plan.

Field Projects

1. Interview five employees at different hierarchical levels regarding the conflicts they experience with their managers. What was the main cause of the conflicts? What did they do to deal with them? Do you see any of the eight styles you have read about reflected in their responses?
2. Interview the HR manager of a company to find out if there are functional conflicts in his/her company. What were the main conflicts and what styles were used in most cases?

What Rides Over— Profit or Ethics?*

Nagesh Iron and Steel Company Ltd, a 6,500-million-rupees project headed by its founder, chairman and managing director, Nagesh Samuel, was established in 1980 with its head office at Delhi. The company's four plants—sponge iron, powerhouse, induction furnace, and rolling mill—were situated in 400 acres of land at Bilaspur in the state of Madhya Pradesh (MP). With an annual turnover of around 10,000 million rupees, the company was recognised as a profit-making unit. The market for the company was exclusively on the domestic front; however, it had to face competition from Jindal, Nova, and Special Steels.

The company had constructed a huge township for the staff and managerial personnel, and almost 70 families including a few workmen resided in the township. Of the company's 3,000 strong workforce, 1,200 workers were on the company's payroll, 600 were staff members, and the remaining contract labour. Most of the workers hailed from Orissa, Bihar, and MP. The workers had formed a union that was affiliated to the INTUC (Indian National Trade Union Congress). The literacy rate was low among the workers and the local antisocial elements often influenced the activities of the union. The relationship between the management and the union had been bitter since the beginning.

Samuel was a qualified engineer from the US, 42 years of age, and dynamic. He believed in quick decision making and autocratic style of leadership. He was directly involved in day-to-day activities, controlling the plants from Delhi and visiting the factory occasionally. He was supported by the president, Satyendra Potdar, vice president—Commercial and Administration, Pratap Verma, and three VPs in the finance, marketing, and technical fields. He had general managers appointed for the plants and divisions at Bilaspur. The recruitment at senior levels was not based on proper procedure, and nepotism was encouraged by giving chance to the relatives of the CMD.

The CMD wanted uninterrupted production at any cost because the working capital involved per day was 3 million rupees. The union took undue advantage of this approach of the CMD and as and when it got an opportunity, it threatened to go on strike and became domineering with the management. These tactics of pressurising were used even for minor demands. Verma and Vaibhav Goyal, manager—Personal and Administration, held several meetings with the union members to build a harmonious relationship.

---

*This case was developed by S. Rangnekar (IIITM, Gwalior), Y.K. Singh (MGCVV, Chitrakoot), Manoj Patwardhan and Hemant Soni (Prestige Institute of Management, Gwalior) in the National Case Writing Workshop at PIM, Gwalior, organized by Prestige Institute of Management, Gwalior. Source: *Prestige Journal of Management and Research*, 5(2): 266–68. Reproduced with permission.

On 2 December 1996, the president of the unit was shocked to receive a fax from the CMD stating that 12 employees including GM—Quality Control, Arnab Roy, and other officers were to be sacked with immediate effect. The CMD said that he had information that there were close links between these people and the union leaders. A meeting was called immediately by the president, which was attended by Verma, Goyal, VP—Technical, and the HR manager. After a long discussion, every member was of the opinion that terminating the officers and managers should be done gradually, in phases, because immediate termination would result in consequences for the company and the process of agreement with the union would take an ugly shape. The CMD, however, did not agree and strongly told the president to sack the 12 employees immediately. The president called Ray and demanded for his resignation on the grounds of lack of confidence. Similar reasons were given to all other employees. Some of them tendered the resignation immediately while others asked for some time to think. Ray and others met the union leaders the same evening to discuss the issue.

As the news of termination spread within the premises, discontent simmered and the atmosphere became tense. Next morning at 6:30 a.m., all workers, at the behest of the union, went on strike. Workers from all the four plants came out to the main gate and even workers from the night shift were not allowed to start their machines. Half the machinery was running without attendants. At 8:30 a.m., the staff members formed a union and associated themselves with the labour union, and a revised charter of demand was served to the management, clearly indicating the reinstatement of the sacked employees. The management refused to accept the new charter of demands, and the situation became violent to the extent that even telephone lines and electricity supply were disconnected. Only six managers stood by the management and they had been gheraoed and locked for 24 hours inside the plant, without food and water. The police was called for maintaining law and order and for protecting the executives. A meeting was conducted by the local management, police, and union leaders, so that the gheraoed managers finally got food from their houses.

The strike continued for the next 8 days and though there were a number of rounds of negotiations, no results were obtained. An application was submitted to the labour court by the local management through their consultants and advocates, and the strike was declared illegal by the labour court and the same was published in the local newspapers. Meanwhile, the CMD started direct dialogue with the union. The local management became powerless and the union stopped listening to and interacting with it.

Since the strike had started in the first week of the month, salaries could not be distributed. Restlessness could be observed among the workers, and the management reached the conclusion that the strike should be called off within a day or two. This was communicated to the CMD, but he did not succumb to this, which he considered as ill advise given by the management, as the company was a facing financial loss of 3,000–4,000 million rupees. On 9 December, the CMD himself reinstated all the sacked employees and bowed down before the union and accepted the charter of demand. In the next 6 months Potdar was called back to the Delhi office, the HR manager and VP (Technical) resigned, and Verma was transferred to another branch at Jabalpur.

Questions for Discussion

1. Analyse the causes of the conflict between the CMD and the union.
2. How did the CMD deal with the conflict?
3. What is the main conflict-management style of the CMD?
4. If you were in the CMD's position, how would you go about managing the conflict?

NOTES AND REFERENCES

1. Pareek, Udai (1992). 'Coercive and Persuasive Power Scale', *Indian Journal of Industrial Relations*, 30(2): 175–89.
2. Sherif, M. and C.W. Sherif (1953). *Groups in Harmony and Tension*. New York: Harper and Row.
3. The following subsection use quotes from Deutsch, Morton (1973), *The Resolution of Conflict*, New Haven: Yale University Press.
4. Vilert, E. Van de (1997). 'Enhancing performance by conflict stimulating intervention', in C. De Dren and E.M. (eds), *Organisational Misconduct*. Van de; Eisenhardt, K.M., J.L. Kahwaji, and L.J. Bourgeois (1977). 'How management teams can have a good fight', *Harvard Business Review*, July–August, 77–85; Lewis, S.A. and D.G. Pruitt (1971). 'Indirect communications and the search for agreement negotiation', *Journal of Applied Social Psychology*, 1: 205–239.
5. Robbins, S.P. (2001). *Organisational Behaviour*, p. 395. New Delhi: Prentice Hall.
6. *Ibid.*
7. *Ibid.*
8. Likert, R. and J.B. Likert (1976). *New Ways of Managing Conflict*. New York: McGraw Hill.
9. Blake, R.R. and J.S. Mouton (1964). *Managerial Grid*. Houston: Gulf.
10. Pruitt, D.G. (1977). 'Indirect communication and the search for agreement in negotiation', *Journal of Applied Social Psychology*, 35(2): 205–239.
11. *Ibid.*, 134.
12. *Ibid.*, 135.
13. Thibaut, J.W. and H.H. Kelly (1959). *The Social Psychology of Groups*. New York: Wiley.
14. Filley, A.C. (1978). 'Some normative issues in conflict management', *California Management Review*, 21(2): 61–66.
15. Walton, R.E. and R.B. McKersie (1965). *Behavioural Theory of Labour Negotiations: An Analysis of a Social Interaction System*. New York: McGraw-Hill Watkinz & Marck.

20
Developing Collaboration

LEARNING OBJECTIVES

After studying this chapter, you will be able to
1. Distinguish between functional and dysfunctional forms of competition and collaboration
2. Enumerate the functions (contributions) of competition and of collaboration
3. Identify the bases of collaboration
4. Explain the roles of perceived power, trust, and the nature of goals in the dynamics of collaboration
5. Suggest interventions to develop collaboration in organizations

The social life of human beings is an interplay between cooperation and competition. Social groups are formed when individuals coming together have some common goals. The relationship between two (and among several) individuals depends on how they approach these goals. If the goal is perceived as unshareable and can be attained only by one party, the two may compete (fight) for the goal. All zero-sum games are situations of this kind. A football match is an example. The two teams playing the match are related to each other by the unshareable goal of winning the match: one must win and the other must lose unless, even after repeated attempts, the match is drawn without either one scoring a victory over the other—a rare happening.

However, if the goal is seen as shareable, the individuals or teams work together to achieve the goal and share it. Situations of external threats to both the groups or those involving superordinate goals are examples of this category. Individuals or teams cooperate in such situations.

There is a third type of situation. Even when the goal is perceived as common to all involved, it may be perceived as achievable by one's sole effort, without the others coming in the way of its achievement. Others, then, are not relevant for either achievement or non-achievement of the goal. Striving to get a first division in an examination is an example of such a situation. Several students can get a first division score, and yet they do not work jointly for attainment of this goal.

The dynamics of these strategies of working for the achievement of goals—sharing (cooperating with others), fighting (competing or conflicting with others), or striving individually for the goal (competing against a standard of excellence)—have important social implications.

Much work has been done by economists and sociologists on cooperative effort. But studies to understand these processes at the micro level, in individuals, and in work organizations, are in their infancy. This chapter discusses various aspects of cooperative and competitive behaviour, and the implications of promoting collaboration in groups and organizations.

LEVELS OF PARTNERSHIP

Organizations with common interests interact with each other and work together. This interaction and working together can take several forms, ranging from networking to collaboration. These forms are mentioned in this section with examples.[1]

Networking   It refers to the exchange of information by companies and individuals for mutual benefit. Networking is the most informal of all inter-organizational linkages. For example, a hospital and a community clinic can exchange information about prenatal services. This phase is characterised by a level of trust, limited time, and a reluctance to share turf.

Coordinating   It refers to the exchange of information and altering organizational processes for mutual benefit and to achieve a common purpose. Coordinating requires a high level of organizational involvement. Uncoordinated services are not considered 'user-friendly' and create access barriers. For instance, in the above example, the hospital and the community clinic can decide to alter service schedules by coordinating their activities. This will help them to meet the needs of common clients more efficiently.

Cooperating   It refers to process of exchanging information, altering activities, and sharing resources for mutual benefit and to achieve a common purpose. Cooperating requires greater organizational commitments and may involve formal agreements among the companies. For example, the hospital and the community clinic—after exchanging information and altering service schedules—can share physical space and funding for prenatal services.

Collaborating   It refers to the process of exchanging information, altering activities, sharing resources, and enhancing the capacity of one another for mutual benefit and to achieve a common purpose. Collaboration is a relationship in which each organization wants to help its partners become better at what they do. For example, the hospital and the community clinic can exchange information about prenatal services, decide to alter service schedules, and share physical space and funding for prenatal services.

THE CONCEPT COLLABORATION

Collaboration between groups within organizations, between organizations, between industrial and business sectors, and between nations has increased and is in great demand today.[2] Public and private sector partnership[3] and inter-organizational networks[4] have increased. Collaboration has been defined as 'the pooling of resources

... by two or more stakeholders to solve a set of problems which neither can solve individually'.[5] Another definition emphasises the 'interactive process, using shared rules, norms and structure to act or decide on issues related to that domain'.[6]

Collaboration can be defined in terms of a person working with another person or other people for the attainment of a goal that is seen as sharable. In this definition, the basic criterion of collaborative behaviour is the perception of the goal. If the goal is seen as shareable, working with other people for the attainment of the goal is collaborative behaviour. When the goal is seen as unsharable, that is, in a situation where two people are involved but only one of them can attain the goal, working for the exclusive attainment of the goal (by implication, against the other person) is competitive behaviour. Both collaboration and competition have their uses.

FUNCTIONAL AND DYSFUNCTIONAL COOPERATION AND COMPETITION

Cooperation (or collaboration) and competition may both be used effectively or ineffectively. Both collaboration and competition can be classified into two categories: functional and dysfunctional, or positive and negative. The terms Comp(+), Comp(–), Coop(+) and Coop(–) are used to indicate the positive and negative, or functional and dysfunctional, uses of competition and cooperation (collaboration), respectively.

Comp(–) is defined as the tendency of a person to deprive the other(s) of the achievement of a goal or to directly or indirectly obstruct in his or her (their) realisation of the goal. When the person is more interested in the competitor than the goal and in preventing the competitor from attaining a goal, it is called negative competition. As posited by Likert, the main criterion of functionality is whether something contributes to the self-worth of a person. Using this criterion, Comp(–) is dysfunctional. Likert has given examples of salespeople who were motivated by this kind of competition and recorded the consequences. Such salespeople withheld information (from their colleagues) that they thought was strategic for achieving the sales target—they did not share information they had about better methods of selling, new markets, new sales strategies, etc.—and their general tendency was to not help their colleagues.

On the other hand, if competition is used to achieve excellence and to search for and create further challenges for oneself, then it is functional or positive competition, or Comp(+). Such competition contributes to the development of a sense of self-worth.

Similarly, cooperation can be either functional or dysfunctional. Coop(–) is the tendency to conform to others' demands in order to ingratiate oneself with them or to avoid the task and associated stress.

When a person collaborates with another person only because the latter is more powerful or he or she wants to please the latter, it is Coop(–). Similarly, if a person enters into a collaborative relationship because he or she finds the demands and pressures of the task too heavy and thinks that by entering into the collaborative arrangement his or her own load will be lighter, it is dysfunctional collaboration.

Functional collaboration or Coop(+) is the tendency to contribute to the joint effort for faster and more effective goal attainment, resulting in mutual trust, respect, and concern. Such collaboration increases self-worth and contributes to the development of various other desirable characteristics. When a group is formed, some members may 'cooperate' by agreeing with the processes and decisions taken by the group because this may help them not to exert themselves to think on their own. Such 'cooperation' for convenience has also been called 'social loafing'.[7] This is Coop(–).

In another group, each member contributes his or her best, supplementing others' efforts and helping others to maximise their contribution. Good teamwork reflects this phenomenon of Coop(+).

Both competition and collaboration are important. However, they perform different functions. In fact, collaboration and competition can be conceived as complementary behaviours. Exhibit 20.1 shows the various functions of competition and collaboration.[8] They are briefly reviewed here.

Exhibit 20.1   *Functions of Competition and Collaboration*

Competition develops	Collaboration develops
Sense of identity	Mutuality
Sense of responsibility	Alternative ideas and solutions
Internal standards	Mutual support and reinforcement
Excellence	Synergy
Individual creativity	Collective action
Individual autonomy	Expansion of resources

Functions of Competition

The main role of competition in an organization is to help develop an individual and his or her psychological world so that he or she develops and attains a distinct identity. The following could be regarded as the main functions of competition in this regard:

Developing a sense of identity   A person functions as an individual and, to be effective, has to develop his or her own identity. The development of this identity is possible through various steps an individual undertakes to realise his or her uniqueness, strengths, capabilities, weaknesses, etc. He or she realises these by testing them in his or her environment, including on other people. Competition helps a person to test the various aspects of his or her personality.

Even in collaboration, competition may be involved, such as when a person wishes to test whether he or she is more collaborative than the other person. A worker who is ready to help anyone who needs help and wants to be 'the most cooperative' member of the group may discover several strengths in himself or herself that he or she was not aware of. In the effort to cooperate, he or she may test various aspects of his or her personality: empathy, tendency to sacrifice personal convenience for group goals, etc.

Developing a sense of responsibility Eventually a person needs to develop a sense of personal responsibility for success and failure. He or she should realistically know how much he or she contributes to the success or failure of any venture. Unless a sense of responsibility is developed, a person's general competence and involvement in work will be low. Competition helps in the development of such a sense of responsibility because it isolates a person to face the consequences of his or her actions. If he or she succeeds in a competitive situation, he or she is happy and attributes this success to his or her own effort and ability. Similarly, if the person fails, he or she analyses and takes the responsibility for the failure. For example, a salesperson who wants to compete for the 'best salesperson of the year' award takes charge of his or her strategy and, if he or she makes a mistake, instead of blaming somebody else, analyses the mistake, corrects it, and works further towards the goal of becoming the best salesperson.

Developing internal standards of behaviour While a person takes the responsibility for the consequences of his or her actions, the person also develops his or her own standards of evaluating what is acceptable and what should be done. A person who merely responds to the outside environment may not have the necessary internal strength to sustain himself or herself. For example, the salesperson aspiring to be the 'best salesperson of the year' would set standards of performance that are challenging for him or her. Such a salesperson does not respond only to the expectations (of higher targets) given by others but sets his or her own targets. This person may also compete with himself or herself (aspire to break his or her own previous record of achieving a high sales figure). Successful competitive experiences help a person to have an internal mechanism of assessing what is excellent, what he or she wants to do, why he or she wants to do it, etc. and increase his or her autonomy for setting the goals and taking steps for their attainment.

Developing excellence The most important contribution of competition is to develop in an individual a concern for excellence, or what has been called achievement motivation. The success he or she achieves produces in him or her a desire to strive for greater success not only as per the standards set by others but also in relation to his or her own standards or past performance. There is a continuous process of competition against oneself because one who has done well in the past and wants to excel. This produces a concern for excellence. All competition, however, does not produce such a concern. Only when competition is properly used can it develop a concern for excellence instead of producing unhealthy competition, the desire to merely pull the other person down in order to move up.

Developing individual creativity Individual identity and a concern for excellence create a desire in the individual to find original and unconventional ways of solving problems, of looking at things, and of acting on decisions. This is the result of the sense of responsibility and concern for excellence. Competition is thus very useful in developing individual creativity.

Developing autonomy Competition helps an individual to develop distinct ways of analysing problems and finding solutions. It helps him or her to be original, think independently, look at different things from a unique point of view, and develop an individual framework and ways of doing things. Autonomy does not necessarily conflict with concern for others or working for a larger cause. The sense of autonomy helps in maintaining the identity of an individual, and if properly used, it may help various persons involved to respect each other's identity. Individual autonomy is maintained even when individuals accept, and work for, a common goal.

For example, in a cricket team, even when all the players play for the common goal of winning the match, each player exercises autonomy, batting or bowling in his or her own unique way. The same is true of a project team.

Functions of Collaboration

Although competition is important for the effectiveness of the individual, collaboration also plays a significant role in both individual and group effectiveness. The following are the main functions of collaboration:

Building mutuality Collaboration helps in building a relationship of mutuality and recognising each other's strengths (the contributions that people can make), accepting these contributions, and maximising the contributions of individuals. Such a relationship helps the organization and the individuals to develop respect for each other and accept each other in a work situation. It also helps them to recognise individual strengths, use them, and contribute to the individuals' further development.

For example, when a project team is constituted, each individual takes responsibility for one part of the project and shares his or her contribution with others. In such an arrangement, each one learns from other members of the team, supplementing each other. This builds mutuality.

Generating ideas and alternatives In a collaborative relationship, people stimulate each other to generate ideas, think about the problem, and develop alternative approaches and solutions. In a collaborative situation, several people generate ideas and alternative solutions. Decision making is facilitated when several alternatives are available.

Building and reinforcing mutual support The collaborative relationship plays a significant emotional role. It reinforces members' efforts for mutual support. Individuals contributing to a particular problem get immediate feedback from their collaborating partners and this helps them not only to use this feedback, but to give feedback to their partners as well. This continuous process of feedback and support reinforces successes and helps in building strong teams.

Developing synergy   A collaborative relationship produces synergy, that is multiplication of talents and resources available in the group. Because of continuou stimulation, the number of ideas produced in a collaborative situation may be much more than the total number of ideas those in the group may be able to contribute to individually. In fact, synergy generates more potent resources in the group and, in that sense, has an effect of multiplying the resources in an organization.

Developing collective action   When people work together in a group or in a team, their commitment to the goal is likely to be high and their courage to stand by that goal and take necessary action is much higher. The difference in the behaviour of an individual in isolation and his or her behaviour as a member of a team is evident in the case of trade unions, representative committees, delegations, etc. A person in such a group feels that the power of several people is behind him or her when the person wishes to present a point of view. This generates greater force and courage and helps in collective action. The success of a trade union lies in the strength of the collective action that it is able to generate. The higher the level of collaboration, the greater the strength a group will have.

Expanding resources   The greatest advantage of collaboration is that individuals go beyond their own limitations. Their lack of expertise in some fields does not come in the way of achieving certain tasks. Different individuals have different strengths and, while working together, they pool the available expertise. As a result, the collaborative group is able to generate multidimensional solutions, unlike an individual working alone, who may be limited to one dimension.

The brief discussion so far has shown that collaboration and competition play their respective roles in an organization. It would not be proper to compare the two. It can only be said that while in some fields collaboration is much more functional, in others, competition is more functional. However, in an organization, much work is done in groups. These groups may be departments, inter-departmental committees, vertical role groups, or horizontal role groups. In many cases, the situation may be of an informal collaborative kind, where two or more people work together on problems. In most cases, people work with other persons most of the time and are, therefore, continuously interacting with others either in a competitive or a collaborative framework. In most such situations, the collaborative framework is more functional than the competitive framework because these situations are based on problems that the organization is facing, the setting of standards, searching for alternatives, etc. Collaboration, therefore, is an extremely important dimension in organizational life. If an organization has a low level of collaboration, the possibility of finding solutions to multidimensional problems that emerge in the organization may be rather low.

Although it is not possible to compare competition and collaboration, many researchers and management professionals have reported that, on the whole, collaboration contributes to better development and has better side-effects than competition. Likert, while analysing various studies done with salespeople, as mentioned earlier, reported that the most successful sales managers were discovering and demonstrating that when a sense of personal worth and importance was used to create competitive motivational forces, the level of productivity and sales performance was not as high as was expected. This was very high, on the other hand, when cooperative motivational forces, rather than competitive, were used. The results showed better performance, lower cost, higher earnings, and certainly higher employee satisfaction. Likert concluded that collaboration releases some motivational forces that build people and also contribute to the effective achievement of targets. Cartwright and Zander, summarising studies done since the famous one by Deutsch on cooperation and competition, reported that the basic conclusion drawn by Deutsch—that cooperation has a much higher pay-off for the organization than competition—was true in most of the studies surveyed. Collaboration contributes to better communication and coordination of efforts and increases the favourable climate of friendliness and pride in one's own group—important qualities for group effectiveness.

Since organizations are increasingly facing multidimensional problems, collaboration becomes very relevant. It is important to find out how collaboration can be further developed in an organization. The first question, therefore, is: Why and how do people collaborate? After understanding this, we can discuss how collaboration should be managed.

Bases of Collaboration

A number of studies have been done on cooperation and collaboration. Experimental social psychologists have devised ways of studying the dyadic relationship of cooperation or collaboration. In these studies, the Prisoner's Dilemma Game has been frequently used. This is a simple game in which a person is required to make a move showing either cooperation or competition (called defection in the game). If the person makes a cooperative move, then he or she helps the other person win, whereas if he or she makes a competing move (defects), he or she makes the other person lose and gains at the other person's cost. The game is manipulated in several ways. Several dimensions are built into it. Extensive research has been done with this game, generating exciting data. The results of these studies are significant for understanding the bases of collaboration. If the different bases of collaboration can be understood, it may be possible to use these bases to develop better cooperation or collaboration in an organization. Some of the factors that contribute to collaboration, or the reasons why people collaborate, are discussed below.

Collaborative motivation There is a basic need in human beings to care for, help, and be useful to others. Relationships with others can be of various kinds. In the need that is called extension motivation, in which the basic urge is to extend oneself to others and be of service, the individual is concerned with the other person and shows this concern by helping him or her. This need is reflected not only in concern for other individuals but in concern for larger groups to which one belongs, including the organization and society. This basic urge of extension motivation is the basis of collaboration. Some individuals may have higher extension motivation and may have a higher tendency to collaborate than other individuals.

The extension motivation or any other motivation is not innate or inborn. It is a product of many forces. Many other factors that are discussed here contribute to either raising or reducing the level of extension motivation. Most of these factors interact with, reinforce, and have implications for one another. The extension motivation is reflected in the general concern a person has for others and his or her desire to forego or postpone gratification of his or her own needs for the benefit of other individuals or groups. If such a motivation operates and if there is reciprocal motivation in individuals or groups, this motivation is further reinforced. On the other hand, if other members do not have a high extension motivation, it may also get reduced. In successful teams (e.g., Tata Cummins, managed by autonomous teams of workers), each member of the team is eager to help other members when required. As a result, every member is prepared to undergo some inconvenience in order to help other members achieve the team goals.

Group norms　The norms prevailing in a group have a strong influence on the behaviour of members and are likely to either raise or lower their motivation. A member with low extension motivation may join a group and may have a tendency to compete. However, if the collaborative norms in that group are high, the same individual's extension motivation will also increase in due course of time. Norms are the standards of behaviour that are accepted by the group. These are implicitly agreed to and become binding on group members. These are not written rules of behaviour but are informally evolved: members implicitly agree with them, agree to conform to these standards of behaviour, and expect others to conform to them. Group norms have the force of the group behind them and therefore are binding on most members of the group. These influence the individual's behaviour a great deal.

Higher pay-off　Generally, an individual behaves according to the perceived reward for the behaviour. If one type of behaviour is rewarded more (or has a higher pay-off), the individual will repeat that behaviour. As a result, his or her motivation will go up and he or she is likely to continue to behave that way. This may then become a habit or a natural part of his or her activities.

A question in this context is how much collaborative behaviour is rewarded in an organization. Rewards may be of various kinds. Most researchers have shown that when the pay-off is higher, people tend to collaborate more. This is particularly so in the case of people who are interested in others. The baffling finding is that competition is not highly correlated with achievement motivation. Conceptually, the achievement motivation (concern for individual excellence and competition) is supposed to have a high correlation with competitive behaviour. But the findings did not bear this out. The reason for such a low correlation seems to lie in the perceived pay-off of competition. A person with a high achievement motivation is interested in results. If he or she perceives that by collaborating he or she can get better results, he or she is likely to collaborate. Similarly, if a person perceives that results are better (pay-off is higher) from competition, the person is likely to compete against others.

Not only those who have a tendency to collaborate but even those who have a tendency to compete are likely to collaborate in due course of time if collaborative behaviour has a higher pay-off. Pay-offs can be in various forms. The various motivators suggested by Herzberg are the various forms of pay-off.[9] If collaborative behaviour, for example, leads to better recognition, more chances for developing one's own abilities, increase of individual creativity, increase in one's influence in the system, more challenges ahead for achieving results, etc., and the individual perceives his or her role as useful or contributing to a cause greater than personal interests, the individual is more likely to collaborate.

The psychological pay-off in terms of such motivators or in terms of role efficacy, supplementing pay-off in monetary or material terms, is likely to reinforce collaborative behaviour. If the reward system in an organization includes rewards for teamwork, development of subordinates, cross-functional collaboration, etc., people with high achievement motivation, who want to be recognized and rewarded for excellence, are likely to show more collaborative behaviour by better cross-functional cooperation, helping others, etc.

Successful organizations collaborate even with their competitors if collaboration is found to yield a high pay-off. The following examples are cited by Shukla.[10]

CMC Ltd and HCL-HP are fierce competitors in the systems integration market. However, they collaborated extensively with each other (in terms of information sharing and training skills) when they were putting the stock exchanges online. The reason for this was that CMC had already developed the software for the stock exchanges but was finding it difficult to sell it. Tandem machines from HCL-HP, on the other hand, had cheaper computers but were finding the development and import of software costly. Hence, the alliance was beneficial to both.

BPL and Videocon are both contenders for dominance in the consumer electronics market. However, when the colour tubes facility of Uptron was put up for sale, both companies joined hands (along with Toshiba) to take it over and run it.

Philips India and Videocon are competitors in the market. However, the semiconductor unit of Philips India supplies components to Videocon for its Bazooka model.

The case of Godrej Foods and Hindustan Lever Ltd selling tomato puree using tomato paste from their competitor Nestle shows that competitors can be collaborators too.

Superordinate goals   Muzafer Sheriff carried out some interesting experiments that demonstrated the value of what he called superordinate goals, that is, goals that are important to all the parties concerned and cannot be achieved by any party working alone. Sheriff's concept of a superordinate goal has contributed significantly to our understanding of cooperation.

Experimental conflict and competition were first created in two groups of adolescents who were taken out camping for several days. Later, situations were created in which the problems faced by the groups could not be solved independently by either group (superordinate goal). It was found that the perception of the superordinate goals by both the groups, which were hitherto involved in conflict and competition with each other, changed their behaviour and they engaged in the maximum possible collaboration.

Several factors contribute to the development of a superordinate goal. First, the goal should be attractive and desirable to all the members. Second, the goal should be seen as a shareable one so that all individuals (or groups) concerned can share it.

Such a situation is called a non-zero-sum game. If the perception is that one party can achieve a goal at the cost of the other party and that the nature of the goal is such that it cannot be achieved jointly by both concerned, then it is called a zero-sum game because the sum of the pay-off to both the parties is zero. All traditional sports are zero-sum games. In a football or a hockey match, the goals secured by one team are its positive pay-off; the team losing the game has a negative pay-off. When the pay-offs of both the parties are added, the result is zero. However, within the same team, members play a non-zero-sum game. Gains by different players on the same team contribute to the higher gain of everyone concerned. This is called non-zero-sum game because the sum total of the pay-off to different members in the team is not zero, it is non-zero: it can be positive or negative.

Third, if the situation is seen as something in which the goal cannot be achieved by a single individual or a group without working with the other(s) involved, then it becomes a superordinate goal. In traditional sports, members of a team competing with other teams have a superordinate goal of getting a score higher than the other team. Within the team itself, members play a collaborative game because they perceive the superordinate goal. The goal of achieving victory is attractive to all members, they see this as a shareable goal, and each one knows that it cannot be achieved single-handedly, that each has to work with the others to be able to achieve this goal.

When people involved in a situation see a goal as having all these three elements, it then becomes a superordinate goal.

Perceived power   Another condition that contributes to the development of collaboration in a group is the perception of power. Power can be of both kinds—power to reward and power to punish. Punishment may be in the form of depriving a person of the rewards that he or she is likely to get. Everyone in the system has at least the negative power of depriving the other person of something desirable. This may be done by holding back information, misleading the other person, and so on. Even the person at the lowest level in an organization can use this negative power to create annoying situations: delaying matters, holding back information, giving information that creates misunderstandings, etc.

Yet every person in the system seems to have some kind of power. If people in the system perceive clearly that they have power which is positive in nature, that they may be able to contribute to and use their influence for the attainment of certain goals, then this is a perception of positive power. At the same time, it is important that they realise that others involved in the situation also have power, both positive and negative.

Power should be perceived clearly and should also be demonstrated. If people do not perceive other people's power, they are likely to use their own power in a competitive way. On the other hand, if someone is not demonstrating power, this can lead to continued exploitative activity (use of competition by the other party).

Unconditional cooperation does not lead to the development of collaboration. Unconditional cooperation by one party may communicate lack of power. If this happens, the other party will find it more and more difficult to get into a collaborative relationship. For collaborative behaviour, a perception of the power of both parties is essential.

This was dramatically demonstrated in an experiment in which the author was involved, along with four groups of educationists from six Asian countries. These groups played a game called 'Win as much as you can'. The game consisted of 10 moves. One of the four groups consistently made cooperative moves and, as was revealed in the later interview and discussion, was fully convinced from looking at the rules that only cooperative behaviour could help all the groups to maximise their gains. However, the unconditional cooperation by this group blocked the emergence of cooperation among other groups. Also, this group was exploited by the other three groups. The final result of the game was that the cooperating group snapped communication with the other three groups and the other groups refused to come forward for negotiation because they saw themselves as being in a more powerful and advantageous position which could be threatened by negotiation.

Many other studies have shown that cooperation emerges after some competitive moves by the group concerned. In this process, the various parties or individuals involved in the situation demonstrate to one another the power they have and their ability to use this power.[11]

The implication of these findings is that collaboration is only possible between two powerful (or resourceful) groups or individuals. It is important for each individual or party involved to have power (special strength) and to demonstrate it. For example, collaboration between unions and managements to achieve high productivity is possible only if the union demonstrates its power of raising or lowering productivity and management demonstrates its prerogative (legitimate power) of evaluating performance. The other conditions necessary are that both respect each other's power and have mutual trust.

Mutual trust Along with a perception of each other's power, it is important that the parties concerned perceive that the power which each party has will not be used against the other. This is a part of trust. Some amount of mutual trust is likely to lead to cooperation. Trust indicates a high probability that the power of the concerned party or individual will not be used in a malevolent way. A combination of perceived power and a minimum level of trust leads to cooperation.

As shown in Exhibit 20.2, collaboration results from a combination of the perceived power of both parties and their minimum trust in each other.[12] In a no-trust condition, there may be coercion and exploitation if the other person is seen as weak or submission and compliance if the other party is seen as powerful. If the perception is that neither has power, there may be indifference towards each other.

Exhibit 20.2   *Cooperation as Function of Perceived Power and Trust*

Trust	Perceived power (who has power?)			
	Only I	Only he/ she/they	Neither	Both
Low	Coercion Exploitation	Submission Compliance	Indifference	Competition or individualistic task achievement
High	Nurturance	Dependence	Mutual sympathy	Cooperation

The perception that both have power may lead to either competition or individualistic behaviour. Under conditions of high trust, a perception of the other party having low power may lead to nurturance (a paternalistic attitude), a perception that it has power may result in dependency, a perception that neither has power may generate mutual sympathy. It is only when both perceive that both have their own power and there is enough trust between them that collaboration emerges. For example, cross-functional collaboration will be effective only when both functional managers are competent and have a special contribution to make in the collaborating situation (in other words, both are powerful in their own functions). However, if one of them is weak, he or she may go along with the other manager and may almost submit to the latter. At the same time, the competent manager may take advantage of the situation to impose his or her views on the colleague who is not so competent (in other words, who has less knowledge power).

Exhibit 20.3 shows that collaboration results from three main factors[13]: the perception that a goal is important to and shareable by both concerned, the perception that both (or all) involved have power, and a minimum level of trust among those involved in the task. Absence of these may result in low cooperation or absence thereof.

Exhibit 20.3   *Cooperation as Function of Shareable Goal, Perceived Power, and Trust*

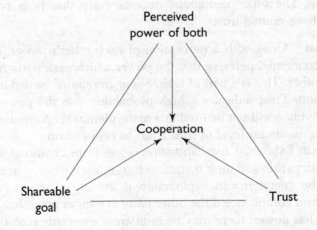

For example, successful collaboration between two teams—marketing and production—will be successful if both teams work for the common goal of expanding the market share of the product, both realise that each one has special knowledge and competence to contribute (their own power), and they trust each other (the marketing people are sure that the promise made by the production people to remove some snags will be carried out and similarly the production people are sure that feedback from the market will be provided immediately to the production team). If all three elements are present (common goals, respect for each other's competence, and mutual trust), collaboration is likely to be successful.

Communication   Another factor contributing to the development of collaboration is communication between or among the various parties involved in the situation. Several experiments have demonstrated that when representatives of the groups or the entire groups have an opportunity to communicate with each other or among themselves, the chances of collaboration increase.[14]

Communication opens up the possibility of discussing the consequences of behaviour. Communication also helps the groups to discuss their perception of each other's power and see that the power they have been using against each other can be turned into a positive force for the benefit of all concerned. In the absence of communication, such sharing of concerns is not possible. When individuals communicate as representatives of a group, it is important that the groups they represent trust them and that the representatives are sure that the commitment they make to the other groups will be honoured by their own.

Fait accompli   If groups or individuals live together and share certain norms, they begin to see good points in each other and collaboration begins to emerge. As long as individuals or groups do not work or live together, they may be prejudiced against each other or even have wrong notions about each other. Poor communication or indifference among individuals or groups could also lead to prejudice. For example, as long as representatives of the management and those of the union do not communicate with each other, the former (management) may think the union representatives unreasonable and the latter (union representatives) may think the management has no empathy for them. The realisation that they have to live or work together contributes to collaboration, and through their sharing of experiences, they evolve common understandings and norms. Sharing a space may help each party to 'experience' and 'see' the other party's strengths and good points.

In a telefilm produced by Doordarshan, a Punjabi is transferred to Kerala and a Malayalee to Punjab. Both hate their new places of residence and find fault with everything there. However, as they continue to live (or are 'forced' to live) there, they begin to see the strengths of the new communities they are exposed to. Finally they find their new places so attractive that the Punjabi marries a Malayalee and settles down in Kerala, which he now considers 'heaven's reflection', and the Malayalee finds a Punjabi spouse and settles down in the Punjab, which he finds 'full of life'.

When a marketing manager discusses with a colleague from the production department the details of a strategy for increasing market share, he or she may become aware of the colleague's strengths. By discussing how the agreed strategy will be implemented, they begin to develop mutual trust and make sure that problems arising in the course of implementation will be sorted out by further discussions.

Risk taking   In the final analysis, cooperation results from the initiative taken by one person or one group to cooperate. This is a kind of risk taking on the part of the individual or the group as it makes one vulnerable. In a non-zero-sum game, the individual or the group making the cooperative move runs the risk of losing a great deal and earns a lower pay-off. This risk of taking the initiative, demonstrating the courage to lose initially for the benefit of all parties concerned, is the key to the development of cooperation. However, this step has to be taken after the other parties concerned perceive the power this group or individual has.

Risk taking becomes significant in combination with trust and demonstration of each other's power. It is only after the latter have been achieved that both mutual trust and mutual power lead to a risk-taking tendency, not the other way round. The risk-taking move leads to cooperation. The person who takes the initiative in making himself or herself vulnerable is able to start the process of change towards collaboration. The inner strength of a person that enables him or her to make such a move helps to build collaborative relationships in a situation. This is shown in Exhibit 20.4.[15]

Exhibit 20.4   *Cooperation as Function of Individual Risk Taking*

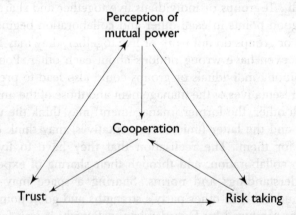

ACADEMIA–INDUSTRY COLLABORATION

One promising area for mutual advantage is academia–industry collaboration. Academicians possess valuable experience and data that the industry can use to deal with several important aspects of the business. In recent times, some innovative models of academia–industry collaboration have emerged. One particularly successful model comes from Porsche. The company has succeeded in bringing the academic brainpower of students and researchers within the company.

A few years ago, Porsche, which produces 10 per cent as many cars as BMW or Mercedes-Benz, beat both the companies in developing and launching a revolutionary ceramic brake system. The company succeeded even though it got a comparably late start on the project, employed about one-tenth as many engineers as its competitors, and had few internal experts in lightweight and composite materials. Its achievements and other R&D advances can be attributed to the company's habit of open collaboration and, in particular, its distinctive academic alliances.

Porsche routinely collaborates with universities on projects for which it lacks the requisite expertise. See Exhibit 20.5.[16]

Such collaboration helps both the students and the industry. Students who love the product or the industry tend to show high performance. For example, Porsche recruited one intern with below average grades, but who had financed his education working part-time at a garage specialising in the company's cars. He was intimately familiar with every part of every model and ultimately became a full-time employee.

To ensure effective collaboration between the staff and the students and to provide

Exhibit 20.5 *Academia–Industry Collaboration*

Every year, the carmaker brings nearly 600 students who are working on their masters' degrees into its R&D facility in Weissach, Germany, where they labor alongside 2,000 staff engineers for four to six months.

An annual budget of up to 30 million US dollars finances paid internships for the students, and also supports external university research or institute-based studies conducted exclusively for Porsche. This arrangement allows the manufacturer to employ just 10 staff specialists in basic research, compared with about 200 each at BMW and Mercedes-Benz. A student costs the company 15 per cent of what a full-time employee costs, so the savings are substantial.

Although the students focus on basic R&D, they participate in every stage of product development— safety and quality remain largely the province of Porche's employees and strategic suppliers. Interns are also involved in commercialising their work, which is not the case in conventional industry or university alliances. Towards that end, students help Porsche identify new suppliers for the technologies they develop, and they collaborate on production techniques that combine the latest research from the universities with suppliers' real experiences.

Porsche's internships are open to students worldwide, but most interns hail from local universities, because the company requires that they labor on its premises. The work is intense sometimes, as much as 60 hours per week, and integration with staff engineers is complete.

Porsche takes great care in selecting its interns from the 2,000 students who apply each year, emphasising passion, creativity and the strategic relevance of their thesis topics to the company's practical R&D problems. The first screening is conducted by the corporate human resource organization; the second by the units that will employ the students.

Porsche's insourcing program also keeps its talent pipeline primed. The company offers its top interns—fewer than 10 per cent—full-time jobs. The possibility of landing one of those prize positions motivates students. Those not asked to stay become part of an alumni network that provides advice on research and technology. Alumni may meet several times a year, sometimes for a weekend at a castle in Southern Germany or Austria, where they enjoy elegant meals and early test-drives of the company's latest models.

the best intern experience, Porsche fully integrates students into development projects, invites them to after-work events, and provides detailed performance assessments. These opportunities are applicable even to those students who are not considered for full-time employment.

To ensure that research results are rapidly absorbed and diffused, Porsche encourages students to make regular presentations to other departments of the company, emphasising on strong visuals rather than detailed written reports.

Porsche gives interns challenging, sometimes sensitive, tasks such as identifying new suppliers and supporting commercialisation. This helps them to experience the full cycle of innovation and help transform the research efforts into business value for Porsche.

The company ensures that students continue to support the brand by providing stimulating and rewarding work during their internships and maintaining active alumni networks.

By insourcing student expertise, Porsche can explore more promising ideas and move these to production faster than its competitors. Companies pursuing innovation should consider following Porsche's example so they too can absorb what the academic world has to offer.

SUPPLY CHAIN COLLABORATION

Recently, substantial research has been done on collaboration in manufacturing. Significant work has been done at Sandia Laboratories in this direction. Some recent books provide guidance and examples of how and why real-time events within the plant floor should be linked online with the supply chain process.[17] These books also discuss manufacturing execution systems and methods for calculating return on investment (ROI) using collaborative techniques. Some books also discuss how companies can form necessary business alliances to combine two of the most versatile and effective business tools of the new century: the power of supply chain and the Internet.[18]

Most organizations operate in a competitive business environment. However, collaboration is more effective in providing positive business results to the companies. Collaborative planning, forecasting, and replenishment (CPFR) has been a very effective tool in retailing. This tool has led to a reduction in stock-outs and also to getting retail chains in a dialogue with product manufacturers over product schedules and delivery. It is the sharing of forecasts and related business information among business partners in the supply chain to enable automatic product replenishment. It is designed to improve the flow of goods from raw material suppliers, to the manufacturer, to retailers' shelves. It is also designed to quickly identify any discrepancies in forecasts, inventory, and ordering data. This helps in correcting problems before they negatively impact sales or profits.

Synchronising inventories across value chains and sharing of product information between suppliers are other effective approaches towards collaboration. There is also great value in a collaborative environment within companies where departments share information. A business can achieve a lot more when its people work together rather than work against each other.

Organizations share their sales history, sales projections, and other important information with their business partners. The business partners, in turn, share their raw material availability, lead times, etc. with the organizations. This information is then integrated, synchronised, and used to eliminate excess inventory and improve in-stock positions, making everyone in the supply chain more profitable.

INTERVENTIONS TO BUILD COLLABORATION IN ORGANIZATIONS

Since collaboration has such a positive role to play, how can it be increased in an organization? Several interventions can be used to help raise the level of collaboration in an organization. The various interventions can be grouped into two broad categories: process and structural.

Process Interventions

Process interventions pay attention to the development and utilisation of the basic processes. They pay attention to 'how' things are being done. For example, they explore questions such as whether the people who have to implement the change are also involved in the development of the strategy of change, whether the leader attends to the feelings of team members, whether the leader checks what difficulties people are experiencing, etc. All these questions relate to the process aspects of the group's work. Such process interventions have been discussed in Chapters 15 and 26.

First, process interventions help to demonstrate and dramatise the dynamics that increase awareness. Even when people experience the behavioural dynamics in a laboratory situation, they may be motivated to change their behaviour.

Second, process interventions help to increase people's awareness of the various processes involved in the situation. Collaboration is a complex phenomenon and, as we have seen, many conditions promote collaboration. Process interventions help people become aware of and recognise such conditions so that they may take action.

Third, process interventions help people look at themselves in what can be called self-confrontation. When an individual is able to analyse his or her own motivation and realise that he or she has a tendency either to use minimal collaboration or that when he or she does use it, it is a dysfunctional type of collaboration, the individual may be greatly disturbed. This may lead to change and the development of real collaborative motivation.

Finally, process interventions help individuals to provide opportunities for experimenting with behaviour and exploring new methods they can adopt.

Structural Interventions

While the main role of process intervention is to create motivation and work on the dynamics, the main role of structural interventions is to consolidate such change and make it a part of organizational life. Role negotiation, the details of which are given in Chapter 28, is a good example of structural intervention. Individuals in different roles share their images of each other, their perception of the other group's strengths, and their expectations from each other. A discussion develops proper understanding of each other and they realise that their effectiveness, to a large extent, depends on the support provided by the 'other' roles. They may become aware of the strengths of the other roles in this way. This realisation helps them to listen to each other and work together.

Structural interventions perform several functions. First, they provide opportunities for the new values and behaviour. For example, when motivation for collaboration is high in some people, structural interventions provide them opportunities to collaborate, which are likely to sustain that motivation before it dies out.

Second, structural interventions reinforce new values in the system. For example, if collaboration is encouraged and rewarded, there will be a greater tendency for people to collaborate. Structural interventions build in higher pay-offs for collaboration in various forms, continuously reinforcing collaborative efforts.

Third, these interventions legitimise new values and behaviour and do not leave it to informal arrangements. For example, by formalising systems in such a way that people are expected to collaborate, the value of collaboration is consciously recognised and communicated by the organization. This process of legitimisation helps in making it a regular part of the organizational life.

Finally, structural interventions help to establish new norms. Norms are important determinants of behaviour.

Both process and structural interventions can be designed to increase collaboration by referring to the various bases of collaboration already discussed.

SUMMARY

Both competition and collaboration contribute to a person's effectiveness. Competition develops a sense of identity, a sense of responsibility, internal standards, concern for excellence, creativity, and the autonomy of an individual. Collaboration, on the other hand, develops mutuality, synergy, collective action, alternative solutions, and expansion of resources. Both competition and collaboration can be functional or dysfunctional.

There are several bases of collaboration: the collaborative motive, group norms, superordinate goals, higher pay-offs for collaboration, perceived mutual power, trust, communication, and risk taking.

Both structural and process interventions can be used to develop collaboration.

GLOSSARY

behaviour modification helping people to become more effective in their individual orientations

collaboration a person working with another person for the attainment of a goal that is seen as shareable

collaborative planning, forecasting and replenishment (CPFR) the sharing of forecasts and related business information among business partners in the supply chain to enable automatic product replenishment

Comp(–) the tendency of a person to deprive the other person of, or directly and indirectly obstruct his or her, achievement of a goal

Comp(+) competing for excellence

Coop(–) the tendency to conform to others' demands in order to ingratiate oneself with them or to avoid the task and related stress

Coop(+) working together, supporting each other to attain a goal

superordinate goals goals that are important to all the parties concerned and cannot be achieved by any party working alone

---

EXERCISES

Concept Review Questions

1. What is competition and what is collaboration?
2. What are the functions of competition and of collaboration?
3. How can collaboration be dysfunctional?
4. What are the bases of collaboration?
5. How can collaboration be developed in an organization?

Critical Thinking Questions

1. From your experience in school/college, recollect some incidents of dysfunctional competition and write about two of them in some detail.
2. Have you had a 'good' experience of collaborating with another student? Why was this experience satisfactory? Explain the experience in terms of the bases of collaboration.
3. If your instructor organized an exercise in which you participated, what were the main lessons you learnt?

Classroom Projects

1. In small groups of two or three, develop from your recent experiences two examples of dysfunctional competition and two examples of dysfunctional collaboration.
2. Based on your reading of business magazines or books, in groups of two or three, prepare a short account of functional collaboration between two companies. How was such collaboration achieved?

Field Projects

1. Interview any executive to find out his or her good and bad experiences with competition (when competition was functional and when it was dysfunctional).
2. Explore with the same or another executive the factors that made collaboration possible and the benefits from such collaboration.

Supply Chain Competency Through Collaborative Relationship*

INTRODUCTION

S.K. Das established ABC Pharma in 1961 in New Delhi. The company marketed antibiotics and became a brand leader in ampicillin and cephalexin orals. It went public in 1973. In 1983, ABC established a plant in Mandideep (near Bhopal, India) with various dosage form facilities. In 2004 it became India's largest pharmaceutical company, manufacturing and marketing world-class generics, branded generic pharmaceuticals, and active pharmaceutical ingredients, and ranked among the top 10 generic companies worldwide. The company's products were sold in over 100 countries with manufacturing operations in 7 countries and ground presence in 44. The company had an expanding international portfolio of affiliates, joint ventures, and representative offices across the globe with joint venture subsidiaries in the US, the UK, Germany, France, Spain, Ireland, Netherlands, China, Brazil, South Africa, etc. While ABC aggressively pursued internationalisation of its business, the growth strategy equally focused on enhancing market share in India. The company had a strong brand marketing team and distribution network in India.

MILESTONES

By the end of December 2004, global sales had reached 1,118 million US dollars and registered a growth of 21 per cent. Overseas markets accounted for 78 per cent of the global sales. The US accounted for 36 per cent, while Europe and the BRIC (Brazil, Russia, India, and China) countries contributed 16 per cent and 26 per cent to global sales, respectively, with a combined turnover of 924 million US dollars. The company's vision was to achieve significant business in proprietary prescription products with a strong presence in developed markets. It also aspired to be among the top five generic players with a 5-billion-dollar sale by the next decade. To translate these objectives into reality and to optimise value creation, the company had adopted a multi-pronged strategy. The major thrust areas for future were acquisition of brands overseas, emphasis on brand marketing in the US and Europe and entering high potential new markets with value added product offerings.

---

*This case was developed by V.K. Jain, Shirish Chowk, Punit Sharma (Prestige Institute of Management and Research, Indore), and Deepak Shrivastava (faculty, Institute of Management Studies, Indore) in the Fourteenth National Case Writing Workshop at PIMR organized by the institute in collaboration with the Association of Indian Management Schools (AIMS), 6–8 May 2005.

The company had established a state-of-the-art multi-disciplinary R&D facility at Gurgaon (near New Delhi), India. ABC Pharma was one of the largest investors in R&D in the Indian pharmaceutical industry, with an outlay of 7 per cent of its sales during 2004. The company's major research focus was in the areas of urology, anti-infective, respiratory, anti-inflammatory, and metabolic disorders segments. The company's continued focus on R&D had resulted in several approvals in developed markets and significant progress in new drug delivery response (NDDR).

FOURTH PARTY LOGISTICS

The company believed in making strong and long-term relationships with a limited number of logistics service providers. They also focused on outsourcing the activities such as warehouse management, packing, and custom clearance through freight forwarders. The company has always believed in its core competencies. The logistics service providers took care of storage and inventory management and ensured the availability of the right product at the right place and at the right time. Through outsourcing, ABC achieved focus on core competencies, cost saving, effective supply chain management, cross-pollination of better available practices, and wider and effective geographical coverage. The company practised Fourth Party Logistics (4PL) services by providing ERP as a backbone system for the third-party logistics service providers. The palette packing services, including packing materials, were outsourced from a local company. The responsibility of complete documentation and custom clearance for import and export of goods had also been outsourced to custom house agents and freight forwarders under the supervision of the general manager – Global Supply Chain.

The warehouse management was done with the help of bar code technology, which facilitated in tracing of materials with a single click of the mouse, resulting in smooth inward and outward flow of materials. In future, ABC was planning to have radio frequency identification (RFID) technology to manage the warehouse activities in a more effective and efficient manner. The company had divided its global operations into four regions: R1—Middle East with headquarters at India; R2—CIS, Africa, and Europe with head quarters at London; R3—Far East and Latin America with headquarters at Singapore; R4—US with headquarters at New York. This division was on the basis of convenience, market potential, and market share.

COLLABORATIVE RELATIONSHIP

The company established its global supply chain hub at Mandideep. They managed their operations with one GM – Supply Chain, one senior manager – Commercial, and four shipment officers. Each shipment officer had four support employees outsourced through freight forwarders. These people were responsible for the day-to-day activities under the administrative control of ABC. The GM was responsible for managing the relations with the supply chain partners, freight forwarders, and custom house agents. The company had been a pioneer in launching the generic versions of products on the same day the products went off patent; this helped the company in getting an edge over competition. ABC managed to maintain dignity, discipline, and business ethics without violating patent laws. This was possible because of the strong and long-term relationship with logistics service providers. There was a strong level of belonging, faith, and trust among the supply chain partners. To maintain good relations, the company practised making timely payments to the service providers. They also opened the account in the same bank in which the service providers had their account so that prompt money transfer could take place. As a result of this, service providers were so concerned about the shipments of the company that they dedicated 25 refrigerated cargos, each equipped with location tracking facility to track the status of the shipments.

The relationship and commitment of service providers was endorsed on 10 January 2003 when Ramipril (an anti-hypertensive drug) was going off patent in Europe. Having strong presence in Germany, ABC wanted to encash the opportunity by making its Ramipril available in the country right on 11 January 2003 so as to take lead in available generic market. However, ABC did not know the number and size of competition they would be facing. The underlying fear of getting the shipment late and thereby losing the advantage of being first was very clear on the faces of ABC's top managers. The task was urgent and important; any delay in availability was to cost heavily. On 10 January 2003, the shipment was to be airlifted from Mumbai so as to reach Germany after the midnight of 10 January, but before the dawn of 11 January. Two Boeings were chartered to lift the goods from Mumbai, but the task was not simple as the goods were to be transported from Mandideep to Mumbai in a caravan of 70 cargos. To worsen things, the transporters had announced strike during that period.

The urgency was briefed to a freight forwarder, who was caught between ABC and the transporters association. He had the option of pleasing only one of them. The long affiliation and the relationship with ABC got priority and the freight forwarder assured ABC's senior commercial manager of carrying out the assigned responsibility. Going against the directives of the association, the freight forwarder contacted the police authorities and obtained a security cover throughout Maharashtra. The freight owner, who considered himself one of the responsible members of ABC, personally received and loaded the cargo at Mumbai. The scheduled departure had a lead-time of 2 days. However, the freight forwarder insisted and stayed in Mumbai at his own cost to see the goods leave India successfully. It was a mission for ABC and the freight forwarder in which collaborative relationship surpassed all limitations and the goods landed in Germany in time.

Questions for Discussion
1. Discuss the role of the 4PL system in view of organizational competitiveness.
2. Analyse the process of collaboration reflected in the case.
3. What factors promoted collaboration to make the supply chain competency successful?

NOTES AND REFERENCES

1. Himmelman, A. T. (1997). 'Devolution as an experiment in citizen governance: Multi-organizational partnerships and democratic revolutions'. Paper presented at the Fourth International Conference on Multi-Organizational Partnerships and Cooperative Strategy. Oxford University, England. 8–10 July.

2. Fryxell, G.E., R.S. Dooley, and M. Vryza (2002). 'After the ink dries: The interaction of trust and control in US-based international joint ventures', *Journal of Management Studies*, 39(6): 865–886.

3. Osborne, Stephen P. (2000). *Public-Private Partnerships: Theory and Practice in International Perspective.* London: Routledge.

4. Ebers, Mark (1997). 'Explaining inter-organizational network formation', in Mark Ebers (ed.), *The Formation of Inter-organizational Networks*, pp. 3–40. Oxford: Oxford University Press.

5. Gray, B. (1985). 'Conditions facilitating inter organizational collaboration', *Human Relations*, 38(10): 911–936.

6. Wood, D.J. and B. Gray (1991). 'Toward a comprehensive theory of collaboration', *Journal of Applied Behavioral Science.* 27(2) (June): 139–62.

7. Comer, D.R. (1995). 'A model of social loafing in real work groups', *Human Relations*, 48(6), 647–667.

8. Pareek, Udai (1992). 'Coercive and Persuasive Power Scale', *Indian Journal of Industrial Relations*, 30(2): 11.

9. Herzberg, F. (1993). *Motivation at Work.* New York: Transaction Publishers.

10. Shukla, Mandhukar (1997). *Competing Through Knowledge: Building a Learning Organisation.* New Delhi: Response Books.

11. See, e.g., Deutsch, Morton (1973), *The Resolution of Conflict*, New Haven: Yale University Press; Shure, G.H., R.J. Meeker, and E.A. Hansford (1965), 'The effectiveness of pacifist strategies in bargaining games', *Journal of Experimental Social Psychology*, 4: 233–46; Bixenstine, V.E., H.M. Potash, and K.V. Wilson (1963), 'Effects of level of cooperative choice by the other player on choices in a prisoner's dilemma game: Part 1', *Journal of Abnormal and Social Psychology*, 66: 308–13.

12. Pareek, Udai (1992). 'Coercive and Persuasive Power Scale', *Indian Journal of Industrial Relations*, 30(2): 175–89.

13. *Ibid.*, 100.

14. Deutsch, M. (1960). 'The effect of motivation orientation upon trust and suspicion', *Human Relations*, 31: 123–139; Greenwood, J.G. (1974), 'Opportunity to communicate and social orientation in imaginary reward bargaining,' *Speech Monographs*, 41(1): 78–81; Loomis, J.G. (1959). 'Communication, the development of tariff and cooperative behaviour', *Human Relations*, 12, 305–315; reviews of several studies on the subject can be found in Pareek, 1992, pp. 78–81.

15. Pareek, Udai (1992). 'Coercive and Persuasive Power Scale', *Indian Journal of Industrial Relations*, 30(2): 175–189.

16. *Business World*, 13 to 26 January 2006.

17. McClellan, Michael (2003). *Collaborative Manufacturing: Using Real-Time Information to Support the Supply Chain.* Boca Raton, FL: St Lucie Press.

18. Poirier, C.C. and M.J. Bauer (2001). *E-Supply Chain: Using the Internet to Revolutionize Your Business.* San Francisco: Berrett Koehler.

21
Leadership Theories and Styles

LEARNING OBJECTIVES

After studying this chapter, you will be able to

1. Distinguish leaders from administrators and managers
2. Describe the evolution of leadership theories
3. Enumerate different theories of leadership, and their main features
4. Discuss the contingency theories, especially the situational theory of leadership
5. Explain the concept of the development levels of a group and how to raise them
6. List steps in the process of delegation

Leadership has long interested psychologists, sociologists, political scientists, and certainly management scientists. There is still a growing interest in leadership, which has been defined in different ways. Leadership can, however, be simply defined as the act of making an impact on others in a desired direction. In this sense, leadership is a broader term than management. Managers can run organizations effectively, but only leaders can build them. Differentiating characteristics for officers, managers, and leaders are shown in Exhibit 21.1.[1]

Exhibit 21.1 *Three Managerial Modes*

	Administration	Management	Leadership
Main concern	Follow procedures	Get results	Excel
Emphasis on	Conformity	Interaction	Creativity
Focus on	Status quo	Stability	Trend setting
Norms	Quantity	Quality	Pushing benchmarks
Assessment criteria	Efficiency	Effectiveness	Boundary management
Driven by	Past (traditions, precedence)	Present (competition)	Future (vision)
Approach	Tactics	Strategy	Vision
Structure	Hierarchy/protocol	Matrix	Network
Response mode	Reactive	Proactive	Pre-active (making others play your game)
Managing by	Developing procedure	Building systems	Building culture
HRD approach	Supervision	Coaching	Mentoring
Dominant need	Control dependency	Achievement power	Power extension
Concept of power	Limited/unsharable	Sharable	Multiplying
Source of power	Status/authority	Competence	Empowerment

The three modes shown in Exhibit 21.1 are illustrated by the following caselet from a premier state government training institute: Three directors at different times functioned differently.

One director continued the work the institute was doing, responding to the training requirements of different departments, maintaining all the records well, and undertaking the various activities for which the institute was established. He was a good administrator.

Another director paid attention to financial aspects, established links with other institutes, developed management systems, and built competence among the faculty. He functioned as an effective manager.

A third director took charge of the institute just after the floods had washed away almost half its grounds and buildings. At the time, the institute was being run in a routine way, depending on an external faculty. After this director, a senior IAS officer took over. He set an example by shifting with his family to the ravaged campus, suffering considerable personal inconvenience, and involved the faculty in the plans for rebuilding, mobilised various stakeholders for the rebuilding process, arranged a grant from the central government, offered almost twice the number of programmes as earlier, established three autonomous centres (for rural development studies, urban development studies, and management studies) by mobilising central government grants, established a memorial park in the ravaged and sunken land where people could plant a tree to commemorate some event or person by paying Rs 100, and so on. This is the leadership mode.[2]

Different approaches have been used to study leadership. Early research on leadership was based on the study of people who were already great leaders. These people were often from the aristocracy, as then few from the lower classes had the opportunity to lead. This contributed to the notion that leadership had something to do with breeding. Later research systematised knowledge in the form of theories. In this chapter, we will review some well-known groups of theories.

TRAIT THEORIES

According to trait theories, people are born with certain inherited traits. The belief in earlier approaches was that some traits are particularly suited to leadership, and people who make good leaders possess the right (or sufficient) combination of these traits, which distinguish them from 'non-leaders'. Therefore, studies have tried to discover those special traits of great leaders.

Stogdill

Stogdill[3] reviewed more than 100 such studies and concluded that while leaders were found to be superior to non-leaders in specific abilities such as intelligence and physical size, there were no specific traits that distinguished leaders from non-leaders. Stogdill's study almost put an end to the trait approach to leadership. However, he did suggest the traits (inborn characteristics) and skills (competencies) of successful leaders. These characteristics are shown in Exhibit 21.2.

Exhibit 21.2 *Traits and Skills of Leaders*

Traits	Skills
• Adaptable to situations • Alert to social environment • Ambitious and achievement oriented • Assertive • Cooperative • Decisive • Dependable • Dominant (desire to influence others) • Energetic (high activity level) • Persistent • Self-confident • Tolerant of stress • Willing to assume responsibility	• Clever (intelligent) • Conceptually skilled • Creative • Diplomatic and tactful • Fluent in speaking • Knowledgeable about group task • Organized (administrative ability) • Persuasive • Socially skilled

McCall and Lombardo

Based on a study of both successes and failures of leaders, McCall and Lombardo[5] identified four primary traits by which leaders could succeed or fail. These traits are explained in this section.

Emotional stability and composure   Calm, confident, and predictable, particularly when under stress

Admitting error   Owning up mistakes rather than covering them up

Good interpersonal skills   Ability to communicate and persuade others without resorting to negative or coercive tactics

Intellectual breadth   Ability to understand a wide range of areas rather than having a narrow area of expertise (and being narrow-minded)

Bennis and Thomas

Bennis and Thomas,[6] based on in-depth interviews of more than 40 leaders, both young and old, have suggested the following four characteristics of effective leaders:

1. Adaptive capacity (hardiness, keen observance, proactive seizing of opportunities, and creativity)
2. Engaging others by creating shared meaning (encouraging dissent, empathy, and obsessive communication)
3. Voice (purpose, self-awareness, self-confidence, and emotional intelligence)
4. Integrity (ambition, competence, and moral compass)

They have also suggested that leaders are characterised by *neoteny*. Neoteny refers to the retention of the qualities of youthfulness, such as curiosity, playfulness, fearlessness, warmth, energy, and 'capacity of uncontaminated wonder'.

BEHAVIOURAL THEORIES

There are two main assumptions underlying behavioural theories: (1) leaders are made, rather than born, and (2) successful leadership is based on definable, learnable behaviour. Instead of searching inborn traits or capabilities, behavioural theories look at what leaders actually do. According to these theories, if success can be defined in terms of describable behaviour, then it should be relatively easy for other people to learn to behave in the same way.

The assumption that leadership capability can be learned provides great hope for leadership development. This approach studies the behaviour of successful leaders. Studies based on large samples can help in identifying statistically significant behaviours that differentiate successful leaders from ineffective leaders. The renewed interest in 'trait' is based on such behavioural research.

Three-dimensional Theory

Kurt Lewin and colleagues carried out leadership–decision experiments in 1939, and identified the following three different styles of leadership, in particular, regarding decision making.[7]

Autocratic   Autocratic leaders take decisions on their own, without consulting others. From the experiments of Lewin et al. it was found that this style resulted in very high level of discontent.

Autocratic leaders are effective when there is no need for others' contribution to the decision making, and where the motivation of the people to implement the decision would not be affected whether they were or were not involved in the decision making.

Democratic   Democratic leaders involve their people in decision making. People usually like democratic decision making. Democratic leadership, however, may be difficult when options differ widely and it is difficult to arrive at an equitable final decision.

Laissez-faire   Laissez-faire leaders have minimum involvement in decision making. They allow people to make their own decisions. The employees are responsible for the outcome of their decisions. Laissez-faire leadership is successful when people are capable and motivated to make their own decisions, and where there is no requirement for a centralised coordination, for example, in sharing resources among autonomous regions in a country.

It was discovered by Lewin et al. that the democratic style was the most effective style of leadership. Excessive autocratic styles led to revolution, while under a laissez-faire approach, people were not coherent in their work and did not put in enough energy in their work. Behavioural characteristics of the three styles are given in Exhibit 21.3.

Exhibit 21.3 *Characteristics of Three Styles of Leadership*

Autocratic (directive)	Democratic (participative)	Laissez-faire
Believes in centralised authority	Involves employees in decision making	Allows employees to have a 'say' in what is decided
Dictates work methods	Delegates authority	Operates in group mode with the leader as a member giving input
Makes unilateral decisions	Encourages participation in deciding work methods and goals	Gives employees complete freedom to take decisions and complete their work as they see fit
Limits employee participation	Uses feedback as opportunity to coach employees	Provides materials and answers questions
	Participation sometimes results in higher satisfaction	
	Greater acceptance of decisions	

Michigan Studies

While the trait approach met a setback with Stogdill's research, the behaviour of leaders has always been a subject of observation and study. Early studies at the University of Michigan, under the leadership of Rensis Likert, suggested that leadership behaviour could be described on a continuum ranging from authoritarian to participative style. Likert identified four main styles of leadership, in particular, around decision making and the degree to which people are involved in the process.[8]

Exploitive authoritative Exploitive authoritative leaders have low concern for people, and use threats and other coercive ways for compliance of decisions. Communication is usually top-down, and managers are least concerned with people's concerns.

Benevolent authoritative Benevolent authoritative leaders are authoritarian, but pay attention to people's concerns. They attend to people's problems and use rewards to encourage appropriate performance. Even though there may be some delegation of decisions, almost all major decisions are still made by the leader.

Consultative Consultative leaders make the major decisions, which remain centralised, although they make genuine efforts to listen to their people's ideas.

Participative Participative leaders involve people at all levels, including lower levels in the decision-making process. People across the organization are psychologically closer together and work well together at all levels.

LBDQ Theory

The Ohio State University, using the famous Leadership Behaviour Description

Questionnaire (LBDQ), conducted landmark research. In this approach, group members describe the behaviour of the leader, or leaders, in any type of group or organization. It is assumed that the followers have had an opportunity to observe the leader in action as a leader of their group. Based on extensive research, 40 items were developed. However, only 30 items are scored, 15 for each of the two dimensions, initiating structure and consideration. These two dimensions accounted for approximately 34 to 50 per cent of the common variance. *Initiating structure* refers to the leader's behaviour in delineating the relationship between himself or herself and the members of his or her group, and in endeavouring to establish well-defined patterns of organization, channels of communication, and ways of getting the job done. *Consideration* refers to behaviour indicative of friendship, mutual trust, respect, and warmth in relationship between the leader and the members of the group.[9]

Continuum of Leader Behaviour

The two contrasting styles of boss-centred leadership, defined by emphasis on the task to be done, and subordinate-centred leadership, defined by attention to the persons doing the task (people-oriented style), were later seen as a continuum from high task orientation. The manager makes a decision and announces it (telling) by convincing people about what should be done. The manager 'sells' a decision (selling), and by discussing the task and its strategy with subordinates, he or she presents ideas and invites questions (consulting). The manager provides the employees the responsibility to plan and achieve results. Thus, by providing enough support, the manager permits his or her subordinates to function within defined limits (delegating).[10]

Managerial Grid

The treatment of task orientation and people orientation as two independent dimensions was a major step in leadership studies. Blake and Mouton proposed the famous managerial grid with these two dimensions, each dimension ranging from low (1) to high (9).[11] This section describes the five styles of the managerial grid, or the leadership grid as it came to be known later.

Impoverished management   It is characterised by low–low (style 1, 1), low task, and low people orientation. Minimum effort is exercised towards getting the work done. It refers to a lazy approach that avoids work as much as possible.

Authority–compliance   It is characterised by high–low (style 9, 1), high task, and low people orientation. There is a strong focus on task, but with little concern for people. The focus is on efficiency, including the elimination of people wherever possible.

Country club management   It is characterised by low–high (style 1, 9), low task, high people orientation, care and concern for the people, a comfortable and friendly environment, and collegial style. However, a low focus on tasks may lead to questionable results.

Middle of the road management   This style of leadership is characterised by medium–medium (style 5, 5), medium task, and medium people orientation. There is a lack of focus on both people and the work. The leader concentrates only on getting the work done and does not push the boundaries of achievement.

Team management   It refers to a leadership style characterised by high–high (style 9, 9), high on task, and high on people orientation. Highly motivated subordinates are committed to the task, and their leader is committed to his and her people and the task.

CONTINGENCY THEORIES

Contingency theories are based on the assumption that the leader's ability to lead is contingent upon various situational factors such as the leader's preferred style, the capabilities and behaviours of followers, etc. Contingency theories contend that there is no one best way of leading and that a leadership style that is effective in some situations may not be always successful in others.

Fiedler's Theory

Another milestone in leadership research was Fiedler's theory of contingency. Fiedler demonstrated that the effectiveness of task orientation and people orientation depends on the situation.[12]

According to Fiedler, relationships, power, and task structure are the three key factors that drive effective leadership styles. He identified the least preferred coworker (LPC) scoring for leaders by asking them first to think of a person with whom they have worked and would now least prefer to work with again. The manager then scores the person on a range of scales between positive factors (friendly, helpful, cheerful, etc.) and negative factors (unfriendly, unhelpful, gloomy, etc.). A high LPC leader generally scores the other person as positive and a low LPC leader scores the other person as negative.[13]

High LPC leaders tend to have close and positive relationships, and act in a supportive way. They even prioritise the relationship before the task. Low LPC leaders put the task first and turn to relationships only when they are satisfied with the progress of the work.

The following three aspects determine the effectiveness of the two leadership styles (high or low LPC):

Leader–member relations   The extent to which the leader has the support and loyalties of followers. The relations with them are friendly and cooperative.

Task structure   The extent to which tasks are standardised, documented, and controlled.

Leader's position power   The extent to which the leader has authority to assess follower performance and give reward or punishment.

As shown in Exhibit 21.4, effectiveness of a leader's style (low or high LPC) will depend on the combination of the three aspects.

Exhibit 21.4 *Leadership Effectiveness Model*

Leader–member relations	Task structure	Leader's position power	Most effective leader
Good	Structured	Strong	Low LPC
Good	Structured	Weak	Low LPC
Good	Unstructured	Strong	Low LPC
Good	Unstructured	Weak	High LPC
Poor	Structured	Strong	High LPC
Poor	Structured	Weak	High LPC
Poor	Unstructured	Strong	High LPC
Poor	Unstructured	Weak	Low LPC

This approach tries to assess respondents' beliefs about people, whether they see others as positive (high LPC) or negative (low LPC).

Cognitive Resource Theory

Cognitive resource theory is another contingency theory.[14] It predicts that (1) a leader's cognitive ability contributes to the performance of the team only when the leader's approach is directive, (2) stress affects the relationship between intelligence and decision quality, and (3) experience is positively related to decision quality under high stress.

Leader's cognitive ability When leaders are better than their people at planning and decision making, in order to implement their plans and decisions, they need to tell people what to do.

When they are not better than the people in the team, then a non-directive approach is more appropriate. For example, such leaders can facilitate an open discussion with the team, where ideas can be aired and the best approach identified and implemented.

Effect of stress Intelligence is fully functional and makes an optimal contribution in situations of low stress. However, during high stress, natural intelligence not only makes no positive difference, but it may have a negative effect. One reason for this may be that an intelligent person seeks rational solutions, which may not be available, and may be one of the causes of stress. In such situations, a leader who is inexperienced in 'gut feel' decisions is forced to rely on this unfamiliar approach. Another possibility is that the leader retreats within himself or herself, to think hard about the problem, leaving the group to their own devices.

Experience and decision quality When there is a high stress situation and the relationship between decision making and intelligence is impaired, experience of the same or similar situations enables the leader to react in the best possible way.

The main implication of the cognitive resource theory is that a leader can be effective and powerful if he or she focuses on the strategic role, is an expert in problem solving, and possesses unique knowledge and skills that nobody else has.

Strategic Contingencies Theory

The strategic contingencies theory, proposed by Fiedler, deals with the concept of organizational power. Intra-organizational power depends on three factors: problem skills, actor centrality, and uniqueness of skill.[15] Fiedler linked the cognitive resource theory with his LPC theory, suggesting that high LPC scores are the main drivers of directive behaviour.

An employee will be in demand if he or she has the skills and expertise to resolve important problems, works in a central part of the workflow of the organization, and is difficult to replace.

For simple tasks, a leader's intelligence and experience are irrelevant. If people work on tasks that do not need direction or support, then it does not matter how good the leader is at making decisions. The manager need not provide any further support to the team.

Vroom–Yetton Theory

Vroom and Yetton, using a decision-making framework, contrasted the autocratic and consultative styles of leadership.[16] They proposed two dimensions: decision quality and decision acceptance. *Decision quality* is the selection of the best alternative and is particularly important when there are many alternatives. It is also important when there are serious implications for selecting (or failing to select) the best alternative. *Decision acceptance* is the degree to which a follower accepts a decision made by a leader. Leaders focus more on decision acceptance when the quality of decision is more important.

Vroom and Yetton defined five different decision procedures. Two of these procedures are autocratic (A1 and A2), two are consultative (C1 and C2), and one is group based (G2).

A1: Leader takes known information and then decides alone.

A2: Leader gets information from followers and then decides alone.

C1: Leader shares problem with followers individually, listens to ideas, and then decides alone.

C2: Leader shares problems with followers as a group, listens to ideas, and then decides alone.

G2: Leader shares problems with followers as a group and then seeks and accepts consensus agreement.

Situational factors that influence the method are relatively logical. These factors are illustrated here.

1. When decision quality is important and followers possess useful information, then A1 and A2 procedures are not the best methods.

2. When the leader sees decision quality as important but followers do not, then G2 procedure is inappropriate.

3. When decision quality is important, the problem is unstructured, and the leader lacks information or the skills to make the decision alone, then G2 procedure is best.

4. When decision acceptance is important and followers are unlikely to accept an autocratic decision, then A1 and A2 procedures are inappropriate.
5. When decision acceptance is important but followers are likely to disagree with one another, then A1, A2, and C1 procedures are not appropriate, because they do not give opportunity for differences to be resolved.
6. When decision quality is not important but decision acceptance is critical, then G2 is the best method.
7. When the whole team, including the leader, feels that decision quality is important, and the decision is not likely to result from an autocratic decision, then G2 procedure is the most appropriate.

Path–Goal Theory

Path–goal leadership theory is a contingency theory proposed by House.[17] It integrates the expectancy theory of motivation. House has suggested four types of leaders: directive (directs subordinates), supportive (shows genuine concern for subordinates), participative (consults subordinates but decides himself or herself), and achievement oriented (sets challenging goals and shows confidence in subordinates). The path–goal theory proposes that the same leader uses all these styles, depending on the situation. The situation is characterised by two main factors: subordinates' characteristics (leader behaviour being accepted to the extent to which subordinates see the behaviour leading to present or future satisfaction) and environmental pressures on subordinates.

The second factor is more important in the expectancy theory of motivation. Subordinates' motivation (increased effort) depends on two factors: the leaders making subordinates' needs contingent on effective performance, and the leader providing support for performance, including guidance and rewards. As proposed in the contingency—expectancy framework, the leader—by influencing subordinates' perceptions and motivation—improves their role clarity, expectancies, satisfaction, and performance. In other words, the leader attempts to make the subordinates' paths to their goals smooth. The leader must use an appropriate style to smoothen the path to the goals. The leader smoothens the path by stimulating subordinates' need for achievement, increasing pay-offs for goal achievement, coaching and guiding, clarifying subordinates' expectancies, reducing functioning barriers, and increasing opportunities for high satisfaction on good performance. This theory has been used extensively in management.

SITUATIONAL THEORY OF LEADERSHIP

Situational theory is the most popular contingency theory, and we shall discuss it in detail in this section. Hersey and Blanchard combined the grid approach and the contingency theories to propose their situational theory of leadership.[18]

According to this theory, leadership is a function of the situation and an effective leader is one who assesses the situation accurately, uses a style appropriate to the situation, is flexible, and is also able to influence and alter the situation. We shall discuss these aspects in some detail.

Leadership Styles

According to Hersey and Blanchard, a leader is concerned with the task to be performed and with building relations with his or her people. However, a leader may have high or low concern for each of these (task and people). A leader may focus mainly on the work to be completed and/or the leader may focus mainly on building the team. Combining concerns for task (low or high) and for people (low or high), Hersey and Blanchard proposed four leadership styles: Style 1 indicating high concern for the task and low concern for people, Style 2 showing high concern for both, Style 3 having high concern for people and low for the task, and Style 4 with both low. According to them, all the four styles are functional; it is their relevance to situations that is important.

Later, Blanchard[19] proposed new terms and his modified model is used here, with the necessary additions. As already stated, leadership style in the situational model is classified according to the amount of task and relationship behaviour the leader engages in.

Task-related behaviour, called directive behaviour by Blanchard, is called regulating behaviour here because a leader's behaviour is focused mainly on regulating his or her group members and their activities for task accomplishment. Other leaders concentrate on providing socio-emotional support and on building personal relationships, which is called nurturing behaviour (formerly called relationship behaviour and also supportive behaviour by Blanchard).

Regulating behaviour This is defined as the extent to which a leader engages in one-way communication; spells out the groups' roles and tells the group members what to do, where to do it, when to do it, and how to do it; and closely supervises their performance. Three words can be used to define regulating behaviour: structure, control, and supervise.

Nurturing behaviour This is defined as the extent to which a leader engages in two-way communication, listens, provides support and encouragement, facilitates interaction, and involves the group in decision making. Three words can be used to define nurturing behaviour: praise, listen, and facilitate.

A combination of high and low directive and supportive behaviour will give four quadrants, each representing four different leadership styles. These are shown in Exhibit 21.5.

Style 1: Directive High regulating and low nurturing leader behaviour is called directive style. The leader defines the roles of group members, telling them what tasks to do and how, when, and where to do them. Problem solving and decision making are initiated solely by the leader. Solutions and decisions are announced, communication is largely one-way, and the leader closely supervises implementation.

Exhibit 21.5 *The Four Leadership Styles*

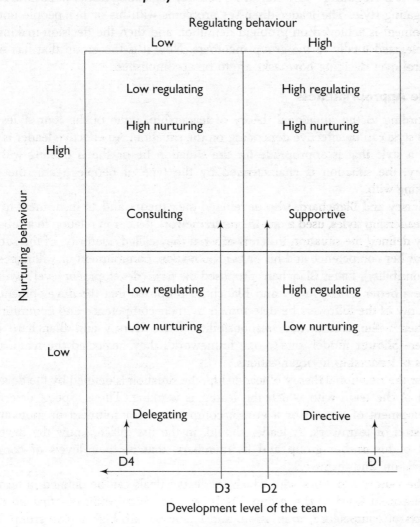

Development level of the team

Style 2: Supportive High regulating and high nurturing behaviour is called supportive style. In this style the leader still provides a great deal of direction and leads with his or her ideas, but the leader also attempts to discover the group's feelings about decisions as well as eliciting their ideas and suggestions. While two-way communication and support are increased, control over decision making remains with the leader.

Style 3: Consulting High nurturing and low regulating leader behaviour is called consulting style. In this style, the focus of control for day-to-day decision making and problem solving shifts from the leader to the group members. The leader's role is to provide recognition and to actively listen and facilitate problem solving and decision making on the part of the group.

Style 4: Delegating   Low nurturing and low regulating leader behaviour is labelled delegating style. The leader discusses problems with his or her people until a joint agreement is achieved on problem definition and then the decision-making process is delegated totally to the group members. Now it is the group that has significant control over deciding how tasks are to be accomplished.

Style Appropriateness

According to the situational theory of leadership, none of the four styles is ideal: each style can be effective depending on the situation. An effective leader is one who uses a style that is appropriate for the situation he or she is dealing with. In this theory, the situation is characterised by the type of people (team) the leader is working with.

Hersey and Blanchard, who developed their theory and an instrument to measure the leadership styles, used a one-to-one framework (leader in relation to a subordinate). They defined the situation in terms of what they called 'maturity' of the subordinate (his or her competence and his or her motivation, commitment or willingness to take responsibility). Later, Blanchard proposed the term 'development level', which seems to be a better term. Hersey and Blanchard proposed that the development level or maturity of the followers be determined by their competence and commitment, that is, their willingness to take responsibility. Since Hersey and Blanchard used the leader–follower model (one-to-one framework), they neglected the team, the main focus of leadership in organizations.

For the situational theory of leadership, the situation is defined by the development level of the team with which the leader is working. Three aspects determine the development of a team or a group: competence, commitment or motivation, and cohesion or teamwork. A leader should, in the first place, know the development level of his or her group and its members, that is, their levels of competence, motivation, and teamwork.

The various situations with which the leader deals can be defined in terms of the development level of the group. D4 level (very high) indicates that all the three aspects of competence, motivation, and teamwork are high in the group. D3 level (moderately high) means two of the three aspects are high, while one is low. D2 (moderately low) means one aspect is high and the other two are low. Level D1 (low) indicates that the group is low on all three aspects.

The effective leadership styles for each development level are shown in Exhibit 21.5. (Style 1 is appropriate for a D1 team, Style 2 for a D2 team, Style 3 for a D3 team, and Style 4 for a D4 team.) An effective leader uses a style appropriate to the development level of his or her team or organization. An example of style appropriateness is given in the next section.

Style Flexibility

Hersey and Blanchard also proposed the concept of style range or flexibility (how easily a leader is capable of using the four styles) in addition to relevance or appropriateness (how appropriately a leader uses the various styles). A leader needs both diagnostic competence to assess the situation (development level of the group) as well as competence to use the various styles with ease, as relevant to the situation or its changing conditions. As already stated, according to this theory, if the situation is D1, characterised by a low level of development (people do not know their jobs well, have low motivation, and do not support each other), the most effective style would be 1, in which the leader defines tasks, monitors performance, and provides the necessary guidance. However, after the group has 'developed' (i.e., they know their jobs, work together, and are able to perform fairly well), the leader needs to change the style, paying attention to group morale, facilitating of work, and so on. On further development of the group, the leader need no longer worry about task requirements (low directive behaviour) but may need to build the group (high supportive). If the group is at D4, that is, highly developed (can work on its own as a team and has relevant competencies), the leader need not be concerned with providing guidance or with providing support (low on both, 4). The leader's main focus may then be envisioning, boundary management, providing facilities needed by the group, and looking after external linkages and relationships.

The leader can decide which leadership style will be more appropriate for the group when he or she knows the development level of the group he or she leads. Diagnosis of the development level may also help the leader to prepare a plan of action for raising the development level by working on the dimensions in which the group is weak.

Leadership Effectiveness

Although the situational theory of leadership suggests that leadership effectiveness depends on the use of a style appropriate to the situation and that there is no best leadership style, the most desirable style is 4. However, in order to move towards this, the leader needs to prepare the group and take them to the D4 level. In this sense, this theory of leadership is a developmental theory.

Raising competence levels   The competence level of a group is made up of the competence of its members. Competence includes the understanding (based on knowledge) and skills required to perform a job. Competence levels of individual members can be summed up and the average gives the group's competence level. Competence building requires providing information relevant to the roles, building skills to fulfil the roles effectively, and planning a proper long-term training strategy.

Raising commitment levels   Commitment or motivation refers to the willingness of individual members to set and accept challenging goals, their eagerness to take responsibility, their involvement in the work, and job satisfaction. Again, the average of individual ratings or scores gives the group's motivational level.

Commitment building (developing motivation) can be facilitated by helping individual members to set realistic and challenging goals, supporting them to achieve these, and recognising their achievement through feedback and rewards.

Raising teamwork levels   The teamwork level can be diagnosed by assessing the level of cohesion, collaboration, and confrontation in the group. Cohesion means that the group functions as a strong team and each member feels that his or her views and concerns are considered by others. Collaboration indicates that some tasks are done by members as small teams and members feel free to volunteer, ask for, and respond to requests for help. Confrontation implies that whenever there is a problem that concerns the group, the group faces the problem and deals with it, generating alternative solutions and taking decisions about a course of action. An instrument on this aspect is available.[21]

Team building can be achieved by making teams responsible for various tasks, allocating resources to them, and recognising the importance of teamwork through team rewards, the high value accorded to teamwork in performance appraisal systems, and special programmes to reduce conflicts and increase collaboration. Various interventions for team building have been discussed in Chapter 18.

Raising development levels through delegation   The movement of a group towards the D4 level can be accelerated through delegation. We shall discuss various processes of delegation and how to ensure their effectiveness in the next chapter.

In short, leadership is the dynamic process of making people more effective, increasing their competence to multiply power, and achieving goals through them. There are different styles of participating in this process. However, the ultimate goal of a leader is to develop his team and people to become more effective and competent to achieve organizational goals as well as their own objectives.

LEADERSHIP FUNCTIONS THEORIES

Two types of leadership functions have been contrasted, transactional and transformational. Transactional leaders maximise efficiency, while transformational leaders emphasise on creativity.

Transactional Leadership

The basic beliefs of transactional leaders are that people are motivated by reward and punishment; social systems work best with a clear chain of command; when subordinates agree to do a job, they cede all authority to their manager; and the prime purpose of subordinates is to do what their manager tells them to do.

The transactional leader works by creating clear structures. The leader provides clear instructions to his or her subordinates regarding their work and the subsequent rewards. Punishments are not always mentioned, but they are well understood. The formal systems of discipline are usually in place.

Transactional leadership is based on *contingency*; rewards or punishments are contingent upon performance. Transactional leadership is still a popular approach with most managers.

Transformational Leadership

While transactional functions are primarily concerned with successful completion of tasks, transformational functions go beyond the immediate task. Transactional functions build the competencies of individuals and groups, and enable them to achieve targets that the organization or the individual would have not expected to achieve. These functions empower various groups and individuals in an organization. The following functions fall in this category: visioning, modelling (setting a personal example of a desirable style and behaviour), setting standards, building culture and climate, boundary management (ensuring continuous availability of resources, support from the major customers and from outside, and developing a strong lobby and networks for the organization), synergising (building teams), and searching and nurturing talent.

Based on their research, Singh and Bhandarkar[22] reported the following six main characteristics of transformational leaders:
1. Empowering
2. Risk taking
3. Clarity of mission
4. Team building
5. Equanimity
6. Evolving trust

Burns' theory

Inspired by the effectiveness of great leaders such as Martin Luther King and Mahatma Gandhi, who 'transformed' millions of helpless people into a formidable force, Burns proposed the concept of transformational leadership. He assumed that people associated with a higher moral position will be motivated by a leader who promotes this quality. Such people are better off working collaboratively than working individually.

Burns defined transformational leadership as a process in which leaders and followers engage in a mutual process of 'raising one another to higher levels of morality and motivation'.[23]

Transformational leaders raise the bar by appealing to higher ideals and values of followers. In doing so, they may model the values themselves and use charismatic methods to attract people to the values and to the leader.

Burns' view is that transformational leadership is more effective than transactional leadership, in which the appeal is to more selfish concerns. An appeal to social values thus encourages people to collaborate, rather than working alone as individuals (and potentially competitively with one another). He also views transformational leadership as an ongoing process rather than the discrete exchanges of the transactional approach.

Bass' theory

Bass defined transformational leadership in terms of how the leader affects followers, who are intended to trust, admire, and respect the transformational leader.[24] He identified three ways in which leaders transform followers: increasing their awareness of task importance and value; getting them to focus first on team or organizational goals, rather than their own interests; and activating their higher-order needs.

Two key charismatic effects that transformational leaders achieve are to evoke strong emotions and to cause identification of the followers with the leader. This can be achieved through stirring appeals, coaching, and mentoring. Bass has recently noted that authentic transformational leadership is grounded in moral foundations that are based on four components: idealised influence, inspirational motivation, intellectual stimulation, and individualised consideration. He also proposed three aspects: the moral character of the leader, the ethical values embedded in the leader's vision, articulation, and process (which followers either embrace or reject), and the morality of the processes of social ethical choice and action that leaders and followers engage in and collectively pursue.[25]

Leader–member exchange theory

A well-known transactional theory is the leader–member exchange theory, also known as LMX, or vertical dyad linkage theory. It describes how leaders in groups maintain their position through a series of tacit exchange agreements with their members.[26]

Leaders often have a special relationship with an inner circle of trusted lieutenants, assistants, and advisers. The members of the inner circle are entrusted with high levels of responsibility, decision influence, and access to resources. The members of the 'in-group' have to pay for their position. They work harder, are more committed to task objectives, and share more administrative duties. They are also expected to be fully committed and loyal to their leader. The out-group, on the other hand, is provided with lower levels of choice or influence.

This also puts constraints upon leaders. They have to constantly nurture the relationship with their inner circle. The subordinates are given power; however, it is ensured that they do not strike out on their own.

LMX process

These relationships, if they are going to happen, start very soon after a person joins the group and follow three stages.

Role taking The member joins the team and the leader assesses his or her abilities and talents. Based on this, the leader may offer them opportunities to demonstrate their capabilities.

Another key factor in this stage is the discovery by both parties of how the other likes to be respected.

Role making In the second phase, the leader and member take part in an unstructured and informal negotiation whereby a role is created for the member. The often tacit promise of benefit and power in return for dedication and loyalty takes place during this stage.

Trust building is very important in this stage, and any betrayal by the employee can result in the member being relegated to the out-group.

This negotiation includes relationship factors and pure work-related ones. A member who is similar to the leader in various ways is more likely to succeed. This perhaps explains why mixed gender relationships are usually less successful than same-gender ones (it also affects the seeking of respect in the first stage). The same effect also applies to cultural and racial differences.

Routinisation   In this phase, a pattern of ongoing social exchange between the leader and the member becomes established.

Successful members are thus similar in many ways to the leader (which perhaps explains why many senior teams comprise of upper caste, upper middle-class, and middle-aged individuals). They work hard at building and sustaining trust and respect. The employees are empathetic, patient, reasonable, sensitive, and are good at seeing the viewpoint of other people (especially the leader). Aggression, sarcasm, and an egocentric view are exhibited by members of the out-group.

The overall quality of the LMX relationship varies with several factors. Curiously, the quality is better when the challenge of the job is extremely high or extremely low. The size of the group, the financial resource availability, and the overall workload are also important determinants of the quality of the LMX relationships.

The leaders also gain power by being members of their superiors' inner circle. These leaders then share this power with their subordinates. People with unusual power at the bottom of an organization may get it from an unbroken chain of circles up to the hierarchy.

SOME RECENT THEORIES

Some new theories of leadership have recently been reported. We shall briefly discuss a few of them.

Level 5 Leadership

Based on an intensive study of 11 most effective leaders, Collins[27] proposed the theory of Level 5 leadership. A Level 5 leader blends genuine personal humility with intense professional will. According to such a leader, Level 5 is the highest level of leadership in a hierarchy of leadership capabilities. Leaders at the other four levels in the hierarchy can produce high levels of success but not enough to elevate organizations from mediocrity to sustained excellence. Good-to-great transformations do not happen without Level 5 leadership. A Level 5 leader can transform a mediocre organization into a great organization. The various levels suggested by Collins are as follows:

Level 1:   The leader is a highly capable individual. He or she makes productive contributions through talent, knowledge, skills, and good work habits.

Level 2:   The leader is a contributing team member. He or she contributes to the achievement of group objectives and works effectively with others in a group setting.

Level 3: The leader is a competent manager. He or she organizes people and resources towards the effective and efficient pursuit of predetermined objectives.

Level 4: The leader is an effective leader. He or she catalyses commitment to and vigorous pursuit of a clear and compelling vision, and stimulates the group to high performance standards.

Level 5: The leader is an executive. He or she builds enduring greatness through a paradoxical combination of professional will and personal humility.

Each level is appropriate in its own right, but none has the power of Level 5.

One does not need to move sequentially through each level of the hierarchy to reach the top. However, to be a fully-fledged Level 5, we need the capabilities of all the lower levels, along with the special characteristics of Level 5.

A Level 5 leader possesses paradoxical combination of professional will and personal humility. Collins has cited Abraham Lincoln as an example of a Level 5 leader. The example of Mahatma Gandhi is more appropriate. In India, the late Ravi Matthai, former director of IIM, Ahmedabad, represented such institutional leadership. Narayana Murthy of Infosys is an example of corporate Level 5 leadership. Collins has suggested the following characteristics of the two aspects.

Professional will

The features of a leader who possesses professional will are as follows:
- Creates superb results, a clear catalyst in the transition from good to great.
- Demonstrates an unwavering resolve to do whatever must be done to produce the best long-term results, no matter how difficult.
- Sets the standard of building an enduring great company; will settle for nothing less.
- Looks in the mirror, not out the window, to apportion responsibility for poor results, never blaming other people, external factors, or bad luck.

Personal humility

The features of a leader exhibiting personal humility are as follows:
- Demonstrates a compelling modesty, shunning public adulation; never boastful.
- Acts with a quiet, calm determination; relies principally on inspired standards, not inspiring charisma, to motivate.
- Channels ambition into the company, not the self; sets up successors for even greater success in the next generation.
- Looks out the window, not in the mirror, to apportion credit for the success of the company—to other people, external factors, and good luck.

Level 5 leadership is an essential factor for taking an organization from good to great.

Succession planning

Level 5 leaders have ambition not for themselves, but for their organizations. They routinely select superb successors. They want to see their organizations become even more successful in the next generation.

The Window and the Mirror: Level 5 leaders, inherently humble, look out the window to apportion credit—even undue credit—to factors outside themselves. If they cannot find a specific event or person to give credit to, they credit good luck. At the same time, they look in the mirror to assign responsibility, never citing bad luck for external factors when things go poorly.

How can a manager become a Level 5 leader? To quote Collins, 'There are two categories of people: those who do not have the capability to become Level 5 leaders, and those who do. The first category consists of people who could never bring themselves to subjugate their egoistic needs to the greater ambition of building something larger and more lasting than themselves. For these people, work will always be first and foremost about what they get—fame, fortune, adulation, power, etc. What they build, create, and contribute is not important to them.

'The great irony is that personal ambition that often drives people to positions of power stands at odds with the humility required for Level 5 leadership. When we combine that irony with the fact that boards of directors frequently operate under the false belief that they need to hire a larger-than-life, egocentric leader to make an organization great, we can quickly see why Level 5 leaders rarely appear at the top of our institutions.'

More people are from the second category and have the potential to become Level 5 leaders. They can be helped to move into Level 5 through self-reflection, conscious personal development, association with a mentor, having a great teacher and loving parents, and working with a Level 5 boss. Of course, a 'crucible' (a significant life experience) may contribute significantly to the transition to Level 5.

Era Theories

Recently, Bennis and Thomas[28] have proposed a theory of leadership as a product of era, 'crucible', and individual factors. Eras 'are characterised by defining events, and may occur every 20 years or so' (p.10). For their study they took two contrasting eras: 1945–54, referred to as the era of limits, and 1991–2000, called the era of options. The researchers were keenly interested in studying 'how era and epiphanic events influenced these leaders worldviews at *similar* points in their lives, i.e., between the ages of 25 and 30. So, in a very real sense, we wanted to compare the effects of era on *two* groups of young people, one that was 25–30 years old in 1950 (roughly) and the other that was 25–30 years old in 2000.'

They contrasted these two eras as analogue and digital worlds: 'The analog world was one that valued linear narrative and thinking. It believed in organizational hierarchy and chain of command. The digital world is nonlinear and has ditched the corporate pyramid for the flat organization. To use psychologist Karl Weick's insightful metaphors, the world born during the Depression and World War II could be understood using a map. To make a sense of the Wild West of the digital world requires a compass. As Weick explains 'Maps, by definition, can help only in known worlds—worlds that have been charted before. Compasses are helpful when you are not sure where you are and can get only a general sense of direction.'

Bennis and Thomas termed older leaders who grew up in the era of limits as *geezers*, and younger leaders who grew up in the era of options as *geeks*. 'Even the controlling metaphors of the two eras differ. Older leaders were trained to think of the world in Newtonian, mechanical terms. Younger ones can look at the world in terms of living organisms and biological systems that are constantly changing and evolving' (p. 12). They found three key differences between geeks and geezers when they compared their aspirations at the same age (roughly 25 to 30). 'First, geeks have bigger and more ambitious roles than geezers; they aspired to change the world and make history, whereas geezers were concerned with making a living. Second, geeks place far more emphasis on achieving balances in their work, family, and personal lives than did geezers at a comparable age. And third, geeks are far less likely than geezers to have heroes' (p.13). They also found some common characteristics in geeks and geezers, which we have discussed earlier in the section on trait theories.

Mayo and Nohria have also given importance to the historical periods to explain leadership styles.[29] They believe that while studies focusing on personal characteristics of leaders and their successes have some merit, they do not explain how people with very different personal qualities have succeeded in creating equally big corporations. These researchers feel that leadership is better examined by understanding the context of the times the leaders operated in. Based on the studies of the greatest business leaders of the twentieth century and their social, economic, and political milieu, in which they were operating, the researchers found that the leaders of each decade had much in common, not in their personal traits, but in their focus. The period of 1910–19 was characterised by pushing the frontiers of operational efficiency; the decade of 1940–49 was characterised by reaching new heights through standardisation, and the decade of 1950–59 saw the era of excessive consumption. According to them the entrepreneurs, CEOs, and managers, who understood their eras correctly achieved spectacular success.

Crucible Theory

As already stated, Bennis and Thomas have given importance to crucibles in the formation of leadership. They have proposed that a 'crucible' (an absorbing event or experience, which transforms an individual) is critical in the development of leaders. A crucible can be a tragedy such as a war, death of a loved one, losing an election; or a joyous experience such as discovering something, a unique achievement, or an apprenticeship with a mentor. Leaders create meaning out of crucibles. Abraham Zaleznik suggested the concept of the 'crucible of leadership' in 1977,[30] while discussing the difference between a manager and a leader. According to him, one difference was whether a person was 'once-born' or 'twice-born'. That is, had they had a traumatic experience in their life (the second birth), requiring, 'a turning into one's self ... following which one emerges with a deepened sense of self, and relatively free of dependency on the social structure.' It may be noted in this connection that in the Hindu tradition a Brahmin boy goes through an initiation process to become *dwij* (twice-born) and, as a part of the ritual ceremony, is symbolically sent away to Kashi (Varanasi)! In the past, a boy had to go for a long time to Kashi (a crucible in terms of 'insertion into foreign territory' and 'enforced reflection') before 'graduating' to the dwij status.

As stated in the earlier section of trait theories, Bennis and Thomas found some common characteristics in all the leaders, both geeks and geezers. These leaders thrive in unstructured settings. They are also characterised by neoteny, adaptive capacity, engaging others by creating shared meaning, voice, and integrity.

Bennis and Thomas derived these conclusions from their detailed interviews with 18 young leaders, 35 years of age and under (referred to as geeks), and 25 persons, 70 years of age or above (referred to as geezers).

Financial Theory

Prince,[31] heading the Perth Leadership Institute, and a former CEO with 20 years of experience in the public and private sector, has proposed an interesting theory by including the construct of 'financial signature'. It refers to a set of innate financial traits that are fundamental to a leader's style. Prince created a taxonomy that financial signatures in order to classify specific leadership traits. Using case studies of successful business leaders, his book illustrates the impact that financial signature combined with the organization's financial mission has on the success or failure of a company. An individual's financial signature can be measured on two continuous axes: value addition and resource utilisation. According to Prince the financial signature is innate. A financial mission is an organizational quality that is also measured along these two axes and is not fixed. Prince argues that it is possible to forecast a company's financial success by analysing these two variables.

All executives have two basic drives: to add value to products or services, and to deploy resources with a certain amount of efficiency. The first drive can be inferred from a business's gross margin and the second by its relative indirect expenses. Together the two numbers constitute an executive's 'financial signature' (p. 5).

Prince proposes four leadership styles, by combining signatures and missions: (1) venture capitalist—both gross margin and expenses are high, (2) buccaneer—high gross margin and low expenses, (3) mercantilist—low gross margin and high expenses, and (4) discounter—both gross margin and expenses are low. Each style has a characteristic set of financial behaviours.

Certain financial signatures are best suited for particular industries. Mercantilists, for example, are ideal for commodity markets with high fixed costs. Moreover, companies might need executives with different financial signatures at various stages in their life cycle. A start-up, for instance, might be better off with a venture capitalist at the helm. Later, that same firm might need to fill its executive suites with discounters. No matter how capable the leader, a mismatch between an organization's requirements and the actual financial signature of its CEO can lead to management problems, possibly even to company failure. Prince also offers a practical guide for human resource and leadership development. Measures have been suggested for self-assessment for leaders to determine their financial signature.

Culture-specific Theories

Some authors have maintained that leadership is culture specific, depending on the special characteristics of the culture.

Nurturant–task theory

J.B.P. Sinha has drawn attention to characteristics of the Indian culture, such as dependence proneness, lack of team orientation, conspicuous use of resting time as a sign of status (late arrival at work and long lunches), preference of the personal over contractual relationships, and *apna–paraya* orientation, in which rules and regulations can be side-stepped to accommodate a friend or a relative. According to Sinha, in such a culture, nurturant–task (NT) leadership is likely to be more effective.[32]

The NT leadership style has two components: concern for the task and a nurturing orientation towards the subordinates. A nurturant task leader demands task performance and maintains a high level of productivity. However, such leaders also show care and affection for the well-being of their people and are committed to their professional growth. The nurturant task leader plays a paternal role and encourages participation. 'He understands the expectations of his subordinates. He knows that they relish dependency and personalised relationship, accept his authority and look towards him for guidance and direction.'[33]

Sinha has contrasted the authoritative style of leadership with the participative style, with task leadership in the middle. According to him the present Indian social ethos is not receptive for participative leadership. He validated his findings by a number of studies of employees' responses in several organizations. He developed a profile of the nurturant task leadership style.

B-C-D theory

Based on his research at the Indian Institute of Management, T.V. Rao[34] has classified the leadership styles into the benevolent, critical, and developmental styles.

Benevolent style   Leaders who practise the benevolent or paternalistic leadership style believe that all their employees should be constantly guided and treated with affection like parents treat their children. Such leaders are relationship oriented, assign tasks on the basis of their own likes and dislikes, constantly guide and protect subordinates, understand the needs of their employees, salvage the crisis situations by active involvement, distribute rewards to those who are loyal and obedient, share information with those who are close to him, etc.

Critical style   The critical leadership style is closer to Theory X, discussed in Chapter 1. Such managers believe that employees should be closely and constantly supervised, directed and reminded of their duties and responsibilities. These managers have short-term goals, cannot tolerate mistakes or conflicts among employees. They are also dominating, keep all information to themselves, work strictly according to rules and regulations, and are highly discipline oriented.

Developmental style A developmental leadership style is characterised by empowerment of subordinates. Such managers believe in developing the competencies of their employees and delegate authority to them. These managers have long-term goals, share information, facilitate the resolution of conflicts and mistakes by the employees themselves.

The developmental style is the most preferred leadership style in organizations. Managers may not be aware of the leadership style used by them and its effects on their employees. Some individuals and some situations may require a combination of benevolent and critical styles. This classification is based on the findings of the responses on Stewart's 35 Psychosocial Maturity model. Rao has developed an instrument 36 to measure these three styles, based on the ways of dealing with nine different situations such as managing rewards, managing conflicts, managing mistakes, assigning tasks, communication, etc. The instrument has been used in 360 degree feedback.

The following results are based on a study of relationship between leadership styles and feelings and reactions of subordinates. ('R' refers to the correlation factor.)

Benevolent or paternalistic style was positively correlated with feelings of loyalty and dependence of subordinates on the manager ($r = 0.51$), feelings of dislike for the boss and tendency to avoid work ($r = 0.54$), and negatively related to feelings of development, empowerment, growth, and independent thinking ($r = -0.5$), learning ($r = -0.4$), morale ($r = -0.5$), and satisfaction ($r = -0.4$).

Critical style was positively related to resentment and dislike for the boss and work ($r = 0.75$), moderately and positively correlated with dependency and personal loyalty ($r = 0.47$), and negatively correlated with empowerment and growth ($r = -0.6$), learning ($r = -0.5$), morale ($r = -0.6$), and satisfaction ($r = -0.6$).

Developmental style was positively related to empowerment, growth, and independence ($r = 0.73$), learning ($r = 0.77$), morale ($r = 0.85$), and satisfaction ($r = 0.84$); and negatively correlated with dependence ($r = -0.4$) and feelings of resentment or dislike for the boss or work ($r = -0.7$).

Performance–Maintenance Theory

The performance–maintenance (PM) theory, proposed by Misumi, is a Japanese culture-specific theory of leadership. Misumi suggested two functions of effective leaders: performance function, referred to as 'P', and the maintenance function, referred to as 'M'.[35] The P function has to do with task accomplishment, while the M function has to do with the maintenance of good working relations among those who are engaged in the task. According to Misumi, the emphasis on P and M will vary from situation to situation. Misumi states that even measures of leadership functions need to be renewed within each substantially different setting in which leadership is studied. Misumi postulates that the exercise of the P and the M functions are not independent, but complement one another. In other words, a leader who places substantial emphasis on both the P and M functions is more effective than a leader who is high on P or one who is high on M. In Misumi's view integrating the followers' view of what is good for them personally with their view of what is good for task accomplishment is a specific form of PM leadership. Misumi's theory is in conformity with the Japanese cultural style. Japanese tend more often to stress the ways in which elements of a situation are interwoven with one another. They evaluate the elements holistically. Consistent with Japanese holistic thinking, Misumi maintained the contextual and configurational themes of Lewin's field theory. Misumi also relied on experimental data to establish causal relationships.

Misumi and his associates have tested the PM theory in a very wide range of Japanese organizations.[36] Leaders high on both P and M were found to be most effective, in terms of both subjective evaluations by subordinates and objective assessments, such as, lower accident rates and higher productivity. Studies have been conducted using tightly controlled laboratory settings, as well as in extensive field studies in large organizations.

The PM theory has been tested in some other countries, such as, the US, China, New Zealand, and Australia. Misumi and his associates claim that the theory works in those settings too, although the theory emphasises the need of situational-specific measurement devices.

Attention has also been drawn to the paternalistic style in Africa. Ahiauzu, based on a study of leadership in African countries, recommended six characteristics of effective African leaders: single management ideology and objective; relational rather than contractual basis of working; attachment to a group rather than a job; importance of age, experience, and wisdom; emphasis on teamwork; and taking care of the total livelihood of employees.[37]

Although culture-specific theories have been postulated, there seems to be a general agreement that the leadership approaches are universally applicable, but with some cultural variations.

Role Theory

Leadership is a function of the era, the individual, the role, and other stake holders or role senders. We shall discuss each one briefly.

Era The era in which a person is born determines his or her leadership style. To use the propositions of Bennis and Thomas, the era in which the older people (geezers) were born was the 'era of limits, and the one in which younger people (geeks) were born was the 'era of alternatives'. This is quite true about India. This is reflected in the leadership styles of the 'old industry' leaders, who were more conservative, and emphasised on stability and consolidation. The 'new industry' leaders, such as those from the IT industry are more outgoing, creative, and expanding. Their search for value added services (VAS) is opening new areas of work. For example, it is estimated that in a TV programme such as the New Indian Idol, the weekly revenue for service providers amounted to 3 crore rupees. The telecommunication industry is busy creating services from calls and short message services (SMS). The next era probably may be the era of affluence, and this may affect styles of people taking leadership role in that era.

Role   Almost every employee is a potential leader. If a person takes or is given the leadership role, he or she is likely to become a leader. As was said earlier, the century of 'great leaders' is over; this is the century of great leadership. This has been shown in recent experiences even at the national level. The role of a leader was almost thrust on late Rajiv Gandhi, and he brought about some new drastic reforms. The same is true of subsequent prime ministers too.

Role senders   Role is an integrating area of the expectations of the role senders, stakeholders, or 'other significant persons' and the individual accepting the role. The significant members of the role set of a leader perform critical functions for his or her success. The functions of the role set members are as follows.

Partnership

Members of the role set need to become partners in order to achieve the goals of a leader. The following functions are important components of partnership.

Positive pressure   The role senders need to put positive pressure on the leader for effective performance. In the current national scenario, the leftist members of the National Progressive Alliance (NPA) are putting continuous pressure on the prime minister to work for the common minimum programme (CMP). Positive pressure communicates expectations of significant persons and groups, as well as reminds the leader about the main agenda for action. Positive pressure also communicates the trust in a leader's competence.

Value orientation   One important dimension of partnership with the leader is to ensure maintenance of ethical standards and respecting key values as guidelines of action. The role senders are the custodians of values and ethics.

Monitoring   One important function of the role senders is to periodically review the leader's work, and monitor both the progress made towards the goal as well as practice of key values in pursuit of the goals. This will help the leader to make midway corrections in various aspects.

Support

The role senders must provide both moral and material support to the leader, without which the leader may not succeed. Such support involves the following functions.

Trust   Role senders must have complete trust in the leader, and should communicate this to him or her. Without such trust, the leader may not progress effectively.

Resources Role senders should also provide necessary material and financial resources to the leader so that he or she can effectively move towards the goals.

Appreciation Support is also reflected in the appreciation communicated by the role senders. The role senders privately and publicly communicate their admiration for the leader when he or she functions effectively on the agreed agenda. Such appreciation strengthens the leader and helps him or her to function more effectively.

Synergy

Role senders can synergise support and effort for achievement of the goals. The following functions come under this category.

Consensus Role senders need to function as a team. Their thinking must reflect in their consensus on various important aspects of the programmes. If they work in different directions, neither they can be effective nor can they help the leader. Consensus should also be built with the leader.

Conflict management It is natural that different role senders have different expectations and different opinions. However, they need to use these differences for creativity and not allow them to result in major conflicts. They need to resolve and manage the differences and conflicts to help the leader.

Collective responsibility The leader is responsible for working and achieving results, but role senders cannot absolve themselves of the responsibility. They need to indicate their willingness to take responsibility jointly with the leader so that both the leader and role senders feel committed to each other.

The individual taking the role is quite perceptive of the expectations of various significant persons and groups, and integrates them, while 'making' his or her role. In this sense, the individual as a person is also important. We shall briefly discuss the characteristics that make a person an effective leader.

SUMMARY

Leadership is primarily concerned with empowerment and goes beyond management, which is different from 'administration'. Leadership theories search for the key elements that make leaders effective. Trait theories looked for basic traits. Then attempts were made to search for consistent patterns of behaviour (styles) in effective leaders. Two styles were contrasted, the task oriented and the people oriented. These were also proposed as two ends of a continuum.

Contingency theories proposed that the effectiveness of a leader's behaviour was contingent on the situation.

The situational theory suggested four styles, all functional, according to the development level of the group in terms of competence, commitment, and teamwork. The development level of the group can be raised through systematic delegation.

Various theories of leadership have been proposed. The two recent prominent theories are by Collins and Bennis and Thomas. The former emphasises the importance of personal humility and professional will. The latter emphasises the role of the era and crucibles in the development of leaders.

Culture-specific theories related to leadership styles have been proposed in India and Japan. Although culture-specific theories have been postulated, there seems to be a general agreement that the leadership approaches are universally applicable, but with some cultural variations.

GLOSSARY

contingency theory effectiveness of an approach depends on the situation

empowering creating conditions in which inner power can be used effectively; expanding choices for the individual and helping him or her to use his or her alternative choices to widen the choices of others

nurturing behaviour the extent to which a leader engages in two-way communication, listens, provides support and encouragement, facilitates interaction, and involves the group in decision making. Three words can be used to define nurturing behaviour: praise, listen, and facilitate

regulating behaviour the extent to which a leader engages in one-way communication, spells out the group's roles, tells the group members what to do and where, when, and how to do it, and closely supervises the performance. Three words can be used to define regulating behaviour: structure, control, and supervise

S1 or **directive** high regulating, low nurturing

S2 or **supportive** high regulating, high nurturing

S3 or **consulting** low regulating, high nurturing

S4 or **delegating** low regulating, low nurturing

trait theory some physical, social, and intellectual traits distinguish leaders from others

---

EXERCISES

Concept Review Questions
1. What is the trait approach to leadership?
2. What is the managerial grid theory of leadership?
3. Enumerate the main contingency theories.
4. Describe the path–goal theory of leadership.
5. What are the four leadership styles according to the situational theory?
6. How can the development level of a group be raised?
7. What are the steps in the process of delegation?

Critical Thinking Exercises
1. Read the following situation. Four choices are given for a leader dealing with the situation. If you are the leader, which *one* action will you choose?

   You have recently taken over a consulting firm as its CEO. You find on your priority list that the firm has got a prestigious consulting assignment. In spite of enthusiasm and rapport among members, you discover that they lack the necessary planning and monitoring competency. What will you do?

   (a) Plan the task in detail and arrange training programmes for them in deficient areas.

(b) Encourage the team to find solutions to their problems.

(c) Plan the tasks, distribute assignments, and supervise their work.

(d) Discuss the situation with members and help them to learn planning and monitoring competencies. *Note:* This situation is at the D3 level (the group has high commitment and teamwork but is low on competence). The most appropriate style to use is S3. The four alternatives listed are respectively S2, S4, S1, and S3. Reflect on your response.

2. Take the example of an effective leader you know. How does he or she work with his or her group? Explain this behaviour using the path–goal theory of leadership.

3. Which of the theories of or approaches to leadership is most appropriate for the society you live in? Why?

Classroom Projects

1. In groups of two or three, examine the development level of your class. Discuss the style your OB instructor follows. Is it an appropriate style?

2. In groups of two or three, develop a plan for effective delegation of the various responsibilities in your institution to the students.

Field Projects

1. Interview two managers to assess the development level of their groups and the leadership styles they are using. Do these match?

2. Interview two managers to diagnose where the delegation process in their organization is weak and how it can be strengthened.

Turnaround at Damodar Valley Corporation*

The turnaround of the Damodar Valley Corporation (DVC) by P.C. Luther at the end of the 1970s illustrates the situational theory of leadership. When Luther took over the chairmanship of DVC, the organization was in a shambles. There were more than 300 strikes, *gheraos*, and sit-ins in a year. Productivity was low and there was very low discipline among the workers. The corporation was at development level 1 (D1), with low competence, commitment, and team spirit. Luther's first act was to instil discipline among the employees, and he did it from the top (including himself as chairman). Norms were prescribed for completing work in time. Disciplinary action was taken on non-compliance. Luther threw out a large number of chairs kept in the chairman's room for workers and officers who came to negotiate with him, and refused to see anyone without an appointment.

He made the general manager (next to the chairman in hierarchy) resign from this role (he was given some other role) after the latter was found not conforming to the norms in spite of several reminders. He set targets for managers and closely monitored their progress. This style of leadership was Style 1 (directive). Managers started taking responsibility as a result of disciplining from the top.

Luther then found that thousands of staff grievances had accumulated and not been attended to. Nobody wanted to touch them because these grievances were filed by workers who were not members of recognised unions. Luther was advised by his lieutenants to keep these grievances under the rug, at least initially. Instead, Luther sent teams of managers to the sites to investigate the grievances, made a public commitment to dispose off the complaints within 6 months, and kept his word.

He took action even without any demand from the union; houses in the colony were repaired, broken street lights were installed, etc. Luther was following Style 2 of leadership, characterised by a supportive leader, with high nurturing as well as high regulating style. So great was the acceptance he gained that a militant union leader who had paralysed the management tried thrice to call a strike but failed each time, and Luther was able to increase productivity by 30 per cent in a single year. During this period, he sent high-performing managers for training, and formed teams to make and execute plans.

Luther had achieved high productivity. The company was able to go beyond the productivity level that a British team had estimated as the maximum possible, with the technology and machines it was using. With his teams of managers functioning well, Luther diverted his attention to building competence and providing facilities. The consulting role performed by the chairman represented Style 3 of leadership.

---

* The story of DVC's turnaround has been narrated in detail by D. Thacore and G. Gupta, 'Miracle at DVC', *Business World* 26–35, 15 October 1981.

This style was appropriate because people now took responsibility (high commitment) and were capable (high competence). However, there were still some problems such as low cohesion or team work among the workers. Luther was paying attention to that aspect when he was replaced by a new chairman!

Luther shared his experiences with students at the Indian Institute of Management, Ahmedabad, and from his responses to questions, it seemed he had been preparing to move to Style 4 (delegating) of leadership.

Questions for Discussion

1. Which leadership theory is illustrated in the case?
2. What made Luther use authoritarian style when he took over the company as its chairman?
3. How did Luther increase his concern for the company's employees?
4. What are the factors for Luther's success in turning around DVC?

NOTES AND REFERENCES

1. Pareek, Udai (2002). *Effective Organizations: Beyond Management to Institution Building.* New Delhi: Oxford & IBH.
2. For details, see Anil Bhatt (1984), 'Creation out of calamity: The case of a training institution', *Vikalpa*, 9: 374–378.
3. Stogdill, R.M. (1974). *Handbook of Leadership: A Survey of the Literature.* New York: Free Press.
4. *Ibid.*
5. McCall, M.W., Jr. and M.M. Lombardo (1983). *Off the Track: Why and How Successful Executives Get Derailed.* Greenboro, NC: Centre for Creative.
6. Bennis, W.G. and R.J. Thomas (2003). *Geeks and Geezers: How Era, Values, and Defining Movements Shape Leaders.* Mumbai: Magna Publishing Company.
7. Lewin, K., R. Lippitt, and R. White (1939). 'Patterns of aggressive behaviour in experimentally created "social climates"', *Journal of Social Psychology*, 10: 271–99.
8. Likert, Rensis (1969). *New Patterns of Management.* New York: McGraw-Hill.
9. Halpin, Andrew W. (1957). *Manual on Leader Behavior Description Questionnaire.* Columbus, OH: Ohio State University.
10. Tannenbaum, R. and W.H. Schmidt (1958). 'How to choose a leadership pattern', *Harvard Business Review*, 36(2), 1958: 95–101.
11. Blake, R.R. and J.S. Mouton (1964). *Managerial Grid.* Houston, TX: Gulf.
12. Fiedler, F.E. (1964). 'A contingency model of leadership effectiveness', in L. Berkowitz (ed.), *Advances in Experimental Social Psychology.* New York: Academic Press.
13. Fiedler, F.E. (1967). *A Theory of Leadership Effectiveness.* New Delhi: McGraw-Hill.
14. Hickson, D.J. et al (1971). 'A strategic contingencies theory of intra-organisational power', *Administrative Science Quarterly*, 16: 216–29.
15. Fiedler, F.E. and J.E. Garcia (1987). *New Approaches to Leadership: Cognitive Resource and Organizational Performance.* New York: Wiley.
16. Vroom, V.H. and P.W. Yetton (1973). *Leadership and Decision-Making.* Pittsburgh, PA: University of Pittsburgh Press.
17. House, R.J. (1971). 'A path-goal theory of leader effectiveness', *Administrative Science Quarterly*, September, 321–338.

18. Hersey, P. and K.H. Blanchard (1982). *Management of Organisational Behaviour.* Englewood Cliffs, NJ: Prentice-Hall.
19. Blanchard, K.H. (1995). 'Situational leadership', in R.A. Ritvo, A.H. Litwin, and L. Butler (eds), *Managing in the Age of Change,* pp. 14–35. New York: Irwin.
20. Khandwalla, P.N. (1992). *Excellent Corporate Turnaround,* p. 259. New Delhi: Sage.
21. Pareek, Udai (2002). *Training Instruments in HRD and OD.* New Delhi: Tata McGraw-Hill.
22. Singh, P. and A. Bhandarkar (1990). *Corporate Success and Transformational Leadership.* New Delhi: Wiley Eastern.
23. Burns, J.M. (1978). *Leadership.* New York: Harper & Row.
24. Bass, B.M. (1985). *Leadership Performance Beyond Expectations.* New York: Academic Press.
25. Bass, B.M. and P. Steidlmeier (1998). *Ethics, Character and Authentic Transformational Leadership,* http://cls.binghamton.edu/BassSteid.html.
26. Graen, G.B. and M. Uhl-Bien (1995). 'Relationship-based approach to leadership: Development of leader-member exchange (LMX) theory of leadership over 25 years: Applying a multi-level multi-domain perspective', *Leadership Quarterly,* 6(2): 219–247.
27. Collins, Jim (2005). 'Level 5 leadership: The triumph of humility and fierce resolve', in *Best of HBR, HBR,* July–August 2005, pp. 136–146.
28. Bennis, W.G. and R.J. Thomas (2003). *Geeks and Geezers: How Era, Values, and Defining Movements Shape Leaders.* Mumbai: Magna Publishing Company.
29. Mayo, Anthony and Nitin Nohria (2005). *In Their Time: The Greatest Business Leaders of the Twentieth Century.* Boston, MA: Harvard Business School Press.
30. Zaleznik, Abraham (1977). 'Managers and leaders: Are they different?' *Harvard Business Review,* May–June.
31. Prince, Ted E. (2005). *The Financial Styles of Very Successful Leaders.*
32. Sinha, J.B.P. (1980). *The Nurturant Task Leader.* New Delhi: Concept.
33. *Ibid,* 63.
34. See www.tvrls.com/360_degree_feedback_and_leadership_development.html.
35. Misumi, J. and M.F. Peterson (1985). 'The performance–maintainance (PM) theory of leadership: Review of a Japanese research program.' *Administrative Science Quarterly,* 3.
36. Khandwalla, P.N. (1992). *Excellent Corporate Turnaround.* New Delhi: Sage.
37. *Ibid.*

22
Developing Leadership for Tomorrow

LEARNING OBJECTIVES

After studying this chapter, you will be able to
1. Discuss the concept of leadership development
2. Identify main characteristics of tomorrow's leaders
3. Elaborate the concept of crucibles
4. Describe various crucibles shaping the leaders
5. List various ways of leadership development

Leadership is attracting a lot of attention. Organizations have realised that it is the most significant competitive advantage. There has been rethinking on the concept of leadership.

PARADIGM SHIFT ON LEADERSHIP

The past millennium has seen many great leaders. By contrast, we are now in a century of great leadership. We need effective leaders in large numbers at all levels in all organizations.

Need for Leadership at All Levels

Indeed, management experts at Wharton and McKinsey say that leadership can be found and must be practised by employees at all levels of an organization. That is the only way in which an enterprise can get the most from managers and employees alike, achieve its strategic goals, fulfil the personal career aspirations of its people, and lay the groundwork for identifying and developing future leaders, including those who may eventually serve at the highest levels. A payroll clerk who recommends a way to streamline the process of cutting a check is demonstrating leadership—given the parameters of his or her place in an organization—in the same way as a CEO who is launching an initiative to transform a corporation.[1]

'Everybody can lead at every level; there are no excuses. It doesn't matter if you're on the front line or the top line. If you are given an office with the powers of that office, what do you add to the office above and beyond those powers? Do you excite and motivate people? Do you bring excellence and vision to what ultimately is the objective of that office or even the whole company? Everybody should be good at leading, whatever their level in the hierarchy.'[2]

'Everyone can exercise leadership by being an individual contributor at any level of an organization ... Ultimately it comes down to looking for opportunities to make the world a better place. That sounds grand, but when people apply that idea to their work situations, it means having a vision of how your unit, or you as an individual, can be more effective and creative, go beyond day-to-day requirements, and energise others around that vision.'

This shift from great leaders to great leadership is a response to the fast-changing environment. As discussed in Chapter 1, the contextual factors of work organization are changing dramatically. The changing environment is characterised by

- Liberalisation (increasing competition)
- Aware and demanding customers
- Educated and impatient employees
- High mobility, careerism, and declining organization 'loyalty'
- Growing unemployment and unemployables
- Glamorisation of designations and consequent meaningless promotions
- Resistance to radical thinking

Organizations earlier witnessed a shift from administration to management and are now beginning to see one from management to leadership. These trends are making organizations move from centralised management and decision making to decentralisation. These complex and fast-changing realities require faster and high quality decision making, which is possible only when there are competent people capable of taking such decisions at all levels.

Faster and quality decision making will lead to de-bureaucratisation, de-hierarchisation, and decentralisation, resulting in empowerment at all levels. The evolution of various approaches to leadership also reflects such a shift.

Developing Leaders

Organizations are realising the need to develop leaders. However, distinction has been made between leader development and leadership development.[3] *Leader development* focuses on the development of the leader, such as, the personal attributes desired in a leader, desired ways of behaving, and ways of thinking or feeling. In contrast, *leadership development* focuses on the development of leadership as a process. Leadership development is the strategic investment in, and utilisation of, the human capital within the organization. Leadership processes will include the social influence process and the team dynamics between the leader and his or her team at the dyad level, and the contextual factors surrounding the team such as the perception of the organizational climate and the social network linkages between the team and other groups in the organization.[4] Both forms of development may mutually influence each other.[5]

Typically, leader development has focused on three main areas: providing the opportunities for development, stimulating the ability to develop (including motivation, skills and knowledge for change), and providing a supportive context for change to occur.[6] Leadership development can build on the development of individuals (including followers) towards becoming leaders. We need a new breed of leaders to manage the future.

PROFILE OF TOMORROW'S LEADERS

The leaders of tomorrow are already emerging. Various organizations in different parts of the world reveal features appropriate to the new era. These organizations have a different kind of culture and a new breed of leaders. What kind of leaders are these? The characteristics of such leaders can be grouped under five clusters: internality, creativity, humility, values, and networking.

Internality

This cluster includes four characteristics: grand vision, internality, optimism, and professional will.

Grand vision

Great leaders have grand vision. Naren Ayyar joined Hewlett-Packard (HP) as their first employee in India in 1986. He started the company's Indian operations from a small room in a hotel. In the first business plan Ayyar prepared, he forecasted that HP India will become the market leader in 10 years. This, however, happened only in 2006. Today Ayyar, as the chief executive officer of Globarena, is dreaming of making the company the market leader in the field of education and career development, and e-learning. In his words, 'Aim for the moon, you will at least reach the clouds.' The role of the leader is to create a unified vision out of the diverse visions of various groups in the organization, articulate it, inspire people with it, and concretise it into action. Core Healthcare in India was set up as just another small-scale business in the IV fluid market. The leaders had a grand vision of the company as a global player. They took several steps to project and concretise that vision. By 1996, Core emerged as Asia's largest and the world's fifth-largest fluid manufacturer, capturing 20 per cent of the domestic market. [7]

When Raghavan took over as the head of the nondescript Minerals and Metals Trading Corporation (MMTC) of the Government of India in 1983, the company was in a shambles. Raghavan redefined the mission of the organization, created a new vision, and de-bureaucratised the company. The exports rose from 2,900 million rupees in 1982 to 7,000 million rupees in 1986 and the total turnover went up from 12,000 million rupees to 28,000 million rupees. [8]

The role of the leader is to strategise and prioritise. A good example of strategic thinking is that of Emannuel Hachipunka, who came to head the loss-making government-owned Zambia Railways in the early 1980s. He sought a reduction in the number of loss-making passenger trains, track rehabilitation, installation of a sleeper plant, upgradation of the telecommunications system, overhauling of the locomotives, workforce training, and a performance-oriented reward system. Between 1983 and 1987, the revenues went up five times and a loss of 10.5 million kwacha turned into a profit of 11.1 million kwacha. [9]

Strategising involves developing priorities of action in a framework geared to the direction of the organization's vision. Great leaders develop the capability of strategic thinking at all levels.

Internality

The new leaders take charge of what happens. They make things happen as they want them to happen. The leaders' internal locus of control is high. They believe that they can influence most things around them.

There are several examples of such leaders turning around organizations. For example, Abhewickrame in Sri Lanka left a good job to take over the loss-making State Timber Corporation. He brought about changes in mechanisation, MIS, pricing, supplies, competence building, etc. Consequently, sales increased from 40 million rupees in 1978 to 300 million rupees in 1980, turning a 4-million rupees loss into a profit of 46 million rupees.[10] Such a sense of internality should prevail at all levels. For example, in the Brazilian company Semco, people on the factory floor decide the monthly production schedule.[11]

Optimism

Optimism has been found to be the key element in leadership effectiveness in business, sports, and politics. Seligman gives the example of Metropolitan Life (Metlife), where insurance agents were tested for an optimistic explanatory style. After a year, it was found that agents with low optimism were twice as likely to quit as those with high optimism. Those who were in the lowest quarter on optimism were three times more likely to quit than those in the highest quarter. The top half in terms of optimism sold 20 per cent more insurance than the bottom half and those in the top quarter sold 50 per cent more than those in the bottom quarter. Then, a 'special force' of optimistic agents was created. Half of the 1,000 selected from 15,000 applicants were optimists and the other half pessimists. In the first year, optimists outsold the pessimists by 8 per cent and in the second year by 31 per cent. The special force of optimists outsold the pessimists by 21 per cent in the first year and by 57 per cent in the second year. This quality of optimism is very critical for leaders.[12]

Seligman's fantastic prediction of the success of candidates for the presidentship of the US on the basis of their scores on pessimism and rumination establishes the key role of optimism in leadership in various fields. Rumination, you will remember, is the tendency to indulge in negative and cynical thinking and obsessive analysis of bad happenings.

Professional will

Collins has suggested that great leaders are characterised by a combination of personal humility and professional will.[13] According to him, professional will consists of stoic resolve and a culture of discipline. People with professional will face brutal facts and take hard decisions without hesitation. It requires professional willpower to take a decision 'without a blink'. The leaders with this quality often make right choices when they handle their 'forks in the road' decision points. Once they have made judgments, they are swift in their decisions and actions. Such leaders do not hesitate to take painful decisions. The following examples of leadership[14] illustrate the concept of professional will.

S. Viswanathan became the operating head of the loss-making Enfield India, a company producing two-wheelers, in 1977. To enforce discipline in the company, he declared a lock-out at a plant for a year; wrote off obsolete inventories; brought in a management consultant; got stakeholders to agree on a bailout; organized brainstorming retreats for top managers; divisionalised and decentralised the organization; started quality circles; strengthened planning, R&D efforts, and marketing; improved relations with unions; and evolved a policy of product and manufacturing flexibility. Sales increased from 127 million rupees in 1976 to 350 million rupees in 1981, and a loss of 34 million rupees in 1976 turned into a profit of 23 million rupees in 1981.

I.S. Kavadia, an IAS officer, took over as the chief of Jaipur Metals, owned by the Government of Rajasthan, India, in 1983. Inheriting a chronically sick unit, Kavadia administered tough medicine. He retrenched hundreds of employees and imposed discipline on a restive labour force. He got the unions to agree to a wage freeze, longer working hours, and acceptance of the company's shares in lieu of bonus. He also brought in participative management within the company. In 5 years, sales quadrupled and profits rose to 30 rupees million from a loss of 9 million rupees in 1983.

M.V. Subbiah joined the loss-making EID Parry, an Indian conglomerate, in 1984. Subbiah acted tough with militant unions, reduced employee strength through golden handshakes, forced out a few incompetent top managers, brought in several outsiders as managers, tightened controls, hived off unprofitable lines of business, terminated unremunerative relationships with vendors, decentralised operations, improved the performance reporting system, identified several strategic business units for special attention, strengthened work ethics, modernised plants, launched new products, and focused on long-term planning. In 1985, the company turned around to enter the fast track of sales and profit growth.

Creativity

Creativity is the set of attitudes, abilities, and mental processes that increase the probability of hitting upon solutions that seem to the well informed both novel and appropriate. The cluster of creativity includes three characteristics: innovation, maverick mindset, and neoteny.

Innovation

Great leaders search new ways of solving problems. They use innovations and promote a culture of creativity. Some examples are given in this section.[15]

C.V. Karthik Narayanan became the head of the loss-making Standard Motors, India, in 1975. He emphasised on innovation, discontinued a loss-making product and vigorously introduced a new product, speeded up indigenisation of a new model, changed the recruitment policy, decentralised processes, strengthened the productivity-linked incentive system, improved personnel management, and built the dealer network. By 1981, sales had tripled, and the company was earning 7 per cent profit on sales.

Mahesh Mansukhani took over the management of Bharat Heavy Plate & Vessels Ltd as its chief in 1978. Despite intense staff hostility, he worked out a wage agreement with the unions, personally solicited orders for the sales starved company, virtually eliminated overtime, installed an incentive system, and strengthened professional management systems. A government enterprise, which had never earlier made profits, not only broke even in a year, but was soon on the fast track of growth and profits.

In 1977, following a change of government, K.L. Puri was transferred from a high position to head Bharat Pumps & Compressors Ltd, a relatively small public sector enterprise. In a faction-ridden, loss-making unit, Puri introduced good human relations management practices, motivated the demoralised management team, insisted that the year's production target be met (and succeeded, though his assistants had pleaded for its downward revision), strengthened professional management systems, and drastically improved profitability. The net operating profit to sales ratio of less than 3 per cent in 1976 rose to 12 per cent in 1978 and 14 per cent in 1979.

Maverick mindset

When Ricardo Semler in Brazil took over Semco from his father in 1980, the company had 100 employees and sales of 4 million US dollars. After 8 years, its manpower went up eight times (to 800), sales rose to 37 million US dollars, and its range of products covered an assortment from marine pumps to commercial dishwashers to digital scanners. It had become the fastest-growing company in Brazil. This miracle was achieved by implementing 'unthinkable' ways of managing: reduction of hierarchical levels to only four (the top five employees were called counsellors, the eight division heads were called partners, the task leaders were called coordinators, and all others were called associates); equal voice of workers in making decisions; people evaluating their bosses and the top management; abolition of rules and introduction of flexitime; 23 per cent of the net profit (post-tax) given twice a year to representatives of the employees, with the latter being left to decide what to do with it; staff functions being made the responsibility of all concerned, and so on.

Semler wrote about his experience in the book *Maverick!*[16] He has now become a representative of such unconventional ways of organizing, a symbol of the paradigm shift in organizational thinking. Following the title of his book, this can be called the maverick mindset. There are several other examples of this mindset.

When Samir Jain took over as joint managing director of Bennett, Coleman & Co. in the mid-1980s, the company was a publisher of more than two dozen periodicals considered touchstones in India. Yet the company's profit (pre-taxation) was less than 2 per cent of its turnover. He adopted an unconventional approach to reorganizing the business. He abolished the post of editor for a daily newspaper, created the post of managing editor (to which a former executive at a cigarette company was recruited), created brand managers for publications, borrowed the idea of marginal onward pricing for advertisements from the airline industry, and introduced a reader–editorial interface. In just a decade, the company emerged as one of the country's most profitable companies—its profit margin going up 14 times! Its English daily, *The Times of India*, became the country's largest selling daily newspaper.[17]

In Cipla, an Indian pharmaceutical firm, there are no functional designations: people are given responsibility in a core area with cross-functional assignments. For example, a cost accountant might also be involved in new product development and launches, pricing, MIS, etc. Cipla went from the eleventh to the third position in the pharmaceutical industry in the country.[18]

The maverick mindset characterises leaders who are vision driven and who develop competence, take moderate risks, learn from various sources, and empower their people to experiment and take responsibility.

Neoteny

As discussed in Chapter 21, Bennis and Thomas found neoteny an important characteristic of leaders, geeks and geezers alike. 'We believe having these childlike attributes are essential to identifying and creating value because they enable people and organizations to embrace the intense change caused by the dynamic effects of technology on our society ... Whatever their physical health, geezers and geeks alike are always discovering the best, most meaningful way to live now. They still wake up every morning and fall in love with the world all over again.'[19]

Humility

The cluster of humility has four characteristics: humility, self-restraint, empowerment, and culture building.

Humility

Collins has suggested the combination of personal humility and professional will as characteristics of great leaders.[20] The concept of personal humility includes aversion to limelight. Such leaders share credit of achievements with their colleagues, develop their successors, and pass on the responsibility as and when subordinates are ready. These leaders generate more and more empowering influence, so that persons working closely with them follow their examples of humility. They admire good qualities in those people and leverage them for the benefit of the organization. These leaders focus on strengthening the organization rather than pursuing their own personal gains. N.R. Narayana Murthy, the chief mentor, founder, and former CEO of Infosys, is a good example of a leader of this kind. Late Ravi Matthai, the former director of the Indian Institute of Management, Ahmedabad, is another example of a leader with personal humility. Organizations can also have a culture of humility (see Exhibit 22.1).[21]

Exhibit 22.1 *Humility in Organizations*

Having heard again and again about how Wal-Mart was dominating and controlling the retail industry and mistreating employees, I was expecting to arrive at a main campus resembling one of the many high tech country clubs I've grown accustomed to seeing in the Silicon Valley. What I found in Bentonville was a collection of buildings that were neither uniform nor impressive, many of which seemed to be converted warehouses and strip-mall quality structures from the 1970s. I loved it! And there was no separate executive suite with a different set of standards. These titans of industry were working in facilities that were no more comfortable or grand than those of the people who worked in their stores around the world. And inside those buildings, the stories were no different. Neat and clean, but more like a DMV than a palace. And the cafeteria where I had lunch reminded me of my junior high school.

But the humility at Wal-Mart went far beyond the physical environment. The people there were uniformly friendly, gracious and unpretentious. But don't misunderstand. They were also very bright and had levels of experience, education and knowledge rivalling any other corporation I had seen. But you would never know it by the way they treated one another. And everyone, from senior executives to the people running the cash registers in the cafeteria, were treated with the same levels of respect and kindness, all of which seemed to create an environment of genuine enthusiasm and commitment among employees.

As for their reaction to the barrage of criticism levelled at them by competitors and the media, they were neither bitter nor angry. Instead, they seemed genuinely open to finding any truth in the accusations so they could address them, and then determined to calmly set the record straight in the many areas where they were being unfairly accused.

Self-restraint

The tendency to postpone gratification of one's immediate needs for a long-term goal is of vital importance anywhere. McClelland and Burnham found self-restraint one of the key characteristics of most successful organizational leaders.[22] This characteristic is a part of the ethos of most Asian cultures. First-generation entrepreneurs and successful business leaders give low priority to their own personal needs and undergo personal hardship in the pursuit of long-term goals.

Empowering

The main role of leaders will be to create an enabling culture and empower people at all levels in the organization. This is done in several ways. Sharing information is one way to empower employees. In Semco, every month each worker gets a balance sheet, an analysis of profits and losses, and a cash-flow statement for his or her division. Education also empowers people. In Semco, workers were taught to read balance sheets and analyse financial statements.

Participation in decision making is another effective means of empowerment. In Semco, employees had a say in their compensation policy. In Petrofils, at a stakeholders' meeting, the top management meet the staff in the canteen to brief them about the company's performance and prospects. At Steel Tubes of India, the management set up a broad-based *jan sabha* (people's forum) consisting of representatives of employees and of senior and top-level managers. Its decisions are binding on the management. Elected representatives of the workers choose the HR manager from among the managers who have been with the company for more than 3 years.[23]

Leadership is increasingly seen as an instrument of empowerment. The influence or power of leaders is in proportion to their ability to confer power on people; such empowerment implies that leaders are prepared to shed their own power in the greater organizational interest. Such behaviour can be referred to as power enhancers. Leaders may enhance their real power by withdrawing somewhat from controlling functions. This is possible only when the leader is released from attending to routine tasks. Leaders who spend a lot of time on allotting houses and vehicles to people will not have enough time to plan a new corporate vision. However, when leaders are relieved from attending to petty details, their real power and influence increases, as they are able to perform more important tasks of envisioning, engaging in boundary management, lobbying for the organization, etc.

What are these power enhancers? Based on published research and interviews with senior Indian managers, a list of power enhancers was prepared. Finally, the following 14 were selected as most significant.[24]

- Developing the competence of employees
- Laying down clear rules and procedures
- Developing systems to generate feedback for individuals
- Providing intrinsically satisfying tasks
- Undertaking advisory and staff functions
- Giving rewards determined objectively by a team rather than by an individual
- Maintaining optimal spatial distance between different key functionaries
- Building strong and cohesive teams
- Encouraging self-government of teams (such as self-sufficient branches)
- Encouraging self-definition of tasks
- Defining a formalised and clear organizational structure
- Initiate schemes to reward employees for ideas/suggestions/creativity
- Nurture a professional orientation
- Developing systems

Culture building

Building an enabling and empowering culture becomes the key role of leaders of the new organization. Culture replaces bureaucracy. The new organizational culture will promote learning, initiative, empowerment, teamwork, and control through a vision. Based on a survey, Shukla has summarised six principles of the new organizations[25]:

- Organize work around an integrated process, not around segmented tasks.
- Create flatter structures, with parallel (instead of sequential) teams.
- Make teams (not individuals) accountable for the task as a whole; empower teams to take all relevant decisions pertaining to their work.
- Make organizational boundaries permeable in order to bring teams in contact with customers, suppliers, and each other.

- Evaluate the performance of the teams on the basis of customers' feedback. Use peer rating to evaluate individual performance.
- Invest in and reward acquisition of new skills by the individual.

Another important part of the new culture is openness. Openness comes from collecting information from several sources. 'Japanese companies have a preoccupation with the actions of their competitors ... Japanese companies' strategic planning process places more of an emphasis on competitor comparisons than do firms in United States, Germany, or Canada. The same holds true for information about foreign nations, and global industries ... Japanese management reads. This simple fact is significant. We observed many senior executives actually reading in their corporate information centres and libraries—something one rarely sees elsewhere. At one large library, we saw an executive with 10 years worth of annual reports from an American competing firm. He was reading the reports annual letter from the CEO because he wanted to get an unfiltered sense of how their CEO thinks.'[26]

New leaders are not satisfied with the traditional hierarchical structure. New structures are necessary to make organizations competitive and to enable them to remain leaders in their fields. Top leaders (in collaboration with others in different parts of their organizations) create structures, which enable people to use power and produce results. Three characteristics of such structures are de-bureaucratisation, de-hierarchisation, and decentralisation. Rules are minimised; in fact, culture replaces rules. Organizations become flatter. The new structure also empowers people to take decisions and act. In place of a hierarchical structure, new networked organizational forms emerge. Such forms are characterised by flexibility, self-designing, self-monitoring, and learning from experiences.

Amtrex Appliances in India moulded itself into a horizontal circular structure consisting of teams. Eastman Chemical Co. changed itself into a circular 'pizza chart' organization: each function, geographic region, or core competence was represented by a slice of pepperoni on a pizza and the white space around the pepperoni represented the space for actual collaborative work.[27]

Values

The cluster of value contains four characteristics: value orientation, ethics, people first, and social concern.

Value orientation

Leaders of tomorrow will be value driven. Values make a significant difference to the image and effectiveness of the organization. Ethical considerations, personal integrity, and a sense of equity and justice are important values for leaders. Effective leaders place high value on empowerment, participation, and sharing of credit and gains.

The BAIF Development Research Foundation, a trust in India following the Gandhian philosophy, has a high commitment to the rural poor and a value-based lifestyle, with a highly professional staff. It is a very successful research organization:

scientists here publish about 40 books in a year. Its founder-president was given the prestigious Magsaysay Award.

To instil an awareness of the dignity of work, young managerial recruits at Indian Hotels, a leading hospitality chain, start with the less 'prestigious' jobs of waiters, dishwashers, porters, and cleaners.[28]

Semler's *Maverick!* is full of examples of the reorganization of Semco around the values of participation, de-hierarchisation, equity, employee's say in decision making, profit sharing, learning through job rotation, autonomy, and empowerment. As already stated, his philosophy has served Semco very well.

Ethics

Great leaders are concerned with ethics. They are concerned with establishing proper norms and fighting corruption. Even at the risk of having temporary setbacks, they pursue the path of ethics, which helps the organizations to gain in the long run. We have already discussed ethics in detail in Chapter 2. In India, organizations such as Tata, Wipro, and Infosys relentlessly pursue ethical practices. Their leaders are role models for other organizations.

People first

The new leaders give high priority to searching, retaining, and developing talent. In the NCNB Corporation of the US, priority is given to the recruitment and development of the brightest young people the bank can find. The mentoring system is one of the ways to nurture talent. Several companies have strong educational programmes and the idea of corporate universities is becoming more popular.

Social concern

Leaders with foresight are not only concerned about the success of their ventures and organization, but are also alive to the needs of the community. Asian countries provide many examples of the involvement of fast-growing industries in socially relevant activities. In the US, the leaders of the First Pennsylvania Banking and Trust Company favoured a highly visible involvement of the bank in the community it served and the creation of a distinctive identity for the bank. The bank played the role of commercial leadership in its community by being the first to lower interest rates, retail mini notes, introduce inflation-fighting deposit certificates, etc. The bank also sought to establish itself in states other than Pennsylvania and bought a share of capital in an Israeli bank. The bank's profitability was the highest for any major company.[29]

While effective leaders become globally oriented, their roots in their own cultures will remain strong. Japanese, Chinese, and various other communities abound in examples of typical ethnic cultural characteristics reflected in managerial styles along with a global orientation. Some authors have suggested that there are special variants of leadership styles in specific cultures, such as the familial style of China and Japan, the nurturing style of India,[30] and the paternalistic style of Africa. These have been discussed in detail in Chapter 21.

Networking

The cluster of networking consists of four characteristics: communication, networking competence, synergy building, and customer orientation.

Communication

Effective leaders communicate with all categories of people with whom they work: employees at all levels, customers, important external collaborators, important government officials, etc. Effective leaders focus on sharing their visions, and fire their people with enthusiasm for the plans of the organization. They share their visions and ideas not only through mass media, but also by personal contact in face-to-face meetings.

T.N. Menon took over as chief of Travancore Cochin Chemicals, owned by the Government of Kerala, in 1978. He embarked on intensive communications with his staff, trained his managers in various aspects of managerial and organizational effectiveness, quickly improved a number of management systems such as maintenance and quality control, introduced new practices in various areas, tackled bad industrial relations successfully, modernised the plants, and redeployed workers. These measures enabled this medium-sized company to change from a chronic loss-making operation to a highly profitable operation, with profits of 27 million rupees on sales of 157 million rupees in 1981.[31]

Networking competence

Great leaders develop networking within their organizations and with strategic outside groups and organizations. Shulka cites examples of companies networking down to the shop-floor level using modern computer technology (Asian Paints), networking warehouses and 3,000 salespersons equipped with laptops, using modems serving 600,000 outlets (Colgate & Palmolive), networking with 24,690 shops in about 350 towns in India (Parle Agro). The structure of the new organization is changing from hierarchical to networked, which reduces bureaucracy and empowers people at all levels.[32]

Leaders also network with key individual and strategic groups outside.

Synergy building

Team building is now a high priority for effective leaders. Organizations are increasingly becoming team oriented. In 1998, Federal Express organized its 1,000 clerical workers into super-teams of 5 to 10 workers with the authority to make improvements. These teams were able to bring down the cost of incorrect billing by 13 per cent. Intel is organized into several dozen small 'councils', which perform a variety of functions.[33] In Tata Cummins, teams of eight workers (called operators) manage everything and six of them are leaders of their own functions.

Leaders also build synergy with other organizations, including competitors. The examples given by Shukla[34] have already been cited in Chapter 20, showing how organizations collaborate with their competitors to sharpen their competitive edge.

In brief, the new leadership is proactive and eager to learn from various sources. It believes in empowering and taking charge. New leaders are assertive, empower their subordinates, and emphasise on individual creativity and team performance. Organizations that do not attempt to create new leadership at all levels are likely to be left behind in the race of excellence and competition.

Customer orientation

All new leaders are concerned about customers. Interaction with customers, feedback from them, and even training of customers is part of their customer orientation. Customising research and offering testing facilities to present and prospective clients helped a small-scale project unit set up by four technocrat friends corner 85 per cent of the distillation and fermentation market in India. Its turnover rose in 10 years, from 4 million rupees to 600 million rupees, 150-fold.[35] The State Street Boston Financial Corporation in the US sought the opinions and ideas of its customers for improving its performance.

PROCESS OF LEADERSHIP DEVELOPMENT: ROLE OF CRUCIBLES

Bennis and Thomas feel that 'crucibles' are important for the formation of leaders.[36] According to them, 'crucible refers to an experiential dimension in the lives of all the leaders we interviewed: an intense, transformational experience that set them on the road to where they are now. For these leaders, the crucible served as a sort of ordeal or test. Surviving the test was an entry or initiation into the life of leadership. True leaders create meaning out of difficult events or relationships, while others may be defeated or even devastated by them. Leaders come out of these experiences with something useful … even a plan of action. Through the crucible, they acquire new insights, new skills and new qualities of mind or character that make it possible to leap to a new, higher level.' As already mentioned in Chapter 21, the idea of crucibles was originally suggested by Zaleznik. Managers who have faced a crucible are referred to as 'twice born', as contrasted with managers who are 'once born'.

Bennis and Thomas identified four major types of crucibles from their interviews.

Mentoring relationships Mentors have always been found to influence their proteges. Bennis and Thomas found two critical elements in almost every mentoring relationship described in their interviews. First, proteges attracted mentors; there was something compelling about them that made them approachable and interesting. Second, mentors were willing to provide care and attention to a particular protege and 'willing to share valuable insight without any expectations of reward for their efforts'.

Enforced reflection This crucible refers to an opportunity for both exploration and reflection, found in such events as going away to a school or to an ashram or a yoga centre. 'Through these crucibles, individuals learn preparedness—an alertness to the rich signals that surround them—and a willingness to experiment in the interest of advancing self-knowledge and, by extension, knowledge of the world around them.'

Experiencing a new world The leaders Bennis and Thomas interviewed demonstrated a remarkable capacity not only to survive their entry in new situations, but also derived profound insights from them. They cite example of Lingyun Shao, a sergeant in the US Army, whose arduous hurricane relief work for several weeks in the mountains of El Salvador led her to shift her career objectives from an exclusive focus on herself to what she could contribute to a much broader community. 'Others might be consumed in the newness, the confusion and the deluge of sensations encountered in foreign territory, but these leaders capture the disorientation and weave it into their own experiential tapestry. More importantly, they continue to seek out new foreign territories, whether a new geography, culture, business, organizational role or idea.' For Mahatma Gandhi, the crucible experience was his stay in South Africa.

Disruption and loss According to Bennis and Thomas, personal loss of a parent, a sibling, close friend, a grown child, bankruptcy, or failure in an important assignment or undertaking can 'stimulate a search for greater understanding of self, of relationships and of larger webs of affiliation. All these events carry the potential to catalyse a search for meaning and develop a far keener ability to extract insights from experience.' For Nelson Mandela, the crucible was the long period of imprisonment in his own country.

The case of Dr R. Balasubramaniam, founder and president, Swami Vivekananda Youth Movement in Mysore, illustrates some of the crucibles discussed in this section. Balasubramaniam wanted to study computer science in one of Karnataka's prestigious engineering colleges. Despite having a high percentage (99.67 per cent), he could not secure admission there. Balasubramaniam was denied admission to the engineering college of his choice, even though he was eligible, and another non-eligible candidate was given admission. This shocking 'loss' was the first crucible he experienced.

He had complained to the Directorate of Engineering Education regarding this injustice and threatened to take them to court in order to seek redressal.

Disappointed, he joined another engineering college in Bangalore. On the first day of attending the engineering college in Bangalore, he was subjected to extreme ragging by the senior students. The ragging was so bad that he did not muster enough courage to attend classes from the next day. He would leave home everyday and spend time at the library in the Ramakrishna Ashram, which was in the same neighbourhood. His long study of Vivekananda's writings during this period changed his outlook, and was to lay the foundation of his subsequent life and thinking.

Based on his earlier complaint, the government admitted him to the engineering college in Mysore. By the time he won the case, and was admitted to the engineering college, he was a changed person (had become a leader), searching to form a group of students to work for the most deprived section of the society. His stay in the tribal society near Mysore (experiencing a new world) exposed him to shocking social reality, which finally shaped him into an effective and committed leader. Today the Swami Vivekananda Youth Movement, the organization he founded, works in all the districts of Karnataka and touches the lives of nearly a million marginalised and deprived rural and tribal people.

MECHANISMS FOR LEADERSHIP DEVELOPMENT

Leadership development may go through several stages, starting from selection of potential leaders to strengthening them with new opportunities and support.

Recruitment

The first stage of leadership development is to select people who can develop the desired qualities of leadership very fast. We have already discussed the characteristics of effective leaders. The selection process may screen people to find potential leaders. Most organizations use psychometric tests, interviews, simulation exercises, etc. to identify potential leaders. A careful selection in the beginning can ensure that efforts are not wasted. Some organizations also use assessment centres for selection of potential leaders.

Training

Development of leaders requires systematic exposure to various experiences, including the vision of the organization, the role of the leaders, strategic thinking, creativity and innovation, team building, change management, etc. The next section illustrates the experiences of a few organizations. Different foci are used for development of leaders at different levels in the organization. The main spirit of leadership is to take charge of situations and innovatively deal with complex issues. Preparing the candidates through several inputs can help achieve the objectives of a leadership development programme. The main elements in training of leaders are internality, creativity, team building, and strategic thinking.

Delegation

Delegation is a very useful device for leadership development. It is based on the assumption that every person has some assets (physical strength, knowledge, interpersonal competence, ability to persuade, etc.). These are sources of power. We can thus say that every person has power. The process of empowering is concerned with creating conditions in which this inner power can be used effectively and the concerned person can take leadership effectively. For example, if we create an opportunity for a person with interpersonal competence to solve conflicts, we have empowered that person. Empowering is thus the process of expanding an individual's choices and helping him or her to use these alternative choices to widen the choices of others. Power can thus be seen as expanding and multiplying.

However, power can never be given; it can only be exercised. Conditions can certainly be promoted to help people use power effectively. One formal way of creating such conditions is delegation. The concept of delegation is not to 'give' power. Senior employees need to evolve (jointly with their junior colleagues) areas in which they would like to use their competencies and ways in which they can use their discretion to make the desired impact. Delegation helps them to work out strategies for doing the same with their junior colleagues. Delegation, then, is a useful way of multiplying power in an organization.

The purpose of delegation will fail, however, if a leader or a senior manager 'gives' the tasks to a junior colleague, which he or she does not like or for which he or she does not have time. It will also fail if the junior colleague feels 'overloaded' with responsibility. Similarly, it cannot succeed in its purpose if the senior person unilaterally does it. It should involve joint decision making. It is therefore a multi-step process.

Steps for delegation

Delegation involves several steps. It is not likely to be effective if we miss any of the following eight steps mentioned below. These steps are stated in terms of action points. We shall cite a simple example of delegation to illustrate the eight steps.

Say, a private bank has been successful in getting customers. Several people are coming in for loans. A senior manager sanctioning home loans finds the work too heavy. She wants to delegate the authority of sanctioning home-building loans up to 100 million rupees to one of the managers working with her.

Jointly define role boundaries Delegation involves two roles, the role of the delegator and that of the delegatee. With delegation, their roles and responsibilities are likely to change. These changes in responsibility must be discussed and decided upon. For example, in our example, the senior manager and the junior manager reporting to her must sit down and discuss what responsibilities will be taken up by the senior manager (e.g., periodic monitoring, guiding, consulting in complex matters, reviewing progress, providing facilities to the manager) and what responsibilities will be taken up by her subordinate (examining the cases, sanctioning loans, following up payment of instalments, etc.).

Delegation is not simply passing on the workload; it is the process of giving more responsibility and challenge to the delegatee. Decisions about responsibilities should be taken jointly and not unilaterally. Since others also need to know about the functions the delegatee will perform, these need to be described fully and made known widely.

Provide needed competencies Most functions delegated will be new to the delegatee and contain higher responsibilities. For example, before sanctioning loans, the junior manager must examine several documents, visit the site, investigate the applicant's profile, etc. He or she was not doing these things earlier and these are his or her new responsibilities. The delegatee should do a self-assessment and openly discuss what new competencies he or she should develop in order to do justice to the new functions. The delegator should then prepare a plan, in consultation with the delegatee, for how the latter will develop these competencies. For example, the manager to whom new responsibilities are delegated may not have much knowledge of insurance procedures. During the discussion, this weakness may be brought up. The senior manager may then arrange for the subordinate's training in insurance procedures before he is delegated the new responsibility.

Provide needed resources   The same is true of resources (financial, material, technological, and human) required for effective performance of the new functions. These should be assessed and provision must be made to provide such support to the delegatee. For example, the junior manager may find that he would need an assistant to help in analysing various documents so that he is able to sanction the loans faster. Such help may then be provided to the delegatee.

Monitor but do not supervise closely   Monitoring of the performance of the delegated functions for some time is essential. This may provide the needed support or help. Monitoring may also indicate the delegator's interest and moral support. If overdone, though, this can be counterproductive. Close supervision of the performance of delegated functions by the delegator may indicate lack of trust in the competence of the delegatee. In this case, the senior manager and her subordinate may decide that they will meet every month to review progress rather than meeting every day or reviewing each case. The delegator should not breathe down the neck of the delegatee.

Reward discretion and initiative   Delegation is an evolutionary and developmental process. It needs to be encouraged and reinforced. Delegation involves taking initiative and using discretion in the delegated functions. If these are rewarded, the process of delegation will be stronger and more successful. For example, if there is a problem with the insurance company in a certain home loan application, the junior manager may take the initiative in working with the insurance company to remove the hurdle and, using his discretionary power, may sanction the loan. This will be taking a calculated risk but leadership involves moderate risk taking.

Respect role boundaries   Once a decision has been jointly taken by the senior and junior colleagues on delegation, the redefined role boundaries must be respected. The delegatee is likely to make mistakes. The delegator may be tempted to rush in to rescue him or her. This may destroy the spirit of delegation. No decision should be taken 'over the head' of the delegatee in matters delegated to the latter. If the decision is to be changed, the delegatee should do it after discussion with the delegator and after being convinced of the need to change the decision. For example, if the junior manager has made a mistake or delayed sanctioning a loan and the customer complains about it, it would be improper for the senior manager to solve the problem. Instead, she should discuss the matter with the manager and provide him any support he needs to solve the problem. This problem often arises when 'influential' clients approach higher authorities to get things done.

Jointly analyse mistakes to plan for future In periodic reviews, mistakes may be used as experiences from which to learn to improve delegation. The mistakes made, difficulties experienced, etc. can be analysed in such review meetings in order to plan how these may be avoided in future. Such experiences may raise many issues that could be useful for improvement of the delegatee. Some mistakes are likely to be made by the delegatee in performing newly delegated functions. Initiative involves risk and the possibility of mistakes. Such mistakes must be regarded as experiences from which to learn to improve performance. The review meetings may therefore include analysis of mistakes and problems so that the future performance level goes up.

Review delegation down the line Often, people want delegation only up to their own level. As we said in the beginning, delegation is a widening process of empowerment. Each senior person involved in delegation should discuss with his or her junior colleagues how the latter can delegate some useful functions to his or her colleagues at the next level. This will help to multiply power through delegation. In the above example, the manager should be asked which of his current functions he would like to delegate so that he can do full justice to his new responsibilities. The manager may then start the same process of delegation with his subordinate.

360-Degree Appraisal

T.V. Rao Learning Systems has developed a model for developing leadership and managerial competencies through 360-degree feedback.[37] This model is referred to as the RSDQ model. This model of leadership and managerial effectiveness views effective management and leadership as a combination of four sets of variables: roles, styles, delegation, and qualities.

Roles The extent to which the individual plays various leadership and managerial roles. This includes both transformational (leadership) and transactional (managerial) roles. Some of these are

- Articulating and communicating vision and values
- Formulating long-term policies and strategies
- Introducing and managing new technology and systems
- Inspiring, developing, and motivating juniors
- Managing juniors, colleagues, and seniors
- Culture building
- Internal customer management
- External customer management
- Managing unions and associations

Styles While effective managers recognise all the leadership roles and perform them well, it is the way (style) they use that is important. As discussed in Chapter 21, Rao has proposed three leadership styles: benevolent, critical, and developmental. The developmental style of leadership is the most desirable style.

Delegation The RSDQ model considers delegation as an important part of a senior executive's effectiveness. Managers who delegate utilise their time to perform higher-level tasks. Managers who do not delegate continue to do lower level tasks and suppress their leadership qualities and managerial effectiveness.

Qualities According to the model, that senior executives should exhibit qualities of leaders and world-class managers. These qualities can be proaction, listening, communication, positive approach, participative nature, quality orientation, etc. Such qualities not only affect effectiveness with which top-level managers perform various roles, but also have an impact on their leadership style.

A study of 26 CEOs drawn from various organizations[38] has indicated that Indian CEOs seem to be good at 'boss management' and weak at managing unions. They also seem to be less effective in transformational roles. While performing transformational roles their strengths lie in articulating vision for the unit and influencing the thinking of their seniors. On a large number of other areas such as culture building, inspiring, developing staff, etc., the leaders need to develop a lot more. Future leadership programmes should focus on change management skills of managers. Their styles are predominantly developmental. They seem to delegate a good deal. High activity level, positive thinking, communication, change orientation, etc. are some of their notable strengths. Proactivity, a cool and composed nature, empathy, patience, and participative nature should be developed to make a significant contribution to the organization.

Mentoring

Role models are the most powerful source of learning in an organization. In some organizations a few senior employees perform mentoring roles, while other organizations have formal mentors who are trained to develop leaders. Mentoring requires careful planning and skills for nurturing hidden talent. Mentors are not advisors; they provide emotional support and encouragement for reflection and learning from experiences. Generally, mentors have special skills of nurturing talent. Mentors need to be selected and developed through training programmes.

Matrix Career Planning

Leadership development requires exposure to a variety of experiences in the organization. If an organization has a divisionalised structure, leadership development would require moving individuals into different divisions and different functions, to expose them to various organizational aspects. A systematic matrix career planning involving the candidates may be useful in providing varied exposure. Such exposure may help the candidates to know the organization closely and gain experience of managing the dynamics at various levels and different sections.

Sabbatical

One way to create a crucible for potential leaders is to encourage them to enter 'a foreign territory'. Employees may go for higher studies, write their experiences, learn new skills, etc. Organizations should encourage their employees to utilise their sabbatical leave to have new experiences and exposures. Such periods may turn out to be critical crucibles. Organizations can also encourage their employees to get involved in community projects or social work. Such exposures are time well spent and help the candidates to reflect on critical aspects.

Reward System

We have already discussed the reward system in Chapter 2. Rewards help to reinforce the desired behaviour in employees. Recognising significant achievement and other behaviours may help to sustain them. This encourages other employees to emulate such behaviours. Organizations are increasingly focusing on group performance and non-financial rewards. The main spirit of rewards is to recognise, applaud, and celebrate desirable behaviours and results. A well-designed rewards system can develop various qualities among a large number of employees.

Group Competition for Creativity and Innovation

While leadership will require development of synergy (team building), competition for excellence and creativity are other important factors in the process. Competition for excellence puts positive pressure on individuals to use their talents to the maximum, and helps them to achieve their potential effectively. Different areas may be identified for excellence and creativity, and objective criteria may be framed to assess people on these dimensions. Such competition may raise the level of quality and creativity in the organization.

SOME MODELS OF LEADERSHIP DEVELOPMENT

Using the example of companies such as Infosys, Wipro, the RPG group, and the JK group, as well as the example of the BPO industry, this section illustrates the various models of leadership development followed in India.

Infosys Model

Infosys is one of the few companies that is transforming the image of India as a country of talent.[39] The vision of Infosys is to create an organization that is 'built to last'. Narayana Murthy saw the need to establish a place to develop leadership on a large scale. The Infosys Leadership Institute (ILI) was established to fulfil this need. The institute was created in early 2001 to assist Infosys in responding to specific challenges of the present and future and to create higher customer value through 'thought leadership'.

The vision statement of Infosys reads: 'We will be a globally respected corporation that provides best of breed business solutions, leveraging technology, delivered by best in class people.' To achieve this vision, leadership competencies have been defined along four broad dimensions: work, people, technology, and business. The following nine pillars are the operational elements for leadership development in Infosys.

360-degree feedback

The 360-degree feedback is a structured method of systematically collecting and processing data about a person's performance and capabilities from a wide range of coworkers. The company provides the employee an opportunity to reflect on this valuable information. Feedback is collected from peers, direct reportees, the manager, and customers (both internal and external). The institute uses a comprehensive tool that is aligned to the leadership competencies.

Development assignments

High-potential employees are given experience in diverse functions through internal job rotations and cross-functional assignments. Development assignments enable employees to gather practical leadership skills outside his or her zone of experience.

Infosys culture workshops

These workshops help participants understand the core values, purpose, and processes followed in the context of leadership development. The design of these workshops allows for extensive interaction among participants leading to reinforcement of the Infosys culture, and ensuring enough empowerment to guarantee adherence and refinement to the culture of the organization.

Development relationships

These are one-on-one relationships in work settings that facilitate the sharing and transfer of knowledge and experience between individuals. The Infosys leadership development model views mentoring as a developmental relationship in the context of leadership development. A 'mentoring for leadership' pilot programme is operational and learning from this programme is used to refine and extend this element of leadership development across the organization.

Leadership skills training

Senior management is fully involved and committed to the development of future leaders. Based on the belief that 'the company is the campus, the business is the curriculum, leaders shall teach', *Leaders Teach Series* workshops are conducted by the board of directors with help from the ILI faculty. This series includes workshops by Narayana Murthy, chairman and chief mentor, and Nandan Nilekani, the managing director and chief executive officer, and other members of the board.

Feedback intensive programmes

Structured behavioural interventions are made to help the participants receive and give feedback in a non-threatening environment and yield a workable plan for setting goals for continued personal and professional development and strategies for attaining them.

Systemic process learning

This is an intervention that enables participants to view an organization as a whole system comprising innumerable interacting sub-systems. It yields plans for continuous improvement in systemic processes and details how an individual will initiate such improvements.

Action learning

This is a team-based real-time experience used to solve real, systemic, and unresolved organizational problems. It is a pragmatic process aimed at yielding a resolution to the problem or issue that has been identified, and a workable plan for setting goals for continued development, with strategies for attaining them.

Community empathy

The institute aspires to create, on a regular and structured basis, opportunities for high-potential candidates to volunteer to work on causes outside Infosys that contribute to the greater good of the less fortunate. The importance of community empathy in overall leadership development is in line with the fundamental belief of the organization that social conscience needs to be nurtured and enhanced in each one of its present and potential leaders.

Leadership journey

The leadership journey commences with the selection of high potential employees of the organization. The top management of Infosys identifies a pool of candidates based on their past performance and an assessment of leadership potential. The formal duration of the leadership journey is 3 years. These identified individuals are classified as 'high potentials'. Each high-potential employee has one ILI faculty member assigned to him or her. The faculty member acts as a guide in the leadership journey with the creation and actionising of the PDP. The faculty member provides support in implementing the individual change objectives. The majority of the high potentials have undertaken at least one or more of the leadership skill training interventions. The high potentials have access to the pilot mentoring for leadership programme. The faculty members in their role as internal consultants enable high potentials to undertake various interventions that help to resolve real business issues.

Wipro Model

Background

Wipro, which was formerly known as Western India Vegetable Products, began its operations in the year 1946.[40] In the late seventies, it began to manufacture mini-computers and followed with attempts to make its own software. By the year 2000, it listed itself on the New York Stock Exchange. Today, the company has 61,000 employees, of which close to 7,000 are spread over 45 nations across the globe. Close to 25 years after it entered information technology markets, Wipro crossed 1 billion US dollars in revenues. It took just 18 months thereafter to reach the 2 billion US dollars mark. It has received several accolades, a recent one being the world's first company in IT services and software to be assessed for People CMM® Version 2, and in 2003 being rated the number one company across Asia Pacific for leadership by Hewitt. In 2004, it also received recognitions from the American Society for Training and Development (ASTD).

Leadership Development

The leadership development programme in Wipro concentrates on developing and promoting talent from within the company.

Leadership qualities After extensive research into literature, understanding best practices, and checking with thought leaders, Wipro identified the following eight leadership qualities:
- Strategic thinking: Anticipating the future through an articulated vision
- Customer orientation: Customer at the centre of the vision
- Aggressive commitment: Pursuing stretched commitments with determination and focus
- Global thinking and acting: Global cultural synchronisation with respect to issues and trends
- Self-confidence: Belief in the abilities of self and team
- Commitment to excellence: Commitment to surpass the best with respect to global standards
- Working in teams: Encouraging harmony and synergy for getting multiplier effect from team
- Building future leaders: Spending time with team; coaching and pursuing developmental needs of team

The impact of global thinking and acting runs across all of these qualities. Wipro has suitably modified people processes so that employee behaviours are seen as consistent with the leadership vision.

Developing leadership talent from within

The process adopted for leadership development follows a lifecycle pattern. There are five programmes that focus on sharpening leadership skills of individual leaders.

Entry-Level Programme This is the first programme a fresh recruit goes through. Country-specific cross-cultural training and the opportunities to work in different nations has made the workforce adaptable and resilient.

New Leaders' Programme This programme is designed for the first-time manager. In the NLP, leaders are particularly trained on aspects of managing virtual teams.

Wipro Leaders' Programme This programme is addressed to the manager or managers who still want to manage the teams directly. From here on, it is a corporation-wide programme. At the WLP, leaders are sensitised on the diversity principle, and mingle with leaders from all parts of the world.

Business Leaders' Programme This programme is for managers-in-waiting who need to look at business as a whole and understand bottom-line implications. It covers relevant elements of finance and environmental scanning. The business leaders' programme (BLP) focuses attention on a single business case, which has a strong international flavour. The programme continues over several days.

Strategic Leaders' Programme The Strategic Leaders' Programme (SLP) is the highest programme and is aimed at the top management. It helps the company's leaders to design and develop strategies in a global environment. From its inception, the SLP has been addressed by thought leaders from all over the world, including luminaries from the Wharton Business School, the London Business School, and the Indian School of Business. Mr Azim Premji, chairman of Wipro, addresses participants of Wipro's Leaders' Programmes, BLP, and SLP.

Advanced experiential learning

Wipro has collaborated a global learning alliance (GLA) with the learning and development divisions of large global organizations, such as, Schneider, L'Oreal, Nissan, and Alcan. Each organization sponsors approximately six senior leaders (at the level of vice presidents in Wipro) from within its multiple lines of business to represent learning and development challenges in a common forum, where facilitation is done by eminent faculty from institutions such as the London Business School and by legends such as Prof. Ikujiro Nonaka. Wipro's corporate HR development team has the custodianship for leadership development in the company. The emerging emphasis of this group has been on facilitated interventions in top management groups across the corporation. Their interventions have facilitated interactions in strategy development between clients and delivery teams, strategic business units, and top management.

Challenges

The various challenges in leadership development are as follows:
- Fostering a climate in which a younger workforce rises to challenges of leadership faster than their predecessors, given the rate at which business opportunities present themselves across diverse business sectors in multiple geographies.
- Ensuring a more comprehensive learning to embrace the diversity of cultures and business sector models in different markets and geographies.
- Helping teams discover their purpose and follow through in performing service operations in lesser time.
- Managing the scale and speed of business growth with a sense of realism and requisite humility.
- Sharpening leadership response to changes in clients' business models for enablement of future business.

RPG Model

RPG, with turnover of 950 million rupees, is a conglomerate with 20 companies.[41] Its core businesses comprise of mature economy businesses such as power, tyres, cables, power transmission, plantations, carbon black, and also new economy businesses such as pharmaceuticals, retail, information technology, and entertainment. The group has 2,000 managers, out of which 170 are at the levels of general manager and above.

Being a large conglomerate it has multiple and diverse industry opportunities. It also faces challenges such as unique requirement of each industry sector, in terms of diverse skill sets, grades and remuneration, and domain knowledge.

The current talent management practices have been initiated with an objective of filling senior management positions from within its own ranks. The RPG talent management process is based on building leadership pipeline by spotting talents early in the career of its employees and providing careers to people based on objective assessment.

Development process

The leadership development process of RPG has three levels. At each level the 'highfliers' are selected on the basis of a combination of performance and potential. Managers who are in the category of high performance and high potential are provided accelerated career growth.

Managers with 3+ rating (for 3 years) participate in the development centre I. It identifies highfliers, develops action plans, and provides one degree change in the job and an opportunity to attend leadership programme at any of the Indian Institute of Management (IIM).

Senior managers with 3+ rating participate in development centre II. It identifies highfliers, develops action plans, provides one degree change in the job and provides an opportunity to attend the leadership programme at IIM. All the highfliers are interviewed by the group's chairman.

All general managers and vice presidents participate in development centre III. These managers plan develop actions and attend leadership programmes at IIM.

There are two main challenges in this regard. The first challenge is the motivation of those who are not highfliers. The HR department and the top management communicate this with a great deal of sensitivity. The company ensures development plans for each of these employees. They are also given opportunity to be considered again by joining the development centre again.

It is equally challenging to manage the expectations of highfliers. The HR department and the top management communicate to them the implications of their selection as highfliers, develop them further, and provide them opportunities for growth.

Competency development is done through customised residential programme at the Indian Institute of Management. Middle management highfliers attend a programme, spread over 15 days, referred to as LDP-I. Senior management highfliers attend a 15-day programme, LDP-II. A 7-day programme, LDP-III, is organized for the top management.

On completion of the development centre, two to three competencies are selected by each participant. These are competencies, which are easy to improve, have high impact on job performance, have viability, and result in action plans for development.

The HR department also prepares training modules on 'specific competencies'. For example, development of competency of analytical skills consists of three modules: a 3-day Classroom session, one and a half months of 'do-it-yourself' sessions, and again a 2-day classroom session.

Competency development is tracked through web-based learning management system and reinforced through 360 degree feedback. Central data is maintained for all highfliers. In the career moves one degree change is made for them. Organizational and management review is done twice in a year for planning and tracking career moves for all managers in middle and senior management. For managers in top management, the management board spends one full day to plan the career moves.

In order to provide opportunities to managers to grow within the group, all vacancies are communicated to all employees through e-mail. They can apply for internal vacancies without going through the boss. Group HR facilitates the process.

The following factors seem to be going well for the company: 100 highfliers have been identified, high credibility of the process, top management involvement and support, career moves of managers 3 years on the job (42 per cent), internal filling of top management vacancies (68 per cent). The company hopes to further strengthen its focus on providing development opportunities after development centres.

JK Model

Leadership development framework

Leadership competency model   There are two models of leadership competency: (1) 'leadership competency model' for presidents, vice presidents, and general managers; and (2) 'emerging leadership competency model' for middle managers and front line executives. Each model has a set of competencies that are required for superior performance in current and future roles.

The models have been developed based on intensive interaction with executives at different levels (from the perspective of a current job holder, a superior, a stakeholder, an internal customer, etc.). The company has focused on current and future challenges, expert inputs from consultants such as M/s SHL and Human Edge, study of best practices, etc. The leadership competencies at senior levels range from 'strategic business perspective' to 'executing strategy'. Similarly, in the emerging leadership competency model for the middle management and front line executives, competencies range from 'business perspective' to 'self-management'.

Each competency comprises of sub-competencies that are defined in terms of exhibited behaviour on the job with unique perspective of the hierarchy level in the organization, i.e., president, VP, GM, manager, and front-line executive.

Leadership (competency) assessment Keeping in view the competency models and the variants within a model applicable to the levels in the organization (such as president, manager, etc.), development centres have been designed using ability tests, psychometric tools, simulation exercises, etc. The development centre is a process involving multiple assessors, tools, dimensions, and participants. It aims at bringing about most objective assessment of an individual's displayed behaviour. At JK, the assessors to participants ratio is 1:2. Each development centre takes 3 days, the first day (about 12 hours) focuses on assessment, the second day is devoted to sensitisation of participants to the development process and feedback, and the third day focuses on the formulation of an action plan to leverage the employee's strengths and developing the critical competency dimensions with a committed plan for break through contribution. The process known as the individual development plan (IDP) is jointly made by the employee, his or her superior, the HR executive, and one of the assessors. The assessor acts as a facilitator.

Ability tests Some of the ability tests used are numerical tests, brainstorming, tests for selection and training (TST), diagrammatical reasoning tests, etc. These tests measure an individual's numerical ability, creativity, mental strength, etc.

Psychological tools These test, also known as personality tests, map an individual's occupational personality attributes. The tools used are occupational personality questionnaires (OPQ), tests to measure emotional intelligence, etc.

Simulation exercises The exercises include group discussion, presentation, role-play, case analysis, 'in tray', etc. These simulation exercises enable the assessor to identify an individual's competency in areas such as customer focus, business perspective, decision making, etc.

Leadership development

The leadership (competency) development at JK is multi-dimensional and uses the following approaches.

Individual development plan The development plan is customised according to the needs of the employees. Various development options for developing a particular competency or sub-competency are provided in the programme. In fact, each individual is evaluated on a learning style inventory and given feedback on his or her preferred learning style, e.g., activist, reflectionist, pragmatist, theorist (how people learn—through action, reflection, application, or concepts and logic). The development options range from 'a personalised individual executive coach' to 'reading books'. Innovative options such as watching television, learning at conferences and seminars, in-house role models, etc. are also used. A typical individual development plan has the following components:
- Personal details
- Learning style
- List of strong and relatively week competencies

- Contribution the individual wants to make in the next 1–2 years with an action plan
- Plan for leveraging the stronger competencies
- Plan for developing the relatively weaker competencies

Development of successors to strategic positions   Each business identifies strategic positions across levels keeping in view the strategic importance of a position in terms of potential to contribute to the business. Keeping in view the potential and performance rating, age, qualification, ambition, and orientation, executives at the next one or two lower levels are identified as successors and groomed. The grooming process involves specialised training, job rotation, sabbaticals, participation in a cross-functional team, additional assignments, etc.

Involvement of young executives in teams and forums   The young leaders are provided with opportunities to work in cross-functional teams (CFT), thereby developing leadership competencies on the job. Some of the companies in the JK group have also created 'young leaders forum' (YLF) comprising of 8 to 10 young bright executives to brainstorm, innovate, and take up breakthrough projects.

Organization-wide common development initiatives   Special development initiatives are organized for different levels of executives. This reinforces and develops certain strategic competencies. Some examples are

- A 6-day strategic leadership programme for senior executives is conducted, with the help of professors from Harvard University.
- A 2-week business leadership programme identifies talent at middle and front-line management. This programme is conducted with the help of IIMB and focuses on both behavioural and functional competencies. These programmes are followed by outbound programmes with the help of companies such as Pegasus to inculcate team spirit and self-awareness.
- A week-long development programme for all general managers at Management Development Institute (MDI), Gurgaon.
- Senior executives are provided special training to acquire coaching and mentoring skills.
- A structured programme on innovation is designed for the top and the senior management.

Evaluation of effectiveness

In order to ensure robust implementation, the development process is integrated with the key result areas of the top and senior management as well as that of the individuals. Status and progress of the programme are evaluated through structured review meetings at various levels including that by the group chairman. Some of the quantified parameters to evaluate the internal process are as follows:

Improvement in talent matrix   The individuals at different levels, i.e., VP, GM, and managers are plotted on a matrix with two parameters. Performance is plotted on the Y axis and assessed potential is plotted on the X axis. The population is divided into talent, emerging talent, dark horse, exit, and solid citizens, based on their position in the grid. The percentage of executives in the talent and emerging talent in the population is an indication of the effectiveness of development plans.

Availability of successors to key or strategic positions   The percentage vacancies filled by internal talent is an indication of better availability of the successors in the organization.

Quantum of break through contribution   The net results of break through contribution planned under the individual development plan are monitored and evaluated on half yearly or yearly basis.

Overall effectiveness of the business   Without prejudice to the contribution made by other processes and initiatives, the growth in the effectiveness in the business or unit is also linked to the success of the development process and also to the improvement in the competencies and performance output of the individual concerned.

BPO Industry

Developing 20-somethings to take up leadership roles in a cut-throat competitive business environment is a challenge of sorts.[42] Fortunately, progressive companies have streamlined their HR processes to convert this challenge into a positive opportunity. The process starts with systematic selection of agents who are ready to make a transition as first-time leaders. And from there on, its training all the way! Young leaders go through a variety of learning programmes, designed with the objective of sensitising them to their new role—supervising and leading teams.

Processes abound

Wipro BPO believes in raising the bar as far as grooming young leaders goes. It has instituted several initiatives targeting at sharpening skills for first-time leaders. The HIGH (How I Grow Here) programme offers grooming sessions to all agents aspiring to be team leaders and acts as a guide to them to prepare themselves adequately for related interviews and group discussions, avoiding common pitfalls and improving their first time success rate. All successful applicants who graduate to the next level of team leaders from the position of calling resources go through a 15 days supervisory training programme. It is mandatory for them to attend an induction session on all policies and practices within the first 1 month of stepping into the new role.

'New manager assimilation' is an intervention for supervisors, who will be handling new teams aimed at gathering the expectations of the team from the supervisor and also introducing the supervisor to the team in a structured manner. Supervisor survival guide is a session conducted by the HR team for all the supervisors, who are briefed about the company values, operating principles, people practices, and their role as supervisors. Another such structured programme is Enhance, which is a 15-day session to enhance technical and behavioural competencies of supervisors.

Apart from structured training programmes, young leaders have access to a number of forums that offer opportunities for practical insights into the intricacies of people management. In the VP Round Table, colleagues meet senior management and share thoughts about the organization. In the Skip Level Meeting, a team meets with the supervisor's supervisor and receives feedback on its performance and style of functioning. As an outcome of this meeting, the supervisor needs to develop an action plan relating to improvements in his or her style of functioning. Policy Bytes is a communication campaign that focuses on highlighting the salient features of various people polices that affect colleagues. One policy is covered every fortnight, and posters and mailers are sent to all spanning this policy.

Many organizations, such as Wipro BPO, are committed to structured training for first-time leaders. In fact, at EXL Service, associate level employees have taken it upon themselves to groom their team members by starting their own mentoring and grooming processes. One such process is 'A day in the life of an AM', where associates play a shadow assistant manager role and spend a day with their supervisors to understand the requirements of the role and their progress is mapped by their supervisors and skips for a certain time period. Periodic developmental inputs are provided based on the monthly performance assessment.

EXL Service has its own share of training programmes for new team leaders. Post promotion, a comprehensive assistant manager module equips team leaders to manage people and process-related aspects of the role. The First Time Leadership Orientation Programme takes team leaders through various stages of leadership inputs required for them to perform their role effectively.

Best practices sharing forums encourage team leaders to learn from each other. Quarterly leadership surveys are used for team members to assess immediate supervisors online and reports are given for each individual on his own scores as well as benchmarking against others.

Every new assistant manager (or team leader) goes through various programmes over the initial period of 6 to 8 months in his or her new role. At the core of these is the induction programme offering an overview of business processes, administration functions, HR policies as well as overview of logistics, facilities, finance, training function, and special programmes related to the quality. The induction mandates the team leader to undergo a 'platform skills programme' and a 'train the trainer programme' (over a period of 3 months).

New team leaders at EXL also undergo a 'first-time leader orientation' (within 3 months of the transition). This three-module programme gets them to understand and appreciate what their promotion to the leadership band means. They can now gain insight into their leadership styles, learn to create and nurture teams, and grasp the basics of giving effective feedback. This is an opportunity to create development plans for themselves and work on it. Participants come back a month after the first module for a review of their learning and actions taken. They take up a project in teams and come back to present it 3 months later. Between the three modules, they have to complete reading the programme material that is sent to them on-line.

Team leaders are required to attend an effective business communication programme within 6 months of having become a team leader. This is a programme focused on honing their communication skills. Yet another crucial input that team leaders require is in the area of performance management. The team leaders must attend the performance management programme before they do the year-end appraisals of their teams. The content revolves around understanding how goals are handed over, creating a buy-in to goals, reviewing performance, working out improvement plans, and learning to have meaningful and wholesome conversations with the team members during the process of appraising. Apart from these programmes, which must be attended as a mandate, EXL customises specific programmes for team leaders, depending on individual needs from time to time.

Convergys grooms young leaders by building on core competencies that are critical to establishing good relationships. And so, training is geared to driving proficiency around elements of 10 core competencies: work ethic, coaching, problem solving, decisiveness, communication, team building, time management, analytical thinking, flexibility, and building relationships.

Convergys believes that a number of key competencies like communication, building relationships, and problem solving must be inherent in a future team leader. These need to be enhanced and developed to enable total success. The organization philosophy: hire for aptitude in core competencies and offer an environment conducive to enabling team leaders to be engaged, challenged, and to continuously learn. Says Karen Crone, vice president – Human Resources, 'It is our job to provide employees with the tools necessary to structure team leader–agent interactions. This involves taking a routine challenge and creating a template structure for addressing this challenge until the appropriate team leader behaviour becomes natural. It is also important to engage the team leader's manager to track team leader's behaviour and provide feedback on his performance.'

Convergys's team leader development programme comprises of a combination of computer-based training, hands-on learning, distance learning, classroom and on-the-job practicum, which provides the variety to keep young talent engaged. According to Crone, the team leader development programme needs to be viewed as a series of events, rather than a single programme. Team leaders go through classroom training, followed by computer-based training in competencies earmarked for further development. They also network with each other and with managers, tracking their individual progress and providing individualised feedback.

All team leaders receive an electronic publication every other month, known as *OutReach*, which discusses team leader performance, as well as challenges they face. They are also encouraged to submit issues for discussion and provide examples of best practices that they have developed.

QAI India Ltd and Nasscom recently launched certification programmes such as Certified BPO Team Leader (CBTL) and Certified BPO Quality Analyst (CBQA), which may be welcome additions for the BPO industry. CBTL covers topics such as operations management, people management, and quality management. CBQA focuses on quality measurement, quality improvement, and quality systems.

SUMMARY

There is a paradigm shift in leadership. New organizations require leaders in large numbers at all levels. The profile of tomorrow's leaders includes internality (grand vision, internality, optimism, professional will), creativity (innovation, maverick mindset, neoteny), humility (personal humility, self-restraint, empowerment, culture building), values (value orientation, ethics, people first, social concern), networking (communication, networking competency, synergy building, customer orientation).

Crucibles play an important role in leadership development. A crucible is a transformational experience. Through the crucibles the leaders acquire new insight. Four crucibles have been identified: mentoring relationship, enforced reflection, experiencing a new world, and disruption and loss.

The mechanisms of leadership development include recruitment, training, mentoring, matrix career planning, sabbatical, reward system, and group competition for creativity. Leadership development models of Infosys, Wipro, RPG, and the BPO industry are presented to illustrate these concepts further.

GLOSSARY

creativity set of attitudes, abilities, and mental processes that increase the probability of hitting upon solutions that seem to the well informed both novel and appropriate

crucible transformational experience that set leaders on the road to where they are now

dark horse one who emerges as a good candidate, without being discussed previously

humility aversion for getting limelight on self

internality the belief that one can influence most things around oneself

leader development development of the leader

leadership development The strategic investment in, and utilisation of, the human capital within the organization

maverick mindset trying out unconventional ways to deal with issues

neoteny retention of childlike attributes into adulthood; qualities of youthfulness

power enhancers leaders' behaviour to shed their own power in the greater organizational interest

professional will stoic resolve; a culture of discipline

self-restraint the tendency to postpone gratification of one's immediate needs for a long-term goal

solid citizen committed person who can be relied on

EXERCISES

Concept Review Questions

1. What is the difference between leader development and leadership development?
2. What are Jim Collin's concepts of personal humility and professional will?
3. Why is creativity called maverick mindset?
4. What are the different crucibles suggested by Bennis and Thomas?
5. What is the difference between Infosys and Wipro models of leadership development?

Critical Thinking Exercises

1. Reflect on your own experiences and write down critical incidents, which you regard as possible crucibles. Also reflect why you regard these experiences crucibles? What kind of changes you experienced and how these increased your effectiveness?

2. Interview one of your friends in detail to identify his/her crucibles. Discuss with him/her changes he/she underwent.

Classroom Projects

1. Read biographies of two effective leaders and discuss what characteristics they show.

2. Form groups of two or three and interview one of your instructons to know the development of his/her leadership style.

Field Projects

1. Interview two managers to find out their crucibles, and how they contributed to the leadership roles.

2. Interview two employees to find the system of leadership development in their organizations.

Leadership Development at Dr Reddy's Laboratories Ltd*

THE CONTEXT

In an era of rapid globalization, intensifying competition and the complexities of business that come with it, business entities across the globe now realise that the 'leadership team' has increasingly become a critical strategic asset.

Dr. Reddy's Laboratories Ltd is an emerging global pharmaceutical company with proven research capabilities and is focused on creating and delivering innovative and quality products to help people lead healthier lives.

With an ambitious vision 'to become a discovery-led global pharmaceutical company', the organization has carefully evolved a strategic roadmap to move up the pharmaceutical value chain. It has transitioned from being a predominantly bulk actives and branded generic formulations player, to mark its presence in the regulated generics market. The organization is steadily progressing towards its vision of being an innovator with its New Chemical Entity (NCE) programme.

The company is working towards building a global specialty pharma business, which will act as a bridge between the transition from generics or branded generics to NCE. The specialty business will be based on incremental innovation on existing molecules to solve poorly met medical needs.

The geographic focus of the company has also changed, with an increasing focus on international markets. Revenues from the international market have grown from 40 per cent in the year 2000 to 64 per cent in 2004. The following priorities arise to execute this strategy:

- Geographic expansion
- Globalization of key businesses
- Transition to a discovery-led global company

These challenges set the stage for the organization to think of methodology to develop internal leaders through a well-defined process, as there is a limit to the number of leaders the organization can absorb from outside.

---

*Slightly abridged and edited version of 'Leadership development in Dr. Reddy's Laboratory Ltd: A case study' by Saumen Chakraborty and D.S. Sengar, published in *Developing Leadership for the Global Era: HRD Perspectives and Initiatives*, edited by Uma Jain, Udai Pareek, and Madhukar Shukla, Macmillan India, New Delhi. Reproduced with permission.

LEADERSHIP DEVELOPMENT

Wave One

Following the merger of Dr. Reddy's Laboratories Ltd with Cheminor Drugs Ltd in the year 2000, issues of integration, change management, and the sheer size of integrated operations necessitated the urgency for strengthening the leadership cadre in the merged entity.

In addition to creating a competency dictionary that defined 23 generic competencies, the company launched two structured processes: the leadership development programme (LDP) and the management development programme (MDP).

Leadership development programme   The leadership development programme was designed for the top 50 position holders in the company. Once the top 50 leadership positions for the company were identified, employees holding these positions were given inputs on the performance ethic and business strategy of the company, in order to bring in a common understanding of the organizations vision and make these employees partners in organization building. Individual development plans for each of these employees were created based on a 360-dgree feedback process. This was followed by focused developmental feedback to position holders.

Management development programme   The management development programme (MDP) used development centres (using the assessment methodology) to identify talent at the middle and junior management levels. Behavioural scientists on the panel ensured unbiased assessment. More than 250 employees were covered in the MDP process, and over 50 were identified as potential leaders. The potential leaders were given increased role responsibilities, customised training and put on developmental assignments.

Competency dictionary   The competency dictionary was evolved as a tool to create a common understanding across the organization on competencies identified as critical to the business. A cross-functional group of 25 executives identified existing technical core competencies in the organization. Subsequently, 23 generic competencies that would support these core competencies were identified. An operational definition along with detailed descriptors for each competency was documented in the competency dictionary.

Key take-aways from wave one   During the course of wave one, it became increasingly obvious that a common thread integrating the organizational initiatives towards leadership development was missing.

To cope with the intense demand for talent, potential leaders at all levels were hired, while also continuing with the focused development of existing employees. Over time, the concept of top 50 positions was changed to top 50 people.

A detailed study to define the future course of leadership development in the company was undertaken. In addition to benchmarking against best practices in leadership development across global companies, Dr. Reddy's also closely studied the Global Champions Initiative conducted by McKinsey.

The highest decision-making body in the company, the Management Council (MC), recognised the criticality of building a strong leadership cadre. The MC also agreed that there was a limit to the number of leaders the organization could absorb from external sources, and hence the requirement for a well-defined leadership engine and designing a leadership model.

Wave Two

With the objective of clarifying the expectations from a leader at Dr. Reddy's, the MC decided to form a subcommittee to work on a leadership model.

The leadership model was evolved using a mix of different approaches. A meticulous study of leadership models used in different companies, along with their long-term strategy and critical success factors was commenced. The team also studied successful leaders within the organization and the leadership traits displayed by them. Using the CEO's personal journal that chronicled various milestones achieved by the company, and the role of leaders at each stage, past trends were analysed in the present context.

The framework used for developing the leadership model used the following steps:

- The company's core values were central to the model, with the vision providing the broad strategic approach.
- Looking at the aspirations of the company, critical success factors, which would help the company achieve its vision, were identified. This future focus was based on the hypothesis that organizations develop leaders in order to further business interests. Therefore if leadership development has to be rooted in business, it is necessary that the expectations from the leader be based upon the future scenario based on the organizational strategy.
- The expectations from a leader were translated into leadership characterisation, specifying differentiating behaviour.

The three dimensions of past successes, vision, and reality demarcate the territory in which leaders revel. However, leaders also need descriptors of observable behaviours and operating principles for self-assessment and development. This was clearly articulated in the DRL leadership model.

EXPECTATIONS FROM A LEADER IN DR. REDDY'S

Having defined the company's core purpose, vision, and values, the next step was to define expectations from the leader of the company. Three key drivers were identified for a leader in the company, which are

Drives organizational building Championing organizational building as preparation for the future and not 'immediate' business results alone will help the company achieve the demanding vision.

Revels in entrepreneurship and innovation   As the vision of the company is to become a discovery-led global company, the importance of entrepreneurship and innovation is unquestionable and hence it is one of the major expectations from a leader in Dr. Reddy's.

Leads by example   In order to meet the challenge of running the present business successfully while building the business and organization for the future, the leader has to lead from the front by accepting and delivering on stretch goals.

CHARACTERISTICS OF THE MODEL

The various characteristics of the model are explained in this section.

Futuristic   The inputs of the MC are taken keeping in mind the future strategy and vision of the company. Understanding the importance of functional leadership in a knowledge intensive organization like Dr. Reddy's, technical or functional experts have the option of choosing to pursue a technical or specialist track.

Framework for self-management   Honest self-assessment and personal awareness of gaps in performance and potential are powerful forces for self-development. The model has been communicated to everyone in the organization and now provides consistent measures for self-management.

Simplicity   HR language or jargon is consciously avoided and business language is used, as the end customer for the model is supposed to be the business leader who has to interpret and act based on his understanding of the model. The nine descriptors in the model are observable behaviours, which can be developed.

Integration lever   The leadership development approach of the company is based on integrating the leadership model with the company values, performance management, coaching with an emphasis on dialogue with the superiors and functional experts for career guidance. The approach is powerful due to the high degree of interdependence of personal development on business requirement. The model is an integrating factor in a company involved in diverse businesses and operates in 40 different countries. Thus the model talks of the same leadership character across businesses and geographies.

Comprehensiveness and ease of evaluation and development   The descriptors in each of the three elements facilitate self-evaluation. For example, in the element 'revels in entrepreneurship and innovation', the three descriptors encompass areas from recognition of opportunity to effective execution.

Based on competency and complexity   The model helps describe the leadership growth path based on competency and complexity with three broad levels: identify leaders, develop them, deploy them.

LEADERSHIP DEPLOYMENT

Having defined a robust and unique company-specific leadership model, the effort was initiated to integrate the model with all other major people processes, while focusing on managing careers of employees.

Identification The identification of employees with leadership potential starts with the important step of checking against the threshold criteria. The threshold criteria are defined in terms of performance history, ability to learn, functional expertise, and value fit of the individual.

Assessment The model provides a tool with diagnostic specificity to assess the demonstrated behaviour of the individual's performance and potential. The process involves a multi-rater system with data and dialogue to substantiate the leadership potential of individuals. All individuals clearing the threshold criteria undergo a 360 Degree Leadership Talent Survey based on the leadership model. A talent management board (TMB) consisting of business managers is formed to discuss each case in detail to finalise the leadership competency rating.

Development and deployment A comparison of an individual's competency rating with the expected standards as per the leadership model serves as an input for development and deployment options. A parallel process of identifying critical positions, position clarification, and position profiling is done by the TMB, using job profile tools. The TMB then identifies potential successors for critical positions. Emerging business opportunities due to business growth are then matched to the identified leaders.

Scalability The approach is scalable, as the 360-degree tool used is web-based and the immediate superior is involved throughout the process.

Continuous process The model evaluates the leadership pipeline on a bi-annual basis and critical positions once a year, based on business requirements.

WAY FORWARD

Leadership development should be viewed as a process evolving over time rather than as an event. Having integrated the leadership model with career management, the company is today involved in an extensive exercise to build awareness through a planned cascading process. Going forward, the plan is also to increase the catchment area of potential leaders within the internal talent pool by continuously developing even those employees not currently meeting the threshold criteria as defined by the leadership model. The development plan includes training programmes as well as job rotation or cross-functional assignments.

The organization also plans to align the RSDQ 360-degree model of T.V. Rao Learning Systems, being used currently, to its leadership model.

CHALLENGES

While the organization is committed to the cause of developing potential leaders through a planned IDP, the business reality of trying to have the best person in the best place is likely to prevail in some cases. The organization needs to convince both potential leaders and their superiors to take intelligent risks, while moving a potential leader from his current assignment to another role, in order to give him the right exposure for a future assignment. The challenge is to ensure that the business continues to run successfully while the development of the leaders is not impacted.

Another challenge is in terms of defining the exit criteria for the presently identified leaders.

CONCLUSION

A robust leadership pipeline is possible only when the focus of the leadership model is on

- Leadership rather than on leaders
- Acquirable skills rather than charisma or checklists

The integrated approach of leadership development is already making an impact at Dr. Reddy's. The company now has significantly ramped up the leadership quotient across lateral levels and potential leaders are willingly accepting stretch assignments.

The process of creating and deploying the leadership model aims at driving towards a desired Dr. Reddy's culture, with the caveat that good judgement and intuition are still essential and cannot be substituted with a process

Questions for Discussion

1. What is the vision of Dr. Reddy's laboratory with regard to leadership development?
2. What is the main emphasis of the leadership development model in Dr. Reddy's laboratory?
3. What structural processes were initiated in the company?
4. How was leadership development model implemented?

NOTES AND REFERENCES

1. Michael Useem, quoted in *Knowledge@Wharton*, Knowledge@Wharton, accessed on 23 December 2003 at knowledge.wharton.upenn.edu/index.cfm?fa=viewArticle&id.
2. Day, David V. (2000). 'Leadership development: A review in context', *The Leadership Quarterly*, 11: 581–614.
3. Wikipedia. http://72.14.235.104/search?q=cache:Kg7LTlVCR2EJ:en.wikipedia.org/wiki/Leadership_development+leadership+development+Wikipedia&hl=en&ct=clnk&cd=1&gl=in.
4. Quinn, R.E. (1996). *Deep Change: Discovering the Leader Within.* San Fransciso: Jossey-Bass.
5. McCauley, Cynthia D. (2001). 'Leader training and development', in S.J. Zaccaro and R.J. Klimonski (eds), *The Nature of Organizational Leadership.* San Francisco: Jossey-Bass.
6. Shukla, Mandhukar (1997). *Competing Through Knowledge: Building a Learning Organisation*, pp. 255–57. New Delhi: Response Books.

7. Khandwalla, P.N. (1992). *Excellent Corporate Turnaround,* p. 248. New Delhi: Sage.
8. *Ibid.,* 247.
9. Semler, R. (1995). *Meverick!* New York: Warner Books.
10. *Ibid.*
11. Collins, Jim (2005). 'Level 5 leadership: The triumph of humility and fierce resolve', in *Best of HBR, HBR,* July–August 2005, pp. 136–146.
12. Khandwalla, P.N. (1992). *Organisational Design for Excellence.* New Delhi: Tata McGraw-Hill.
13. *Ibid.*
14. Semler. *Meverick!*
15. Shukla. *Competing Through Knowledge,* pp. 261–263.
16. *Ibid.,* 277.
17. Bennis, W.G. and R.J. Thomas (2003). *Geeks & Geezers: How Era, Values and Defining Movements Shape Leaders.* Mumbai: Magna Publishing Company.
18. Collins, Jim. 'Level 5 leadership'. www.izmanage.com/methods_collins_level_5_leadership.html.
19. Lencioni, Pat (1960). Tabe Group News.
20. McClelland, D.C. and. D.H. Burnham (1976). 'Power is the great motivator', *Harvard Business Review,* 54(2): 100–110.
21. Khandwalla. *Organisational Design for Excellence,* p. 253.
22. Pareek, Udai (2002). *Effective Organizations: Beyond Management to Institution Building.* New Delhi: Oxford & IBH.
23. Shukla. *Competing Through Knowledge.*
24. Quoted in Shukla, *Competing Through Knowledge,* p. 266, from a commissioned study by Ernst and Young about Japanese management.
25. Shukla. *Competing Through Knowledge.*
26. Khandwalla. *Organisational Design for Excellence,* p. 253.
27. *Ibid.,* 99.
28. Sinha, D.P. (1986). *T-Groups, Team Building and Organisation Development.* New Delhi: ISABS.
29. Khandwalla. *Organisational Design for Excellence,* p. 119.
30. *Ibid.*
31. Shukla. *Competing Through Knowledge,* pp. 285–6.
32. *Ibid.,* 302.
33. *Ibid.,* 299.
34. *Ibid.,* 270–2.
35. Bennis, W.G. and R.J. Thomas (2003). *Geeks & Geezers: How Era, Values and Defining Movements Shape Leaders.* Mumbai: Magna Publishing Company.
36. *Ibid.*
37. Rao, T.V. and M. Vijayalakshmi (2000). 'RSDQ model for 360 degree feedback for leadership & managerial competence building', in T.V. Rao, Raju Rao, and M. Vijayalakshmi (eds), *360 Degree Feedback and Performance Management Systems.* New Delhi: Excel Publications.
38. Rao, T.V., Raju Rao, and Soumya Dixit (2002). 'A study of leadership roles, styles, delegation and qualities of Indian CEOs', in Udai Pareek, Aahad M. Osmani, S. Ramnarayan, and T.V. Rao (eds), *Human Resource Development in Asia: Trends and Challenges.* New Delhi: Oxford & IBH.
39. Culled with permission from www.thehindubusinessline.com/praxis/pr0304/03040380.pdf.

40. Culled with permission from a paper by Acharya, Ranjan and J.G. Anjilvelil (2006), Leadership Development in India: An Experiential Perspective, WIPRO Ltd ODN, GD-13.
41. Based on a PowerPoint presentation by Arvind Agrawal, management board member and president – Corporate Development and HR, RPG Group.
42. Based on inputs by P.V. Bhide, G.P. Rao, and Sudhansu Pathak of JK Oraganisation.
43. Reproduced with permission from *Human Capital*, 2006, 10(4): 21–23.

The Organization

- Power and Politics

- Organizational Culture and Climate

- Organizational Communication

- Organizational Learning and the Learning Organization

- Organizational Change

- Organization Development

23
Power and Politics

LEARNING OBJECTIVES

After studying this chapter, you will be able to
1. Define the concept of power and politics in the organization
2. Distinguish between cohesive (controlling) and persuasive (empowering) power
3. Spell out steps in empowering of individuals and organizations
4. Discuss the dynamics of power in organizations
5. List various ways of enhancing and using power in organizations

Organizational scholars and practitioners have neglected to confront the issues of power and politics in organizations. An organization is an uneasy coalition of different interest groups and individuals, which compete and/or co-operate as they pursue a variety of goals and ends. One of the main objectives of development is to empower various persons, roles, and teams in an organization and increase their ability to deal effectively with various organizational issues. However, empowerment has been confined mainly to 'process' aspects, or what has been known as psychological empowerment.[1] We will explore the concepts and nature of power, politics, and empowerment in this chapter.

The challenges faced by strategic leaders in implementing complex and long-term decisions relate to issues of leadership, power, and politics. The changes that shape the nature of work in today's organizations require leaders to develop the political will, expertise, and personal skills to become more flexible, innovative, and adaptive. Without political awareness and skill, managers face the inevitable prospect of becoming immersed in bureaucratic infighting, parochial politics, and destructive power struggles, which greatly retard organizational initiative, innovation, morale, and performance.[2]

CONCEPT AND BASES OF POWER

Power has been defined in many ways. Kotter[3] seems to capture the spirit of most definitions when he defines power as 'a measure of a person's potential to get others to do what he or she wants them to do, as well as to avoid being forced to do what he or she does not want to do'. It is the capacity to affect people, things, situations, and decisions.[4]

Kurt Lewin defined power as 'the possibility of inducing forces of a certain magnitude on another person'.[5] It has also been defined by researchers and thought leaders as the potential to influence (individuals and groups),[6] and as 'the capacity to effect or affect organizational outcomes'.[7] Influence can be both on the covert (attitudes, values, thinking) and on the overt part (behaviour and action) of the persons. Interpersonal power has been defined as 'the ability to get one's way in a social situation'.[8]

Ever since Machiavelli suggested fear and love as bases of power, many suggestions have been made to dichotomise power bases. Flanders, in his seminal work on classroom strategies of teachers, differentiated 'direct' influence from 'indirect' influence on the basis of how much freedom the teacher (through his or influencing behaviour) gave to the student.[9] Talking (lecturing) by the teacher, scolding, criticising, disapproval, etc. were classified as 'direct' influence, because these 'coerced' the students into accepting what the teacher wanted them to do or think. Influencing behaviour that gave freedom to students to think and experiment (encouragement, compliments, open questions with alternative answers, sensing, voicing individual and group feelings, etc.) were put in the category of 'indirect' influence. Flanders thus seemed to use a classification similar to Machiavelli: coercion (fear) or persuasion (love).

Hersey and Blanchard researched on situational leadership and proposed seven bases of power: coercive, legitimate, expert, reward, referent, information, and connection. They accepted the dichotomy of *position power* and *personal power*, although they pointed out the limitation of dividing 'the pie always into two pieces'.[10] Two influence strategies, *push* and *pull*, have also been suggested by the researchers; the first being located in the system and the second being a part of the spirit of the individual that influences others.[11] These are similar to position and personal power, respectively. Another dichotomy of overt and covert has been proposed, the first being concerned with 'preferred outcome in conflict', and the second (which is unobtrusive) 'ensuring no conflict through use of symbols and myths to manage meaning'.[12]

All the suggested dichotomies have a common thread. Should influence be used to force the other individual into accepting what the influencer wants him or her to think or do (fear power, direct influence, position power, push energy, and overt influence), or will it help the individual to choose to think or do things (love power, indirect influence, personal power, pull energy, and covert influence)? The first has the element of coercion, and the second that of persuasion. It seems to be useful to classify the bases of power into coercive and persuasive bases. The bases and types of power are illustrated in Exhibit 23.1.

Exhibit 23.1 *Bases and Types of Power*

Coercive power		Persuasive power	
Base	**Type**	**Base**	**Type**
Organizational position	Status	Expertise	Expert
Closeness to power source	Reflected	Competence	Competence
Charisma	Charismatic	Role modelling	Referent
Punishing	Coercive	Rewarding	Reinforcing
Personal relationship	Emotional	Helping or caring	Extension
Withholding or depriving information	Manipulative	Information	Logical

Coercive Bases

From the literature on power bases it is clear that power and punishment are coercive bases. Six bases of power are included in the coercive power group: organizational position (legitimate power), personal relationship (emotional power), punishment (coercive power), charisma (charismatic power), closeness to a source of power (reflected power), and withholding information or resources (manipulative power).

Legitimate power It refers to the power drawn from the organizational position (legitimate power in the role or power due to allocation of resources) that coerces people to accept influences. Punishment deserves to be listed separately as coercive power.

Emotional power Personal relationship can also act as a power base if the person being influenced needs to maintain the relationship and therefore accepts to do what the other person wants him or her to do. In this case the relationship is 'manipulated' to get things done. For example, a fond mother may give her child pocket money or permission for watching TV if the child refuses to eat, or if the mother is afraid that the child will be cross with her.

Coercive power It refers to the power derived out of close affectionate bonds, which (relationships) often acts like coercion, because the person accepting influence does so more out of an emotional bond, rather than by making a conscious choice. Such power has been put in the category of coercive power. The main rationale is that when people accept an act of influence because of an emotion, such as fear or excessive love, they are being coerced and manipulated.

Charismatic power Charisma is included in coercive power for the same reasons. A charismatic leader arouses strong emotions and gets things done. The leader does not treat his or her followers as mature people with competence to make their own choice.

Reflected power Another base included in coercive power is the power derived from a person with larger power bases. For example, the private secretary of the chief executive may use her association with the officer as a source of influence. This example illustrates the concept of reflected power.

Manipulative power Another type of power is exercised by withholding from, or depriving a person of information, or by delaying action. Some role occupants exercise power by delaying decisions and withholding critical information.

Persuasive Bases

There are six bases of power in the category of persuasive power: reward (reinforcing power), expertise (expert power), competence (competence power), role modelling (referent power), empathy, caring and helping others (extension power), and information and its rationale (logical power). The bases and types of power are shown in Exhibit 23.1.

Personal power is accepted as the opposite of coercive power and comes under the category of persuasive power. There are three main sources of personal power: expertise (special knowledge), competence (general effectiveness to produce results), and modelling (setting example by behaviour). We accept the suggestion of mechanics because they are experts in their field. A competent manager influences because he or she is capable of getting results. A person who 'lives' certain values, such as not smoking, encouraging others to speak, listening, giving credit for new ideas, etc., may influence others into behaving the same way, or at least attempting such behaviour. This is also referred to as referent power.

Reward has also been included in the category of persuasive bases because reward encourages people to experiment and gives them more autonomy, unless, of course, it is manipulated, as in the case of operant conditioning. Another base included is the concern for others, caring for them, and helping them develop. This helps in widening the autonomy of the individuals.

Raven suggested information as a base of power,[13] but this was subsequently dropped because his co-author French did not agree.[14] It was listed only as a form of influence in 1959, but was subsequently included as a base of power. Many people are influenced by the given facts and logic behind the information. This can be referred to as logical power, as the base is a rational aspect of information.

Relevance of Power Bases

Some studies have reported on the compliance of people to different power bases, and the relationship of power bases with employee satisfaction and productivity.[15]

In the use of power bases, a person's perception of the power he or she has, and how much more he or she needs, may be quite relevant. Perception of having and using power empowers a person, while the need for power shows a sense of lack of power.[16]

The various studies on the relationship of power bases with satisfaction have shown a positive relationship with persuasive bases, and negative relationship with coercive bases.[17]

The relationship of bases of power with productivity shows the importance of persuasive bases. Referent and expert power were positively related with four measures of performance.[18]

It can thus be concluded that persuasive power bases contribute to managerial effectiveness, development of human resources, and creation of an enabling climate in the organization, while coercive bases have the opposite effects.

Multiplying Power in Organizations: Empowering

Empowerment has attracted a lot of attention recently. The major differences have been between organization-related scholars and practitioners on the one hand, and community-related thinkers and interventionists on the other. The latter groups emphasise collective power as the central theme. Empowerment is defined as 'the mechanism by which people, organizations, and communities gain mastery over their lives'[19]; 'a process through which people become strong enough to participate within, share in the control of an influence, events and institutions affecting their lives'[20]; 'a social-action process that promotes participation of people, organizations, and communities towards the goal of increased individual and community control, political efficacy, improved quality of life and social justice'. Its definition as 'the ability to act collectively to solve problems and influence important issues'[21] seems to be closer to the organization-related concept of empowerment.

In OD literature, empowerment has been defined as 'giving people the skills and the information they need to make good decisions and take informed deliberate actions ... so organizational members can solve problems and manage change on their own'.[22] Empowerment has been defined in a simple equation of direction × support × autonomy,[23] where all the three elements are equally important in enhancing or reducing empowerment. If any one of them is 0 (zero), there will be no empowerment (it will become zero). Empowerment will be weak if any one of these is low in value.

A distinction has been made between psychological empowerment (subjective experience of self-efficacy) and community empowerment (modified structural conditions for the purpose of reallocating resources).[24] 'Psychological empowerment can be defined as a feeling of greater control over their own lives ... Community empowerment includes a raised level of psychological empowerment ... a political action component ... and the achievement of some redistribution of resources or decision-making favourable to the community or group in question.'[25] Many lessons can be learned by OD interventions from the study of community empowerment. In fact, for our purpose, a distinction can be made between individual empowerment and team empowerment.

Three components of empowerment have been proposed[26]: micro factors (interpersonal aspects), mediating structures (raised critical consciousness through active participation and shared knowledge), and macro factors (social and political reality). A three-stage model of empowerment has been proposed[27]: critical consciousness of powerlessness, strong feeling about inequity and discussion with like-minded people, and group work in changing the social conditions creating powerlessness. Community empowerment has evolved over the last four decades with the ideology of social action in the 1960s, self-help orientation of the 1970s, community psychology (the individual being recognised as a citizen) in the 1980s, and citizens' control of most matters in the 1990s.[28]

To summarise, power is the central concept in politics and empowerment. It is the capacity to shape outcomes significant to oneself or the group. Politics, as a neutral term, is the management of power dynamics to facilitate development and use of power. Empowering is the process of enabling individuals or groups to use power for achieving agreed goals. Empowerment is both individual and collective. It is also related to the organizational processes and structures, both of which are important for effective empowerment. Das[29] has developed a scale of individual empowerment. The three important aspects of empowerment are the process of empowerment, the enabling culture and conditions of empowerment, and the structural interventions to bring about redistribution of power.

Empowerment culture

Individual and team empowerment would require a culture of trust and collaboration. The concept of OCTAPACE (openness, confrontation, trust, authenticity, proaction, autonomy, collaboration, and experimentation) has been proposed as the ethos for empowerment, and an instrument (OCTAPACE Profile) has been prepared for this purpose.[30] Where interdependent individuals or teams are involved, there are potential conditions of conflict. The goals of these individuals or teams may be incompatible. The resources may be scarce or limited, and the access to resources may be uneven. The mutual trust among group members may be low. To overcome these possible problems, 10 bases of collaboration and the related interventions have been suggested.

Structured empowerment

Structured interventions are required to ensure decentralisation and delegation. Chapter 22 has already discussed delegation as an empowering mechanism for multiplying power in the organization.

Power enhancers   The main function of a leader is to multiply power in the organization, which means empowering people at all levels. Every person has enough power within him or her. The process of empowering is concerned with creating conditions in which this inner power can be used effectively. Empowering is the process of expanding choices for individuals and helping them to use their alternative choices to widen the choices of others. Delegation is a useful and structured way of multiplying power in an organization.

Leadership is increasingly seen as a catalyst, and the influence or power of a leader may be in proportion to his or her ability to 'dispossess' the organization, or become 'dispensable'. Withdrawing from or giving up controlling functions is a power enhancer for the leadership, enhancing the leader's real power—not the coercive power but his indirect influence (becoming a role model of empowering sudordinates). This is possible only when the leader is released from attending to routine tasks and from the use of his or her discretion in most routine matters. Let us take the example of house or vehicle allotments. A leader has directive influence if she uses her discretion to allot vehicles or houses to people. In that case she will not have enough time to plan for a new vision. However, if clear rules are made so that the leader does not play any role and has no discretion, her real power and influence will increase, as she will be able to perform the more important tasks of visioning, boundary management, lobbying for the organization, etc. In this sense, these can be seen as power enhancers rather than as leadership substitutes.

Based on research literature and interviews with some senior managers, a list of power enhancers was prepared and then edited. Finally, the following 14 power enhancers were selected[31] to develop the competence of employees:

1. Clear rules and procedures
2. System to generate feedback to individuals
3. Intrinsically satisfying tasks
4. Advisory and staff functions
5. Rewards determined objectively by a team rather than by individuals
6. Spatial distance of different key functionaries
7. Strong and cohesive teams
8. Self-governing teams (such as branches)
9. Well-defined tasks
10. Formalised and clear organizational structure
11. Schemes to reward employees for ideas, suggestions, or creativity
12. Professional orientation
13. Development of systems

A factor analysis of these power enhancers in one organization gave five factors. These are, therefore, briefly mentioned under the five heads suggested by the factor analysis. A few factors appear in more than one category.

Professionalism Four enhancers fall within the category of professionalism. These are competence building, rewards system, feedback system, and professionalism.

Competence building Professionalism is attained through competent people in the organization. An organization can focus on competence development through various programmes and HRD practices. A leader will have greater opportunities to exercise higher leadership functions if there are more competent people in the organization.

Rewards system Rewards play an important role in building a positive organizational culture and in multiplying power. If creativity, innovation, and initiatives are rewarded, people develop power relating to these. The leaders then have greater resources available to them, adding to their overall power. Thus, rewards are very effective power enhancers.

Feedback system A well-developed system of giving feedback to the employees on their performance develops professionalism and reduces the subjective element in decision making. In fact, the feedback system in a way releases time to leaders to perform this function.

Many organizations are examining work processes to streamline customer service. They develop new procedures that ensure that people closest to the work have immediate access to the tools and information they need. In traditional organizations, information is power and is often kept away from those who need it the most.

Professionalism A professional orientation in the organization develops several substitutes or enhancers of power. Developing professionalism in an organization involves recruiting trained and competent persons with expertise in their fields, use of appropriate technology, and periodic competence building of personnel at various levels. Leadership in a professional organization deals with functions at higher levels.

Teamwork It is an effective power enhancer as it relieves the leader of attending to many routine matters and multiplies power in the organization by increasing the effectiveness of teams. This factor has five enhancers: professionalism, strong teams, self-governing teams, satisfying tasks, and rules and procedures. The concept of professionalism as a power enhancer has already been discussed. The concepts of satisfying tasks and rules and procedures have been discussed later in the section.

Strong teams A strong and cohesive team is a major power enhancer. The more cohesive the team, the more the leader is able to exercise high-level power, leaving most of the internal matters to the teams.

Self-governing teams When teams can function on their own, with minimum direction from the top, leadership can focus on strategic issues. Strong teams help the process of decentralisation. For example, autonomous work groups reduce the role of supervisors as the teams make most of the decisions themselves. The teams add value to the supervisor's role by helping him or her to become a real leader by resolving issues relating to resource mobilisation, boundary management, competence building, and consultation. Branches of organizations with enough autonomy have the same effect. Companies such as Conrail pull together talented people from the middle of the organization and empower them to tackle pressing business challenges. These teams are more than task forces—they have the power to recommend and implement change.

Formalisation Informality in organizations functions as a lubricant. However, too much of it may create a mess. Some formalisation is needed to increase the effectiveness of leaders and their subordinates, in terms of better use of discretion by them. Of the four enhancers in this group, two are common with the previous factor (tasks and roles) and are discussed first, followed by the other two factors.

Satisfying tasks Intrinsically satisfying tasks are likely to promote both formalisation and team building. Well-designed tasks that are seen as worthwhile by employees build employee motivation and involvement. The leader will not need to spend energy on this aspect. These will also contribute to the effective use of discretion by the concerned employees and thereby enhance power in the system.

Rules and procedures Clear rules and procedures for most routine matters, an important element in formalisation, reduces the need for attention and time to be given by the leaders to such matters. Moreover, they minimise the anxiety level of employees about these matters, and this helps in increasing their own sense of power. For example, most organizations have clear-cut rules and procedures for compensation, perks, facilities, amenities, etc. Although not directly related to team building, such rules reduce bickering and help in team building.

Organizational structure A clear well-defined structure helps in formalisation. It reduces the leader's discretion in many matters and 'forces' the leader to pay attention to other important functions. This allows the leader to use the power available to him or her to increase expertise in the organization.

Management systems   In effective organizations, well-designed systems replace leaders' roles in most matters. For example, good planning, budgetary allocation, and information systems generate most processes of decision making. Recruitment and other human resource systems ensure that these functions are performed well, without any need for the leaders to attend to them.

Expert power   Development of expert power in an organization multiplies power within the organization. This relieves leaders of the necessity of paying attention to most matters that can be taken care of by the experts. There are three enhancers in this category: staff functions, objective rewards, and spatial distance.

Staff functions   Advisory and staff functions develop formalisation by introducing structured and formalised special functions. These functions help to develop expertise. Power is distributed and gets multiplied, and this in turn strengthens the leader's ability to lead the organization.

Objective rewards   Rewards become more objective when they are decided on the basis of clear criteria, developed by a team, and managed by a group of persons (teams). Experts are involved in such decision making. The leader gives up his or her role of deciding about rewards and passes this responsibility to a team. This releases the leader's time and energy for higher-level tasks.

Spatial distance   Divisionalisation and decentralisation contribute to the development of expert power. When functionaries are located away from the head office, they have to use more autonomy. This enhances power in the system and the leader. Sharing of power and responsibilities are consequences of divisionalisation and decentralisation.

Task clarity and autonomy   Self-governing teams and task clarity are included in this section. The concept of self-governing teams has been explained earlier in the section.

Task clarity   Well-defined tasks are important for autonomous functioning of individuals. This increases the power of the leader and his or her employees. The leader can divert his or her time on other issues. In brief, leaders can empower people and teams at various levels, thereby multiplying power in an organization.

Empowerment process

Based on their work with 10 companies, Blanchard et al. have suggested a three-step approach to empowerment.[32] Three key concepts have been suggested as the core of empowerment[33]: sharing information with everyone, creating autonomy through boundaries, and teams becoming the hierarchy. The researchers have also suggested a three-stage action plan for empowerment: starting and orienting the journey; change and discouragement; and adopting and refining empowerment. Action recommendations for the three key concepts at each stage are given in Exhibit 23.2.

Exhibit 23.2   *The Concepts and Stages of Empowerment*

The empowerment process

1. Share information
    - Share company performance information.
    - Help people understand the business.
    - Build trust through sharing sensitive information.
    - Create self-monitoring possibilities.
2. Create autonomy through structure
    - Create a clear vision and clarify the little pictures.
    - Clarify goals and roles collectively.
    - Create new decision-making rules that support empowerment.
    - Establish new empowering performance management processes.
    - Use heavy doses of training.
3. Let teams become the hierarchy
    - Provide direction and training for new skills.
    - Provide encouragement and support for change.
    - Gradually have managers let go of control.
    - Work through the leadership vacuum stage.
    - Acknowledge the fear factor.

Action recommendations

I   Share Information with Everyone

Stage 1
- Help people understand need for change.
- Avoid misinformation.
- Explain how the company makes money.
- Teach company financials.
- Share some sensitive information.
- Ask what information you would want as an employee.
- List information people have and need.
- Locate where information is now.
- Start small.
- Stretch but do not break your comfort zone.
- Share good and bad information.
- Use a variety of means to share information.
- Share location or site-specific information.
- Share the same information that managers use.
- Use information to make people accountable.
- View mistakes positively.

Stage 2
- Use information to align expectations with reality.
- Share information to build pride in people's work.
- Encourage information sharing from employees up to management.
- Train managers to listen better.
- Expect tough questions from employees.

Exhibit 23.2   (*Contd*)

- Do not shy away from sensitive information.
- Show people how their work has impact.
- Encourage team members to share information with each other.
- Praise improvements in performance.
- Praise teams that identify problems.
- View mistakes as learning opportunities.
- Share information regarding change process and progress.
- Share even more sensitive information than in the first stage.
- Use technology to efficiently share information.
- Hold meetings with IT so that it learns what information is needed where.
- Show impact of small changes.
- Help teams see results of using new skills.
- Create better links of rewards to performance.

Stage 3
- Let teams determine what information is needed.
- Trust teams with information they request.
- Ask teams to inform senior management how they use information.
- Let teams work directly with IT to improve systems.
- Stress that complete information sharing is vital to continuous building of responsibility and trust.
- Let teams use information to hold themselves accountable.
- Use information to indoctrinate new team members.
- Continue to teach and reinforce values and expectations.
- Use information sharing to keep everyone knowledgeable of new changes.
- Praise people who facilitate information sharing.
- Continue to share information regarding mistakes so that everyone can learn.

II   Create Autonomy Through Boundaries

Stage 1
- Recognise the hierarchy mind-set; boundaries limit action and responsibility.
- Define boundaries to clarify what people can and must do.
- Define desired responsibilities.
- Clarify decisions employees will make and will not make.
- Explain company's business goals.
- Explain company vision and values.
- Set clear performance goals for people.
- Clarify priorities.
- Teach employees business basics.
- Teach managers to be coaches.
- Teach decision-making skills.
- Clarify small decisions people can make.
- Teach problem-solving skills.

Stage 2
- Use collaborative goal setting.
- Discuss role of managers in relation to goal accomplishment.
- Use team member ideas to set goals.
- Use a mix of team and individual goals.

Exhibit 23.2 (*Contd*)

- Get teams involved in determining problems for focus.
- Focus on continuous improvement.
- Set skill goals as well as performance goals.
- Begin to revamp the performance management system.
- Build a performance partnership among team members.
- Listen to concerns of people regarding performance management system.
- Begin to devise a pay system to treat employees like owners.
- Create a team-based performance management system.
- Broaden scope of decisions made by teams.
- Move to creation of profit centres.
- Facilitate teams solving problems.
- Draw out ideas to change old policies and procedures.

Stage 3

- Expand the teams' scope of decision making.
- Replace old hierarchical boundaries with vision and values in people.
- Include team members in setting new boundaries.
- Let team goals replace individual goals.
- Let teams monitor impact of their actions.
- Let teams be free to set goals that relate to company's strategic goals.
- Have teams use information to identify areas for improvement.
- Encourage team members and team leaders to act as true partners.
- Use an ongoing performance management system built on team member and team leader partnership.
- Let teams make HR decisions that used to be taken by HR managers.
- Be sure teams and management stay on the same measurement 'page'.
- Let teams help create new business opportunities.
- Encourage teams to continue to seek operational improvements.
- Reinforce team members as full partners in the business.
- Encourage teams to create goals that stretch management.

III Let Teams Become the Hierarchy

Stage 1

- Understand that teams can do more than individuals.
- Begin to use team diversity.
- Do not expect too much success early.
- Teach team skills to managers and employees.
- Teach consensus decision making.
- Teach team communication skills.
- Teach how to conduct team meetings.
- Help teams see small successes.
- Teach team members to hold each other accountable.
- Start early with teams using information.
- Hold team information-sharing meetings.
- Give teams small decisions to make.
- Begin to hold teams accountable.
- Share issues and involve teams in solutions.

Exhibit 23.2   *(Contd)*

Stage 2

- Have team leaders provide support and direction.
- Encourage team leaders to expect more from teams.
- Encourage teams to use their new skills.
- Be sure teams tackle challenging but solvable problems.
- Encourage team members to take leadership roles.
- Draw out from team members ideas for improvement.
- Allow teams to tackle more complex decisions.
- Anticipate and work through stalls in team involvement.
- Continue to hold teams accountable for results.
- Allow team goals to drive performance.
- Reduce department meetings; increase team meetings.
- Anticipate team fear of failure; help teams stay focused.
- Expect a lot from teams but not full synergy of effort yet.
- Help teams see what they are accomplishing.

Stage 3

- Let teams use information and skills to play vital business role.
- Have teams begin to focus on strategic goals as their own accountability.
- Encourage teams to integrate new team members.
- Encourage teams to continue to work hard to stay as a fine tuned unit.
- Encourage teams to reach out to other teams regarding company-wide empowerment.
- Cross-train all team members for greater flexibility.
- Be sure that teams value and seek diversity of members.
- Have teams work with senior management on new strategic initiatives.
- Encourage teams to ask how to improve the company empowerment culture.
- Let teams continue to raise performance standards.
- Have teams fully included in benefits and risks of business partnership.

Summing up the essence of empowerment is a quote from *Sunday Times*, 'A Japanese worker produces, on average, twenty seven improvement ideas a year. A US worker produces one idea every thirty seven years.' Edgell has suggested that an empowered organization is characterised by

- A strong sense of direction and purpose, shared by all staff
- Well-understood values and beliefs, explicitly or implicitly stated, that form the basis for management behaviour
- A focus on customers, processes, and improvement techniques, so that people can concentrate on adding value and pleasing customers
- Pro-activity, learning, problem solving, and innovation at all levels
- A high degree of trust in each other, in management, and in other functions and departments
- People who are highly motivated and who possess a great sense of self-worth and achievement
- Managers who listen, encourage, develop, and help their people[34]

ORGANIZATIONAL POLITICS

Politics, the study of the dynamics of power in a group, and its management, has been defined in various other ways. It is 'the art of using power'[35] or 'the management of influence to obtain ends not sanctioned by the organization or to obtain ends through non-sanctioned influence means'.[36] Organizational politics 'involve intentional acts of influence to enhance or protect the self-interests of individuals or groups'.[37] French and Bell treat politics as illegitimate power.

Harold Lasswell's definition of politics[38] as who gets what, when, and how, is quite relevant for the concept of organizational politics. Politics involves the exercise of power to get something done. It enhances and protects the vested interests of individuals or groups. Political activity is used in an organization to overcome resistance and to challenge the opposition in a priority decision situation. We can define organizational politics as the use of power, with power being a source of potential energy to manage relationships.

Four 'frames' for viewing the world have been proposed[39]: structural, human resources, political, and symbolic. The political frame is an excellent tool for examining the concept of organizational politics. The following assumptions can be made about organizations in this context:

- Organizations are coalitions of individuals and interest groups, which form because the members need each others' support. Through a negotiation process, members combine forces to produce common objectives and agreed upon ways to utilise resources, thus, aggregating their power. Power bases are developed that can accomplish more than individual forces alone.

- There are enduring differences among individuals and groups with regard to values, preferences, beliefs, information, and perception of reality. Such differences change slowly, if at all.

- Most of the important decisions in organizations involve allocation of scarce resources: these are decisions about who gets what. This activates political behaviour.

- Due to scarce resources and enduring differences, conflict is central to organizational dynamics. Power is the most important resource. Conflict is more likely in decentralised systems. In centralised and authoritarian systems, politics remains underground. While organizations play the political game within the broader governmental context, individuals also play politics within organizations. Power is key in both cases, the ability both to allocate resources and to consolidate power by bringing others with similar goals and objectives into the inner decision-making core.

- Organizational goals and decisions emerge from bargaining, negotiating, and jockeying for position among members of different coalitions. Building large dams in India is an example of a complex coalition consisting of the central government, state governments, Parliament, scientific organizations, the media, and even portions of the public. The recent controversies regarding Narmada Dam is a good example of organizational politics.

Organizational politics need not necessarily consist of negative, dysfunctional, or aggrandising behaviour. It helps us to realise that organization diversity, interdependence, resource scarcity, and power dynamics will inevitably generate political forces, regardless of the players. Organizational politics cannot be eliminated or wished away. Leaders and other organizational members with a healthy power motive, however, can learn to understand and manage political processes.

Political Frame of Decision Making

Rational models of decision making were proposed, based on two main strategies. The *planning approach*, proposed by Ansoff,[40] is based on formal procedures, and training and analysis, and quantitative models. It has been popular with managers seeking direction. The *design approach* was proposed by Chandler.[41] He advocated the need to achieve a fit between the internal capabilities of an organization and the external possibilities it faces. While Ansoff sees strategy as almost totally concerned with the relationships between the firm and its environment, Chandler takes a broader view and includes internal as well as external factors. New developments brought attention to some other important elements in strategy formulation.

For example, Mintzberg and Quinn's *analytical approach* suggested that strategies are more 'emergent' than 'deliberate'.[42] The approach of *discontinuous change*, suggested that styles and strategies change according to the specific situation.[43] Change sometimes needs to be made fast and in short, sharp bursts of activity, followed by periods of consolidation. The strategies required will change according to the change in the situation.

Political strategy goes beyond these frames. It can be based on some assumptions. Four assumptions have been proposed.[44]

1. Organizations are characterised by pluralism and the existence of multiple goals. 'In micro politics, there is no dominant actor, but rather a number who vie with each other to control organizational outcomes, or else who challenge vulnerable actors.'[45]

2. Resources are scarce and will be much sought-after by organizational members for their own ends. Important decisions, therefore, will be concerned with the allocation of these scarce resources.

3. Rational models, which claim it is possible to collect all information necessary to make a decision that will produce an optimal solution, are impractical. The political school assumes that more often decision makers are governed by short-term considerations, their own self-interests, and a commitment to well-entrenched ideologies, norms, and values.

4. People will form coalitions and interest groups with other like-minded individuals in order to control outcomes in organizations, even though these people may have very little in common in other ways. The assumption is people can put aside their differences when united by a common cause that is sufficiently important to them.

These assumptions suggest that one important part of the political framework is acquisition of power by the decision makers. Several strategies have been suggested in this regard.

Strategies of Acquiring Power

Luthans[46] has given a comprehensive list of strategies, suggested by DuBrin, which 'provides important insights into power and politics in modern organizations'. These are as follows:

- Maintain alliances with powerful people.
- Embrace or demolish, reflected in some corporate takeovers.
- Divide and rule.
- Manipulate classified information.
- Make a quick showing.
- Collect and use IOUs. While doing favours, make it clear that they owe something to you in return.
- Avoid decisive engagement (Fabianism)—an evolutionary rather than a revolutionary approach to change.
- Attack and blame others.
- Progress one step at a time (camel's head in the tent).
- Wait for a crisis (things must get worse before they get better).
- Take counsel with caution.
- Be aware of resource dependence.

Cross-cultural differences have been studied in the perceived effectiveness of various influence tactics for gaining approval from a boss for a proposed change, or for resisting a change initiated by a boss. A comparative study of American, Swiss, and Chinese managers showed that the cross-cultural differences in rated effectiveness of tactics were consistent with cultural values and traditions. Direct, task-oriented tactics were rated more effective by Western managers than by Chinese managers, whereas tactics involving personal relations, avoidance, or an informal approach were rated less effective.[47]

A positive approach to political processes in organizations is more important. As discussed by several authors recently,[48] power at the strategic organization level is manifested and executed through three fundamental elements: consensus, cooperation, and culture.

'An organization is high in consensus potential when it has the capacity to synthesise the commitment of multiple constituencies and stakeholders in response to specific challenges and aspirations.' In this area, strategic leader power is derived from the management of ideas, the management of agreement, and the management of group and team decision-making processes.

'Cooperative potential refers to an organization's capacity to catalyse cooperative interaction among individuals and groups.' Power is employed by a strategic leader in the management of organization structures, task designs, resource allocation, and reward systems that support and encourage this behaviour.

'Cultural/spiritual potential refers to a sense of timeless destiny about the organization, its role in its own area of endeavour as well as its larger role in its service to society.' Strategic leaders use power in this area to manage and institutionalise organizational symbols, beliefs, myths, ideals, and values. Their strategic

Exhibit 23.3   *Turnaround of Indian Railways*

Economics Behind IR's Turnaround Saga

Indian Railways coined it's own homegrown economic principle to work its much talked about turnaround. 'Milk the cow fully, otherwise it will fall sick.' According to a member of Team Lalu, the principle as slogan was the cornerstone of the revival. In fact, the railways played on volumes, and reduced the unit cost to increase its internal generation of resources to Rs 13,000 crore in 2005–06.

The target for 2006–07 is as high as Rs 20,000 crore, and according to early estimates by the Rail Bhawan, it may even go up further. Significantly, expert group on IR, headed by Dr Rakesh Mohan noted that IR would be in a terminal debt trap. Shifting its focus from an increase of tariff to increase revenue, the railways stressed on reducing the unit cost. In fact, freight unit cost (paise per Net Tonne Kilometers or NTKMs) was reduced from 61 in 2001 to 53 in 2005–06. The freight operating margin was increased from 22 per cent in 2000–01 to 57 per cent 2005–06.

These were possible with an improved wagon turnaround and axle load, tariff rationalisation and targeted investment. Similarly, passenger losses were contained by increasing length, seating capacity and occupancy, and enhancing non-passenger fare income. Also, the ticket upgradation option improved the occupancy rate considerably.

The fundamental principle for yet-to-be-launched Garib Raths is also the same—increase volume and reduce costs. Though fares of these AC trains will be 25 per cent less than standard AC trains, it is likely to be a profit making venture for the railways because of the economy of scale. Four Garib Raths will be operational by October this year.

While a standard AC train coach has 64 berths in 3AC, it will be 74 in Garib Rath. Similarly, a Garib Rath coach will accommodate 102 chair cars, 32 more than a conventional AC train coach. Thus, a 17-coach Garib Rath will accommodate 1,254 passengers, whereas a standard AC train will carry just 799 passengers. 'It's a simple economy. The cost per passenger km (paise) in a 17-coach Garib Rath is just 39 paise whereas it is 58 paise for a standard AC train. In case of a 24-coach Garib Rath, the unit cost will be as low as 34 paise per passenger per km. We will make profit once the unit cost is contained below 41 paise,' said an official.

In fact, IIM-A is studying the Indian Railways turnaround story to make it a case study for its students.

aim is to create a strong culture that connects the destiny of the organization to the personal goals and aspirations of its members.

The turnaround of Indian Railways is a good illustration of the positive use of politics. The turnaround has been engineered by Lalu Prasad Yadav, a political leader from Bihar, who remained the chief minister of the state for a long time and was criticised for keeping it backward. After his party was voted out in the state of Bihar, he was elected to the Parliament and became the Union Minister of Railways. His use of political power in turning around Indian Railways is illustrated in Exhibit 23.3.[49]

SUMMARY

Power is the central concept in politics and empowerment. It is the capacity to shape outcomes significant to oneself or the group. Politics, as a neutral term, is the management of power dynamics to facilitate development and use of power.

Empowering is the process of enabling individuals or groups to use power for achieving agreed goals. Empowerment is both individual and collective. It is also related to the organizational processes and structures, both of which are important for effective empowerment. Three important aspects of empowerment are the process of empowerment, the enabling culture and conditions of empowerment, and the structural interventions to bring about redistribution of power.

Organizational politics involve intentional acts of influence to enhance or protect the self-interests of individuals or groups. Organizational politics cannot be eliminated or wished away. Leaders and other organizational members, with a healthy power motive, can learn to understand and manage political processes. The following strategies provide important insights into power and politics in modern organizations: (1) maintain alliances with powerful people, (2) embrace or demolish, as reflected in some corporate takeovers, (3) divide and rule, (4) manipulate classified information, (5) make a quick showing, (6) collect and use IOUs, (7) avoid decisive engagements, (8) attack and blame others, (9) progress one step at a time, (10) wait for a crisis, (11) take counsel with caution, and (12) be aware of resource dependence. A positive approach to political processes in organizations is very important. Power at the strategic organization level is manifested and executed through three fundamental elements: consensus, cooperation, and culture. The turnaround of Indian Railways is a good illustration of the positive use of politics.

GLOSSARY

charismatic power controlling and manipulating emotions

coercive power reducing alternatives in decision making

direct influence reducing alternatives in decision making

emotional power using personal relationship to control and influence

empowerment the process of helping to realise and use the power within

extension power influencing through helping and developing people

indirect influence increasing alternatives in decision making

logical power influencing through rational discussion

manipulative power withholding or depriving information for controlling and influencing others

persuasive power increasing alternatives in decision making

politics the study of the dynamics of power in a group and its management

power a measure of a person's potential to get others to do what he or she wants them to do, as well as to avoid being forced to do what he or she does not want to do

power enhancer away of reducing controlling power to perform transformational functions

referent power influencing through role modelling

reflected power using closeness to power source to gain influence

reinforcing power rewarding people to influence

status power using organizational position to influence

Concept Review Questions

1. What is power?
2. How does power define politics?
3. What is structured empowerment?
4. What are the effects of coercive and persuasive power?

Critical Thinking Questions

1. Why is coercive power dysfunctional?
2. How to increase the bases of power?
3. How can political process in organizations be used for enhancing organizational effectiveness?
4. What approaches can be used to empower people and groups?

Classroom Projects

1. Interview your two friends to find out their needs for coercive and persuasive power.
2. Analyse the political processes in the classroom, elaborating what strategies are adopted by your teachers to gain and use power.

Field Projects

1. Interview two managers to analyse their experiences in using both coercive and persuasive bases of power.
2. Interview an HR manager to find out the empowerment processes followed in his or her organization.
3. Collecting data from the Internet, analyse the political aspects and processes of Tata's acquisition of Corus.

Acquisition of Arcelor[*]

The acquisition of Arcelor Steel by Mittal Steel led to the creation of Arcelor–Mittal, the largest steelmaker in the world. It has been one of the most controversial business deals ever. When European steelmaker Arcelor bowed to an improved 25.6-billion-euro (32.2 billion US dollars) takeover offer from Mittal Steel, it went on to create a world giant three times larger than its nearest rival.

BACKGROUND

Mittal Steel was the largest producer of steel in terms of volume. Despite the fact that Mittal Steel is based in Netherlands, it is perceived that the company is non-European because its CEO, Lakshmi Mittal, is Indian. Headquartered in Luxembourg, Arcelor was created by the merger of three steel companies: Aceralia, Arbed, and Usinor. In 2005, Arcelor had revenues of 32 billion euros.

THE ORIGINAL BID

In January 2006, Mittal Steel launched a 22.7-billion dollars offer to Arcelor's shareholders. The deal was split between Mittal Steel's shares (75 per cent) and cash (25 per cent). Under the offer, Arcelor shareholders would have received four Mittal Steel shares and 35 euros for every five Arcelor shares they held. (Ultimately the power to buy or sell the shares rests with the shareholder and the company management can at best advice its shareholders whether to accept or reject the bid.)

CONSOLIDATION IN STEEL INDUSTRY

The steel industry is highly fragmented, the top five manufacturers in the steel industry account for less than 25 per cent of the market (to put that in perspective, the corresponding figure for the automotive industry is 73 per cent). Mittal believes that the consolidation will end with three of four major companies dominating the industry around 2010.

Bigger steel manufacturers have better bargaining powers against customers (such as auto manufacturers) and against suppliers (such as iron ore suppliers). Consolidation will help companies to improve their raw material sourcing. It will also lead to access to more markets, better utilisation, more flexibility in production scheduling, and better efficiency.

[*]Culled from **http://8questions.wordpress.com/2006/11/23/5/** November 23, 2006 at Indian Business, Business http://www.ft.com/cms/3065e6f0-e981-11da-a33b-0000779e2340.pdf

CONTROVERSY

The Arcelor management believed that it should acquire other companies rather than the other way around. The management was extremely hostile to Mittal Steel's bid from the beginning. Arcelor repeatedly played the patriotic card to convince shareholders to reject the bid. The CEO of Arcelor dismissed Mittal Steel as a 'company of Indians' and unworthy of taking over a European company. All these attempts were going on despite most industry analysts and investment banks pointing out that the deal was in the best interests of Arcelor.

The French government (despite not being a shareholder) was against the deal because of worries over the future of 28,000 Arcelor employees. Despite repeated assurances from Mittal that the deal would not lead to layoffs, the Government of France was never convinced. The Government of Luxembourg (a stakeholder) was against the deal as well for a variety of reasons. The European Union, however, approved of the Mittal–Arcelor deal.

MOVES BY ARCELOR TO COUNTER BID

On 16 February, Arcelor declared a dividend of 1.2 euros, which was 85 per cent higher than the previous dividend in 2004. This was seen as an attempt by the company to convince shareholders that the situation under the current management was extremely positive. Many analysts accused the company of 'creative' accounting.

In an attempt to thwart the offer from Mittal Steel, Arcelor released a 13-billion-euro merger plan with Severstal, a Russian company. This merger would have made the new Severstal–Arcelor entity too big for Mittal Steel to buy. Despite the merger plan being fraught with loopholes, the Arcelor management tried to convince shareholders that this was the best deal for them. The shareholders, however, rejected the merger with not one shareholder voting in favour of the merger.

ROLE OF GUY DOLLE

The reaction of Guy Dolle, the then CEO of Arcelor, to the Mittal Steel bid led to widespread criticism of his actions. Analysts believe that Dolle had issues with the personality of Mittal.

As the controversy raged on, Dolle raised several issues including the management of Mittal Steel (Aditya Mittal, son of Lakshmi Mittal, is on the board). Dolle also raised a number of issues about the safety record of Mittal Steel and also repeatedly pointed out that Arcelor was an absolute key to Europe's economic health. Guy Dolle is not a part of the new Arcelor–Mittal organization.

INDIAN GOVERNMENT'S STANCE

Most Indians were of the opinion that the deal was not getting pushed through because of Mittal's nationality. The Indian government raised the issue at several forums, especially through Commerce Minister Kamal Nath. There were allegations that India had threatened not to ratify a taxation accord with Luxembourg due to the latter's opposition to the deal. The irony is that Mittal himself felt there was no case of 'racism' here as Mittal Steel was a European company and not an Indian one.

END RESULT

The deal was finally clinched when the shareholders of Arcelor agreed to Mittal Steel's offer. This ended transactions that had dragged on for months. Mittal Steel had to considerably sweeten the initial offer. Under severe pressure to counteract the Arcelor–Severstal merger, Mittal Steel had to raise its valuation of Arcelor to 32.9 billion US dollars. The Mittal family holds 43 per cent of the combined group. The combined company holds 10 per cent of the global market for steel. The consolidation phase is well and truly underway.

CURRENT POSITION

Arcelor–Mittal, the new entity, will be based on Arcelor's industrial model. It has been decided that the management board will have seven members—four from Arcelor, including the CEO Guy Dolle, and three nominated members from Mittal Steel.

The board of directors will comprise 18 non-executive members. Six members will be nominated by Mittal Steel, of whom three will be independent. Six members will be nominated from the existing Arcelor board, three from the existing Arcelor shareholders, and three members from employee representatives.

Mittal Steel's CEO will be the president of the new company. The chairman of Arcelor, Joseph Kinsch, will be the chairman of the new group, and will be succeeded by Mittal upon retirement. Kinsch was to propose a new president after Mittal becomes the chairman.

The management board of the new company will comprise four members from the Arcelor management board, including the chief executive, and three members nominated by Mittal, including Aditya Mittal.

The Mittal family will own 43 per cent of the group and has agreed to a 5-year lock-up period. During this period it will not increase its stake above 45 per cent. The sequence of events leading to the merger are given here:

27 January 2006:   Mittal Steel unveils 18.6-billion-euro cash and share offer for Arcelor.

29 January 2006:   Arcelor directors reject Mittal's offer as '150 per cent hostile', saying the companies 'do not share same vision, business model, and values'.

31 January 2006:   Jean-Claude Juncker, the prime minister of Luxembourg, which holds 5.6 per cent of Arcelor, vows to use 'all necessary means' to fend off Mittal's unsolicited offer.

16 February 2006: Arcelor raises 2005 dividend by 85 per cent.

4 April 2006:	Arcelor says it will distribute 5 billion euros to shareholders. Raises 2005 dividend to 1.85 euros.
28 April 2006:	Arcelor chairman says supervisory board would think again if Mittal made a cash bid.
9 May 2006:	Mittal Steel says it is willing to revise terms if the Arcelor board recommends its bid.
12 May 2006:	Arcelor says it will implement a 5-billion-euro share buy-back.
17 May 2006:	Mittal launches offer after regulators approve terms of the deal.
18 May 2006:	Mittal raises offer by 34 per cent to 25.8 billion euros with a 57 per cent increase in cash component. New deal would relinquish Mittal family's control over the group.
25 May 2006:	Arcelor agrees to join forces with Russian steelmaker Severstal.
30 May 2006:	Leading Arcelor shareholders speak out against the proposed Severstal merger.
31 May 2006:	More than a third of Arcelor investors sign a letter demanding the right to vote on a deal.
7 June 2006:	Arcelor agrees to meet representatives from Mittal Steel.
11 June 2006:	Arcelor formally rejects Mittal's 25.8-billion-euro bid and reiterates plans to press ahead with Severstal merger, but leaves the door open for an increased offer from Mittal and gives shareholders the chance to vote.
18 June 2006:	Arcelor cancels shareholder vote on Severstal.
20 June 2006:	Spanish investor forces Severstal rethink after calling for management changes at Arcelor.
21 June 2006:	Severstal changes terms of its proposed merger with Arcelor to counter shareholder fears.
25 June 2006:	Arcelor recommends the upgraded 26.9 billion euro Mittal offer after intensive talks.

Questions for Discussion

1. Why did the French government oppose the acquisition of Arcelor by Mittal Steel?
2. How did Arcelor try to block the acquisition by Mittal Steel?
3. What influence tactics did Mittal employ to clinch the deal?
4. Discuss Mittal's tenacity in the power struggle for the acquisition.

NOTES AND REFERENCES

1. Swift, C. and G. Levin (1987). 'Empowerment: An emerging mental health technology', *Journal of Primary Promotion*, 8: 71–94.
2. Kotter, J.P. (1985). *Power and Influence: Beyond Formal Authority*. New York: Free Press.
3. Kotter, J.P. (1979). *Power in Management*. Saranac Lake, NY: American Management Association.
4. Lee, R. and P. Lawrence (1991). *Politics at Work*, p. 119. Cheltenham: Stanley Thornas.
5. Raven, B.H. (1993). 'A power interaction model of interpersonal influence: French and Raven thirty years later', *Journal of Social Behaviour and Personality*, 7(2): 217–244

6. Rogers, Carl (1951). *Client-centred Therapy*. Boston: Houghton Mifflin; Heresey, P. and K.H. Blanchard (1982). *Management of Organisational Behaviour*. Englewood Cliffs, NJ: Prentice-Hall.

7. Suggested by French, W.L. and C.H. Bell (1995), *Organization Development: Behavioural Science Interventions for Organization Development*, 4th edn., p. 280. New Delhi: Prentice-Hall of India.

8. French, W.L. and C.H. Bell (1995). *Organization Development: Behavioural Science Interventions for Organization Development* (4th edn). New Delhi: Prentice-Hall of India.

9. Flanders, N.A. (1970). *Analyzing Teacher Behavior*. Reading, NJ: Addison-Wesley.

10. Hersey, P. and K.H. Blanchard (1982). *Management of Organisational Behaviour*. Englewood Cliffs, NJ: Prentice-Hall.

11. Berlew, D.E. (1986), in S. Srivastava and Associates (eds), 'Managing human energy: Pushing versus pulling', *Executive Power*, pp. 33–50. San Francisco: Jossey-Bass.

12. Pettigrew, A.M. (1986). 'Some limits of Executive Power in Creating Strategic Change', in S. Srivastava and Associates (eds). *Executive Power*, pp. 132–54. San Francisco: Jossey-Bass.

13. Raven, B.H. (1993). 'A power interaction model of interpersonal influence: French and Raven thirty years later', *Journal of Social Behaviour and Personality*, 7(2): 217–44.

14. *Ibid.*

15. Based on a study of 40 production groups and using the five power bases of French and Raven. Legitimate, expert, reward, referent, and coercive power, in this order, were stated as reasons for compliance of employees with their foremen. Another study found the rank order of power bases for compliance of salesmen of a large firm as expert, legitimate, reward, referent, and coercive powers. The rank order of the importance of power bases among students has been reported as legitimate, coercive, expert, reward, and referent; among graduates, expert, legitimate, reward, coercive, and referent.

16. Based on the distinctions between coercive and persuasive bases, and between using and needing power, an instrument has been prepared (Pareek, unpublished). In a study of 209 managers, using this instrument, it was found that internals (using Levensen's scale) used more persuasive power, whereas the externals wanted more coercive power, and externals (chance) used less persuasive power. The study also reported significant positive correlation between perception of having persuasive power and negative correlation between need for persuasive power with enlarging life style. No significant correlation was found with coercive power. Using Rotter's scale for interpersonal trust, the study found negative correlation between need for coercive power and interpersonal trust. Other correlations were not significant. One non-government service organization ranked the 10 bases for compliance as follows: development, competence, expertise, referent, relationship, organizational position, reward, closeness to authority, charisma, and punishment. Expert and legitimate power were in most organizations, and in a variety of organizations.

17. Coercive base was strongly and negatively associated with satisfaction among all the three groups of students, as well as a variety of five organizations (manufacturing farms, sales organizations, life insurance companies, utility firms, and liberal arts colleges), and in several offices of a utility company. Expert and referent power have been reported to be associated with employee satisfaction.

18. Rappaport, J., C. Swift, and R. Hess (1984). *Studies in Empowerment: Steps Toward Understanding and Action*. New York: Haworth.

19. Torre, D.A. (1986). 'Empowerment Structured Conceptualization and Instrument Development', Ph.D. dissertation, Cornell University.

20. Wallerstein, N. (1992). 'Powerlessness, Empowerment, and Health: Implications for Health Promotion Programs', *American Journal of Health Promotion*, 6: 197–205.

21. Karl, N. and P. Michels (1991). 'The Lazarus project: The politics of empowerment', *Annual Journal of Occupational Therapy*, 45: 719–725.

22. Smith, W.J. and J.A. Temer (1995). 'Adoption', in W.J. Rothwell, R. Sullivan, and G.N. McLean (eds), *Practicing Organisation Development: A Guide for Consultants*. San Diego: Pfeiffer & Co.
23. Koestenbahm, P. (1991). *Leadership*. San Francisco: Jossey-Bass.
24. Swift and Levin. 'Empowerment: An emerging mental health technology'.
25. Rissel, Christopher (1994). 'Empowerment: The Holy Grail?' *Health Promotion International*, 9(1): 41.
26. Forre, Saimon (1986). Speech at INTRAC Regional Conference.
27. Swift and Levin. 'Empowerment: An emerging mental health technology'.
28. Rissel. 'Empowerment: The Holy Grail?'
29. Das, G.S. (1992). 'Development of an empowering scale: Item analysis and factor structure', *ASCI Journal of Management*, 22(2–3): 138–45.
30. Pareek, Udai (2002). *Effective Organizations: Beyond Management to Institution Building*, Chapter 98. New Delhi: Oxford & IBH.
31. *Ibid*, Chapter 88.
32. Blanchard, K., J.P. Carlos, and A. Randolph (1996). *Empowerment Takes More Than a Minute*. San Francisco: Benet-Koehler.
33. *Ibid.*
34. Edgell, Roger (2005). *Empowerment*. London: Develin & Partners.
35. Lee, R. and P. Lawrence (1991). *Politics at Work*, p. 4. Cheltenham: Stanley Thornas.
36. Mayes and Allen (1977) quoted in French and Bell, *Organizational Development*, p. 283.
37. Allen et al (1979) as quoted in French and Bell, *Organizational Development*, p. 283.
38. Laski, Harold (1932). *A Grammar of Politics*. London: Allen & Unwin.
39. Bolman, L.G. and T.E. Deal (1997). *Reframing Organizations*. San Francisco: Jossey-Bass.
40. Ansoff, H.I. (1965). *Corporate Strategy*. New York: McGraw-Hill.
41. Chandler, A.D. (1962). *Strategy and Structure: Chapters in the History of American Industrial Enterprise*. Cambridge, MA: MIT Press.
42. Mintzberg H. and J.B. Quinn (1991). *The Strategy Process: Concepts, Contexts, and Cases*. London: Prentice-Hall.
43. Dunphy, D. and D. Stace (1988). 'Transformational and coercive strategies for planned organizational change', *Organization Studies*, 9(3): 317–334.
44. Lewis, Dianne (2002). 'The place of organizational politics in strategic change', *Strategic Change*, January–February 2002: 25–34.
45. Mintzberg H. (1990). 'Strategy formation: Schools of thought', in J.W. Frederickson (ed.), *Perspectives on Strategic Management*. New York: Harper Business.
46. Luthans, Fred (2002). *Organisational Behaviour*. New York: McGraw-Hill.
47. Yukl, Gary, Ping Ping Fu, and Robert McDonald (2003). 'Cross-cultural differences in perceived effectiveness of influence tactics for initiating or resisting change', *Journal of Applied Psychology*, 52(1): 68.
48. This, as well as the following quotes, is from Berlew, D.E. (1986), 'Managing human energy: Pushing versus pulling', in S. Srivastava (ed.), *Executive Power*, San Francisco: Jossey–Bass.
49. S.N. Sharma in *Times News Network*, 4 June 2006, http://economictimes.indiatimes.com/articleshow/1611991.cms.

24
Organizational Culture and Climate

LEARNING OBJECTIVES

After studying this chapter, you will be able to
1. Identify various dimensions of organizational climate
2. Discuss the implications of different motivational climates for organizations
3. Define organizational culture and related terms
4. Explain the different approaches to organizational culture
5. Suggest interventions to improve organizational culture and climate

The number of studies on organizational culture is steadily increasing. Sometimes such studies have used different terminology and sometimes the same terms have been used with different meanings. There is hence a need to clarify some terms and to evolve a common understanding of their use.

The various terms used in the context of organizational culture include values, ethics, beliefs, ethos, climate, and culture. Ethics refers to the normative, to what is socially desirable. Values, beliefs, attitudes, and norms are interrelated. Interaction between beliefs and values results in attitude formation (attitudes = beliefs × values), which then produces norms. Values and beliefs are the core of an individual's self, while attitudes are the next layer, followed by norms of behaviour. When these get institutionalised or when they accumulate and integrate, social phenomena are formed.

The culture-related concepts can also be seen as multi-level concepts. At the core (first level) are the values that give a distinct identity to a group. This is the ethos of the group. *The Random House Dictionary* defines ethos as 'the fundamental character or spirit of a culture … dominant assumptions of a people or period' (p. 489).

At the second level is climate, which can be defined as the perceived attributes of an organization and its sub-system as reflected in the way it deals with its members, groups, and issues. The emphasis is on the perceived attributes and the working of the sub-systems.

The third concept is culture—the cumulative beliefs, values, and assumptions underlying transactions with nature, and important phenomena, as reflected in artefacts, rituals, etc. Culture is reflected in the ways adopted to deal with basic phenomena.

ORGANIZATIONAL ETHOS

As already suggested, ethos can be defined as the underlying spirit or character of an entity or group and is made up of its beliefs, customs, and practices. At the base of ethos are core values. The eight important values relevant to organizations are openness, confrontation, trust, authenticity, proactivity, autonomy, collaboration, and experimentation. In addition to being an acronym for these values, OCTAPACE is a term indicating the eight (*octa*) steps (*pace*) needed to create a functional ethos.[1] We shall briefly discuss each aspect—its meaning, its outcome for the organization, and its indicators—to show whether and to what degree each exists in the organization.

Openness Openness can be defined as a spontaneous expression of feelings and thoughts and the sharing of these without defensiveness. Openness applies in both directions, receiving and giving. Both these types of openness may relate to ideas (including suggestions), feedback (including criticism), and feelings. For example, openness means receiving without reservation and taking steps to encourage feedback and suggestions from customers, colleagues, and others. Similarly, it means giving— without hesitation—ideas, information, feedback, feelings, etc.

Openness may also mean spatial openness (in terms of accessibility). Installing an intranet may be a step in this direction: everyone having a computer terminal has access to information, which may be retrieved at any time. Offices without walls are a symbolic arrangement promoting openness. In some organizations, even the chief executive does not have a separate cabin, and floor space is shared by colleagues at different levels in the organization. For example, P.P. Gupta, when he was chairman of CMC Ltd, a public sector company, shared his office with managers at three levels. This willingness to share, this openness, results in greater clarity of objectives and free interaction among people. As a result of openness, there should be more unbiased performance feedback as well. Indicators of openness in an organization are productive meetings and improved implementation of systems and innovations.

Confrontation Confrontation can be defined as facing rather than shying away from problems. It also implies a deeper analysis of interpersonal problems. All this involves taking up challenges. The term confrontation is used with some reservation and means putting up a front, as contrasted with turning one's back to (escaping from) the problem. A better term would be confrontation-cum-exploration (CE).

Let us use the term confrontation in this sense of confrontation and exploration, that is, facing a problem and working jointly with others to find a solution to the problem. The outcome of confrontation can be better role clarity, improved problem-solving, and willingness to deal with problems and with 'difficult' employees and customers. There will be willingness in teams to discuss and resolve sensitive issues. These indicators, which are the outcomes, can be increased by periodic discussions with clients, bold action, and refusal to postpone sticky matters.

Trust Trust is not used in the moral sense here. It is reflected in maintaining the confidentiality of information shared by others and in not misusing it. It is also reflected in a sense of assurance that others will help when help is needed and will honour mutual commitments and obligations. Trust is accepting what another person says at face value and not searching for ulterior motives. Trust is an extremely important ingredient in organizational building processes.

The outcomes of trust include high empathy, timely support, reduced stress, and reduction and simplification of forms and procedures. Such simplification of procedures, reduced paperwork, effective delegation, and higher productivity are indicators of trust.

Authenticity Authenticity is the congruence between what one feels, says, and does. It is reflected in owning up to one's mistakes and in an unreserved sharing of feelings. Authenticity is similar to openness. The outcome of authenticity in an organization is reduction in distortion of communication. This can be seen in the correspondence between members in an organization.

Proactivity Proactivity means taking initiative, pre-planning, taking preventive action, and calculating the pay-offs of an alternative course before taking action. The term 'proact' can be contrasted with the term 'react'. In the latter, action is in response to (and in the pattern of) an act from some source; in the former, the action taken is independent of the source. For example, if a person shouts back at a friend's accusation, he or she shows reactive behaviour. However, if he or she responds calmly and suggests that they discuss the problem together, the person is showing proactive behaviour.

Proactivity gives the person initiative to start a new process or set up a new pattern of behaviour. In reactive behaviour, the initiative lies with the source and the person merely acts according to the pattern set by that source. In other words, the usual response pattern is reactive. Proactivity involves unusual behaviour. In this sense, proactivity means freeing oneself from, and taking action beyond, immediate concerns. A person showing proactivity functions at all the three levels of feeling, thinking, and action.

At the level of feeling, the person transcends the role boundary and sees things from the point of view of the other (the role sender). This is empathy. He or she appreciates the other person's point of view (understands it even if he or she does not agree) and is able to feel empathy with the other person. This also means that the person transcends logic and reasoning and is able to reach into feelings. Things may then acquire a new meaning.

At the thinking level, the person may transcend his or her own immediate feelings, emotions, and reasons to understand a problem. He or she may transcend time and think of the future in terms of long-term implications; he or she may also transcend individual events and see a pattern, leading to his or her own action theory.

At the action level, proactivity means transcending the immediate cause, that is, taking initiative. There are three ways in which this can be done transcending symptoms (i.e., looking for the causes of a problem), transcending traditional and uniform ways of acting (i.e., searching several alternative modes of action), and transcending content (i.e., initiating a new process—e.g., the process of joint exploration). In transactional analysis, proactivity is stressed in terms of transcending circularity (being sucked into a game). Instead of falling into the 'game' trap, a proactive individual makes a new move that stops the game and starts a new set of adult–adult transactions.

Proactivity thus shows a high level of maturity. Both individual employees and the organization can do a lot to promote it. There are four ways in which an organization can respond to environmental changes. These, adapted from McNamara's concept, include inaction (maintaining the status quo), reaction (responding to change as it occurs and fire-fighting), transaction (adapting after anticipating and confronting change), and proaction (a strategy planning to influence events and, in a way, cause change).

A good example is tennis. A poor player simply responds from his or her 'best position', leaving balls not coming to that position. A better player tries to run around and hit back all the balls his or her adversary throws at him. An even better player anticipates where the adversary is likely to throw the ball and is already there to send back the ball, saving a lot of energy. The best player is the one who studies the strengths and weaknesses of his or her adversary to prepare himself or herself for the game. Such players study video clippings of the adversary's playing style, and decide their own strategy—where to place the balls to tire the adversary out, placing most of the balls in areas that are the adversary's weak spots. They make the adversary play 'their' game, rather than they playing the adversary's game themselves.

The outcome of high proactivity is greater initiative in anticipating problems and issues, planning, developing strategies, ensuring faster response, and processing information about national and international competitors, the market, collaborators, raw materials, etc. The outcome is early problem detection, detailed planning, analysis of successes and failures, reduction of surprises, improved time management, reduction of 'emergency' meetings in organizations and with customers, willingness to enter new areas of work, and timely curtailing of unprofitable business. All these can also be used as indicators of proactivity, including better capital management.

Autonomy Autonomy is using and giving freedom to plan and act in one's own sphere. It means respecting and encouraging individual and role autonomy. Autonomy develops mutual respect and is likely to result in willingness to take responsibility and individual initiative, and better succession planning. The main indicator of autonomy is effective delegation in an organization and reduction of references to seniors for approval of planned action.

Collaboration Collaboration is giving help to, and asking for help from, others. It means working together (both individuals and groups) to solve problems and developing a team spirit. The outcomes of collaboration include timely help, teamwork, sharing of experiences, improved communication, and improved resource sharing. The indicators could be productivity reports, frequent meetings, involvement of staff in decision making, more joint decisions, better resource utilisation, and 'quality' meetings.

Experimentation Experimentation means using and encouraging innovative approaches to solve problems, using feedback for improvement, taking a fresh look at things, and encouraging creativity. We are so caught up with our daily tasks that we often use only the traditional tried and tested ways of dealing with problems. While such methods save time and energy, they also blind us to perceiving the advantage of new ways of solving problems. The more we work under pressure, the less our inclination to try a different approach, as the risk seems too high. And yet complex problems require new approaches for their solutions. Organizational learning does not imply repetitive action; it implies applying past experience to current problems to reach beyond the usual solutions. This can be called creativity. Other terms such as innovation, experimentation, and new approach also convey the same meaning.

There are several kinds of creativity in an organization. Creativity is reflected in new suggestions generated by employees, attempts at improving upon older ways of working, trying out a new idea to which one has been exposed, originating new methods, and ignoring the so-called constraints while thinking about a problem. It is also called lateral thinking, that is, thinking aimed at generating alternatives. There is evidence that such thinking contributes to the development of new products, new methods, and new processes.

An instrument, Octapace Profile, is available to study organizational ethos.[1]

ORGANIZATIONAL CLIMATE

Climate can be defined as the perceived attributes of an organization and its sub-systems as reflected in the way an organization deals with its members, groups, and issues. The emphasis is on perceived attributes and the working of sub-systems. One conceptual framework of climate emphasises motivational linkages.[2] This framework seems to be quite relevant for studying organizational climate.

Motivation

Six motives, already discussed in Chapter 7, are particularly relevant for organizational climate.

Achievement This motive is characterised by a concern for excellence, competition against standards set by others or by oneself, the setting of challenging goals for oneself, an awareness of the obstacles that might be encountered in attempting to achieve these goals, and persistence in trying alternative paths to one's goals.

Influence This motive is characterised by a concern for making an impact on others, a desire to make people do what one thinks is right, and an urge to change situations and develop people.

Control This is characterised by a concern for orderliness, a desire to be and stay informed, an urge to monitor events and to take corrective action when needed, and a need to display personal power.

Extension   This is characterised by a concern for others, an interest in superordinate goals, and an urge to be relevant and useful to large groups, including society as a whole.

Dependency   This motive is characterised by a desire for the assistance of others in developing oneself, a need to check with significant others (those who are more knowledgeable or have higher status, experts, close associates, and so on), a tendency to submit ideas or proposals for approval, and an urge to maintain a relationship based on the other person's approval.

Affiliation   This is characterised by a concern for establishing and maintaining close personal relationships, an emphasis on friendship, and a tendency to express one's emotions.

Dimensions and Processes

Likert proposed six dimensions of organizational climate: leadership, motivation, communication, decisions, goals, and control.[3] Litwin and Stringer (1968) proposed seven dimensions[4]: conformity, responsibility standards, rewards, organizational clarity, warmth and support, and leadership.

A review of various studies and discussions with managers suggested the following 12 processes:

Orientation   This is the main concern of the members of an organization. If the dominant orientation or concern is to adhere to established rules, the climate will be characterised by emphasis on control; on the other hand, if the orientation is to excel, the climate will be characterised by achievement.

Interpersonal relationships   An organization's interpersonal relations are reflected in the way informal groups are formed. If groups are formed for the purpose of protecting their own interests, cliques may develop and a climate of control may result. Similarly, if people tend to develop informal relationships with their supervisors, a climate of dependency may result.

Supervision   Supervisory practices contribute significantly to the climate. If supervisors focus on helping their subordinates to improve personal skills and chances of advancement, a climate that is characterised by the extension motive may result. If supervisors are more concerned with maintaining good relations with their subordinates, a climate characterised by the affiliation motive may result.

Problem management   Problems can be seen as challenges or irritants. They can either be solved by the supervisor alone or jointly by the supervisor and the subordinate(s) concerned, or they can be referred to a higher level. These different perspectives and ways of handling problems contribute to the creation of an organizational climate.

Management of mistakes   A supervisor's attitude towards a subordinate's mistakes develops the organizational orientation towards shortcomings and errors, which is generally one of annoyance, concern, or tolerance. An organization's approach to mistakes influences the climate.

Conflict management   Conflicts may be seen as an embarrassing annoyance to be covered up or as problems to be solved. The process of dealing with conflicts has a significant effect on the organizational climate, as does that of handling problems or mistakes.

Communication   The process of communication is concerned with the flow of information, its direction (top-down, bottom-up, horizontal), its disbursement (selectively, to those concerned, or to everyone), its mode (formal or informal), and its type (instructions or feedback on the state of affairs).

Decision making   An organization's approach to decision making can be focused on maintaining good relations or on achieving results. In addition, the issue of who makes the decisions is important: it could be people high up in the hierarchy, experts, or those involved in the matters about requiring a decision. These elements of decision making are relevant to the establishment of a particular climate or atmosphere.

Trust   The degree of trust or its absence among various members and groups in the organization affects the organizational climate. The issue of who is trusted by the management and to what degree is also relevant.

Management of rewards   Rewards reinforce specific behaviours, thereby arousing and sustaining specific motives. Consequently, what is rewarded in an organization influences the organizational climate.

Risk taking   How people respond to risks and whose help is sought in situations involving risk are important determinants of organizational climate.

Innovation and change   Who initiates change, how change and innovations are perceived, and how change is implemented are all critical to establishing the organizational climate.

Effectiveness Profile

Motivational climate of an organization can be assessed with the help of an instrument especially designed for this purpose. One such instrument is Motivational Analysis of Organizations—Climate or MAO–C.[5] MAO–C provides a profile for an organization based on the six motives mentioned earlier.

The profile includes scores on six motives. The two highest scores are generally used to interpret the climate: the highest score shows the dominant climate and the next highest the back-up climate. The combination of these two motives thus characterises the organizational climate. Generally, there are six different kinds of dominant climate characterised by different motives as shown in Exhibit 24.1.

Exhibit 24.1   *Six Motives Characterising Dominant Organizational Climates*

Motives	Characteristic organization
Achievement	Industrial and business organizations
Expert power (corresponding to the influence motive)	University departments, scientific organizations
Control	Bureaucracy (as in government departments)
Dependency	Traditional or one-man organizations
Extension	Community service organizations
Affiliation	Clubs

Combinations of the six motives as dominant and secondary climates give 30 profiles. We briefly mention below the nature of the organization associated with each of the 30 profiles. Some of these are based on research.[6] By and large, dominant climates characterised by achievement, expert power, and extension are conducive to the achievement of results and those characterised by control, dependency, and affiliation retard achievement of results.

Achievement–expert power   People are involved in challenging tasks and are highly stimulated by challenges and specialists dominate in determining action. The organization rewards specialisation.

Achievement–control   Most people are involved in challenging tasks, but they face a lot of constraints because of rigid procedures and inflexible hierarchy.

Achievement–dependency   In spite of the emphasis on high achievement shared by most people, there is a tendency to postpone critical decisions pending approval from a higher authority. The organization discourages decision making without approval from the higher level, resulting in a sense of frustration.

Achievement–extension   People work on challenging tasks with equal attention to the social relevance of such tasks. The organization has a high sense of social responsibility and also pays attention to employee needs.

Achievement–affiliation   While people work on challenging goals, they form strong groups based on speciality, department, language, region, etc. The organization, with so many in-groups or cliques, must pay a lot of attention to maintaining good relations among the groups.

Expert power–achievement   The organization attaches high value to specialisation and specialists influence most decisions. At the same time, there is emphasis on high quality of work and unique contributions.

Expert power–control   The organization is controlled by experts, with cumbersome procedures resulting in lack of job satisfaction, and relatively low output.

Expert power–dependency   The organization is dominated by experts, with a rigid hierarchy. Decisions are passed up the hierarchical line. Bright employees may remain highly dissatisfied.

Expert power–extension   Specialists play a major role in organizational matters, working in a planned way on socially relevant issues. The organization pays attention to the employees' needs and welfare.

Expert power–affiliation   This results in an expert-dominated organization, with in-groups based on specialities, languages, religions, etc. The organization's attention is more on maintaining a friendly climate and results often suffer.

Control–achievement   The organization is bureaucratic, laying down detailed procedures, with a rigid hierarchy. The organization emphasises quality of work but most employees with achievement orientation get frustrated due to the higher emphasis on control. Some public sector organizations have this kind of climate.

Control–expert power   This implies a bureaucratic organization in which specialists' opinions are valued but with rules being treated as more important.

Control–dependency   Here we have a bureaucratic organization with rigid hierarchy, where all actions are referred to higher levels for approval, and decisions get delayed. Following rules and ensuring proper protocol adherence to regulations are more important than achieving results. Senior staff protect subordinates who do not make procedural mistakes. Most government offices function in this way.

Control–extension   This creates a hierarchical organization with social concern, paying attention to the needs and welfare of the employees.

Control–affiliation   The climate is that of a hierarchical organization with low concern for results and greater emphasis on good relations. However, informal groups based on relationship have an important place here. Some voluntary organizations are of this type.

Dependency–achievement   The organization emphasises respect for people in power and all major decisions are referred to them. However, achievement of results is rewarded and enough freedom is given with key decisions being controlled by a few, who have the last word on all matters. Many family-owned organizations have such a climate.

Dependency–expert power   The organization has a rigid hierarchy, decisions being referred to higher levels for approval. Experts play an important role in the various aspects of the working of the organization.

Dependency–control   This is an organization controlled by a few individuals, who have clear-cut channels of communication and are referred to for final approval of all decisions.

Dependency–extension A traditional organization working in socially relevant areas, this is dominated and controlled by a few individuals demanding all respect from other members and taking care of the members' needs in return.

Dependency–affiliation This makes for a traditional organization with the top management controlling all matters using their own in-group members, who have high loyalty to their leaders.

Extension–achievement The organization aims to be relevant to society, with emphasis on achieving results. Employees are selected for their competence and are given freedom to work. See Exhibit 24.2.[7]

Extension–expert power This organization has social awareness, with experts influencing all the major decisions.

Extension–control An organization with the goal of serving a larger cause, this has a bureaucratic structure, with rules and regulations to be followed strictly.

Extension–dependency An organization in the area of community service (such as education, health, or development), it emphasises conformity to policies laid down by the top management, who require all matters to be referred to them for the final decision.

Extension–affiliation In this organization in the area of community service, members with a similar background (in terms of caste, ideology, specialisation, region, language, kinship, etc.) work with strong linkages with one another.

Affiliation–achievement The organization accords high importance to relationships and draws people with similar backgrounds (in terms of language, caste, region, etc.). The organization also values achievement of results and excellence of performance.

Affiliation–power The organization, mainly consisting of experts, emphasises good relations, and either consists of persons of the same background or has in-groups (cliques) based on some common links.

Affiliation–control This organization is involved in maintaining good relations, but has a bureaucratic form. A club with strict rules and procedures would be in this category.

Affiliation–dependency The organization puts a high value on friendly relations among the members. One or two people make most of the decisions. People are rewarded on the basis of their closeness to the person(s) at the top.

Affiliation–extension The main goal at this organization working on socially relevant issues is a good relationship between its members. The Lions Club and similar organizations would be in this category.

Exhibit 24.2 *Developing Extension–Achievement Climate at Excel Industries*

Ever since Excel Industries was started in the 1940s, headquartered in Mumbai, western India, its mission was to develop indigenous technology to produce world-class chemicals, a mission that reflected the patriotic urges of the founding family. By the 1990s, Excel had had plants in five locations and was producing highly sophisticated chemicals for industrial and agricultural applications. It had developed in-house over a hundred alternative processes for manufacturing chemicals, all without any foreign technology, collaboration, or agreement, and, in fact, had supplied technology not only to Indian companies but also to foreign companies. It had won several awards for export performance, excellent plant management, and fair business practices. In 1990, Excel re-committed itself for the next 50 years to technological excellence and contribution to the development of the country, industry, and rural society through what the Japanese call *rentai*, or 'togetherness', and extended its vision to develop responsible, creative, and productive persons to serve society. In this 50-year vision of excellence, Excel committed itself to the dignity and capability of every human being and to creating an environment where everyone was motivated to realise her/his full potential. The stress was on teamwork, academic learning environment, and maternal concern for the stakeholders.

Excel worked hard to make its vision a reality. Group brainstorming was widely used in problem solving for generating fresh ideas, and for this purpose temporary inter-functional teams were formed. A blackboard was installed in every office to instil a learning culture, and was used widely for presentations or explanations. No need was seen for a suggestion scheme, as it was expected that employees would feel free to discuss their ideas with higher-ups. If an idea was accepted, the proposer became a member of the team formed to implement the idea. To facilitate informal interactions, employees, including the CEO, lunched together in the company canteen. Formal designations and status symbols were discouraged. Socialisation of new members involved not only exposure to technical subjects, but also to talks by seniors on the history and culture of the organization, innovativeness, and teamwork. Right from the start, young recruits were assigned to teams and tasks that might not be related to their past experience and training.

No one was sacked at Excel. There was planned job rotation. The Excel Institute of Technology, Environment, and Management provided in-house training, although employees were also sent for outside courses. There were even courses on yoga and meditation, and the company funded the higher education (including doctorates) of staff members. The gap between the emoluments of top- and bottom-level employees was kept modest. Before a formal promotion, the employee was tried out for a while in the new job. Excel frequently induced innovation through overloading. Employees were challenged with targets like halving the cost or doubling the production.

Regarding R&D, Excel's philosophy was of exploring the possibilities of impossibilities—by taking up only those projects that were difficult and challenging. Excel's R&D was geared to providing it with the first-mover advantage in new, high-quality products. Most of the R&D work was done in teams and their work was reviewed by task forces. A forum called 'Innovation 1992' was formed for teams to present their innovative ideas. It was fairly commonplace to appoint groups to brainstorm on alternative uses of the technologies developed at Excel, including some 'failures'.

By 1992, Excel had become one of the top five Indian private sector chemicals companies in size. It was the most profitable of the top 10.

ORGANIZATIONAL CULTURE

As you saw in Chapter 2, culture can be defined as the cumulative beliefs, values, and assumptions underlying our transactions with nature and various important phenomena (collectives, the environment, context, time, biological differences, power, etc.). Culture is reflected in artefacts—rituals, design of space, furniture, and ways of dealing with various phenomena.

Power Model of Organizational Culture

Distribution and concentration of power can be one basis of classifying cultures. From this point of view, organizational culture can be of four types: autocratic (or feudal), bureaucratic, technocratic, and entrepreneurial (or organic and democratic).

Autocratic or feudal culture is characterised by centralised power concentrated in a few individuals and observation of proper protocol in relation to the people in power. Bureaucratic culture is characterised by primacy of procedures and rules, hierarchy, and distant and impersonal relationships. Technocratic culture emphasises technical and professional standards and improvement. Entrepreneurial culture is values, achievement of results, and quality customer service.

Two related concepts relevant to organizational culture are organizational climate and organizational ethos. As stated earlier, there are six types of organizational climate, based on the dominant motive:

- Achievement (dominant concern for excellence)
- Expert power (concern for impact through expertise)
- Extension (concern for relevance to larger goals and entities)
- Control (concern for orderliness)
- Affiliation (concern for maintaining good personal relations)
- Dependency (concern for approval and maintenance of hierarchical order)

The first three motives (achievement, expert power, and extension) and the corresponding organizational climates fostered by them have been found to be functional, contributing to organizational effectiveness. The last three (corresponding to control, affiliation, and dependency) have been found to be dysfunctional for organizational effectiveness.

Ethos is primarily concerned with values and is the fundamental character of the organizational spirit. As already discussed, the OCTAPACE ethos is characterised by the eight values of openness, confrontation, trust, authenticity, proactivity, autonomy, collaboration, and experimentation. The respective opposite poles of the eight values are closeness, avoidance, suspicion, manipulation, inertia, role-boundness, conflicts, and playing safe.

Based on data, observation, and discussions, certain hypotheses have been proposed about the four organizational profiles in terms of the climate and ethos variables. These are shown in Exhibit 24.3.

Let us briefly discuss these profiles as hypotheses.

Autocratic An autocratic or feudal culture is primarily concerned with following proper protocol and is dominated by dependency ('de'), and a climate with affiliation ('af') as its secondary. People are recruited on the basis of relationship, and they are trusted. In the 'deaf' (dependency–affiliation) climate, as already indicated, the top managers control the organization and employ their own in-group members, who

Exhibit 24.3 *Profile of Organizational Cultures*

Cultures	Focus	Climate	Ethos
Autocratic/feudal	Proper protocol	Deaf (dependency–affiliation)	Rammassic (all opposite values of OCTAPACE)
Bureaucratic	Rules and regulations	Code (control–dependency)	Sick (playing safe, inertia, conflict, and closeness)
Technocratic	Perfection	Expex (expert power–extension)	Pace (proactivity, collaboration, and experimentation)
Entrepreneurial/ democratic/organic	Results and customers	Ace (achievement–extension)	OCTAPACE (all eight values)

are extremely loyal to these leaders. The ethos of such a culture is closed, mistrustful, and self-seeking.

Bureaucratic   A bureaucratic culture is concerned with following proper rules and regulations. Its climate is dominated by control ('co'), backed up by dependency ('de'). Such a 'code' climate shows that bureaucracy and a rigid hierarchy dominate the organization. Because actions are generally referred to the higher levels for approval, decisions are usually delayed. It is more important to follow rules and regulations here than to achieve results. Senior employees protect those subordinates who do not make any procedural mistakes. The ethos of a bureaucratic organization is characterised by playing it safe, inertia, lack of collaboration, and being closed.

Technocratic   A technocratic culture generally has an 'expex' climate—expert power (exp) being dominant, with a back-up climate of extension ('ex'). Specialists play the major roles in the organization, working in a planned way on socially relevant matters. The organization pays attention to the employees' needs and welfare. The ethos is positive, featuring proactivity (initiative), autonomy, collaboration, and experimentation.

Entrepreneurial   An entrepreneurial culture (also called organic or democratic) is primarily concerned with results and customers. Its 'ace' climate is generally that of achievement (ac), or concern for excellence, and extension ('e'), or concern for larger groups and issues. In such a climate, employees work on challenging tasks and devote equal attention to the social relevance of these tasks. The organization has a highly developed sense of social responsibility as well as a strong sense of its responsibility to fulfil employee needs. The ethos is positive and characterised by the eight values of OCTAPACE.

Organizational Culture: A Comprehensive Framework

Schein defines culture as 'a pattern of basic assumptions—invented, discovered, or developed by a given group as it learns to cope with its problems of external adaptation and internal integration—that have worked well enough to be considered valid and, therefore, to be taught to new members as the correct way to perceive, think, and feel in relation to those problems'.[8]

Sathe and Davidson has also included shared behaviour patterns, shared beliefs, and shared values in his conceptual model of culture.[9] According to him, beliefs and values, although subconscious, can be altered once they are raised to the level of consciousness. As beliefs and values are expressed through rationalisation and justifications, they can be uncovered through insight, challenged, and consciously changed.

Quinn and McGrath have suggested four types of organizational culture: rational (market), developmental (adhocracy), consensual (clan), and hierarchical (hierarchy).[10]

The author, as discussed in Chapter 3, has defined culture as cumulative preferences of some states of life over others (values), predispositions towards several significant issues and phenomena (attitudes), organized ways of filling time (rituals), and ways of promoting desired behaviours and preventing undesirable ones (sanctions).[11]

The well-known conceptual framework of values proposed by Kluckhohn and Strodtbeck has been quite frequently used in studying cultures.[12] This framework has been discussed in detail in Chapter 3. The 15 dimensions of culture emerging from this framework and that of McClelland, also discussed in Chapter 3, are given in Exhibit 24.4.[13]

The various dimensions of culture can be used to prepare profiles. The profiles can broadly fall into categories on a modern–traditional continuum. The question before developing societies is whether their characteristics are dysfunctional for moving towards modernity, with the implication that if this is so they need to adopt characteristics of the cultures of developed societies. Experience in managing development has shown that developing countries need not adopt (or copy) the

Exhibit 24.4 *Dimensions of a Comprehensive Framework of Culture*

Concerns	Dimension of culture
Relationship with nature	Internality (vs externality)
Orientation to context	Ambiguity tolerance Contextualism
Time orientation	Temporality
Orientation to collectivities	Collectivism (vs individualism) Particularism (vs universalism) Narcissism Role-boundedness Other-directedness (vs inner-directedness)
Orientation to sex differences	Androgyny
Orientation to power	Power distance tolerance
	Expressive Conserving Assertive Expanding

culture of the developed world. There are many functional aspects in their own cultures. Similarly, there are many dysfunctional aspects in the cultures of industrialised societies. Developing countries can contribute significantly to evolving future societies capable of meeting new challenges. However, following long periods of colonisation, developing countries often have low self-confidence and a negative self-image. It is not surprising that members of such societies do not see many strengths in their cultures and tend to use the framework of the colonising power.[14]

Sometimes the opposite view is taken in reaction by people who eulogise the past and create delusions about the functionality of their culture. This revivalist tendency—which assumes that the past was glorious and must be restored in order to achieve glory once again—is more dysfunctional than lack of awareness of one's own strengths. What is needed is a critical attitude, sifting the functional from the dysfunctional aspects of a culture.

Hofstede's framework of organizational culture As mentioned in Chapter 3, Hofstede, based on a cross-national study of a large sample (more than 100,000), suggested a comprehensive framework of four dimensions to study cultural differences: individualism vs collectivism, uncertainty avoidance, power distance, and masculinity vs femininity.[15] He has also prepared an instrument to measure these aspects both in societies and in organizations.

Three-perspective framework Panda and Gupta[16] have drawn attention to Martin's framework.[17] Martin proposed that culture operates at three levels: integrated (common characteristics), differentiated (different characteristics in different subgroups), and fragmented (containing contradictions and confusion in the complexity of the dynamics). Martin proposed that the culture of an organization can be (or, rather should be) studied from all the three perspectives: integrated, differentiated, and fragmented. This may help to have a deeper understanding of the organizational culture.

While the other frameworks discussed earlier have used instruments, in this framework qualitative anthropological type of study is more relevant. Panda and Gupta studied culture of one organization and found that while employee welfare reflected differentiated perspective (region/branch/department-wise differences), customer care, employee care, and ethics showed both integrated as well as fragmented perspective (showing integrated culture with weak sub-cultures). They have identified three roles of a leader from a symbolic interpretative perspective: leader as a symbol, leader as a hero in the organizational stories, and leader as manager of rituals.[18]

SUMMARY

Several terms have been used for organizational culture and related phenomena. While organizational culture comprises the cumulative and shared values, attitudes, rituals and sanctions in a group, organizational ethos is the profile of core values, and organizational climate is the pattern of perceived and experienced attributes of an organization.

A framework of eight values (OCTAPACE) can be used to study organizational ethos (openness, confrontation, trust, authenticity, proactivity, autonomy, collaboration, and experimentation). Twelve organizational processes (orientation, interpersonal relationship, supervision, problem management, management of mistakes, conflict management, communication, decision making, trust, management of rewards, risk taking and innovation, and change) in a framework of six motives (achievement, expert power, extension, affiliation, control, and dependency) make up the different climates of organizations.

Several frameworks are available to study organizational culture (the power model, Hofstede's four dimensions, a comprehensive framework of 15 dimensions, and a qualitative three-perspective framework). Any of these frameworks can be used to study organizational culture.

GLOSSARY

authenticity   congruence between what one feels, says, and does

autonomy   using and giving freedom to plan and act in one's own sphere

climate   the perceived attributes of an organization and its sub-system as reflected in the way it deals with its members, groups, and issues

collaboration   giving help to and asking for help from others; working together (individuals and groups) to solve problems; team spirit

confrontation   facing rather than shying away from problems

culture   the cumulative beliefs, values, and assumptions underlying transactions with nature and

important phenomena, as reflected in artefacts, rituals, etc.

ethos   the fundamental character or spirit of a culture; dominant assumptions of a people or period

experimenting   using and encouraging innovative approaches to solve problems; using feedback for improvement; taking a fresh look at things and encouraging creativity

proactivity   taking initiative, pre-planning, taking preventive action, and calculating the pay-offs of an alternative course before taking action

EXERCISES

Concept Review Questions
1. What is the difference between organizational ethos and organizational climate?
2. Discuss different approaches to understanding organizational culture.
3. Which organizational processes are covered in the study of organizational climate?
4. How can you classify cultures using the power framework?
5. What is Martin's three-perspective framework of organizational culture?

Critical Thinking Questions
Consider the organization (or institution) where you do full-time work or study. Answer three sets of questions about it.
1. **Organizational climate** Six statements are given below. Rank the statements from 6 (most like the situation in your organization or unit) to 1 (least like the situation in your organization or unit). Do not give the same rank to more than one statement.

(a) People here are mainly concerned with following established rules and procedures.
(b) The main concern of people here is to help one another develop greater skills and thereby advance in the organization.
(c) Achieving or surpassing specific goals seems to be the main concern of people here.
(d) Consolidating one's own personal position and influence seems to be the main concern here.
(e) The dominant concern here is to maintain friendly relations with others.
(f) The main concern here is to develop people's competence and expertise.

From the above responses, find out the motivational climate (the most characteristic feature). The various statements represent (a) dependency, (b) extension, (c) achievement, (d) control, (e) affiliation, and (f) expert power.

2. **Organizational ethos** Eight statements given below reflect some organizational values. Rate how much the spirit shown in the statement is valued or practised in your organization (or institution). Use the following key to give your responses:

Key
Write 4 if it is highly valued or practised.
Write 3 if it is given fairly high value.
Write 2 if it is rather given low value.
Write 1 if it is given very low value (or not practised).

1. Free interaction among employees, each respecting others' feelings, competence, and sense of judgment.
2. Facing and not shying away from problems.
3. Offering moral support and help to employees and colleagues in a crisis.
4. Congruity between feelings and expressed behaviour (minimum gap between what people say and do).
5. Preventive action on most matters.
6. Taking independent action relating to their jobs.
7. Teamwork and team spirit.
8. Trying out innovative ways of solving problems.

Add all your responses. This is the score for organizational ethos (ranging between 8 and 32). Are you satisfied with it? Where would you like to improve?

3. **Organizational culture** Below are given two sets of characteristics, each containing four statements. Read the statements in each set and then rank them. Give the rank of 1 to the statement that describes your organization most closely or accurately; give the rank 2 to a good description of your organization; rank 3 to a statement not too true of your organization; and rank 4 to the statement that is least true of your organization.

Set 1
A. The dominant belief here is that things do not happen; you make them happen.
B. The belief here is that most things depend on the top management.
C. People believe that the major constraints are managerial.
D. People believe there are too many external constraints, which are difficult to fight.

Set 2
A. The leaders here expect to be implicitly obeyed.
B. The leaders here are role models for their people.
C. People are expected to follow the proper channels as per procedures that have been laid down.

What kind of culture does your organization have? (1a + 2b = Entrepreneurial; 1b + 2a = Autocratic; 1c + 2d = Technocratic; 1d + 2c = Bureaucratic)

Classroom Projects

1. Form groups of two or three and discuss what kind of organizational climate prevails in your OB class. The various groups may share their perceptions. How much commonality is there in these perceptions?
2. Using Martin's three-perspective framework, discuss in groups of two or three the different aspects of your institution/organization's culture under the three categories integrated, differentiated, fragmented.

Field Projects

1. Interview one or two people in a successful organization. What kind of culture does the organization have in terms of the power framework?
2. Interview one or two HR executives in an organization and collect ideas on how to improve the motivational climate of an organization.

Netscape's Work Culture*

INTRODUCTION

On 24 November 1998, America Online Ltd (AOL) announced the acquisition of Netscape Communications, a leading Internet browser company, for 10 billion US dollars in an all-stock transaction. With this acquisition, AOL got control over Netscape's three different businesses—Netcenter portal, Netscape browser software, and a B2B e-commerce software development division. According to the terms of the deal, Netscape's shareholders received a 0.45 share of AOL's common stock for each share they owned. The stock markets reacted positively and AOL's share value rose by 5 per cent just after the announcement. Once shareholders and regulatory authorities approved the deal, Netscape's CEO James Barksdale was supposed to join AOL's board.

Many analysts felt that this acquisition would help AOL get an edge over Microsoft, the software market leader, in the Web browser market. Steve Case, chairman and CEO of AOL, remarked, 'By acquiring Netscape, we will be able to both broaden and deepen our relationships with business partners who need additional level of infrastructure support, and provide more value and convenience for the Internet consumers.'

However, a certain section of analysts doubted whether AOL's management would accept Netscape's casual and independent culture. Moreover, they were worried that this deal may lead to a reduction in Netscape's workforce, the key strength of the company. A former Netscape employee commented, 'People at Netscape were nervous about the implications of AOL buying us.' Allaying these fears, in an address to Netscape employees, Case said, 'Maybe you joined the company because it was a cool company. We are not changing any of that. We want to run this as an independent culture.'

In spite of assurances by Case, it was reported that people at Netscape were asked to change the way they worked. In July 1999, Netscape employees were asked to leave if they did not like the new management. By late 1999, most of the key employees, who had been associated with Netscape for many years, had left. Barksdale left to set up his own venture capital firm, taking along with him former chief financial officer, Peter Currie. Marc Andreessen stayed with AOL as chief technology officer till September 1999, when he left to start his own company, Loudcloud. Mike Homer, who ran the Netcenter portal, left the company while he was on a sabbatical.

*This case was written by D. Sirisha under the direction of Vivek Gupta, ICFAI Center for Management Research (ICMR). Slightly abridged and modified version reproduced with permission of ICFAI Center for Management Research (ICMR), Hyderabad, India.

Analysts remarked that Netscape's ability to respond quickly to market requirements was one of the main reasons for its success. The ability to introduce new versions of products in a very short span of time had made the company stand apart from thousands of start-up dotcom companies that were set up during that period. Analysts said that Netscape's culture, which promoted innovation and experimentation, enabled it to adapt quickly to changing market conditions. They also said that the company's enduring principle 'Netscape Time' (see Exhibit I) had enabled it to make so many product innovations very quickly.

NETSCAPE'S CULTURE

Netscape promoted a casual, flexible, and independent culture. Employees were not bound by rigid schedules and policies and were free to come and go as they pleased. They were even allowed to work from home. The company promoted an environment of equality—everyone was encouraged to contribute his opinions. This was also evident in the company's cubicle policy. Everyone, including Barksdale, worked in a cubicle.

Independence and hands-off management were important aspects of Netscape's culture. There was no dress code at Netscape. So employees were free to wear whatever they wanted. Barksdale laid down only one condition, 'You must come to work dressed.' The company promoted experimentation and did not require employees to seek anyone's approval for trying out new ideas. For example, Patrick O'Hare, who managed Netscape's internal human resources website, was allowed to make changes to any page on the site without anyone's approval.

Netscape's management reposed a high degree of trust in its employees, which translated into empowerment and lack of bureaucracy. Beal, a senior employee said, 'Most organizations lose employees because they don't give them enough opportunities to try new things, take risks and make mistakes. People stay here because they have space to operate.' Realising that some experiments do fail, Netscape did not punish employees for ideas that did not work out. However, to maintain discipline at work, employees were made accountable for their decisions. They were also expected to give sound justifications for their actions.

Job rotation was another important feature of Netscape's culture. By doing so, the company helped its employees learn about new roles and new projects in the company. For example, Tim Kaiser, a software engineer, worked on four different projects in his first year of employment. The company believed in letting its staff take up new jobs—whether it was a new project in the same department or a new project in another department. Moreover, related experience was not a requirement for job rotation. Netscape played a proactive role in identifying new positions for its employees inside the company.

Employees were offered a wide range of training options and an annual tuition reimbursement of US $6,000. This opportunity to expand their skills on the job was valued by all employees. The company also helped employees learn about the functioning of other departments. There were quarterly 'all-hands' meetings in which senior managers of different departments gave presentations on their strategies. These efforts created a sense of community among employees. An employee remarked, 'They really try to keep us informed so we feel like we are involved with the whole company.'

Netscape offered a wide range of on-campus services to its employees. The standard package of health and vision benefit included medical benefits, vision care, life insurance, income protection, disability benefits, business travel accident insurance, vacation, paid holidays, 401(k) retirement savings plan, employee stock purchase plan (ESPP), tuition assistance program, Hyatt Legal, employee services, employee assistance programme (EAP), Concierge Service, onsite services, ClubNet, child and elder care referral service, and credit unions and banking. Netscape also offered a 'Total Health and Productivity' plan. The on-campus services programme was introduced through an agreement with a San Francisco-based service provider, LesConcierges. Under the programme, employees were able to get some of their routine work done, like dry cleaning, paying bills, getting the oil changed in their automobiles, etc. They could also consult a dentist or even have a massage. The programme also helped employees to plan for holidays as well as order gifts. Sick children of employees were also looked after at a child-care facility near the campus for US $10 a day.

Since employees worked for long hours, Netscape gave them paid vacations. Employees were given a 6-week paid sabbatical after the completion of 4 years of full-time employment. Incentives were given to employees at all levels, not just senior employees. Employees earned bonuses on the basis of individual or group performance. Senior executives were entitled to bonuses in the range of 1–30 per cent of their annual salaries. There was also an annual company-wide bonus plan based on revenues per employee and customer satisfaction figures. Employees also qualified for bonuses, based on their manager's discretion, for specific projects/assignments.

Netscape developed innovative methods of reducing employee stress and preventing them from shifting to rival companies. The company was one of the pioneers in introducing the 'canines-in-the-cubicle' policy, which allowed employees to bring their dogs to work. The company believed that this policy increased productivity by reducing stress. The company also felt that pets were good icebreakers for shy workers and that they forced employees to take breaks from their work.

Another element of Netscape's success was its quick recruitment process. The company's employees strength had increased from 2 to 330 in just 15 months between April 1994 and July 1995. The company attracted promising students, fresh out of college, by offering them a lot of incentives, including beach parties, free clothes, signing-on bonuses, and free computers. Once they joined, to keep up morale, employees were offered stock options, which translated into huge profits when the company performed well. Netscape launched an aggressive recruitment campaign: it went to some of the most popular campuses like UC Berkley, MIT, Stanford, Cornell, Michigan, and Carnegie Mellon in the US.

Netscape's efforts to build a flexible and supportive culture seemed to have motivated employees and made them highly productive. According to an analyst, employee retention is the key to success in the IT industry. Compared to the industry attrition rate of 30 per cent, Netscape's attrition rate was 20 per cent. Netscape's management believed that more than the pay check, employees were interested in meaningful work, independence, flexibility, and a desire to learn on the job. Tim Garmager, principal of the Human Resources Strategies Group at Deloitte & Touche LLP in Chicago, confirmed this belief: 'There is less emphasis on pay today than ever. In today's job market, employers need to look closely not only at the benefits they offer but at the culture they engender.'

SETBACK

After the acquisition, AOL planned to integrate Netscape's Web browser products and Netcenter portal site with its Interactive Services Group. The company created a Netscape Enterprise Group in alliance with Sun Microsystems to develop software products ranging from basic web Servers and messaging products to e-commerce applications. However, overlapping technologies and organizational red tape slowed down the process of integration.

Within a year of the acquisition, Netscape browser's market share fell from 73 per cent to 36 per cent. Andreessen, who had joined AOL as chief technology officer, resigned only after 6 months on the job. His departure triggered a mass exodus of software engineering talent from Netscape. Soon after, engineers from Netscape joined Silicon Valley start-ups like Accept.com, Tellme Networks, Apogee Venture Group, and ITIXS. Former Netscape vice president of technology Mike McCue and product manager Angus Davis founded Tellme Networks. They brought with them John Giannandrea. As chief technologist and principal engineer of the browser group, John Giannandrea was involved with every Navigator release from the first beta of 1.0 in 1994 to the launch of 4.5 version in October 1998.

Ramanathan Guha, one of Netscape's most senior engineers, left a 4-million-dollar salary at AOL to join Epinions.com. He was soon joined by Lou Montulli and Aleksander Totic, two of Netscape's six founding engineers. Other Netscape employees helped start Responsys. Some employees joined Accept.com and others AuctionWatch. Spark PR was staffed almost entirely by former Netscape PR employees.

Market watchers were surprised and worried about this exodus of Netscape employees. Some of them felt that the mass exodus might have been caused by monetary considerations. Most of the employees at Netscape had stock options. Once the acquisition was announced, the value of those options rose significantly. David Yoffie, a Harvard Business School professor said, 'When AOL's stock went up, the stock of most of the creative people was worth a fortune.' Most of them encashed their options and left the company.

But some analysts believed that there were other serious reasons for the exodus. Netscape employees always perceived themselves as an aggressive team of revolutionaries who could change the world. Before resigning from AOL, Jamie Zawinski, the twentieth person hired at Netscape, said, 'When we started this company, we were out to change the world. We were the ones who actually did it. When you see URLs on grocery bags, on billboards, on the sides of trucks, at the end of movie credits just after the studio logos—that was us, we did that. We put the Internet in the hands of normal people. We kick-started a new communications medium. We changed the world.' Another ex-employee said, 'We really believed in the vision and had a great feeling about our company.' But the merger with AOL reduced them to a small part of a big company, with slow-moving culture.

Some employees felt that AOL was more interested in the Netscape's brand name. An ex-Netscape executive said, 'AOL always turned its nose up at technology— what Netscape was trying to do. The opportunity AOL had was to make Netscape the technology arm of AOL. As rich of a resource as Netscape was for technology, equally notable is at AOL the lack of that resource. AOL had a hard time understanding how to best tap into it.' They felt that AOL had just paid lip service to Netscape's technology by naming Andreessen its chief technology officer. According to Rob Enderle, vice president of Giga Information, 'All Andreessen got was a corner. All they wanted was Web presence … They got the [Netscape] name, they just had to figure out how to get rid of the people.'

AOL's corporate philosophy was also completely different from the Netscape philosophy. That difference made many employees feel that they were working in the wrong place. So most of the engineers left and Netscape was transformed from a technology to a media company. Zawinski said, 'AOL is about centralisation and control of content. Everything that is good about the Internet, everything that differentiates it from television, is about empowerment of the individual. I don't want to be a part of an effort that could result in the elimination of all that.'

Would Netscape have survived on its own had AOL not bought it in 1998, when the company was reeling under huge losses? The ex-employees of Netscape did not care to answer that question. They only knew that their old company and its culture had gone forever. An analyst remarked, 'Unfortunately, AOL is a good technology company that doesn't know what to do with good technology. It's sad, what they did to Netscape.'

Exhibit I   *Netscape Time*

Netscape Time was Netscape's most enduring principle. It was about the speed at which the employees worked and delivered new products. It concerned the mindset of employees rather than the business model of the company. Netscape Time had six core principles:

The first principle was 'fast enough never is'. Ever since its inception, Netscape maintained a lightening speed in whatever it did. Analysts felt that the company could move quickly because it knew what it wanted. It hired programmers from the best schools and from companies like Oracle, Silicon Graphics, etc. The company wanted them to get used to Netscape's code-writing culture.

'The paranoid predator' was the second principle. Netscape knew that even a predator could become a prey. The company's management believed that their role was to instil urgency at all levels. They always portrayed Netscape as a start-up that had to compete with industry giants like Microsoft and Oracle.

The third principle was 'all work, all the time'. Netscape's employees seemed to be habituated to non-stop work. For example, to launch the company's first product, employees worked round-the-clock for 8 months. Even at 1 a.m., there were employees to give ideas, talk code, or discuss a problem. Jim Sha, general manager, worked 11 hours a day at the office, went home for dinner and then came back to office and worked till late night.

'Just enough management' was the fourth principle. Netscape seemed to consciously under-manage. Neither Clark nor Andreessen played major roles in the management. Andreessen said, 'If you over manage software, the result is paralysis.'

Another principle of Netscape Time was doing things 'four times faster'. Netscape described Netscape Time as 'turning out new product releases four times faster than the competition'. In less than 9 months, Netscape launched three versions of its browser as well as servers.

The last and most important aspect of Netscape Time was 'Web squared.' Netscape placed Web at the heart of its operations. Andreessen believed that 'worse is better', and released usable software quickly, without waiting for perfection. He believed in using the Web to access the source of perfection. The company did not use any retail outlets or resellers. Interested users could download an 'evaluation copy' from the Internet. A fully supported version of the software was later sent to interested users. This helped increase the company's interaction with the customers. Their feedback was utilised to design the next version.

Questions for Discussion

1. Analyse and describe the culture of Netscape and comment on its strengths and shared assumptions. How far do you think the culture contributed to Netscape's success as a leading Internet browser company?
2. Andeerssen's exit from Netscape triggered a mass exodus of software engineering talent from the company. Did the cultural incompatibility of AOL and Netscape cause the mass exodus of key persons in a short time? Were there any other reasons for this exodus?
3. What could AOL have done to retain Netscape employees? Did AOL miss an opportunity to make Netscape the technology arm of AOL?

NOTES AND REFERENCES

1. Pareek, U. (2002). *Training instruments for HRD & OD*, Chapter 98. New Delhi: Tata McGraw-Hill.
2. Litwin, G.H. and R.A. Stringer (1968). *Motivational Organizational Climate*. Cambridge, MA: Harvard University Press.
3. Likert, Rensis (1967). *The Human Organisations*. New York: McGraw-Hill.
4. Litwin, G.H. and R.A. Stringer (1968). *Motivational Organizational Climate*. Cambridge, MA: Harvard University Press.
5. Pareek, U. (2002). *Training instruments for HRD & OD*, Chapter 96. New Delhi: Tata McGraw-Hill.
6. *Ibid.*, for review of these studies.
7. Khandwalla, P.N. (1992). *Excellent Corporate Turnaround*. New Delhi: Sage.
8. Schein, E.H. (1985). *Organisational Culture and Leadership*, p. 9. San Francisco: Jossey-Bass.
9. Sathe, V. and E.J. Davidson (2000). 'Towards a new conceptualization of culture change', in N.M. Ashkanasy, P.M. Celeste, and M.F. Peterson (eds), *Handbook of Organizational Culture and Climate*, pp. 279–296. New Delhi: Sage.
10. Quinn, R.E. and M.R. McGrath (1985). 'The transformation of organizational cultures: A competing values perspective', in P.J. Frost et al (eds), *Organizational Culture*. London: Sage.

11. Pareek, U. (2002). *Training instruments for HRD & OD*. New Delhi: Tata McGraw-Hill.
12. Kluckhohn, F. and F.L. Strodtbeck (1961). *Variations in Value Orientation*. Evanston, IL: Rowe Peterson.
13. Pareek, U. (2002). *Training instruments for HRD & OD*, Chapter 100. New Delhi: Tata McGraw-Hill.
14. For an analysis of this phenomenon, see Nandy, A. (1983), *The Intimate Enemy: Loss and Recovery of Identity Under Colonization*, New Delhi: Oxford University Press.
15. Hofstede, G. (1980). *Culture's Consequences: International Difference in Work-Related Values*. Beverly Hills: Sage; Hofstede, Geert (1991). *Cultures and Organizations: Software of the Mind*. New York: McGraw Hill.
16. Panda, A. and R.K. Gupta (2001). 'Understanding organizational culture: A perspective on roles of leaders', *Vikalpa*, 26(4): 3–19.
17. Martin, J. (1992). *Cultures in Organization: Three Perspectives*. Oxford: Oxford University Press.
18. Panda, A. and R.K. Gupta (2001). 'Understanding organizational culture: A perspective on roles of leaders', *Vikalpa*, 26(4): 3–19.

25
Organizational Communication

LEARNING OBJECTIVES

After studying this chapter, you will be able to
1. Define organizational communication
2. Enumerate the various goals of organizational communication
3. Explain the different forms of communication networks
4. Suggest ways of improving horizontal, vertical, and other directions of communication
5. Analyse the role and dynamics of rumours
6. Discuss the importance of external communication and ways of making it effective

Over the past years, communication has attracted increasing attention. Many problems in organizations arise because of the inadequate attention given to the organizational communication process. Organizational communication can be defined as 'the process of the flow (transmission and reception) of goal-oriented messages between sources, in a pattern, and through a medium or media'.

What has been discussed in Chapter 17 on interpersonal communication about the source, the target, and the message applies to organizational communication also. An additional element not present in interpersonal communication, as defined in Chapter 17, is the flow pattern of messages. Thus, there are seven elements in organizational communication: the transmitting source, the receiving source (the target), the transmitted message, the received message, the goal of the message, the medium or media, and the flow pattern (which is called the network). The transmitting and receiving sources are the people sending and receiving the message.

Media, as in interpersonal communication, can be verbal or non-verbal, oral or written. Verbal media can be classified using the following dimensions: whether it is oral or written, and whether it takes place in a small group or is meant for a large group (Exhibit 25.1).

Written communication is more effective in the transmission (and reception and comprehension) of cognitive messages. On the other hand, oral—especially face-to-face—communication is more effective in bringing about changes of opinions and attitudes.

Exhibit 25.1 *Different Verbal Media in Organizational Communication*

	Oral	**Written**
Small group	Conversation/telephone	Letters/memos Telex/e-mail
Large group	Lectures Meetings Radio Closed-circuit TV Teleconferencing	Circulars Newsletters Handbooks/manuals Posters/bulletin boards/e-mail

Telecommunication technology has changed the mode of meetings. Teleconferencing has become more common. People from different parts of the world can now confer without meeting each other. While this has facilitated communication, it has also affected social interactions adversely. Telecommunication is still in the early stages of development, but it has tremendous potential for the future.

GOALS OF ORGANIZATIONAL COMMUNICATION

Organizational communication has several goals.

Information sharing The main purpose of communication is to transmit information from a source to a target (individuals or groups). Various types of information are transmitted in the organization, such as policies, rules, changes, and developments in the organization. There may be a need to disseminate some information in the organization quickly, such as that pertaining to special rewards and awards given, a settlement with a union, or a major change in the organization. An effective use of information sharing is in induction of new employees: their orientation, including policies and procedures, employee benefits, etc. Information is also shared in meetings held for briefings or discussion of projects or issues concerning a group.

Feedback It is necessary to give feedback to employees on their achievements, to departments on their performance, and to the higher management on the fulfilment of goals and any difficulties encountered. Communication of feedback makes it possible to take corrective measures and make the necessary adjustments, and motivates people to develop challenging and realistic plans.

Control The management information system (MIS) is well known as a control mechanism. Information is transmitted to ensure that the plans are being carried out according to the original design. Communication thus helps in ensuring such control and serves as a monitoring mechanism. Ensuring that critical information reaches people at the appropriate level in the organization helps in directing action and events properly.

Influence Information is power. One purpose of communication is to influence people. This is very clear in the case of communication by a trainer to a training group. The main purpose there is to influence the participants. Similarly, the higher the management level, the more important is the influencing role of the manager. The manager communicates to create a good climate, the right attitudes, and congenial working relationships. All these are examples of influencing.

Problem solving In many cases, communication aims to solve problems. Communication between the management and the union on various issues takes the form of negotiation aimed at finding a solution. Group meetings are held to brainstorm alternative solutions to a problem. Such communication can take place in small groups (dyads or triads) or large groups.

Decision making Several kinds of communication are needed for arriving at a decision—for example, exchange of information, of views, of available alternatives, of favourable or unfavourable points for each alternative. Communication helps a great deal in decision making. It plays an important role in the sharing of alternative solutions and exchanges of views on various matters.

Interviews are used for decision making in selection, performance management, career planning, etc.

Facilitating change The effectiveness of a change introduced in an organization depends to a large extent on the clarity and spontaneity of communication. Communication between consultants and managers, between managers and subordinates, and between peers helps in uncovering the difficulties in a change planned, and in taking corrective action.

Group building Communication helps in building relationships. Even under conditions of severe conflicts, good relations can be restored only if the communication process is continued. If communication breaks down, the group may disintegrate. Communication provides the necessary lubrication for the proper functioning of a group. The communication of feelings, concerns, and support is particularly important in this context.

Gate keeping Communication helps to build linkages between the organization and the outside world. The organization can use its environment to increase its effectiveness. It can also influence the environment, the government, its clients, its resource systems, etc. Communication plays a critical role in this respect.

COMMUNICATION NETWORKS

Organizational communication has a pattern of flow or a network. In an organization with several sources and targets (people at various levels), the messages transmitted and received may adopt a consistent pattern. Such patterns are very useful and may be good indicators of organizational culture, climate, and ethos.

Extensive research has been done on communication patterns. This has come to be known as communication network research. Most such studies have involved small groups under controlled conditions.

A network is a system of several points of communication for the purpose of decision making. In most network research, a small group (usually of five people) is given a task to perform and the group functions under controlled conditions of communication. The direction of communication is variously controlled in different networks. The effect of each network on performance and satisfaction is then studied.

The general conclusion arrived at from studies done for over two decades seems to be that wheel and all-channel networks are the most effective and the circle the least effective for simple tasks. However, the circle gives the highest satisfaction to participants. The peripheral members of the wheel are the least satisfied communicators. The findings of other studies on the effects of various networks on the three variables—performance, satisfaction, and effective organization for the task—showed that wheel groups got organized fastest, all-channel groups took longer to get organized although they eventually performed as well, and wheel groups had the most difficulty in getting organized.

Dubin[1] applied the findings of communication network research to organizations and suggested 'linkage systems'. These are given in Exhibit 25.2. He used the three main linkage patterns, serial, radial, and circular, to develop a number of linkage systems through their vertical or horizontal positions and combinations. The serial is the simplest system. In a vertical position, it is a chain of commands; in the horizontal position, a work-flow system operates (e.g., an assembly line). Similarly, in a vertical position, radial linkage gives coordination or direction, while in the horizontal position, service and staff functions are enabled.

Communication network research has indicated that efficiency and satisfaction are positively related to the number of links in the network and inversely to the number of links through the centre. These findings have significant implications for the organization of groups and units. The more opportunities are provided to the various members of a unit to communicate with each other for specific tasks (with a minimum coordination), the higher the efficiency and satisfaction are likely to be. However, this relationship will depend on several other factors, including the nature of a task. For simple, routine tasks, the wheel pattern seems to be the most efficient.

All these findings are from network studies done under laboratory conditions. Communication network research has been done on large natural groups also. Different types of communication networks are useful at different stages of adoption—a wheel type at the trial stage, a chain type at the deliberation stage, and an unfinished-star type at the evaluation stage.[2]

Exhibit 25.2 *Linkage Systems in Organizations*

Serial linkage	Radial linkage

Levels of authority

Work flow

Coordination or direction

Service, control, and reporting

Circular linkage	Radial and serial linkage

Representative governing board

Coordination or direction of related units

Service, control, and reporting among related units

Radial and circular linkage	Serial–radial–serial linkage

Representative advisory board

Typical line organization

DIRECTIONS OF COMMUNICATION

Organizational communication may be vertical, horizontal, or circular. Vertical communication may be either from the senior levels to the junior levels (downward) or vice versa (upward). Circular communication in organizations is very rare.

Sometimes communication may be bi-directional, messages being exchanged between two sources.

Exhibit 25.3 *Purposes and Mechanisms of Different Directions of Communication*

Purposes	Mechanisms
Downward communication	
Diffusion of routine information	Circulars, bulletin boards, wall magazines
Diffusion of procedural information	Circulars, handbooks, manuals
Socialisation	Special publications, lectures, meetings
Providing job-related information	Conversations
Feedback	Conversations, memos
Employee development	Conversations, group meetings
Upward communication	
Control	Periodic information, special reports
Feedback	Questionnaires, exit interviews
Problem solving	Periodic meetings, grievance procedures
Ideas for improvement	Suggestion box, exit interviews
Catharsis and group building	Review meetings (mecom)
Horizontal communication	
Experience sharing	Joint forum
Problem solving	Task force, problem clinics
Coordination	Periodic meetings
External communication	
Image building	Annual reports, balance sheets, brochure advertisements
Credibility building	Balance sheets, correspondence
Influencing	Conferences, dialogues

Here, mainly three directions of intra-organization communication are discussed: downward, upward, and horizontal. A fourth type of organizational communication is between the organization and the external environment. Each of these types of communication has its purpose and relevant mechanisms are used, or can be used, to make communication effective for those purposes. The purposes of the various types of communication and the relevant mechanisms are summarised in Exhibit 25.3.

Downward Communication

Communication from the higher to the lower levels of an organization may serve several purposes. Six purposes are suggested in Exhibit 25.3.

The first two relate to the diffusion of information. Such communications are quite frequent in most organizations. Information is disseminated through several media or mechanisms: circulars, bulletin boards, handbooks, manuals, etc.

The purpose of downward communication may also be to give job-related information. Often, routine information of what is expected from the job and what facilities are available are communicated thus. The rationale of the job (why the employee is doing the job, what contribution it is making to a larger task and to the organization, and how important it is) is usually not communicated.

Feedback to the employee on performance and ways in which he or she can learn further and improve can contribute to the employee's development. The purpose of feedback is a very important one. Effective managers must therefore spend some time with every employee on this process. The main mechanisms used are face-to-face discussion (here termed 'conversation') and written communication. An important application of communication in developing employees is performance feedback and employee counselling.

The most neglected aspect is the communication of the values, ethos, and ideology of the organization. The main purpose of such communication would be to educate the employees in the organizational ethos and values. This can be done by a special induction policy for new employees, helping them to meet other employees in groups and giving them written material that they may read. The purpose should not be to brainwash them but to help them to be clear in their minds about the values and ethos of the organization. This may help develop an integrated organization of which the employees may be proud. They may also communicate similar messages about the organization when they meet outsiders.

One problem in downward communication is that of message distortion. One study of 100 business firms reported a very high degree of loss of information in downward communication. Between the boards of directors and the levels below, the loss in terms of the original information was as shown in Exhibit 25.4.

Exhibit 25.4   Loss of Information in Downward Communication

Levels	Loss
Vice presidents	37%
General supervisors	44%
Plant managers	60%
General foremen	70%
Workers	80%

Exhibit 25.5 gives some down-to-earth suggestions for downward communication.[3]

Exhibit 25.5   Downward Communication

1. Ensure every employee receives a copy of the strategic plan, which includes the organization's mission, vision, values statement, strategic goals, and strategies about how those goals will be reached.
2. Ensure every employee receives an employee handbook that contains all up-to-date personnel policies.
3. Develop a basic set of procedures for how routine tasks are conducted and include them in the standard operating manual.
4. Ensure every employee has a copy of their job description and the organization chart.
5. Regularly hold management meetings (at least every 2 weeks), even if there is nothing pressing to report. If you hold meetings only when you believe there is something to report, then communications will occur only when you have something to say—communications will be one way and the organization will suffer. Have meetings anyway, if only to establish and affirm the communication that things are of a status that there are no immediate problems.

Exhibit 25.5 (*Contd*)

> 6. Hold full staff meetings every month to report how the organization is doing, major accomplishments, concerns, announcements about staff, etc.
> 7. Leaders and managers should have face-to-face contact with employees at least once a week. Even if the organization is over 20 employees (large for a non-profit), management should stroll by once in a while.
> 8. Regularly hold meetings to celebrate major accomplishments. This helps employees perceive what is important, gives them a sense of direction and fulfillment, and lets them know that leadership is on top of things.
> 9. Ensure all employees receive yearly performance reviews (including their goals for the year), updated job descriptions, accomplishments, needs for improvement, and plans to help the employees accomplish the improvements. If the non-profit has sufficient resources (a realistic concern), develop a career plan with the employee, too.

Upward Communication

Most communication in organizations is downward. Upward communication is rarer. Upward communication may be used for several purposes. The first two purposes shown in Exhibit 25.3 are control and monitoring of an action. A popular method for this purpose is the survey, used to identify problems and get feedback that helps in taking action. Such information can also be collected through exit interviews to find out what problems people face and how they feel about their jobs.

Upward communication can also be used for solving problems and generating ideas. The mechanisms for transmitting ideas include the well-known suggestion box and grievance committees. In many cases, the proper use of such methods increases people's involvement in work and results in excellent ideas being put forward and implemented.

This leads to the last purpose, namely, group building. Special review meetings can be organized to build up a better rapport between the employees and managers. In BHEL, Bhopal, a special mechanism has been developed—Management and Employee Communication (acronym mecom). These are periodic meetings in which employees express their feelings and give feedback to senior managers. Evaluation of the workings of mecom has indicated the great success of this experiment. The case study at the end of this chapter gives details.

Organizations use different mechanisms to encourage upward communication. Some of these are suggestion boxes, use of e-mails, grievance collection procedures, an open-door policy, and open meetings.

Exhibit 25.6 gives some practical suggestions for upward communication.[4]

Exhibit 25.6 *Upward Communication*

> 1. Ensure all employees give regular status reports to their supervisors. Include a section for what they did last week, will do next week, and any actions/issues to be addressed.
> 2. Ensure all supervisors meet one-on-one, at least once a month, with their employees to discuss how it is going, hear any current concerns from the employee, etc. Even if the meeting is informal, it cultivates an important relationship between the supervisor and the employee.

Exhibit 25.6 (*Contd*)

> 3. Use management and staff meetings to solicit feedback. Ask how it is going. Do a round-table approach to hear from each person.
> 4. Act on feedback from others. Write it down. Get back to it, if only to say you cannot do anything about the reported problem or suggestion, etc.
> 5. Respect the 'grapevine'. It is probably one of the most prevalent and reliable forms of communications. Major 'movements' in the organization usually first appear when employees feel it safe to venture their feelings or opinions to peers.

Horizontal Communication

Horizontal communication is necessary to develop a collaborative and proactive culture in an organization. People communicate with others at their own level, in their own departments or other departments, to solve problems and to share experiences. Devices such as problem clinics and task forces are used for this purpose.

A problem clinic is conducted by people concerned with a problem to diagnose and generate alternative solutions. A task force is constituted of persons from different departments or different sections to work on a particular problem over a length of time and make recommendations on solving the problem.

External Communication

An organization has communication interfaces with the external environment as well. One of the objectives of an organization is to make an impact, to be known for something unique. Organizations communicate with the outside world through advertisements via mass media, annual reports, balance sheets, and brochures specially prepared for this purpose. This helps in image building. More and more professional attention is being given to the preparation of the chairman's annual report. Recent annual reports from various companies—Hindustan Lever, Punjab National Bank, Larsen & Toubro—are interesting in this regard.

Communication with customers, vendors, suppliers, etc. has also become increasingly important. Many service organizations are conducting regular communication programmes with their customers. Many banks are organizing meets with cocktails and dinners for their 'valued' customers. Such methods have very high pay-offs for the organization. There are several purposes behind such meets: to communicate to the customers that they are valued, to give them information about new products and new services, to identify areas for further improvement of products and services, and to invite ideas and suggestions for new initiatives and/or projects.

For instance, the chairman of a large bakery in Japan installed a toll-free telephone for customers to send messages. As soon as he came to his office in the morning he listened to all the messages received the previous day. One morning, he heard a child's message. She did not give her name or telephone number, but said that she could not eat any of the pastries because she was allergic to the pastries made at the bakery. The chairman asked the R&D department to investigate the matter and prepare a cake that would be free of allergens. After the new product was developed, it was released with a big ad in the papers, dedicating the product to an unknown child who stimulated the company to work on the product! The sales of the bakery suddenly increased a great deal.

An organization also communicates with the government, financial institutions, and large clients. The main purpose of such communication is to influence these systems and secure the maximum advantage for the organization. The chief executive of an organization plays the external affairs role, which is quite critical. Some organizations have special roles, like director – external relations, principal public relations officer, business intelligence officer, etc., to get the necessary information for taking quick decisions on expansion, diversification, etc.

DYNAMICS OF COMMUNICATION

More recently, the field of organizational communication has moved from acceptance of mechanistic models (e.g., information moving from a sender to a receiver) to a study of the persistent, hegemonic, and taken-for-granted ways in which we not only use communication to accomplish certain tasks within organizational settings (e.g., public speaking), but also to study how the organizations in which we participate affect us.[5, 6]

These approaches include postmodern, critical, participatory, feminist, power/political, organic, etc. and draw from disciplines as wide-ranging as sociology, philosophy, theology, psychology, business administration, institutional management, medicine (health communication), neurology (neural nets), semiotics, anthropology, international relations, and music.

Thus the field has expanded or moved to study phenomena such as

Constitution

- How communicative behaviours construct or modify organizing processes or products
- How the organizations within which we interact affect our communicative behaviours
- Structures other than organizations that might be constituted through our communicative activity (e.g., markets, cooperatives, tribes, political parties, social movements)

Narrative

- How do group members employ narrative to acculturate/initiate/indoctrinate new members?
- Do organizational stories act on different levels?
- Are different narratives purposively invoked to achieve specific outcomes, or are there specific roles of the 'organizational storyteller'?
- If so, are stories told by the storyteller received differently than those told by others in the 'organization'?

Identity

- Who do we see ourselves to be, in terms of our organizational affiliations?
- How do communicative behaviours or occurrences in one or more of the organizations in which we participate effect changes in us?
- Do people who define themselves by their work–organizational membership communicate differently within the organizational setting than people who define themselves more by an avocational group?

Interrelatedness of Organizational Experiences

- How do our communicative interactions in one organizational setting affect our communicative actions in other organizational settings?
- How do the phenomenological experiences of participants in a particular organizational setting effect changes in other areas of their lives?
- When the organizational status of a member is significantly changed (e.g., by promotion or expulsion), how are other organizational memberships affected?

Power

- How does the use of particular communicative practices within an organizational setting reinforce or alter the various interrelated power relationships within the setting?
- Do taken-for-granted organizational practices work to fortify the dominant hegemonic narrative? Do individuals resist/confront these practices? If yes, through what actions/agencies, and to what effects?
- Do status changes in an organization (e.g., promotions, demotions, restructuring, financial/social strata changes) change communicative behaviour?
- Are there criteria employed by organizational members to differentiate between 'legitimate' (i.e., endorsed by the formal organizational structure) and 'illegitimate' (i.e., opposed by or unknown to the formal power structure)?
- Are there 'pretenders' or 'usurpers' who employ these communicative behaviours?
- When are they successful?

Rumours—Distortion in Communication

Rumours play a critical role in communication during periods of stress and unrest. A rumour is usually a belief that is passed on as an item of information from one person to the other person, without verification of the relevant evidence. A thorough study of rumours suggested two conditions for rumour-mongering: importance of a topic to people and lack of correct and definite information about it.[7] The study proposed that intensity (incidence) and diffusion (rapidity and expansiveness) are multiplicative functions of the two conditions.

Chorus added a third factor, critical sense. This is the tendency to take several factors into account and make decisions after reflection, on the basis of data or verified information. He proposed that rumour could be expressed by the following formula:

$$R \sim I \times a \times \frac{1}{C}$$

This is to say that rumour (R) depends directly on importance (I) and ambiguity (a) and inversely on critical sense (C). Rumours become weak if the critical sense is high in people. This formula has interesting implications for organizations wishing to minimise rumours and cope with them.

Transparency seems to be an effective way of dealing with rumour. In denial of rumour, honesty and appropriateness had an additive effect, such that the denial was most successful in reducing belief when the source was perceived as high on both honesty and appropriateness.[8]

SUMMARY

Organizational communication is the flow of goal-directed messages between sources, in a pattern, through some media. There are several goals for organizational communication, from information sharing to facilitating change. Several media are employed in organizational communication, which follows several patterns in its flow.

Organizational communication is both internal (multidirectional) as well external. The main problem in communication is distortion, reflected in the rumours, which need to be managed.

GLOSSARY

communication network the process of the flow (transmission and reception) of goal-oriented messages between sources, in a pattern, and through a medium or media

rumour usually a belief that is passed on as an item of information from one person to another without verification of the relevant evidence

EXERCISES

Concept Review Questions

1. What is the definition of organizational communication?
2. What are the goals of organizational communication?
3. How do media affect the quality of communication?
4. What contributes to efficiency and satisfaction of communication in communication networks?
5. Why is upward communication necessary and how can we improve it?
6. Why do rumours spread and how can we minimise them?

Critical Thinking Questions

1. Take the prospectus/handbook of your institution and identify its strengths and weaknesses from the point of view of external communication of the institution.

2. What different mechanisms are available to students to communicate with the administration of your institution?

Classroom Projects

1. In groups of three, discuss and develop effective ways of external communication to ensure better placement for students.
2. In small groups, develop ideas for improving communication between students and teachers.

Field Projects

1. Analyse balance sheets issued publicly by two contrasting (high and average performance) companies. Do you find any differences?
2. Interview two customers at a bank. Find out which aspects of communication they like and why. Also collect ideas on how communication can be improved.

Management and Employee Communication at BHEL*

The Bhopal unit of BHEL set up with British aid had started out with excellent systems, only to find itself sliding into a bureaucratic culture by the early seventies. A consultant from the UK spent a month at the plant and advised the management against any organizational development (OD) effort as, in his view, the people were not ready for it. So the organization development exercise, which should have started somewhere in 1974, got postponed till September 1976, when a human resource committee (HRC) comprising members of the plant management was formed. It organized a workshop of line managers to analyse the major problems facing the organization. The workshop concluded that labour productivity was falling because of two reasons: withdrawal of the incentive scheme and the communication gap that existed between the management and the employees.

Taking off from this perception of the line managers, an all-out effort was made to seek the views of a larger cross-section of employees. A consultant from the Delhi University interacted with groups of workers, supervisors, labour union representatives, executives, and top management to elicit their perceptions about major problem areas and about the strengths and weaknesses of the organization. On the positive side, there was a strong feeling of belonging and pride in the organization, backed by fellow feeling in the township and confidence in the capabilities of the workforce. The complaints related to lack of opportunity for free expression, 'one-sided downward communication', lack of leadership and teamwork among the seniors. A lot of hostile feelings towards management were thrown up by the interactions, and employees wondered whether the feedback process 'could lead to any kind of improvement'.

It was obvious that all groups were focussing on the human side of the organization and so a major intervention was planned, which was destined to change the management–worker interface in the Bhopal unit of BHEL.

Besides concentrating on training and development as a mechanism for raising quality awareness and increasing managerial effectiveness, management–employee communication meetings (mecoms) were started on a regular basis from August 1978. It was decided that the meetings would be held in rotation every month, with workers, supervisors, and executives.

Starting with small groups of about 125 participants, these meetings soon grew in numbers (today there are about 700 participants in a mecom) and an open-house atmosphere came to be established.

*From *Human Resource Development: The Indian Experience* by D.M. Silvera, New India Publications, New Delhi, 1988, pp. 112–115. Reproduced with permission.

In the early days the atmosphere was quite tense, with the executive director of the plant, the general managers and heads of department being subjected to the pent up feelings of anger and frustration that had been bottled up for years. Questions were raised about the promotion policy, dearness allowance differences between supervisors and executives, delegation of powers, and so on. The management's patience and understanding paid dividends, because the outpourings led to a catharsis and the atmosphere at the meetings began to change gradually. The clarifications and explanations on the issues raised at the mecoms were given wide publicity.

The mecoms soon began to fulfil the intended objective of providing 'a platform for mutual sharing and developing better understanding between management and employees'. Vital organizational issues like the bane of overtime, ineffectiveness of incentive schemes, etc. were raised. mecoms also helped in smoother implementation of decisions, because the intent and purpose was first shared with the employees and their reactions analysed before implementing a decision.

In their present format, the agenda of mecoms involves sharing of information by the management through a presentation on themes like quality, productivity, growth plans, welfare, performance review, and so on. After this it is open house, with the discussion on the presentation freewheeling into questions on any issue that may be agitating the minds of the participants. Any specific information sought by participants, e.g., on the promotion policy, incentive scheme, feedback survey data, etc., is provided at subsequent mecoms.

Today the meetings are marked by an atmosphere of cordiality and bonhomie. The tea session that follows makes for even more informal interactions between the management and those who could not get a turn at the mike earlier. There is a widespread awareness of the functionality of such meetings. Individual grievances and bargainable issues that predominated in the earlier meetings have been replaced by problems of work groups and of the entire organization. The managers note them for corrective action.

Mecoms have indeed emerged as a bridgehead of mutual understanding and appreciation, trust and confidence through very candid, open, and even blunt talk. As BHEL's A. Madhava Rao, director – Personnel, puts it, 'There have been constructive and creative suggestions from the employees. The acceptance of suggestions, ideas, and problems brought up before mecoms with an open mind by the chief executive have generated trust and confidence in the management's sense of fair play and justice. Several pressing problems of the unit have been tackled effectively in this spirit. These include stopping of overtime, change in shift timings, and introduction of a new reward scheme for increasing productivity. Employees actively come forward with suggestions for capacity utilisation, production planning, after sales service, human relations, etc., many of which spell a big difference to productivity of the plant.'

The mecoms at Bhopal are not being held in isolation. This OD exercise is backed by feedback surveys to assess changes perceived by the employees and to obtain their perception about the health of the organization. The human resource committee summed up the thrust areas through a slogan coined in the early eighties: Achievement through participation.

The OD department was formed in 1981. Programmes were held to reinforce team building, to put across the concept of task forces, and so on. Thereafter task forces were constituted and their functioning constantly reviewed. OD workshops were held for senior managers on organizational excellence through achievement motivation. Simultaneously, the mecoms took up the theme of 'excellence through human development'.

Questions for Discussion

1. What is the concept of mecom?
2. What were the objectives of mecoms?
3. Describe the evolution of mecoms.
4. What contributed to the success of mecoms?
5. What more can be done to make such mechanisms effective?

NOTES AND REFERENCES

1. Dubin, R. (1959). 'Stability in human organizations', in M. Hasne (ed.), *Modern Organization Theory*, pp. 218–253. New York: Wiley.
2. Pareek, Udai and Y.P. Singh (1969). 'Communication nets in the sequential adoption process', *Indian Journal of Psychology*, 66: 33–35.
3. Basics in Internal Organizational Communications by Carter McNamara, 2007, www.managementhelp.org/mrktng/org_cmm.htm.
4. Basics in Internal Organizational Communications by Carter McNamara, 2007, www.managementhelp.org/mrktng/org_cmm.htm.
5. wikipedia.org/wiki/Organizational_communication, April 2007.
6. For example, see Redding, W. Charles (1985), 'Stumbling Toward Identity: The Emergence of Organizational Communication as a Field of Study', in McPhee and Tompkins, *Organizational Communication: Traditional Themes and New Directions*, Thousand Oaks, CA: Sage; Gergen, Kenneth and Tojo Joseph (1996), 'Organizational Science in a Postmodern Context', *Journal of Applied Behavioral Science*, 32: 356–378.
7. Allport, G.W. and L. Postman (1947). *The Psychology of Rumour*. New York: Holt.
8. Bordia, P., N. DiFonzo, and C.A. Schultz (2000). 'Denying rumours of organizational closure: Honesty is the best policy', *Journal of Applied Social Psychology*, 11: 2309–2321.

26
Organizational Learning and the Learning Organization

LEARNING OBJECTIVES

After studying this chapter, you will be able to
1. Define organizational learning (OL) and the learning organization (LO)
2. Explain organizational learning processes
3. Identify the mechanisms of organizational learning
4. Expand the role of policy in promoting organizational learning
5. Discuss the characteristics of a learning organization

The concept of learning has traditionally been used in the context of individual persons (and animals). Recently, however, this concept has been extended to organizations, a distinction being made between individual learning and organizational learning.

WHAT IS ORGANIZATIONAL LEARNING?

Chris Argyris, using his 'theory-in-action' concept originally developed for individuals, defines organizational learning in terms of restructuring of the organizational theory-in-action. According to him, 'Organizational learning occurs when: members of the organization act as learning agents for the organization, responding to changes in the internal and external environments of the organization by detecting and correcting errors in organizational theory-in-use, and embedding the results of their enquiry in private images and shared maps of organization.'[1]

Argyris proposed the concept of qualitative learning. Contrasted with traditional learning, which he called 'single-loop' learning (involving incremental change within an existing framework), 'double-loop' learning emphasised the testing of underlying assumptions and achieving transformational change. This concept was later extended to organizations.[2]

Senge contrasts adaptive learning (solving problems in the present without examining the appropriateness of current learning behaviours) with generative learning (emphasising continuous experimentation and feedback in an ongoing examination of the way organizations define and solve problems).[3] Kolb's cyclic model of learning[4]—concrete experience, reflective observation, abstract conceptualisation, active experimentation (CE–RO–AC–AE)—has been applied to organizational learning with some modification.[5]

Several definitions of organizational learning have been proposed. Some other definitions of organizational learning are given below:

- A process of detecting and correcting error[6]
- Increased intelligence and sophistication of thought, and linked to it, increased effectiveness of behaviour[7]
- The process of improving actions through better knowledge and understanding[8]
- Encoding inferences from history into routines that guide behaviour[9]
- Building on past knowledge and experience (i.e., on memory) through shared knowledge, insights and mental models[10]
- Change in the range of the potential behaviour of an entity through its processing of information[11]
- The capacity or process within an organization to improve performance based on experience[12]
- An increased shared understanding involving the organization, its environment and the relationship between the two[13]
- The capacity (or process) within an organization to maintain or improve performance based on experience[14]

As will be evident from these definitions, the concept of organizational learning integrates both the cognitive/conceptual and the behavioural perspectives of learning. Organizational learning has been proposed by most researchers as a normative function (i.e., it is desirable for all organizations). Some authors have proposed it as a descriptive category, assuming that all organizations learn in their own way, and studied what and how they learn.[15]

Process of Organizational Learning

Organizational learning has been proposed as a development process for individuals, groups, and organizations. Three processes have been suggested at the levels of the individual (interpreting), group (integrating), and organization (institutionalising) and also the respective outputs (cognitive map, shared belief structures, and organizational structure and systems).

Organizational learning has been defined in terms of seven orientations, each being a continuum on a bi-polar scale.[16]

1. Knowledge source (internal–external)
2. Focus (product–process)
3. Documentation (personal–collective)
4. Dissemination (formal–informal)
5. Learning (adaptive–innovative)
6. Value chain (design/make–market/deliver)
7. Self-development (individual–group)

A combination of any two orientations can suggest four learning styles. This model has been applied, for instance, to healthcare systems.[17] Based on extensive study, a slightly modified eight-orientation model has been proposed:

1. Knowledge source (internal–external)

2. Focus (content–process)
3. Knowledge reserve (individual–public)
4. Dissemination (formal–informal)
5. Knowledge focus (improvement of existing–development of new services)
6. Learning time (immediate needs–long-term use)
7. Learning focus (individual performance–group performance)
8. Learning mode (practice–reflective activities)

An instrument called the Learning Advantage has been prepared incorporating these orientations.

Huber identified four constructs of organizational learning, implying sequential stages: knowledge acquisition, information distribution, information interpretation, and organizational memory.[19]

Although Schein drew attention to the need for organizations to learn at a faster rate,[20] Guns has developed the concept of a faster learning organization (FLO).[21] He defines an FLO as 'an organization that fuses hard assessment of its reality with unbounded conviction about its future into a stimulating climate for learning and performance'. He suggests five key characteristics of such organizations:

1. Openness to exploration (learning)
2. Competitive challenge (stimulating leadership; supporting challenge and change)
3. Clear and compelling vision (commitment of resources to the vision)
4. Entrepreneurialism/Adventure (dedicated fast learners)
5. Opportunities to spin off innovations

Here we propose a normative concept of organizational learning as a continuum from no learning (insensitive or closed to experiences and realities) to full learning (effective use of experiences for action). We define organizational learning as 'the process by which an organization acquires, retains, and uses inputs for development, resulting in an enhanced capacity for continued self-learning and self-renewal'.

The above definition has five main elements:

1. Organizational learning is a process, continuous series of interlinked activities producing several changes. It is not seen as a product although OL results in a product, that is, learning (effective use of experiences for action).
2. It has three main systems or sub-systems (Exhibit 26.1). The first is that of acquiring an input and examining it. The new input may be a new structure, a new planning and control system, new technology, new ways of dealing with problems, etc. Any change being introduced in an organization, small or large, is an input. The organization acquires a new input and examines it for suitability to its needs by reflecting on its feasibility, advantages, cost consequences, etc.

Exhibit 26.1   *Organizational Learning Systems*

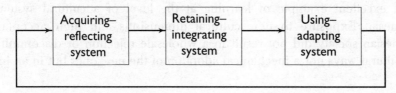

3. The second system or sub-system is concerned with retaining the input. Not only does an input need to be acquired quickly, it also needs to be retained and/or sustained in the organization over time. Retention of an input would depend on how well it gets integrated into the existing systems in the first place. An organization is not interested in simply collecting a large number of inputs. If inputs remain independent of each other, the organization may become schizophrenic. For example, if a new performance appraisal system with self-assessment elements is introduced and employees continue the previous practice of not meeting their bosses for appraisal feedback and counselling, the new input cannot become a ritual. Organizational learning is effective only when new inputs get integrated with current practices.

4. Once the acquired inputs get integrated in and internalised by the organization, they should be used whenever needed. If what has been acquired (say, a new technology) is only ornamental and not used, learning is not effective. Use also implies adaptation of the new input in the light of experience gained in its use. This is another indicator of organizational learning. For example, the various behavioural dimensions of a new performance appraisal system may be altered or the rating system may be modified to suit the needs of the organization after experiencing certain difficulties in its implementation.

5. Finally, learning increases the ability of an organization to learn more on its own. Self-learning may not necessarily involve an outside stimulus or input. An organization may develop mechanisms of examining its experiences, retaining functional processes, and discontinuing dysfunctional ways of dealing with issues. This is self-learning leading to self-renewal.

As already stated, organizational learning has three sub-systems. Each sub-system has a relevant learning phase, involves certain learning processes, requires a specific climate, and is associated with some values and norms.

Phases of organizational learning

Organizational learning is a continuous evolutionary or growth process. It involves three phases corresponding to the three sub-systems. These are innovation, implementation, and stabilisation. They are similar to the well-known Lewinian phases of change: unfreezing, moving, and refreezing.

Innovation is concerned with the exposure of the organization to a new idea or practice, acquiring the new input, and reflecting on its costs and benefits. The second phase of retaining moves to a new qualitative level, when the organization integrates the input and retains it. The third phase of stabilisation is concerned with the continued use of the innovation and its internalisation by the organization, mainly reflected in the adaptation of the innovation.

An excellent example of learning at the level of a cultural system is that of Indonesia. Exposure to new cultural dimensions and their acceptance by the Indonesian society did not result in a wholesale rejection or discontinuation of the old cultural ways nor a mechanical adoption of the new ones but in an integration of the new with the existing forms, resulting in a new synthesis that is reflected in highly aesthetic forms of artistic creativity and a society with high value for synthesis, mutual support, and openness to innovation.

Learning processes

Different learning processes are involved in the three sub-systems of organizational learning.

In the first sub-system (acquiring–reflecting), an inflow of new ideas/practices (or the exposure of the organization to them) is an important element. This is followed by the trying out of the innovation on a small scale. Finally, the organization arranges for an analysis of the results of the experiment so that concerned organizational members may reflect on the costs and benefits.

In the second sub-system of retaining–integrating, three learning processes are involved. The new ideas or practices are first assimilated by the organization. Assimilation involves acceptance of the new notion as a regular feature of the organization. Whatever experiences are generated during the experimentation are put together (cumulated) so that the organization may be able to use this experience. Finally, the top levels in the organization provide support to build the innovation into an acceptable practice. For example, a new performance appraisal system, after trial and positive feedback, is accepted for regular use (assimilation). The person monitoring the system collects all the employees' experiences with it periodically (cumulation) and organizes periodic meetings with the top management, where these experiences are shared and the management provides encouragement and support for the new system (building). The top managers' ideals and support thus play a critical role in organizational learning.

In the third sub-system (using–adapting), the main emphasis is on stabilisation and internalisation of the innovation. This is made possible by continued use. The experiences gained while using the innovation need to be reviewed and critiqued. Such a critique–review will help in identifying what changes are required to make the innovation serve a useful function in the organization. Then the innovation will be adapted to the organization and not remain a stand-alone phenomenon. All these steps contribute to make an innovation a part of the organization (internalisation).

Organizational climate

An appropriate organizational climate creates the necessary conditions for organizational learning and then sustains and enhances it. Different kinds of climate are needed for the three phases. During the first phase of innovation—when acquiring a new idea or practice, experimenting with it, and reflecting on its costs and benefits are important—the climate needs to be innovative, encouraging the trying out of new ideas and open examination of its feasibility.

During the second phase of implementation—when the processes of assimilation and integration of the innovation into the existing system and the building up of support for it are important—a climate of rigour and discipline is more desirable.

Those concerned with incorporating the innovation should work meticulously on its proper implementation. They also need to keep proper records of the initial trials. Lapses during this phase may adversely affect the learning process. This is similar to the drill or practice required for individual learning. The climate should emphasise and encourage rigour in implementation of the innovation at this time. Those involved in the implementation may be freed from some of their regular responsibilities at this time to ensure they have sufficient opportunity to carry out these function. In review meetings, emphasis should be laid on thoroughness and reviewing of details.

In the last phase of stabilisation—when the process of continued use, critiquing, and adaptation of the innovation are important—a supportive–critical climate is conducive for organizational learning. The climate for this phase needs to be characterised by both critical examination of the consequences and support from senior managers for using the innovation, trying out its various forms, and examining them critically. The conditions required for its continued use must also be created. A small group may be given the responsibility of monitoring implementation, collecting experiences and data, analysing and examining these, and suggesting any modifications in the details of the implementation plan.

Values

Appropriate values sustain a system. Awareness of these values may help in planning to make a system effective.

For the first sub-system (acquiring–building), three values are important. The value of openness, welcoming new ideas, and being ready to try them out can help the organization acquire new inputs more successfully. The second relevant value is that of taking initiative in trying out a new idea (experimentation) and in searching for different ways of solving problems (creativity). The third value conducive to the acquiring–building process is that of mutuality—accepting others' points of view or ideas and contributing one's own without any reservations.

For the second sub-system (retaining–integrating), the values of rigour, thoroughness, and meticulous work cannot be overemphasised. In addition, mutual support helps in retaining the innovation. Members of the organization should also be rooted in the organization, which is reflected in the value of respect for its traditions. Such respect helps in building a positive critical attitude towards the innovation. Finally, the value of integration (blending the new with the old) helps in the process of retention.

In the third sub-system (using–adapting), three main values are relevant. The first is the value of perseverance—continuing work in spite of problems. Often, organizations fail to use an innovation because they get discouraged with initial difficulties. For example, when a new open system of performance appraisal is introduced in an organization, some problems are likely to surface because of the new climate of openness. If these problems are not seen in the proper perspective, the organization may discontinue the new system. However, if the organization perseveres in its use of the new system and gives it enough time to get over initial

Exhibit 26.2 *Processes in Organizational Learning*

Phases	Sub-systems		
	Acquiring–reflecting (innovation)	Retaining–integrating (implementation)	Using–adapting (stabilisation)
Learning processes	Inflow Experimentation Exchange	Assimilating Cumulating Building	Continued use Critiquing Adapting
Organizational climate	Innovative	Encouraging rigour and discipline	Supportive–critical
Values	Openness Creativity Experimentation Mutuality	Thoroughness Mutual support Respect for traditions	Perseverance Objectivity (analysis of experiences) Criticality Creative adaptation
Norms	Respect for innovation Exposure to outside experts Sharing experiences informally Learning from others	Thoroughness in preparation Detailed planning Volunteering Search for common links between the new and the old	Perseverance Quick feedback Support for implementation No hesitation in modifying plans

problems, the innovation will get internalised by the organization. The second relevant value is that of questioning—asking relevant questions, looking for both advantages and disadvantages of the innovation, and analysing experiences without bias. The third value is that of creative adaptation—making changes in the innovation to suit the reality and special nature of the organization.

An overall summary of the processes of organizational learning is shown in Exhibit 26.2.

Mechanisms of Organizational Learning

Here we propose some mechanisms to be used by organizations during the three phases of organizational learning. These can also be used to diagnose the state of the learning system and the areas where interventions are needed. A mechanism is a specific action an organization takes to achieve a purpose. However, it may be useful to discuss the general areas in which such mechanisms operate. We suggest below five such areas and further suggest a number of mechanisms under each area.

Experimentation and flexibility

An organization needs to develop flexibility and a positive attitude towards experimentation, trying out new ways to deal with issues and problems. Several mechanisms can promote this. Here are some suggestions:

- Invite experts and experienced and creative practitioners to share their ideas and experiences with selected members of the organization.
- Encourage employees to try out new ways of dealing with problems even if these do not always succeed.
- Reward new methods that are successful in solving a problem. The reward may be related to the benefit. For example, if an innovation results in a substantial benefit, about 10–15 per cent of the savings can be given to the innovator as a reward.
- Hold periodic meetings to share the results of experiments. Such meetings will encourage people to learn about innovations, create a climate conducive to experimentation, and show the way to legitimate experimentation and flexibility.
- Hold periodic meetings to share the objectives and designs of and experiences with innovations being tried out. The same purpose as suggested in the point above is accomplished.
- Organize employee seminars on new developments. This educational measure will help members of an organization to become aware of new developments in a particular field and create a positive attitude towards experimentation. Employees may be encouraged to raise relevant questions and issues in such seminars.
- Set up an implementing and monitoring task group for new projects/experiments. The task group will have the responsibility of educating organizational members about the purpose and progress of an experiment. This mechanism would indicate that the organization is serious about the experiment or project.
- Set up a task group to identify common elements between old practices and the innovation. The findings may help employees perceive the innovation as a useful evolutionary step rather than a supplanting of old practices.
- Hold periodic reviews of experiences and share your own experiences hitherto. This serves the purpose of sharing experiences widely at all stages of change.
- Modify the plan of implementation if needed. In a large and complex organization, adoption of an innovation may require some modification in the innovation itself or in its proposed method of implementation. For example, an organization may decide to first introduce the innovation in one department, review the results, and then introduce it in other departments. Another organization may like to introduce it in one region and modify it slightly for another region. A third organization may want to introduce some parts of a new system first and move on to others after these get internalised. Sharing the rationale and *modus operandi* of these modifications and experiences with the new system may create a climate of experimentation rather than of adherence to one accepted way of doing things.
- Encourage preparation of alternative plans of implementation. If different groups have the freedom to adapt a proposed change to suit their own needs and requirements, a general message of openness and experimentation is generated in the organization.

Mutuality and teamwork

Organizational learning requires mutual support, mutual respect, learning from one another, collaborative work, and effective teams to solve problems. Without teamwork, it cannot be effective. The concept of organizational learning includes team-based learning by a group of people to deal with certain problems and their capacity as a group to sustain it for future use. Several mechanisms promote teamwork and mutuality. We mention some of these below (those already discussed are mentioned without comments):

- Invite experts and experienced and creative practitioners to share their experiences.
- Share your own experiences, concerns, ideas, etc. with outside organizations. When a change is introduced in an organization, different organizations have different experiences. Mutuality can be enhanced if the organizations concerned build mutual trust and openly share their experiences (happy and unhappy): futher plans, concerns, problems, and how problems were overcome.
- Hold periodic meetings to share the results of experiments.
- Hold periodic meetings to share details of ongoing experiments.
- Organize employee seminars on new developments.
- Set up an implementing and monitoring task group for new projects/experiments.
- Set up a task group to examine common elements between the old practices and the innovation.
- Hold periodic review meetings chaired by top/senior management. Such meetings not only enhance the importance of the innovation but also produce a collaborative relationship between those responsible for implementing the change and the top management. The top management will thus both understand the process of implementation and contribute to this process.
- Set up a task group to critique the innovation based on data collected during the trials. The task group will use experiences to look at different aspects of the innovation and to increase collaborative arrangements.
- Hold periodic reviews to share experiences.
- Set up a task group to follow up the experiment. The task group will collect experiences on various aspects of the implementation: intended and unintended consequences of the innovation, factors contributing to the speed of implementation (both organizational and innovation related), further competencies needed to stabilise the change, adaptations needed in the innovation, etc.
- Hold widespread debates on experiences during the implementation. This may legitimise open and uninhibited participation by members of an organization in understanding, analysing, and adapting the innovation to suit the organization.

Contingency and incremental planning

Organizational learning is enhanced by an attitude of learning rather than by an attitude of certitude. The planning process can vary on this continuum, with certitude and rigidity on the one end and tentativeness and flexibility on the other. A blueprint represents the first end of the continuum (reflecting the assumptions that the planners know all the dimensions fully, that the same plan is equally relevant to all parts of the organization, and that a foolproof plan can be prepared and should not require any change). An incremental model of planning represents the other end of the continuum, based on the assumptions that a plan can be prepared with the known variables, that these may undergo changes requiring further change in the plan, that a better plan should use new learning and should therefore be an evolutionary and developmental phenomenon, and that the different parts of the organization may require some variations on the plan. The incremental approach is more learning based. This approach promotes organizational learning. The following mechanisms both reflect this approach to planning and are likely to strengthen it:

- Prepare a detailed plan reflecting the contingency approach. PERT is a good example of detailed contingency planning. Time-bound commitments may be prepared with contingency plans indicating what alternative action will be taken if a particular thing is not done or if an expected result fails to be achieved. Contingency planning will help the organization to think of possible difficulties and handicaps and to take steps both to prevent these as well as take alternative action if they become impediments.
- Link the new practices proposed with the known ones. Learning of new inputs is faster if these are seen as related to existing practices/ideas. Then the new does not produce a threat to most members of the organization; the new then builds on rather than supplanting the old.
- Maintain records of your own and others' experience. Effective planning would require continuous review and learning from experiences. This may not be possible unless experiences are properly recorded and analysed.
- Hold periodic review meetings chaired by top/senior management. The meetings are likely to produce ideas for better implementation planning.
- Hold periodic reviews and share experiences. Sharing of experiences produces ideas that can be used to modify parts of the plan prepared.
- Set up a task group for evaluation. This task group may prepare detailed reports on the progress of an innovation, positive and negative effects in the organization, conditions needed to make the innovation successful, etc.
- Hold widespread debates on experiences with the implementation.
- Realistically appraise the support needed for continued use of an innovation. Planning is also concerned with reviewing at the stage of implementation what resources need to be provided to ensure effective internalisation. This may be in terms of structural changes, competence building, setting up of temporary systems, etc.
- Modify the plan of implementation if required. This shows an attitude of incremental planning.
- Encourage preparation of alternative implementation plans by different groups in an organization. This helps to select the most functional ones and to decide whether several forms of a programme should coexist.

Use of temporary systems

Temporary systems are effective mechanisms to generate ideas and take quick action. Some examples of temporary systems are task groups, task forces, special committees, project groups, problem identification teams, etc. There are several advantages to temporary systems: inter-functional, inter-departmental, or inter-regional groups can be formed to incorporate diverse points of view as more individuals get exposed to other departments/regions/functions, etc.; work is done faster because of the time-bound nature of a temporary system; there is a more objective view of the problem; more risks can be taken because members of a temporary system do not have vested interests; there is more flexibility because these systems are not part of the organizational structure and can be created and dissolved according to need.

Effective use of temporary systems may enhance organizational learning. These can be used at different stages of implementation as already mentioned above. However, they are listed again as follows:
- Set up an implementing and monitoring task group for the innovation.
- Set up a task group to examine common elements between the old practices and the innovation.
- Hold periodic review meetings chaired by the top/senior management.
- Set up a task group for data-based critiquing of the innovation.
- Set up a task group for evaluation and reporting of the plus and minus points.
- Set up a task group for following up the experiment.

Competency building

To make organizational learning effective, it is necessary to build resources that the organization can use when needed. Building necessary resources may ensure the continuity of organizational learning. Competencies are the primary resources in this regard.

Competency building can be achieved if training facilities are provided by the organization for both external and internal programmes, members of the organization are exposed to new ideas and experiences, opportunities are created for sharing experiences and plans, and existing competencies are effectively used by the organizations. Several mechanisms relevant for competency building have already been mentioned. These and two new ones are listed below:
- Invite experts and experienced creative practitioners.
- Encourage employees to attend external training programmes. This may be done after examining the programmes that will be relevant for the purpose of the organization.
- Hold periodic meetings to share results of experiments.
- Hold periodic meetings to share ongoing experiments.
- Organize employee seminars on new developments.
- Utilise relevant existing skills for implementation of change. The more existing skills are utilised, the more such competencies develop. Unutilised competencies get atrophied and discourage people from acquiring new competencies, as it is highly frustrating not to be able to use one's strengths.

ORGANIZATIONAL LEARNING: POLICY IMPLICATIONS

An organizational policy is an accepted guideline for action to move in a direction predetermined by the organization. If developing organizational learning systems is a direction that an organization has accepted as worthwhile, it needs to develop action guidelines or policies that will facilitate this process.

Policy Foci

Policies can achieve several purposes. We suggest the following main foci for policies promoting OL:

Enhancing functional autonomy with accountability   Policies should both promote the autonomy of a sub-system as well as emphasise its accountability for the tasks it agrees to undertake. Without functional autonomy, a system cannot be innovative and loses the motivation to take initiative and solve problems. However, the autonomy of a system cannot be without defined limits. Mostly, autonomy is needed in relation to the introduction of innovation—the changes needed for the innovation to work, the changes needed to adapt the innovation to the organization, the internal distribution of responsibilities, procedures to implement the change successfully, etc. Functional autonomy thus also demands accountability—taking responsibility for results. Without autonomy, the basic motivation for initiative and creativity is lacking; without accountability, the positive pressure to be effective remains low. Both need to be emphasised through organizational policies.

Availability of support and resources   For making a change, several kinds of resources are needed. Accountability is possible when the resources needed are provided. Providing resources indicates interest in the system and its members, as well as high expectations for them. These promote learning.

Competence building   Organizational policies need to promote and upgrade the various competencies needed to work on the various objectives of an organization.

Networking   Various sub-systems involved in a particular area of work need to learn from one another and collaborate. The development of a network of experts, groups, and organizations enhances learning. Organizational policies need to promote such networking.

In the light of the above four policy foci, we may briefly look at some examples of policies corresponding to the three phases or the three sub-systems of organizational learning.

Policies at the Innovation Phase

The first phase of organizational learning can be effective if the policies promote experimentation, openness, and exposure of members of the organization to new developments. Some examples of such policies are mentioned as follows.

Exchange of experiences without pressure for conformity If an innovation is being tried out in a large system, different sub-systems may have different experiences. Sharing such experiences may be very useful and stimulating, but there may be a temptation to pick up a successful experience and make it an accepted pattern for all sub-systems. Such an approach inhibits experimentation. Experience shows that given encouragement and patience, the various sub-systems can come up with a number of innovative and functional ideas independently.

Defining of areas of national and regional collaboration In a country involved in developing new areas of industry, collaboration at various levels is conducive to organizational learning. Areas of such collaboration can be defined formally at the national, regional, and state levels, for instance.

National and regional participation in innovation Usually those at national and regional levels of the country lose contact with the real practices in the field, especially at the grassroots level. Yet actual organizations at lower levels (e.g., provinces or institutions) are involved in the hands-on use of innovations to solve problems. This imbalance can be rectified if the national and regional levels are encouraged to participate in the field where innovations are happening. This can, for example, be done with a few representatives of these two levels being made members of temporary systems in a province to plan and implement innovations. This may facilitate provincial-level learning nationwide in the long run.

Encouraging experimentation and feedback Two important conditions of learning, whether in the case of individuals or organizations, are experimentation and feedback. The sub-systems of an organization concerned with implementation of change need to experiment with different ways of implementing it. The policy implication is that communication from a higher (central) level needs to be in the form of guidelines rather than detailed prescriptive instructions. Prescriptions prevent experimentation and at best ensure conformity. If experiment is encouraged, feedback on the experiment from the experimenting group given to the policy formulation group helps improve the process of policy making. It contributes to an understanding of the various levels of policy formulation. Conversely, feedback from policy-formulating unit(s) to operational systems (on how the experiment is perceived, what positive and negative consequences it is producing, etc.) contributes to the latter's learning.

Policies at the Implementation Phase

At the implementation level, policies are needed to develop competencies for implementing the change, promote functional autonomy of the implementing systems, and provide support to the system. Some examples of such policies are mentioned below:

Functional autonomy of temporary systems As it is important to ensure autonomy of the implementing sub-organizations, so also the functional autonomy of temporary systems involved in an implementation is essential. If an implementation task group has been set up, it should have the freedom to work out its plans and pursue an agreed course of action. A task group can be given functional autonomy by investing the group with defined powers and functions.

Budget for temporary systems   Along with functional autonomy, a temporary system needs resources—competent members, a budget, secretarial help, etc. Specific provisions for an adequate budget are necessary to facilitate the work of temporary systems.

Developing multi-level consultants   Organizational learning should result in enhancement of the self-learning capability of an organization. Self-learning requires diagnostic and remedial competencies in the organization. Such competencies are also needed for effective consultation (providing help to the organization in understanding and dealing with its problems). If an organization develops these competencies to a high degree, its future learning capability will be quite high. In a large organization, consulting competencies need to be developed at various levels. For example, in a countrywide organization, consulting competencies are needed at the apex level, at the regional levels, and at the local organizational levels.

Product-oriented rewards   Behaviour that is rewarded gets reinforced and stabilised in individuals and in the organization. If people are rewarded for results and concrete achievements, their urge to take responsibility and initiative is likely to be high and they are likely to learn faster, contributing to raising the level of organizational learning.

Policies at the Stabilisation Phase

The policies at the stabilisation stage are mainly concerned with providing needed support to those who are implementing a change so that it gets internalised by the system. Attention to competency building and networking also needs to be continued. Some examples of such policies are mentioned below.

Budget for follow-up and implementation   Even after successful acceptance of a new system, it is necessary to monitor its working for some time and review experiences periodically. Follow-up is very important for the successful internalisation of a change in an organization. It is also necessary to provide an adequate budget for its implementation.

Involvement of the higher-level management   Interest from and participation of higher-level management at the stabilisation stage sends a clear message that the organization supports innovation. For example, when experiences are periodically reviewed, the top managers should be present to raise questions, offer comments, and indicate their support for the innovation. Involvement of the top management in the review and further planning of an innovation provides great support to the introduction of the change.

Financial support for stabilisation of change   An innovation takes some time to be internalised and stabilised. An 'experiment' (working under controlled conditions with necessary modifications from time to time) needs to be protected and supported for some time before it becomes a part of the ongoing system. A budget is needed for supporting experimentation with the innovation for about 3–4 years, until it stabilises. The budget should also make it possible to critique the innovation, report experiences and allow for debate on them at various levels, and analyse the results for final consideration by the top management.

Multi-level sharing of experiences   Experiences in the implementation of an innovation need to be shared at all levels—national, regional, and local. Conferences can be organized to discuss experiences and results and the implications of these for adaptation or use of the innovation for various purposes.

Organizational development competencies   Good organizational learning programmes should result in enhanced capabilities to diagnose problems, set priorities, search for alternative interventions to work on an issue/problem, develop an appropriate organizational culture, build strong teams, evaluate results and replay successes in an organization. All these are part of organization development (OD). At some stage, systematic attention needs to be given to the development of OD competencies in the organization as well as to the introduction of an OD system.

ORGANIZATIONAL LEARNING IN LARGE SYSTEMS: DIFFUSION AND INSTITUTIONALISATION

There are special problems of organizational learning in large systems. Two main concerns in large systems are how to multiply learning fast and how to make the new practice a regular part of the system. These are respectively the issues of diffusion and institutionalisation. Diffusion is concerned with the fast proliferation of an innovation so that various sub-systems are able to adopt and use it. Institutionalisation is concerned with internalisation and stabilisation of an innovation so that it can continue to be used in the system regularly without being dependent on external resources (such as expertise or special budgets).

Diffusion

The main function of diffusion is to accelerate change and development so that the use of an innovation is widespread. Diffusion involves replication; hence the issue of replicability of an action is often raised in connection with diffusion. It is worth clarifying the nature of diffusion here.

People may use one of the two models of diffusion or multiplication and these seem to be opposed in spirit. These are the cloning and development models. The former emphasises multiplication of a product and the related norms and procedures; the latter gives importance to the diffusion of processes (not products), values (not norms), and approaches (not procedures). The underlying belief in the development model is that an innovation needs to develop within a given culture and experiences elsewhere can help the culture to learn how to facilitate the relevant processes, develop values conducive to the use of this innovation, and use the appropriate approaches. These are all (processes, values, and approaches) seen as replicable. The cloning model of diffusion emphasises the mass copying of a prototype, replicating an action in all its details.

When an innovation is adopted by one sub-system, tested for its utility, and finally accepted for continued use, there is a natural eagerness on the part of other sub-systems to share the benefits of the change. Diffusion makes innovation an economical effort. Diffusion also achieves faster learning by the units of an organization from one or more of sister units. It thus propels the organization in the direction of self-learning. There are at least four types of diffusion of organizational learning and we need to pay attention to all these types while attempting diffusion or multiplication of a change.

Horizontal diffusion Horizontal diffusion is the multiplication of a change across the various units of an organization. For example, if the use of case studies in management training is found useful in an institution or a province, there would be understandable eagerness to adopt this approach at other institutions or provinces also. When this teaching methodology is adopted by more institutions, we have an example of horizontal diffusion.

Vertical diffusion An innovation is usually introduced in a system for improving a specific dimension. For example, task analysis may be adopted by an organization to clarify and delineate various roles and role responsibilities. If task analysis is found useful for this purpose and is also adopted by other sub-systems of the organization, we have horizontal diffusion. However, this success may lead to task analysis being used by the organization for other purposes also. This we call vertical diffusion—the spread of an innovation for use in areas not originally envisaged in the application programme.

Action diffusion An innovation may be introduced for use by a specific group. For example, teaching through case studies may be introduced as an innovation in management training. However, the real impact of the case methodology may be reflected in the use of some dimensions of the approach in the operational sphere. For example, people who are trained in the case methodology may collect more information about different individual points of view, may respect and empathise with the feelings of other people, and may look for alternative approaches to deal with a problem. This application of the case study approach (primarily meant to re-orient management training) in the performance of a job is an example of action diffusion: the innovation diffuses (or spreads) to the actions of people doing various jobs in an organization.

Networking If horizontal, vertical, and action diffusion has been taking place, linkages among units that are using the innovation are needed to enable them to share experiences, continue to learn from one another, and critique their experiences to renew the innovative approach periodically. Networking is the interlinking of individuals, teams, or organizations interested in the use of a particular approach/ practice in order to share their experiences, share expertise, help each other out, motivate each other, and develop collective resources for use by all members of the network.

Institutionalisation

When a change is accepted by the organization and is made a part of the regular working of the organization, we call it institutionalisation. An innovation starts in the form of an experiment. It is tried out under special conditions: the necessary financial resources are provided, the relevant expertise is procured, and the sub-system in which it is being used gets special treatment (e.g., transfer of personnel to other departments may be frozen and regular workloads may be lowered). However, if the innovation is to survive in the organization, after some time the special treatment should be withdrawn and the innovation should become part of the regular organizational functioning. Then it gets institutionalised. There are several forms of institutionalisation and attention needs to be given to all of them.

Institutional commitment When an innovation is incorporated in an existing institution, an important step has been taken in the direction of institutionalisation. For example, if the case study methodology is introduced in an organization, a major training institution may adopt this as a part of its curriculum. This shows the latter institution's commitment and is one form of institutionalisation.

Use in action An innovation gets institutionalised if it is used regularly in an organization. For example, we read earlier that task analysis was found useful as a management tool in a province in Indonesia. The provincial training system then decided to incorporate it into the management training curriculum of healthcare personnel. This ensured its continued use.

Competency building An innovation cannot be sustained without competencies in its proper use. If case studies are introduced as an innovation in management training, it is necessary to develop competencies to write and teach from case studies to ensure their continued use. In fact, competency development programmes should be prepared well in advance.

Financial commitment A special budget may be needed for initial experimentation. However, after the innovation has been found to be relevant and useful by an organization, some financial provision needs to be made in the organization's regular budget. For example, if evaluation and follow-up are found useful, a provision in the training budget for follow-up and evaluation may help in the continued use of the innovation.

Formalisation Some innovations may require structural modifications or the creation of an appropriate structure for making the innovations effective. For example, if a package of HRD practices is introduced in an organization, it may be necessary to create an HRD unit or department so that the changes can be sustained. Similarly, to ensure systematic attention training, a separate training department may be needed. Many changes need to be formalised through appropriate structures, systems, and mechanisms.

Making Diffusion and Institutionalisation Effective

Two sets of organizations are usually involved in the processes of diffusion and institutionalisation: those undertaking the task of diffusion (usually experts or central/national organizations) and those using the innovations (client organizations). Their roles are complementary. While most activities by the change-generating system are concerned with diffusion, those of the target systems or adopting systems are more concerned with accepting and institutionalising the change. Several mechanisms may help the process of diffusion and institutionalisation in the different phases of organizational learning. These are summarised in Exhibit 26.3 and briefly discussed below.

Innovation phase The main contribution of the agent of change in the initial phase is to communicate experiences, difficulties, special process dynamics, expected and unexpected consequences of the innovation, and resources required for successful implementation of change to the adopting systems. The adopting system maximises learning during this phase by critical examination of the various inputs received, preparation for action, and utilisation of external help. Some specific action suggestions are given in Exhibit 26.3.

Exhibit 26.3 *Action Areas in Diffusion and Institutionalisation*

Phase	Agency of change	Adopting system
Innovation	• Share experiences and process dynamics • Share difficulties • Share resources needed • Share consequences (of innovation)	• Prepare, select, and invite a group • Hold in-group discussions • Examine relevance, consequences, and problems • Raise questions • Prepare plans • Obtain needed resources (for follow-up) • Experiment • Invite outsiders to check
Implementation	• Provide consulting help (and training) • Share tools, mechanisms, etc. • Learn from the new experience	• Create a temporary system • Provide a special budget • Provide top-level support • Plan relevant training

(Contd)

Exhibit 26.3 (Contd)

Stabilisation	• Share the latest experiences • Provide consultation help • Develop collaboration and a strategy for further diffusion	• Create a temporary system • Examine and modify structures (if necessary) • Modify roles (if needed) • Examine and modify systems (if needed) • Incorporate the action in the regular budgeting list • Build competencies

Implementation phase   During the next phase, the system that is the agency of change both learns from the experiences of adopting systems and provides them support and technical help. The adopting systems complement this by creating the necessary conditions for successful implementation of the change, including creating a special group to take responsibility for and pay full-time attention to the implementation. Relevant competencies are also developed.

Stabilisation phase   In the last phase, the agency of change pays attention mainly to building linkages, critically examining its experiences and organizing support for stabilisation. The adopting organizations pay more attention to formalisation and financial support to ensure effective implementation and continuity. Various suggestions for this phase are summarised in Exhibit 26.3.

Organizational learning mechanisms seem to facilitate organizational excellence. (See Exhibit 26.4 for learning mechanisms in Indian organizations.)[22] The organizational learning mechanisms that statistically correlated with at least 7 out of the 10 indicators of organizational performance (as subjectively assessed by the respondents on another questionnaire) were

- Maintaining detailed records of the organization's successes and failures
- Realistic appraisals of the support needed for stabilising innovations
- Identification and use of employees with the necessary skills and expertise for implementing changes
- Modification of implementation plans based on experience
- New practices proposed by the management incorporating the strengths of old or well-known practices
- Holding of periodic meetings chaired by the top or senior managers to review innovations and changes
- Creation of task forces for data-based evaluation of innovations
- Holding of seminars on new developments for the staff
- Encouraging departments and task forces to consider alternative ways of implementing changes and innovations

It is noteworthy that only two of the learning mechanisms used most frequently are also on the list of the most effective.

Exhibit 26.4 *Learning Mechanisms in Indian Organizations*

In an ongoing study of organizational learning practices at the Indian Institute of Management, Ahmedabad, senior managers from over 50 relatively progressive private and public sector organizations were asked to fill up a questionnaire. The responses of managers from each organization were averaged to develop organizational scores for each of the 23 different learning mechanisms. The six most widely used mechanisms appeared to be the following:
- Sending employees to external training programmes, conferences, etc.
- Identification and use of employees with relevant skills and expertise for implementing changes
- Modification of implementation plans for projects and innovations on the basis of actual experience
- Holding of periodic staff meetings for sharing results of organizational experiments, innovations, etc.
- Inviting experts and innovative practitioners to share their ideas with members of the organization
- Creation of task forces for implementing and monitoring new projects, experiments, etc.

Facilitating and Hindering Factors

The following 10 facilitating factors have been suggested for organizational learning[23]:
1. Scanning imperative (awareness of the environment and outside world)
2. Performance gap (between actual and desired performance)
3. Concern for measurement
4. Experimental mindset
5. Climate of openness
6. Continuous education
7. Operational variety
8. Multiple advocates (employees from all levels)
9. Involved leadership
10. Systems perspective

Exhibit 26.5 gives facilitating and hindering factors, identified on the basis of an analysis of a large number of case studies of Indian organizations.[24]

Exhibit 26.5 *Facilitating and Hindering Factors*

Facilitating factors
- Commitment to well-defined organizational priorities
- Effective HRD systems
- Mechanism of collective thinking and reflection
- Flexible and participative leadership styles
- Collaboration and teamwork
- External orientation for learning
- Measuring devices for hitherto neglected aspects

Hindering factors
- Frequent changes at the top, leading to loss of continuity and absence of a long-term orientation.
- A culture of complacency arising out of past success, inadequate efforts for improvement leading to the setting in of a slow decline.
- Excessively bureaucratic and centralised methods of working, leading to delays in decision making, missed opportunities, and loss of energy and enthusiasm at operational levels.

Exhibit 26.5 (*Contd*)

- With a community of functional specialists, having little appreciation of each other's area, learning gets fragmented and this leads to functional myopia. This tunnel vision of information sharing blocks learning.
- In hierarchical organizations with strong command and control orientation, roles of organizational members become too narrowly defined and, as a result, they merely ensure implementation of decisions. Organizations thus lose employees' ideas and inputs.
- Due to preoccupation with day-to-day fire-fighting, time and attention do not get allocated to issues of change and innovation. As a result, changes are not backed up by visible support or energetic action.

A climate conducive to experimentation and learning, transformational leadership, and empowerment can promote organizational learning. A correlation of organizational learning diagnostics scores with climate variables suggests that climate and ethos are very important in the implementation phase, that trust and the extension motive (with its corresponding climate) play a very positive role, and that a climate of dependency is detrimental to organizational learning.[25]

Organizations need to develop action guidelines or policies to facilitate the process of organizational learning. Focusing on the following concerns has been helpful to policy making in organizations:

Enhancing functional autonomy with accountability Organizational policies should promote the autonomy (within defined limits) of the sub-system (e.g., a department or unit) and emphasise accountability for the tasks that the sub-system agrees to undertake. Without functional autonomy, a system cannot be innovative.

Availability of support and resources Implementing change requires resources. Accountability is possible only when the necessary resources are provided. Providing resources also shows interest in employees and the system, and indicates high expectations from them.

Competency building Organizational policies should promote and upgrade the competencies needed to meet the objectives of the organization.

Networking The various sub-systems involved in a particular area of work need to learn from one another so that they can collaborate. The development of a network of experts, groups, and organizations enhances learning. Organizational policies need to promote such networking.

LEARNING ORGANIZATIONS: CONCEPT, PROCESSES, AND DEVELOPMENT

The concept of the learning organization is not new—many authors have talked about organizations learning from others and their own past experiences. Probably Garratt was the first to publish a book on the subject.[26] However, the term was popularised by Senge, whose book[27] triggered a great deal of interest in learning organizations. It was soon followed by another volume.[28]

The concept of the learning organization is a natural extension of organizational learning. How can an organization remain a learning organization? 'An organization skilled at creating, acquiring, and transferring knowledge, and modifying its behaviour to reflect new knowledge and insights'[29] can remain a learning organization. It has been suggested that the learning organization is one that 'can respond to new information by altering the very "programming" by which information is processed and evaluated' (p. 5) through 'internal reframing of process and managerial practices that put these ideas into action' (p. 10).[30]

Learning organizations have been defined in terms of various characteristics.[31]

Senge popularised the term 'learning organization' through his popular book.[32] Since he has influenced most thinking on organizational learning, the five characteristics suggested by him are given in Exhibit 26.6. According to him, the fifth characteristic (systems thinking) is the most critical one. He therefore titled his book *The Fifth Discipline*.

Exhibit 26.6 *Peter Senge's Framework*

Personal Mastery

Personal mastery applies to individual learning, and, according to Senge, organizations cannot learn until their members begin to learn. Personal mastery has two components: defining what one is trying to achieve (a goal), and having a true measure of how close one is to the goal. People learn to use both reason and intuition to create. They become systems thinkers who see the interconnectedness of everything around them and, as a result, they feel more connected to the whole. One needs this type of individual at every level of an organization for the organization to learn. Traditional managers have always thought that they had to have all the answers for their organization. The managers of the learning organization know that their staff has the answers. The job of the manager in the learning organization is to be the teacher or coach who helps unleash the creative energy in each individual.

Mental Models

A mental model is one's way of looking at the world. It determines how we think and act. A simple example of a mental model comes from an exercise described in *The Fifth Discipline Fieldbook*. In this exercise, pairs of conference participants are asked to arm wrestle. They are told that winning in arm wrestling means the act of lowering their partner's arm to the table. Most people struggle against their partner to win. Their mental model is that there can be only one winner in arm wrestling and that this is done by lowering their partner's arm more times than their partner can do the same thing to them. Argyris contends that these people have a flawed mental model. An alternative model would present a framework where both partners could win. If they stop resisting each other, they can work together flipping their arms back and forth. The end result is that they can both win and they can win many more times than if they were working against each other.

Team Learning

Senge defines team learning as 'the process of aligning and developing the capacity of a team to create the results its members truly desire. It builds on the discipline of developing shared vision. It also builds on personal mastery, for talented teams are made up of talented individuals.' Senge describes a number of components of team learning. He identifies three conditions that are necessary for dialogue to occur: All participants must 'suspend their assumptions'; all participants must 'regard one another as

Exhibit 26.6 (*Contd*)

colleagues'; and there must be a facilitator (at least until teams develop these skills) 'who holds the context of the dialogue'.

Shared Vision

The shared vision of an organization must be built of the individual visions of its members. The vision must be created through interaction with the individuals in the organization. The shared vision can be created only by integrating the individual visions and the development of these visions in a common direction. The leader shares his own vision to encourage others to share their vision too. The organization's vision should evolve from these visions.

Systems Thinking

Senge calls systems thinking as the fifth discipline because it integrates all the four disciplines. At the heart of a learning organization is a shift of mind—from seeing ourselves as separate from the world to seeing ourselves as connected to the world, from seeing problems as caused by someone or something 'out there' to seeing how our own actions create the problems we experience. A learning organization is a place where people are continually discovering how they create their reality; and how they can change it. At the foundation of systems thinking is the identification of circles of causality or feedback loops of systems. These can be reinforcing or balancing. The essence of systems thinking lies in seeing interrelations rather than linear cause–effect chains.

Watkins and Marsick have presented a model, reflecting the common features of learning organizations.[33] The model depicts two interacting triangles, the lower one representing the people in the organization and the upper one representing the organizational structure and culture. In the interacting space between the triangles is the team and the top area beyond the organization is the global environment, with which the organization needs to be connected. They have subsequently recorded 22 cases of learning organizations: five on changing the whole systems, seven focusing mainly on individual learning, five on team learning and action, and five on organizational restructuring.[34] To summarise, they suggest that the learning organization should

- Create continuous learning opportunities (individual)
- Promote enquiry and dialogue (individual)
- Encourage collaboration and team learning (team)
- Establish systems to capture and share learning (organization)
- Empower people towards a collective vision (organization)
- Connect the organization to its environment (global)
- Use leaders who model and support being at the individual, team, and organizational levels

Based on a survey of earlier studies and in-depth interviews with leaders of three learning organizations, we suggest the following eight characteristics.

1. Holistic framework This includes systems thinking, mainly the perceiving of interconnections and patterns among key variables. Organization members are able to connect the organization to the environment. They are aware of the interconnections of the various systems and functions within the organization, between their organization and other organizations and agencies, and between the organization and the society. They are able to see not only the trees, but also the forest—seeing patterns rather than discrete events. This is possible only if the organization takes a long-term view, seeing beyond the immediate and the present. Problems are seen and solved in the futuristic framework, and by working on the root cause rather than dealing with symptoms. The organization practices double-loop learning, critically examines its theories or premises, by using boundary workers, customers, vendors, etc. as scanners of the environment.

2. Strategic thinking Another step to move towards action, strategic thinking involves thinking of the consequences/implications of each action, preparing patterns of things to be done in a certain order, and choosing the most important actions and the key variables making the most impact—prioritising. This may mean, for example, willingness to close down unprofitable or irrelevant units/activities. This is possible only when the organization reframes information at the strategic level. This involves double-loop learning—questioning the current thinking, and not resting on past and current success. Sometimes success becomes the beginning of failure. Exhibit 26.7 contains several examples of this.

3. Shared vision Examining and developing vision is an important function of the top management. It involves developing a vision through participation from all

Exhibit 26.7 *How Success Breeds Failures*

1. HMT was once a leader in the watch market. In the 1980s the watch market started changing from mechanical to quartz technology and redefined the product as a personal accessory rather than a utility item. HMT, however, continued to focus on its success formula and produce durable mechanical watches meant to be utility items. HMT had started producing quartz watches in 1983, but even in 1993, mechanical watches formed 75 per cent of its production (as compared to 15 per cent share of mechanical watches worldwide). It took a newcomer, Titan, to redefine the product and snatch away the market from HMT. By 1994, HMT had a market share of less than 10 per cent as against 70 per cent of Titan-Timex.[35]

2. In 1965, Nelco (then known as National Ecko) was one of the leaders in the radio market. When transistors started making an entry, the company ignored it and stuck to its diode sets. Within a few years, the diode was out of the market and by the time the company realised this, its market share was down to 2 per cent.[36]

3. Till the 1980s, Remington Rand of India was the leader in the manual typewriter market. Its brand was synonymous with the product, and its factories at Howrah, Faridabad, and Mysore kept producing at high capacity. In the mid-1980s, the market started shifting to electronic typewriters and word-processing equipment; Remington Rand, however, continued with its manual versions. Things did not change till it started losing to competition, but by then it was too late. After changing ownership twice, and continuing to register losses, in 1993 it was forced to withdraw from the market.[37]

Strategic thinking also involves differentiating roles in terms of policy, strategy, and operations, sharing strategy at all levels, inviting comments and suggestions, and providing support at the individual, team, and organizational levels.

levels, inspiring members by linking the vision with their personal goals. The top management not only creates an inspiring vision, but they also communicates the vision, and commits people to the vision by concretising it. It involves transformational leadership.

4. Empowerment   Empowerment has already been discussed in Chapter 23. It includes creating enabling structures, and decentralisation and delegation. As discussed in Chapter 23, empowerment requires clarity of the proper direction, trust, and providing the needed support. Empowerment also requires the use of persuasive (rather than coercive) power, and rewarding initiative and decisions.

5. Information flow   There is enough sharing of information in a learning organization. Critical and authentic information is shared at all levels. There is free flow of information, willingness to pass on even negative information. Rumours get minimised by opening up formal channels of communication (in the absence of which outside sources of information are more likely to be used).

Internal exchange of ideas is encouraged. Information is used for planning and control. Monitoring and scanning capability is developed in the organization. Some examples of effective use of scanning capability are given in Exhibit 26.8.

6. Emotional maturity   Learning organizations are high in emotional intelligence. This includes a sense of control over the better part of one's destiny, optimism, self-discipline, commitment, and moderate risk taking. The organization inspires self-confidence (as against helplessness), and the belief that people can influence events. It encourages people to take responsibility (self-monitoring). It encourages people to learn postponement of immediate gratification of one's own needs for a larger goal. People become bold and moderate risk taking. They develop tolerance for and ability to manage ambiguity, and the faith that they have the critical competitive edge.

7. Learning   Learning obviously is at the heart of the learning organization. It includes several mechanisms and sources, like valuing and encouraging self-development, learning from outside, interdisciplinary functioning, and creating a climate conducive to learning. A learning organization encourages dialogue and discussion, and rewards flexibility. It results in openness. Learning is reflected in and promotes self-reflection. Exhibit 26.9 contains some examples of such capabilities.

Exhibit 26.8   *Use of Scanning Capability*

1. ITC uses remote sensing data provided by IRS-IA and IRS-IB satellites. This data provides the company with advanced intelligence on the tobacco harvest in Andhra; hence it can better predict the price of tobacco even before it comes to the market.[38]
2. Modi Xerox conducts an annual employee satisfaction survey of all employees. The survey data is analysed to identify areas for improvements and to develop improvement plans. The action planning process directly or indirectly involves almost half the total workforce. Implementation of these action plans is then assessed in the next survey so that the impact of the action taken can be monitored and evaluated.[39]

Exhibit 26.9 *Self-reflection and Problem-solving Capabilities*

1. At Jolly Boards, each of the 160 employees is given 6 minutes every month to talk to the entire company about how improvements can be brought about in work systems and practices. He can suggest improvements even in jobs not related to his own. On an average, there are 20 suggestions given by each employee every month. The company has found that of the total suggestions given every month, about 600 yield tangible results.[40]

2. Mukund, a 3,700-strong steelmaker, has about 200 Juran quality improvement teams and 64 quality circles. These are cross-functional teams, fully empowered to identify and implement process improvements across the organization. Through regular brainstorming, these groups identify projects, calculate the cost of poor quality, implement solutions, and monitor the savings made through improvements.[41]

8. Synergy Learning organizations generate synergy through collaboration and teamwork. The basic quality for teamwork is empathy. Empathy requires each party to suspend its own assumptions and think together. Emphasis is on consensus building, through continued use of dialogues and debates. The different teams accept and make commitment to consensual decisions. Enough attention is given to process—spending time on working through differences, negative feelings, etc. The learning organizations use cross-functional teams. They develop networking capability. Exhibit 26.10 contains some example of networking through information sharing.

Several instruments have been developed to access organizational learning and learning organizations.

- Organizational learning diagnostics (OLD) measures key learning mechanisms at the three phases of change in an organization.[42]
- Organization Learning Inventory (OLI).[43]
- Learning Advantage measures learning orientations and facilitating factors.
- Organization Learning Climate Questionnaire.[44]

Exhibit 26.10 *Information Dissemination and Sharing*

1. One of the increasingly popular methods of improving information flow in organizations is through networking computers. Asian Paints Ltd, for example, uses e-mail to instantly communicate production figures, sales targets, etc. to its 14 production plants and distribution centres across the country. Its information system allows it to keep track of the 56 million packs it produces annually (in 40 shades of more than 100 types, sold through thousands of dealers). This helps the company keep the shop-floors completely responsive to market information.[45]

2. In 1992, HCL-HP started using a groupware, which allowed it to tap and pool the knowledge of its service engineers on an on-line basis. Any service engineer could hook into this countrywide data network to find out if a similar problem had been solved earlier by any of his colleagues. Not only did this reduce the solution from about 3 days to just 4 hours, it also gave the company a better service edge over its competitors.[46]

3. In M&M, the shop-floor engineers visit customers across the country twice a month. They videotape their interactions with them, and then play them back to the workmen on the shop floor. So, a complaint or reaction from a customer that would normally have reached the shop floor via the Internet memos from the service engineer is now heard live by the technical staff.[47]

- Two questionnaires—a 25-item questionnaire on the five aspects of learning organizations suggested by Senge and another 44-item questionnaire on the four aspects suggested by Garvin, viz., systematic problem solving, experimentation, learning from past experience and from others, and transferring knowledge.
- Faster Learning Organizations(FLO).[48]
- Learning Organization Process Survey (LOP Survey)[49] is based on the eight main characteristics of learning organizations suggested above. Half the items in this survey are stated in positive form and half in negative.

SUMMARY

Organizational learning is the process of acquiring, retaining, and using inputs for development, leading to an enhanced capability of self-learning in an organization. Organizational learning has three main sub-systems: acquiring–reflecting, retaining–integrating, and using–adapting. These relate to the three phases of innovation, implementation, and stabilisation, respectively.

There are relevant processes, climates, values, and norms for each system. There are also five mechanisms of organizational learning (experimenting and flexibility, mutuality and teamwork, contingency and incremental planning, use of temporary systems, and competency building) and certain policy implications as well.

A learning organization is one that is skilled in creating, acquiring, and transferring knowledge and modifying its behaviour to reflect new knowledge. Characteristics of learning organizations have been listed under eight heads: a holistic framework, strategic thinking, a shared vision, empowerment, information flow, emotional maturity, learning, and synergy.

GLOSSARY

adaptive learning   solving problems in the present without examining the appropriateness of current learning behaviours

generative learning   emphasising continuous experimentation and feedback in an ongoing examination of the way organizations define and solve problems

learning organization   an organization skilled at creating, acquiring, and transferring knowledge and modifying its behaviour to reflect new knowledge and insights

organizational learning   the process by which an organization acquires, retains, and uses inputs for development, resulting in an enhanced capacity for continued self-learning and self-renewal

EXERCISES

Concept Review Questions

1. What is organizational learning?
2. What are the sub-systems of organizational learning? What are their underlying processes?

3. What are the main mechanisms of organizational learning?
4. Discuss the process of diffusion and institutionalisation of organizational learning in large systems.
5. How do you define a learning organization?
6. What are the main characteristics of learning organizations?

Classroom Projects

1. Discuss in small groups (of two or three) how you would rate your institution/organization as a learning organization (low, medium, or high capability of learning), using the eight aspects suggested in this chapter.
2. Discuss in the same group which aspects of organizational learning are strong and which are weak in your institution/organization.

Field Projects

1. Discuss the various mechanisms of organizational learning. Find out if these are useful to assess an organization's learning capacity.
2. Interview an HR manager in the IT industry to find out what learning mechanisms are adopted in the industry. Do these match those discussed in this chapter?

Core Healthcare*

The story of growth at Core Healthcare Ltd (CHL), based in Ahmedabad, is almost a fairy tale. CHL has come a long way since its inception in 1988 as Core Parenterals. The company achieved overwhelming success in a wide range of healthcare products. During the past 9 years, the sales turnover of the company has swelled from a humble turnover of 21.7 million rupees and a profit of 1.1 million rupees in 1988 to about 2,610 million rupees in 1995–96. In terms of manpower, the growth has been from 30 employees to more than 3,000 employees. From a small IV fluid unit in 1988, today CHL has transitioned into an international pharmaceutical and healthcare company, spread over a sprawling campus of over 2.5 million square metres of land. CHL has created an astonishing capacity of 600 million units of IV fluids, 2.5 billion ampoules of SVPs, injectables, and topicals, 240 million IV sets and variants, 2.75 billion units of syringes and other disposables, and 1.5 billion tablets with 15 million bottles of formulations per annum. This capacity is supported by a country-wide distribution network comprising of over 5,000 distributors and stockists. In strict financial terms, the company has established a tradition of doubling sales and profits every year, and has an asset of 3 billion rupees and market capitalisation of over 10 billion rupees.

CHL has earned a reputation for quality products, state-of-art technology, and an aggressive marketing mindset. Banking upon the established management principle of cost reduction through economies of scale, CHL made super-normal profits at a time when the industry was scattered with small-size local operators. This the company did with panache, evolving a work ethic of high quality, zero bacteria, untouched-by-hand products. Within the company, the commitment towards stringent process controls and adherence of standard operating procedures to consistently deliver international quality products has been constantly reinforced.

The rewards of enterprise to CHL have not been distant. The company made an Euro issue offering in June 1994 with road shows across the world including Southeast Asia, US, UK, and Switzerland. CHL successfully completed the issue for 70 million US dollars (including the green shoe option of 10 million US dollars) for part-financing the on-going expansion-cum-diversification projects. CHL has thus been able to create a global investor base.

SHIFT FROM PARENTERALS TO HEALTHCARE

'Parenterals' referes to generic nutrients delivered to human beings through routes other than the mouth and intestines.

---

*Prepared by Dr Arun Kumar Jain, CEO and principal researcher, Jain-Bond Strategy Research. Reproduced with permission of All-India Management Association.

Till early 1990s, CHL was just an IV fluid manufacturer. With addition of several new products such as total parenteral nutrition, blood products, irrigation solutions, renal care products, pharmaceuticals, small volume parenterals, surgical products, medical disposables and devices, Core moved beyond the definition of parenterals, shifting towards total healthcare systems. In 1994, Core Parenterals Limited changed its name to CHL to reflect the new realities.

During the year 1995–96, CHL achieved appreciable growth in sales. There was also a significant increase in costs, overheads, and fixed charges. According to Mr Sushil Handa, managing director of CHL, the high incidence of overheads and fixed charges was a result of a strategic plan to invest simultaneously in technology, a series of new products, and large capacities in order to give a major growth thrust. This strategic plan involves major investments and would necessarily reflect on margins in the short-run. But then it would push the company from a medium-scale IV fluid company into the league of international scale healthcare companies with high margins and surplus in future.

CORE BUSINESS PHILOSOPHY

The governing work and quality philosophy at Core is both emotional and rational: Core marketed only those products that we would confidently use on our own dear ones. They called it Emotional Pharmacopoeia. They attribute it all to their philosophy.

Following the quality philosophy, CHL has articulated its core purpose thus:

It is our endeavour to contribute to saving life worldwide by achieving and maintaining excellence and leadership in the fields of healthcare, both, within India and internationally. This we shall achieve through maintaining continuously technological edge over competition, manufacturing products of world-class quality standards, being the most cost efficient manufacturer of our products world-wide, thereby making our products available at affordable prices and ensuring the highest standard of excellence in all aspects of our work.

ORGANIZATION

As an organization, Core was highly focused till recently on IV fluids. It has a flat, profit-centre-based structure built around specific products and markets. In line with growth of operations, the company has undergone structural changes. The functional structure has been dispensed with and a focused profit-centre-based organization structure has been installed. To improve efficiency of operations and remove wastages, the company has embarked on professionalising the functions with particular emphasis on market research, information technology, budgeting and control, re-engineering, TQM, and other scientific management techniques.

Human Resource Development

As can be expected for any company growing rapidly, CHL faced multiple challenges. In the initial years, the company lacked the means to draw highly qualified professionals, mainly because they were reluctant to join a new, fragile company. Since people were going to be the core strength for managing growth, Core adopted a multi-pronged strategy to develop in-house reservoir of managerial talents. Initially, the criterion was to check young and qualified persons for their ambitions, urge, and desire to achieve success. The second was to create an environment within the company so that people enjoyed work. In this process, a culture has come about wherein good performance is rewarded and publicly announced. The third element was to rotate the job-content of persons periodically and establish cross-functional teams to enrich their knowledge base and empower them to shoulder higher responsibilities. The fourth was to update learning through seminars and programmes of premier management institutions. This strategy of initial years has become a part of the organizational philosophy. A visibly young team manages prestigious projects, travels around the world, and manages a multinational business.

Training and Development

One of the key strengths of CHL is the concept of information sharing and cross-functional innovative training. In 1995–96, the company invested 15,221 man days in HRD activities at the corporate level, including training for field sales personnel. On an average, each employee at Core undergoes 45 man hours on various HRD inputs each year. Further as a technology and research driven company, it invests in the knowledge base of the employees through participation in international conferences and seminars.

The way CHL grooms and trains fresh recruits is fascinating. Through extensive HRD inputs, and empowerment with critical and significant responsibility and authority at a young age, the company has been able to create a bank of professionals who are young, ambitious, and have either grown with the company or are in the process of developing and shouldering high responsibilities. The company has created role models from the Indian mythology, such as Ekalavya of Mahabharatha. The story in Mahabharatha is that Ekalavya had the desire to be an ace archer, but was denied the opportunity by guru Dronacharya because of his humble background. This did not deter him from self-learning and development and achieve his ambition through hard work, self-experiments, and unending practice. He learnt without a guru and told himself 'I will persists until I succeed.' The training-cum-discussion halls at Core headquarters in Ahmedabad are a continuous reminder of the value of self-development through inspiring names, such as Ekalavya Hall, Persistence Hall, Excellence Hall, etc.

Another popular symbol of CHL's market aggressiveness is the tiger programme. The emphasis is on transforming a pussy-cat salesman into a tiger salesman, with the motto being, 'in the long run, tigers make more friends and close more sales, too.' According to the trainers, the pussy-cat salesman does a fine job of prospecting and establishing the initial contact. He makes a good presentation, but is not sharp at replying to sales objections and closing the deal. In his eagerness to be good and polite, he loses sight of his main objective, i.e., bagging the order. The tiger salesman, an end-product envisaged from this programme, is persistent and does not give up. He is trained to view every sales objection as an opportunity for telling more about his product, and at the end he does not hesitate to ask for the final order.

The training programme envisages each employee to develop all-round ground dynamism like Maradona, having the ability to play equally well from various positions on the field. He is at ease as a defender, forward, or in the mid-field and has the vision and intuition to find out open spaces, i.e., create opportunities and tactically send the ball through dribbling, dodging, kicking, or passing as the need arises. He has to be an excellent team builder, always passing the ball to get the goal and in the process never keeping the ball to himself for too long. Another important aspect of his play is his control of the ball and the belief that 'my head always rules my legs'. And, as in the other stories, Maradona too had a very humble beginning and achieved his status through sheer hard work, determination, and commitment to excel.

Latest addition

The latest addition to the training programmes is 'Vishwakarma'—for persons working on project sites. In the Hindu mythology, Vishwakarma is depicted as the master craftsman whose creations are artistic, beautiful, and supreme in quality. He is believed to be the first person who passed on the knowledge of architecture and its mechanics to future generations. The main objective of this programme is to develop creative capabilities among the participants, which should result in outstanding performance, better aesthetics, and codification of knowledge.

INTERNATIONAL OPERATIONS

Core has a vision to be a global company. Its international presence is extended to more than 63 countries, both developed and underdeveloped. During 1995–96 it consolidated its position in most of the export markets with more products getting registered, which would help achieve higher sales and profits. The strong quality equity of CHL has enabled the company to reduce the time lag in launching of new products. For example, within a span of 9 months, the disposable syringes and needles are being exported to more than 20 countries. Presently, exports constitute 40 per cent of total sales making it truly an international company.

At the next stage of internationalisation process, CHL is working towards setting up a strong international distribution and marketing network. It has already opened warehouses on certain markets and has been scouting for global managers to handle its international activities.

Simultaneously, Core Healthcare plans to invest in manufacturing operations abroad. In 1995–96, it had finalised joint ventures for manufacturing plants at Dubai, CIS (Commonwealth of Independent States, consisting of 11 former Soviet Union Republics), and China. At Dubai, Core Healthcare proposed to manufacture IV fluids, tablets, and liquid orals. Started in 1985 with an investment of 4.5 million rupees, Core Healthcare grew at a 75 per cent compound annual growth rate between 1988 and 1995, and at its peak, the company had a market capitalisation in excess of 15,000 million rupees. In 2002 it touched the one billion mark in terms of intravenous (IV) fluid bottles produced.

AWARDS

In its very first year of operation in 1995, Core's manufacturing facility for IV fluids at Sachana, near Ahmedabad, won the prestigious IDMA award, the highest recognition of quality excellence in the Indian pharmaceutical industry. The same facility also received the ISO 9002 approval from BVQI, London. It may be recalled that the IV fluid plant at Rajpur had already received ISO 9002 certification in 1994. The company's various manufacturing facilities have also been certified from GMP (good manufacturing practices) as per norms set by the World Health Organization.

NEW COMPETITIVE REALITIES

The prime competition for Core in international markets for its IV fluids came from the world's largest manufacturer, Baxter. It is reported that just as Core would study Baxter's strategies, the latter too had sessions on the former's scenario building and likely strategies in its strategy rooms. Of late, however, apparently inadvertently, the company was stepping on the toes of another Fortune 500 company, Becton Dickinson (or BD, as more popularly known), that was into blood transfusions and disposal syringes business. In effect, CHL had entered product markets dominated by two global giants, who not only had the financial muscle, marketing set-ups, and a high historical learning curve, but also the latest innovative products in their portfolios. Simultaneously, CHL's share has been discounted heavily at the bourses—from a peek of around Rs 300 to Rs 23 for a 10-rupees chip. CHL's main problem seemed to be the almost total absence of a widely experienced top management, an entrepreneurial organization that did not have the necessary experience in handling very large products (and business) having international ramifications, a heavy financial gearing resulting in heavy interest and depreciation outgo, a young relatively inexperienced middle management that still had to learn a different set of skills other than the Rambo culture of getting the work executed no matter how. Further, the markets for IV fluids had matured in India. The early first-mover advantages of CHL in terms of technology, high quality, and safety were being equaled or surpassed by almost every large-scale manufacturer. The distribution and dealers held a powerful hold on the manufacturers and were now more aggressive since the final buyer had choice and information about other companies products. A powerful wholesaler of North India said, 'Late 1980s Core came to us for dealership and set all sorts of terms and we had to agree. But now, those days are over when a IV fluid costing Rs 7.50 could be sold at Rs 32 per bottle. Now, equally or more reputed companies such as Wochardt and Albert Davis are selling at margins of just 25 paise and giving us credit.'

Questions for Discussion

1. What was the trigger for CHL to become a learning organization?
2. What is the approach of CHL to develop core competency in the company?
3. How did CHL use the Indian cultural heritage for inspiring its people to develop expertise?
4. What should, in your opinion, CHL do to continue to remain a learning organization in a new competitive context?

NOTES AND REFERENCES

1. Agyris, C. and D.A. Schon (1978). *Organizational Learning: A Theory of Action Perspective*, p. 29. Reading, MA: Addison-Wesley.
2. Argyris, C. (1977). 'Double loop learning in organisations', *Harvard Business Review*, (5); Agyris, and Schon. *Organizational Learning*.
3. Senge, P.M. (1990). *The Fifth Discipline: The Art and Practice of the Learning Organization*. New York: Double Day.
4. Kolb, D.A. (1984). *Experiential Learning: Experience as the Source of Learning and Development*. New Jersey: Prentice-Hall.
5. Carlson, K.D., B.P. Keane, and J.B. Martin (1976). 'R&D organizations as learning systems', *Sloan Management Review*, 17(3): 1–15.
6. Argyris, 'Double loop learning in organisations'.
7. Etheredge, L.S. and G. Short (1983). 'Thinking about government learning', *Journal of Management Studies*, 20(1): 41–58.
8. Fiol, C.M. and M.A. Lyles (1985). 'Organizational learning', *Academy of Management Review*, 10(4): 803–13.
9. Levitt, B. and J.G. Merch (1988). 'Organization learning', *Annual Review of Sociology*, 14: 319–40.
10. Stata, R. (1989). 'Organizational learning: The key to management innovation', *Sloan Management Review*, 39(3): 32–49.
11. Huber, G. (1991). 'Organizational learning: The contributing processes and literature', *Organization Science*, 2, 88–115.
12. Nevis, E.C, A.J. DiBella, and J.M. Gould (1995). 'Understanding organization as learning systems', *Sloan Management Review*, 36(2): 73–85.
13. Inkpen, A.C. and M.M. Crossan (1995). 'Believing is seeing: Joint ventures and organizational learning', *Journal of Management Studies*, 32(5): 595–617.
14. DiBella, A.J. (1996). *Organizational Learning Inventory*. Natick, MA: Organization Transitions.
15. For example, *Ibid.*
16. Inkpen, A. and M. Crossan (1995). 'Believing is seeing: Joint ventures and organizational learning' *Journal of Management Studies*, 32(5): 598.
17. Cavaluzzo, L. (1996). 'Enhancing team performance', *Health Forum Journal*, 5: 61–99.
18. Huber, G.P., (1991). 'Organizational learning: The contributing processes and literature,' *Organization Science*, 2(1): 88–115.
19. Schein, E. (1993). 'On dialogue, culture and organizational learning', *Organizational Dynamics*, 22(2): 40–51.
20. Guns, Bob and Kristin Anandsen (1996). *The Faster Learning Organization: Gain and Sustain the Competitive Edge*. San Franscisco: Jossey-Bass.
21. Khandwalla, P.N. (1992). *Organisational Design for Excellence*. New Delhi: Tata McGraw-Hill, p. 223.

22. Nevis, E.C, A.J. DiBella, and J.M. Gould. 'Understanding organization as learning systems', *Sloan Management Review*, Winter: 73–85

23. Ramnarayan, S. and J. Bhatnagar (1993). 'How do Indian organizations meet learning challenges?' *Vikalpa*, 18(1): 39–48.

24. Pareek, Udai (2002). *Effective Organizations: Beyond Management to Institution Building*, pp. 731–3. New Delhi: Oxford & IBH,

25. Garratt, Bob (1990). *Creating a Learning Organization: A Guide to Leadership, Learning and Development*. Cambridge: Director Books.

26. Senge. *Fifth Discipline*.

27. A large number of publications appeared on the subject during the 1990s. Two important journals— (M. Cohen, and L. Sproull (eds) (1991). 'Organizations learning' *Organization Science* (special issue), 2(1) and *Organizational Dynamics* (1993)—published special numbers on this subject.

28. Garvin, D.A. (1993). 'Building a learning organization', *Harvard Business Review*, 4: 80.

29. McGill, M.E., J.W. Slocum, and D. Lei (1992). 'Management practices in learning organization', *Organizational Dynamics*, 21(1): 5–17.

30. Garratt. *Creating a Learning Organization*.

31. Senge. *Fifth Discipline*.

32. Watkins, K.E. and V.J. Marsick (1993). *Sculpting the Learning Organization*, San Francisco: Jossey-Bass.

33. Watkins and Marsick. *Sculpting the Learning Organizations*.

34. Krishnamurthy, 1995, quoted in Shukla, M. (1997). *Competing Through Knowledge*. New Delhi: Sage.

35. Sharma, 1994, quoted in Shukla, *Competing Through Knowledge*.

36. Bose and Ghosh, 1991, quoted in Shukla, *Competing Through Knowledge*.

37. Kanavi, 1994, quoted in Shukla, *Competing Through Knowledge*.

38. Parker and Krishnamoorthy, 1993, quoted in Shukla, *Competing Through Knowledge*.

39. Sharma and Gupta, 1994, quoted in Shukla, *Competing Through Knowledge*.

40. Dhawan, 1995, quoted in Shukla, *Competing Through Knowledge*.

41. Khanna, 1992, quoted in Shukla, *Competing Through Knowledge*.

42. DiBella, A.J. (2001). *Learning Practices: Assessment and Action for Organizational Improvement*. Upper Saddle River, NJ: Prentice Hall.

43. Cavaluzzo, L. (1996). 'Enhancing team performance', *Health Forum Journal*, 5: 61–99.

44. Deshpande, M. and U. Pendse (undated). Organization learning questionnaires from personal communications with this author.

45. Lahiri, 1993, quoted in Shukla, *Competing Through Knowledge*.

46. Viswanathan, 1994, quoted in Shukla, *Competing Through Knowledge*.

47. Pareek, Udai (2002). *Training Instruments in HRD and OD*, Chapter 90. New Delhi: Tata McGraw-Hill.

48. Guns, Bob and Kristin Anandsen (1996). *The Faster Learning Organization: Gain and Sustain the Competitive Edge*. San Franscisco: Jossey-Bass.

49. Pareek, Udai (2002). *Training Instruments in HRD and OD*. New Delhi: Tata McGraw-Hill, Chapter 91.

27
Organizational Change

LEARNING OBJECTIVES

After studying this chapter, you will be able to
1. Define the sequential process of organizational change
2. Identify the main roles in change management
3. Elaborate the dynamics of the implementation of change in organizations
4. Suggest ways of ensuring effective implementation
5. Explain the phenomenon of resistance to change and suggest ways of dealing with it

Organizational change is a complex phenomenon. A recent book makes a distinction between changing reality, which is a continuous process, and changing perception, which is essentially a sporadic process. These have been proposed as two levels of change.[1] It has been suggested that we need to become 'the driver of change rather than being nailed by the multiplicity of influences that a change of external circumstances can wield'. The author emphasises the need for deciphering the early signals of change to be able to ride the crest.

Another recent book has proposed a model of change comprising four core tasks that are crucial to the success of any change initiative in organizations. These are appreciating change, mobilising support for change, executing change, and building change capability.[2]

Change has also been studied as turnaround of organizations. Khandwalla has made significant contributions on this phenomenon.[3]

We shall take up a few critical ones in this chapter, namely, the sequential process, the main roles in change, the dynamics of implementation, and resistance to change.

SEQUENTIAL PROCESS

There have been several models of the process of organizational change. All these models envisage change as a continuous process involving several stages. Eight stages are identified and detailed here:

1. **Initiation** Initiation is the stage for the vocalisation of the need to change. Organizational change starts when someone at the level of the corporate management, where the concern for a certain dimension of organizational functioning is shared and discussed, takes the initiative of proposing that something has to be done. The idea is mooted at the level of the corporate management, either being based on observations or recommendations from some other level of the organization

or being a result of discussion at the corporate management level. This usually leads to the hiring of a consultant or discussion with the appropriate set of people within the organization.

2. **Motivation** Motivation is the stage where people are involved in detailed consideration of the proposed change. At this stage, both the corporate management and the expert who helps with organizational change takes the necessary steps to involve a large section of the organization in thinking about the various dimensions of the change.

3. **Diagnosis** Diagnosis is the attempt to search for the main cause underlying the symptoms encountered.

4. **Information collection** At this stage, detailed information is collected about the dimension indicated by the diagnosis and alternative approaches are developed in relation to the problems or issues.

5. **Deliberation** The deliberation stage is concerned with evaluating various alternatives generated for dealing with the problem or the issues related to the change.

6. **Action proposal** This is the stage for framing a proposal in relation to the problems or issues identified.

7. **Implementation** Implementation is concerned with translating the proposed ideas into action.

8. **Stabilisation** Stabilisation is the stage of internalising the change and making it a part of the organization's normal life.

It may be useful to pay attention to the details of these processes as reflected in the various stages of change in the beginning. This makes it possible to pay less attention to the process as organizational change proceeds further and reserve more attention for the main task of implementing change.

MAIN ROLES

Several roles are involved in organizational change and these can help ensure a smooth and speedy transition. These include both internal and external roles. Organizational change is a collaborative effort in which several roles and individuals are involved. Various roles perform various functions. They make their specific contributions to the design and implementation of organizational change. The six main roles are discussed below in this connection.

Corporate Management

The corporate management includes the chief executive and several top executives who are involved in making policy decisions. The following are the main functions of the corporate management in relation to organizational change:

Legitimising function The corporate management legitimises the change being planned, recommended, and implemented. The more actively the corporate management promotes the change, the more legitimate it becomes and the quicker it is likely to be accepted. If the corporate management does not clearly indicate its interest in and support for the change, the implementation is likely to be slowed down. Concern on the part of the corporate management and the visibility of such concern are very important for smooth organizational change.

Energising function The corporate management energises the whole organization towards a common goal. The top team of 100 people evolved Larsen and Tubro's vision of being a world-class professional organization. The draft was shared with a large number of people. Based on these discussions, the final vision evolved. It was then widely disseminated.

Organizational change is a very difficult process. It may be slowed down at several stages. Often, enthusiasm flags. Sometimes difficulties arising in the natural course of the process may discourage members of the organization, who may find it difficult to deal with problems and prefer to take the course of least resistance by reverting to older methods or ways of management. The role of the corporate management is crucial at such critical points. The management revives the slackening pace and interest by taking up problems for discussion and by showing concern.

Communicating function The corporate management must communicate the proposed change to the rest of the organization, so that people are enthused and give full co-operation and commitment. They must convey a sense of urgency to the organization. Change fails in many organizations because the corporate management does not establish a great enough sense of urgency. The role of the chief executive is important in this context (see Exhibit 27.1).

Two communication consultants, who have helped large organizations communicate major changes to employees, have made very useful suggestions on communications:
- Communicate only facts—stop communicating values.
- Communicate face-to-face—do not rely on videos, publications, or large meetings.
- Target front-line supervisors—the responsibility of introducing the change to front-line employees is too important to be delegated.[4]

Exhibit 27.1 *Importance of Communication*

Allied Signal, a 13-billion-dollar American company making aerospace systems, automotive parts, and chemical products, with 58 business units, had grown rapidly through mergers and acquisitions, but the earnings had become stagnant. The company had developed an insular culture with centralised decision making. In 1991, the company was losing cash and was in dire need of transformational change. At that time Lawrence Bossidy took over as the chief executive. He talked to 5,000 employees in the first 60 days of his tenure. His message was simple: 'Here's what I think is good about us. Here's what I am worried about. Here's what we can do about it. And if we don't fix the cash problem, none of us is going to be around.' His message got through.

The company went through a radical transformation. It combined business units, closed factories, increased working-capital turnover, and generated substantial free cash. In all, 19,000 salaried jobs were cut and the company reduced the number of suppliers from 9,000 to 3,000. Net income went up from 359 million US dollars in 1991 to 708 million US dollars in 1994.

Exhibit 27.2 *Turnaround of Crompton Greaves Ltd*

Most of CGL's production was concentrated in Mumbai, where wage and real estate costs were among the highest in the country. CGL's sales were growing at a slower rate than the industry average and its profitability started to decline. The company's performance dipped to its lowest level in 1985.

Kewal Krishan Nohria (KKN) took over as president and managing director of CGL in 1985. He saw two challenges facing the company. First, the company needed to adapt to the changed conditions in the electrical equipment industry. It needed to respond to a buyer's market by emphasising quality and service in addition to controlling costs. Second, it had to diversify into new business areas to maintain growth and profitability. Both these challenges required a new mindset. KKN articulated these ideas in terms of a new vision for the company. According to the new vision, the company needed to adopt a new attitude for success, which would involve concern for customers, people, product, cost, and innovation. KKN visited all the divisions and regional offices of CGL to communicate his vision and values for the company. At each location he met with groups of about 40 employees and reached out to about 1,000 executives during the year. Managers attending these meetings were encouraged to repeat the same process with workers at lower levels. In these fora, employees were given opportunities to voice their views. The employees discovered that the top management was not only accessible but also had a clear vision and strategy. Arising out of these meetings, a simple statement of the strategy for change was evolved: excellence through a concern for quality, productivity, cost, and employees. This was widely displayed throughout the organization. CGL also diversified into electronics and telecommunications areas.

According to them values are best communicated through actions, not through words. When change requires front-line employees to do their job differently, that information must be conveyed face-to-face. Front-line supervisors are critical for the success of any change effort.

Exhibit 27.2 is another illustration of the importance of communication.[5]

Gate-keeping function The corporate management helps in establishing a relationship between the consultants and the various groups in the organization. This is usually done by calling meetings in which the purpose of the change is explained and the consultants are invited into the organization.

Consultant(s)

A consultant or a team of consultants usually comes from outside to help with the change, but he or she can also be an insider. The consultant's role is that of an expert who has both knowledge and experience in the field in which change is proposed. There are some advantages in having an outside consultant for some time. Internal members, even if they have the necessary expertise, are likely to be biased by their own perceptions of the problem. Also, they may be restrained by internal dynamics. This may make them less effective. Therefore, even organizations with high-quality expertise in a particular field initially invite outside consultants. The following functions are performed by the consultant:

Implanting function The consultant does not supplant available internal expertise but supplements and implants such expertise. It is necessary that the consultant carries the various people along with him or her during the different stages of organizational change. Then the consultant is able to make change a part of the organization.

Transcending function   One great advantage of having an external consultant is that he or she is not bound by the constraints governing members of the organization. He or she takes an independent overall view. The consultant transcends both the ecology of the organization—that is, the various units and departments—to be able to take this overall view of the organization as well as transcending time and the people not yet attuned to the future of the organization. This transcending function makes the role of the consultant more creative. He or she thinks about the organization as a whole—not only as it is now but as it is likely to be in the future. This helps to give a wider perspective to the organizational understanding of the change.

Function of generating alternatives   The consultant is not there as much to work out a specific solution as to help the organization develop the capability of evolving solutions. The consultant does this by generating several alternatives, out of which the organization can choose one or two. The more the consultant generates and helps to generate various alternatives, the more creative and useful his or her role becomes and the more the organization develops the ability to design interventions and ways of solving problems on its own.

Process facilitating function   The consultant is primarily a process facilitator. He or she has to be perceptive of the reality in the organization. There is no ideal or best solution. Even if one solution is technically the best, a consultant may see the repercussions of the solution and wish to make the necessary modifications to suit the situation. The consultant also helps in developing various roles as the programme of change proceeds and change begins to be implemented. The process-facilitating role helps the consultant to move towards self-liquidation. He or she also helps the relevant people in the organization to take over the role of consultant when the programme is being implemented.

Shock-absorbing function   During the planning of change and making of necessary recommendations, much unpleasant feedback may have to be given to the organization. It is sometimes difficult for internal people to do so. They cannot take the risk necessary to make certain things explicit. An external consultant can take such a risk. He or she can afford to absorb the shock created by the change and help the system to confront reality and discuss certain processes, which may be quite unpleasant but without which it may not be possible to move towards the solution.

Resource-sharing function   The consultant brings with his or her background the latest knowledge and a wide variety of experience, which he or she uses in making organizational change effective. The consultant collects these resources and shares them with internal members so that the knowledge can be utilised for making the change effective.

Resource-building function   The consultant helps in generating resources within the organization by building the necessary expertise as he or she works with the organization. This does not mean that the consultant makes people dependent on him or her. By sharing his or her knowledge and experience and by continuously discussing issues with the concerned people, he or she helps in building internal resources.

Self-liquidating function   By building internal expertise and resources, the consultant is working towards withdrawal from the organization and liquidating his or her role and indispensability. In many cases, the consultant enjoys the influencing function so much that he or she may continue to play this role in the organization. This is bad both for the organization and the consultant. The consultant must hence deliberately refrain from using undue influence on internal executive decisions.

As the work of the organizational change draws to a close, he or she takes definite and deliberate steps to withdraw and wean the organization off depending on him or her. The self-liquidating function is very difficult to carry out. Once a consultant is successful and effective, he or she faces the temptation to continue to influence organizational decisions. If the consultant is not perceptive enough, in his eagerness to be helpful, he or she may make the organization dependent on him or her. If he or she enjoys this dependency, the results may be bad for the organization as well as for the consultant.

The organization should have the capacity to assimilate the influence and expertise of the outside consultant. Necessary preparations should be made to make use of the consultant in the organization. It is important that continuous communication is maintained with the consultant at all the stages of the process of change.

Counterpart

Even if the expert is from outside, some people from the organization must work with him or her. They represent the same expertise the consultant has or, at least, they propose to develop that expertise. This role we shall call the counterpart role. This may already exist in an organization or may be created. For example, if a new management information system is to be introduced, people with technical experience and expertise need to be involved. If such expertise does not exist in the organization, new people may have to be recruited.

The counterpart helps in implementing the policies and activities worked out and accepted and in stabilising these in the organization. It is only through the counterpart that the change becomes a part of the organization. Several issues need to be explored in relation to the counterpart: whether the counterpart should be an independent individual or group, whether members from different groups constitute a team that functions as the counterpart, how to legitimise the counterpart role in the system, the length of time required for the counterpart to develop the necessary expertise, etc. In many cases, jealousy develops when the counterpart becomes successful and effective. His or her success may produce some threat to other members of the organization, leading to various prejudices and jealousies. All such issues require careful attention and proper handling.

Implementation Team

The implementation team consists of a group of people from various departments or areas of the organization who have been given the responsibility for monitoring, deliberating on, and making recommendations on the programme from time to time. The team must ensure proper motivation of people throughout the organization and take steps to ensure effective implementation. The following are the main functions of the implementation team.

Collaboration-building function The implementation team helps to build collaboration among various sections and departments of the organization. It should therefore be a cohesive team, every member having respect for the others and collectively evolving a consensus in spite of differences in views. An effective team is one that has a representation from various kinds of expertise and diverse experiences relevant for the change. Yet people in this team must be prepared to listen to each other and take collective decisions that are not necessarily unanimous or even endorsed by the majority although consensus is developed.

Gate-keeping function The implementation team helps keep the communication channels between those who are planning and implementing change and the rest of the organization open. This is done by developing a liaison between all the various departments and sections of the organization. Since the team has representatives from these departments and sections, it is able to convey various matters to the departments and raise various questions there. Similarly, it receives feedback from the departments for discussion with the implementation team in its entirety.

Reviewing function The implementation team reviews the progress of the change programme from time to time and makes the necessary adjustments so that the implementation is efficient. The reviewing function involves both stock taking as well as making the necessary modifications so that implementation is not hampered.

Policy-formulating function The implementation team makes recommendations and formulates policies in the light of the review to ensure that the programme of change is both effective and smooth. This helps in making the programme more realistic.

Chief Implementer

Organizational change need not be implemented by those who are working in one particular area. In fact, it is much better to make such implementation independent of functional responsibility in an organization. The chief implementer is usually the chairperson of the implementation team. But his or her responsibility is not confined only to discussing the problems and making recommendations. The chief implementer takes the responsibility of monitoring the programme and ensuring proper implementation. The main difference between the role of the chief implementer and the implementation team is that a group can never take on executive responsibility. This can be taken on only by an individual. However, the group can help the chief implementer to perform his or her function more effectively in several ways. The following are the main functions of this role:

Monitoring function   The chief implementer monitors the programme of change. He or she has to be a tough person, a go-getter, in order to relentlessly keep the programme on schedule. He or she ensures that the programme design and the time schedule are followed.

Diagnostic function   The chief implementer reviews the programme from time to time to find out whether anything is preventing its smooth functioning and progress. This is the diagnostic function of the chief implementer. He or she collects the necessary information through specially designed questionnaires or interviews and uses these to discuss the need to either modify the programme or provide additional input for its proper progress with the implementation team.

Executive function   The chief implementer has the responsibility of implementing the programme. This is an executive function. It involves not only making recommendations but ensuring that action is taken on whatever has been decided. He or she thus mobilises the necessary resources and works on the implementation of the programme.

The chief implementer should be systematic in his or her approach and should concern himself or herself with systematic planning, going into the details of the various steps planned. At the same time, he or she should be flexible. If the individual has strong views and ideas and so finds it difficult to accept others' points of view, he or she would not make a good implementer.

The chief implementer needs to be creative and imaginative. He or she will come across several problems and have to find solutions for them. He or she should search for various ways of dealing with problems, sometimes unconventional ones. He or she should also be resourceful and should be known for the ability to implement and for concern for the organization and the employees.

Task Forces

Task forces are set up for specific purposes—to prepare material, collect information, generate ideas, and take on a specific responsibility, which is time bound. Many task forces get dissolved as soon as their particular task is over. Task forces make use of the various kinds of expertise and skills available in the organization.

The relationship between these roles and their involvement in organizational change is presented in Exhibit 27.3. As the exhibit shows, all the roles contribute to

Exhibit 27.3 *Key Roles in Sequential Process of Organizational Change*

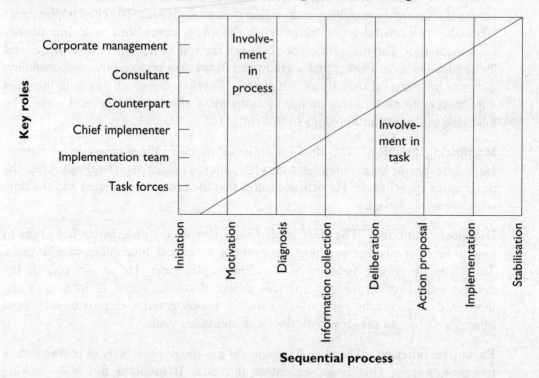

the process and to the task. For example, the corporate management and the consultant are primarily contributing to the process: their major function is to facilitate the process so that the necessary movement towards organizational change is possible. The counterparts also contribute to the process, although they experience increasing preoccupation with the task. The maximum concern for and involvement in the task is that of the task forces and implementation team. The chief implementer of the organizational change is certainly involved in the achievement of the task. He or she is also involved in smoothening the process.

Every role is concerned, to some degree, with the process as well as with the task. However, there are differences in terms of relative emphasis: some roles are primarily involved in the process while others are involved in the task. It would, for example, be dysfunctional if the chief executive or the corporate management were concerned directly with the task. Similarly, the focus of the external consultant may be on developing the necessary understanding of the process through diagnosis and preparation of recommendations but his or her involvement in implementation of the task may not be useful. This does not mean that the corporate management and the consultants are indifferent to the task or the implementation of recommendations. They are not directly involved in taking action, nor do they take the primary responsibility for implementation, but they do provide the necessary climate and support.

Exhibit 27.3 also indicates the relative involvement of the different roles in the process or task that is likely to make them effective at different stages of the change process.

In the initial phases, the involvement required with the process is much greater than that in the subsequent phases when, gradually, greater involvement in the task may become possible. When the process of change has begun, all the roles concerned with it should pay more attention to processes. If this is properly done, task performance becomes easier. Towards the end, all roles can pay attention to the task. The exhibit also indicates that, even towards the end, the top management has to be concerned with the process, though the intensity and the time spent will be less. As a matter of fact, the involvement of the top management will always be predominantly with the process, whereas the task force(s) would need to pay attention mainly to the emergent tasks.

EFFECTIVE IMPLEMENTATION

Change is alien to an organization yet needs to be accepted. Unless a change is internalised and integrated, it remains 'alien'. Introduction of change in an organization is akin to the transplantation of an organ in a body. An organism (a body) and an organization have some common features. The transplanted part in a body has to be integrated with that body. It may be rejected, and so a watch has to be kept to ensure that it is not and steps have to be taken to facilitate integration. The same applies to an organization. It is necessary to ensure that the change gets integrated into the organization, is stabilised, and becomes a part of the working of the organization. This is a part of the implementation process.

Implementation can be defined as the institutionalisation and internalisation of a change after it has been accepted by an organization and a decision has been taken to accept and make it an ongoing activity. Implementation starts after a decision has been taken to plan a programme of change. Several contextual factors have been found significant to the success of implementation.

Fullen and Pomfret have suggested four different dimensions of implementation.[6] These relate to the characteristics of the innovation (its explicitness and the complexity, or degree and difficulty, of change), strategies and tactics (in-service training, resource support, feedback mechanisms, and participation in decision making), characteristics of the adopting unit (the adoption process, the organizational climate, environmental support, and demographic factors), and characteristics of macro socio-political units (design issues, incentive system, evaluation, and political complexity). Implementation has been treated as an issue of control versus decentralisation and facilitation of change through participation.

Implementation may be seen as a multidimensional process. Paul[7] has proposed the concept of strategic management for the implementation of public programmes as an interaction between four dimensions—environment (opportunity, needs, constraints, threats, scope, diversity, and uncertainty), strategy (service–client sequence and demand–supply resource mobilisation), process (planning and allocation, monitoring and control, human resource development, and motivation–compliance), and structure (differentiation–integration of tasks, structural forms, degree of decentralisation, and degree of autonomy).

The end result of implementation is the institutionalisation and stabilisation of change. Institutionalisation implies making the change a permanent part of an organization; internalisation means stabilisation of the change so that it becomes a natural part of an organization's working style—the former is more structural and the latter more processual.

In order to achieve the end results, one starts with planning the whole process of implementation. Implementation primarily consists of monitoring the change, taking action in relation to the change, and making the necessary adjustments in the programme that has been accepted for implementation (which may be called adaptation). This three-phase implementation process (monitoring, action, adoption) is possible if the necessary support is provided at the various stages. This gives us a basic model of the implementation process, which is shown in Exhibit 27.4. As the exhibit indicates, planning is the initial process followed by the circular process of implementation, in which the feedback loop goes from adaptation to monitoring. This leads to institutionalisation and stabilisation of change. The various aspects of this process are briefly discussed in this section.

Planning

The main purpose of planning is to have an overall understanding of the nature of implementation. Here, 'planning' refers to the planning of the implementation process after a decision has been taken on making a change. Reviewing several Asian experiences in implementation of curriculum change, a group of experts have suggested that the preparation should include broad-based participation by people involved in the implementation of the programme itself, public support, and adequate resources for implementation of the programme. The following three dimensions are involved in planning.

Phasing   Planning may be focused on the phasing of implementation. Implementation may be a short-term or a long-term programme. Depending on the nature of the change, the implementation process may have to be phased. Phasing may be either temporal (in terms of time) or spatial (in terms of the various parts or locations of an organization).

Temporal phasing would involve preparation of a plan in which some elements of the innovation may be introduced later. For example, in some organizations, when a new system of human resource management is introduced, performance appraisal is implemented first; then, after it gets stabilised, the potential appraisal system is implemented. Thus the whole system may not be implemented at one time. Phasing allows some elements of the change programme to stabilise before the next elements are introduced.

Phasing can also be in relation to the various parts of the organization. For example, the programme of change may be implemented in some parts of the

Exhibit 27.4   Model of Implementation of Change

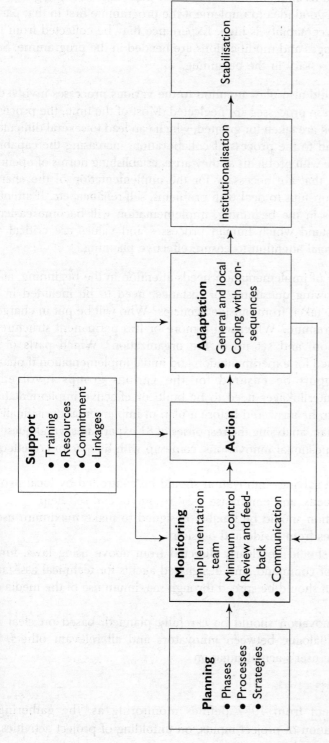

organization first, followed by implementation in other parts later. If the organization is a large one, it may be a good idea to implement the programme first in that part of the organization where acceptability is high. Experience may be collected from that part to see what new changes and modifications are needed in the programme. Such attention to phasing is necessary in the beginning.

Processes Planning should also play attention to the various processes involved in implementation. Often these processes are neglected. Most of the time, the processes underlying implementation are taken for granted, which can lead to several difficulties. Attention needs to be paid to the process of collaboration, increasing the capability of the organization to cope with problems as they arise, establishing norms of openness and various other values that are necessary for the implementation of the change, developing creative relationships to deal with problems, self-reliance, etc. If attention is paid to these processes in the beginning, implementation will become easier. It may be useful to understand which human processes and values are critical and therefore will require special attention to ensure effective planning.

Strategies The strategy of implementation needs attention in the beginning, at the planning stage. The following questions, for instance, need to be included in the strategy: Will any help be taken from outside agencies? Who will be put in charge of the implementation programme? When will a more or less permanent structure be evolved (institutionalisation) and set up in the organization? Which parts of the organization will be selected for experimentation and initial implementation if phasing is used? How will support be ensured for the various groups involved in implementation? What interlinkages need to be built for effective implementation? All such questions need to be answered before a plan of implementation is finalised.

Havelock and Huberman, analysing the responses of 81 experts to several questions on implementation of educational innovations, came up with five factors of effective strategy formulation[8]:

1. Participative problem solving—innovation should be controlled by local people, responsive to their needs, and emphasise local resources and self-help
2. Open input—innovation should be flexibly designed to make maximum use of all ideas and resources from inside and outside
3. Power—innovations should be clearly directed from above using laws, formal procedures, a chain of command, and designated agents for technical assistance
4. Diffusion—innovation should be spread through maximum use of the media and informal networks
5. Planned linkage—innovation should be carefully planned, based on clear and realistic objectives, dialogue between innovators and all relevant others, and high sensitivity to the user's actual situation

Monitoring

A World Bank document from 1977 defines monitoring as 'the gathering of information on the utilisation of project inputs, on unfolding of project activities, on timely generation of project outputs, and on circumstances that are critical to the effective implementation of the project'.[9] A document issued by the United Nations in 1978 on monitoring and evaluation defines the concept of monitoring as follows: 'The term monitoring usually refers to the process of routine periodic measurement of programme inputs, activities and outputs undertaken during programme implementation. Monitoring is normally concerned with the procurement, delivery and utilization of programme resources, adherence to work schedules or progress made in the production of outputs.'[10] Both these definitions agree that the function of monitoring is to provide early warnings concerning shortfalls in inputs or outputs in order to enable the programme management to undertake timely corrective measures.

Monitoring is necessary to make implementation effective. Monitoring means ensuring that a plan proceeds according to the original design. It is necessary to set up a mechanism of monitoring and reviewing a programme of change and its implementation.

Monitoring and institutionalisation may be kept independent for some time in an organization. Further, the monitoring function may precede institutionalisation of the change (in the form of setting up a permanent or semi-permanent unit to take over the programme) so that the advantages of monitoring may be fully utilised. There are several reasons why monitoring and institutionalisation should be kept independent for some time. While a monitoring group may be a temporary system, the group that takes over the programme of change and through which the programme is institutionalised in the organization will be a permanent or a semi-permanent system.

First, it is necessary to involve a wide cross-section of people in the monitoring function. This is not possible if the programme is institutionalised too quickly and a permanent unit or department takes over this function and the monitoring function. In order to make the monitoring broad based, it may be useful to have a representation of various groups in the implementation team, which should be a temporary system.

Second, if the function is institutionalised too early, the new department or unit will have a need to justify its existence and may therefore not pay attention to several factors that can create problems in the implementation of the change. An independent and temporary group, not having any vested interest in the programme, is more likely to pay attention to acknowledging and sorting out these difficulties.

Third, if the monitoring group continues to be an independent one, it may be able to attend to the several dimensions which require continuous attention that might be neglected by a permanent or semi-permanent group (because it would be too busy with day-to-day activities and may thus neglect some important dimensions in favour of the urgent issues, hoping to come back to those later and never finding time).

Lastly, being a broad-based group, the implementation team may be able to garner support from others in the organization more easily.

The following dimensions of monitoring require attention.

Implementation team A broad-based task group or implementation team should be set up to implement and to monitor such a programme effectively. It is useful to have an almost whole-time coordinator for such a group. This group may have representation from several parts of the organization. It should include people who are known for their creativity, who are positive while critical, and who are interested in providing support to new ideas. The convenor of the team should have a high enough status in the organization to be able to garner the necessary support for the group. He or she should also enjoy high acceptance in the organization, should have high task concern with an eye to being effective, should enjoy creative work in which there is no authority involved, and should be interested in the field of the change in question.

In one organization where a new human resource development system was being implemented, a task group for implementation was set up even before the new department was created. This task force continued for some time. The convenor of the task force was well known for his implementation skills and for his high task orientation. The task group had representation from several units of the organization. After the task group had functioned for some time, a new department was created in order to institutionalise the HRD system and a senior person, a director, was put in charge of this new function (the convenor of the task group was a general manager). However, the task group still continued to function and the chief of the new department attended the meetings of the task group as a permanent invitee. Although he was from a senior grade, he continued to attend the meetings and provide the necessary information about the functioning of the HRD system, while the implementation team continued to work on new dimensions and transferred to the HRD department those dimensions on which stability had been reached.

The above experience indicates that in some organizations it is acceptable to continue to have a parallel temporary system for some time in order to provide support and critical feedback to a new permanent unit.

Minimum control Monitoring will be most effective when it is able to keep track of what is happening at various levels in the organization, provide support for local experimentation, and make any necessary modifications in the programme. Monitoring is a delicate affair. In one sense it is a control function, getting feedback from time to time in order to take decisions, ensuring that the programme is carried out according to the design, and reminding people and communicating to them the need to meet schedules. On the other hand, it also attempts to develop new norms of creativity, diversity, and experimentation. This combination is possible if the implementation team uses minimum formal controls and yet is able to keep control of the implementation of the programme.

Review and feedback Implementation requires getting data and experiences about the use of a particular innovation. Periodic reviews may be based on continuous feedback. Monitoring also involves providing feedback to people on how well they are implementing the programme. The function of a review is to know what difficulties people are experiencing in implementing a programme so that the necessary support can be provided.

Dissemination of information   As a result of review and feedback, the implementation team collects information about what is happening in various parts of the organization with regard to the change being implemented. It may prepare its own strategies of collecting information and disseminating information on experiences of success to reinforce confidence and optimism in other people. Information that is needed to implement the programme may also be disseminated from time to time. The implementation group may wish to prepare a programme of how such information is to be disseminated and what will be the form of the dissemination in advance. It may issue written instructions and send written communication. It may also convene special seminars and meetings in order to discuss problems and experiences.

Action

A programme of change requires certain steps to be taken. 'Action' covers all the details of actual implementation, which involves various phases and the steps people take.

Adaptation

Fullen and Pomfret have suggested two main dimensions of implementation[11]—what they call fidelity (the actual use corresponding to the intended or the planned use) and mutual adaptation (flexibility, so that a programme develops and changes during the process of implementation). Adaptation has been suggested as being one of the two main criteria for the effectiveness of implementation of a change. A programme in which no modifications are introduced later does not indicate effective implementation. Implementation requires understanding and analysis of the experiences people have with the programme as well as learning from them. This should be reflected in the modifications that are made in the programme. Adaptation may be both general (in the sense that some modifications may be made in the original plan) and some may be local (indicating that while the programme is being implemented throughout the organization, some units in the organization may make the necessary modifications in it to suit their own requirements). Such an approach gives flexibility.

Dealing with consequences of change   Change introduces an alien element and causes some disturbance. When a change is introduced in an organization, it may produce a threat for some people. Such threats are more imaginary than real. It may also produce some 'negative' results in the short term. For example, the introduction of a job enrichment programme or work redesign programme may result in an initial fall in productivity, initial dissatisfaction among people who have to learn new things, and initial concern among the supervisors about their functions. (The term 'initial' has been used to indicate that these are temporary symptoms of the disturbance which is a necessary part of change.) The organization has to deal with such consequences. If attention is not paid to the consequences, the symptoms may accumulate and contribute to a rejection of the change.

This is similar to the problem of organ transplantation in a human body. Transplantation produces some disturbances, shown in the form of a high temperature, change in blood pressure, etc. These symptoms have to be controlled. If the early post-operative period can be managed properly, the transplantation may be successful.

It has been reported in cases of new job enrichment and work redesign systems that immediately after the change is introduced in the organization, there is a fall in production. In work redesigning efforts, the dissatisfaction of supervisory staff increases gradually when they perceive that their roles are becoming redundant. Unless the new programme does something about this dissatisfaction (e.g., redesigning their roles, involving them in critical decisions, etc.), the change may not succeed as the supervisory staff create obstacles.

In one organization, a new human resource system was introduced that included a new performance appraisal system. As a result of open discussion of the employees' objectives with their managers and later discussion of favourable and unfavourable factors for performance (which were part of the new appraisal system), the employees wanted to know more about ratings. Some managers felt uneasy and thought that the new system was increasing 'indiscipline'. The problem was solved by organizing training programmes for employees (appraisees) and managers (appraisers) on how to receive and give feedback and counselling (coaching). In another organization, similar consequences were anticipated and similar action was taken as a preventive prior to the introduction of the new system. This helped to reduce the problem considerably.

Support

Support of various kinds is required for the implementation of a programme. The main sources of support are administrative and managerial groups. Some important dimensions of support are suggested below:

Training New skills are needed for the implementation of a programme. It is necessary to provide training for such skills. This may include process skills such as collaboration, openness, problem solving, and decision making, or these may be specific technical and work-oriented skills such as those of planning and using information and collecting information for specific purposes.

Resources Implementation requires support in terms of various types of resources, such as human, financial, and material resources. The implementation team provides such support by identifying needs from time to time. Resource support may be needed for all the three aspects of managing organizational change—for monitoring, for implementing an action, and for bringing about modifications and adaptations.

Top management's commitment A critical dimension is support from the top management. The involvement of the top management is necessary for effective implementation of change. This may come about as signals from the top management that they consider the change important, that they are interested in its implementation, and that they themselves are involved in the change.

In one organization where a new HRD system was being implemented, there was little enthusiasm during the first year. Next year, it was reported that the chief executive had sat down with his secretary himself and had helped him to prepare the next year's plan and spent some time on performance review. The implementation of the HRD system was much faster this year. This was a mode of top management support in which the top management does what it wants other managers to do. In another instance, the chief executive attended seminars organized to discuss the problems in the implementation of the HRD system. This sent a signal of support from the top management.

Linkages Support may also be required in terms of building linkages both with external experts and various other agencies and with internal departments and groups who may provide the necessary help in the implementation of the programme. While the programme may officially be the responsibility of one group, it should be the responsibility of the whole organization to implement it. The development of internal linkages between the implementation team and the permanent department or unit, between the implementation team and the line management, between the implementation team and top management, etc. helps to provide the necessary support for the change.

Linkages are also needed between the internal people (or the internal facilitator) and the external consultants. An external consultant does not work alone. The implementation team depends to a great extent on vital linkages between the external consultant and internal people.

A caselet on effective planning and implementation of change in a large organization (see Exhibit 27.5) illustrates several of the points discussed above.[12]

Exhibit 27.5 *Restructuring the State Bank of India*

The State Bank is India's largest bank. The old Imperial Bank was nationalized in 1955 to promote rural development, broadbase entrepreneurship, and provide finance to the public sector. The State Bank grew phenomenally after its nationalisation, and by 1970 it had increased the number of its offices from about 400 to over 2,100 (in the early eighties it had some 6,000 offices and over 100,000 employees). In 1969, several other banks were nationalised, and from having a monopoly over public sector business, the State Bank was suddenly confronted with a lot of competition for this sector of business. Huge size, bureaucratic structure, the lack of expert staff support to the branch manager lost near the bottom of the vast managerial hierarchy, and having to compete compelled the State Bank of to reorganise its structure with the help of outside consultants. The objective was to devise a structure that could facilitate the pursuit of profitability and growth but keeping in mind the bank's social responsibility.

A SWOT analysis was performed to identify the strengths and weaknesses of the organization and it was agreed that organization change should be implemented to improve the bank's competitive position, facilitate decentralization (with accountability for performance), develop resilience and challenge taking

Exhibit 27.5 (*Contd*)

[sic] capacity in the organization, and bring about greater clarity in the staff about the bank's tasks, thus facilitating the development of managers. Several 'principles' of reorganization were articulated, such as greater emphasis on catering to different market segments, increasing performance orientation by adopting performance based budgeting and review of performance, bringing about greater unity of command over the branch managers, and the separation of operations from planning and staff function.

A participative process was used to usher in the changes. The following major changes were made:

- Accounting was now done on market segment basis and managers of market segment divisions were appointed to report to each branch manager. These included the commercial and institutional banking, small industries and small business, agricultural banking, and personal banking divisions.
- Annual budgeting was introduced with monthly performance reporting and review from branch level upwards.
- A unified chain of command was introduced starting from managers of divisions reporting to branch manager, who in turn reported to the regional chief, who in turn reported to the general manager (operations) at the local head office, who in turn reported to the chief general manager of the local head office, who in turn reported to the managing director at the central office. A regional manager controlled about 75 branches and a general manager (operations) controlled 5–6 regional managers. There were 12 local head offices.
- Specialized staff and functional support at local head offices was provided under a general manager (planning). Development managers who were specialists in each market segment, a planning manager, a personnel manager, specialists like the organization and methods officer, and other service functionaries reported to this general manager. At the central office, the managing director was assisted by deputy managing directors (in charge of operations, development and planning, personnel and services, and associate banks) and these were assisted, in their functional areas, by specialists in their fields.
- Overall corporate coordination was provided by the Central Management Committee consisting of the chairman, managing director, and deputy managing directors. Similarly, at each local head office there was a 'Circle' management committee consisting of the chief general manager, general manager (planning), general manager (operations), and chief regional managers as invitees, and a 'Circle' Coordination Committee of the same officials. At each branch there was a Branch Management Committee consisting of the branch manager, managers of sectoral divisions, and accounts manager.

A RADICAL APPROACH: DOMAIN RESHUFFLING

Organizations operate in an environment with which they have a close relationship in terms of getting human, material, technological, and financial resources. When the operating environment of an organization becomes unfavourable or hostile (e.g., due to a change in the governmental policy of not using a particular raw material or a High/Supreme Court ruling that bans mining), the organization may resort to what Khandwalla[13] has called 'domain reshuffling'. This is the strategy of giving up some domain (area of business) and adopting some other(s) that seem to be favourable. Exhibit 27.6[14] demonstrates how Third World organizations were able to manage change.

Exhibit 27.6   *Domain Reshuffling*

Organizational sickness is frequent in the Third World. A common response to sickness in the West is for sick organizations to exit from depressed domains and enter buoyant domains. But in many Third World countries there are legal and other restrictions on choosing what domains or business the organization can operate in. And yet, there are many examples, some ingenious ones, of how sick Third World organizations have successfully sought to get into more buoyant environments and/or out of unfavourable environments:

- Gambia Produce and Marketing Board owned by the government of Gambia, Africa, was originally set up to trade in oilseeds, cotton, rice, etc. It also operated oil mills and river transportation facilities, and traded in fertilizer, lime, soap, etc. The company began to make losses. As part of its turnaround effort, it withdrew from the loss-making import of rice and fertilisers and from dealing in other loss-making products.
- Richardson and Cruddas, India, a producer of structurals and various machineries, began to make losses in the mid-seventies. As part of its turnaround strategy, it sought to get out of the highly competitive and loss-making low-valued structurals business, reversed its proposed expansion of structurals making capacity, and moved more aggressively into high-valued structurals. It also doubled sales of scrap, moved aggressively into foreign markets, capitalising in part on Indian aid to other countries, and pressured various government bodies for orders.
- Jamaica Railway Corporation, operating in Jamaica, West Indies, was a loss-making railway. It sought to make its environment more buoyant by helping to reopen a port, and by organizing luxury and educational tours and excursion trips. It also aggressively sought to carry greater passenger traffic and bulk cargo, such as petroleum products.
- Sylvania and Laxman, an Indian producer of lamps and bulbs, began to lose money in the mid-seventies. It aggressively penetrated the hitherto neglected rural market as part of its turnaround strategy.
- Standard Motors, an Indian producer of cars and a loss-making unit, moved away from producing vehicles that used petrol, and into vehicles using the much cheaper diesel, the latter being a growth segment of the automobile industry.
- Enfield, an Indian producer of two-wheelers and agro-engines, sought to diversify into the high growth chemicals and electronics industries. Based in South India, Enfield had hitherto neglected North Indian markets. Enfield aggressively sought to penetrate these markets.
- State Timber Corporation, owned by the Government of Sri Lanka, a producer of timber, sought forward vertical integration into such buoyant product markets as teak paneling, doors and window frames, and charcoal.
- Tinplate, India contracted with its holding company, Tata Steel, a giant steelmaker, to galvanize the latter's steel sheet.
- Air India embarked on a major image revamping exercise to turn into a truly international airline from being mainly an ethnic airline catering mostly to Indian passengers. It aggressively sought to tap the first class and business class travellers businesses, and also sought new routes.
- Bharat Heavy Plate and Vessels, a Government of India owned producer of sophisticated heat exchangers, pressure vessels, and cryogenic equipment, and loss making since its inception did an ABC analysis of its orders, and found that small orders contributed the bulk of its losses. Accordingly it decided not to take small orders. It sought to expand business in the lucrative area of systems selling (as opposed to marketing pieces of equipment).
- Bharat Heavy Electricals, a producer of electrical equipment, another Government of India undertaking, made losses in the early seventies. As part of its revival strategy, it set up an exports division, and sought and landed foreign turnkey projects. It began to emphasize the marketing of energy systems rather than of just electrical equipment.

DEALING WITH RESISTANCE TO CHANGE

An organization often has to deal with resistance to change. There may be several reasons for resistance to change. If these reasons are understood, effective steps can be taken to reduce resistance. Most of these steps can be of a preventive nature, reducing resistance to a great extent. Some action can also be taken when resistance is experienced. We present below some ideas on dealing with resistance to change. Exhibit 27.7 summarises the sources of resistance and the steps that can be taken to deal with such resistance.

Perceived peripherality of change If executives perceive that the change being introduced in the organization is not critical for them or their units, they are likely to resist such a change. Implementation of change can be effective if the change introduced is seen as critical and useful. This can be achieved by involving the concerned managers in the diagnosis of the issues or problems so that they appreciate the need for change. The attitude to the innovation introduced will then be positive.

Perception of imposition Similarly, if the managers in an organization see the change as being imposed upon them by the corporate management or the head office, they are likely to resist the change. Such resistance can be reduced by involving them in the introduction of change at several stages. This can be done through seminars, work groups to evolve the various parts of the strategy, task forces to work out details of implementation, etc. Participation of managers at the various stages increases their commitment to the change.

Indifference of the top management The behaviour and attitudes of the top management are critical factors in the implementation of change. If the top management do not show much enthusiasm or interest in the change, people at the lower levels will have increased resistance to it. The top management can show their interest by frequently requesting information and feedback on the progress of the programme, participating in seminars organized to discuss experiences with the new system, meeting the occupants of new roles created as part of the change, providing

Exhibit 27.7 *Sources of Resistance and Coping Mechanisms*

Sources of resistance	Coping mechanisms
Perceived peripherality of change	Participation in diagnosis
Perception of imposition	Participation and involvement
Indifference of the top management	Active support from the top
Vested interests	Fait accompli
Complacency and inertia	Fait accompli
Fear of large-scale disturbance	Phasing of change
Fear of inadequate resources	Support of resources
Fear of obsolescence	Development of skills
Fear of loss of power	Role redefinition and re-orientation
Fear of overload	Role clarity and definition

positive strokes (encouragement and appreciation) on success experiences, mentioning the experiment in significant documents such as the annual report, etc.

Vested interests Change produces some disturbances, and sometimes some dislocations. For example, if an organization creates new units that are located in small towns, people moving there from capital cities will face problems and experience some inconvenience. As a result, they are likely to resist the change. They may, of course, formally give other reasons that appear logical. However, once they go and work in the small towns, they may find they enjoy the change and see its positive aspects.

Complacency and inertia As a general rule, change produces discomfort. People develop a complacency from being in one state. A change of state is somewhat painful. The solution to the problem is to introduce the change and help people experience the new conditions. Then the resistance usually goes down.

Fear of large-scale disturbances Resistance may also increase if the implementation of a change requires additional resources in the form of new skills, additional recruits, or a considerable budget. Provisions for such resource support may reduce resistance. However, it is necessary to examine whether there is a genuine need for the resources. For example, if a new unit is created with considerable autonomy, the support of planning, personnel, and technology must be provided to help the unit to succeed in meeting its objectives.

Fear of obsolescence Resistance to change may also be high if the change requires new skills. Existing employees may feel that they may become obsolete because of the lack of these skills. This may be a real threat. Resistance can be partly reduced if the concerned people are given an orientation and are trained in the new skills needed. For example, introduction of HRD may succeed if the existing functionaries in the personnel or organizational planning departments are given enough training in the new functions so that they feel confident in carrying these out effectively.

Fear of loss of power Sometimes resistance to a change is high because there is a feeling that, as a result of the change, some roles will lose power. For example, creation of new planning roles may raise such a fear as the planning functionaries may not get operational powers. Creating a new unit may 'deprive' the existing top managers of the operational powers being delegated to the units. Such resistance can be reduced if the roles are redefined and redesigned so that the concerned role occupants can perceive that they may have different kinds of power that may be of a higher order, although different in nature. The involved roles may be helped to realise their potential power and develop ways of effectively using the power.

Fear of overload If some people feel that the change will increase their workload, they are likely to resist change. This may happen if they perceive new functions being assigned to their roles. However, if their roles are defined, and they are able to prioritise the functions, and decide which functions can be delegated to their subordinates, the resistance can be reduced. This would require seminars on role definition and clarity, and negotiation for delegation of some functions.

SUMMARY

Organizational change is a complex and continuous process, having several sequential aspects. In the process of planned change, several actors are involved—the corporate management, the external consultant(s), the counterpart, the implementation team, the chief implementer, and the task forces. Every actor performs specific functions.

The investment of time and energy in the process work in the beginning helps to smoothen progress on task achievement later. The implementation of change is itself a complex process and requires a great deal of attention. Planning is followed by action, leading to the institutionalisation and stabilisation of change. The monitoring of progress is necessary and forms a small feedback loop in correcting action (adaptation).

There is always resistance to any change being introduced. Sometimes resistance plays a positive role in warning the organization of possible consequences. Generally, resistance is caused by various kinds of fear and lack of attention to the actual process. Effective strategies for coping with resistance can be achieved by understanding and dealing with the sources of resistance.

GLOSSARY

deliberation stage evaluating the various alternatives generated for dealing with the problems or issues associated with the change

diagnosis an attempt to search for the main cause of the symptoms encountered

domain reshuffling giving up certain domains (areas of business) and adopting others that seem to be favourable

fidelity actual use corresponding to the intended or the planned use

implementation translating the proposed ideas into action

initiation the stage of vocalisation of the need for a change

stabilisation internalising a change and making it a part of the system

EXERCISES

Concept Review Questions

1. What are the main sequential phases of organizational change?
2. List the functions of the external consultant and the implementation team in managing organizational change.
3. What are the main aspects of the process of implementing change?
4. Who are involved in monitoring an effort to make a change and how can it be made more effective?
5. What are the sources of resistance to an effort to implement change?
6. Take any two sources of resistance and suggest ways of dealing with them.

Classroom Projects

1. In groups of two or three, identify one recent change that has been successfully accepted/adopted at your institution and prepare a note on the process elements of its success.
2. The idea of student participation in the management of institutions has been much discussed but rarely implemented. Form groups of three and prepare a plan of implementation for your institution. Give a brief outline of the sequential process you would adopt.

Field Projects

1. All the banks are now computerised. Interview the manager of a bank in your neighbourhood to find out how this change (computerisation) was introduced and how it got institutionalised. Trace the whole process of successful implementation of this change.
2. VAT (value-added tax) has been proposed as a major economic change. Interview some businesspersons to find out why there has been resistance to this change. Find out which processes were overlooked in the introduction of this change.

Change Management at ICICI*

In May 1996, K.V. Kamath replaced Narayan Vaghul as CEO of India's leading financial services company, Industrial Credit and Investment Corporation of India (ICICI). Immediately after taking charge, Kamath introduced massive changes in the organizational structure, and the emphasis of the organization changed—from a development bank mode to that of a market-driven financial conglomerate. Kamath's moves were prompted by his decision to create new divisions to tap new markets and to introduce flexibility in the organization to increase its ability to respond to market changes. Necessitated because of the organization's newfound aim of becoming a financial powerhouse, the large-scale changes caused enormous tension within the organization. The systems within the company were soon in a state of stress. Employees were finding the changes unacceptable as learning new skills and adapting to the process orientation was proving difficult.

The changes also brought in a lot of confusion among the employees, with media reports frequently carrying quotes from disgruntled ICICI employees. According to analysts, employees began feeling alienated. The discontentment among employees further increased, when Kamath formed specialist groups within ICICI like the 'structured projects' and 'infrastructure' group. Doubts were soon raised regarding whether Kamath had gone 'too fast too soon', and more importantly, whether he would be able to steer the employees and the organization through the changes he had initiated.

ICICI was reported to be one of the few Indian companies known for its quick responsiveness to the changing circumstances. While its development bank counterpart IDBI was reportedly not doing very well in late 2001, ICICI had major plans of expanding. This was expected to bring with it further challenges as well as potential change management issues. However, the organization did not seem too much perturbed by this, considering that it had successfully managed to handle the employee unrest following Kamath's appointment.

CHANGE CHALLENGES—I

ICICI was a part of the club of developmental finance institutions (DFIs)—ICICI, IDBI, and IFCI—who were the sole providers of long-term funds to the Indian industry. If the requirement was large, all three pooled in the money. However, the deregulation beginning in the early 1990s allowed Indian corporates to raise long-term funds abroad, putting an end to the DFI monopoly. The government also

---

*An abridged and modified version of the material compiled by ICFAI Press Research Center, Hyderabad. Reproduced with permission.

stopped giving DFIs subsidised funds. Eventually, in 1997, the practice of consortium lending by DFIs was phased out.

It was amid this newfound independent status that Kamath, who had been away from ICICI for 8 years, working abroad, returned to the helm. At this point of time, ICICI had limited expertise, with its key activity being the disbursement of 8-year loans to big clients like Reliance Industries and Telco through its nine zonal offices. In effect, the company had one basic product, and a customer orientation, which was largely regional in nature. Kamath, having seen the changes occurring in the financial sector abroad, wanted ICICI to become a one-stop shop for financial services. He realised that in the deregulated environment, ICICI was neither a low-cost player nor was it a differentiator in terms of customer service. The Indian commercial banks' cost of funds was much lower, and the foreign banks were much more savvy when it came to understanding customer needs and developing solutions. Kamath identified the main problem as the company's ignorance regarding the nuances of lending practices in newly opened sectors like infrastructure. The change programme was initiated within the organization, the first move being the creation of the Infrastructure Group (IIG), Oil and Gas Group (O&G), Planning and Treasury Department (PTD), and the Structured Products Group (SPG), as the lending practices were quite different for all of these. Kamath picked up people from various departments, who he was told were good, for these groups. The approach towards creating these new skill-sets, however, led to an unintended consequence. As these new groups took on the key tasks, a majority of the work, along with a lot of good talent, shifted to the corporate centre. While the zonal offices continued to do the same work—disbursing loans to corporates in the same region—their importance within the organization seemed to have diminished. An ex-employee remarked, 'The way to get noticed inside ICICI after 1996 has been to attach yourself to people who were heading these [IIG, PTD, SPG, O&G] departments. These groups were seen as the thrust areas and if you worked in the zones it was difficult to be noticed.'

Refuting this, Kamath remarked, 'This may be said by people who did not make it. And there will always be such people.' Some of the people who did not fit in this set up were quick to leave the organization. However, this was just the beginning of change resistance at ICICI.

Another change management problem surfaced as a result of ICICI's decision to focus its operations much more sharply around its customers. In the prevailing system, if a client had three different requirements from ICICI, he had to approach the relevant departments separately. The process was time consuming and there was a danger that the client would take a portion of that business elsewhere. To tackle this problem, ICICI set up three new departments: Major Client Group (MCG), Growth Client Group (GCG), and Personal Finance Group. Now, the customer talked only to his representative in MCG or GCG. And these representatives in turn found out which ICICI department could do the job.

Though the customers seemed to be happy about this new arrangement, people within the organization found it unacceptable. In the major client group, a staff of about 30–40 people handled the needs of the top 100 customers of ICICI. On the other hand, about 60 people manned the growth client group, which looked after the needs of mid-size companies. Obviously, the bigger clients required more diverse kinds of services. So working in MCG offered better exposure and bigger orders. The net effect was that the MCG executive ended up doing more business than the GCG executive. A middle-level manager at ICICI commented, 'The bosses may call it handling growth clients but the GCG manager is actually chasing Non-Performing Assets (NPA) and Board of Industrial and Financial Restructuring (BIFR) cases.' Kamath was quick to deny this allegation as well: 'Just because somebody is within the MCG does not guarantee him success. And these assignments are not permanent. Today's MCG man could easily be tomorrow's GCG person and vice versa.'

Complaints against these changes continued and ICICI was blamed for not putting in adequate systems in place to develop the right people. The manner in which ICICI recognised an individual's efforts—the feedback process—was also questioned.

With Kamath's stated objective to make ICICI provide almost every financial service, separating the customer service people from the product development groups was another problem area. In the current scheme of things, an MCG or GCG person acted as a clients' representative inside ICICI. The MCG or GCG person understood the clients' needs and got the relevant internal skill department to develop a solution. Unlike foreign banks, there were no demarcations between these internal skill groups and client service person. (Demarcation helped in preventing an internal skills person from cannibalising business being developed by the client service group.) With no such systems in place at ICICI, this distorted the compensation packages between the competing divisions. Exhibit I summarises the patterns of employee behaviour over time.

While Kamath's comments in the media seemed to dismiss many of the employee complaints, ICICI was in fact putting in place a host of measures to check this unrest. One of the first initiatives was regarding imparting new skills to existing employees. Training programmes and seminars were conducted for around 257 officers by external agencies, covering different areas. In addition, in-house training programmes were conducted in Pune and Mumbai. During 1995–96, around 35 officers were nominated for overseas training programmes organized by universities in the US and Europe. ICICI also introduced a 2-year Graduates' Management Training Programme (GMTP) for officers in the junior management grades. Along

Exhibit I *'Post-merger' Employee Behavioural Pattern*

Period	Employee behaviour
Day 1	Denial, fear, no improvement
After a month	Sadness, slight improvement
After a year	Acceptance, significant improvement
After 2 years	Relief, liking, enjoyment, business development activities

Source: www.sibm.edu

with the training to the employees, management also took steps to set right the reward system. To avoid the negative impact of profit-centred approach, wherein pressure to show profits might affect standards of integrity within an organization, management ensured that rewards were related to group performance and not individual performances. To reward individual star performers, the method of selecting a star performer was made transparent. This made it clear that there would be closer relationship between performance and reward. However, it was reported that pressure on accountability triggered off some levels of anxiety within ICICI, which resulted in a lot of stress in human relationships. Dismissing reports of upsetting people, Kamath said, 'Much of the restructuring plan has come from the bottom.' ICICI also reviewed the compensation structure in place. Two types of remuneration were considered—a contract basis, which would attract risk-takers, and a tenure-based compensation, which would be appealing to employees who wanted security. Kamath accepted that ICICI had been a bit slow in completing the employee feedback process. Soon, a 360-degree appraisal system was put in place, whereby an individual was assessed by his peers, seniors, and subordinates. As a result of the above measures, the employee unrest gradually gave way to a much more relaxed atmosphere within the company. By 2000, ICICI had emerged as the second largest financial institution in India with assets worth 582 billion rupees.

CHANGE CHALLENGES—2

ICICI had to face change resistance once again in December 2000, when ICICI Bank was merged with Bank of Madura (BoM). Though ICICI Bank was nearly three times the size of BoM, its staff strength was only 1,400 as against BoM's 2,500. Half of BoM's personnel were clerks and around 350 were subordinate staff.

There were large differences in the profiles, grades, designations, and salaries of personnel between the two entities. It was also reported that there was uneasiness among the staff of BoM because they felt that ICICI would push up the productivity per employee to match the levels of ICICI. BoM employees feared that their positions would come in for a closer scrutiny. They were not sure whether the rural branches would continue or not as ICICI's business was largely urban oriented.

The apprehensions of the BoM employees seemed to be justified as the work cultures at ICICI and BoM were quite different and the emphasis of the respective managements was also different. While BoM management concentrated on the overall profitability of the Bank, ICICI management turned all its departments into individual profit centres and bonus for employees was given on the performance of individual profit centre rather than profits of the whole organization.

ICICI not only put in place a host of measures to technologically upgrade the BoM branches to ICICI's standards, but also paid special attention to facilitate a smooth cultural integration. The company appointed consultants Hewitt Associates to help in working out a uniform compensation and work culture and to take care of any change management problems. ICICI conducted an employee behavioural pattern study to assess the various fears and apprehensions that employees typically went through during a merger. Based on the findings, ICICI established systems to take care of the employee resistance with action rather than words.

The 'fear of the unknown' was tackled with adept communication and the 'fear of inability to function' was addressed by adequate training. The company also formulated a 'HR blueprint' to ensure smooth integration of the human resources.

To ensure employee participation and to decrease the resistance to the change, management established clear communication channels throughout to avoid any kind of wrong messages being sent across. Training programmes emphasised on knowledge, skill, attitude, and technology to upgrade skills of the employees. Management also worked on contingency plans and initiated direct dialog with the employee unions of the BoM to maintain good employee relations.

By June 2001, the process of integration between ICICI and BoM was started. ICICI transferred around 450 BoM employees to ICICI Bank, while 300 ICICI employees were shifted to BoM branches. Promotion schemes for BoM employees were initiated and around 800 BoM officers were found to be eligible for the promotions. By the end of the year, ICICI seemed to have successfully handled the HR aspects of the BoM merger. According to a news report, 'The win-win situation created by ... HR initiatives have resulted in high level of morale among all sections of the employees from the erstwhile BoM.' Even as the changes following the ICICI–BoM merger were stabilising, ICICI announced its merger with ICICI Bank in October 2001. The merger, to be effective from March 2002, was expected to unleash yet another series of changes within the organization. With Kamath still heading ICICI, analysts were hopeful that the bank would come out successfully in the task of integrating the operations of both the entities this time as well.

Questions for Discussion

1. Analyse the changes implemented by Kamath in mid-1990s to make ICICI a one-stop shop for financial services.
2. What factors contributed to the success of the change efforts?
3. How was resistance to change in ICICI, and BoM's merger with ICICI managed?

NOTES AND REFERENCES

1. Brabandere, Lucde (2006). *The Forgotten Half of Change.* New York: Dearborn Publishing.
2. Nilkant, W. and S. Ramnarayan (2006). *Change Management.* New Delhi: Response Books.
3. Khandwalla, P.N. (1992). *Organisational Design for Excellence.* New Delhi: Tata McGraw-Hill.
4. Larkin, T.J. and Sandar Larkin (1994). *Communicating Change: Winning Employee Support for New Business Goals.* New York: McGraw-Hill.
5. Khandwalla. *Organisational Design.*
6. Fullan, M. and A. Pomfret (1977). 'Research on curriculum and instruction implementation', *Review of Educational Research,* 47(2): 337–97.
7. Paul, Samuel (1980). 'Strategic management of public programmes'. Cambridge, MA: Harvard University, Kennedy School of Government. mimeographed.

8. Havelock, R.G. and A.M. Huberman (1977). *Solving Educational Problems,* p. 308. Paris: Unesco.
9. World Bank document, 1977.
10. United Nations document, 1978.
11. Fullan, M. and A. Pomfret (1977). 'Research on curriculum and instruction implementation', *Review of Educational Research,* 47(2): 337–97.
12. Reproduced with permission from Khandwalla, *Organisational Design.*
13. Khandwalla. *Organisational Design.*
14. Reproduced with permission from Khandwalla, *Organisational Design,* p. 163.

28
Organization Development

LEARNING OBJECTIVES

After studying this chapter, you will be able to
1. Define organization development (OD)
2. Enumerate the various phases of OD and the conditions for its success
3. Suggest guidelines for effective OD
4. Present different OD interventions, using a framework for their classification
5. Explain ways of developing internal OD facilitation

Organization development (OD) has been widely used in recent years as an approach to introducing planned change in organizations. Several researchers have defined OD in different ways. Although there are several points of agreement across definitions, special emphases are also reflected in them. The following definition is proposed by the author[1]: OD is a planned effort initiated by process specialist(s) to help an organization develop its diagnostic skills, coping capabilities, linkage strategies (in the form of temporary and semi-permanent systems), and a culture of mutuality.

DEFINITION OF OD

Several important dimensions of OD are contained in the above definition. Some elaboration of these dimensions may be useful.

Planned effort   OD is a planned effort and therefore requires a great deal of thinking and planning on the part of the OD expert.

Initiated by process specialists   Knowledge and skills of the applied behavioural sciences are used in OD. It is, therefore, best initiated by an expert who has both knowledge of the applied behavioural sciences and the skill of applying this knowledge in the organizational situation. This effort may be taken over by the organization in the long run and an internal resource be developed to carry on the work. However, in the beginning, behavioural science consultants are usually called in.

Diagnostic skills   The emphasis in OD is on planning change on the basis of data. Data is collected over a period of time about several aspects of the organization and its problems as part of this effort. OD tries to develop the organization's capacity to diagnose its problems. The emphasis is not only on the diagnosis of current problems but also on developing these skills in the organization so that it can diagnose its own problems in the course of its regular functioning.

Coping capabilities The main thrust in OD is on the organization's problem-solving abilities. The organization is thus helped to develop its ability to confront and cope with problems it faces, but OD does not stop there.

Linkage strategies OD emphasises the building of links between individual goals and organizational goals, between individuals who work in the various roles, and between various groups that function in the organization. Problems in the organization can be resolved only through collaborative effort. One emphasis of OD, therefore, is on building such collaboration in the organization. This is done, among other ways, by setting up temporary systems such as task forces and by making structural changes that ensure continuing collaboration.

Culture and mutuality OD is based on certain values that are important for the development of organizations as open and proactive systems. OD fosters a set of specific values: openness, confrontation, trust, authenticity, proactivity, autonomy, collaboration, and experimentation (OCTAPACE). Openness implies confronting problems rather than avoiding them. Confrontation means exploring ways of improving relationships among individuals and searching for solutions to the problems the organization faces together. Trust is both the result of these values and an aid to generating mutuality in the organization. Authenticity is the value underlying trust— it is the willingness of a person to acknowledge his or her own feelings and accept both himself or herself and others. This value is important for the development of a culture of mutuality. Another value emphasised by OD is proactivity. Instead of merely reacting to situations, the organization should take the initiative in influencing the situation. Autonomy is another value emphasised. An individual who does not feel threatened in seeking help from others to cope with problems is an autonomous person. Autonomy involves collaboration and mutuality, because only an autonomous person can collaborate and not perceive his or her collaborative initiative as a sign of weakness or inferiority. Collaboration is itself emphasised as a value so that individuals work in teams instead of working independently to solve their problems and develop commitment to their roles and to the organization.

OPERATIONAL GOALS OF OD

The OD approach to change treats the organization as a system. In this respect, OD is different from action research. While the latter may attempt to find solutions to a problem without much regard for related issues in the organization, the former takes a view of the organization as a whole. This means understanding the organization in relation to the environment as well as the internal dynamics of the organization. A systematic view of the organization would imply understanding the various dynamics of the organization: its interface with the environment; the stable systems in the organization; interteams, that is, the collaborative working relationships among various groups in the organization; teams, that is, groups of which the organization consists; interpersons, that is, the relationship among the various members of a team; and finally, the most important, the individuals who work in the organization. To accomplish all this, OD has to work with certain operational goals.

Person The individual is the central entity in OD. Although the goal of OD is to produce change in the organization, the individual working in the organization is the most important vehicle of change and hence the best target. The development of self-awareness and self-acceptance is the main goal in working with the individuals in an organization.

Often, individuals are alienated and OD must focus on their integration into the organization. It then focuses on the individuals' motivation by helping them to learn how to set realistic and challenging goals so that they have a sense of satisfaction and a taste of challenge. This helps individuals develop the skills of planning so that goals can be divided into smaller, achievable units. OD thus attempts to develop the skills, knowledge, and ability of individuals.

Interperson The individual's competence depends on his or her interpersonal effectiveness. OD tries to open up communication among the various people working in the organization with a view to increasing their interpersonal competence. It tries to foster what we have called the OCTAPACE values.

Teams 'Teams' implies both temporary systems as well as permanent or semi-permanent groups in the organization. By developing teams, OD tries to work on establishing continuous improvement mechanisms in the organization. These are mainly in the form of temporary systems. These mechanisms can help the organization build its ability to cope with problems.

Interteams Regarding the interface between teams and groups in the organization, OD aims at developing the ability of teams to manage conflicts and developing collaboration among them in order to further the attainment of individual and organizational goals.

Organization The organization is the stable entity that uses the individuals and the various teams for the attainment of its goals. OD helps the organization as a whole in its goal-setting process. It also helps the organization develop internal resources to carry on the work, which may be started by an outside expert. However, the new role of an internal OD facilitator is important for the continuing growth or development of the organization.

Interface with environment OD deals with the organization's ability to transact with the environment through both adaptive as well as proactive behaviours.

Adaptation is not the same as adjustment. The changing environment may demand certain changes within the organization so that it can continue an effective transaction with the environment. Proactive behaviour is equally important when the organization needs to produce change and initiate new action. Compared to several other countries, India seems to be in a better position given that several of its organizations, especially those in the public sector, are in a position to influence national issues and policies that may have long-term and widespread effects. Organizations should realise their potential for taking proactive action and help to develop a congenial environment in the country.

CONDITIONS FOR THE SUCCESS OF OD

Before we discuss the various phases of OD programmes and how OD works in organizations, it may be useful to consider the various conditions necessary for successful use of OD in an organization. In the absence of these conditions, OD is not likely to succeed. One way to create these conditions is to start an OD programme. OD may then attempt to create the preconditions for full-scale OD work. These conditions are as follows:

Commitment from top   OD cannot succeed unless the people at the top are committed to what is being done. By definition, OD has to begin from the top. In many organizations, the top people may be in favour of OD but are not in favour of making changes in certain aspects and avoid getting involved themselves in the effort of change. In the absence of such a commitment, OD cannot succeed.

Strong linkpins   OD can succeed only if what Likert describes as 'linkpins' are strengthened. These are the roles that connect various levels and various parts of the organization. These roles are extremely important because change can flow through these key roles and they can become the main media of communication in the organization. In some organizations, these roles may not be visible and several parts of the organization may be functioning almost independently of each other, with only the head of the organization coordinating the various parts. An absence of strong linkpins is not conducive to the use of OD in the organization.

Willingness and resources in a department   OD can be successful if at least one department in the organization is both willing to experiment and has resources that can be used to stabilise the changes introduced through OD. It is necessary to stabilise change in the organization and this can be done by making sure that the innovation will continue in at least one part of the organization. If at least one department is ready for this kind of work, OD can make an entry into the organization and later be spread out when other departments see the effect of OD in that one department. If an organization does not have any department in which there are willingness as well as resources to effect this kind of change, OD is not likely to succeed.

Involvement of external consultant   In the beginning, for various reasons, an external consultant is necessary for a successful OD effort. He or she not only brings expertise, but is helpful in confronting several issues in the organization that an internal person may find difficult to deal with, even though he or she has the skill and ability to do so. An external OD consultant can take certain risks and can confront the organization to some extent. In due course, however, the external consultant withdraws from the organization and internal members can take over.

Strong internal resources One of the objectives of OD is to develop strong internal resources in the organization, enabling it to continue the work the external consultant may start. For this, it is necessary that such internal resources are identified. These people should be able to replace the external consultant. Such a replacement has to be properly phased so that there is an overlapping between the external consultant and the internal facilitator. In organizations where such people have been identified and developed, OD efforts are stabilised and the organization is able to continue to develop along the lines laid down by the consultant.

PHASES OF ORGANIZATION DEVELOPMENT

The OD programme develops through certain phases. The purpose of discussing these phases is to see how the OD programme flows. Although there will be variations, and some elements of these phases may either overlap or come in a different order, OD generally goes through the following phases.

Entry into the Organization

The first phase of OD is the establishment of a rapport between the external consultant and the organization. During this phase, the external consultant enters an organization and establishes both his or her identity and understanding with the organization regarding the purpose of OD. There are several ways in which a consultant enters an organization. He or she may either be called in by the organization for a specific problem or may be called to discuss the possibility of a general OD programme leading on to various kinds of OD activities. In any case, the following may occur during the first phase:

Obtaining preliminary information The external consultant collects preliminary information about the organization in order to understand its nature. In order to have an overview of the organization, he or she may look at various reports and other papers or may go round the organization so as to acquaint himself or herself with its technology and get a general view of its size and type, etc.

Interviewing key persons The consultant collects information not only through a general survey and reading of the available material but also through interviews with those who determine the culture of the organization. The main purposes of interviewing these key people is to understand their value systems and the various roles in the organization and to develop a shared understanding about mainly two things: first, the assumptions on which they are operating and performing their roles and second, the chief actors in the organization. It is necessary for the organization to understand the assumptions on which the consultant will operate and for the consultant to understand how the chief people in the organization operate. This helps to develop a healthy relationship between the consultant and these key people.

Getting a glimpse of the process   The consultant may also have an opportunity to look inside the OD process. One useful way to do this is to sit in on a few meetings of top people, in the organization as well as some other groups. Discussions in meetings and the way differences are voiced and resolved sometimes give much more insight than an interview can. It may therefore be useful for consultants to find an opportunity to observe the dynamics of the interactional process.

Making a presentation on the OD approach   Finally, before OD is taken up in the organization, the consultant makes a presentation on what OD is and what it involves. The presentation may be made to the top people in the organization so that they have an opportunity to ask questions and raise doubts. Such a meeting is very useful to allay any fears about OD. In some cases, a top person from another organization where OD has been used can be invited to informally share his or her experiences with the group on how OD was introduced in his or her organization and what it did and did not do. As a result of such a meeting, the consultant may either be finally invited to initiate the OD programme or the top group may feel that their organization is not yet ready for OD programmes.

Problem Identification

After the first phase is over and if the OD consultant has been invited to work with the organization, the second phase begins. The main purpose of the second phase is to understand the main problems facing the organization. This understanding has to be developed by working with several people in the organization. In addition to collecting preliminary data, the consultant now gives his or her detailed attention to OD strategy. The following elements are involved in this phase.

Interview   The consultant interviews people at several stages. In addition to interviewing the top people, he or she interviews people at various other levels and collects information based on these interviews. The consultant keeps his or her eyes open to see what would ordinarily be neglected in the organization. For example, while crossing the shop floor to interview the supervisor, the consultant may observe behaviours such as that of a person shouting at another person or of people busy in a hurried conversation in a small group, etc. The consultant notes down important observations.

Data collection   As a result of interviews with several people, the consultant will have obtained enough information to select certain aspects of the organization to work on. He or she may, for example, find that the main problem in the organization is lack of trust in one another, or may find that people feel they do not get enough responsibility in their roles. The consultant then collects more data in order to go into the details of the problem. The usual way of data collection is to use various instruments to be filled out by individuals. Such instruments may yield data about individuals as well as group processes.

The instruments used may focus on such aspects of the organization as climate, motivational patterns, perception of leadership styles, perception of various kinds of problems, delay, work satisfaction and role tension. They are either available as standard instruments[2] or are especially prepared by the consultant. Data collection through structured instruments helps in systematically getting information about the organization. Many things that may not come out in the interview can be learnt from such data. In many cases, it may not be possible to interview the large number of people in the organization, and data collection through instruments may be more convenient.

Diagnosis   After data collection, the consultant tries to diagnose the main problems. Diagnosis takes into account not only the data collected through the instruments but also the data from the interviews as well as observations and notes made. The consultant gains a preliminary understanding of the diagnosis, prepares notes on it, and obtains some understanding of what the problems are and which of them are more important than others.

Strategy planning   The consultant then sits with the main people in the organization in order to give feedback to them first and work with them on deciding what to do. During this part of the second phase, a shared understanding of where the organization will go from here is necessary. During strategy planning, the first step is giving feedback on the consultant's diagnostic understanding to the top people.

Then the consultant works out various alternatives for dealing with the problem that was identified and agreed on. He discusses the consequences of using different alternatives. This helps the client group get involved in the decision about the intervention to be used. At this stage, the choice of terminating the relationship with the consultant is always open. The consultant helps the client to commit himself or herself to the OD work. Once the strategy is planned, it is a strategy to which the client is committed; the client can commit to a particular action plan only when he or she is clear about what is involved.

Specific Intervention

After planning the strategy for change, specific intervention should be designed/selected and implemented. An intervention is a planned structural group of activities to achieve the goals of OD. Such an intervention may be in the form of specific structural changes, working on conflicts, team building in a particular department, work at the top level, etc. Each intervention requires a detailed plan. Two main aspects of interventions are as follows:

Team building   One of the goals of any intervention used in an organization is to build the teams in it. Team building may be done either through special programmes or through specific activity on which they have to work together. Sometimes team-building exercises are held in quick succession so that a shared understanding and a culture of mutuality may be developed and the teams may be able to function effectively in the intervention chosen.

Collaborative work on intervention Both as a result of team building and for continued work on team building, it is necessary that the work on the intervention is done jointly by the consultant and the various teams that have been identified and are able to collect data, and work out the details. In practice, such collaborative work may result in further strategy planning.

Building a Collaborative Culture

While work on the intervention is going on, it is necessary to build a collaborative culture in the organization. This is both the culmination of and a necessary part of the OD effort. The following steps are involved during this phase:

Data collection After the use of an intervention, the consultant and the various teams that have been formed jointly collect data in order to see whether any change has taken place and to what extent if yes. Data may be collected again, through interviews and/or through the use of specific instruments.

Review The consultant looks at all the data collected and holds joint meetings with the groups of the client organization in order to review and assess what OD work has been effective so far. In such reviews, either the top people or members of the various teams are involved. It depends on what is being reviewed and for what purpose.

Formation of temporary teams As a result of the review work to sustain the OD efforts, teams are formed with the responsibility of continuously collecting data and planning a strategy to continue OD by having subsequent and frequent meetings.

Planning of next phase The organization and the consultant together plan the next phase. This is done mainly by the top people and the consultant in a joint meeting. They may, for example, decide that the next phase should have more to do with process work, that specific structural changes are needed, or that a particular department should be taken up for more intensive work. At this stage, it is necessary for the consultant to decide how much involvement he or she would like to have in the process and to ensure that an internal person is able to take on some responsibility.

Development of Internal Resources

Although this has been mentioned as the last phase, this in fact continues through the four phases already mentioned. The consultant identifies an internal resource person in the beginning and works with him or her so as to ensure his or her acceptability as a consultant on various aspects of OD programmes. If the person is not strong enough in terms of his or her professional abilities, plans are worked out to help the person develop professionally as an OD consultant. Investment of the external consultant's time and energy in the development of an internal resource person for OD is paid off in terms of speedy work and sustained efforts. HRD managers and trainers are often effective OD resources. In one major bank, HRD managers and trainers in its training institutions have been extensively involved in functioning not only as internal OD resource people but also as external consultants to various branches and other sub-systems of the bank.

SOME GUIDELINES FOR ORGANIZATION DEVELOPMENT

Experience has shown that certain considerations are important in a pragmatic approach to OD programmes in an organization. These may help to increase the probability of success of an OD effort. The following suggestions may be made in this regard:

Choose receptive points for entry   Only a few points of entry should be chosen for OD. Instead of either attempting to introduce change in the entire organization at once or taking up departments in which there are difficulties, it may be useful to enter an organization through those departments that are willing to change and want to do something about their problems. These are the healthy parts of the organization and may, therefore, provide greater facility for introducing change.

Focus on the linkpins   It is important to identify the linkpins in the organization. If these people are taken into confidence first and built into a team, they will facilitate a great deal of the work planned.

Work with forces supportive of change   It may be useful for the consultant to identify those roles and those people in the organization who want change and are, therefore, enthusiastic about it. These people are likely to be of great help to the consultant. However, their help must be sought judiciously, without arousing suspicion or without it appearing as if the consultant has a preference for some people over others.

Work with autonomous parts   It may be useful for the OD consultant to work with a department that is more autonomous than others and that can introduce changes without necessary approval from the other departments. Initially, it may be difficult to introduce changes in a department that has a visible link with another department and therefore cannot introduce the changes without approval of and disturbance in the relationship with the other department.

Use internal resources and develop them   It may be necessary to identify and develop internal resources for OD and use them continuously.

Begin at the top and get commitment   It is necessary for the consultant to begin at the top level—getting the management's support for the OD programme by making sure it understands the implications of the work, and by ensuring its active participation in the programme. This may in turn ensure sustained action as a result of OD. Beckhard has put this down as a necessary part of OD.[3]

Achieve minimum critical concentration   The principle of critical concentration is important in achieving effectiveness.[4] In any department, it is necessary to have a minimum level of concentrated effort in order to achieve success. For example, in team building, not just a few people but several should be targeted in a department so that there is a minimum critical concentration of a certain kind of culture and this is built up to help in further achieving the objectives of OD.

Multiple entry points   Instead of attempting only one OD intervention in one department, it may be useful to have several entry points (although OD can start with only one department). Through multiple entry points, the consultant can focus attention on several interrelated problems.

Work on felt needs   The organization may be having certain problems of which it is aware. On many occasions, such problems are found to be on the surface, while there are other, real problems underlying these 'felt' problems. However, it may be useful for the consultant to rely on and trust the perceptions of the organization. If the consultant starts with its felt needs, he or she may soon be able to confront the organization with what its real needs may be and help it perceive these. However, a consultant who thinks that the needs felt by the organization are not its real needs may get into trouble if he or she is seen as imposing his or her judgment on the organization.

Use proactive behaviour   The main role of the OD consultant and of OD is to establish a new culture—an OCTAPACE culture, with new norms of solving problems—in the organization. This can be done by the consultant himself or herself showing some proactive behaviour. For example, the consultant may establish new norms of functional leadership rather than traditional hierarchical leadership by forming teams in which the convenorship is given to a person who is able to perform a particular role well even though he or she is of a lower rank. The consultant's attempt at establishing such norms may help the organization develop a new tradition and a new culture.

In what has been said above, it is necessary for the consultant to see that there is a continuous reinforcement of the various interventions. It is necessary to provide various experiences of psychological successes to the organization. Positive reinforcement in terms of perceived successes goes a long way in establishing a culture of mutual trust. The role of the external consultant becomes less prominent and visible as the OD programme progresses. The consultant has somehow to phase himself or herself out so that both the internal agent of change and various other people in the organization are able to take on the responsibility of continuing the work.

OD INTERVENTIONS

It is important to look at the various OD interventions that can be used during various phases of OD work. The most important factor in the choice of intervention is an understanding of the culture of the organization. It may be useful to look at the organization's past history for this. If the organization is a highly traditional one, which has grown out of past successes based mostly on traditional ways of achieving results, unstructured interventions focused on the process may threaten it and its top people may not know how to deal with the consequences. As a result, OD may be seen as threatening, resulting in the rejection of OD programmes. There are three factors that are involved in the culture of an organization.

Ambiguity tolerance   It may be useful to see to what extent the organization is prepared to live with ambiguity in a situation. Some organizations have functioned only on the basis of clear-cut and specific directions received from the top in the past. This tradition may continue, so that any ambiguous situation threatens the organization.

Risk-taking capacity   It may also be assessed to what extent the organization is prepared to take risks in terms of dealing with problems that may arise from opening up the system and introducing elements of the OCTAPACE culture.

Openness   It may be necessary to see whether the organization has a climate of support and mutual trust or whether it is one in which the people function only as roles and have no consideration for each other.

Another important dimension in the choice of an intervention is the background of the OD consultant himself or herself. Some consultants are more comfortable with one rather than another kind of intervention. The consultant will and should work with the interventions with which he or she is familiar and comfortable. Certainly, the consultant should experiment and try out different interventions, but he or she may not be able to use those effectively interventions with which he or she is uncomfortable.

The choice of intervention will also depend on the problems initially identified by the organization. If the problems 'felt' require somewhat structured interventions, it may not be useful to use highly unstructured ones. The consultant has a wide choice of interventions. In fact, all the steps he or she takes from the point of meeting the top people onwards are interventions. The sequencing and planning of interventions needed at the various stages form the basis of strategy planning.

A large number of interventions have been designed. Several methods have been proposed for grouping them. Some of the suggested classification systems are as follows:

OD cube   Schmuck and Miles proposed a $9 \times 6 \times 8$ cube, suggesting the following dimensions[3]:

- Diagnosed problem (9): Goals/plans, communication, culture/climate, leadership, authority, problem solving, decision making, conflict/co-operation, role definition, and 'other'
- Focus of attention (6): Person, role, dyad/triad, team/group, interteam, and whole organization
- Mode of interventions (8): Training (education, process consultation), coaching, confrontation, data feedback, problem solving, plan making, OD task force establishment, and techno-structural activity

Consulcube Blake and Mouton proposed a comprehensive system covering a large number of interventions at different levels.[4] Theirs is an excellent sourcebook for interventions. They classified intervention using three dimensions to make it a cube ($5 \times 4 \times 5$).

- Consulting approach (5): Acceptant, catalytic, confrontation, prescription, theories and principles
- Focal issues (4): Power/authority, morale/cohesion, norms, and goals/objectives
- Units of change (5): Individual, group, intergroup, organization, and larger social systems

Intervention families French and Bell[5] have proposed 13 families, or types, of intervention in terms of activities: diagnostic, team building, intergroup, survey feedback, education and training, techno-structural change, process consultation, grid OD, third-party peacemaking, coaching/counselling, life and career planning, planning and goal setting, and strategic management.

Four quadrants French and Bell have also suggested a classification of interventions in four quadrants by combining two dimensions: the target of intervention (individual or group) and the focus of intervention (task issues or process issues).

We are proposing another way of classifying interventions, based on two dimensions: the focus of the intervention and the nature of the intervention. The focus of the intervention may be on the statics (structure) or on the dynamics (process) of the organization or it may be on both. The nature of the intervention may be either structured or unstructured or it may be a mixture of both. With a combination of these three different ways of looking at the two dimensions, we have a 3×3 classification table. This is shown in Exhibit 28.1. Objectives and steps in implementing five interventions are given in the appendix to this chapter.

Exhibit 28.1 *Focus of Intervention*

Nature of Intervention	Statics (structure)	Dynamics (process)	Both
Structured	Reorganization Organizational designing MBO Work review Differentiation integration	Motivation development Role negotiation Organization mirroring Interaction process analysis	Survey feedback
Unstructured	Team development Development of internal facilitators Job enrichment	L-groups Counselling Conflict resolution Managerial grid	Process consultation Confrontation meetings
Both	Task force		Inter-role exploration

Detailed interventions have been proposed for various levels:

Person (five participant-active interventions—encounter groups, role playing, instrumentation, self-study and reflection, and awareness expansion; and five facilitator-active interventions—psychodynamic methods, motivation arousal, training, feedback, and coaching and mentoring)[6]

Role (role analysis technique, role analysis process, comprehensive role analysis, role efficacy lab, role stress and coping, role negotiation, role contribution, and team roles)[7]

Team (understanding team dynamics, stages of team development, team process, team building, intergroup team building)[8]

Large group (organization–environment relationship, internal design analysis, open system planning, network organizations, socio-technical systems, structural design, reward systems, high involvement organization)[9]

Organization (structure change, culture and climate building, change management, etc.)[10]

Whole systems (Some examples of whole system change are appreciative enquiry, future search, open space technology, whole system transformation. These can be found in the recent OD volume)[11]

DEVELOPMENT OF INTERNAL OD FACILITATORS

The development of the internal resources for OD in the organization is extremely important. Without such resources, the organization may not be able to stabilise changes and continue OD work. Several important aspects of the development of an internal resource deserve attention. The following are some of these important aspects:

Support of the community The role of the internal OD facilitator has to be legitimised in the organization. It is necessary for occupants of various important roles in the organization to sit together and define the role of the OD facilitator. The legitimisation process can be accelerated by discussing the role openly in the organization rather than the head of the organization appointing a person to this role arbitrarily. A role analysis technique can be used to clarify and work out the role in detail. It is also useful for various members in the organization to project their expectations on to such a role. The person to be selected for such a role should have qualities enabling him or her to function as an agent of change. There should be enough time allowed for the preparation of the person for this role.

Linkage with consultants The person who grows into an internal facilitator should have links with several outside consultants. The initial linkage should be with the external consultant associated with the OD effort from the beginning. The external consultant can help the person through several programmes as well as give him or her graduated readings. The linkage can be further established by the internal resource person becoming a member of a professional body such as the Indian Society for Applied Behavioural Sciences.

- Participative mode
- Collaborative work

Currently different approaches are being used in OD. *Practicing Organization*[16] represents the current concepts of OD. OD has been treated as a planned, systematic, and designed change to improve organizational performance. In the definition of OD, some key themes are—OD is long range in perspective; OD should be supported by top managers; OD effects change through education; OD emphasises employee participation in assessing the current and future state, making free and collaborative choice on how to implement change, and empowering the system to take responsibility for evaluating results.

OD competencies have been studied in details through factor anasysis. An OD competency is a personal quality that contributes to successful consulting performance.[17] Analysis of the underlying structure found three basic competencies: self-mastery (the most important), the ability to apply research methods, and skills in change management technology. Structural interventions have also been suggested, like HRD audit. Assessment tools have been developed to measure the OD competencies.

New interventions have been developed and used. In addition to person-focussed and team-focussed interventions, role-focussed interventions have been developed. There has been significant work on interventions in large systems, and whole system transformation.

Importance is being given to organization culture.[18] With increasing globalization the need for global OD has emerged.[19]

Future of OD

Unprecedented and rapid changes are posing challenges for OD to search new ways of dealing with them. The limitations of the current OD concept and practice are the pointers for future developments.[20] Several issues have been raised for consideration of an OD community. Some of these and other issues are listed below.

1. The gap between theory and practice has increased in OD, although some significant attempts are being made to bridge this gap.
2. The emphasis on 'organization' seems to be inadequate, and a question is raised: where is *organization* in OD?
3. The ability of self-renewal through double-loop learning seems to be missing.
4. OD is a logical and systematic approach, with less scope of creativity (out-of-the-box thinking).
5. OD relies on diagnosis (focus on past) vs projection (focus on future).
6. It is more analytical and diagnostic vs synthetic and appreciative of strengths.
7. OD is a top-down team-building strategy vs everyone getting involved in change.
8. In OD process and group work is confined within the organization vs involving outsiders also.
9. Although the need to put OD in the cultural context has been voiced, OD continues to remain divorced from larger social realities. For example, the issues

of discrimination, poverty, equality, etc. at the societal level are not considered in OD.

Some scholars see crises in OD, which point to the need for a new paradigm shift. The future of OD should address all such needs. There is already a shift in the direction of positive scholarship—for example, appreciative inquiry, creativity, diversity of interventions, whole system change, large group interventions, etc. Hopefully, process work will also take social realities into account, while working on organizational issues. If social activists are involved in OD work, OD will respond to such social realities.

These challenges need to be taken up by OD consultants, scholars, practioners, and institutions like ISABS. ISABS, like NTL, is already experimenting in broadening the process work, by including new ways of developing human processes. The future of OD seems to be promising.

SUMMARY

Organization development (OD) is a planned, process-oriented effort at self-renewal by an organization. Its operational goals concern all HR units—individuals, roles, teams, interteams, and the whole organization.

OD can succeed under certain conditions: commitment from the top, strong linkpins, commitment of the department or unit, and an external consultant resource and strong internal resources. There are phases covering entry, diagnosis, interventions, and culture building in OD.

Several OD interventions have been developed and have been classified in various ways.

Internal resource building is especially important to make OD a self-renewing process.

With rapid changes in the societies and organizations, new challenges are emerging, requiring some paradigm shifts in OD. OD is a promising approach to change and development.

GLOSSARY

intervention   an integrated group of activities to bring about a change

organization development (OD)   a planned effort initiated by process specialists to help an organization develop its diagnostic skills, coping capabilities, linkage strategies in the form of temporary and semi-permanent systems, and a culture of mutuality

EXERCISES

Concept Review Questions

1. What is the definition of OD? Explain the various elements of the definition.

2. What are the conditions for a successful OD effort?
3. Enumerate the different phases of OD and their main foci.
4. How can OD interventions be classified? Give examples of some interventions, using the interaction between the focus (structure, process, and both) and the nature of the interventions (structured, unstructured, and both) to classify them.
5. How can internal OD facilitators be developed?

Critical Thinking Questions

1. In a training institution, there is a problem between the faculty group (responsible for training) and the administrative group (responsible for resources, arrangements, and maintaining accounts). The former (the faculty group) accused the latter of delayed response, insensitivity to priorities, and insensitivity to participants' needs. The administrative group accused the faculty of not planning well, being too demanding, and being insensitive to the problems of the administrative group. This conflict resulted in various other problems, affecting their quality of work.

   What OD intervention will you use in this situation? Give the sequential steps of the intervention.

2. The Ignorant Farmers

   In the early 1950s, the Indian Agricultural Research Institute designed and developed a small biogas plant, at that time called 'the cowdung gas plant'. The plant was for the use of a family who had about four heads of cattle.

   The plant was a simple one. A family with five heads of cattle could get sufficient gas for cooking and lighting purposes.

   The main features of the cowdung gas plant were very attractive. It eliminated smoke and the problems of drying and storing cowdung cakes. In addition, the cowdung could also be used as manure. The slurry (digested cowdung) was released as the gas was emitted and could be directly put out into the field as manure. It had a higher percentage of nitrogen than raw cowdung and was therefore a richer manure. Raw cowdung cannot be put out into the field directly—it has to be treated and digested; otherwise it attracts white ants, which can damage the crop. The slurry did not smell and was both fly-repellent and mosquito-repellent. The cooking gas released was non-toxic and had no smell. Thus the advantages of the cowdung gas were so numerous that adoption of this innovation was quite logical. The farmers could use the cowdung as fuel and, at the same time, they could have it back as manure for their fields.

II

The institute installed six plants on the premises of six families, free of charge for the purpose of demonstration. The total cost of the plant at that time was about Rs 500. The institute announced a scheme of subsidising the plant so that it could be installed for half the usual cost. The family had to provide the labour. The institute was to provide the know-how, help, and material for Rs 250. It gave the subsidy for the installation of the plant and free services to help the farmers to learn how to use the gas.

   In one of the houses where the plant was originally installed, the housewife proudly showed others how the gas could be used for cooking. Visitors who came from different places and from outside the country were usually taken to this house where the housewife proudly demonstrated how chapatis and rotis could be cooked on the gas flame. The family had also installed some filament lamps for the purpose of lighting and at night they had a good time sitting in the light from the cowdung gas plant, which was much brighter than the kerosene lamps used by other villagers. Upon visiting the house and having seen how the cowdung gas was used, one was highly impressed. And there was no doubt that this was a panacea for the villagers and would solve many of their problems.

III

Several families got the cowdung gas plants at the subsidy provided by the institute. In the mid-1950s, however, the diffusion of this innovation stopped. There was no more demand for the cowdung gas plants. On the other hand, some families who had got these installed at a subsidy got the cowdung gas plants removed. Of the six families to whom the cowdung gas plants had been given free of charge, three of them got them removed. This was quite disturbing.

A team of three senior scientists, consisting of a psychologist, a sociologist, and a home scientist, visited these villages and the families. Our team saw the gas plant and interviewed several people and came to the conclusion that the innovation introduced was indeed a panacea for the villagers. We all concluded that the villagers were ignorant, irrational, and did not know the advantages of this innovation. The villagers were pitied for their lack of rationality. However, it was thought necessary to probe deeper into the problem to understand why the villagers did not adopt such a useful device. We spent long hours in the villages and stayed with the families who had the cowdung gas plants installed in order to learn the reason behind the rejection.

What do you think were the reasons for resistance to this change introduced in the villages (cowdung gas plant)? Write these down. Now read the following sections of the case.

IV

Based on the various interviews in the villages and after living with the families and observing what was happening, we, the experts, were converted and our team concluded that it was us rather than the villagers who were ignorant. The villagers were quite rational. In fact, it was concluded that, in the prevailing circumstances, if we were villagers living in that part of the country, we ourselves would not use the cowdung gas plant! We were again shocked and disillusioned with ourselves, getting acquainted with the ignorant social scientists! The tables had turned!

V

Let us now turn to the life in the villages. *Jats* form the dominant caste in these villages. They are tall, strong, and sturdy people, engaged in agriculture and dairying operations, and very proud of their association with the land. They have fertile land to cultivate and usually have about six to 10 buffaloes per family; they supplement their income through selling ghee. Both men and women work hard. Indeed, women work harder than men. They go and help the menfolk in the fields in various agricultural operations during the better part of the day. In the morning, they cook. After they return from the fields in the evening, they cook for the family, boil milk, and keep it away for making curd. In the morning, they usually have a breakfast of leftover *rotis*. They churn the curd to make *ghee* and attend to other chores before they go off to their fields. Both men and women work the whole day in the field. In the evening, when they get home, they bathe in hot water, even in summer.

The women, before they go to the field, attend to the cooking. They use cowdung cakes, which are dried in the sun and stored. They set up seven to eight small fires with the cowdung cakes. They light these, and let them smoulder the whole day. On one such small fire they put a big clay pot in which milk slowly simmers throughout the day. As a result, a thick cream is formed in the evening, giving good *ghee* next morning. On another fire, they put a big container of water so that it is slowly heated and hot water is available in the evenings when they return from the fields. On the third, they put a big pot with some fodder to boil for the cattle and this also cooks the whole day. On a fourth, they put some *dal*—usually they cook whole rather than split *dal* and it cooks for several hours. On a fifth fire, they put some vegetables (mustard leaves, etc.), which also take several hours of slow cooking, and so on. Thus, before the women go out to work in the fields, they set up these small fires and put out the things that they have to heat or cook. In the evening, when they come back, they do not need much time to make *rotis* or *chapatis*. With all the dal and vegetables ready, they quickly make *chapatis*, give the men their hot water for a quick bath and, in the meantime, the meals are ready. After the men have eaten, the women take their bath and have their dinner. Later, they sit and talk untill they retire for the night.

The lifestyle of the villagers in this part of the country is quite interesting. The team of social scientists now had more insight into their living and working. And we were a little more educated about people's lives and their thinking. Our ignorance was reduced to some extent!

What lessons do you learn from this case regarding dealing with resistance to change?

Classroom Projects

1. Form three-member groups. Your goal is to make your group the best or one of the best classes in the country. Discuss whether this is a realistic goal. Then diagnose the situation using forcefield analysis, listing both pushing and pulling forces.
2. In new groups of three, take up the above diagnosis and develop an OD strategy, suggesting appropriate intervention for this work.

Field Projects

1. Work with a small group of people from a small organization that wants to improve. Do a SWOT analysis with them. Note down the analysis.
2. Take the next step of using the above analysis to do an ABCD analysis of the same data. Discuss this strategic analysis with the concerned members.

Appendix: Five OD Instruments

1. SWOT Analysis

Objectives

1. To help an organization in undertaking a quick managerial diagnosis
2. To help it plan action for improving its effectiveness

Steps

(i) Introduction by the chief on the need for openness in the joint effort to look at the organization in the context of the present and the future. Introduction by the consultant/facilitator on the concept of SWOT (strengths, weaknesses, opportunities, and threats) (1 hour)

(ii) Small group work (heterogeneous groups of six to eight members) in SWOT analysis (1 hour)

(iii) Plenary session chaired by the chief, for discussion of reports from the groups and developing consensus on SWOT analysis in four of five major areas (1 hour)

(iv) (a) Create two groups, each not exceeding five members (volunteers or those nominated by the chief). Both groups are given the lists of opportunities and threats. One group, in addition, gets the list of strengths and another the list of weaknesses.

(b) The group with the strengths generates two new lists, combining strengths with opportunities (SO or A list), and with threats (ST or C list). The A list is created by asking what strengths can be used to utilise which opportunities for immediate *action*. The group also prepares a C list, asking what strengths can be used to convert threats into *challenges* to be taken up by the organization.

(c) Similarly, the group with the list of weaknesses prepares two lists, B and D. List B contains what opportunities can be used to remove which weaknesses to *build* the organization. List D uses threats and weaknesses to see what should be *dumped* for now (not doing anything about them).

(d) We shall thus have A, B, C, and D lists of priorities, in that order. These can be put into the following format (30 to 45 minutes, preferably during the break):

	Strengths	**Weaknesses**
Opportunities	Act	Build
Threats	Challenge	Dump

Break for tea or lunch

(v) Plenary session for discussion of the new classified list (ABCD) for consensus (45 minutes)

(vi) Small work groups of three or multiples of three, such as six or nine, each group working on one aspect (A, B, or C), developing specific action suggestions in that area (1 hour)

(vii) Plenary session to discuss the reports, with assignment of specific responsibilities to the various departments/sections/groups (1 hour)

(viii) Meeting of the departments/sections/groups to discuss the plan of implementation and evaluation/follow-up (1 hour)

(ix) The plans to be followed by a person or small team nominated by the chief

2. Confrontation Meeting (originally developed by Richard Beckhard)

Objectives

1. To help an organization generate information about its major problems
2. To help diagnose the main problems (underlying causes)
3. To help the organization develop action plans and action schedules to deal with problems

Steps

(i) Introduction by the chief on the need for joint diagnosis and search for an appropriate action strategy and the need for openness. Also, introductory remarks by the consultant/facilitator (1 hour)

(ii) Small group work (heterogeneous groups of six to eight members) on generating information about problems causing lack of motivation (policies, procedures, attitudes, behaviour) and what would make the organization more effective (1 hour)

(iii) Plenary session for sharing reports from each group and the comprehensive list of problems categorised by the chief or facilitator into broad categories (1 hour)

(iv) Duplication of the categorized problems (preferably during the break)

Break for tea or lunch

(v) Natural functional groups, headed by the chief of the group, work on
   (a) Priority-setting among problems related to them and action steps they commit themselves to take
   (b) Priority issues/problems for the top management
   (c) Ways of communicating the results of the confrontation meeting to the subordinates (1½ hours).

All participants except top team leave

(vi) Meeting of the top team to review reports and discuss follow-up action steps on the basis of the reports (2 to 3 hours)

(vii) Written communication of the action steps suggested to all participants (within a few days)

(viii) Follow-up meeting (after 2 to 3 months) of all participants to review the progress of commitments of action and replanning new action (2 hours)

3. Role Negotiation (originally developed by Roger Harrison)

Objectives

1. To help individuals or groups develop better understanding of each other's roles
2. To develop ways of increasing collaboration between roles and/or teams
3. To develop common goals for individuals/teams to which all concerned are committed

Steps

(i)   Unfreezing: Micro lab (1½ hours) plus introduction (1½ hours).

(ii) Image building: 10 adjectives or phrases for themselves (self-image) and other roles/groups (mirror image) and guessing what images 'others' have made for them (fantasy image)

(iii) Image sharing: The images are exchanged and the members in each group reflect on the reciprocity, pecking order in the images, and also congruence with own images and empathy reflected in images (1 hour).

(iv) Empathy building: Groups on 'home base' develop positive images (strengths) about other groups. These should feature genuine appreciation of the strengths. These are read out alone (½ hour).

(v)   Introduction to role negotiation: The consultant/facilitator elaborates the philosophy of role negotiation, emphasising that one's effectiveness depends on the help given by others, who will give help only when they also receive help to be effective. The facilitator/consultant also spells out the conditions of role negotiation (1 hour).

(vi) Developing expectations: List of expectations/demands from the other group(s) are prepared for maximising one's own effectiveness. Three lists are prepared—(a) continue to do, (b) stop or reduce, (c) start, increase, or do better (2 hours).

      These are exchanged for classification (no discussion) (½ hour).

(vii) Preparation for negotiation: The groups on their 'home bases' discuss which demands to accept in return for which of their demands (or a new demand). They may not accept demands that are beyond their scope or those with which they do not agree on (1 hour).

(viii) Role negotiation in the community (fish-bowl design) (1 hour).

(ix) Checking and working out details in home groups (½ hour).

(x)   Role negotiation continued (fish-bowl design) (1 hour).

(xi) Finalisation of the agreement by a small intergroup team and signing of the agreement (½ hour).

(xii) Agreement on mechanisms of implementation and follow-up (½ hour).

(xiii) Sharing with the chief and closing (1 hour).

(xiv) Review and renegotiation after every 3 months (1 hour).

4. Intergroup Conflict Management

Objectives

1. To increase mutual understanding between two conflicting groups
2. To help the conflicting group develop action plans to reduce conflict and develop cooperation

Steps

(i)   Micro lab (1 hour)

(ii) Preparation of images of own group and the other group and guessing 'what they think of us' (1 hour)

(iii) Sharing of the images and clarification (½ hour)

(iv) Developing positive images (strengths) of the other group and a list of the priority issues to be settled with the other group (1 hour)

(v)   Sharing the strengths and discussion of the priority issues to develop a consensus list with priority setting (1 hour)

(vi) Formation of small teams (with equal number of members from each group) for each issue, to develop action suggestions, with responsibilities for each group (1 hour)

(vii) The same process of feedback and discussion as in (iii) and (iv) above to be repeated for the various parts of the organization and the two other hierarchies, but feedback to be confined only to the results for the concerned part or hierarchy. Each division to discuss what they propose to do by themselves and what they recommend to the top management (2 hours each)

(viii) After feedback and discussions, a meeting of representatives of all parts and hierarchies of the organization to review proposed action, chaired by the chief (3 hours)

(ix) Follow-up by one person or small team nominated by the chief for this purpose

7. Role Efficacy Lab

Objectives

1. To help participants take charge of increasing efficacy of their roles
2. To develop action ideas to increase efficacy of 'reporting roles' of the participants
3. To develop top commitment for increasing efficacy of various roles in the organization

Steps

(This is a 3-day intervention—steps are suggested for each day)

Day 1: 1. Writing an essay on 'My Role', completion of role efficacy scale for subordinate roles and other instruments (1 hour)
   2. Micro lab (1 hour)
   3. About the REL (½ hour)
   4. The concept of role efficacy, its aspects, and scoring method, the concept session with discussion and examples (1½ hours)
   5. Scoring one's own essays (¾ hour)
   6. Exchange of essays in threes and scoring (1 hour)
   7. Plenary session, discussing some essays (¾ hour)
   8. Scoring of RES (½ hour)

Day 2: 1. Small group work on own and subordinate's roles to identify areas for strengthening (½ hours)
   2. Plenary session, reporting and integrating (¾ hour)
   3. Work on increasing one's role efficacy (1 hour)
   4. Work on increasing efficacy of subordinate roles (¾ hour)
   5. Forcefield analysis for role efficacy in the organization (small groups) (¾ hour)

Organization Development in a Voluntary Organization*

This paper is based on an OD project conducted by the Behavioural Science Centre (India). It presents the experience of the authors in an OD effort in an unusual setting—an organization whose members were bonded through ideology rather than economic relationships.

THE SETTING

The organization was governed by a central coordinating authority (CCA), with a chief. The CCA coordinated the activities of six sectors. Each sector also had a chief, who was guided by the Board of Sector Representatives (BSR). Each sector was divided into divisions. Each division had a divisional chief with a Board of Divisional Representatives (BDR). Each division was further subdivided into local units (LUs). Each member of the organization was essentially a member of an LU. The members of the LUs elected their chief. These chiefs were members of the BDR, all divisional chiefs were members of the BSR, and all sector chiefs were members of the CCA.

The organization was committed to its ideology and served the ideology by working for the people. All over the world, this organization was known for its service to humanity in distress. It also ran a number of specialised institutions. Initially, they concentrated upon individualised care in the institutional framework. The activities of all these institutions were not performed by members of this organization only. Many other people of different backgrounds were employed in the institutions.

The sources of income for the organization were charity, gifts, endowments, and the like. Institutions managed by them generally had two systems: free and paid service. The payment charged was linked to the paying capacity of the person. These were non-profit institutions; money collected from payments was spent on the running of the institutions.

The CCA had a clear structure and authority pattern. Its administration was guided by a constitution. At the end of every 6 years, the constitution of the CCA was reviewed to see whether any changes were necessary. We had the impression that the organization chose bureaucracy as their method of administration. Power was extremely centralised in the hands of the chiefs at each level, the communication flow was almost one-way from the top down, decisions were taken at the top in each level, and members were expected to follow, implement, and work according to them. There were a number of implications of this system that could be easily visualised. A few years ago, there was a special review of the CCA constitution and

*Abridged version of a longer paper by Somnath Chattopadhyay and Udai Pareek, and published in *Managing Organisational Change*, edited by Somnath Chattopadhyaya and Udai Pareek. New Delhi : Oxford & IBH, 1982. Published with permission.

drastic changes were brought about. Essentially, the changes centred round a more democratic, participative management. At that time, the CCA took a close look at the organization and redefined its objectives, mainly in terms of greater emphasis on total development orientation.

Controversies and differences of viewpoints, often blended with reasons and intense feelings, filled up every LU meeting during the following 2 years. Some of the differences were voiced loud and clear; some were muffled and whispered. To some, the new trend was the reviving breeze that energised and liberated; to some it was the dreaded storm that uprooted everything that came in its way and left behind only destruction. There was utter confusion. The confusion, however, did not lead to any sharp, organised polarisation.

During this period, the organization realised that changing the constitution per se was not enough. Operationalising the new constitution needed a series of activities. Accordingly, a concerted effort in terms of a new scheme (we shall call it plan of renovation, or PR) was thought up and discussed. The spirit of and the expectations from PR were necessarily vague. Its unstructuredness and ambiguity matched the uncertainty that followed the new constitution. One of the tasks of PR, we understood, was to remove the fear and apprehension of rootlessness, supportlessness, and shifting anchors that were inadvertently generated as a consequence of the new constitution; to reduce the level of anxiety and channellise it for creative problem solving; and, most importantly, to find out ways and means not only to operationalise the new constitution but stimulate the desire to live with all changes. No one was very clear about the objectives of PR, the ways and means of achieving them, the barriers and blocks it would face, or its results. One decision was, however, taken—instead of taking directions from the central authority, each sector should find its own answers.

Around this time, we were invited by one sector to help it formulate and implement PR. Before we describe our entry, it would be worthwhile to consider a few details about our client sector.

CLIENT SYSTEM

The sector geographically comprised two countries and had two divisions, each division having several local units. Numerically, this sector had the largest membership in the organization.

The number of members and consequently the strength of the LUs were evidently not equal. The numbers depended upon convenience, availability of regular work, or special work assignments. Migration from one LU to another, dictated by the requirements of work, was quite common.

Life in the LU was marked by austerity and plain living—this also meant group living. Domestic activities were shared by members on the basis of competence and accommodation. Every morning, after breakfast and after completing domestic chores, they went to their workplace. At the end of the day's work, they came back to the house again for tea, relaxation, cooking, dinner, studies, meditation, and sleep.

Guests came quite often—members from other countries or from other LUs, who might stay for a few days. Callers from outside communities visited occasionally in the afternoons or evenings. The members were not socially insulated from the external community but had set up for themselves an implicit boundary on social mixing at home. Their involvement in their ideological work and their work schedules made them economical with time. Besides food and shelter, the LU provided them with a small allowance for personal necessities, which included the simplest of clothes and sandals, toothpaste, and books. One could buy anything one liked within the budget limit. We did not see anybody complaining about the modesty of the allowance—far from it. Their acceptance of plain living had developed ease, grace, and simplicity.

To become a member of the organization, one had to apply to the chief of the LU. If one was a minor, explicit permission of the parents was necessary. The candidate was not immediately accepted as a member and was required to spend quite some time in learning and training. If the applicant chose a particular vocation with which the society agreed and if that vocation required the person to pursue academic studies, the member was free to do so. After the candidate had passed through the final phase of training and had had a taste of what membership of the organization would mean, he or she had to make promises and pledges at three stages. After the third stage, which was the stage of final commitment, the person became a full member. A member had the freedom to leave the organization, although psychologically it was a difficult option to exercise.

The sector had, at the time of this exercise, 188 members, mostly below the age of 50. There were only 11 members above the age of 50. The majority were in their 30s (79), followed by those in their 20s (51) and 40s (47). It was obvious that younger members were more in number than the older. But if one divided the range into three—young (below 30), middle-aged (between 30 and 39), and older (above 40)—one got a real feel of the forces behind the composition. The number of those in these three categories were 51 (young), 79 (middle age), and 58 (older), respectively. The implication is that none of these three groups was a 'minority'—each had sufficient strength. Only if one group joined with another did the third became a minority. The organization could thus be divided into two age camps of almost equal strength, with 35 as the median age.

The members ranged from one who had just joined the organization to one who had spent 38 years with it. The quartiles fell on 5 years, 10 years, and 15 years, that is, about one-fourth of the members had spent 5 years or less with the organization, about half the members had spent 10 years or less with the organization, and about one fourth had spent 15 years or more.

In terms of vocations, the nursing profession had the highest numbers, followed by midwifery. Many of the members were also in education, public health, or administration at various levels. Some were also students.

Members came from 13 different geographical backgrounds: eight countries and five different parts of one country.

To gain some insight into their interpersonal orientation styles, we subsequently administered the FIRO-B. The scores showed that the members of this organization did not have extremely high (7, 8, 9) or low (0, 1, 2) scores except on control dimensions. It seemed that they had a tendency not to express control. Their desire to be controlled by (to receive instructions, ideas, and decisions from others) was higher than their need to exercise control. By and large, the data showed that the community as a whole was a psychologically mature group.

ENTRY OF OD

One fine morning, N came up the narrow stairs of the Behavioural Science Centre (India), or BSC(I), office. She discussed the purpose of this visit with the executive director of the BSC(I) with one of the authors present. N enquired about our willingness to help her organization.

When these discussions were going on, one of the authors was invited by the apex body of the organization to participate in a 3-day international meeting in Europe to work out the dimensions of PR. We had several meetings with N, the contact person for the organization. The main purpose of meeting with N, and with a few other members, was to understand the organization. On the basis of these meetings and discussions, we prepared a working paper on the project.

The working paper consisted of four parts dealing (a) our understanding, at that time, of some of the key issues involved, (b) a conceptual framework developed to formulate interrelations, (c) some hypotheses, assumptions, and propositions that were to be the basis of the OD programme design, and (d) a outline of the intervention plans.

We were invited to the sector meeting. Half a day in the 2-day meeting agenda was reserved for the discussion of the working paper. The main stand taken was that of tentativeness, both in terms of the contract as well as the proposal.

Incubation Period and Contracting

A shorter version of the working paper was circulated to all the members of the organization before a decision was taken. There was complete silence for almost 6 months. It was decided by the organization that the decision to implement an OD programme would have to be taken not from above but by each member and that the decision of each member would be communicated upwards. This then became an issue by itself. A system that usually followed the norm of decision making from the top was now required to reverse the norm and initiate a new practice. The result was indecision.

At the same time, an important process began: A good deal of questioning started. Questions were raised not only on whether to accept or reject the working paper but also on the various norms and practices associated with the governance of the system. Such questions were raised by the members individually, in small groups, and in the LUs. All the LUs were buzzing with these questions. It may be noted here that the consultants did not actively generate the process, but the task performance (of discussing the working paper) made this process almost inevitable.

We were satisfied with the process. We clearly indicated that we were not at all eager for a hasty decision. We could wait. During this phase, S showed a great deal of leadership, courage, determination, and above all, a sense of positive patience. She was under strong pressures. Some people were eager to start OD; others were reluctant to have anything to do with it. To some it would be a process of rejuvenation; some thought it would be a sure road to chaos and confusion. So we waited.

After a period of 6 months, we thought it would be necessary to churn things up a little. First of all, it was necessary that a final decision—yes or no—emerge and that the members should have the success experience of being able to arrive at a decision. In order to facilitate the process, we offered to meet the representatives of the houses for a couple of days. So a 2-day programme was arranged.

The programme was attended by representatives of all LUs. The programme design provided opportunity to the members to discuss the new constitution, the emergent issues facing them since the introduction of the constitution, the meeting, the implications of PR and societal changes, adaptability, etc. We presented various aspects of change: how we face issues of change, what change means to us personally and professionally, and how we cope or fail to cope with the demands of change. We gave a demonstration of laboratory training in micro form and presented a possible outline for the OD programme and its financial implications.

After this programme, the representatives went back to their LUs and vigorous discussion ensued. We did not hear anything, one way or the other, for 2 months until most of the LUs became ready to participate in the OD programme and it was sensed that the entire community of members might, by and by, choose to participate in the programme. Finally, a draft contract was prepared, which was readily accepted. We waited for another 3 months, by which time a few more members expressed their willingness. At this stage we thought our entry phase was over and we started planning the interventions.

INITIAL DIAGNOSIS

We had clearly mentioned to our client that the working paper was based to some extent on our limited understanding of the organization and mostly on our general understanding of OD. To gain a thorough understanding, we did the following:

- Visited a few LUs and saw the normal way of life there
- Observed some of the formal meetings, both at the LU level as well as the division level
- Acquainted ourselves intensively with the organizational process in the members' workplaces

Visits to the LUs were informal. Sometimes these were in response to their requests, sometimes on our own initiative. During the visits we talked freely about a number of things. We had no particular question in mind, yet we had so many questions! We were aware of our ignorance of the organization. So we sat there for long, lazy hours with cups of coffee in hand, talking and listening. We imbibed, slowly and quietly, the life that easily flowed in the house. And we did not take any notes!

We went to their formal meetings on invitation. Our role was that of a learner rather than that of an observer. We were interested in the content of their discussion as well as in the processes of discussion and decision making. Sometimes we also took part in the discussions, despite our limitations.

We observed their functioning at work quite thoroughly. We undertook an organizational diagnosis of the workplace and analysed the role of the members of the BDR. With all this data and understanding, we agreed among ourselves that we had developed enough insight to help us go ahead with planning the interventions.

The process of initial diagnosis we undertook was rather unorthodox. The nearest standard method to our approach was the anthropological method of observation. Our view is that too much reliance on instrument-generated data tends to shadow the holistic nature of the client system. Attention tends to be given to the quantitative picture and the consequent interpretation of data.

INTERVENTION PLANNING

Some of the parameters of intervention planning had been presented earlier in the working paper that we discussed with our clients and these remained unchanged even after the initial diagnosis, although we were ready to change them if needed.

We conceived of interventions at four levels: person, interperson, intragroup or team, and interteam or the total human system of the organization.

The specific objectives of the inteventions would be to help them move towards the positions they valued and become self-actualised, to help them function as optimally as possible, and to help them use freedom and responsibility in being relevant to the world and its needs today. These three objectives included other objectives, such as

- Developing an orientation of alertness concerning what is happening in the organization and why it is happening. This would presumably strengthen both religious motivation and concern for others.
- Fostering a tendency to help others and receive help from others (interdependence of growth).
- Instilling comfort with discussing things, including differences, openly (openness).
- Working towards continual growth.
- Developing tolerance and flexibility at all levels.
- Creating awareness and improving sensitivity to one's own strengths so that better utilisation of resources for the community takes place.

Phasing, sequencing, and linkage The nature of the task and the objectives of the programme were such that the interventions had to target the living systems. For example, all members participated—after their participation in the basic lab (see below)—in organizational diagnosis of their houses and in preparation and implementation of action plans.

Before our withdrawal, stabilisation and consolidation of the effort for change had to be planned. This would technically be an attempt to refreeze and would obviously be the last input. Accordingly, the interventions were attempted in the following order:

- Basic laboratory
- Internal resource development
- Organizational diagnosis
- Review laboratory for internal resource people
- Stabilisation

The entire OD programme was to be completed in a period of 12–15 months. The basic laboratories were to be provided within the first 6 months, followed by internal resource development. It was planned to have organizational diagnosis after 4 months and continue the practice thereafter. At the end of the year, the review laboratory was to be conducted. And after the review laboratory was over and the internal resource persons went back to their respective houses, the terminal phase was to start.

The following are brief descriptions of the interventions, notwithstanding the obvious and understandable difficulties of verbalising unstructured interventions.

BASIC LABORATORY

The basic intervention was a 5-day laboratory. All the members of the organization had the opportunity to participate in such a laboratory. In all, 15 basic laboratories were conducted and all of these were completed within 6 months.

Personal structured data   As mentioned earlier, instruments were used for the purpose of giving feedback on the data. One of the forms required the participants to state what they expected from the programme. The responses related to the self (more self-knowledge, self-acceptance, more self-confidence, reduced oversensitivity, increased listening, seeing others' strengths, and self-discipline), the community (openness and sensitivity, learning to recognise each other's strengths, increase in individual responsibility, mutual understanding and love, greater participation by all, a better climate, and mutual support and help), and solving problems (practical guidance to problems, choosing better leaders, and working out definite changes in the community).

As already stated, FIRO-B and six cards of TAT were used by the participants to write stories. The concept sessions were very short and mostly grew out of the needs of the groups. Themes included conditions of learning, feedback, defensive behaviour, sensitivity, congruence, authenticity, levelling, collaboration–competition–conflict, role analysis, motivation, motivating others, helping relationships, working effectively in groups and in organizations, effective membership behaviour and leadership functions, and dynamics of planned change.

The basic skills emphasised in the laboratory for practice were mainly effective speaking, effective listening, giving and receiving feedback, giving and receiving help, confrontation, and action planning.

Several exercises were incorporated in the programme to facilitate the process of movement, specially in acquiring new knowledge, and developing insights, attitudes, and skills. Structured exercises were focused on perception, trust and mutuality, self-motivation and motivating others, planning and communication, decision making, and life and society goals.

Panel discussion of PR About the third day, a panel discussion used to be arranged on plan renovation. Generally, the panel was constituted of one representative from each L-group. Each member put before the community his or her own ideas as well as the ideas of other members of his or her L-group on PR. A single chair was used for any member of the community to occupy when stating a point for the consideration of the panel. On the whole, the discussions brought out in the open many hidden agendas, fears, apprehensions, as well as hopes about PR. The session was usually followed by a period of free time, in which the discussion continued in small groups of twos and threes.

Action plan As stated in one of the propositions in the working paper presented earlier, we strongly believe that behavioural changes are better sustained in the context of actual action. Resolutions, howsoever pious they may be, tend to remain in ether, losing their vigour and becoming mere wishes or fantasy, if they are not reinforced continually by commitments in the work sphere. Accordingly, we place a great deal of emphasis on action plans. Work on action plans was started towards the end of the third day, followed by night assignments, which was again followed by considerable time spent on this on the fourth day. Essentially, the action plan module started with a concept discussion on the dynamics of planned change. For the exercise of action plans, participants worked not in L-groups but in new groups composed on the basis of geographical proximity of their living quarters, often coming from the same house. Each participant prepared two action plans—one for the LU and one for himself or herself.

These plans were presented by the planning module to the whole group in the community session for critical review and, later, revision. After revision, the group committed themselves to working on the action plan on their return. Strategies to involve other members of the house (who were not present) were also discussed.

Evaluation At the end of the programme, the whole experience was evaluated. Different methods were used. Typically, the participants worked in six groups to discuss the various aspects of the programme and presented their conclusions to the community. For example, six groups were formed for different aspects.

The programme ended with songs on commitment and energising the learning obtained with the transferring it for the good of all. Usually, it was a very intensive programme, highly packed with events both at the rational as well as the emotional level. The working day started at 8:00 a.m. and often closed in the small hours of the following day.

ORGANIZATIONAL HEALTH SURVEY

At a much later stage and as a part of an intervention to help the members develop some skill in organizational diagnosis, we undertook a survey with the help of the members. We believe that interventions themselves are not enough in the OD facilitation process. What happens during the intervening phase between two interventions is also important. To sustain the momentum gained in the basic laboratories, we thought that an intervention would be necessary at the level of each LU. This took the form of organizational diagnosis. This was one of the OD interventions.

Unit health survey   This intervention was named the unit health survey. This exercise required the would-be facilitator to enter into a dialogue to assess the health of the LU. What was meant by 'organizational health', the characteristics of a healthy organization, and the action steps to be followed were explained in a letter written by coordinator N and sent to each house. In the absence of a facilitator, it was decided that any person nominated by the LU could undertake this exercise.

The procedure suggested is as follows:

Step 1. Interview as many members (one at a time) as you can.

Step 2. Then arrange small group discussions to discuss the issues mentioned in the objectives.

Step 3. Organize a conference of all (most) [sic] members of the LU. List all issues raised. Evolve a consensus of the issues.

The survey helped in integrating the various action plans prepared by the members for the LUs during the basic labs, as described in a later section. We hoped that the organizational diagnosis itself would throw up important issues for the LUs and motivate the members towards their management.

The following picture came out of the survey regarding the organizational climate:

- There was lack of involvement of members in making decisions in the community (or, all members did not participate in making decisions in the community).
- There was a felt absence of an atmosphere of complete trust, openness, and acceptance in which the most timid might feel free to speak.
- There was a feeling of inadequacy in some members.
- There was a lack of sufficient information.
- There was a fear of hurting and being hurt.
- There existed a feeling among members that small groups would be the answer to all the problems, while at the same time realising that this was not physically possible.
- Communications did not always get through, though there had been improvement in this area.
- Members did not feel entirely free to express their feelings and opinions.

INTERNAL RESOURCE DEVELOPMENT (IRD)

In the plan of process facilitation, it was conceived that the role of the external consultants should be self-liquidating. In order to do so, it was decided that a self-supporting system would be developed within the organization. This included:

- Developing a group of persons who might acquire the expertise to become agents of change from within the organization. They might be termed internal change agents, internal resource persons, or internal facilitators. The term, 'internal facilitators' was most acceptable to the organization.
- Developing, from among the internal facilitators, a few who had some knowledge of the behavioural sciences further in terms of acquiring more knowledge and expertise in application through higher education and training.
- Contracting young behavioural scientists to work full time within the organization, in close liaison with the internal resources, on problems requiring the application of the behavioural sciences. This was a suggestion made to N for putting up for consideration before the governing board.

Internal Resource Development Programme

Selection of internal resources turned out to be a very potent intervention in itself. In almost all the LUs, many a battle was fought in the open and under cover; armistices were signed; peace was made, broken, and remade. An intense confrontation process came into operation. Many a tear was shed and much laughter rolled in, literally.

As soon as the task became apparent, a reply was sent to the consultants, however, which said 'nothing doing'. The parallels of this behaviour in laboratory situations are too frequent to require elaboration. When the consultants did not relieve members of their responsibility to do the task and the task had to be done, three courses were open: confront the situation and do the task as conscientiously as possible; avoid the situation, and express bottled-up emotions in an indirect fashion; or, instead of doing the task properly, distort it and go through the motions and rituals of doing it. All these things happened.

At a certain stage, when the organization communicated to us that they understood the position we had taken and asked us for help in selecting the resource persons, we agreed to join them in evolving certain criteria that might be used in the selection.

One of the latent concerns was whether the resource persons selected would become too powerful—by the fact of their selection by the assembly and by the advanced expertise generated out of specialised training—and replace, in effect, the chief of the LU. This did disturb the existing power equations. The entire issue of power distribution came under scrutiny. Backed up by experience from the basic laboratory and the members' newfound energy for verbalising, sharing, opening up, and owning, there was vigour and strength enough to deal with the issue. However, the task became very involved and difficult indeed.

The list ultimately did arrive, but only just before the start of Phase 2. The list contained names, which included one facilitator from each house and a few more members who could look after the process facilitation for special tasks at the corporate level.

The basic programme was a 10-day laboratory, which included consultant–client group (C-group), participants concept session (PCS), your choice time (YCT), modules, faculty concept session (FCS), L-group, reinforcement lab.

The content of the programme essentially revolved around the role of the facilitators—the skills needed in performing the role effectively and in identifying and resolving their dilemmas facilitators while working in their LUs.

The first part of the programme focused on sharing their experience as facilitators in the respective houses during the preceding 9 months.

The reinforcement laboratory spent most of its time in discussing the issues brought out thus by the facilitators from their experience in working as facilitators. They themselves formulated the schedule of the programme.

Every day, the facilitators had one extended session on skill practice. Work was done on skills of communication, collaboration, conflict management, consensus building, commitment and involvement, help giving, help receiving, and trusting. The duration of the laboratory was 4 days.

STABILISATION AND TERMINATION

One of the thrusts of the reinforcement lab was to bring in maturity in place of an exuberance of enthusiasm resulting in over-ambitious planning of action. Notwithstanding the shortcomings in the original selection of internal facilitators and the subsequent struggle, after the reinforcement lab we had renewed faith in the strength of the internal facilitators and their self-confidence was reinforced. We thought it was time for us to plan our withdrawal. Before we withdrew finally, we thought it was necessary to attend to a few issues. One of these issues was helping to resolve some conflicts that arose at the management level of plan renovation. One of us spent quite some time in an LU to counsel on this issue and arrange confrontation meetings between the conflicting parties. The confrontation proved very useful and resolution was achieved through the hard work of the conflicting parties.

At almost the same time, the members of the LU had reinforcement and psychological rewards from other sectors. There was praise and appreciation (and a little bit of jealousy also!) that this sector had moved ahead of the other sectors in their work. In the meantime, an international meeting of representatives from all over the world was held. One of us agreed to provide process help to the meeting and four internal resource persons were selected for help. We spent time in planning the process feedback strategy, and a few days on back-up help to the internal facilitators, who took on the main process work. Almost everyone in the meeting was highly impressed by the superb professional work the internal facilitator did. And we were naturally very proud of it.

The central authority was also keeping itself informed about the activities of this sector and they had witnessed their work and professional competence. Happily, they did give positive reinforcement. A professionally competent person visited the sector several times, met the members almost in every LU, and entered into detailed dialogue in each LU. His visits had a stimulating effect on the members in their new pursuit.

In our gradual withdrawal process, we made it clear to the organization that we did not think any other direct intervention was needed now, but that we would like to visit and help any LUs and the coordinator if it was needed. However, we made it clear that such requests for help must be channelled through their coordinator and they should approach the external consultants only when they had done all that they could do to help themselves. These criteria were set forth to underscore the need for self-help and self-reliance. We are glad to say they did not need much outside help. They really depended on their own skills and abilities. A year later, however, we received a request for help in training a group of members on certain specific aspects of management. But that is another story.

OD IN VOLUNTARY ORGANIZATIONS: TOWARDS ORGANIZATIONAL MATURATION

We have described one long-term attempt to implement OD in a voluntary organization. Our experience has been very rewarding. We learnt a great deal from this association. Voluntary organizations have some special features that distinguish them from enterprise. While these can be regarded as their main strengths, they also pose some problems. In our experience, these problems can be resolved through effective OD interventions and their special features can be turned into their greatest strengths. We would like to comment on three main features.

Commitment In the first place, voluntary organizations work in a climate of commitment. In most voluntary organizations, the members come together on the basis of some ideology and a high level of commitment to the goals that they share in common. This level of commitment is not found in other organizations. While this may be a great strength of these organizations, this may also create some problems. Since commitment is the main distinguishing feature of these organizations, individuals may become manipulative through their high level of commitment to the cause and thereby may control the organization. If this happens, a great deal of dependency may be generated in the organizational culture. It often happens that those who start as sources of inspiration feel that they have—and they may, in fact, have—a much higher commitment to the goals of the organization. This may give them a sense of ownership of the organization, with the right to direct and control. This may be done in good faith and with noble intentions. However, this does cause a problem when more people begin to join the organization and a differential strata of psychological membership begins to emerge. OD in such organizations, then, has to deal with the problem of dependency.

Extension motivation Another feature of these organizations is that the level of extension motivation—concern for others and a desire to serve others—is quite high. Compared to other organizations, the stress on service and working for others is a great strength of these organizations. However, the stress on service may lead to the tendency to use oneself for others rather than to work for others without necessarily sacrificing one's own self.

We make a distinction between self-sacrifice (giving precedence to larger goals over immediate individual goals and integrating the self with the goals) and sacrificing or using the self (denying the self in the name of serving the goals by splitting the two and taking the role at the cost of the self). While in the concept of self-sacrifice, an integration of the self and the higher goals is involved, in using the self, a split and denial of the self is implied.

This is likely to be the problem in India, where denying oneself is a prime value. There may be two consequences if the self is used for, rather than integrated with, service to others. On the one hand, it may lead to self-rejection and an escape into the role of a helper. This may disturb mental health and the individuals working in voluntary organizations with this tendency are likely to relish self-rejection and escape the problem of confronting their personal problems with the members with whom they work. On the other hand, excessive stress on serving others may lead to lack of affection and personal relationships among members of the organization. As a result of these, there may be a lack of mutuality and collaboration. One problem, therefore, which OD has to deal with in voluntary organizations is that of working towards mutuality and collaboration.

Empathy A corollary of a high level of extension motivation is that members of these organizations may have a high level of empathy. This in itself is a great strength. However, it may create problems if empathy makes people over-sensitive and may result in the tendency to avoid hurting the feelings of others. If this happens, people are likely to try to be 'good' and would generally avoid confrontation. This may create issues that OD may have to deal with.

As discussed earlier, some of the strong points that these organizations may have are likely to become problems if the organization does not mature as an organization. Organizational maturation (and not organizational maturity)—a state of becoming and not of being—is likely to be an issue in voluntary organizations, since their main emphasis is on service and commitment to goals rather than on organizational effectiveness. Over-emphasis on such goals may make them insensitive to organizational issues. It may be important for OD to work towards organizational maturation—a process of developing a rational and empirical approach to the understanding of the problems of the organization and its functioning and finding a systematic way of dealing with these problems, working towards a high commitment and positive confronting culture on the organization. A combination of these two is likely to result in the maturation of an organization.

For working towards organizational maturation, it is necessary that the consultants help the organization deal with the problems of dependency, independence, and counter-dependence and enable it to move towards mutuality and collaboration.

Questions for Discussion
1. How was diagnosis made in the organization?
2. Which interventions were used to introduce change, and with what effects?
3. What were different phases in the OD work?
4. What was the role of the external consultants and how were internal resources developed?

NOTES AND REFERENCES

1. Pareek, Udai (1975). 'The concept and the process of organization development', *Indian Journal of Social Work*, 36(2): 109–25.
2. Pareek, Udai (2002). *Training Instruments for HRD & OD*. New Delhi: Tata McGraw-Hill.
3. Schmuck, R.A. and M.B. Miles (eds) (1971). *Organization Development in Schools*. Palo Alto: National Press Books.
4. Blake, R.R. and J.S. Mouton (1976). *Consultation*. New York: Addison-Wesley.
5. French, J.R.P. and B. Raven (1989). 'The bases of social power', in D. Cartwright (ed.), *Studies in Social Power*. Ann Arbor: University of Michigan, Institute for Social Research.
6. Pareek, Udai (1995). 'Person-focused interventions', in W.J. Rothwell, R. Sullivan, and G.N. McLean (eds) *Practicing the Art of Organization Development*, pp. 265–310. San Diego: Pfeiffer & Co.; also in S. Ramanarain, T.V. Rao, and Kuldeep Singh (eds) (1998). *Organisation Development: Interventions and Strategies*, pp. 76–102. New Delhi: Sage.
7. Pareek, Udai (1998). 'Role-focused interventions', in S. Ramanarain, T.V. Rao, and Kuldeep Singh (eds), *Organisation Development: Interventions and Strategies*, pp. 103–135. New Delhi: Sage.
8. Dyer, William G., W. Gibb Dyer, Jr., Jeffrey H. Dyer, Edgar H. Schein (2005). *Team Building: Proven Strategies for Improving Team Performance*. San Fracisco: Jossey-Bass.
9. Cummings, T.G. and C.G. Worley (2005). *Organization Development and Change*. Mason, OH: South-Western College Publishing.
10. French, W.L. and C.H. Bell (1995). *Organization Development: Behavioural Science Interventions for Organization Development* (4th edn). New Delhi: Prentice-Hall of India.
11. Cady, S.H. and K.D. Dannemiller (2004). 'Whole system transformation: The five truths of change', in W. Rothwell, R. Sullivan, and G.N. McLean (eds), *Practicing OD*, Chapter 18, pp. 548–571. San Francisco, CA: Jossey-Bass Pfeiffer.
12. Corey, Stephen M. (1953). *Action Research to Improve School Practices*. New York: Teachers College Press, Columbia University.
13. De, Nitish R. (1984). *Alternative Designs of Human Systems*. New Delhi: Sage.
14. Sinha, D.P. (1986). *T-Groups, Team Building and Organisation Development*. New Delhi: ISABS.
15. *Ibid.*
16. Rothwel W.J. and R. Sullivan (eds) (2005). *Practicing Organisations Development: A Guide for Consultants*. San Francisco, CA: John Wiley.
17. Worley, C.G., W.J. Rothwel, and R. Sullivan (eds) (2005). 'Competencies of OD practitioners', in W.J. Rothwel and R.L. Sullivan (eds), *Practicing Organisations Development: A Guide for Consultants*, Chapter 5. San Francisco, CA: John Wiley.
18. Schein, E. (2005). 'Taking organization culture seriously', in W.J. Rothwel and R.L. Sullivan (eds), *Practicing Organisations Development: A Guide for Consultants*, Chapter 14. San Francisco, CA: John Wiley.
19. McLean, G.N., K.J. Davis, M.N. Baker, and J. Anguita (2005). 'Global Organizational Development', in W.J. Rothwel and R.L. Sullivan (eds), *Practicing Organisations Development: A Guide for Consultants*, Chapter 20. San Francisco, CA: John Wiley.
20. Bradford, D.L. and W.W. Burke (eds) (2005). *Reinventing Organization Development*. San Francisco, CA: Pfeiffer.

Index

F/Boxtool/90305782/8/08